# LAW TEACHING STRATEGIES FOR A NEW ERA

# Law Teaching Strategies for a New Era

## BEYOND THE PHYSICAL CLASSROOM

Edited by

TESSA L. DYSART & TRACY L. M. NORTON

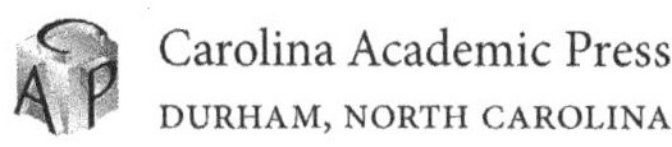


Carolina Academic Press
DURHAM, NORTH CAROLINA

LIBRARY OF CONGRESS CATALOGING-IN-PUBLICATION DATA
Names: Dysart, Tessa L., editor. | Norton, Tracy, editor.
Title: Law teaching strategies for a new era : beyond the physical classroom / edited by Tessa L. Dysart, Tracy Norton.
Description: Durham, North Carolina : Carolina Academic Press, LLC, [2021] | Includes index.
Identifiers: LCCN 2021021424 (print) | LCCN 2021021425 (ebook) | ISBN 9781531007294 (paperback) | ISBN 9781531015640 (ebook)
Subjects: LCSH: Law--Study and teaching. | Law--Automation. | Internet in education--Law and legislation. | Distance education--Law and legislation.
Classification: LCC K100 .L393 2021 (print) | LCC K100 (ebook) | DDC 340.071/1--dc23
LC record available at https://lccn.loc.gov/2021021424
LC ebook record available at https://lccn.loc.gov/2021021425

Carolina Academic Press
700 Kent Street
Durham, North Carolina 27701
(919) 489-7486
www.cap-press.com

Printed in the United States of America

*To all the teachers and students who survived (and even tried to thrive) during pandemic teaching—this book is for you. To a brighter future!*

# Contents

## SECTION TWO · Designing the Course of the Future

PREFACE I

# To the Future

Tessa L. Dysart*

I taught my first fully online asynchronous class in the spring of 2017. It was a masters-level law class on legislation and regulation. It ran eight weeks, and I had fifty students. As soon as the class started, I realized how unprepared I was to teach online. For example, my syllabus did not specify what time zone assignments were due in, which was an immediate problem since I had students all over the world in my class. I had also assigned a significant number of discussion board posts and essays, not realizing how much time those assignments would take for me to grade on top of an existing heavy in-person teaching load. Looking back now with even more perspective, I suspect that my videos were not that great and certainly were not appropriately short for the asynchronous model.

When I had finished teaching that course, I was convinced that online teaching should remain where it was at that time—a teaching style used mostly for legal masters-level courses. At the same time, I knew that there was a robust discussion in the law school community about online JD-level courses. In fact, when I interviewed for my current job, I remember talking about my online teaching experience—which was considered a plus.

Fast-forward three years to the spring of 2020. In addition to teaching a section of Constitutional Law I, I was creating a fully online asynchronous Constitutional Law II class that would run that summer. Despite my previous unpleasant experience with online teaching, I had answered a general call from our dean to consider offering doctrinal classes online. But, in my mind, this online class would be different. This time I had a professional studio in which to record my lectures and a team of expert online course designers available to back me up. I was ready.

And then COVID-19 hit.

---

* Assistant Director of Legal Writing and Clinical Professor of Law. University of Arizona James E. Rogers College of Law. Professor Dysart began full time teaching in January 2012 and taught her first online class in 2017.

My school was just finishing spring break when our University president announced that classes were moving online. As I pondered how I would teach my Spring 2020 classes online, I did not stress too much about Constitutional Law. It seemed relatively easy to lecture over Zoom, even if I could not execute all of the formative assessments that I had planned. My moot court class that included an intramural competition presented a different challenge, which I have blogged about.[1]

The planning of my asynchronous online class changed, too. Instead of recording in the studio, I recorded each video from my home office with a rotating set of virtual backgrounds, one for each case. Our studio team edited my videos, and our online course designers still built the course, but the video quality certainly did not match what could have been filmed in the studio.

As the summer progressed, the topic of remote learning and returning to the in-person classroom was one of the many COVID-related topics that dominated the news. News story after news story reported that students did not like online learning.[2] Many of these stories focused on the "pandemic teaching" that was happening in schools across the country, and some seemed to consider "pandemic teaching" and online teaching to be functionally equivalent. I even saw stories that appeared to conflate distance learning at the K-12 level with collegiate or graduate distance learning. Despite my earlier reticence about online teaching, each time I saw a story conflating the different types of online teaching, I loudly complained to my spouse that these news stories were comparing apples to oranges. I knew that the "pandemic teaching" that I had done in the spring was vastly different from the planned asynchronous Constitutional Law II class that I was teaching that summer.

Whether based on my experiences teaching during the pandemic or my realization that legal education was in for a profound change, I developed this need to defend online teaching—not pandemic-teaching, but real online teaching. And thus, the concept for this book was born. This book is the first comprehensive look at online law teaching. It starts with the premise that COVID-19 has forced lasting change on the practice of law. How we conduct trials and appellate arguments, depose witnesses, staff offices, and meet with clients has changed, and many of these changes will be

1. Tessa L. Dysart, *Moot Court in the Age of Coronavirus*, App. Advocacy Blog (Mar. 23, 2020), https://lawprofessors.typepad.com/appellate_advocacy/2020/03/oral-advocacy-in-the-age-of-coronavirus.html; Tessa L. Dysart, *My Final Thoughts on Moot Court in the Age of Coronavirus*, App. Advocacy Blog (Apr. 27, 2020), https://lawprofessors.typepad.com/appellate_advocacy/2020/04/index.html.

2. Joe Nocera, *College as We Know it Coming to an End? Don't Bet on it*, Bloomberg (May 22, 2020), https://www.bloomberg.com/news/articles/2020-05-22/college-students-parents-professors-hate-online-classes; Erin Richards, *'This is hell': Parents and kids hate online classes. Going back to school likely will include more of it*, Bay St. Parent (June 29, 2020), https://www.baystateparent.com/news/20200629/this-is-hell-parents-and-kids-hate-online-classes-going-back-to-school-likely-will-include-more-of-it; Larry Ferlazzo, *Student: Online Learning Is 'Stressful and Irritating'*, Educ. Wk. Tchr. (May 7, 2020), https://blogs.edweek.org/teachers/classroom_qa_with_larry_ferlazzo/2020/05/student_online_learning_is_stressful_and_irritating.html.

permanent. Even the bar exam has gone digital! Therefore, how we teach students to become lawyers must also change.

Even before the pandemic, the ABA Standards and Rules of Procedure for Approval of Law Schools were starting to acknowledge that change. The 2018–2019 Standards changed the number of distance education credits that a student could earn toward graduation from fifteen credits to one-third of the total credits.[3] But legal education changes slowly—look at how long the Langdellian case method has stuck around! While the ABA granted variances to law schools to teach online during the COVID-19 pandemic, at the time of this writing, it remains unclear if the ABA will be as flexible post-pandemic, or, at a minimum, continue to conflate synchronous and asynchronous classes under the heading of "distance education" despite the fundamental differences between the two approaches.

Our hope is that this book will help law teachers navigate this fundamental transition occurring in our profession. This book is designed to be a comprehensive look at developing the law school curriculum of the future. It is not a book on emergency remote teaching or pandemic teaching. Instead, it is a book that looks to the future of legal education and practice and recognizes that the future is, to a greater degree, digital.

The book contains thirty-four chapters written by law professors who have navigated the transition beyond the physical classroom. Some transitioned pre-COVID-19, while others made groundbreaking changes when the pandemic hit and are continuing to innovate.

The book starts with chapters on innovation and inclusion—how do we get started with this transformation to new modalities of learning and how do we make sure that classes of students are not left behind, including students with poor technology access and disabilities. Next, we look at designing courses and building community in these new "classrooms." Finally, we look at specific course design, from traditional first-year courses to upper-year electives and skills courses.

While this book may up your pandemic teaching game (assuming that there is still pandemic teaching going on when this book is released), we hope that it does so much more than that. We hope that it radically transforms how you view the law school classroom. The future of legal education is now, and that future includes a digital component. Furthermore, as many of our authors point out, the future also includes increased formative assessment and education in the interpersonal and professional

---

3. *Compare* A.B.A. Sec. Leg. Educ. & Admis. to the Bar, *Standards and Rules of Procedure for Approval of Law Schools*, Standard 306(e), at 19 (2017–18), https://www.americanbar.org/content/dam/aba/publications/misc/legal_education/Standards/2017-2018ABAStandardsforApprovalofLawSchools/2017_2018_aba_standards_rules_approval_law_schools_final.authcheckdam.pdf, *with* A.B.A. Sec. Leg. Educ. & Admis. to the Bar, *Standards and Rules of Procedure for Approval of Law Schools*, Standard 306(e), at 19 (2018–19) https://www.americanbar.org/content/dam/aba/publications/misc/legal_education/Standards/2018-2019ABAStandardsforApprovalofLawSchools/2018-2019-aba-standards-rules-approval-law-schools-final.pdf.

skills that are so essential to lawyering. Breaking out of the physical classroom, as our authors point out, presents myriad opportunities to experiment with formative assessment and professional skills teaching.

Welcome to the future. It may not include flying DeLoreans or true hoverboards, but it will include video calling and conferencing, online course materials, online meetings, and frequent requests to unmute yourself.

PREFACE II

# Lessons Learned

Tracy L. M. Norton*

*If you can't be a good example, then you'll just have to be a horrible warning.*

— Catherine Aird

In December 2020, over the course of a week, I replaced all the light bulbs in my house with smart bulbs and programmed them all to respond to voice commands through Google Home. I explained to my husband and three daughters—ages 20, 17, and 6—how the lights worked, what each was named, and which Wi-Fi network the lights were on. It went off without a hitch if you ignore the one time my 6-year-old daughter, Lizzie, was found standing in front of Google Home saying, "Google, you're not very good at this," when Google failed to turn on the light she had asked for.

My point is this: my family is used to the way I—a benevolent technology dictator—conduct a forced march through new tech. To be honest, how I approach my family with new technology is just a variation on how *I* experience new technology. I hear about the next big thing and often read the description as an edict: "There's a better way to do what you've been doing—get hoppin'!"

I bring this same energy to my law teaching, where it collides with the truth that legal education is slow to change. So I was delighted when the American Bar Association adopted standards requiring ongoing formative assessment of the program of education.[1] It seemed that overnight we no longer just *aspired* to be better teachers; circumstances *required* that we be better teachers. We learned new words and con-

* Associate Professor, Touro College Jacob D. Fuchsberg Law Center. Professor Norton began designing and teaching online courses in 2013. She has taught synchronous, asynchronous, and blended online courses.

1. A.B.A. Sec. Leg. Educ. & Admis. to the Bar, *Standards and Rules of Procedure for Approval of Law Schools*, Standards 314–15, at 23–24 (2014–15), https://www.americanbar.org/content/dam/aba/publications/misc/legal_education/Standards/2014_2015_aba_standards_and_rules_of_procedure_for_approval_of_law_schools_bookmarked.pdf.

cepts: spaced repetition, research-validated assessment, evidence-based teaching, instructional design. I approached this the way I approached new tech: if there is a better way, we must do it! I read *Make It Stick*[2] and *A Mind for Numbers*[3] and went to teaching workshops[4] and joined the Team-Based Learning Collaborative.[5] I flipped my classroom. I joined a group of law professors to learn how to use a research-validated peer review platform. I upended twenty years of teaching experience, re-examined everything, and implemented it right away. I turned everything around on a dime.

The thing about turning on a dime is that the Laws of Physics are not on your side. And while legal education was changing, it was not turning on a dime. I had a painful couple of years—during which I met resistance from students, colleagues, and administrators—but learned so much: about what had been missing in my teaching up to that point; about how hard it is to change the presumption that individual achievement—and not teamwork and leadership—are what students should be rewarded for; and about how much of a forced march through new territory I can orchestrate without an institutional commitment or, at least, a critical mass of faculty on the same page. Being an early and enthusiastic adopter, particularly as a female professor, can take a toll on course evaluations as students question whether you are doing things the "right" way.[6] Fortunately, the pain of being an early adopter has eased somewhat as the A.B.A. standards have required changes that are becoming more commonplace in law schools.

Cut to March 2020. All legal education experienced what I had experienced over the past four years. Suddenly, legal education had to turn on a dime. Thousands of law professors—myself included—spent the summer in online workshops learning to teach online. Although I had taught courses in all three modes of online teaching, I had never taught my 1L courses online. Fortunately, armed with my hard-won experience of how not to approach new challenges in teaching, I went into this challenge with some lessons in mind that I want to share with you as you read these chapters.

This is exactly the book I wish I had when I started online teaching in 2013. It is probably best that I did not, though, because I would have tried to implement every single good idea in one semester. And with thirty-four chapters of great ideas, that could have been dangerous. As you read about new strategies that excite you and maybe overwhelm you a little bit, I offer these five hard-won suggestions. Take what you need; leave the rest.

---

2. Peter C. Brown et al., Make It Stick (2014).

3. Barbara Oakley, A Mind for Numbers: How to Excel at Math and Science (Even If You Flunked Algebra) (2014).

4. Thanks to the Touro College Graduate School of Education for bringing in authors Peter C. Brown, Barbara Oakley, and Dylan Wiliam to conduct hands-on workshops.

5. Team-Based Learning Collaborative, www.teambasedlearning.org (last visited Mar. 27, 2021).

6. *See, e.g.*, Colleen Flaherty, *Even 'Valid' Student Evaluations are 'Unfair'*, Inside Higher Ed, Feb. 27, 2020, https://www.insidehighered.com/news/2020/02/27/study-student-evaluations-teaching-are-deeply-flawed.

## I. Be Kind

To yourself. To your students. To your colleagues. To administrators. It will be a while yet before we know what the new era of law teaching looks like. Some things will seem obvious to you that are not obvious to others, and the reverse is true. Recently, I talked to a student who snickered while looking down throughout the class. Every class. All semester. I told him that it was distracting me and that it had to stop. He was shocked that it distracted me and at a loss as to how to prevent it from happening. I softened when I realized it had honestly never occurred to him to put the phone away in a Zoom session. He seemed genuinely grateful for the suggestion.

The thing about technology in education is that it provides some marvelous solutions but can also dehumanize us. The more time we spend online, the less we see each other as three-dimensional people. For me, technology can reduce people to one-dimensional characters in my head. For that reason, it helps to make sure that as many interactions as possible are face-to-face so I can connect with my students, my colleagues, and my administrators as real people who are not, in fact, out to make my life more difficult. Those face-to-face interactions help me be kinder to myself by avoiding frustration, and they help me be kinder to others, whose faces remind me of their humanity and the fullness of their lives beyond my experience with them.

## II. Easy Does It

Learning to teach online and, at the same time, incorporate strategies like team-based learning or backward course design is like drinking from a fire hose. Prior to the dramatic move online in March 2020, I had already (mostly) learned my lesson. So I have limited how much information I have taken in over the last year. The temptation to learn more and implement more is strong sometimes, but I am not effective when I try to implement the "best" techniques all at once. I am instead a frantic, overwhelmed crank. My suggestion is to do what you can when you can. Try out one technique instead of three. Convert one course instead of all of them. Use a new assessment tool in one unit of your course instead of the whole thing.

## III. Help Your Students Get on Board

Perhaps, like me, you have labored under the misapprehension that young people like the best new thing. Why would they not want to use cool, new technology for formative assessment? Why would they not want the best evidence-based teaching they can get? I have no idea why they do not, but my experience has been that they do not. Orienting students to new tech and to evidence-based teaching strategies that are unfamiliar can smooth the way for you and ease their concerns considerably.

You can orient students with written instructions, short videos, or in-class demonstrations. For example, for evidence-based teaching strategies, record a short video containing data showing the differences in long-term memory between traditional study techniques and evidence-based techniques. For some tech, a simple one-page instruction sheet with screenshots is helpful. You might also record a short, simple demo video and explain how the tech makes their lives easier as compared to the non-tech option. For tech that is more complex or that will ultimately have a grade associated with its assessments, consider an in-class, hands-on demo.

## IV. Don't Reinvent the Wheel

Because legal education is later to the digital education party than other areas of education, resources in other disciplines abound. Expand your network of resources and experts. In addition to the usual listservs and blogs that law professors might rely on for help, consider social media groups. Facebook has an array of teaching groups for different disciplines, all of which grapple with online teaching challenges.[7] Remember to look beyond just teachers. Instructional designers have become an incredible resource for law schools.[8] When you cannot figure out how to accomplish something online, or you want feedback for an idea you are considering, reach out on social media if your immediate network is not able to help.

Expand your network beyond higher education also. K-12 educators are well organized in sharing teaching ideas, and they share those resources in places law professors may not think to look. For example, I have been surprised at how useful Pinterest is for online teaching, particularly if you are looking for how to complete a class activity online.[9] Another K-12 resource called Teachers Pay Teachers,[10] has recently added a suite of digital tools.

## V. Get a Buddy

In 2016, my colleague Jack Graves asked if I was interested in working with Jane Winn to explore using a research-validated peer review platform that Jane had been using for a few years with law students.[11] In my first conversation with Jane, she introduced me to the idea of a "community of practice."[12] The community of practice that Jane and Jack put together consisted of about seven law professors who met weekly over the summer to learn how to use the peer-review platform in a law school setting.[13] We took turns being the "professor" so we could explore the platform as both stu-

---

7. Two that have been very helpful for me in online teaching recently have been Pandemic Pedagogy and Pandemic Pedagogy: Law Teaching in a Time of COVID-19.

8. One Facebook group of instructional designers is Instructional Designers in Legal Education (IDLE).

9. PINTEREST, www.pinterest.com (search in search bar "online teaching") (last visited Mar. 27, 2021).

10. TEACHERS PAY TEACHERS, www.teacherspayteachers.com (last visited Mar. 27, 2021).

11. PEERCEPTIV, www.peerceptiv.com (last visited Mar. 27, 2021).

12. CREATING A COMMUNITY OF PRACTICE, www.communityofpractice.ca (last visited Mar. 27, 2021).

13. While a number of undergraduate institutions use Peerceptiv, Jane Winn pioneered its use in law schools.

dents and instructors. While I learned a lot from Jane and the rest of the group about research-validated peer review, the idea that has stuck with me the most is using a community of practice to improve my teaching.

Since that summer, this has been my go-to strategy anytime I want to explore something professionally. I collect a handful of professors who are interested in exploring the same thing, organize us so we can work through problems and solutions, and then let the group continue organically until it comes to a natural end. I have made new friends, expanded my professional network, and learned more than I ever could on my own. Fun loves company, too.

A law professor friend tells a story about a visit she and her husband had with a financial planner. One of his first questions was, "At what age do you want to retire?" She was stumped: "I'm a law professor. I think about things that interest me, write about them, and see them published. I serve my institution and my community. I share my passion with young people and mentor them as they develop their own passions. That's retirement."

This is a great job, and we are fortunate that it has such longevity. No matter how you have come to online teaching—whether you had already embraced it or were forced to catch a curveball in March 2020—adapting your teaching for online delivery can breathe new life into both your online and in-person teaching. For me, it has been an opportunity to rethink everything—but not all at once!—as we head into this new era of law teaching beyond the physical classroom.

# Distance Education Terms

Distance education was a quickly-changing landscape even before March 2020. Since March 2020, the landscape has evolved even more quickly as students and teachers from Kindergarten to graduate school have transferred education online and back, with stops in between. To prevent confusion in the following chapters, this book uses the following terms and definitions to refer to the marvelous array of opportunities before us since we have opened up the places, times, and modes of instruction.

*Locations of instruction:*

**In-person.** This refers to an experience in which students and the teacher occupy the same physical space while working together.

**Online.** This refers to an experience in which students and the teacher occupy different physical spaces while working online.

**Concurrent.** This refers to concurrently teaching two groups of students—one online and one in-person—by one teacher. This is also referred to as HyFlex teaching.

*Times of instruction:*

**Asynchronous.** This refers to an experience in which the students or the students and teacher interact with one another at different times.

**Synchronous.** This refers to an experience in which the students or the students and teacher interact with each other simultaneously.

*Modes of instruction:*

**Blended.** This refers to a course that is taught with a combination of in-person and online experiences that may include experiences that are synchronous, asynchronous, or a combination.

**Flipped.** This refers to the strategy of "flipping" traditional in-class content with traditional out-of-class content. Lecture is provided outside of class through videos, readings, or activities. Class time is then used for hands-on, collaborative activities that the teacher can observe and provide feedback on.

# SECTION ONE

## The Move Beyond the Physical Classroom—Getting Started and Fostering Inclusion

ONE

# We Are in this Together: A Faculty-Led Approach to Fostering Innovation in Online Instruction

Courtney Selby*
Rachel H. Smith**

After reviewing this chapter, readers will understand how to:

- Implement a faculty-led approach to improving online instruction at their institutions;
- Convene a faculty task force to spearhead that approach;
- Engage faculty members in productive discussions about the pedagogy of online law teaching;
- Prepare a set of institution-specific recommendations for improved online teaching; and
- Foster a faculty culture invested in innovating online instruction well beyond emergency use.

As so many platitudes tell us,[1] challenges present opportunities. And the challenges of teaching law in a pandemic certainly created an avalanche, a flood, a—pick your natural disaster—of opportunity. Indeed, the sudden switch to online teaching occa-

* Associate Dean for Library Services and Associate Professor of Legal Research. Professor Selby began teaching legal research in 2002 and taught her first fully online course in 2020. She teaches both an online synchronous introductory legal research course and a concurrent advanced legal research course.

** Associate Dean for Experiential & Skills-Based Education and Professor of Legal Writing. Professor Smith began teaching legal writing in 2007 and taught her first online course in 2020. She has since designed and taught synchronous and concurrent courses.

1. You know these: When the universe shuts a door, it opens a window. Every cloud has a silver lining. When life gives you lemons, make lemonade.

sioned by COVID-19 was a unique opportunity to start a discussion about law school pedagogy and technology that was, for at least some law faculties, long overdue.[2]

But how to approach this discussion with faculty members, some of whom have taught the same classes in largely the same ways for decades, was not an easy question. Some law professors may have wanted to wait things out, hoping that life and teaching would return to "normal" in short order. For those professors, the switch to emergency remote teaching[3] risked entrenching old teaching approaches — lecturing, cold calling, assessing students through single summative assessments — and casting everything created in the spring of 2020 as a halfhearted approximation.

For other professors and administrators, those already hip to the ways online course delivery could expand the reach of legal education, the switch was a chance to shepherd everyone toward a new future where law school classes were taught in a variety of modalities for students spread across the globe. For those already comfortable with online instruction, online law teaching was long overdue and is an essential part of the future of legal education.

Between these two camps there is a middle way: a faculty-led approach to help law professors make incremental but significant progress over the course of one summer and then forever toward becoming more effective and engaging teachers both in person and online. This approach accepts that the need for quality online instruction for law students will remain beyond any emergency need but does not reject outright the in-person teaching techniques that many law professors have developed over their careers. It seeks to meet faculty members where they are and accommodates a spectrum of mindsets, preferences, and deeply held beliefs about the best way to prepare students for the practice of law.

## I. The Goals & Benefits of a Faculty-Led Approach

We will describe our process in greater detail in part II, but here is an overview. Near the end of the Spring 2020 semester, the dean of our law school convened a faculty task force to explore online and concurrent pedagogy.[4] The task force's charge was to take the lead in thinking through the pedagogical challenges of teaching in both remote and synchronous concurrent environments, identify the "better practices" that faculty

2. Michael L. Perlin, *Online, Distance Legal Education as an Agent of Social Change*, 24 PAC. MCGEORGE GLOBAL BUS. & DEV. L.J. 95, 98 (2011) (describing online courses as a "pivotal development in the history of American legal education").

3. Some scholars refer to this by its initials, ERT. *See* Charles Hodges et al., *The Difference Between Emergency Remote Teaching and Online Learning*, EDUCAUSE REVIEW (March 27, 2020), https://er.educause.edu/articles/2020/3/the-difference-between-emergency-remote-teaching-and-online-learning [https://perma.cc/8BZ3-JTBW].

4. We use the term "concurrent" to refer to a single teacher leading online and in-person students simultaneously.

should be using in various course settings, and develop a plan for getting the faculty as a whole up to speed on those practices. The task force worked all summer to listen to faculty, collect and review resources, and prepare recommendations for better practices in fully remote and concurrent teaching. Those recommendations were released to the faculty (and the world) as a work-in-progress.[5] Then, the task force held listening and sharing sessions with faculty in preparation for the Fall 2020 semester.

This process was informed at every step by a primary institutional goal of fostering broad faculty buy-in for improving the faculty's approach to teaching online. Having survived the abrupt transition to fully online courses, we wanted to generate faculty engagement with online pedagogy that was collaborative, positive, and ongoing. We wanted to incentivize and empower faculty members to experiment with online teaching tools and strategies. We wanted the faculty to feel supported in efforts to improve their online teaching by providing resources and materials that allowed them to try new things and build up experience and judgment about the tools that worked best for them. And we wanted to create a faculty culture that was open to innovation and invested in discussing and sharing pedagogical advancements.

As we reflected on our experiences from the necessary move to remote teaching, we considered various models for gathering, digesting, and disseminating useful resources for remote and concurrent instruction. A top-down model with required approaches to online teaching seemed like the least effective way to reach our goals and had the potential to minimize faculty buy-in. External solutions, such as hiring instructional designers and technologists to guide us through intensive summer work, were both cost-prohibitive and risked leaving valuable faculty voices and experiences out of the process. Instead, we believed we could best meet our goal with a faculty-led approach.

While the faculty task force approach yielded innumerable benefits, we saw three particularly noteworthy outcomes. First, our shared responsibility for identifying the path forward provided an opportunity for an already-collegial faculty to communicate with and support each other at an extraordinarily difficult time. It quickly became clear that participants wanted to express their frustrations, concerns, uncertainties, and needs. By making space to talk about these things, we were better able to craft recommendations that were responsive to our needs and reflective of our hopes.

Second, our collaborative exploration of both practical and theoretical resources about online pedagogy allowed us to identify opportunities to improve student experiences without setting standards for the transformation of every course that would be impossible to achieve. By talking and listening to each other as a faculty, we created realistic "better practices" that could be implemented on a continuum depending on the priorities and resources of each individual professor and had the potential to improve the student experience in every course.

---

5. St. John's University School of Law Online & Hybrid Teaching Task Force, *Recommendations for Online Teaching* (June 26, 2020), https://scholarship.law.stjohns.edu/faculty_publications/310/ [https://perma.cc/C7ZS-JWX7].

Finally, and perhaps most importantly, the collaborative creation of recommendations for "better practices" gave those involved some sense of control during uncertain times. Despite our inability to change our circumstances, we did have the ability to shape the experience we and our students would have in the coming semester and beyond.

## II. The Process

### A. CONVENE A FACULTY TASK FORCE WITH DIVERSE TEACHING EXPERIENCE AND CLEAR DELIVERABLES

Our task force included eight faculty members teaching in a variety of course types: clinical, large 1L, large upper-level, skills, seminars, and writing. The task force members had different teaching and learning backgrounds and included junior faculty and senior faculty.[6] It also included a few faculty with online teaching experience that predated the pandemic and some with online learning experience. Finally, the faculty members had differing degrees of familiarity with educational technology. This diversity of teaching experiences gave the faculty as a whole a sense that the issues we shared were being explored, while the issues unique to specific types of courses would not be overlooked.

The faculty who served on the task force were all professors known for caring deeply about teaching. In addition, they all have personalities that make them well suited for working collaboratively. And perhaps most important, the task force was a relatively diverse and inclusive group, which allowed us to think about the challenges faced by a broad range of students and faculty. We knew that the task force would often need to meet virtually during an extremely stressful time, and so we wanted the experience to be one that was at least pleasant, and maybe even fun.

In preparation for our first meeting, we asked the task force members to think about three ways we could improve the teaching and learning experience for faculty and students. We contemplated fully online classes as well as classes taught in a concurrent model, i.e., with low-density, simultaneous in-person and online instruction. Answers ranged from providing faculty access to specific hardware and software to engaging in extensive educational technology training. Some ideas focused on physical changes to our classrooms for socially-distanced or concurrent in-person teaching. Others contemplated a more conceptual re-working of the way we engage in legal education. It quickly became clear that our charge, identifying ways in which we could improve our remote and concurrent teaching and learning, would require an exploration much broader than we first imagined.

---

6. The task force faculty included tenured professors, tenure-track professors, skills professors with contracts of different statuses and lengths, and administrators who also teach.

We agreed on an ambitious timeline and set of goals that would, in twelve short weeks, provide us an opportunity to learn, synthesize, and share an incredible amount of information. We set weekly meetings to identify action items and review our progress, worked collaboratively in shared folders and documents to assemble our findings, and sought to experiment with as many tools and ideas as possible. Ultimately, we aimed to provide the following deliverables: We would curate a collection of resources focused on online pedagogy, find and share opportunities for professional development related to online and concurrent teaching and learning, and prepare written recommendations for our faculty based on what we learned from these resources and from our colleagues.

## B. HOLD LISTENING SESSIONS THAT ALLOW FACULTY TO VENT AND BRAINSTORM

Central to the task force's work was listening to the faculty. We knew that if our recommendations were going to be helpful, they had to respond directly to faculty feelings about online teaching. And they had to meet the faculty where they were in terms of both pedagogy and logistics. So we organized virtual listening sessions with small groups of faculty. The discussion groups were guided by two prompts — looking back at Spring 2020 and looking forward to Fall 2020 and beyond.

To no one's surprise, we heard a lot of gripes at these listening sessions.[7] Many related to technological glitches and limitations. Others were about the things that all educators struggled with in the shift to online teaching — it takes longer, it feels lonely, and it is vastly different than in-person instruction. Sharing those common complaints set the stage for the faculty to think about ways, even small ones, to improve the teaching and learning experience for the fall and afterward. And as much as we could, we tried to steer the discussion to what worked well and what we had learned.

From these sessions, we were able to identify several objectives that most, and maybe all, professors had for their continued online teaching. In particular, faculty repeatedly expressed that they wanted (1) for the technology to work seamlessly during class, including audio, video, chat, slides, and interactive tools; (2) to see the students as much as possible; (3) to encourage student engagement and participation; (4) to prepare classes effectively to suit online teaching and learning; and (5) to build community in classes, connecting with students and helping them connect with each other. The task force then focused on these objectives and ways to achieve them in preparing our recommendations.

---

7. To be fair, the emergency remote teaching of the spring semester was difficult and stressful for everyone involved. It was, without question, a sub-par teaching and learning experience. Part of the task force's work was to help the faculty understand that there is a chasm between ERT and thoughtful, well-executed remote instruction, and that our efforts were intended to help bridge that gap. *See* Charles Hodges et al., *supra* note 3.

## C. USE STUDENT FEEDBACK TO ASSESS WHAT WORKED AND WHAT DIDN'T

In addition to listening to faculty, we also needed to listen to students. To do so, we decided to use the course evaluations from the spring semester, which included the following new question: "If this course were going to be taught again in an online format, are there any improvements that could be made?" We extracted the answers to this question from all evaluations and anonymized them. We then grouped responses for similar types of courses together. We shared these answers with the task force, hoping that in the aggregate we would get an accurate view of our students' responses to online teaching and ideas for how it could be improved.

Perhaps not surprisingly, the student answers in many ways tracked the faculty objectives from the listening sessions. Students wanted (1) the technology to work seamlessly; (2) to see their professors and classmates; (3) for the classes to be interactive and engaging with visual elements, especially slides, that were distributed in advance of class and prepared with online delivery in mind; and (4) to feel connected to their professors and classmates so they could still be part of the law school community even while learning remotely.

## D. COLLECT, ORGANIZE, AND SHARE EXISTING RESOURCES

While we engaged with our faculty colleagues and reviewed student feedback, we collected resources and information from beyond our community. We began by putting useful articles, webinars, resource lists, blog posts, and teaching tools into a shared folder. In a matter of days, it was clear that we would need to impose some sort of organizational structure for these resources to be truly useful. Broad categories emerged in our collection and included pedagogy in online education, online teaching specific to legal education, assessment in online teaching, educational technology tools and techniques, and open educational resources.

There seemed to be an endless supply of resources and tools related to online learning generally, but a dearth of guidance specific to online and concurrent teaching in legal education. A vocal minority of law faculty and law librarians has been calling for and assembling tools for online instruction in law schools for several years, but we found relatively few examples of robust and broad-based initiatives to integrate online instruction into legal education.[8] This, it appeared, was the moment that those voices would be heard and new initiatives would gain traction.[9] Members of the task force participated in webinars, conferences, and intensive courses and then we shared our

8. Suffolk Law School and Mitchell Hamline School of Law stand out as early adopters.

9. The AALS Section on Technology, Law & Legal Education created a series of weekly webinars for the summer of 2020 focused on remote instruction in legal education. CALI created a 7-session intensive course designed to touch on major issues and practical applications in online legal education.

take-aways with each other. In hopes of disseminating our collection as broadly and efficiently as possible, we created a guide using the LibGuide software licensed by the law library.[10]

## E. DRAFT SPECIFIC RECOMMENDATIONS FOR ALL TYPES OF CLASSES

Once the task force had listened to faculty and students, reviewed and collected resources, and coalesced around a set of ideas that it would be worthwhile to share, we set out to draft written recommendations that we could distribute to the faculty before the start of the fall semester. We felt that our faculty would be best served by recommendations specific to our law school with its unique culture, student profile, geographic location, and technology infrastructure.

The process of collaboratively drafting the recommendations required planning and collegiality. The recommendations begin with the following short introduction that explains their perspective, purpose, and scope:

> This is a collection of recommendations drawn from a variety of sources, including our colleagues, students, webinars, books, articles, podcasts, and our own experimentation. It is not our expectation that any individual professor would adopt all of these suggestions and indeed no one of us intends to. Instead, we hope that some of these are helpful to you. Some suggestions deal with the nuts and bolts of teaching online while others with how to accomplish broader goals.
>
> Many of the suggestions are intended to deal with the same set of particularly troublesome problems for online classes: holding student attention, facilitating calling on students and discussions, increasing student engagement with the material outside of class, and making it possible for students to get to know and work with each other.[11]

We decided to write general recommendations that would be useful to all faculty and specific recommendations for each type of class: large 1L, legal writing, large upper-level, upper-level seminars, upper-level skills, and clinics. Using the faculty objectives as a roadmap, we structured the general and specific recommendations to have the following five sections: (1) Logistics & Technology, (2) Synchronous Classes,[12] (3) Student Engagement, (4) Assessment, and (5) Social Presence & Building Community.

---

10. This collection continues to evolve and grow, and its current iteration can be found at https://law.stjohns.libguides.com/sjulawremote/pedagogy. A separate collection of open educational resources for legal education can be found at https://law.stjohns.libguides.com/sjulawremote/oer.

11. St. John's University School of Law Online & Hybrid Teaching Task Force, *supra* note 5.

12. In the recommendations, "synchronous classes" refers to fully online classes with synchronous instruction. These classes usually take the form of the professor and students all logged on at the same time with their cameras on and the professor alternating between lecture and colloquy with students. *See id.*

The general recommendations reflected the task force's consensus about the best ways to improve our online teaching. Often, there was not a single answer that would work for every faculty member or every course. For example, faculty and student opinions about the chat function ranged from love to hate and everything in between. So rather than recommending that faculty use the chat function in one particular way, the task force recommended that every faculty member make a decision about chat and communicate that decision and any expectations clearly in the syllabus.

For the specific recommendations, members of the task force paired off to work on recommendations for the type of courses they were most familiar with teaching. The specific recommendations were written to capture the particular concerns that come with teaching certain types of courses and were informed by the common pedagogy and practices of the professors who wrote them. For example, the recommendations for large 1L classes were written by professors who teach Civil Procedure and focused on the best ways to engage new law students in the first semester of law school. In contrast, the recommendations for upper-level skills courses were written by professors who teach a variety of skills courses and focused on the best ways to create community in small classes and offer realistic experiential opportunities online.

Once everything was written, each member of the task force had the opportunity to offer edits and suggestions. We wanted to make sure that the document read as informed recommendations, not fiats or demands. We also wanted the recommendations on the whole to be encouraging, non-judgmental, and readable so the faculty would read and use them immediately. We also stressed that they were a work in progress and that we were open to feedback.

### F. SHARE THE RECOMMENDATIONS

We delivered our written recommendations and resource collection to the faculty just eight weeks after our first task force meeting and invited the faculty to engage in a second round of smaller and more targeted discussions. The groupings for these conversations aligned with the types of courses faculty were preparing to teach in the fall semester.[13] The primary goals of these targeted discussions were to engage with the entire faculty about the recommendations, explore concrete ideas for individual courses, and answer questions about the task force's work.

As with the first set of conversations, we tried to steer the discussion toward building on positive experiences from the spring, fleshing out new ideas for fall class sessions, and identifying remaining questions that would need to be answered before the start of classes. During these sessions, we discovered that faculty members who were not part of the task force had also been actively engaged in learning about online and concurrent instruction and had made thoughtful plans for their fall classes. So in

13. Of course, faculty members were invited to participate in as many of the small group meetings as they wanted.

addition to fresh ideas, this second set of discussions provided us with a list of logistical and technological questions that needed answers before the fall semester began. To help with these, the task force facilitated technology rehearsals for certain classes, created user guides for technology tools, and recommended the law school make certain purchases that would allow for the kind of teaching the recommendations had envisioned. The plans that grew out of these discussions gave us hope that our work would result in a better fall experience for everyone.

### G. REVISE THE RECOMMENDATIONS AND OFFER ADDITIONAL SUPPORT

A month into the fall semester, we scheduled a third round of conversations to see how classes were going and whether our recommendations were useful. Again, our faculty discussions resulted in helpful ideas for revising our work — a process that is ongoing and will continue as faculty members continue to gain comfort and fluency with online and concurrent teaching.

## III. Lessons

There are many lessons that we learned from this faculty-led process. Virtual meetings should be short; personalities and perspectives matter when working as a team during a stressful time; teams that are diverse and inclusive are better problem solvers; technology will fail no matter how much you test it; and many more. But the most important lesson, and the one that makes this faculty-led approach a blueprint for improving the online education offered by law schools, is that law professors are at their best when asked to do the simultaneous teaching and learning that is at the core of being a member of a law school faculty. Each of us had knowledge and insights to share and so, so much to learn. And our work was better because we taught and learned from each other.

TWO

# The Art of Cutting Yourself Some Slack: Reinventing Yourself as an Online Teacher

Meredith A.G. Stange*

At the conclusion of this chapter, readers will have:

- Strategies for accepting the uncertainty of learning how to teach in an online environment;
- Ideas for creating an online teaching style; and
- A better understanding of what students are looking for with the online educational experience.

Like most of us, I never intended to be an online teacher. I love the energy of an in-person classroom. I love seeing the smiles and nods when students are understanding things and being able to gauge by furrowed brows and blank looks when they are confused. I love feeling like my students and I are all on an educational journey together, connected by the space we share in the classroom. Also, after nearly two decades of teaching, I love the comfort and familiarity I feel when I teach a class I have taught for years. I have a tool kit of ready strategies should an exercise not work or if students need to learn in a different way. Online teaching was always a foreign, slightly alien concept best done by professors with far more technological savvy than I. However, with law schools actively trying to broaden their online course offerings, law professors who never anticipated becoming online teachers, myself included, want to broaden their skillset by teaching typically in-person courses online. But the change is not an easy one. This chapter includes the lessons that I learned, often the hard way, as an online teacher.

* Director of the Legal Writing Program at Northern Illinois University College of Law. Professor Stange joined NIU Law in August 2003. She began teaching online courses in 2020. Since then, she has designed and implemented multiple synchronous online classes, including Health Law and Legal Writing I and II.

In addition to my own experience, this chapter also features those of my students. Since I had a group of students with a front-row seat to all my first online teaching struggles and successes, I sent them a survey asking for their thoughts about what makes online courses and online teaching effective.[1] Their responses will be incorporated throughout the chapter.

## I. Online Teaching is Different

The first thing to do as an online teacher is let go of the idea that you can recreate the in-person classroom online. You cannot, and you will only frustrate yourself—and the students—by trying. I speak from experience, having spent an inordinate amount of time fighting against the differences between online and in-person teaching. I taught two online courses, consecutively, in the summer of 2020, Health Law and Legal Writing II. In preparation for teaching these classes, I took a course in online teaching through our Center for Innovative Teaching and Learning. The course addressed best practices for online learning, how to make a visually pleasing online course, and how to engage students. Yet despite the information learned during this course, when I started teaching, instead of adapting my teaching to fit the online format, I initially focused on trying to make my online teaching exactly the same as the in-person experience. I spent the first two weeks of my Health Law class feeling frustrated. Every technological glitch was just another roadblock keeping me from that connection and from being the teacher I was supposed to be. But, as is so often the case, my students helped me put everything in perspective. After one of those early summer classes, I was talking with a group of students about how frustrating the online format was and one student responded, "Don't worry. We're learning all of this too." That recognition that the students were adapting too really helped me relax a bit and stop stressing when everything was not working perfectly. Although I still felt frustrated when things did not go as planned, I always reminded myself that my students and I were all adapting together.

Another piece of advice that has helped me tolerate the inevitable technical stumbles that are part of teaching online came during the 2021 AALS Annual Meeting.[2] Professor Elizabeth Emens, Director of the Mindfulness Program at Columbia Law

---

1. During the summer 2020 semester I taught twenty students in Legal Writing II and thirty students in Health Law and received responses from nine Legal Writing II students and sixteen Health Law students. The questions that I asked in the survey were:

> What makes an effective online teacher?
> What did we do in class that made the online class effective?
> What part or parts of the online class worked?
> If something/s didn't work, what could have been done to make it work better?
> What was your favorite part of the online class this summer?
> What was your least favorite part of the online class this summer?
> What could I have done to make your online learning more effective?

2. *Mindfulness in Legal Pedagogy*, Section on Teaching Methods & Balance in Legal Education, AALS 2021 Annual Meeting—The Power of Words (Jan. 5, 2021) (recording available to AALS members at https://am.aals.org/past/am20/).

School, commented that she views technical interruptions as an opportunity for a mindfulness technique called a "forced pause." She incorporates these unexpected breaks into her classroom and uses them to give her and her students an opportunity to take a moment away from the classroom and refocus. Framing technical problems this way makes them a helpful part of the teaching experience as opposed to an unwanted interruption to fight against. Regardless of how you view this part of your learning curve, accepting the adaptation required for a new teaching platform is your first opportunity to cut yourself some slack.

## II. Welcome to Your Second First Year of Teaching

Building on that, part of cutting yourself some slack involves the acknowledgement that, with a new teaching format, you must become a different teacher. Online teaching is a new experience, regardless of how many years of teaching you have under your belt. For example, despite years of teaching and being comfortable in the classroom, I was nervous before each online class. In addition to technical concerns, I worried that I would not be able to reach the students; that my class plans, often dependent on interaction between me and the students, would not work in an online format; and that I had no online teaching tools to fall back on if students had difficulty connecting with the material. Yet as I struggled, it all felt oddly familiar.

It finally dawned on me that I had not felt this insecure since my first year of teaching. I had been a litigation associate prior to teaching and, for a variety of reasons, my two weeks' notice from the law firm ended on a Friday and I started teaching in 1L Orientation the following Monday. To say it was a trial by fire is an understatement. I had no classroom experience and only the textbook and materials my colleagues shared to guide me. Although my colleagues were excellent mentors, I did not have the chance to watch experienced teachers in action before being responsible for a classroom in my own right because we all taught at the same time. As a result, I entered every class petrified. Since I had no frame of reference for teaching, I never knew if I was explaining information well, if the students were understanding the material, or if I was even conveying the right information. When I realized my reactions to the shift to online teaching mirrored that first-year experience, I reached the uncomfortable conclusion that I was starting over. Starting over meant that I had to create new teaching strategies based on trial and error, just as I had in my first year.

My biggest error when starting to teach online was mistaking a lack of a camera for a lack of engagement. Although it was difficult to adapt to the fact that I was not seeing my students' faces anymore, I did not feel comfortable requiring my students to turn their cameras on since many of them are using private spaces, like bedrooms, to do their work. As a result, for both of my summer classes, I only rarely saw students' faces and usually only if the student verbally asked a question or responded to one. But while I missed seeing their faces, I got used to talking to the silent, unblinking eye of the computer camera and almost forgot students were on the other end of it. Given that, the first few times students typed comments in the chat, showing they were not only listening but invested in the class, I was a little taken aback. I soon discovered that even with the cameras off and the chat function on, many of my students were very engaged. Even students who typically did not speak up in class felt much more empowered to do so when we shifted to online learning. One of my students explained it perfectly, saying, "Things are actually less intimidating online." Students seemed to feel especially comfortable about using the chat function and that was often where most discussions took place. Not only did I notice this, but other students did as well, noting that, "Engaging in the chat box [in class] can also be critical because a lot of students seem to be more comfortable being involved that way. We have very intelligent students who we would never hear a peep from in in person classes, however, when they can communicate easier through text, they share their insights."[3]

However, although some students feel more comfortable contributing via the online chat, these chat boxes can be difficult to navigate. If you find it difficult to have the chat running throughout the class, turn it off at times. For example, if you usually save some time at the end of a section or at the end of class for questions, open the chat then as well. Whether you keep the chat open during the whole class or only for some part of it, controlling the chat is important. Not only can chat conversations sometimes go quickly and the stream of conversation be distracting, it is easy to forget that there is a person on the other side of the computer screen and students can be less professional in a chat than they would be in person. One example of this occurred in my summer Health Law class. Due to a schedule change, I had more time in the 2020 summer session than I had when I taught the class the prior summer; as a result, I decided to add a section discussing abortion. At the time that I created my class plan, it was unclear that we were going to be online in the summer as well. Once the decision was made to shift to online, I debated discussing such a difficult topic online but ultimately decided to keep it on the schedule. During the class discussion, a more conservative student spoke up about his views, which were consistent with Justice Scalia's. Most of the vocal students in the classroom had more liberal views along the lines of Justice Ginsburg. After the conservative student voiced his views in the chat, multiple students immediately began challenging it, often by making emotional points that were not grounded in the law.

When I saw this happening, I interrupted the lecture and immediately took the conversation out of the chat. I started discussing the issues I saw in the chat, including the fact that, although the conservative student's view did not seem to be commonly shared by the class, it was one that Justice Scalia not only wrote on but used law to support. By doing this, I redirected the discussion to one focused on the legal issues that we were discussing and reminded the students of the importance of making points that had sup-

3. For a more in-depth discussion of how online teaching increases participation from quiet students, see Chapter 4: *Understanding and Lifting Up Our Quiet Students: Reimagining "Participation" in the Remote Classroom* by Heidi Brown.

port in the cases we were reading. This diffused the emotionally-charged atmosphere of the chat and ended a situation where a student was made to feel like a target. Having this experience was an important initiation into using the chat effectively. Now if I see a chat discussion that is moving toward incivility or where one student's comments or views appear to be the subject of an inordinate amount of attention, I immediately bring it out of the chat and start talking about it. Very often talking about the chat conversations out loud reminds students not only that their words are being seen but that arguments need to have a legal basis in order to be effective. Monitoring the chat can be a challenge but part of navigating this new method of in-class communication requires trial and error and cutting yourself slack to make mistakes and learn from them.

Despite the need to monitor the chat, I was pleasantly surprised to discover my summer students were talkative, especially since, when I was planning my online Health Law course, I had been terrified that no one would talk. Having only taught the class in person, I knew that part of its success was ensuring student discussion. However, aside from cold-calling students or sitting in painful silence while I waited for someone to say something, neither of which I wanted to do, I had no idea how to get online students talking. I decided to use one of the tools the instructors for my online teaching course had used: discussion questions. However, I neither wanted to give students questions just for the sake of asking questions nor did I want to spend time reviewing them when I was not sure they would help move the class discussion along. I decided to require one short discussion question to be answered in only two to three sentences each week. The questions were all based on the readings for that week. Further, to ward against a series of, "I agree with that" comments, I set the discussions up so that students could not see their classmates' answers until after they posted themselves.

Since the questions involved the readings for the week, it was easy to incorporate those questions and answers into the in-class conversations. By referencing specific comments made, usually without the students' name to ensure no one was made uncomfortable, the class became a conversation even when students did not want to talk. Plus, referencing student comments made students feel like the discussion questions served a purpose and were not separate from the class. This was important as many students noted that discussion questions can often seem like busy work unless they see a direct connection between the questions and the classes for which they are used. Of course, when creating these questions, remember to cut yourself some slack. The questions will not all be perfect and that is okay. The point is to draft questions that get the students thinking so you have a starting place for in-class discussion.

## III. What Do Students Want?

Although I discovered a lot about myself as a teacher while teaching online over the summer, the teacher's experience is only half the equation. The students are the ones who have to listen to us every day, and they certainly have an idea about what makes online learning and teaching effective. When asked what makes an effective teacher, the students' overwhelming response was that a teacher should be engaging. Engaging does not, however, mean that the classroom should be turned into a circus with excitement every moment. According to the students, engagement can be demonstrated in a variety of ways, from starting classes with jokes or movie quotes to merely modulating tone. As one student noted, "The voice of the teacher is everything, basically." Further, when students are learning from home, "[t]eachers are competing for our attention against every distraction that comes up in the comfort of your own home. So a professor speaking in monotone for an hour is not going to be a strong contender for that attention." These comments are a reminder that although professors are engaged by the process of teaching, students are usually just sitting and staring at a computer screen.

Because they are just staring at the screen, the students all noted that it is easier to "zone out" online. My students universally commented that it was hard to pay attention or focus with online classes. Professors who use a PowerPoint or another presentation program help focus by giving students something to look at while also providing a structure for the class. Further, classes that encourage discussion and participation, either via chat or audibly, tend to be more successful from a student perspective. The main consensus is that frequent breaks, either via polls, group work, or class breaks, are important. Students note that, "[i]t is so easy to get distracted and detach from the online learning so I think the more interactive and involved the students are, the better." Given the number of potential distractions for students learning at home, it is more important than ever to encourage student engagement by building breaks or other active learning activities into longer classes. Frequent breaks are necessary for learning[4] and even more so for students who are sitting in front of a computer screen.[5] Studies have shown that even momentary breaks can help students retain more information,[6] so don't be afraid to build breaks in for online classes, even where you would not do so in-person.

For shorter-term breaks, in-class polls can often serve as a way to break up long classes and test students' understanding. Launching a poll or two in the middle of class can be used to determine how well students are connecting with the material and help you learn students' opinions on lecture topics. If you do not want to use a polling feature, you can ask questions out loud and have the students respond in the chat. Polls can even be used at the start of class to help engage the students early. For

---

4. Avraham Z. Cooper & Jeremy B. Richards, *Lectures for Adult Learners: Breaking Old Habits in Graduate Medical Education*, 130 Am. J. of Med. 376, 378 (2017) (using adult learning data showing attention span dwindles after 20 minutes, this article focuses on the importance of active learning to improve information retention in adult learners).

5. Atsunori Ariga & Alejandro Lleras, *Brief and Rare Mental "Breaks" Keep you Focused: Deactivation and Reactivation of Task Goals Preempt Vigilance Decrements*, 118 Cognition 439, 443 (2011) (study participants required to memorize four-digit numbers and recall them after a 40 minute task performed better when the task was briefly interrupted); *The Science of Taking a Break*, OnlineSchools.org, https://www.onlineschools.org/science-of-study-breaks/ (last visited Dec. 8, 2020) (discussing the importance of computer screen and study breaks for college students to aid in information retention).

6. Ariga & Lleras, *supra* note 5, at 443.

example, one colleague likes to start classes with a quick poll asking everything from the students' favorite candy to what season is their favorite.

Group work can also be helpful, not only to encourage interactivity but also because students miss the socialization of in-person classes just as much as we do. In fact, while most students surveyed appreciated it when cameras were not required, others lamented the lack of cameras because it limited that personal interaction. Students agreed that using breakout rooms and small group work can encourage more socialization and participation while also allowing a break in longer classes. However, some students cautioned that breakout rooms can quickly become "silence zones" where students do not talk without encouragement. To counteract this, make sure the group sessions are not too long and that group members are constantly changing.

Finally, the one thing that was the most surprising when I read the students' comments about what makes for an engaging class was how similar they were to comments I had heard for years from students during in-person learning. We have all seen students' eyes glaze over during a particularly long or complicated class, just as we have all seen students pretend to pay attention while they surf the web on their laptops instead. It turns out that online, their struggles and expectations are just as they were in person, albeit now without having to worry that we will see them. Just like in-person learning, not every class will be perfect. So while creating an engaging classroom online is important, realistic expectations are important as well. Some of our classes will not lend themselves to group work or polls or breaks, and we will not be able to foster the kind of engagement we want. When that happens, we need to cut ourselves some slack and plan to do better next time. If you are anything like me, however, you cannot always rely on memory to ensure you do better next time. I create a document and make notes about the class while I am teaching it and save it to a folder for the next time I offer the class. For example, my Health Law notes from Summer 2020 are in a folder marked Summer 2021, when I plan to teach the course next. Leaving myself notes in this way gives me the opportunity to see the document while I am prepping the course, instead of relying on myself to go back to materials from a prior semester.

## IV. Professor Accessibility and the Online Classroom

In addition to familiar in-class expectations, another thing that has not changed with online learning is that students want their professors to be accessible. Unlike in-person learning, where professor accessibility tends to be gauged by time spent in the office, with online learning, this accessibility can take a variety of forms. Some of my colleagues have virtual office hours each week, logging into an online room and waiting for students to come and ask questions. Whether they attend or not, many students like this form of office hours because they know that their professor is available at a set time and in a set place. Plus, for the students who do attend, these virtual office hours provide an opportunity to form a relationship not only with the professor but with other students who attend as well. As is the case during in-person office hours, students often want to listen to other students' questions and hear the answers, so they will remain in an online office hour with their classmates to get more information. Depending on the personalities of the students and the professor, these office hours can be very well attended and informative, even turning into mini-classes at times.

For other professors, myself included, the idea of waiting in an online classroom with the hopes that someone will attend is not particularly palatable. Even though a professor can do other work while waiting for students, when teaching online, it can be difficult to spend yet another hour, or more depending on the time period of the office hours, sitting in front of a screen. For me, although I have set office hours when I am available to my students, scheduling student meetings on an as-needed basis is far more manageable. That is also true if some students are unable to meet during the typical workday due to issues with their schedule. I have scheduled meetings in the evenings and on weekends to accommodate students. So even though I do not sit in an online course room for a set number of office hours a week, my students still know that I am available to them.

In addition to office hours, whatever form they take, more informal meetings can also provide accessibility. For example, a few weeks after our law school first moved online in March 2020, I started hosting online meetings that I called Meltdown Meetings. My thought was that, since we were quarantined in addition to being online, students might need the opportunity to not only socialize with each other but also provide an outlet for frustrations. Originally these meetings were scheduled during the school day, usually over the lunch hour. However, at the request of students, these meetings moved to Friday evenings instead. Although originally designed to be a stopgap measure to connect us until we were back in school in person, as the pandemic wore on, these meetings became part of our weekly routine. While conversations often center around school-related issues, more often than not these Meltdown Meetings function like a Happy Hour. They provide an opportunity for people to get together for some casual conversation at the end of the week, often with a cocktail.

Through word of mouth, enough students are aware of the Meltdown Meetings that I can post the link and reminders on Facebook, and a core group of students and my fellow Legal Writing colleagues attend regularly. The meetings typically last an hour, but attendees are certainly welcome to stay longer and often remain in the room to continue meeting. These informal Meltdown Meetings have provided the students, my colleagues, and me with some much-needed social interaction while at the same time helping us rebuild the community that we lost during the shift to online learning. Additionally, these meetings allow us all to talk about our online experiences and realize that we are not alone when we struggle or when we succeed. That knowledge that we are not alone in our successes and struggles helps all of us cut ourselves some slack.

## V. Becoming the Online Teacher You Want to Be

Regardless of how you teach or how you hold your office hours, when teaching online it is important to stay true to the kind of teacher that you want to be. Shifting from in person to online teaching requires change, but with that change comes a freedom to try new things and become a different kind of teacher. While I was reflecting on my online teaching experiences, I read an article in which Soprano Stephanie Blythe was interviewed by her friend F. Paul Driscoll about embracing reinvention.[7] After a discussion surrounding her career and the inevitable changes that were likely to occur post-COVID-19, she noted,

> Everyone knows how frightening transition is in life—regardless of what they do, regardless of how they identify themselves, regardless of what kind of job they have, where they come from, what language they speak. It doesn't matter. We all go through transitions.... And I think that especially now, this is very real and very poignant for every person on the planet. And the fact that I am saying that out loud to you is terrifying and exhilarating at the same time.[8]

That quote resonated with me because "terrifying and exhilarating" typifies what it is like to be teaching online. Most of us never planned on teaching online since we were happy and comfortable in person. But, as Blythe aptly notes, we are all in the midst of a transition. For those of us who are reinventing ourselves as online teachers, mentors, and scholars, we need to embrace the terrifying and exhilarating nature of that transition. And, of course, cut ourselves some slack.

7. F. Paul Driscoll, *Dynamic Force*, Opera News, Nov. 2020, at 16.

8. *Id.* at 22.

THREE

# Helping Traditional Students Become Effective Online Learners in Both Synchronous and Asynchronous Environments

Rachel Croskery-Roberts*
Queena Mewers**

After reviewing this chapter, readers will be able to do the following:

- Provide students concrete guidance regarding how to maximize learning in the online synchronous classroom (Part One);
- Teach students how to effectively engage with and learn from asynchronous video lectures, while avoiding common pitfalls (Part Two);
- Explain to students the most common categories of time-management issues and how to address them by developing effective time-management strategies (Part Three); and
- Teach students how to create and maintain a home study and learning space that allows them to be as productive and focused as possible (Part Four).

Because most of our students are digital natives, it is tempting to assume that students will encounter little difficulty transitioning from an in-person classroom to an online learning environment. Unfortunately, this assumption is both inaccurate and does a disservice to our students.

It is inaccurate for two reasons. First, even students who have grown up using computers rarely have much experience using technology in the ways we expect

* Associate Dean and Professor of Lawyering Skills, UC Irvine School of Law. Professor Croskery-Roberts has been teaching since 2002 and began teaching online in Spring 2020. She has designed and taught synchronous skills courses and created asynchronous content for online delivery.

** Associate Director of Academic Skills and Lecturer, UC Irvine School of Law. Professor Mewers began law teaching in 2012 and began teaching online in Spring 2020. She has designed and taught synchronous courses and both synchronous and asynchronous academic-skills workshops.

for a rigorous online law school environment. Second, it is our observation that many of the solutions to challenges students face in the online classroom are not, in fact, technology-based. Thus, many digital natives may overlook "obvious" tech-free solutions.

Assuming students can easily transition to an online environment also does a disservice to students because we risk exacerbating inequities among students and increasing the likelihood that students miss the substance as they struggle with the course-delivery system.

Take a student who was in one of our courses that finished online in the Spring 2020 semester. This course, which covers drafting and negotiating contracts, is heavily exercise-based and requires students to spend significant time in small groups. Students access the exercises either in the textbook or on Google Docs. The instructor also uses PowerPoints and other visuals.

The first part of the semester was in-person, and the student performed well. When we transitioned online in March 2020 due to COVID-19, the student turned off her camera and stopped participating. Concerned, I reached out to the student. What I found was a student still eager to learn the course material but wholly overwhelmed with the online course environment. The student was accustomed to taking notes on her laptop and accessing a digital copy of the casebook via her laptop as well. When we added online lectures and in-class activities, all on the same laptop screen, the student found herself struggling to manage course materials and unable to focus on the substantive information. I quickly realized that students need our guidance as educators not just on the substantive course material but also on how to effectively learn in new educational environments.

This chapter addresses key areas where we can help prepare our students to be better online learners. It also addresses issues related to equity and inclusion that may arise when faculty make assumptions about students' access to technology or quiet, safe, private study spaces.

## I. Helping Students Engage Effectively in the Synchronous Online Classroom

One of the most challenging things in transitioning to online education is that many students simply do not know how to learn in this space. Professors jumping directly into the substantive information for their course without ensuring students are equipped to manage the online classroom may find students appear ill-prepared, more confused than usual, and disengaged. However, it pays dividends to spend time guiding students through adjustments to the way they engage in the online classroom. There are three key areas in which students and faculty seem to struggle the most: (1) managing multiple demands on screens; (2) deciding whether to require cameras on and ensuring students remain engaged even when cameras are off; and (3) maximizing time in breakout rooms.

## A. MANAGING MULTIPLE DEMANDS ON A STUDENT'S SCREEN

First, some students may struggle with managing multiple demands on their screen in an online class environment. When overwhelmed, some of these students fail to speak up and just subtly fade out of the classroom, decreasing voluntary participation and appearing unprepared and disengaged when called on. It is true that there are real problems with some students' lack of focus in the online classroom and ability to prepare as diligently for class as they might have done in the in-person classroom. But it would be a mistake to assume that students are simply ill-prepared without first troubleshooting their classroom set-up. Often, students are simply trying to engage with their laptops in the same way they would have done in the in-person classroom. Without minor adjustments, that strategy is unlikely to prove successful, and students may flounder.

In the in-person classroom, many students take notes on laptops.[1] Increasingly, students are also using online textbooks. But everything else—the professor's presentation, any small-group discussion, handouts, and visual learning aids—exists in distinct spaces outside the students' computers. Thus, at most, students are placing two classroom-based demands on their laptops.

In the online classroom, however, everything gravitates to the students' laptops, including watching the lecture, viewing visual aids or handouts the professor provides, engaging in small-group work, accessing online textbooks, and taking notes. At our institution alone, students have reported to faculty, to the Academic Skills Program, and to our Dean of Student Services that they are becoming overwhelmed trying to keep up with everything, missing critical content, and finding themselves anxious and distracted.

To non-digital natives, solutions may seem obvious. But our experience is that this is far less obvious to some digital native students. In an age where students routinely arrive at conferences or office hours without a pen and paper to take notes, it should be unsurprising that simple fixes like handwritten notes may elude some digital natives. Providing students the following explicit guidance can help them engage more effectively in class by reducing the demands on their laptops.

### 1. Rent or purchase print copies of books

First, advise students to rent or purchase print versions of books rather than just online versions. Consider asking your school to explore ways to help students struggling to pay for textbooks; it is a small but critical support you can provide.

---

1. *See, e.g.*, Colleen P. Murphy, et al., *Note-Taking Mode and Academic Performance in Two Law School Courses*, 68 J. Legal Educ. 207, 207, 218–19 (2019).

### 2. In the alternative, use a second screen for the textbook

Second, if students cannot purchase a print version of any textbook (or handout) and only have access to an online version, advise them to use a second screen to display the textbook. One option for doing so is to purchase a second monitor, which can be done for under $100. Alternatively, students can use their smart phone or a tablet to move either the lecture or the textbook onto a second screen.

### 3. Take notes by hand

Finally, consider advising students to take notes by hand. Many students are out of practice in doing this and are used to basically taking dictation on their laptops rather than triaging what information is important. It may help to model good note-taking techniques[2] and to inform students that it may help learning and retention to handwrite notes.[3]

## B. DECIDING WHETHER AND WHEN TO REQUIRE STUDENTS TO HAVE VIDEO CAMERAS ON

The question of whether to require video cameras on in the online classroom is one that professors have debated heavily.[4] Participation in class with cameras on has the potential to greatly enhance the online teaching and learning experience, particularly when engaging in group work and presenting in class. Among other things, live video enables the instructor to assess student understanding more effectively than is possible with video off. Furthermore, keeping cameras on facilitates community building.

Nevertheless, there are significant downsides to requiring students to have their cameras on. First, video takes more bandwidth, so many students (and professors) have problems with freezing screens, choppy audio, and even ejection from the class when they keep their videos on. Thus, it is critical if you do require cameras on that

---

2. *The Cornell Note Taking System*, CORNELL UNIV. LEARNING STRATEGIES CTR., http://lsc.cornell.edu/how-to-study/taking-notes/cornell-note-taking-system/ (last visited Dec. 28, 2020).

3. *See, e.g.*, Pam A. Mueller & Daniel M. Oppenheimer, *The Pen is Mightier Thank the Keyboard: Advantages of Longhand Over Laptop Note Taking*, 25 PSYCH. SCI. 1159, 1159–68 (2014) (errors reported in Pam A. Mueller & Daniel M. Oppenheimer, *The Pen is Mightier Thank the Keyboard: Advantages of Longhand Over Laptop Note Taking: Corrigendum*, 29 PSYCH. SCI. 1565, 1565–68 (2018)). *But see* Kayla Morehead et al., *How Much Mightier is the Pen Than the Keyboard for Note-Taking? A Replication and Extension of Mueller and Oppenheimer*, 31 EDUCATIONAL PSYCH. REV. 753, 753–80 (2019).

4. *See, e.g.*, Madeline Will, *Most Educators Require Kids to Turn Cameras On In Virtual Class Despite Equity Concerns*, EDUCATION WEEK (Oct. 20, 2020), https://www.edweek.org/teaching-learning/most-educators-require-kids-to-turn-cameras-on-in-virtual-class-despite-equity-concerns/2020/10; Tabitha Moses, *5 Reasons to Let Students Keep Their Cameras Off During Zoom Classes*, THE CONVERSATION (Aug. 17, 2020), https://theconversation.com/5-reasons-to-let-students-keep-their-cameras-off-during-zoom-classes-144111; Matt Reed, *Should Showing Faces Be Mandatory*, INSIDE HIGHER ED BLOG: CONFESSIONS OF A COMMUNITY COLLEGE DEAN (May 13, 2020), https://www.insidehighered.com/blogs/confessions-community-college-dean/should-showing-faces-be-mandatory.

you convey that you understand if students must occasionally turn the camera off due to bandwidth issues.

Perhaps an even more significant concern is one related to equity and inclusion. Not all students are similarly situated. Classes may include wealthy students, poor students, students with their own apartments, students sharing a space with multiple other household members, homeless students, students who are caregivers for children or other individuals, students with disabilities (and therefore accommodations that permit them to keep their cameras off), and the list goes on. Requiring cameras on potentially places our most vulnerable students in an uncomfortable (and unfair) learning environment.

On balance, we conclude the most humane policy is a cameras-optional one. Consider why you want students to have cameras on. Are there workarounds? Could you require cameras in only limited situations, ones that you give students ample notice of? For example, could you limit the requirement to times when students are engaging in small-group work or when learning skills that require face-to-face interaction (negotiation simulations, interviews, etc.)? In truth, there are ways to engage students who have their cameras off and ways to help students maintain privacy when they must turn their cameras on.

### 1. Engaging students who have cameras off

For those of us accustomed to gauging student engagement or comprehension by scanning the classroom and looking at students' facial expressions and reactions, it can be unnerving to transition to the online environment, where allowing students to keep cameras off results in teaching to a sea of black boxes. But this, quite frankly, is a professor problem, not a student one. There are ways to both engage students and to assess understanding without seeing their faces.[5] For example, if you are using Zoom or some other similar platform, you can regularly use the polling feature to ask questions that demonstrate whether the class is following the discussion. There are freestanding polling applications as well.[6] Another simple option is to require students to answer in the chat window and then review the chat transcript after class. The chat function is also a really good way to coax more timid students into participating,[7] so consider encouraging or requiring participation via chat in addition to more traditional forms of participation.

---

5. If it feels too impersonal to teach to a window of tiny black boxes, consider requiring students to upload a photo or personalized avatar.

6. *E.g.*, Poll Everywhere, https://www.polleverywhere.com/ (last visited Jan. 8, 2021) (free and paid options); Survey Monkey, https://www.surveymonkey.com/ (last visited Jan. 8, 2021) (free and paid options); Kahoot, https://www.kahoot.com/ (last visited Jan. 8, 2021); Google Forms, https://www.google.com/forms/about/ (free) (last visited Jan. 8, 2021).

7. For a more in-depth treatment on engaging quiet students in online courses, see Chapter 4: *Understanding and Lifting Up Our Quiet Students: Reimagining "Participation" in the Remote Classroom* by Heidi Brown.

### 2. Helping students maintain privacy in a class where cameras must be on

If you determine that there are times when students must have their cameras on, provide them with affordable ways to maintain their privacy and that of their family members or roommates. If the student's laptop can support virtual backgrounds, encourage them to use this option. If a student's laptop is too old to support virtual green screens, an actual physical green screen is necessary. This does not require spending a lot of money. In fact, some solutions are inexpensive enough that you could likely convince your school to provide them for students. For example, a simple piece of green poster board or a green tablecloth purchased from a dollar store and temporarily pinned to a wall will permit students to display a virtual background image of their choice behind them. For students who have enough space and can afford around $60, a simple privacy screen can be found on Amazon and through other retailers. Another solution available with some online platforms is to place students in a virtual scene like a classroom, hiding most of their backgrounds and preserving the "seating."

### 3. Sample camera policies

Regardless of what you decide regarding cameras, clearly set out your policy in the syllabus. Here is sample language for cameras-optional and cameras-required policies.

***Start either policy with this language.*** "Student participation in class with video cameras on has the potential to enhance the online teaching and learning experience. Some of the reasons are as follows. First, as the instructor, I find it easier to assess student understanding when I can see students' facial expressions. Second, having cameras on also facilitates vital community-building and student-engagement aspects of the online classroom."

***Add this language if cameras on not required.*** "Nevertheless, there are legitimate reasons why you might be unwilling or unable to turn on your camera during a synchronous class, including privacy concerns or issues related to bandwidth. Thus, although I encourage you to consider participating with your camera on when possible, [it is not required] [it is only required when you are on-call and during small-group work]. If you choose to participate in class with your camera off, make sure to get my attention either by using the raise-hand feature or the chat function so you are able to remain fully engaged in the class. [If I call on you while your video is off and it is clear you are not actually present, I will count the class as an unexcused absence.]"

***Add this language if cameras on required.*** "In this course, therefore, I require students to have their cameras turned on during all synchronous class sessions and small-group meetings. If you cannot appear on camera for some reason, it is your responsibility to contact me promptly (preferably in advance of the class session) to explain the reason for not having your camera turned on. Unless you have an accommodation of some sort, it is solely my decision whether to grant the requested excuse from appearing on camera."

## C. HELPING STUDENTS EFFECTIVELY ENGAGE IN BREAKOUT SESSIONS IN A SYNCHRONOUS CLASS SESSION

Breakout rooms provide an excellent opportunity for student engagement and small-group exercises. But to be effective, the exercises must be structured properly, and the students may need some assistance in how to use the rooms. First, you want to ensure that they know how to access relevant handouts or exercises while in breakout rooms. Second, teach them how to watch for announcements, comments, or visits from the professor while in a breakout room. Third, provide students with ways to ask for help while engaging in online small-group work. Finally, do not assume that students will know how to effectively manage their time in a breakout room. Because you cannot circle the room in the same way you might in the in-person classroom, you may have to give much more explicit guidance regarding your expectations for small-group sessions.

### 1. Ensure students know how to access relevant handouts or materials while in breakout rooms

One unfortunate feature of breakout rooms is that any PowerPoint or other visual available in the main class session disappears when students join breakout rooms. Thus, to ensure your students have a seamless experience in small-group sessions requiring access to documents, you should either (a) share PowerPoints or other necessary documents before class; or (b) post links in the chat window to any material (like Google Docs) that students need to access during the breakout sessions.

### 2. Teach students to watch for announcements, comments, or visits from the professor while in breakout rooms

Depending upon the platform you use, you may be able to broadcast announcements or to visit individual breakout rooms to see how students are doing and whether they need any help. For example, on Zoom, you can broadcast time warnings, questions, or instructions that will appear in each room. You can also drop in on various rooms, simulating walking around the in-person classroom. Warn students that you will be doing this. Unlike in the in-person classroom where they can see you coming, you will simply appear out of nowhere. We have found students are startled by this and sometimes do not even notice the professor's presence if they are working without the panel of participants maximized.

Another way to drop in on students is to have them work on a shared document (like Google Docs) in the small group, and then you can communicate by typing into each document rather than jumping into various breakout rooms. This also allows you to monitor progress and see where various groups are getting stuck. We have found that students find this method of communication quite helpful, perhaps more so than visiting the breakout room.

### 3. Teach students methods for asking for help from the professor while in breakout rooms

When students are working on a small-group assignment during class and have a question, they can simply raise their hands. This is not so with breakout rooms. Familiarize yourself with the options in the platform your school uses. On Zoom, for example, students can click on an "ask for help" button, and it will send a note to you in the main room. For platforms that do not have this feature, simply include in your instructions for small group work that students should drop back into the main room if they have questions.

### 4. Provide students with necessary guidance to ensure effective use of time in breakout rooms

Do not assume that students will manage their time as effectively in breakout sessions as they do in small groups in person. First, many may be craving human interaction, so it may make sense to build in a minute or two (and let them know you have done so) to allow them to informally chat. Second, they may need extra time to access relevant materials and to get settled. Finally, they may struggle with what roles each member of the group should play.

To ensure students effectively engage in a breakout session, give students explicit instructions about how to structure their time. If you are giving them several questions to work on, give them guidance as to precisely how long to spend on each question. Moreover, tell groups to assign everyone a role at the outset. Tell students they must have at least one person designated to take notes (creating Google Docs for this is a great way for you to track their progress later) and another to report out to the class after the session ends. If it is a large group or a contentious topic, consider also assigning someone the role of facilitator to make sure that the discussion remains respectful and that everyone has a chance to participate.

## II. Helping Students Learn Effectively from Asynchronous Lecture Videos

Another challenge that online students frequently face is figuring out how to learn effectively from watching asynchronous lecture videos. This is a critical skill that law students must master because asynchronous lecture videos are a common feature of many online courses as well as live or blended courses using a flipped classroom model.

Two of the most common reasons why students find it difficult to learn from watching asynchronous lecture videos are that (1) it is a passive activity; and (2) students may feel they do not need to pay close attention to these videos because they can always re-watch the recording later. Above all, students struggle with learning from asynchronous lecture videos for the same reason they struggle with learning from live lectures—i.e., they mistakenly believe that learning primarily occurs from their intake of information during a lecture.[8] Faculty can effectively teach students to better engage with asynchronous video content and persuasively explain to students that actual learning depends not just on watching a lecture, but on what students themselves *do* with the information *conveyed* in that lecture.

## A. TEACH STUDENTS TO ACTIVELY ENGAGE WITH THE CONTENT BOTH DURING AND AFTER WATCHING

In an ideal world, all asynchronous lecture videos tackle content that is riveting, engage students using an interactive format, and appeal to all students' senses with high-production value. But the reality is that many asynchronous lecture videos feature just a talking head, with or without slides as a simple visual aid. This type of content naturally leads students to treat watching lecture videos as, at best, a passive learning activity. At worst, students watch lecture videos the same way they watch television shows or random YouTube videos—barely paying attention and often while multitasking.

Faculty should remind students to treat asynchronous lecture videos like a live, in-person lecture for maximum effect. Instruct students to avoid watching lecture videos while lying in bed or leaving the video running in the background while doing other activities like exercising or household chores. Instead, advise students to set up an appropriate learning environment that creates positive cues that prompt their brains to treat the lecture video as a serious learning activity. For example, students should place their computer screen on a desk or table and sit upright; wear real clothes rather than pajamas; take action to avoid distractions; and get ready to take notes, preferably using pen and paper. If additional external motivation is desirable, students can also watch the video at the same time as a classmate and then schedule a meeting to review or discuss the material together.

During the lecture itself, students should avoid transcribing everything, just like during a live lecture. Instead, faculty should advise students to focus on identifying, processing, and summarizing the most important points. Remind students that they ultimately engage more deeply with the content when they work to differentiate between critical and non-critical information; paraphrase the information in their own words; and impose structure to organize the information and explain the relationships between various concepts (including how the newly learned information connects to previously learned information). Even if students are not able to do this while the

8. Celeste Pilegard, *So Your Classes Are All Online Now: 3 Keys to Success*, YouTube (March 26, 2020), https://www.youtube.com/watch?v=1IIUVU-d1DM&t (explaining, at 2:36, the "illusion of fluency" that occurs when watching lecture videos); *see also* Henk G. Schmidt et al., *On the Use and Misuse of Lectures in Higher Education*, 1 Health Profs. Educ. 12, 14 (2015) (explaining that lectures are only partially effective for student learning because of the "information transmission fallacy"); Diane F. Halpern & Milton D. Hakel, *Applying the Science of Learning to the University and Beyond: Teaching for Long-Term Retention and Transfer*, Change: The Mag. of Higher Learning, Jul./Aug. 2003, at 36, 40 (explaining that lectures work badly for fostering deep learning or understanding).

professor is actively speaking, students can either pause the video to complete these thought processes in the moment (which is a real benefit of asynchronous lecture videos compared to live lectures) or wait until afterwards to meaningfully review and synthesize their notes.

Faculty should also encourage students to ask questions and engage in class discussions about content covered in asynchronous lecture videos, such as via an online discussion forum, during group or individual office hours, or through writing short reflection papers or follow-up assignments. Even though the video is pre-recorded, students should still generate and note questions they have about the material to follow up on later. Actively questioning, analyzing, or evaluating the material will help students learn the material better than just passively listening to absorb the information.

One active note-taking method that can help students better engage with the content both during and after a lecture is the Cornell System, which instructs students to take notes on a piece of paper that is divided into three sections: (1) the largest section for note-taking (in the top two-thirds of the page, on the right side); (2) a narrower column for writing down keywords, questions, or cues that can be used for recall later (in the top two-thirds of the page, on the left side); and (3) a small section for summarizing the key points (in the bottom one-third of the page, spanning across the whole page).[9] Faculty can advise students to use the note-taking section to record information during lecture; then, after class, review those notes and write down in the left-side column questions for office hours or for later self-testing (like flashcards, which help the student more actively review the material). Then, after the student has fully internalized the material, the student can use the bottom section to reflect upon and summarize the main takeaways from the lesson. Using this method of note-taking not only helps students record and make notes but also builds in the opportunity for students to interact with and reflect upon their notes for more effective learning.

### B. ADVISE STUDENTS TO AVOID RE-WATCHING VIDEOS LATER TO LEARN OR REVIEW MATERIAL, AS OTHER STRATEGIES RESULT IN MORE EFFICIENT AND EFFECTIVE LEARNING

As noted above, one benefit of asynchronous lecture videos is the ability to pause, rewind, and re-watch so students can catch a point that was discussed too quickly or clear up a muddy point. While there is certainly value in re-watching portions of a video in the moment for these purposes, students should not rely on the ability to re-watch a video to justify not fully focusing on the video the first time through.

Re-watching videos in full is typically a far more time-intensive activity than reviewing one's written notes summarizing the most important points from the video; this is because most people can read faster than a person can speak. It is also much harder to visualize the overall structure or organization of a lecture video's content

9. *The Cornell Note Taking System*, *supra* note 2.

while the video is playing and to navigate to exactly the right spot that addresses points needing further review. Faculty can demonstrate these points by engaging in the following exercise with students: First, provide students with a short, written handout that summarizes a video's content in an organized fashion (e.g., using headings and hierarchical bullet points or even a flowchart). Then, ask students to compare how long it takes them to read the handout versus re-watching the video. Also, ask students whether the video format or the handout format gives them a better big-picture overview of how different points relate to one another, as well as whether the video or handout format allows students to more quickly jump directly to a specific point for additional review.

After the exercise, faculty should encourage students to create their own organized summaries of each video's content, which will not only produce a more user-friendly resource for later reviewing or studying the substantive course content but also require students to engage in the thinking processes that help them to truly learn and understand the material.

Faculty can also help students understand the illusion of fluency that can come from simply re-watching a lecture video. Students may mistakenly believe that they know the material just because they have seen the video before and the material is familiar. But re-watching the professor successfully explain a concept is not the same as the student being able to successfully explain the concept using his or her own words or, more importantly, apply the concept to solve a new problem, which is what the student will likely need to be able to do on an exam or other major graded project. Therefore, faculty should encourage—or perhaps even require—students to engage in more effective and active learning strategies, such as creating portions of course outlines or working through practice problems. Providing students with feedback on these activities will also help students better identify what they think they know versus what they actually know.

## III. Helping Students with Effective Time Management for Successful Online Learning

Given the amount of challenging work and effort law school requires, students must have excellent time-management skills to succeed in law school generally. This is even more true for students who are working full- or part-time or have other significant obligations like family caretaking. These students also frequently opt for asynchronous online programs, which require even better time-management and self-regulated learning skills because of the flexibility such programs offer. Without proper time management, online learning can also create challenges such as more acute feelings of isolation and burnout.[10]

---

10. *See* Janette R. Hill, *Overcoming Obstacles and Creating Connections: Community Building in Web-Based Learning Environments*, J. of Computing in Higher Educ., Sept. 2002, at 67, 72–73; Nour Mheidly

While some students may already be familiar with basic time-management strategies like creating a schedule, scheduling backwards from deadlines,[11] setting "S.M.A.R.T. Goals,"[12] or using the Pomodoro Technique®[13] (all discussed below), some students may arrive at law school without any formal training on time management. Even if they have heard of or practiced some of these techniques, they may not know when precisely to use which technique(s) to best address the different kinds of time-management issues that will arise.

As with effectively implementing any strategy to solve any problem, students must first correctly identify the root cause of any time-management issues they are struggling with before they can select the "right" strategies to address those specific issues. Faculty can help guide students in selecting the appropriate strategies by first explaining the following major categories of common time-management issues:

- Difficulty with keeping track of important dates and assignment deadlines, including building in sufficient time to adequately prepare;
- Uncertainty about how to create a realistic schedule, including how much time to allocate to each task;
- Inability to stick to a created schedule due to external or internal factors, including but not limited to the following:
    - Feeling overwhelmed by the amount of work required, and not knowing where to start or how to prioritize;
    - Having trouble staying focused because of external or internal distractions; and
    - Finding insufficient time to complete everything on one's to-do list; and
- Burnout resulting in decreased productivity.

Once students have identified the specific issue or issues they are facing, faculty can then offer more targeted advice with specific recommended strategies.

---

et al., *Coping with Stress and Burnout Associated with Telecommunication and Online Learning*, FRONTIERS IN PUB. HEALTH (Nov. 11, 2020), at 2–3, 5, https://doi.org/10.3389/fpubh.2020.574969.

11. *E.g.*, MICHAEL HUNTER SCHWARTZ & PAULA J. MANNING, EXPERT LEARNING FOR LAW STUDENTS 27 (3d ed. 2018).

12. *E.g.*, K. Blaine Lawlor & Martin J. Hornyak, *Smart Goals: How the Application of Smart Goals Can Contribute to Achievement of Student Learning Outcomes,* 39 DEV. IN BUS. SIMULATION & EXPERIENTIAL LEARNING 259, 259–67 (2012).

13. THE POMODORO TECHNIQUE®, https://francescocirillo.com/pages/pomodoro-technique (last visited Dec. 28, 2020).

### A. DIFFICULTY WITH KEEPING TRACK OF IMPORTANT DATES AND ASSIGNMENT DEADLINES, INCLUDING BUILDING IN SUFFICIENT TIME TO ADEQUATELY PREPARE

Advise students to keep a paper or digital calendar, whichever better suits their lifestyle. Paper calendars are typically easier to use when inputting events or adding annotations, while digital calendars provide easier access across multiple devices and can also generate pop-up reminders. Students should also consider which calendar "views" or styles to use for different purposes—e.g., semester-long or monthly view (good for longer-term or big-picture review of major events and deadlines), weekly view (good for shorter-term planning), or daily view (good for hour-by-hour scheduling). Using color-coding or different font styles or icons may also be beneficial.

Students should start by inputting all fixed-time commitments like class times, work hours, and dinnertime with children, as well as all fixed-date deadlines for assignments and exams, consulting their course syllabi and other relevant sources.

Then, explicitly instruct students to add in designated time for preparation work in advance of any deadlines. For each class, this would include prep time for completing any reading or other tasks assigned by the professor as well as reviewing notes. For major writing assignments, this would include time for researching, drafting, revising, editing, and proofreading. For exams, this would include time for reviewing notes, outlining, and doing practice questions. Adding in designated time for preparation involves working backwards from deadlines. Students may struggle with identifying all the individual tasks that must be completed as part of a larger project; therefore, faculty can be especially helpful in guiding students through this process of breaking down a larger project into smaller chunks, perhaps even by providing specific interim deadlines to help students better manage their work process and time allocations.

### B. UNCERTAINTY ABOUT HOW TO CREATE A REALISTIC SCHEDULE, INCLUDING HOW MUCH TIME TO ALLOCATE TO EACH TASK

When we have not done something before, it is hard to estimate how long it will take us to do that thing. For this reason, students may struggle with creating a schedule in the first place—and then they may also struggle with successfully following or implementing that schedule due to frequently underestimating and/or overestimating the amount of time required to complete certain tasks.[14] In our experience, students then tend to stop planning schedules when those schedules "don't work" because students feel like planning becomes a waste of time.

---

14. *See* Christine P. Bartholemew, *Time: An Empirical Analysis of Law Student Time Management Deficiencies*, 81 U. Cin. L. Rev. 897, 933–34, 946 (2013).

Faculty can be especially helpful here by offering estimates for how long different study tasks or assignments should take. Whenever possible, base your estimates on reports from actual students on how long it takes to complete the task; remember that students are less experienced than you are at legal reading, analysis, and writing, so the average student likely requires more time than you might expect to complete a "satisfactory" assignment. Students can also become better estimators of their own time by tracking how long it actually takes them to perform different types of study tasks, including by using time-tracking applications.[15]

Faculty can also help students determine how much time is appropriate to allocate to each task by reminding students to consider the relative importance or weight of different assignments. This is true not only for tasks associated with coursework but also for extracurricular tasks, as students also may not realize the consequences that can occur when they miss important extracurricular deadlines (like submitting clerkship applications at the earliest opportunity).

### C. INABILITY TO STICK TO A CREATED SCHEDULE DUE TO EXTERNAL OR INTERNAL FACTORS

Even with the best of intentions, students may not be able to follow or implement a pre-planned schedule because of external factors like family emergencies or internal factors like depression or anxiety. Faculty should not feel like they need to solve, or have the expertise to solve, all the students' potential problems; instead, faculty should be familiar with and freely refer students to available on- and off-campus resources as appropriate.

That said, below are three common reasons why students may have trouble sticking to a created schedule that can be addressed by application of common time-management techniques or strategies.

#### 1. Feeling overwhelmed by the amount of work required and not knowing where to start or how to prioritize

Students may feel overwhelmed by the amount of law school work they have to complete when they do not take the time to pre-plan a study schedule—i.e., identify all the tasks that must be completed and block off time to complete each task. To assure ourselves that we *can* do it all, we typically need to be able to visualize everything that needs to be done and when specifically we can do those things. That's why, as discussed above, faculty should encourage students to keep a calendar, break up larger projects into smaller chunks, and schedule backwards from deadlines to input prep time for completing each task.

15. *E.g.*, TOGGL TRACK, https://toggl.com/track/ (last visited Jan. 7, 2021).

Even the project of creating a study schedule can be made less overwhelming by breaking it down into smaller, more manageable chunks or steps.[16] For example, students may find it helpful to initially create just an overall to-do list for each class or project. Then, as a separate step, they should prioritize[17] or otherwise logically order the individual tasks on each to-do list so students know exactly where to start and what to do next. Third, as another separate step, students should estimate how long each task should or will take before completing the final step, which is to transfer each task from the to-do lists to their main calendar by assigning each task a specific time block based on the estimates. Again, faculty can use their experience to help guide students on each step or even provide students with checklists and interim deadlines for larger assignments.

Faculty should also advise students to be as specific as possible when describing the tasks added to their calendars. Avoid generalities like "study for Torts"—instead, specify the study tasks to be performed during the designated study period (e.g., "review notes from Classes 9 and 10, and update outline on causation"). For reading assignments, include the page numbers. Identifying specific study tasks to be performed during each time block on their calendar will make it much easier for students to simply follow or implement their study plan because it obviates any further decision-making processes that could delay or distract students right when they should just get started.

For students who tend to procrastinate when they are feeling overwhelmed, oftentimes the best solution is to force or trick themselves into just getting started. Advising students to apply the Pomodoro Technique® can help here:[18] Set a timer[19] for 25 or so minutes, which helps to create a sense of urgency; 25 minutes is also a short enough period of time to seem doable to the student. Assign a manageable[20] task to start with,

---

16. *See, e.g.*, SCHWARTZ & MANNING, *supra* note 11, at 18–22, 24–27; Albert Bandura & Dale H. Schunk, *Cultivating Competence, Self-Efficacy, and Intrinsic Interest Through Proximal Self-Motivation*, 41 J. OF PERSONALITY & SOC. PSYCHOL. 586, 586–98 (1981).

17. This may be a good time to teach students about prioritizing tasks based on the "Eisenhower Decision Matrix," invented by President Dwight D. Eisenhower. The matrix is comprised of two axes (urgency and importance), creating four quadrants: (1) important and urgent (which should be done first); (2) important but not urgent (which should be scheduled for later completion); (3) urgent but not important (which should be delegated to someone else to do, if possible); and (4) neither urgent nor important (which should be disregarded). *See, e.g.*, Drake Baer, *Dwight Eisenhower Nailed a Major Insight About Productivity*, BUS. INSIDER (Apr. 10, 2014), https://www.businessinsider.com/dwight-eisenhower-nailed-a-major-insight-about-productivity-2014-4.

18. The Pomodoro Technique®, developed by Francesco Cirillo, uses a timer to break down work into 25-minute intervals or "pomodoros." Four pomodoros make up a set. Each pomodoro is followed by a break—i.e., a five-minute break follows each of the first three pomodoros in a set, while a longer 15- to 30-minute break occurs after the fourth pomodoro. THE POMODORO TECHNIQUE®, *supra* note 13.

19. *E.g.*, TOMATO TIMER, https://www.tomatotimerapp.com/ (last visited Jan. 7, 2021); POMODOR, https://pomodor.app/timer (last visited Jan. 7, 2021).

20. This may be a good time to teach students about setting "S.M.A.R.T. Goals" that are clear and reachable. The acronym was first used by George T. Doran and is now known to commonly stand for "specific," "measurable," "achievable," "relevant," and "time-bound." *See* Lawlor & Hornyak, *supra* note 12, at 260–61.

like reviewing one class session's worth of reading and lecture notes, pulling out all the relevant black-letter rules, and typing them into a separate document. Then, after a five-minute break, set another 25-minute timer, and tackle the next logical task, such as listing out concrete examples of how this rule works by writing short, one- to three-line summaries of relevant cases or hypotheticals, as well as key policies implicated. Voilà, you completed part of an outline!

### 2. Trouble staying focused because of external or internal distractions

Distractions can be external or internal. Students may be familiar with how to minimize external *digital* distractions like putting phones out of reach, turning off notifications on phones and computers, and downloading applications to assist.[21] But students may forget about non-digital or *physical* external distractions like family members, roommates, friends, or pets interrupting a study session. Remind students to communicate with their family and friends by sending out a copy of their study schedule or physically hanging up a "do not disturb" sign near their workspace. Doing so can also result in family and friends helping to hold the student accountable for staying focused on studying.

Even if students recognize the need to minimize external distractions, students may overlook *internal* distractions—i.e., the students' own thoughts and emotions. These can include the students' thoughts about other tasks they need to accomplish, important or tangential questions they want to research about the material they're studying, or feelings of fear or inadequacy. One common strategy for managing these thoughts and emotions[22] during class or a study session is to acknowledge them by writing them down on a sticky note, but then resolving to deal with them later so that they do not interrupt the current task. For this reason, faculty can suggest to students to always keep a small pad of sticky notes nearby.

Faculty should also teach students about the myth or pitfalls of multitasking—i.e., when you try to do two tasks at once, you are really doing neither; after all, you are simply reducing the amount of attention paid to each task, so you end up doing both tasks more slowly and less well.[23] Therefore, advise students that the better practice is to focus their undivided attention on just one task at a time, allowing them to accomplish it more efficiently and effectively.

---

21. *E.g.*, FocalFilter, https://www.focalfilter.com/ (last visited Jan. 7, 2021); SelfControl, https://selfcontrolapp.com/ (last visited Jan. 7, 2021); StayFocusd, https://chrome.google.com/webstore/detail/stayfocusd/laankejkbhbdhmipfmgcngdelahlfoji?hl=en (last visited Jan. 7, 2021); LeechBlock, https://www.proginosko.com/leechblock/ (last visited Jan. 7, 2021); AppBlock, https://www.appblock.app/ (last visited Jan. 7, 2021).

22. Faculty should refer students with more serious forms of anxiety or depression to other expert resources, including the Dean of Students, the student health center, or another medical professional.

23. *See* Sanjay Gupta, *Your Brain on Multitasking*, CNN Health (Aug. 1, 2016), https://www.cnn.com/2015/04/09/health/your-brain-multitasking/index.html.

3. Insufficient time to complete everything on one's to-do list

There are many reasons why a student may not actually have enough time to complete everything on their to-do list.[24] There are two reasons that can be addressed with time-management techniques or strategies.

First, some students may be overextending themselves by agreeing to too many commitments. Faculty can remind these students that there is a finite amount of time each week (168 hours) and encourage students to calculate exactly how many hours they really have "leftover" for different types of activities. Here is an example:

| **168 hours** | |
|---|---|
| -48 hours | minimum for 16 units of course work (based on ABA Standard 310) |
| - 5 hours | or so for other law school obligations (e.g., attending workshops) |
| -56 hours | for sleeping (at 8 hours/day) |
| - 7 hours | for exercise or other wellness activities (at 1 hour/day) |
| - 21 hours | for basic life upkeep (e.g., eating, showering, chores, etc.) |
| **31 hours** | left for family/friends, hobbies, extracurricular activities, pro bono, etc. |

Second, some students may also fall victim to perfectionism, spending more time than necessary on a task. Here again, faculty can be especially helpful by providing time estimates to help students better determine how much time they should be spending on different study tasks or assignments. Faculty can also remind students about Parkinson's Law: work expands to fill the time allotted.[25] Therefore, a critical part of creating an effective study schedule is setting time limits for each task and sticking to those limits; otherwise, students will not be able to accomplish *all* of the tasks on their to-do list. Applying the Pomodoro Technique® and setting a physical timer or alarm can also help students implement appropriate time limits.

## D. BURNOUT RESULTING IN DECREASED PRODUCTIVITY

Burnout occurs when we do not balance our work obligations (including schoolwork) with our personal wellbeing. When students plan out their weekly or daily schedules, advise them to take care to schedule "downtime" to unwind and take care

---

24. For example, some students may be strapped for time because they are using ineffective or inefficient study strategies; or they may be underprepared for law school and lack some foundational skills in reading, critical thinking, or writing. Addressing these types of issues is beyond the scope of this chapter. Whenever possible, faculty should strive to work one-on-one with these students to help them build their skills, and faculty should also refer these students to other available resources for additional help (e.g., academic support programs).

25. Cyril Northcote Parkinson, *Parkinson's Law*, Economist (Nov. 19, 1955), https://www.economist.com/news/1955/11/19/parkinsons-law.

of themselves physically, mentally, and emotionally. Faculty can help highlight the importance of self-care and wellness by explicitly discussing these topics with their students.

The Pomodoro Technique® can also help combat burnout and productivity decreases by incorporating both (1) a short five-minute break after every interval of 25 minutes of focused work; and (2) a longer 15- to 30-minute break after every four intervals of focused work.[26] Breaks are also particularly important in an online learning environment to help reduce "Zoom fatigue," avoid eyestrain, and reduce feelings of isolation from spending too much time just sitting in front of a computer screen.[27]

## IV. Helping Students Set Up a Workspace for Successful Online Learning

Finally, it is important to help students create a home workspace or find an appropriate study space that is as ideal as possible for studying and for attending class. In doing this, we must not forget issues related to equity and inclusion that arise when faculty assume all students have access to quiet, safe, private study spaces.

The in-person classroom is designed to optimize learning. Typically, college-level classrooms are carefully planned spaces, with everything from room organization that ensures all students can easily view the professor and any visual aids, to desk set-ups that provide ergonomic seating, ample space to lay out materials, easy and reliable Wi-Fi access, and power outlets for laptops. Moreover, in the in-person classroom, there are few distractions. It is a dedicated educational space.

In the online classroom, however, students are learning from a wide variety of locations with varying levels of privacy and unequal access to technology. Thus, while some students have access to a quiet, dedicated study space, others are learning in nearly impossible situations, setting up in their car outside a restaurant to borrow Wi-Fi, sitting in closets for the only quiet space in their homes, or sharing a study space with multiple family members or roommates. Without taking this into account and offering solutions for students, professors may find that student performance levels relate more to income and privilege than to ability or willingness to learn the material.

Thus, advice we give students should not assume privilege. Of course, it makes sense to give routine advice for those who have a single bedroom with a door that closes. But when providing feedback about workspace functionality, it is equally important to normalize the fact that many do not have such accommodations.

For those students who are working in the same place in which they sleep, one of the best pieces of advice to give is to create as much of a divide between relaxation

---

26. The Pomodoro Technique®, *supra* note 13.

27. *See* Nour Mheidly et al., *supra* note 10, at 3, 5, https://doi.org/10.3389/fpubh.2020.574969; *Eyestrain,* Mayo Clinic, https://www.mayoclinic.org/diseases-conditions/eyestrain/diagnosis-treatment/drc-20372403 (last visited Dec. 28, 2020).

space and study space. Advise students to avoid attending class or studying in the same place in which they relax, sleep, or watch television. (This means no setting up in bed!) If they have access to a space in which they can set up class or study materials regularly (rather than having to clean up materials after each class or study session), advise them to keep that space organized and clean so they can easily find things they need. Suggest that they keep a notebook and a pen or pencil for taking notes in addition to their laptops.

Some students, however, may be studying or attending class in much less ideal settings. Rather than asking students to self-identify before you give advice for such scenarios, just provide advice upfront for various situations. So, for example, one thing professors might suggest is that students who have to move their study space around a lot prepare a small kit of the materials they regularly need (pen, paper, sticky notes, mini-stapler, etc.) in an accordion folder or plastic bag that they can easily grab and transport with them wherever they might be setting up for the day. Acknowledge upfront that you know many may be studying in cramped spaces with little privacy. Allow cameras off whenever possible so that students do not have to worry about focusing in class while hiding an embarrassing work environment. Do just a bit of research and provide them with suggestions of quiet free locations in your community or on campus with Wi-Fi access. If they are located outside the community, just make the suggestions more general (public libraries, coffee shops with outdoor seating, etc.). Identify inexpensive noise-cancelling headphones that students might be able to purchase. If students can use financial aid for required items, consider requiring them for class, or find out whether your university will provide equipment for those who can demonstrate need.

Taking even a little time to craft such advice for students will help them be better learners and will help equalize the playing field. As educators, we want to believe that we are testing mastery of material. Helping students find appropriate study and learning spaces regardless of their financial situation is critical to ensure that we are testing what we mean to be testing.

FOUR

# Understanding and Lifting Up Our Quiet Students: Reimagining "Participation" in the Remote Classroom

Heidi K. Brown*

After reviewing this chapter, readers will be able to:

- Better understand the role of positive quietude in our students and classrooms;
- Discern differences among introverted, shy, and socially anxious students;
- Consider how the remote classroom increases the number of communication modalities for naturally quiet students;
- Activate more communication modalities in the classroom; and
- Enhance inclusivity and belonging in classroom dialogue.

Midway through pandemic lockdown in New York City, my television was tuned to CNN one Saturday morning while I exercised in my kitchen. My ears perked up at hearing an elementary school principal in Washington, D.C.—Dr. Sundai Riggins—relay in an interview how students who were not talkative in in-person classes were expressing themselves more frequently in distance learning. I thought, *Wow, I wish every educator in the country (especially law professors) could hear that message!* Remote learning offers a prime opportunity to change our definition of "participation" in the classroom and help our quiet students amplify their voices *authentically.* Let's grow as teachers, let go of outdated practices, and make our classrooms more inclusive.

---

* Professor of Law, Brooklyn Law School. Professor Brown began law teaching in 2008 and began teaching courses online in 2020. She has designed and taught synchronous classes (with several asynchronous classes designated within the course progression).

As an introvert and someone who has grappled with public speaking anxiety throughout a 30-year arc from law student to construction litigator to law professor, I often falter when cold-called in classrooms and meetings, though I am unfailingly substantively prepared. I have always needed time to reflect on and process complex principles before speaking aloud. I do not thrive when put on-the-spot. Even as a tenured law professor now, I blush and my heart races when I am quizzed in public settings (faculty meetings, for example). This does not mean I am unprepared or disengaged, or "just need to be pushed out of my comfort zone." I care deeply about legal education and the profession, and I have been propelling myself into uncomfortable experiences and studying my performance anxieties for years now. In researching my books, *The Introverted Lawyer*[1] and *Untangling Fear in Lawyering*,[2] I learned that I—like many of our naturally quiet students—need a pause for contemplation before jumping into the fray. And then, when I do speak, it is because I have something to say, and I have thought it through. I never speak just for the sake of speaking.

When the law school where I teach shifted to "emergency remote learning" in March 2020, I observed quiet students embracing virtual communication tools to contribute insights more frequently than they had in our in-person classroom. Students who rarely raised their hands in our in-person classroom began activating the "raise hand" feature on Zoom, enabling their participation without having to interrupt their classmates or me to be heard. They also posed and answered questions in the "chat" function, expressing their ideas in writing. Following my quiet students' lead, I began using those electronic tools in Zoom meetings, noticing heightened comfort in articulating my thoughts in writing, not having to interrupt multiple competing voices to be heard.

As we evolve as educators in online spaces, let's seek to set aside "traditional" models of teaching and offer more "modalities" for student participation. The end result will be more inclusive classrooms where all voices are heard—by choice rather than by pressure—and more students can enjoy and thrive in the learning process.

## I. Remote Learning Can Increase Quiet Students' Participation

In-person classrooms can be over-stimulating, chaotic, unpredictable, and disruptive for quiet students who need time to think, process, and reflect on substantive material before sharing ideas aloud. Multiple competing stimuli, constant interruption of thought flow, social pressures, and perceived enhanced scrutiny by peers and teachers

1. Heidi K. Brown, The Introverted Lawyer: A Seven-Step Journey Toward Authentically Empowered Advocacy (2017).

2. Heidi K. Brown, Untangling Fear in Lawyering: A Four-Step Journey Toward Powerful Advocacy (2019).

in in-person classrooms can pose challenges for introverted, shy, or socially anxious students (three different categories that often are conflated).

Early in the pandemic, teachers at various levels of education anecdotally described an uptick in participation from quiet students in distance learning. Instructional coach, Angela Watson, asked teachers to share observations about remote learning on her Facebook page.[3] Her follow-up blog post relayed that "[q]uiet and shy kids are more likely to ask questions and participate."[4] One teacher reported, "I've noticed my quiet students are starting to shine. They are participating in Zoom. They are asking questions. They are offering ideas."[5] Another relayed that "[k]ids who might not ask questions in class are messaging me with their questions."[6]

Sari Beth Rosenberg, an award-winning U.S. History teacher at a public high school in New York City, remarked on an increase in her quiet students' participation, by highlighting that "shy kids actually want to share."[7] She observed:

> Students who rarely chimed in when we had class discussions in the physical classroom have been more communicative in online classes. They use the chat feature... to share their thoughts. A lot of times, I mistakenly assumed that the quiet students were just not interested in participating. This online learning experience has made me realize that some students prefer to write down their thoughts and might be too shy or uncomfortable to say them out loud in class. Sometimes they even email me after class or throughout the day with questions about the work.[8]

Similarly, Professor John Watkins, who teaches English at the University of Minnesota, noted that "[s]hy students seemed to have an easier time speaking up online than in a crowded lecture hall."[9] Barbara Gartner, an English Language Learner specialist at Brooklyn Law School, indicated in an email to me that one international student felt more empowered in the Zoom classroom than in "the big lecture hall."[10] The student confided that she could hear and understand the professor better, and she "felt freer to ask questions, since other students weren't turning around to look at her."[11] *The New*

---

3. Angela Watson, *Some Parts of Teaching Are BETTER with Remote Learning. Here's How to Leverage That*, Angela Watson, Cornerstone for Teachers (Apr. 19, 2020), https://thecornerstoneforteachers.com/truth-for-teachers-podcast/benefits-teaching-remotely/.

4. *Id.*

5. *Id.*

6. *Id.*

7. Sari Beth Rosenberg, *Teaching in the Age of Coronavirus: Week 4—Spring Break*, PBS NewsHour Extra (Apr. 24, 2020), https://www.pbs.org/newshour/extra/2020/04/teaching-in-the-age-of-coronavirus-week-4-spring-break/.

8. *Id.*

9. *CLA Recreates the "Classroom" During COVID-19*, U. Minn. C. Liberal Arts (May 13, 2020), https://cla.umn.edu/news-events/story/cla-recreates-classroom-during-covid-19.

10. E-mail from Barbara Gartner to Heidi K. Brown (May 5, 2020, 1:16 p.m.) (on file with author).

11. *Id.*

*York Times* reported, "Introverts who are the last to volunteer an answer in class even when they know it, are now making themselves heard."[12]

Traditional approaches toward mandating and measuring class "participation" underserve our quiet students. Remote education invites us to adjust our understanding and definition of "engagement," activating and valuing different communication modalities. If we construct alternate pathways for quiet students to amplify their voices *authentically*, we (and our more loquacious students) will reap the vast benefits of our quiet students' intellectual contributions.

## II. Student Silence ≠ Certain Disengagement

We must avoid automatically equating student silence with lack of participation or engagement. Katherine Schultz, Dean and Professor of Education at the University of Colorado Boulder, wrote an impactful book called *Rethinking Classroom Participation: Listening to Silent Voices.*[13] Schultz points out that "[t]eachers often define classroom participation as a verbal response that fits into a routine or a teacher-established pattern of classroom discourse."[14] Indeed, in most classroom settings, "students are only given the opportunity to participate by speaking out loud."[15] Yet Schultz contends that silence is a form of student participation.[16] Instead of viewing student silence as an educational failure, she calls on teachers to examine and investigate the important role of silence in a classroom. She explains:

> Educators tend to have limited understandings of silence in the classroom. Silence is generally viewed as an individual characteristic and educators assume, for instance, that a quiet person is intrinsically shy. Alternatively, teachers assume that silence means a student either does not know the answer or has made a[] conscious decision not to participate in the discussion. In fact, student silence in the classroom can carry multiple meanings.[17]

Silence can symbolize "thoughtfulness" or "strategic timing."[18] Schultz eloquently defines silence as "a container for ideas that cannot be expressed in words."[19] She advocates that students can, and should, use silence "as a space in which to build their imag-

12. Elizabeth A. Harris, *Not Everyone Hates Remote Learning. For These Students, It's a Blessing*, N.Y. Times (May 20, 2020), https://www.nytimes.com/2020/05/20/nyregion/coronavirus-students-schools.html.

13. Katherine Schultz, Rethinking Classroom Participation: Listening to Silent Voices (2009).

14. *Id.* at 3.

15. *Id.*

16. *Id.* at 4.

17. *Id.* at 3.

18. *Id.*

19. *Id.* at 19.

inations or to solidify knowledge."[20] Schultz urges educators to seek to understand the various forms and *positive* roles of silence in the classroom.[21] For example, one (loud) student's silence can create space for another (quiet) student's participation.[22] Schultz advises educators to refrain from trying to eliminate silence from the classroom, and instead understand how it can be a powerful teaching and learning tool.[23]

In her book, Schultz shares vignettes of quiet students who intentionally choose silence as an affirmative act—to think. When they ultimately *opt to* speak after a period of quietude, they make "consequential" contributions to class discussions and help other classmates learn.[24] A student's silence may represent a conscious preference (or decisive need) for reflection and contemplation, and "a desire to choose his words carefully."[25]

As educators, as a *first step*, we should answer Schultz's call to give more thought to why some of our students choose to be quiet in our learning environments. As Schultz illuminates, a student's silence certainly may be a form of resistance, but alternatively it may represent power, self-protection, a trauma response, or an arena for creativity and discovery.[26] Schultz cautions, "There are potentially grave consequences for students when teachers do not understand their silence as a form of participation."[27]

As a *second step*, to enhance inclusivity and a sense of belonging in our classrooms, we should—as Schultz encourages—experiment with multiple modalities of class participation.[28] Deep student engagement can manifest in oral, visual, and written forms, *and* in intentional silence.[29] Professors Viji Sathy and Kelly A. Hogan concur, stating, "Not all participation and engagement in your course needs to be spoken."[30]

In this time in our collective lives marked by chaos, confusion, and a cacophony of competing voices, let's acknowledge the important role of silence in learning, and in life. Indeed, "[s]ilence is the sound of thinking."[31] Gillian Drake, who teaches acting workshops for lawyers in Washington, D.C., remarks how "[l]awyers often pick the

---

20. *Id.* at 25.
21. *Id.* at 26.
22. *Id.* at 3.
23. *Id.* at 26.
24. *Id.* at 29.
25. *Id.* at 34.
26. *Id.* at 29; *see also* Valerie Strauss, *Why Introverts Shouldn't Be Forced to Talk in Class*, WASH. POST (Feb. 12, 2013), https://www.washingtonpost.com/news/answer-sheet/wp/2013/02/12/why-introverts-shouldnt-be-forced-to-talk-in-class/ (posting an article by Katherine Schultz).
27. SCHULTZ, *supra* note 13, at 5.
28. *Id.* at 84–85.
29. *Id.* at 85.
30. Viji Sathy & Kelly A. Hogan, *How to Make Your Teaching More Inclusive: Advice Guide*, CHRON. HIGHER EDUC. (July 22, 2019), https://www.chronicle.com/interactives/20190719_inclusive_teaching.
31. Jordan Catapano, *Classroom Management: Helping Introverts Thrive*, TEACHHUB EDUCATION BLOG (May 2016), https://web.archive.org/web/20190526050210/http:/www.teachhub.com/classroom-management-helping-introverts-thrive.

easiest voice, which is to be louder."[32] She notes, "There [are] some people who could dwell in silence a little bit."

## III. Introverted Students Naturally Need Time to Think and Process

Extroverted teachers, and introverted ones who may never have grappled with shyness or social anxiety, should consider the multiple shades of quiet in our students. Introversion is distinct from shyness and social anxiety, yet our society tends to conflate these labels and lump all quiet individuals into one (often misunderstood) category.[33]

"Introversion" and "extroversion" embody the differences in how humans react to and manage stimuli, information, and energy.[34] Introverts absorb and process sounds, voices, lights, movement, language, questions, and sensations *internally* and deeply.[35] We like to ponder and contemplate, vetting and testing our feelings, thoughts, ideas, solutions to problems, and reactions *internally* and as *fully* as possible before sharing them aloud.[36] In contrast, extroverts shape thoughts, ideas, answers, and decisions *externally*. An extrovert's reaction time to a stimulus, sound, question, or situation appears—on the surface—faster than an introvert's. Yet the extrovert's initial outward contribution often is not fully formed; extroverts sculpt and mold their nascent ideas out loud. Conversely, we cannot see or hear the introvert's internal gears turning. The mistake is to assume nothing is happening. Rather, the introvert is delving deeply, moving pieces of a puzzle around, honing, chiseling. The introvert is seeking the "right" response, not just "a" response.[37]

Introverts resist interruption—to themselves and others. Interruptions derail our train of thought.[38] Many of us also prefer writing to speaking; writing affords us valuable time to think, ponder, examine, draft, edit, and articulate without interruption.[39] As Jordan Catapano, a Chicago high school English teacher, notes, "Introverts are naturally self-reflective, which leads to the cultivation of strong convictions and principles."[40] To flourish in educational and professional environments, introverts need "time to think and process," and "space to exist away from others."[41] Dr. Kate Earle, Chief Learning Officer of The Quiet Leadership Institute, echoes this principle,

---

32. Debra Bruno, *Inside DC's Acting School for Lawyers*, WASHINGTONIAN (Jan. 7, 2020), https://www.washingtonian.com/2020/01/07/inside-acting-for-lawyers-school/.

33. BROWN, *supra* note 1, at 3.

34. *Id.* at 5–6.

35. *Id.* at 7.

36. *Id.* at 7–8.

37. *Id.* at 9.

38. *Id.* at 12.

39. *Id.* at 47.

40. Catapano, *supra* note 31.

41. *Id.*

reiterating that "introverts thrive in learning situations that enable solitude, independent thinking, and time to process."[42]

Many introverts ramp up energy to perform at peak levels in highly-stimulating environments like classrooms, but ultimately our vigor depletes, and we must retreat to quietude to replenish.[43] In contrast, many extroverts gain energy in such environments.

## IV. Shy and Socially Anxious Students Grapple with a Fear of Judgment

Many people assume introverts are shy or socially anxious, but these are distinct concepts. Shy individuals experience worry, apprehension, or fear in interpersonal interactions; this is vastly different from an introvert's natural preference for internal reflection before speaking, and for quietude to replenish energy.[44] Shyness can stem from a fear of judgment, criticism, exclusion, or rejection.[45] Shy individuals can experience uncomfortable or even painful *physical* sensations such as blushing, sweating, rapid heartbeat, shortness of breath, and shaking.[46] Social anxiety disorder—a recognized mental health condition[47]—is a more intense version of shyness marked by severe physical symptoms, avoidance of interactive situations, and interference in an individual's personal or professional life.[48]

Sathy and Hogan emphasize that, in the classroom, several "of the most traditional and common teaching methods" such as calling on students to respond to questions "aren't very inclusive, at least as they are commonly done."[49] For a shy student who is "uncomfortable raising her hand or blurting out answers the way other students do," persistent unease can interfere with learning.[50] Moreover, "her ideas are not part of the conversation, so others aren't learning from her."[51] In classrooms with only one participation highway—speaking aloud—extroverted or confident students dominate the conversation. Quiet or fearful students can feel "overwhelmed."[52] Teachers must realize the risk of such a dynamic: "quiet students [may] prematurely accept other

---

42. Taryn Oesch, *Using E-Learning to Engage Introverts*, Training Industry (Feb. 16, 2017), https://trainingindustry.com/articles/e-learning/using-e-learning-to-engage-introverts/.

43. Brown, *supra* note 1, at 6.

44. *Id.* at 16.

45. *Id.* at 17.

46. *Id.*

47. *See* Richard G. Heimberg et al., *Social anxiety disorder in DSM-5*, 31 Depress. & Anxiety 472–79 (2014).

48. Brown, *supra* note 1, at 18.

49. Sathy & Hogan, *supra* note 30.

50. *Id.*

51. *Id.*

52. *Id.*

people's ideas before considering their own, and... those dominating the discussion [may] think their contributions are more valuable."[53]

The good news is: in remote learning settings, students may feel relief from social intimidation.[54] A high school psychology teacher in Alabama, Blake Harvard, noted that "[t]he online environment may allow for voices to be heard without the added bit of social anxiety."[55] *The New York Times* reported how "[s]ome students have found it easier to participate in remote classes without the social pressures of a physical classroom."[56] Mike Drosos, a seventh-grade math teacher at Voice Charter School in New York, similarly reported that "[k]ids who would not have put a hand up at the end of a lesson are now emailing me."[57] He surmised that these students feel more comfortable engaging "when the teacher isn't making direct eye contact six inches from their desk."[58] Further, Kymbra Li, an American professor who has been teaching for seven years in China, reiterated how online courses can "give shy students, who normally feel anxious or scared to speak out in class, an opportunity to express themselves, build more language confidence and interact more with their teacher and peers behind the privacy of a computer screen in the comfort of their own home."[59]

## V. Remote Learning Can Reduce Classroom Disruptions and Overstimulation

Remote classrooms can reduce the overstimulation and distractions present in live classrooms that can disrupt quiet students' thinking. Education writer Nora Fleming reported that several groups of learners, including shy, hyperactive, and highly creative students, "are suddenly doing better with remote learning than they were doing in the physical classroom" because of the reduction of "everyday distractions."[60] Instructional coach, Elisabeth Bostwick, similarly explained, "Although many learners flourish in a busy classroom, some benefit from a quieter space with fewer distractions. I've worked with learners who feel overstimulated in the classroom and others who seek attention from peers by trying to be funny."[61] Watson shared that "[k]ids who need quiet in order to concentrate dislike the distractions of the classroom....

53. *Id.*

54. Nora Fleming, *Why Are Some Kids Thriving During Remote Learning?*, Edutopia (Apr. 24, 2020), https://www.edutopia.org/article/why-are-some-kids-thriving-during-remote-learning.

55. *Id.*

56. Harris, *supra* note 12.

57. *Id.*

58. *Id.*

59. Kymbra Li, *How Teachers Are Responding to Online Classes*, China Daily (Mar. 6, 2020), https://global.chinadaily.com.cn/a/202003/06/WS5e61c14ba31012821727ce93.html.

60. Fleming, *supra* note 54.

61. Elisabeth Bostwick, *5 Reasons Some Learners Are Thriving During Remote Teaching & Learning*, Elisabethbostwick.com (May 18, 2020), https://elisabethbostwick.com/2020/05/18/5-reasons-some-learners-are-thriving-during-remote-teaching-learning/.

Many students will do far better quality work when they aren't physically surrounded by their peers."[62]

As Catapano points out, "When students are socially and even physically separated from others, it gives them a chance to buckle down and zero in on their work... and get it done."[63] This is especially true for introverts. Catapano emphasizes that introverts "are more prone toward deep thinking. Thinking happens in slow, non-linear paths. The fewer interruptions, the more depth those thoughts can access."[64]

## VI. Quiet Students Thrive When We Offer Different Participation "Modalities"

Teachers perceiving a boost in participation from quiet students in remote learning point to the increased number of communication "modalities" in online classrooms—beyond the blanket approach of on-the-spot public speaking.

Two years before the pandemic, Ruth Chisum, Executive Director of Online Operations at Sam Houston State University, wrote that "[r]ecent explorations of the introversion dynamic in relation to learning have started to produce mounting evidence of a potential benefit for introverted students in online courses."[65] Remote classrooms offer participation modalities beyond the expectation of *immediate* answers to questions in front of a sea of peers. As Cinthia Fabian wrote, "As a former bashful student myself, I always appreciated when teachers gave me multiple points of entry."[66] In the online classroom, communication channels can include the "chat" feature, polling, discussion forums, reflection assignments, the "hand-raise" feature, and email.

### A. THE CHAT FEATURE

An assistant professor at the UCLA School of Theater, Film, and Television, Michelle Liu Carriger, shared the value of enabling quiet students to participate through the *chat feature* in remote classes.[67] Reflecting on her seminar course, *Art and Performance in the Time of Coronavirus*, Carriger noted, "Professors are discovering that some really quiet students who we might have suspected were tuned out or didn't care, are actually just quiet; they participate a lot more via the chat function in the class-

62. Watson, *supra* note 3.

63. Catapano, *supra* note 31.

64. *Id.*

65. Ruth Chisum, *Introversion and The Online Classroom*, SHSU Online Campus (May 29, 2018), https://online.shsu.edu/news/2018/may/introversion-and-the-online-classroom.html.

66. Cinthia Fabian, *How to Engage Shy Students in the Virtual Classroom*, UPchieve (Apr. 15, 2020), https://upchieve.org/blog/2020/4/15/how-to-engage-shy-students-in-the-virtual-classroom.

67. Noela Hueso, *Teaching Theater in a Time of Quarantine*, UCLA Newsroom (June 9, 2020), https://newsroom.ucla.edu/stories/teaching-theater-in-a-time-of-quarantine (interview of Professor Michelle Liu Carriger.)

room."[68] Similarly, Taryn Oesch conveyed how "[c]ommunicating via an online chat for example, may be more comfortable and impactful for an introvert than speaking up in a classroom full of other learners."[69] Indeed, many introverts prefer writing to speaking, and articulate their ideas and thoughts more fluidly in written form.[70]

## B. POLLING

Professor Tiffany Atkins uses *polling* programs[71] to increase the diversity of voices in her law classroom, empowering her quiet students.[72] She explains, "Students can ask questions anonymously, share how they are feeling about an upcoming assignment, take a quiz, or give live feedback on a piece of legal writing they are working on as a class."[73]

## C. ONLINE DISCUSSION FORUMS

Further, as Chisum explains, *online discussion forums* "level the playing field for participation. While face-to-face classroom discussions may often be dominated by outgoing extroverts who frequently take the lead in open discourses, the online discussion forum provides an opportunity for *all* students to participate equally in dialogue."[74] Discussion forums afford quiet students much-needed "time to process through the questions presented, and more time for unhurried reflection of the topic before a response is elicited."[75]

## D. REFLECTION ASSIGNMENTS

Any opportunity to *reflect and write* about substantive topics, rather than the immediate pressure to speak about such content, allows introverts to shine. As Chisum points out, "since online coursework inherently thrives on written over verbal communication, introverts may not only favor the communication modality, but may also

---

68. *Id.*

69. Oesch, *supra* note 42.

70. BROWN, *supra* note 1, at 47.

71. For additional resources on integrating polling systems into online classes, see Chapter 8: *From Ground to Cloud and Back Again: Modern Tactics to Improve Your Teaching* by Katherine Brem (discussing polling system options and uses when designing a course for online delivery); Chapter 20: *A Whole New Meaning to Cybercrimes: Teaching Criminal Law and Criminal Procedure in an Online Learning Environment* by Tonya Krause-Phelan (uses in Criminal Law & Procedure); and Chapter 24: *Teaching Civil Procedure Online with Active Learning* by Cynthia Ho (uses in Civil Procedure).

72. Tiffany D. Atkins, *Amplifying Diverse Voices: Strategies for Promoting Inclusion in the Law School Classroom*, SECOND DRAFT, Fall 2018, at 13.

73. *Id.*

74. Chisum, *supra* note 65.

75. *Id.*

perform better academically, since their preference and skills trend toward the written word."[76]

### E. ELECTRONIC HAND-RAISING

Some quiet students resist, and might even fear, interrupting someone else's dialogue—either the teacher's or their classmates'—by raising their hands in an in-person classroom to ask a question or share a thought. Further, in a remote classroom, quiet students likely will be reluctant to simply unmute themselves to interrupt others and chime in. The *electronic hand-raise feature* in remote learning platforms permits quiet students to signal that they have a thought, idea, or answer to share, without the stress of interrupting someone else. Electronic hand-raising also fosters an orderly progression of speakers; this sense of order can mitigate feelings of unpredictability and lack of control that can agitate (and further silence) quiet students in a live classroom.

### F. EMAIL COMMUNICATIONS

*Email communications* from quiet students reflecting on substantive course content also should be valued as "participation"—and can serve as a stepping-stone toward helping these students gain confidence in amplifying their voices in more public venues. In her book, Schultz shares a vignette about inviting a silent student to write an email describing "her reflections on the conversations in class so that I could gauge her understanding and engagement with the material."[77] Schultz and the student commenced an email correspondence. Schultz reported that, over time, "perhaps as a consequence of [the student's] practice through writing the email messages, I began to notice that she was willing to offer her opinion more frequently to the large group.... [T]he private email correspondence helped to build a stronger relationship between the teacher and the student, which, over time, was translated into broader participation."[78] Schultz surmised that possibly the student "gained confidence through these one-on-one interactions, that we developed trust with one another, and that the email exchanges provided her with practice and a space to try out her ideas, allowing her to verbally enter into the public space of the classroom."[79] Teachers can establish guidelines for email communications that are appropriate for the educational setting.

* * *

76. *Id.* (citing Isabel Briggs Myers & Peter B. Myers, Gifts Differing: Understanding Personality Type (1980)).

77. Schultz, *supra* note 13, at 114.

78. *Id.*

79. *Id.* at 114–15.

Overall, as we plan our online curricula, it is heartening to envision how "the online learning environment can mean richer participation, deeper and more meaningful discussions, as well as a higher opportunity to utilize and develop writing skills."[80]

## VII. Asynchronous Classes Afford Critical Reflection Time

Online learning in the asynchronous classroom offers much-needed reflection time for quiet students. The Working Group on Distance Learning in Legal Education issued a report in 2015 called *Distance Learning in Legal Education: Design, Delivery and Recommended Practices*.[81] The report reiterates that "[i]n a live class, typically the most outgoing and verbal students are well known by the professor."[82] However, "in an asynchronous classroom all voices are heard."[83] Asynchronous learning offers flexible timelines, reduced distractions, and an emphasis on written discourse; these "are all things that satisfy the introvert's innate need for independence and often very considered responses to communication."[84] The Working Group's report indicates that, when students can access a class on their own time and at their own pace, "faculty hear from students who are hesitant to speak in class. Often this favors thoughtful, thorough, and shy students who use careful contemplation to generate excellent written responses."[85]

In in-person educational settings, introverts are "less likely to put their hand up in a classroom, but might go home with many unanswered questions. This is one of the main reasons introverts benefit from online learning and remote tutelage."[86] Time for reflection "takes pressure off the 'raise your hand' moment, where introverts often withdraw."[87] Oesch reiterates that "any type of asynchronous e-learning provides that crucial processing time for introverts."[88] Indeed, "[a] blended learning or flipped classroom approach in which learners first access content online and then participate in instructor-led training can be especially helpful for introverts, considering their preference to have time to prepare."[89]

---

80. Chisum, *supra* note 65.

81. Working Grp. on Distance Learning in Legal Educ., Distance Learning in Legal Education: Design, Delivery and Recommended Practices (2015).

82. *Id.* at 17.

83. *Id.*

84. Editorial, *Is Online Learning Better for Introverts?*, TNT Mag. (Jan 11, 2017), http://www.tntmagazine.com/lifestyle-career/is-online-learning-better-for-introverts#:~:text=The%20benefits%20of%20online%20learning,to%20think%20before%20they%20speak.&text=Online%20learning%20allows%20students%20to,the%20relevant%20topic%20or%20answer.

85. Working Grp. on Distance Learning in Legal Educ., *supra* note 81.

86. *Is Online Learning Better for Introverts?*, *supra* note 84.

87. *Id.*

88. Oesch, *supra* note 42.

89. *Id.*

Catapano likewise emphasizes that educators can help introverts thrive by incorporating multiple opportunities and platforms for asynchronous communication, such as discussion boards, reflection assignments, and self-paced collaborative work.[90] He stresses that "[i]ntroverts are less inclined towards small talk group interactions, and quick social responses. So don't demand these from them—at least not all of the time."[91] Catapano further indicates that "research has shown that, while synchronous group collaboration isn't as powerful as we recently thought, asynchronous interactions across time and space actually produce more powerful thoughts."[92]

## VIII. To "Walk the Walk" of Inclusivity, Our Teaching Must Evolve

As introversion expert Susan Cain illuminated in her renowned TED Talk, *The Power of Introverts*, "Our most important institutions, our schools and our workplaces, ... are designed mostly for extroverts and for extroverts' need for lots of stimulation."[93] Lynette Guastaferro, CEO of Teaching Matters, urges educators to recognize that "[t]here's no reason for all learning to be built for extroverted, socialized kids."[94] As we shift to more *intentional* online teaching, this is our opportunity to build communication systems and structures that truly foster inclusion and belonging, rather than further entrenching outdated educational models that only favor extroverts and confident students.

Schultz emphasizes that "[r]apid-paced classrooms privilege students who can respond quickly and accurately (preferably with the teacher's answer)."[95] She reinforces the point that many students need time and space to think and reflect before speaking, first testing their thoughts, ideas, and theories in writing or perhaps in smaller groups.[96] Schultz asks us to consider, "Do we encourage students to guess at answers, offering incorrect and incomplete thoughts in order to gain the teacher's recognition, rather than supporting careful (and sometimes slower and more deliberate) thinking?"[97] If so, we are contributing to introverts' and other quiet students' "frustration with settings that demand an extroverted approach to communication."[98] As Sathy and Hogan note, "Teaching inclusively means embracing student diversity in all

---

90. Catapano, *supra* note 31.
91. *Id.*
92. *Id.*
93. Susan Cain, *The Power of Introverts*, TED (Feb. 2012), https://www.ted.com/talks/susan_cain_the_power_of_introverts.
94. Harris, *supra* note 12.
95. SCHULTZ, *supra* note 13, at 51.
96. *Id.*
97. *Id.*
98. Oesch, *supra* note 42 (quoting Chris von Baeyer of the online training platform, The Ariel Group).

forms—race, ethnicity, gender, disability, socioeconomic background, ideology, even personality traits like introversion—as an asset."[99]

If we are unsure of how best to reach our quiet students, we should *ask them* specifically. I hear reports from faculty that "students *want* to be cold-called"; indeed, extroverted and confident students may complete surveys indicating a desire for cold-calling but this does not capture the sentiment of all our students. As Christine de Denus, a chemistry professor at Hobart and William Smith Colleges, encourages in the context of work settings, we must "[g]o to the people and say, 'How can I help you thrive?'"[100] Professor de Denus underscored, "Just because I'm quiet in a meeting doesn't mean I don't have ideas."[101]

As a law professor, I routinely hear legal academics rationalize their persistence in cold-calling students with statements like these:

- "Cold-calling is the only way to ensure my students are prepared for class; it keeps them on their toes."
- "My classroom isn't scary; also, if students don't know the answer, I just move onto someone else."
- "Cold-calling *is* inclusive; it forces everyone to speak."
- "The traditional Socratic method of Q&A is the best way to teach students how to 'think like a lawyer.'"
- "The law classroom should mirror the courtroom; students need to learn how to think on their feet so they might as well start now."
- "Students need to be pushed out of their comfort zone."

I urge professors to understand that these mindsets and approaches do *not* help our quiet students amplify their voices in a healthy, meaningful, and lasting way. And worse, they risk sending the erroneous message to quiet students who chronically struggle with cold-calling that they are not "cut out" for this type of intellectual discourse, or a career in the law. Instead, I suggest a *Field of Dreams* approach: "If you build it, they will come."[102] Let's first provide proper guidance and modeling for Socratic dialogue—including how to stay in the moment when you are prepared but are not sure how to answer the question—*before* pressing students into the arena. But more importantly, let's identify, encourage, and truly value alternative forms of classroom communication, participation, and engagement so students can exper-

---

99. Sathy & Hogan, *supra* note 30.

100. Maria Cramer & Mihir Zaveri, *What if You Don't Want to Go Back to the Office?*, N.Y. Times (May 5, 2020), https://www.nytimes.com/2020/05/05/business/pandemic-work-from-home-coronavirus.html.

101. *Id.*

102. Field of Dreams (Gordon Company 1989).

iment with their intellectual voices in lower stakes settings, thereby building up to public Socratic exchanges.

Three points merit emphasis here: (1) this approach does not mean giving quiet students a "pass" to opt out of class participation; (2) in most circumstances, helping quiet students stay "in the moment" in a class dialogue is more valuable to their long-term well-being than moving on to another student too quickly; and (3) simply cold-calling *every* student (without the guidance and support mentioned above) and thinking that is a healthy approach to accomplishing "diversity" is a flawed notion.

## A. OFFERING (AND TRULY VALUING) ALTERNATIVE MODES OF PARTICIPATION IS TRANSFORMATIONAL

Access to alternative modalities for contributing to class discussion can be transformational for a quiet student; allowing the student to routinely "take a pass" on participation is not.[103] In assessing class participation, teachers must consider two key questions: First, are students quiet *but otherwise contributing* "to the classroom learning community," or are they *not otherwise contributing*?[104] Second, are quiet students *engaged* or *disengaged*?[105] Schultz clarifies that "[t]eachers need to be careful not to let students opt out of participation, while at the same time supporting them to remain silent if that silence is a form of participation that may lead to verbal engagement or participation in another modality."[106]

Next, Schultz asks us to self-assess: "If the student is silent because she is disengaged, then the teacher might examine his own teaching and the classroom dynamics to look for ways to draw the student into the classroom conversations through talk."[107] On the other hand, "If the student is engaged, yet silent, the teacher might simply work out a way for the student to stay in touch with the teacher through other modes than verbal participation, such as writing notes, meeting with the teacher to talk on an individual basis, talking regularly with a peer, or expressing ideas in another modality."[108]

## B. LET'S HELP A STRUGGLING STUDENT STAY IN A SOCRATIC DIALOGUE TO BEGIN TO TRUST THEIR VOICE (AND US)

It is important for educators to help struggling students stay in a classroom dialogue to a reasonable degree—rather than moving on too quickly to another student simply to defuse (everyone's) discomfort—so students can develop trust in their voic-

---

103. Of course, in appropriate circumstances such as student accommodations, we should honor student requests to be excused from classroom participation.

104. Schultz, *supra* note 13, at 132.

105. *Id.* at 138.

106. *Id.* at 132; *see also id.* at 142.

107. *Id.* at 138.

108. *Id.*

es, their teacher, and their classmates. We must signal that a classroom interchange does not need to proceed "perfectly" for it to be a "success." As Oesch notes, "While it's important to get introverts and extroverts outside their comfort zones by challenging them to communicate in new ways, it's also important that they feel valued and encouraged to participate."[109] Sathy and Hogan echo the theme that we must "build trust and help students gain confidence."[110] This is an *incremental* process. As Fabian emphasizes, "While we certainly want to encourage students to go beyond their comfort zones, it's also critical that we create the space for them to gradually build their confidence and elevate their voice."[111]

Throwing quiet students into the deep end of classroom participation before we teach them to swim does not work; it is unfair and, frankly, unkind. Instead, let's model Socratic dialogue and then create space for initially hesitant students to experiment with their voices. Let's also encourage them to vet and test their emerging ideas through short email exchanges, discussion boards, "chat" features, and written reflections. When they do speak in class, let's guide them through a dialogue—even a bumpy one—to completion. With positive reinforcement and encouragement from teachers and peers, students will gain confidence in their voices and ultimately step into the participation arena with enhanced fortitude.

### C. SIMPLY COLD-CALLING ALL STUDENTS DOES NOT PRODUCE AN INCLUSIVE CLASSROOM

Some law professors have cited a study conducted in 2001–2002 at Yale Law School to justify the assertion that cold-calling all students ensures "diversity of voices" in the classroom.[112] I respectfully disagree with the notion that universal cold-calling is the plain solution to upping diversity in class participation.

I admit, when I learned of the Yale article summarizing the study in the way it was hyped by some (extroverted, confident, and intimidating) law professors, my instinct was to resist and emphatically disagree with it. But after reading and reflecting upon the article, I believe most of its principles *complement* rather than contradict my mission to amplify the voices of our introverted, shy, and socially anxious students in an authentic rather than forced manner.

The article summarizing the Yale study notes that "law schools cultivate and reward patterns of behavior that are more likely to be found among men than among women even though these behaviors do not necessarily reflect the skills students need to be good lawyers, judges, and legal academics."[113] The study of the educational experiences

109. Oesch, *supra* note 42.

110. Sathy & Hogan, *supra* note 30.

111. Fabian, *supra* note 66.

112. Sari Bashi & Maryana Iskander, *Why Legal Education is Failing Women*, 18 YALE J.L. & FEMINISM 389 (2006).

113. *Id.* at 391–92.

of women at Yale Law School—conducted in 2001–2002—showed that "female students participate in law school class discussions less than male students."[114] Further, the article states that "women at Yale Law School report less engagement when they speak up in class."[115] Male students "dominate class discussions."[116] Professors queried in the study conveyed "that male students tend to speak more often, more quickly, and in a more aggressive manner than female students, and that male students tend to speak for a longer period of time."[117] Further, "men, particularly white men, are more likely to volunteer to participate, whether or not they have something interesting or insightful to say."[118] Female students also "are less likely than men to interrupt classroom discussions."[119]

Some law professors' reliance on the Yale article to validate universal cold-calling seems to stem from two references therein. First, in a footnote, the article states that "not being called on makes students less likely to volunteer. *Some* professors report that they reinstituted cold-calling in response to the silence of female students and students of color. According to *these* faculty members, once students were compelled to speak, they began to volunteer."[120] The footnote does not indicate how many Yale Law School professors comprise "some" professors, or delve into any more detail (number, personality type) about the students "compelled to speak" who subsequently volunteered. Second, in its recommendations, the article contends:

> a volunteer-only regime, in which professors fail to solicit broad participation, will result in male-dominated class discussion.... Professors should ensure that active learning occurs, *whether they do so through* non-coercive cold-calling, panel discussion, "on-call" systems, response papers, chat rooms, or other creative means.[121]

As the foregoing excerpt shows, this article does *not* assert that universal cold-calling is the one solution for inclusive class participation. The article does make the point that "at Yale, many professors have successfully diversified class participation by requiring all students to speak in class."[122] Yet as the article articulates, "speaking in class" can have many definitions and forms.[123]

Moreover, with regard to dominance of class discussions by one cohort (whether comprised of the white male students described in the Yale study, or extroverts or

---

114. *Id.* at 396.
115. *Id.* at 399.
116. *Id.* at 403.
117. *Id.* at 407.
118. *Id.* at 409.
119. *Id.* at 413.
120. *Id.* at 411 n.83 (emphasis added).
121. *Id.* at 437 (emphasis added).
122. *Id.* at 438.
123. The article emphasizes that "[c]old-calling can be effective *especially when combined with other methods*, but it should not be an exercise in which faculty members coerce students into giving the answer that they seek and punish students who fail to comply." *Id.* at 437 (emphasis added).

confident students in other classrooms), we should be teaching those students *how to self-regulate*[124]—rather than demanding that our quiet, thoughtful students jump into the fray and mirror the loquacious students' behavior. Our students monopolizing airtime need to understand that their periodic silence will make space for classmates' voices. Indeed, the Yale article asserts that "the current practice of rewarding loud, emphatic classroom participation" is poor pedagogy.[125] Instead, we should value "depth and thoughtful reflection."[126] As Professor Atkins advocates, we and our loquacious students should actively *listen* to and *pay attention* to minority voices in our classrooms, credit their ideas, reiterate the value of those ideas, and create space for others to apply those ideas more fully.[127]

Accordingly, it is a mistake for educators to default to universal cold-calling and think that is enough to foster inclusivity in the classroom because every student is eventually "heard." This approach only serves to nurture the ego, well-being, and comfort level of the already confident students (and the teacher). Cold-calling all students—without proper understanding of and empathy for our students' diverse personalities, learning styles, and stressors—can further marginalize students who arrive at our classrooms with little historical or institutional guidance and support for navigating this type of public performance. As Schultz states:

> These strategies allow more voices to be heard in a classroom discussion and are meant to hold students accountable. They do not, however, necessarily shift the dynamics of a classroom, nor do they interrogate or address the possible reasons for a student's silence. Further, these techniques focus on increasing the number of students who speak in class; they may not draw in those students who elect to remain silent, nor do they address the conditions that prompt them to participate through silence. Finally, they do not ensure that students respond in ways that increase their learning or the learning of their peers.[128]

Schultz emphasizes, "It is not enough simply to hear every person's voice in a classroom."[129] Instead, we should mindfully construct and value multiple channels of communication, participation, and engagement. We can encourage students to experiment with different modalities, ultimately *choosing* those that amplify their voices in the most healthy, productive, and lasting way.

---

124. "[W]omen are more likely to be aware of their classroom environment and to regulate their own participation in order to listen and to give others an opportunity to speak." *Id.* at 413; *see also id.* at 407. We should be teaching *all* students how to increase their emotional intelligence and make space for others' voices.

125. *Id.* at 415.

126. *Id.* at 434.

127. Atkins, *supra* note 72, at 12.

128. SCHULTZ, *supra* note 13, at 8.

129. *Id.* at 109.

## IX. Conclusion

Instead of just "talking the talk" of inclusion, let's "walk the walk." As Watson wrote about emergency remote teaching in the pandemic, "Many students whose home language and culture are devalued by the school system are thriving right now in ways that the school system is not designed to measure."[130] Let's pay attention to our quiet students and notice when, why, and how they "speak" in the remote classroom. Let's be intentional about opening more channels of communication and participation, acknowledging and appreciating the diverse ways that our students learn, think, process, and share.

Further, let's infuse our remote classrooms with higher doses of humanity. As Professor Cathy Davidson wrote in her poignant article, *The Single Most Essential Requirement in Designing a Fall Online Course*, "our students are learning from a place of dislocation, anxiety, anger, and trauma. So are we."[131] She urges us, as educators, to "build our courses thinking about... empowerment [and] agency... designing ways for students to interact with one another and with us."[132] Let's reimagine participation and communication. Let's consider the value of quietude and silence in learning, and in life.

Quiet is where the magic happens. Let's create space for it.

130. Watson, *supra* note 3.

131. Cathy Davidson, *The Single Most Essential Requirement in Designing a Fall Online Course*, HASTAC (May 11, 2020), https://www.hastac.org/blogs/cathy-davidson/2020/05/11/single-most-essential-requirement-designing-fall-online-course.

132. *Id.* A creative idea suggested by Professor Joy Kanwar is to empower students to select an avatar as a vehicle for communication when learning about persuasion. *See* Joy Kanwar, *Avatars, Acting and Imagination: Bringing New Techniques into the Legal Classroom*, 43 J. LEGAL PROF. 1, 3 (2018).

FIVE

# Integrating Digital Wellness into Online Legal Education

N.E. Millar*

After reviewing this chapter, readers will be able to:

- Recognize the health and wellness challenges posed by online education;
- Identify and introduce solutions to those health and wellness challenges;
- Integrate digital wellness concepts into law school courses in order to bolster student engagement and learning;
- Teach students about the value of health and wellness in the context of ethical law practice; and
- Teach students about mindfulness and the mindful use of technology as tools to address mental and physical wellness issues.

Online legal education is not only about intellectually engaging and teaching students. Instead, a more holistic perspective takes into account online learning's broader impact on law students' health and well-being—in other words, their digital wellness. Addressing the impact of technology on law students' already precarious health and wellness will enhance student engagement and learning, while simultaneously safeguarding students against personal and professional fallout stemming from problems with mental health, physical health, substance abuse, and overall wellness issues.

Across the profession, law students and lawyers are under enormous stress and have disproportionately high levels of depression, anxiety, suicide, substance abuse, and other challenges.[1] The intense pressures to achieve high grades and prestigious

* Assistant Professor of Law, Widener University Delaware Law School. Professor Millar began teaching law in 2011 and first started studying online teaching in 2014. She integrates many of the concepts discussed in this chapter into her legal writing and ethics classes.

1. Patrick Schiltz, *On Being a Happy, Healthy, and Ethical Member of an Unhappy, Unhealthy, and Unethical Profession*, 52 Vand. L. Rev. 871, 920 (1999).

positions, meet billable hours requirements, and achieve career success—while balancing financial demands, family responsibilities, and personal lives—have led, predictably, to what has been called an "unhappy, unhealthy, and unethical profession."[2]

Moving more legal education online presents the risk that these issues will be exacerbated. In addition to the already challenging burden of being a law student, increasing technology use through online or hybrid classes can contribute to students' health and well-being in negative ways. For example, increased use of technology can disrupt sleep, increase anxiety, reduce access to friends and community, and decrease physical activity.[3] Technology overuse and addiction can lead to problems with mental health and social interaction, and studies have demonstrated that the distractions provided by smartphones can interfere with daily activities like studying.[4] These wellness issues, in turn, can negatively impact learning and academic performance, including class attendance and grades.[5] After graduation, mental and physical wellness issues also impact lawyers' ability to practice law ethically, implicating the duties of competence and diligence, among others.[6] Thus, any discussion of online education must consider the impact of online learning on law students, the role of faculty and administration in addressing this impact, and creative solutions for helping our students lead happy, healthy, and ethical lives.

## I. What Is Digital Wellness?

Wellness is a concept that has evolved from a simplistic historic definition—the absence of illness—to a holistic modern definition incorporating six dimensions: occupational, physical, social, intellectual, spiritual, and emotional.[7] In the digital context, digital wellness refers to measures aimed at regulating and improving the healthy use of technology, resulting in balanced attention to the body, mind, and spirit. Digital wellness can include strategies like taking regular breaks from technology, turning off unnecessary notifications, managing and organizing incoming email effectively, limiting social media use, and maintaining social engagement both online and offline.

---

2. *Id.*

3. *See* Amrita Balram, *How Online Learning Can Affect Student Health*, Johns Hopkins News-Letter (John Hopkins Univ., Baltimore, Md.), Aug. 24, 2020, at 2.

4. Griffin Wiles, *Students Share Impact of Online Classes on Their Mental Health*, The State News, July 30, 2020, https://statenews.com/article/2020/07/students-share-impact-of-online-classes-on-their-mental-health?ct=content_open&cv=cbox_featured.

5. *See* Jacklyn J. Thompson & Stella C.S. Porto, *Supporting Wellness in Adult Online Education*, 6 Open Praxis 17, 23, 26 (2014) (noting the positive impact of exercise on grades and the link between health and attendance).

6. Alex Yufik, *Evaluating an Impaired Attorney's Fitness to Practice*, Law Practice Today (Sept. 14, 2018), https://www.lawpracticetoday.org/article/evaluating-impaired-attorneys/.

7. *See* Thompson & Porto, *supra* note 5, at 18–19; *Defining Lawyer Well-Being*, Nat'l Task Force on Law. Well-Being, https://lawyerwellbeing.net/ (last visited Oct. 29, 2020).

In educational and other contexts, the *mindful* use of technology leads to greater digital wellness.[8] Use is mindful when students are aware of how and when they are using technology, thoughtful about their choices, and able to identify their own healthy and unhealthy use. Mindful use might include screen-free breaks, for example, and a specific time when technology is turned off at night. By integrating these strategies, technology users can better achieve balance and wellness in their personal and professional lives.

## II. Ideas for Law Schools

### A. WHAT FACULTY CAN DO IN THE CLASSROOM

Faculty play an important role in increasing student self-awareness around health and wellness issues, and we can easily integrate health-boosting exercises and activities into our courses. For example, taking time for just one group breath can calm the energy of the classroom and help students focus on the present moment. A simple reflection question can create opportunities for increased self-awareness. Increased presence and mindfulness, in turn, lead to greater digital wellness.

#### 1. Integrate wellness education and principles into the classroom

Wellness should be a routine topic of conversation in law school, in light of the high rates of mental health problems among both law students and lawyers. Professors can integrate wellness topics into their classes to better educate students about how to stay healthy in law school and to encourage them to begin preparing for the increased stress of practice. By establishing good habits and discovering effective tools during law school, students set themselves up for success both before and after graduation.

Because humans are social animals and the human brain is a "social organ, . . . much of what we learn about the world is due to our witnessing the different ways people interpret the same event."[9] Online education can be isolating, and isolation from other humans can impact learning and mental health. To help students escape the isolation that accompanies frequent technology use and off-campus learning, faculty can assign group work and encourage students to form study groups that meet outside of class.[10] Creating groups or "law firms" that last for an entire semester or year can lead to deeper relationships and, perhaps, informal study groups or friendships.[11] During class,

---

8. *See* Andy Puddicombe, *The Mindful Use of Technology*, PSYCH. TODAY (July 9, 2013), https://www.psychologytoday.com/us/blog/get-some-headspace/201307/the-mindful-use-technology.

9. TRACEY TOKUHAMA-ESPINOSA, MAKING CLASSROOMS BETTER: 50 PRACTICAL APPLICATIONS OF MIND, BRAIN, AND EDUCATION SCIENCE 69 (2014).

10. For a discussion of the importance of community in learning, see Chapter 11: *The Importance of Building Community in Online and Blended Courses* by Sophie Sparrow.

11. For a more in-depth treatment of using teams in online learning, see Chapter 10: *Team-Based Learning in an Online Teaching Environment* by Joy E. Herr-Cardillo and Melissa H. Weresh.

breakout rooms or similar tools transform a large classroom into intimate smaller groups where students feel less intimidated and more empowered.[12] Simply "opening" the virtual classroom thirty minutes before the official start of class allows students to chat and compare notes before the professor arrives. When I join my class at the start time, I often have to wait a few moments before the excited pre-class chatter ends. Some professors also hold virtual "coffees" or "village halls" with students, where smaller groups can socialize in a relaxed setting.

Numerous studies have demonstrated the positive effects of physical exercise on cognitive functioning, including protection from cognitive decline, improved memory, and increased academic achievement.[13] Prolonged sitting is a serious health risk and predictor of increased mortality and chronic disease; in addition, reducing sitting time can improve mood and decrease back and neck discomfort.[14] On campus, students walk between classes, sometimes stand to answer questions or deliver oral arguments, and may have access to nearby workout facilities. While we cannot replicate all of these experiences during online learning, certainly we can sometimes ask students to stand if they are able when speaking to the class, offer frequent stretch breaks, and remind students of the importance of physical movement. In law school, a friend of mine power-walked while listening to bar-prep CDs; similarly, students could listen to professor-made or professor-recommended podcasts, lectures, or other audio materials while walking, jogging, or working out.

In addition to incorporating wellness into existing courses, law professors can propose and teach courses specifically focused on lawyer wellness. In its comprehensive 2017 report, the National Task Force on Lawyer Well-Being recommended that law schools include well-being topics in courses on professional responsibility, provide educational opportunities on topics related to well-being, and take other steps to encourage wellness among students.[15] Many schools have heeded the call. The University of Tennessee College of Law, for example, offers a course called Thriving as a Lawyer that introduces students to positive psychology and goal-setting, among other subjects.[16] The University of Miami School of Law's Mindfulness in Law Program offers classes on mindful ethics, mindful leadership, and more.[17] By creating these innovative courses, faculty introduce students to important tools and elevate wellness to a school-wide goal.

---

12. For the particular benefits to quiet students, see Chapter 4: *Understanding and Lifting Up Our Quiet Students: Reimagining "Participation" in the Remote Classroom* by Heidi Brown.

13. *See, e.g.*, Laura Mandolesi et al., *Effects of Physical Exercise on Cognitive Functioning and Wellbeing: Biological and Psychological Benefits*, Frontiers in Psychology (2018), https://www.ncbi.nlm.nih.gov/pmc/articles/PMC5934999/.

14. *See* Thompson & Porto, *supra* note 5, at 21.

15. *See* Nat'l Task Force on Lawyer Well-Being, The Path to Lawyer Well-Being: Practical Recommendations for Positive Change 35–40 (2017), https://lawyerwellbeing.net/wp-content/uploads/2017/11/Lawyer-Wellbeing-Report.pdf.

16. *Institute for Professional Leadership: Curriculum*, U. Tenn. Knoxville C.L., https://law.utk.edu/programs/leadership/curriculum/ (last visited Nov. 15, 2020).

17. *Mindfulness in Law Program*, U. Miami Sch. L., https://www.law.miami.edu/academics/mindfulness-in-law-program (last visited Nov. 15, 2020).

Finally, faculty can encourage students to limit their technology use outside of class times and help to educate them about the issue. We can require students to purchase print copies of textbooks and other class materials and give offline assignments, such as research exercises in a local library or courtroom observation reports, to mandate time away from the computer.

### 2. Incorporate mindfulness into law school courses

Derived from Buddhism, mindfulness is the secular practice of paying attention to one's present experience.[18] The American Psychological Association defines mindfulness as "a moment-to-moment awareness of one's experience without judgment."[19] Research has linked the practice of mindfulness to enhanced working memory capacity, reduced anxiety and stress, heightened awareness of one's cognition, reduced risk of depression relapse, reduced emotional reactivity, and increased attention and awareness.[20] Mindfulness can be learned and practiced through meditation or through a simple daily practice of noting what we are doing and what is going on around and within us. It is the opposite of mindlessly scrolling through the Internet or being so lost in thought that we don't hear or notice what is happening around us.

Faculty can integrate mindfulness into the law school classroom in many ways. In my Professional Responsibility class, I assign a Computer-Assisted Legal Instruction (CALI) lesson on mindfulness,[21] conduct a short in-class meditation exercise, and ask students to complete a confidential stress management plan to assess their challenges, goals, and resources.[22] The response from students is overwhelmingly positive, and every piece of this exercise could be integrated—individually or collectively—into any law school course, whether virtual or in person.

Other law professors seamlessly integrate mindfulness into courses throughout the 1L and upper-level curriculum. For example, a former colleague regularly began her Business Associations class with a short meditation, using a jar of water and sand

18. Matthew Nisbet, *The Mindfulness Movement: How a Buddhist Practice Evolved into a Scientific Approach to Life*, Skeptical Inquirer 41 (May/June 2017), https://web.northeastern.edu/matthewnisbet/2017/05/24/the-mindfulness-movement-how-a-buddhist-practice-evolved-into-a-scientific-approach-to-life/.

19. Daphne M. Davis & Jeffrey A. Hayes, *What Are the Benefits of Mindfulness*, Am. Psychol. Ass'n (July–Aug. 2012), https://www.apa.org/monitor/2012/07-08/ce-corner.

20. *See* Shailini Jandial George, *The Cure for the Distracted Mind: Why Law Schools Should Teach Mindfulness*, 53 Duq. L. Rev. 215, 220–36 (2015); Patrick Palace, *Mindful Technology: Can Well-Being Be Improved with Tech? (Or Is That Just Crazy Talk?)*, GP Solo Magazine (June 24, 2019), https://www.americanbar.org/groups/gpsolo/publications/gp_solo/2019/may-june/mindful-technology/; Meagan B. MacKenzie & Nancy L. Kocovski, *Mindfulness-Based Cognitive Therapy for Depression: Trends and Developments*, Psychol. Res. Behav. Mgmt. (2016), https://www.ncbi.nlm.nih.gov/pmc/articles/PMC4876939/.

21. Mindfulness Practice for Law School, CALI, https://www.cali.org/lesson/18209.

22. I adapted the plan from Ann D. Foster, Practicing Law and Wellness: Modern Strategies for the Lawyer Dealing with Anxiety, Addiction and Depression 9–13, https://www.texasbar.com/AM/Template.cfm?Section=Wellness1&Template=/CM/ContentDisplay.cfm&ContentID=15158 (last visited Oct. 29, 2020).

scooped from the Grand Canyon to illustrate students' thoughts whirling and then settling. A professor at The George Washington University School of Law incorporates a three-minute "Mindfulness Moment" into the beginning of each Civil Procedure class.[23] And a professor at the Florida International University College of Law uses techniques like a needs-assessment poll ("do I have what I need to be present in today's class?") and intentional brain breaks in her courses.[24]

Outside of the classroom, students can enhance their case and textbook reading by engaging in mindful reading, which is the process of not only paying attention to what the text says, but also noticing how they are reading.[25] Are they skimming or reading carefully? Are they focused and paying attention, or are they distracted? When they pause at the end of a paragraph or page, can they recall what they just read? When engaged in mindful reading, students learn not just legal doctrine, but also more about themselves as readers and learners. Faculty can create self-awareness reading exercises—with prompts asking students to evaluate their methodologies and pause to notice their focus—that boost mindfulness and help to establish this technique as a regular practice.[26]

In my Professional Responsibility class, students submit a time log for one week of the term, carefully monitoring time spent in class, at work, and on homework. Professors teaching online could integrate questions about technology use, social interaction, physical activity, and other topics into the assignment. This could be transformed into a mindfulness exercise by encouraging reflection on the time spent on these various components, asking students to set goals for how they spend their time, and incorporating questions like, "How do I feel when I'm online?" or "Am I satisfied with the amount of time I'm spending online?"

Finally, even small mindful moments during the day—pausing before replying to an email or taking an intentional breath before signing into an online class—can help to increase focus and decrease stress. By sharing these techniques with students and building opportunities for self-reflection into law school classes, faculty help to educate students about practices that can benefit their academic, personal, and professional lives.

## B. WHAT LAW SCHOOL ADMINISTRATORS CAN DO OUTSIDE OF THE CLASSROOM

Law school administrators can support students learning online by addressing problems in the law school culture that extend beyond the online environment. The competitive law school environment discourages vulnerability, and "[s]eeking help is

23. Jordana Alter Confino, *Where Are We on the Path to Law Student Well-Being?: Report on the ABA CoLAP Law Student Assistance Committee Law School Wellness Survey*, 68 J. Legal Educ. 650, 689 (2019).

24. Rosario Lozada, Associate Professor of Legal Skills and Values, Florida International University College of Law, Featured Presenter at The Language of Well-Being in the Law School Classroom (Sept. 16, 2020).

25. Ellen C. Carillo, A Writer's Guide to Mindful Reading vi, viii (2017), https://wac.colostate.edu/docs/books/mindful/reading.pdf.

26. For more ideas, *see generally id.*

an acknowledgment of vulnerability."[27] One study found that third-year law students were significantly less likely to seek help with mental health and substance abuse problems than first-year law students because of concerns that seeking assistance would negatively impact their ability to be admitted to a state bar and their job or academic status, lead to social stigma, or otherwise impact them financially.[28] Thus, law schools should devote resources to educating students about the importance of seeking assistance and why doing so will not hurt their futures.

As online education exacerbates existing issues, law schools should increase resources to assist students with health and wellness. In addition to making free counseling available online, law schools should consider offering free or low-cost gym memberships, yoga and meditation classes, and other opportunities to engage in physical activity, such as virtual or in-person 5Ks. During orientation and at other times, law schools should anonymously survey students on their mental and physical health status, as well as substance use, to normalize these topics as part of the legal-education discourse and identify the need to address any widespread issues. Many law schools and universities provide anonymous online screening tools to help students self-identify issues, and some offer access to innovative services like financial and wellness coaching.[29]

Law schools also need to identify ways to encourage student interaction by supporting student groups, law reviews, and school-wide events. Hosting online "town halls" and other programs—perhaps with smaller breakout discussion groups—will help to reduce isolation and ensure a sense of community. Schools might create, or encourage students to create, support groups or discussion boards. Law schools can provide workshops and speakers on wellness issues, and they can look for ways to collaborate with local lawyers' assistance programs or bar associations.

As law schools move toward more online education, increasing wellness-related programming and services will help students navigate the impact of technology use and virtual education on their health and wellness. Providing these tools and resources to students, in turn, will have a lasting impact on the well-being and ethics of the legal profession.

---

27. Jerome M. Organ et al., *Helping Law Students Get the Help They Need: An Analysis of Data Regarding Law Students' Reluctance to Seek Help and Policy Recommendations for a Variety of Stakeholders*, Bar Examiner, Dec. 2015, at 8, 13, http://www.ncbex.org/pdfviewer/?file=®assets®media_files®Bar-Examiner®issues®2015-December®BE-Dec2015-HelpingLawStudents.pdf.

28. *Id.* at 10–12.

29. *See, e.g.*, Financial Coaching, Student Wellness Services, Ohio State Univ., https://swc.osu.edu/services/financial-education/financial-coaching/; Services, Student Wellness Services, Ohio State Univ., https://swc.osu.edu/services/; Weekly Wellness Coaching, William & Mary Law School, https://law.wm.edu/studentlife/wellness/coaching/index.php.

## RESOURCES TO SHARE WITH LAW STUDENTS

### Podcasts and websites

- "The Path to Law Student Well-Being" podcast series https://www.americanbar.org/groups/lawyer_assistance/events_cle/path_to_law_student_well-being_podcast_series/.
- The National Task Force on Lawyer Well-Being, https://lawyerwellbeing.net/.
- State Lawyer Assistance Programs, https://www.americanbar.org/groups/lawyer_assistance/resources/lap_programs_by_state/.
- "Help Yourself. Help Others.," anonymous mental health screening tool, https://www.helpyourselfhelpothers.org/.
- University of Pennsylvania Authentic Happiness Test Center, https://www.authentichappiness.sas.upenn.edu/testcenter.
- Academic Mindfulness Programs, such as https://www.law.miami.edu/academics/mindfulness-in-law-program and https://mindfulnesscenter.asu.edu/.
- Center for Mindfulness, https://www.umassmemorialhealthcare.org/umass-memorial-center-mindfulness.

### Books

- Heidi K. Brown, Untangling Fear In Lawyering: A Four-Step Journey Toward Powerful Advocacy (2019).
- Jeena Cho & Karen Gifford, The Anxious Lawyer: An 8-Week Guide to a Joyful and Satisfying Law Practice Through Mindfulness and Meditation (2016).
- Scott L. Rogers, Mindfulness for Law Students: Using the Power of Mindfulness to Achieve Balance and Success in Law School (2009).
- Kathryne M. Young, How to Be Sort of Happy in Law School (2018).

SIX

# The Persistence of Distance Education: Low(er) Tech Options for Remote Learning

Stephen A. Rosenbaum*

After reviewing this chapter, readers will be able to:

- Design an appropriate online course with less reliance on large web-based platforms or on the need for stable internet access;
- Create assignments that foster student engagement in a low-tech environment;
- Incorporate individualized assessment and guidance strategies;
- Consider collaboration with peer teachers at other institutions; and
- Anticipate associated technology challenges.

I explore below the use of online and other low-tech methods of remote learning that I have considered in teaching law students abroad in technologically distressed communities. The lessons learned can help instructors anywhere teach students for whom (1) internet connectivity is not always reliable, (2) video-conferencing options may be limited to applications not suitable for class settings because phone or tablet screens accommodate a limited number of participants, (3) students lack adequate privacy or space for study, (4) the dominant educational system has not transitioned from lecture mode to interactive teaching and critical thinking, or (5) any combination of these conditions.

* Frank C. Newman Lecturer, University of California, Berkeley; Part-Time Lecturer, University of Washington (2020–21). Professor Rosenbaum began adjunct law teaching in 1985 and has trained law teachers on clinical pedagogy in developing countries where many students earn degrees through "distance" or "open" education. He has also conducted periodic video-conference workshops and courses for law students in Togo, Iran, Indonesia, and Trinidad & Tobago, and taught a U.S. legal studies course during the pandemic on a video-conferencing platform.

# I. Low-tech Online Teaching Abroad

*The distance education students meet their "teacher" only once or twice per academic year for "crash courses" before the exams which last[] for a few days.*[1]

Introduced in 1975 by the military regime in Myanmar (aka Burma), distance education was meant to address university overcrowding and allow students in remote areas to earn a higher education degree for lower tuition. What was originally labeled "correspondence courses" had the added advantage of preempting student protest gatherings on campus.[2] At last count, almost twice as many students attend the country's distance education programs than in-person postsecondary education institutions.[3] All of this predates the COVID-19 pandemic,[4] and the teaching and learning suffers.[5]

The experience in Myanmar is not unique. Once home to the Arab world's most prestigious law schools, Egypt has relied for decades on an "open education" program for student overflow in certain fields, including law.[6] This has permitted students with lower grades, those with full-time work or family obligations, and those unable to afford supplemental fees, to earn a postsecondary degree while attending classes in the evenings, weekends, or during vacation periods.[7] The program, which can lead

1. Myint Zan, *Legal Education in Burma Since the 1960s*, 12 J. Burma Studies 1, 16 (2008).

2. Hla Tint, *Present Situation of Distance Education in Myanmar* 4 (Int'l Council for Open & Distance Educ., 2014) https://www.icde.org/knowledge-hub/distance-education-in-myanmar. Law students were key protagonists in the pro-Democracy movement, resulting in killings by the armed forces and long-term university closures. *Id.* A new military coup d'etat, which took place on February 1, 2021, once again calls into question the fate of the nation's educational and political institutions. As this book goes to press, the Yangon University Distance Education's website has had no new postings since February 2. Yandon University Distance Education, https://www.yude.edu.mm (last visited May 19, 2021)..

3. Myan. Ministry of Educ., *National Education Strategic Plan 2016–21* at 35, Brit. Couns., https://www.britishcouncil.org/sites/default/files/myanmar_national_education_strategic_plan_2016-21.pdf.

4. While preparing a group of Myanmar law students in 2020 for the upcoming Jessup International Law Moot Court Competition, through regular, but unstable, Zoom and Google GoToMeeting platforms, I learned that there had been no in-person classes and no attempt to establish a temporary means of conducting classes or communicating with the law faculty since the inception of the COVID-19 lockdown. In essence, no "distance education" was available for students enrolled in the on-campus East Yangon University Law Department.

5. *See* Stephen A. Rosenbaum et al., *The Myanmar* Shwe*: Empowering Law Students, Teachers and the Community through Clinical Education and the Rule of Law*, 28 Indiana J. Global Legal Studies 153, 199–201, 210–12 (2021). Enrollment qualifications are minimal, students are fed exam questions in advance, and "lawyers and legal faculty hold [distance education] in very low regard." Int'l Comm'n of Jurists, Right to Counsel: The Independence of Lawyers in Myanmar 32 (2013), http://www.burmalibrary.org/docs16/ICJ-MYANMAR-Right-to-Counsel-en-red.pdf.

6. *See, e.g.*, Stephen A. Rosenbaum, *The Legal Clinic is More than a Sign on the Door: Transforming Law School Education in Revolutionary Egypt*, 5 Berkeley J. Islamic & Middle Eastern L. 39, 60–62, 67 (2012); Assiut University, Open Education System, http://www.aun.edu.eg/fr/open_education.php (last visited Jan. 31, 2021) (since 1998, program in place for law students to "catch up," based on "concept of guided self-education" and weekly meetings with faculty).

7. Rosenbaum, *supra* note 6, at 67 and n. 109.

to a dead end in a discriminating labor market, has been under reconsideration for several years.[8]

In Myanmar, Egypt, and elsewhere, distance learning is not simply a temporary instructional mode, but a fixture of the higher education system and the only option for students who, by reason of geographic location, socio-economic class, scholastic record, and/or employment status, are unable to participate in a campus-based, full-time university program.[9] These students are limited (exclusively) to off-site attendance and—just like their on-campus peers—their instructors are typically wedded to stagnant teaching methods and materials that do not often translate well to remote instruction: formal lecture, outdated textbooks, a modicum of questions-and-answers, and an assessment limited to a final written examination.[10]

The overseas options for "distance" and "open" education have often been fraught with problems due to both pedagogy and technology. In an online workshop exchange during the height of the COVID-19 pandemic, students at the University of Tehran Faculty of Law and Political Science ticked off a list of limitations to video-conferencing technology that they experienced in other classes:

- "I can't see the professor's face because his web cam is off."
- "I'm using my phone because I can't get a connection on my laptop."
- "I don't have enough bandwidth."
- "It's time-consuming because I need to go back and listen to a recording of the professor's lecture to understand what he was saying."
- "There is no interacting except for some questions and answers in the chat box."

Even where the cyber infrastructure may be unreliable, many of today's law students across the globe are part of a generation of "digital natives"[11] who access the

---

8. *See* Ahmed El Shamy, *Egypt Reconsiders "Open Learning,"* AL-FANAR MEDIA (Jan. 12, 2016), https://www.al-fanarmedia.org/2016/01/egypt-reconsiders-open-learning/; Walaa Ali, *An End to Old Open Ed Program in Egypt*, EGYPT TODAY (June 11, 2018), https://www.egypttoday.com/Article/1/51944/An-end-to-Old-Open-Education-program-in-Egypt.

9. Despite its appearance in some contexts as a second-class form of education, the concept of OFDL ("Open, Flexible, and Distance Learning") has a long and reputable history, as evidenced by the establishment in 1938 of the International Council for Open and Distant Education, having evolved in curricular scope, geography and technology. INTERNATIONAL COUNCIL FOR OPEN AND DISTANT EDUCATION, https://www.icde.org/about-us (last visited Feb. 22, 2021). Perhaps the international gold standard for robust postsecondary open education is The Open University (OU), chartered in the United Kingdom. Promoting "flexible learning" for students located throughout the world, OU offers personal tutors, special advisors, group tutorials, online conferencing, and study networks at one's own pace and own place. THE OPEN UNIVERSITY, http://www.openuniversity.edu (last visited Feb. 21, 2021).

10. *See, e.g.*, Rosenbaum et al., *supra* note 5, at 161–62, 166; Rosenbaum, *supra* note 6, at 56–60.

11. Michele Pistone & Warren Binford, *Implementing Effective Education in Specific Contexts (Use of Technology)* (citing Marc Prensky, *Digital Natives, Digital Immigrants* Part 1, 9 On the Horizon, no. 5, 2001, at 1), *in* BUILDING ON BEST PRACTICES: TRANSFORMING LEGAL EDUCATION IN A CHANGING WORLD 130–31, n. 10 (Deborah Maranville et al., eds., 2015).

internet but often on small platforms like mobile phones, if only intermittently. This is the case of the group of Iranian students who encouraged their professor to set up a "Legal Clinic" on WhatsApp and to sponsor periodic virtual workshops, months before COVID-19 was part of the Farsi speaker's vocabulary.[12] A junior member of the law faculty at Togo's University of Lomé hosted client interview simulation *ateliers* via Skype for his student clinicians.[13]

It may be years before the cyber infrastructure permits enough exchanges between students and teachers, or the reigning pedagogy prompts faculty to engage with their counterparts across the country and outside their borders. While these phenomena are most pronounced in the Global South, the digital divide in the United States and elsewhere in the Global North can have a similar impact on pockets of marginalized learners.[14] Therefore, when creating online courses, it is important for professors who teach these marginalized learners to consider low-tech solutions that make online education more accessible.

## II. Course Content Delivery

Marginalized learners may only have a mobile phone or tablet to use for online education. While using telecommunication apps on a mobile phone may not be ideal for group work due to the small screen size, educators can still structure online course delivery if they keep the platform size in mind. There is no reason to settle for an outmoded instructional strategy whereby students work independently on written materials, separated from the instructors and their peers, when they have some ability for connecting via their mobile devices. Email and other mobile-based apps can help professors deliver quality online education.

12. The University of Tehran students have a greater command of technology and the English language than their professor and are eager for a forum where they can speak outside the confines of a rigid jurisprudence-based curriculum. What began as Skype workshops with in-person classrooms morphed into group Skype and Zoom meetings, with erratic connectivity and sometimes more chats than aural discussion. One of the sessions was dubbed a "Virtual Workshop on 'Virtuous Lawyering.'" A WhatsApp group also served The Open University law students, working remotely on group projects, to "accelerate the building of good working relationships, to improve informal group communication and to provide peer support." Hugh McFaul et al., *Taking Clinical Legal Education Online: Songs of Innocence and Experience*, 47 Int'l J. Clinical Legal Educ. 6, 27 (2020).

13. The Clinique d'Expertise Juridique et Sociale, one of the few law school *cliniques juridiques* in francophone Africa, serves poor clients in Togo's capital. Clinique d'Expertise Juridique et Sociale (CEJUS), Facebook, https://www.facebook.com/cliniquejuridiquecejus (last visited Feb. 22, 2021). The sound quality for the Skype sessions was inconsistent and internet connectivity unreliable. *See also* Stephen A. Rosenbaum, *Clinique ToGo: Changing Legal Practice in One African Nation in Six Days,*17 Int'l J. Clinical Legal Educ. 59, 93–97 (Appendix II: *Bleu*print for a Francophone African Law School Clinic) (2012).

14. Benjamin Mueller & Mitra Taj, *Schools Worldwide Are Relearning the Value of TV Lessons*, N.Y. Times, August 18, 2020, at A8.

## A. EMAIL, APPS, AND SMARTPHONES

*By focusing on the learning outcomes, exams, lesson content, scaffolded assignments, and promoting student learning via engaging assignments and good feedback instructors can create rich experiences without the use of more complex technology.*[15]

Instructors can use email to connect with remote students and deliver content. Where the internet is unreliable, professors should anticipate the students' difficulty in accessing it on-demand and start by sending the syllabus out before the term begins, with as much detail as possible about the direction of the course and the assignments. Emails can be sent to students in all sections, or tweaked from section to section, and used again the next term with modifications. For example, sending three emails per week or per lesson may be a way to start:

- An initial email with the lesson;
- A follow-up email and feedback on how the week is progressing; and
- A clarifying email at the end of the week.

While one can "drip each lesson out over a period of time," an email can contain instructions and lessons for one class or one week, which, when added up, constitute a full course.[16] Student expectations on frequency of contact will vary from institution to institution, but the focus should be on creating clear lesson plans, evaluated as necessary for low-tech distance learning, and a personal feel to the course.

Assignments should take only a few minutes to read through and end with a solid, actionable step that students can take, e.g., an assignment, a project to complete, a chapter to read, or a video to watch on the internet. To transform this educational mode from self-study for the truly motivated and advanced student, the materials delivered by the instructor should be complemented by some semblance of teacher-student engagement, as set out below.

15. E-Learning Center, Borough of Manhattan Cmty. Coll., https://www.bmcc.cuny.edu/about-bmcc/mission-statement-and-goals/ (last visited Feb. 21, 2021). I have drawn upon the Center's commonsensical and cogent guidance, offered early in the pandemic to legal educators adjusting to remote teaching in tech-distressed communities. Its focus is on teaching style, personality, and mastery of subject matter over mastery of technology. *See* BMCC Course Continuity, *Low-Technology Distance Learning*, Google Sites, https://sites.google.com/bmcc.cuny.edu/emergency-preparedness/low-tech (last visited Feb. 21, 2021).

16. *Low-Technology Distance Learning*, *supra* note 15.

## B. TEL-EDUCATION

*[D]ebates over how to make online classes engaging and interactive... [are] sheer fantasy for many of the world's students, including millions in affluent nations, who do not have broadband connections or computers.*[17]

Educational television, a closed-circuit medium relied on by an earlier generation of remote educators and learners, is enjoying some resurgence as the next best thing to cybernetic communication, at least in communities where bricks-and-mortar schools, teachers, and/or internet access are in short supply. Today's broadcasts are slicker and more engaging than the old school productions. They are perhaps most popular for early childhood learners and primary school pupils but also reach secondary school students[18] and have the potential to serve postsecondary learners, including those studying the law, in newer, more engaging formats.

There are some obvious economies in this methodology. This medium is not dependent on high tech infrastructure. It can reach most households where a TV set is more likely to be found than a laptop and where the curriculum is uniform throughout a nation and can be delivered by a small cadre of teachers. Broadcasts may be accompanied by smartphone apps to provide support.[19]

Similar to televised broadcasts are publishers' websites or video recordings with scripted lecture or exercise content.[20] With this more recent technological advance, students learn individually, at their own pace. Clinician and digital specialist Warren Binford notes that with video recordings, particularly those prepared by others and available at no cost, "teaching efficiencies could create significant savings at a time when they are most needed. And faculty could devote more of their time and energy to more personalized, hands-on instruction of students."[21]

This methodology works best when executed by a dedicated corps of distance learning faculty who are released from other significant teaching obligations. In some localities, teachers can monitor students in real-time through cell phone contact.

---

17. Mueller & Taj, *supra* note 14.

18. *See generally* Raissa Fabregas, *Broadcasting Human Capital? The Labor Market Effects of Mexico's Telesecundarias* (working paper, 2018) (reviewing rural secondary programs in Mexico and other long-standing programs in Latin America, Africa, Europe, and U.S. Pacific Islands), https://www.dropbox.com/s/6jylpe3edru9r34/Telesecundaria_2018.04.29.pdf?dl=0.

19. *See, e.g.*, Shule Direct, https://www.shuledirect.co.tz/ (last visited Feb. 21, 2021) (delivering educational content for students in Tanzania and elsewhere in East Africa through mobile apps).

20. LegalED, for example, is a program that focuses on law student learning. "Students can view at their own pace, from anywhere, review lessons as often as they want for mastery, go deeper into topics of particular interest, and hear diverse perspectives on legal concepts." LegalED, http://legaledweb.com/home (last visited Feb. 19, 2021). *See also Zero-L*, Harvard Law School, https://online.law.harvard.edu/ (online course modules developed by Harvard Law School for incoming first year students across law schools) (last visited Feb. 19, 2021).

21. Warren Binford, *Envisioning a Twenty-First Century Legal Education*, 43 Wash. U. J. L. & Pol'y 157, 173 (2013).

Where there are no bureaucratic or cultural hurdles, those engaged in traditional, synchronous instruction would do well to be in sync with the online curriculum, so that distant learners would be "on the same screen" as their on-campus peers. This also frees up instructors to make one-on-one or small group contact outside of class time with students via email, video conferencing platforms, speakerphone, or text messaging.[22]

In post-pandemic times, or when complying with public health mandates—such as social distancing and masking—it is also possible for off-campus students enrolled in closed circuit television and other broadcast or video-recorded classes to meet neighboring or nearby students informally for peer-to-peer learning or to gather in local learning centers under the guidance of local educators or para-educators.[23]

## C. CHANGING THE PEDAGOGY AND THE CULTURE

> *[O]ur challenge is not to merely replace (or offer substitutes for) face-to-face instruction, but to find new and innovative ways to engage students in the practice of learning.*[24]

Perhaps as important as the technological means of instruction is the cultural transformation of the educational enterprise: Shifting from two-dimensional, one-way proscenium-framed lectures to applied learning, interactive teaching, critical thinking and individualized assessment, mentoring, or other forms of engagement.[25] Law teachers' skills can be increased through peer exchanges with other institutions, which can lead to better educational outcomes and improved standing for university faculties.

Collaboration with academic and other professional peers, both in-country and abroad, can be accomplished virtually by lower tech means:

---

22. *See, e.g.*, Azar López Bernardo Anwar, *Técnicas de Enseñanza del Derecho en la Educación a Distancia. Unas Cuantas Líneas de Reflexión*, *in* Nuevas Tendencias de la Enseñanza del Derecho en la Era Digital 273, 281–83 (2019) (use of audio podcasts, WhatsApp groups, YouTube videos and other small platforms for teacher-student and student-student contact in UNAM law school); Enlace Jurídico Académico, http://enlacejuridicoacademico.com (last visited May 31, 2021); *Class Clips—PSHE/Citizenship KS3 & GCSE: Young Legal Eagles*, BBC Teach, https://www.bbc.co.uk/teach/class-clips-video/pshecitizenship-ks3-gcse-young-legal-eagles/zmpbscw (programming for secondary school students, including mock trials) (last visited Feb. 22, 2021). *See also* Tia Ebarb Matt et al., *The Silver Lining in the Black Cloud of Covid-19*, 47 Int'l J. Clinical Legal Educ. 135, 143–45 (2020) (British law students' reliance on communication with peers when internet connectivity is unstable).

23. *See, e.g.*, Mueller & Taj, *supra* note 14 (informal student meet-ups in Lima, Peru shantytown). Under Myanmar's current five-year education strategic plan, one higher education goal is to "[e]nhance the status of e-learning centres and e-libraries." Myan. Ministry of Educ., *supra* note 3, at 35.

24. Jesse Stommel, *Hybridity, pt. 2: What is Hybrid Pedagogy?*, Hybrid Pedagogy (Mar. 9, 2012), https://hybridpedagogy.org/hybridity-pt-2-what-is-hybrid-pedagogy/.

25. *See, e.g.*, David I.C. Thomson, *Defining Experiential Legal Education*, 1 J. Experiential Learning 1, 20 (2014) (experiential learning integrates theory and practice by providing numerous opportunities for students to learn and apply lawyering skills).

- Legal educators can guest teach or co-teach classes with local faculty on a simple video-conferencing platform.
- These educators can also offer workshops or one-on-one support in critical thinking, research skills, clinical methodology, or other forms of interactive teaching or classroom management techniques.
- A listserv or Facebook closed group page can be launched for inter-university faculty members and their professional partners to share ideas about teaching methodologies, curriculum, research, and related activities.[26]

Transforming classrooms—virtual or physical—may require a transformation in culture and bureaucracy.

## D. ASSESSMENT & GUIDANCE

*[E]ducators and students alike have found themselves more and more flummoxed by a system that values assessment over engagement, learning management over discovery, content over community, outcomes over epiphanies.*[27]

Good pedagogy includes instructor and student interactions. At a minimum, the course instructor must be available to answer questions and conduct some form of individualized evaluation, beyond assignment of a numeric or letter grade. This is more challenging in situations where time is limited, due to other teaching or administrative duties, and where the instructor can only communicate with students *one-by-one* via laptop or phone. The communication is even less efficient when the internet or phone line connectivity is unstable or the screen and keyboard are small—for either teacher or learner.

There are perhaps two fundamental tasks for the instructor in this domain in technologically distressed environments:

- Instructor monitoring: Set a standard number of student discussion posts that require a response from you to in any given discussion and the number of daylight hours that can pass before posting your responses.

---

26. The Myanmar Law Teachers Network (https://www.facebook.com/groups/347164726105917) was established as a closed group Facebook page, making it affordable, culturally appropriate, and technologically accessible to Myanmar teaching staff as a means of pedagogical exchange where other modes of communication are not reliable or there are greater administrative hurdles. *See also Pandemic Pedagogy Facebook Group*, FACEBOOK, https://www.facebook.com/groups/pandemicpedagogy1/files (group composed of several thousand educators, students, and others "sharing insights, best (and worst) practices, advice, successes, challenges, and research about converting to fully remote/online instruction.").

27. Jesse Stommel, *Critical Digital Pedagogy: a Definition*, HYBRID PEDAGOGY (Nov. 17, 2014), https://hybridpedagogy.org/critical-digital-pedagogy-definition/.

- Mentoring and Advice: Call students who are struggling, schedule conference calls instead of office hours. Ask students to share their phone number with their assigned groups and collaborate verbally, if not visually.

Digital teacher and pedagogue Sean Morris reflected on this process:

> [T]o let these students know they had been heard... to listen and respond, to prod and embolden, to cheer.... Weaving your way down the thread of discussion was also a weaving my way through the relationships you establish with each student. Had they engaged deeply? Did they ask technical questions seeking high marks? Did they make deeper inquiry, delving past the material of the course to the act of learning itself? Could I sense in their words the need for a reply? Could you read within the exchanges between students a need for my interruption, interjection, or redirection?[28]

There are variations on how to organize and operationalize the monitoring, mentoring and advising tasks, notwithstanding the suggestions above. The same may be said about the assessment of students' work product and overall performance. Assessment is an important part of any instructor's role—whether the teaching-learning mode is in-person, online, synchronous, or asynchronous and whether the course content is primarily doctrinal or clinical.

## III. Communication Between Students

### A. PEER EDUCATION À LA PEN PAL

The other form of engagement to complement self-study and interaction with the instructor is peer-to-peer connection. One asynchronous exercise meant to allow participation from multiple voices is writing letters between "pen pals" in class. This can help students feel more connected to their peer community and provide some of the feedback and dialogue that is not frequently available from the instructor. In these letters, students may discuss readings, review assignments, or they may work together—virtually or not—on a project. These letters are both a variation and extension of reflective journals, which are a core component of clinical legal education.[29] "Pen pal

---

28. Sean Michael Morris, *Fostering Care and Community at a Distance*, SEAN MICHAEL MORRIS (May 28, 2020), https://www.seanmichaelmorris.com/fostering-care-and-community-at-a-distance/. Morris, who has more than twenty years of experience in instructional design, networked learning, digital composition and publishing, collaboration, and editing, dutifully undertakes this daily task "with my tea in hand, unbreakfasted, and usually still in my pyjamas." Yet, he resists the quality control rubrics and monitoring established by his educational institution and derides the efforts of instructional designers, such as Quality Matters, who "corner the market on best practices" with a business model "predicated on overreaching and infantilising teachers." *Id.*

29. There is a vast body of literature on reflective journaling. *See, e.g.*, J.P. Ogilvy, *The Use of Journals in Legal Education: A Tool for Reflection*. 3 CLINICAL L. REV. 55 (1996); Carolyn Wilkes Kaas et al., *Delivering Effective Education in Externship Programs, in* BUILDING ON BEST PRACTICES, *supra* note 11, at 235–36.

letters have a personal immediacy to them that can foster trust and collegiality, or give insights into significant differences in background and perspective."[30]

Any combination of digital teacher and pedagogue Sean Morris's guidelines can be adapted for students studying law remotely, whether or not they ever meet on screen in a synchronous class. These include:

- Establishing norms and boundaries for the letters to which students will hold each other accountable.
- Encouraging reflection on learning and writing that goes beyond the class material.
- Promoting creative expression.
- Relying on students to write each other "enough to be effective communicators."

Students should choose their own pen pal—or you can suggest a match or be a pen pal yourself—and not be monitored to see if they are writing to one another. Pen pal letters are a form of correspondence that is made public if the writer consents.[31]

## IV. Conclusion

There is no remote learning substitute for reliable, quality video and telecommunications in a course overseen by an instructor schooled in the best practices of teaching, mentoring, giving feedback, and fostering student engagement. That said, in technologically distressed environments, where highly trained teachers are in short supply or there is a lack of congregate meeting spaces, learners face a different reality. We must persist in efforts to advance the education of these students in ways that are neither overly reliant on online connectivity nor forgetful of human connection.

---

30. Sean Michael Morris, *Love Letters and Pen Pals: Community Through Correspondence*, Sean Michael Morris (May 4, 2020), https://www.seanmichaelmorris.com/love-letters-and-pen-pals-community-through-correspondence/.

31. *Id.*

SEVEN

# Using Blended and Online Learning Strategies to Provide Innovative Academic Support to All Students

Susan Landrum*

After reviewing this chapter, readers will be able to:

- Identify ways in which academic support programs (ASP) can develop blended resources, programming, and courses to support law students;
- Summarize several benefits to providing ASP content in blended formats;
- Explain how blended approaches to ASP can be used to increase collaboration between ASP professionals and other faculty and integrate ASP throughout the law school curriculum;
- Consider how blended approaches to a pre-orientation program for incoming law students could improve students' readiness for their first semester; and
- Identify several best practices for designing online content for students with disabilities.

Academic support programs (ASP) have become increasingly important over the years as law schools have committed to accepting students from diverse backgrounds.[1]

* Assistant Dean of Academic Success & Professionalism, Nova Southeastern University Shepard Broad College of Law. Dean Landrum began her teaching career in 1992, first as a historian and later as a legal educator. She has been designing and teaching hybrid courses since 2000 and online asynchronous and synchronous courses since 2013. Dean Landrum also consults with law schools regarding online teaching and learning, academic support, and disability access projects.

1. For a brief overview of the history of academic support programs, see Russell A. McClain, *Bottled at the Source: Recapturing the Essence of Academic Support as a Primary Tool of Education Equity for Minority Law Students*, 18 U. Md. L.J. Race, Religion, Gender & Class 139, 140–55 (2018); Rebecca Flanagan, *The Kids Aren't Alright: Rethinking the Law Student Skills Deficit*, 2015 B.Y.U. Educ. & L.J. 135, 172–74 (2015); and Louis N. Schulze, Jr., *Alternative Justifications for Law School Academic Support Programs:*

Academic support has primarily come in three formats: academic skills workshops, academic success and bar-related courses, and individual counseling.[2] Traditionally, all of those things have happened in in-person environments. Technology, if used appropriately, can revolutionize the delivery of academic support to law students, increasing ASP accessibility for all students—including those with disabilities. Online ASP components can and should effectively implement current best practices in teaching and learning, including teaching skills tied to self-directed learning and metacognition, memory, and executive function,[3] while maximizing the limited resources available to those programs. Moving ASP into blended formats will also help to integrate ASP more fully into the rest of the law school curriculum.

This chapter explores some of the ways in which twenty-first century ASP can use blended and online learning tools and strategies to maximize the support provided to all law students. First, the chapter explains how online, asynchronous ASP modules could be used to ensure that all incoming law students have the same basic foundation of background knowledge and academic skills. Second, the chapter identifies how ASP can make academic support more flexible and broadly accessible by taking at least some programming and instruction into the asynchronous online environment. Finally, the chapter advocates that ASP professionals—as well as all legal educators—ensure that any online materials meet legal requirements and educational best practices for accessibility. Even as law schools move more ASP programming and other course content online, we must prioritize design decisions that make legal education accessible for students with disabilities. Moving more of legal education onto online platforms provides both an opportunity and an imperative to better support law students with disabilities. Because online materials are usually designed for repeated reuse, and in advance of any notice of students' accommodations, legal educators must apply best practices in designing their online courses, programs, and resources, and ASP professors should lead the way in these efforts.

---

*Self-Determination Theory, Autonomy Support, and Humanizing the Law School*, 5 Charleston L. Rev. 269, 274–78 (2011).

2. *See* Susan Landrum, *Drawing Inspiration from the Flipped Classroom Model: An Integrated Approach to Academic Support for the Academically Underprepared Law Student*, 53 Duq. L. Rev. 245, 263–64 (2015).

3. For more discussion of these best practices, see, e.g., Louis N. Schulze, Jr., *Using Science to Build Better Learners: One School's Successful Efforts to Raise Its Bar Passage Rates in an Era of Decline*, 68 J. Legal Educ. 230 (2019); Elizabeth M. Bloom, *Creating Desirable Difficulties: Strategies for Reshaping Teaching and Learning in the Law School Classroom*, 95 U. Det. Mercy L. Rev. 115 (2018); Jennifer M. Cooper, *Smarter Law Learning: Using Cognitive Science to Maximize Law Learning*, 44 Cap. U. L. Rev. 551 (2016); Elizabeth M. Bloom, *Teaching Law Students to Teach Themselves: Using Lessons from Educational Psychology to Shape Self-Regulated Learners*, 59 Wayne L. Rev. 311 (2013) [hereinafter *Teaching Law Students*]; Michael Hunter Schwartz, *Teaching Law Students to Be Self-Regulated Learners*, 2003 Mich. St. DCL L. Rev. 447 (2003) [hereinafter *Self-Regulated Learners*]; Michael Hunter Schwartz, *Teaching Law by Design: How Learning Theory and Instructional Design Can Inform and Reform Law School Teaching*, 38 San Diego L. Rev. 347 (2001).

## I. Using Online, Asynchronous ASP Modules to Provide a Basic Foundation for Students Starting Law School

Online, asynchronous ASP content can be a way of "leveling the playing field" for students entering law school from diverse educational and personal backgrounds—especially if content is made available prior to the first weeks of law school. Incoming students are usually excited to start law school, and they often want to know what they can do to be prepared. Using technology, we can re-envision what we do with orientation, teaching those motivated incoming students the academic skills they need for early success in law school.

Think about the traditional model for law school orientation. Most schools offer a short orientation program that lasts from a single day to several days. In that time, students are inundated with information and events: sessions about law school policies and graduation requirements; financial aid presentations; technical support appointments; social opportunities and student mentoring programs; professionalism panels; wellness initiatives; and student activity fairs. In the midst of this information onslaught, we introduce students to critical skills for preparing for class—how to read and brief cases. The amount of time spent on academic skills development in most orientation programs is relatively small, as little as an hour or maybe a few hours at most. How much are students likely to retain when they are experiencing information overload?

### A. THE PRE-ORIENTATION ASP MODEL

With ASP content included in the traditional orientation module, there are limited opportunities to build incoming students' knowledge base and foundational academic skills. But what if we pulled this instruction out of the orientation schedule and made it a pre-orientation, online, asynchronous "course"? What might this new pre-orientation ASP approach look like? The starting point is to consider the basic knowledge and academic skills we believe law students need for success as they begin law school. Law professors often assume that students already have a basic knowledge of civics and the structure of the judicial system, but most students have some gaps in their knowledge. In fact, we know that some incoming students' knowledge and skills gaps are significant and can potentially adversely affect their success in law school. First, students come from diverse backgrounds. Students educated in elite school systems have a different framework for what they are learning. Students whose parents are college-educated or professionals draw from different contexts than first-generation students. Immigrants and international students may not have the same educational context as those who were educated in U.S. schools since childhood, and even students' majors in college may affect what context they have for their legal studies.

To address these gaps, law schools could develop asynchronous ASP modules that first-year students would complete in the weeks prior to the start of their first semester. An online ASP pre-orientation "course" could provide some foundational knowledge, such as: (1) a general introduction to what lawyers do and how law school and the bar exam relate to becoming a lawyer; (2) "civics"-related content, such as the structure of state and federal governments, balance of powers, and sources of law; (3) the structure of state and federal court systems; (4) an explanation of how cases work their way through the civil and criminal judicial systems; and (5) an introduction to foundational legal concepts including precedent, stare decisis, and mandatory versus persuasive authority. Students could complete modules at their own pace, depending on their prior education and experience.

Beyond the "knowledge" content, additional modules could begin new students' academic skills training, establishing a foundation for additional academic skills they will learn during the first year of law school. These modules could begin the process of building a specific learning "culture" for the incoming class and introduce students to learning concepts that underpin successful learning, such as self-regulated learning, effective memory strategies like spaced repetition, growth mindset, and active learning strategies.[4] There is an opportunity to have incoming students think about what they want to accomplish in law school, how they believe they learn best, and what strategies they have used in the past that may transfer to their law school learning. It is also a chance to challenge wrong assumptions about effective learning strategies and replace those assumptions with sound, research-supported approaches. Modules on reading and briefing cases would allow students to practice critical reading skills, introduce effective notetaking strategies, and engage students in the process of learning how cases—and therefore the law found in those cases—is constructed. Further modules could introduce classroom methodologies like Socratic Method and team-based learning, as well as logical reasoning skills.

How could these pre-orientation ASP modules be constructed? The modules could be built into the law school's learning management system as an ASP "course." Each module would start with an introduction. The modules' substantive content could then be presented in a series of short videos, and each module would offer opportunities for self-assessment and reflection and provide suggestions for students who want to improve further.

## B. CURRENT APPROACHES TO PRE-ORIENTATION PROGRAMS, BOTH IN-PERSON AND ONLINE

The concept of pre-orientation learning opportunities for law students is not new. Some law schools have had summer programs or extended orientation programs for

4. *See generally* Cooper, *supra* note 3; Bloom, *Teaching Law Students*, *supra* note 3; Schwartz, *Self-Regulated Learners*, *supra* note 3.

conditionally-admitted students,[5] targeted groups of first-year students,[6] and even all incoming 1Ls[7] for years. Those programs have usually taken place in person and have not had the level of flexibility that an asynchronous, online pre-orientation ASP program would have.

More recently, two different approaches to online pre-orientation programs have begun to emerge. The first approach is a commercial model, with two options leading the field. Harvard Law School introduced their Zero-L course in 2018. Zero-L was created for Harvard students but has since been marketed broadly to administrators at other law schools.[8] Zero-L primarily provides incoming students with basic knowledge that will aid in the transition to law school, although students do read and brief a case as part of the course.[9] Course modules are taught by Harvard Law School faculty, not ASP professors, and do not emphasize learning concepts rooted in educational psychology or self-directed learning.[10] The main focus of Zero-L appears to be on the "what" and "why" of law school learning, rather than the "how." BarBri has introduced the second commercial option, further extending its products into the legal education market with a one-credit asynchronous online course package they began offering

5. *See, e.g.*, Judith J. Devine & Jennifer D. Odom, *Do Academic Support Programs Reduce the Attrition Rate of First-Year Law Students?*, 29 T. Marshall L. Rev. 209, 227 (2004) (noting law schools with conditional admission programs that offered voluntary or requires ASP programming for students).

6. I created a five-week ASP course at St. John's University School of Law for incoming law students who, based on their applications, were identified as benefiting from an extended introduction to the academic skills required for success in law school. That course is titled Foundations of American Law & Analysis. *See also* Louis N. Schulze Jr., *Alternative Justifications for Academic Support II: How "Academic Support Across the Curriculum" Helps Meet the Goals of the Carnegie Report and Best Practices*, 40 Cap. U. L. Rev. 1, 22–23 (2012) (describing the benefits of targeted pre-Orientation programs). The CLEO Summer Institute, which is not focused on students at a single law school, is another example of a pre-Orientation program. *See* Council on Legal Education Opportunity, Inc., Pre-Law Summer Institute, https://cleoinc.org/programs/plsi/ (last visited Nov. 6, 2020).

7. For example, the University of Oklahoma College of Law has a First-Year Summer Start Program, where students have the option of taking a "legal foundations" course along with one doctrinal law course in advance of the Fall semester. *See The First-Year Law Summer Start (1LS) Program: A First-Look at Law School*, The University of Oklahoma College of Law, https://law.ou.edu/admissions/jd-program/first-year-law-summer-start-1ls-program-first-look-law-school (last visited Nov. 6, 2020). Other schools have shorter pre-Fall semester courses, such as St. John's University School of Law's two-week Introduction to Law course, which is taught by doctrinal faculty but also includes some basic law school academic skills instruction, such as briefing cases, outlining, and writing essays. *See Introduction to Law Course Enhances St. John's 1L Experience*, St. John's University (June 15, 2017), https://www.stjohns.edu/about/news/2017-06-15/introduction-law-course-enhances-st-johns-1l-experience (last visited Nov. 6, 2020).

8. A few law schools used Zero-L in Fall 2019, but then Harvard offered the course free to all law schools who wanted to use it for incoming students during the COVID-19 pandemic in Summer 2020. *See Harvard makes online course for incoming students available to all law schools for free this summer*, Harvard Law Today (May 20, 2020), https://today.law.harvard.edu/harvard-makes-online-course-for-incoming-students-available-to-all-law-schools-for-free-this-summer/.

9. *See Zero-L*, Harvard Law School, https://online.law.harvard.edu/ (last visited Feb. 18, 2021) ("Zero-L is an online course designed to ensure all incoming students, whatever their backgrounds and previous areas of study, start with foundational legal knowledge that enables them to thrive in law school.").

10. In fact, I would argue that Zero-L is not an ASP course at all, as its primary focus is really on basic knowledge acquisition rather than skills development.

to law schools in 2020 called Lawyering Fundamentals.[11] Unlike Harvard's Zero-L program, which puts most of its emphasis on a student's knowledge acquisition, Lawyering Fundamentals is designed to teach students "foundational lawyer-like thinking, reasoning, analytical, and problem-solving skills."[12] I expect the field of commercially available pre-orientation programs to grow in the next several years.

The second online pre-orientation approach is one designed by faculty, both ASP and doctrinal, at individual law schools. This in-house approach is much more labor-intensive for law schools than the commercial model to create, but it gives schools the flexibility to tailor content to what the school has identified as most important for its admitted students and establish the law school's own faculty as learning experts for their students. If done well, this customized model has several advantages over the commercial model:

- the pre-orientation course can be aligned with the law school's larger programmatic learning objectives;
- incoming students will be introduced to some of the faculty they will work with during their time in law school, including ASP professors;
- pre-orientation course content can reference the specific courses and even professors that students will have during their first semester of law school, as well as law school policies, procedures, and customs that may be relevant;
- although there may be significant initial labor costs to creating an in-house program, there are minimal costs to maintaining it afterwards; and
- law school faculty and administrators can regularly assess the course and modify content as necessary to address student needs.[13]

In addition to the benefits to online ASP programming already mentioned in this chapter, there are other significant benefits to offering this type of pre-orientation ASP course for incoming law students. This approach offers more opportunities for students to practice the skills they are learning by using formative assessments. For example, a module introducing students to reading and briefing cases could instruct students to apply what they are learning to brief a specific case, and then ask a series

11. *See* Email from Thomas Stenson to Susan Landrum (Mar. 6, 2020) (on file with author) (introducing BarBri's Lawyering Fundamentals course).

12. *See id.*

13. I designed a short asynchronous online ASP pre-orientation course, which my department implemented for the first time for our Fall 2020 entering class at Nova Southeastern University Shepard Broad College of Law. After a successful first run, we are adding additional modules for future entering classes. I also consulted with the University of Memphis Cecil C. Humphreys School of Law in creating a similar online pre-orientation course for that school's students. In addition, Yale Law School professor Ian Ayres has created a free course for incoming law students on Coursera titled "A Law Student's Toolkit" which includes some ASP-related content. *See* Ian Ayres, *A Law Student's Toolkit*, COURSERA, http://www.coursera.org/learn/law-student (last visited May 29, 2021).

of multiple-choice questions to assess whether they properly identified the parts of the case. Finally, an asynchronous online pre-orientation ASP course gives law schools the opportunity to start identifying students who may have academic challenges early on—getting accommodations set up more quickly in advance of the school year for students who have disabilities; identifying knowledge and skills deficits that may require remediation; identifying students who lack sufficient access to technology, Wi-Fi access, or home study environments that will help set them up for success (a particularly important benefit if more law school courses are online in the future, which seems both possible and increasingly likely); and identifying issues with motivation, executive functioning, and other things that could affect long-term academic success.

## II. Making the ASP Department Virtual: Designing Academic Support Programs to Make ASP More Flexible and Broadly Accessible

There is one thing that has become evident as law schools have navigated the COVID-19 pandemic: the ASP program of the future should have an online base. This conclusion does not mean that the brick-and-mortar ASP department will disappear entirely. After all, there are some aspects of teaching that may be both easier and more effective in-person; in most circumstances, individualized academic counseling fits in this category. But, in a modern, technologically-driven world, where our students have grown up regularly using technology and engaging online, it is important that ASP have a strong online presence. That online presence will allow ASP professors to engage effectively and flexibly with students, even when unusual circumstances like natural disasters or pandemics affect the law school's traditional methods of communicating and delivering instruction.

### A. USING LEARNING MANAGEMENT SYSTEMS AND UNIVERSAL DESIGN FOR LEARNING GUIDELINES TO PROVIDE EFFECTIVE AND ACCESSIBLE VIRTUAL ACADEMIC SUPPORT

Accepting that it is good for law school ASP programs to have a virtual platform, what might this online presence look like? At a minimum, ASP programs should use their universities' learning management systems to create a virtual academic support department. Students could go to the online platform to access curated ASP resources such as handouts, short videos, and links to helpful blogs and websites.[14] ASP could

14. For example, the Academic Success & Professionalism Department at Nova Southeastern University Shepard Broad College of Law has created an ASP Canvas "course" for all students. The ASP Canvas course contains curated academic success resources for students, including blog posts, recommended supplements, and other guides; links to mental health and physical health resources for law students; suggestions of useful study apps; writing and grammar resources; bar exam resources; and videos, podcasts, and asynchronous ASP workshops. It can serve as a platform for ASP programming announcements and discussions, and we can set up live online workshops and meetings integrating Canvas and Zoom.

also offer asynchronous workshops in this virtual platform and create discussion boards for student questions. Putting the virtual ASP program into the university's learning management system ensures that students access it in the same way they access online content from other courses they may be taking. Many learning management systems also have apps, offering access to virtual ASP materials on tablets and cell phones, not just computers.

Virtual ASP programs should be created using Universal Design in Learning (UDL) principles.[15] UDL "is a framework to improve and optimize teaching and learning for all people based on scientific insights into how humans learn."[16] UDL guidelines focus on developing "expert learners" who are (1) purposeful and motivated, (2) resourceful and knowledgeable, and (3) strategic and goal-directed, by providing learners with multiple alternative ways to engage, act, and express what they are learning in a variety of formats.[17] UDL guidelines should affect the development of virtual ASP programs in a variety of ways, and in the process could make online ASP content a model for other law school courses. For example, UDL requires that information be presented in multiple formats, such as providing scripts or captioning for audio and video files.[18] This approach ensures that the online course is compliant with the Americans with Disabilities Act and Section 504 of the Rehabilitation Act of 1973, making materials fully accessible to students with disabilities,[19] but it also improves accessibility for *all* students. UDL-based virtual ASP platforms can also offer students multiple alternatives for how to develop academic skills, granting students more autonomy over their own learning in the process.[20]

A virtual ASP platform can provide more support to students who may be underserved by traditional in-person ASP programming. In part, this is because asynchronous courses are not constrained by the clock. One of the ongoing challenges for ASP is providing support to part-time evening or, increasingly, blended program students, who usually are unable to participate in daytime workshops and whose course and work schedules may make it difficult to schedule alternative ASP sessions. Moving at least some academic support online and making it asynchronous gives part-time students access to ASP content on demand, when it fits best into their busy schedules.

---

Previously, I created a more limited ASP "course" with curated content on Westlaw's TWEN platform for students at St. John's University School of Law.

15. *See* Jason S. Palmer, *"The Millennials are Coming!": Improving Self-Efficacy in Law Students Through Universal Design in Learning*, 63 CLEV. ST. L. REV. 675 (2015).

16. *About Universal Design for Learning*, CAST, http://www.cast.org/impact/universal-design-for-learning-udl (last visited Nov. 7, 2020).

17. *See The UDL Guidelines*, CAST, http://udlguidelines.cast.org/ (last visited Nov. 7, 2020).

18. *See id.*

19. For a detailed explanation of the legal requirements of these two statutes in the context of online-based educational content, *see Legal Obligations for Accessibility*, UDL ON CAMPUS: UNIVERSAL DESIGN FOR LEARNING IN HIGHER EDUCATION, http://udloncampus.cast.org/page/policy_legal (last visited Nov. 6, 2020).

20. *See id.*

For programs that have sufficient resources to provide only individualized support to students identified as academically at-risk, a virtual ASP department provides at least some support, at low cost, for those outside of that group.

There is also the opportunity to think of creative alternatives to traditional presentations of information—videos for students with lengthy commutes on public transportation, or podcast-style content for students who drive long distances to get to work or school. Of course, videos and podcasts are more suitable for certain aspects of ASP than others. Videos or podcasts can introduce students to new learning concepts, such as self-directed learning, growth mindset, and spaced repetition and other memory techniques. They can even introduce new academic skills, such as outlining or synthesizing legal rules or taking multiple-choice or essay exams. Students would still need to practice the concepts they are learning, but moving information delivery into an asynchronous, online format could be beneficial.

In addition, online ASP materials could benefit law students for whom English is a second language or who were educated outside of the United States, whether those students are J.D. or LL.M. students.[21] Many law schools admit immigrants and international students. There is a significant benefit of online materials for these students, especially well-designed video content. Because students can watch videos on their own schedule, allowing them to pause, rewind, and even re-watch content, students can work at their own pace. Closed captioning or accompanying scripts for videos provides additional resource tools for these students to improve their reading and listening comprehension skills.

Finally, offering students a virtual ASP platform could reduce the stigma some students feel in seeking academic support. ASP online content would be available to all students, even those who might not normally come to our offices for help. Offering virtual appointments, through Zoom or other video-conferencing platforms, could be another way to reduce feelings of stigma. A student who might hesitate to come to an ASP professor's office for help might not feel the same way about scheduling a virtual appointment on Zoom, which can feel more private. Ultimately, technology has the potential to normalize academic support, making it something that everyone has access to and uses on a regular basis.

It will take time and significant effort to create a robust virtual ASP platform, and that prospect can make such a goal seem overwhelming at first. After all, high quality videos require a well-written script, the time to record the video, and time and skill to edit and caption it. ASP faculty will have to learn best practices for setting up their materials in the learning management system. Thought must go into how traditional workshops can be translated to an asynchronous, online environment. It is not necessary to offer all components of such a program at one time, however. ASP faculty

21. Most law school ASP programs only provide academic support to J.D. students, often because of limited resources. A virtual ASP platform could provide basic ASP resources to all students at a law school, not just J.D. students, without further taxing the ASP department's limited resources.

can determine which resources they would like to include in such an online platform and then identify which items are highest priority and work on those first. Because the virtual platform can be used indefinitely, more content can be added over time, ultimately building a rich set of resources for students.

### B. USING A BLENDED APPROACH TO TURN ASP CLASSROOMS INTO LEARNING LABORATORIES

Technology can also transform ASP courses. ASP professors can use a blended learning approach to turn classrooms into learning laboratories. A flipped classroom, also known as an inverted classroom, is one in which students complete what traditionally would happen during class, such as listening to lectures, asynchronously outside of class, leaving in-person class time to practice what they have learned.[22] Some law professors, including ASP professors, have incorporated flipped classroom strategies into their teaching in recent years.[23]

What would a flipped classroom approach to a first-year ASP course look like? Each face-to-face class session would be the heart of a learning module, focused on one academic skill or a cluster of related academic skills. Students would prepare for the class session by going into the learning management system and watching one or more short videos introducing the academic skill for that session and exploring strategies for maximizing that skill. There might also be additional preliminary homework, such as review of specific doctrinal content from one of their other courses prior to attending the ASP class session. After students complete practice exercises or hypotheticals in class, students could debrief those questions as a class or in smaller groups or pairs. Completing practice exercises in the classroom gives students the opportunity to ask questions immediately, rather than having to schedule an appointment with the professor at a later point to get clarification.[24]

This flipped classroom approach allows students to spend class time applying what they are learning, developing the skills they need for academic success. For example, a key skill for law school exams, whether multiple choice or essay, is issue spotting. Stu-

---

22. *See* MARY BART, FACULTY FOCUS SPECIAL REPORT, BLENDED AND FLIPPED: EXPLORING NEW MODELS FOR EFFECTIVE TEACHING AND LEARNING 2 (July 2014); Barbi Honeycutt & Jennifer Garnett, *Expanding the Definition of a Flipped Environment*, *in* FACULTY FOCUS SPECIAL REPORT, BLENDED AND FLIPPED: EXPLORING NEW MODELS FOR EFFECTIVE TEACHING AND LEARNING 12 (July 2014).

23. *See, e.g.*, Landrum, *supra* note 2; Catherine A. Lemmer, *A View from the Flip Side: Using the "Inverted Classroom" to Enhance the Legal Information Literacy of the International LL.M. Student*, 105 LAW LIBR. J. 461 (2013); Peter Sankoff, *Taking the Instruction of Law Outside the Lecture Hall: How the Flipped Classroom Can Make Learning More Productive and Enjoyable (For Professors and Students)*, 51 U. ALBERTA L. REV. 891 (2014).

24. I have designed and taught ASP courses in a "flipped classroom" format and found that approach increased student engagement with the course materials and the ASP department in general, as well as helped students connect academic skills to the substantive law they learned in other courses. For a more detailed discussion of how that course was designed and how it functioned, see Landrum, *supra* note 2, at 271–77.

dents could start by watching a video about issue spotting and reviewing their outline for specific topics in a doctrinal course before coming into the ASP classroom. Then, in class, everyone could work through some issue spotting exercises, comparing what each student spotted in a fact pattern and brainstorming ways to make it easier to spot missing issues in the future. This would only be one part of a series of class sessions on exam skills, but the later class sessions could build on what students learned in this session. And, because students had the opportunity to practice issue spotting rather than just learning about it in the abstract, they will have a better understanding of how to exercise that skill again in the future. This approach could be used for teaching any academic skill, whether in a first-year ASP course or a more targeted upper-level course for students whose first-year academic performance suggests that additional skills development would be helpful.

Like the virtual ASP platform described earlier in this chapter, a flipped classroom approach to an ASP course requires some time investment at the beginning. The ASP professor must identify what content is best presented online, in an asynchronous format, versus what will be most effective in the physical classroom. Once those determinations are made, the professor must create video scripts and record and edit video content for the online portion of the modules. After that content is created once, however, it will be reusable in subsequent semesters. And, in addition, students can go back and review videos for skills that they find particularly challenging, both during that semester and even at later times.

## C. MOVING ACADEMIC SUPPORT OUT OF THE ASP SILO AND INTO THE BROADER LAW SCHOOL CURRICULUM

Traditionally, ASP has been entirely separate from other parts of the law school curriculum. This reality has been reinforced by several factors: ASP content has often been presented as workshops rather than courses; ASP courses have often been zero-credit courses, even when required, and are usually graded Pass/Fail; and ASP professors have often been classified as staff rather than faculty at most law schools. What is the problem with ASP being kept so separate from other parts of the law school curriculum? First, this approach signals to students that what ASP courses teach is less important than their other courses, rather than encouraging them to view those academic skills as an essential foundation to their academic success. Second, when ASP content is taught separately, many students struggle with transferring the things they are learning in those ASP workshops and courses to their other classes.[25] Third, without connecting academic skills to substantive content, those skills are taught and learned in the abstract; doctrinal course content really is essential for practicing many of the academic skills students learn in their ASP courses.

---

25. This is a general problem for student, who often do not recognize how skills learned in one context can apply in other, multiple contexts. *See generally* Tonya Kowalski, *True North: Navigating for the Transfer of Learning in Legal Education*, 2010 SEATTLE U. L. REV. 51 (2010).

In the past several years, there have been increased efforts to integrate ASP content with substantive courses, particularly in the first-year curriculum.[26] To this point the number of ASP programs that are fully integrated with doctrinal courses is still limited,[27] although there have been a few professors who have advocated for an "ASP across the Curriculum" approach for some time.[28] Some ASP programs coordinate on a more limited basis with doctrinal faculty, for specific class sessions or skills.[29] But these efforts to integrate ASP with doctrinal courses have generally been focused on the in-person classroom and have not usually integrated online content.

Going forward, blended and online learning models create even more opportunities to move ASP into the broader law school curriculum. This can be done by pairing online ASP content with in-person, blended, or online substantive courses, rather than teaching skills separately. As with earlier in-person integration efforts, collaboration between ASP professors and faculty teaching those doctrinal courses is necessary for effective student learning. For students to take the ASP content seriously, their doctrinal law professors must communicate its importance. It is also a chance for ASP professors to showcase their specialized knowledge and expertise—focusing on learning theory, educational psychology, pedagogy, and, in this context, best practices in online teaching and learning.

One way that integration could occur is for the ASP professor to coordinate with a doctrinal law professor and pair online academic skills instruction and practice with the doctrinal class. This approach could be particularly effective in the first semester in law school. Students could complete an online module on critical reading and case briefing, and then apply what they have learned to a reading assignment for the doctrinal course. When the professor finishes one topic and moves on to the next in the syllabus, that would be the perfect time for an online module on rule synthesis and outlining. The accompanying assignment could be for the students to outline the recently completed topic. Other modules could cover additional academic skills traditionally taught in first-semester ASP courses and workshops, but once again integrated with substantive course content. This type of approach could work for upper

---

26. *See generally* Schulze, *supra* note 6.

27. For example, McGeorge School of Law at the University of the Pacific requires a one-semester Fall Semester Skills Lab for 1Ls, which is integrated with a substantive law course such as Property or Torts. *See* ACADEMIC SUPPORT SERVICES—MCGEORGE, https://law.pacific.edu/law/students/academics/academic-support/academic-support-services (last visited Nov. 5, 2020).

28. *See generally* Schulze, *supra* note 6; Melissa J. Marlow, *It Takes a Village to Solve the Problems in Legal Education: Every Faculty Member's Role in Academic Support*, 30 U. ARK. LITTLE ROCK L. REV. 489 (2008); Deborah Zalesne & David Navordney, *Integrating Academic Skills into First Year Curricula: Using Wood v. Lucy, Lady Duff-Gordon to Teach the Role of Facts in Legal Reasoning*, 28 PACE L. REV. 271 (2007); *see also* Schulze, *supra* note 1, at 283–85.

29. I have done this at each school I have taught at: Savannah Law School, St. John's University School of Law, and Nova Southeastern University Shepard Broad College of Law. Sometimes that has meant coordinating with a doctrinal professor to identify a topic that will be used to teach skills in an ASP class session like issue spotting, outlining, or essay writing. At other times, I have gone into the doctrinal professor's class to teach a session on reading and interpreting statutes or exam skills.

level courses as well, providing the opportunity to teach advanced academic skills or bar skills as part of students' other courses.[30]

ASP professors could also use online resources to take a broader approach to integrating academic skills instruction throughout the law school curriculum. Because most of the skills ASP professors teach are applicable to almost all law school courses, ASP professors could create short skills videos that have general applicability and share them with doctrinal faculty for use in their courses.[31] With this approach, students would get the same messaging from multiple sources, reinforcing the fact that the skills they are learning are transferrable from one course to the next.

## III. Ensuring Twenty-First Century Legal Education is Fully Accessible for Students with Disabilities

Because law schools have had to move to online and blended learning during the COVID-19 pandemic, an ongoing transition to more and more online legal education is likely to be accelerated. This trend provides an opportunity to implement thoughtful, accessible online course design across the law school curriculum. ASP professors, who for the reasons already discussed in this chapter can both maximize the benefits of online learning and need to make their instruction accessible to all students, can be leaders in this process. ASP at its core is about increasing access to legal education, and therefore all types of access must be considered. And if a law school has a commitment to a diverse legal profession, then accessibility for students with disabilities must be a priority.

Moving forward, there are both real educational opportunities and a legal mandate[32] to think differently about accessibility for law students with disabilities. In the in-person classrooms of the past, law school administrators, as well as most faculty, have had a tendency to only think about support for students with disabilities in terms of legal status, asking the question of whether a student was entitled to accommo-

---

30. As one example, I created a set of online modules that upper-level seminars use at St. John's University School of Law. In those seminars, students must complete a research paper, but not all students have experience in this type of scholarly writing. The seminar courses focus on a particular area of substantive law, but they generally do not teach how to write the paper. I created a set of five modules that took students through the process of choosing a topic and developing a thesis, developing a research plan, organizing their research, meeting professional and ethical standards in scholarly writing, drafting, and editing. The online modules had a strong ASP focus, reinforcing time management skills, project management skills, critical thinking, and organization, among other applicable academic skills.

31. For example, I created a series of short videos focused on final exam skills and shared them with faculty at my law school. Video topics included creating a final exam study schedule, studying for open book exams, avoiding plagiarism in open book and take-home exams, and strategies for taking online exams. Professors have then shared the videos most relevant to their exam format. Students learned other exam strategies, specific to multiple choice and essay exams, in their ASP course.

32. Accessibility requirements for online educational content are mandated by the Americans with Disabilities Act and Section 504 of the Rehabilitation Act of 1973. *See Legal Obligations for Accessibility*, UDL On Campus: Universal Design for Learning in Higher Education, http://udloncampus.cast.org/page/policy_legal (last visited Nov. 6, 2020).

dations.[33] Online and blended learning, in contrast, use a different lens. The design approach to online course content must be proactive, considering universal design principles that create accessibility from the outset, as the Office for Civil Rights of the U.S. Department of Education has stated that students with disabilities "must be afforded the opportunity to acquire the same information, engage in the same interactions, and enjoy the same services as [nondisabled] students."[34] In addition, it should be no more difficult for students with disabilities to access online classroom materials than it is for any other student.[35] The professor should try to anticipate student access needs in advance and design online materials to support as many different students' needs as possible from the outset, rather than reacting after the professor receives notice of an accommodation. This approach is important because online resources are usually meant to be reusable. There is a lot more work up front, before a course begins, in creating online resources, and having to go back to recreate learning materials to make them accessible for a student with an accommodation later can be a poor way to approach resource use. It may also lead to a delay in student access to important materials that have had to be remade.

In the future, law professors should apply Universal Design for Learning (UDL) principles from the outset to online and blended course design, ensuring that course content is accessible in multiple ways, using multiple formats.[36] That design process should begin with checking to see what the accessibility features are for the platforms the professor plans to use, in particular making sure that screen readers work with text-based platforms and synchronous video platforms have captioning capability.[37] If professors intend to put content online, they need to understand what the law requires for accessibility, and they should have a basic grasp of online educational best practices.[38] If creating videos, professors should present video content in multiple formats, captioning the videos and preferably offering a script as well.[39] If a professor assigns

---

33. The American Bar Association's Commission on Disability Rights offers a Law School Disability Programs Directory, which collects information from law schools about disability programming and accommodations processes. *See Law School Disability Programs Directory*, AMERICAN BAR ASSOCIATION (April 24, 2020), https://www.americanbar.org/groups/diversity/disabilityrights/resources/law_school_programs/.

34. U.S. Dep't of Educ., Off. for Civ. Rts., *Frequently Asked Questions about the June 29, 2010 Dear Colleague Letter* (May 26, 2011), at 2, http://www2.ed.gov/about/offices/list/ocr/docs/dcl-ebook-faq-201105.html.

35. *Id.*

36. *See* Kristina Wilson, *Five Ways to Incorporate Universal Design for Learning into Your Online Course*, NORTHWESTERN SCHOOL OF PROF. STUDIES DISTANCE LEARNING (Feb. 28, 2018), https://dl.sps.northwestern.edu/blog/2018/02/five-ways-incorporate-universal-design-learning-online-course/. For some practical guidance for making online law school course materials accessible for students with disabilities, see Susan Landrum, *Best Practices and Practice Tips for Designing Accessible Hybrid and Online Law School Courses and Academic Support Programming*, THE LEARNING CURVE 13 (Summer 2020).

37. *See generally* Landrum, *supra* note 36.

38. *See id.*

39. Deque University, *Design Considerations for Disabilities*, at 1, https://dequeuniversity.com/assets/pdf/module-design/dq-design-considerations.pdf (last visited Nov. 10, 2020);

videos created by someone else, or audio recordings like podcasts, that content should be available in an alternative format as well.[40] Images such as graphs or photographs should be narrated if they convey important content to students, and documents, such as PDFs, Microsoft Word documents, and PowerPoint slides, should provide alt-text captions for images.[41]

What are the benefits to this approach to online course design? Taking a proactive approach will mean that many student accommodations will be anticipated, minimizing the amount of modification that will have to be made to any online course materials. As stated previously, it also benefits students who may not have a disability but will still benefit from alternative material options. But there is also a significant benefit for the many law students with disabilities who do not get accommodations, either because they do not seek them (perhaps because of concerns about stigma or lack of knowledge of the accommodations process); have accommodations requests denied because of outdated diagnoses or insufficient documentation; or have undiagnosed disabilities. Using UDL guidelines for online course materials ensures all students have full access to course materials, increasing their opportunity to achieve academic success in law school.

## IV. Conclusion

The future of legal education is undoubtedly connected to online learning, and online and blended strategies will be an important part of ASP programs as well. If approached thoughtfully, applying science-based teaching and learning practices, online and blended instruction has the potential to make legal education accessible to more students and integrate the teaching and learning of academic skills, legal analysis, and knowledge of substantive law. But success in this approach will also require collaboration among ASP professors and other faculty and demand that legal educators become learners again themselves, seeking to understand more about educational best practices in both the in-person and online learning environments.

---

40. Disability Resource Center, Univ. of Ark. Little Rock, *Captioning How-To and Resources*, https://ualr.edu/disability/faculty/captureaudiocaptionvideo/ (last visited Nov. 10, 2020); Kristina Wilson, *Five Ways to Incorporate Universal Design for Learning into Your Online Course,* Northwestern School of Prof. Studies Blog (Feb. 27, 2018), https://dl.sps.northwestern.edu/blog/2018/02/five-ways-incorporate-universal-design-learning-online-course/; *UDL Guidelines, Offer Alternatives for Auditory Information,* CAST, http://udlguidelines.cast.org/representation/perception/alternatives-auditory (last visited Nov. 20, 2020).

41. Deque University, *Design Considerations for Disabilities*, at 4, https://dequeuniversity.com/assets/pdf/module-design/dq-design-considerations.pdf (last visited Nov. 10, 2020); Deque University, *Accessibility Checklist*, at 2, https://accessibility.deque.com/website-accessibility-checklist-download (last visited Nov. 10, 2020).

SECTION TWO

# Designing the Course of the Future

EIGHT

# From Ground to Cloud and Back Again: Modern Tactics to Improve Your Teaching

Katherine Brem*

After reviewing this process-based chapter, readers will be able to:

- Summarize the benefits and challenges inherent in systematically modernizing course content in any course, online or otherwise;
- Identify learning objectives that would most benefit from modernization;
- Cull the multitude of learning activities and methods of assessment now available to select those most suited to meeting modernized curricular needs; and
- Implement fresh learning objectives and modern teaching and assessment methods to reinvigorate course content.

The unexpected transition from the physical classroom to the virtual one in Spring 2020 caused me to reexamine my course structure and content, realign course objectives, and find new and innovative ways to deliver course content. As a result, I have updated learning objectives in each of the courses that I teach and adopted alternative learning methods and means of assessment that have revolutionized my students' learning and significantly improved my teaching. These methods are useful in the online classroom but equally so in the physical classroom. This chapter is process based, intended to offer a plan you can easily follow to reassess your own learning objectives and update your teaching and assessment methods as you transition from ground to cloud and back again.[1]

---

* Associate Professor, University of Houston Law Center. Professor Brem has been teaching law for twelve years and began teaching courses online in 2020. She has designed and taught synchronous and hybrid courses.

1. For a discussion of implementing backward design in specific courses, see Chapter 22: *Flexing Your Muscles: Using Backward Design to create a Property Course That Can Be Taught in Multiple Modes* by Kimberly E. O'Leary (casebook course); Chapter 30: *Backward Design: Course Design for Online Simulation Classes* by Christine Church (skills course).

Initially, I recommend that you carefully consider course content and modernize learning objectives. Transitioning online helped me to see that some of my learning objectives were, if not out-of-date, certainly stale. Over the years, I had combined some, left others by the wayside, and emphasized some in ways I had not anticipated when I first drafted the learning objectives. Developing courses for online delivery provided an unexpected opportunity to reconsider what I *was* teaching versus what I *wanted* to teach. This modernization of my teaching objectives provided a meaningful first step as I transitioned from the physical classroom to a virtual one.

Next, following advice from colleagues who were experienced asynchronous teachers, I divided my teaching objectives—and their associated learning activities—into modules.[2] It is far less daunting to revise a discrete module than an entire course.

Finally, after significant research and experimentation with new technology, I crafted a syllabus designed to facilitate modernized teaching objectives with reimagined assessment and learning activities appropriate to the virtual classroom. Along the way, I realized that many of these same assessment and learning activities would be useful also for the traditional classroom. They are innovative and designed with Gen Z[3] in mind and so tailor-made for our current cohort of students. Moreover, because they provide timely and efficient feedback delivered in a format that is easy to consume and digest, quite surprisingly I find them more effective than the assessment and learning activities I left behind.

---

2. Hat tip to Allison Martin, Clinical Professor of Law at Indiana University Robert H. McKinney School of Law, and Kenneth Swift, Clinical Professor of Law and my colleague at the University of Houston Law Center. I had the pleasure of working with both of them in preparing the Association of Legal Writing Director's guide *Teaching LRW in a HyFlex Classroom, available at* https://www.alwd.org/images/resources/ALWD_HyFlex_Guide.pdf. Their combined experience developing high-quality asynchronous course offerings positively impacted my transition to the online classroom.

3. "Gen Z" is a common abbreviation for Generation Z, a cohort born between 1995 and 2010. Laura P. Graham, *Generation Z Goes to Law School: Teaching and Reaching Law Students in the Post-Millennial Generation*, 41 UALR L. Rev. 29, 43 (2018) (addressing research described in Corey Seemiller & Meghan Grace, Generation Z Goes to College (2016), particularly as it relates to law students). Generational theorists posit that, because Gen Z's lives have always been saturated with technology, they have shorter attention spans and an unrealistic belief in the merits of multi-tasking that may hamper their ability to think critically and thoroughly analyze complicated legal issues. *Id.* at 52–53.

## I. Step 1: Consider Course Content and Modernize Learning Objectives

As you embark on your own journey to modernize learning objectives, embrace the concept of backward design.[4] What I mean by this is, "begin with the end in mind."[5] In moving from ground to cloud, I thought deeply about what I was teaching for the first time since developing my classes. I realized I was teaching what *I* wanted to teach, not necessarily what *my students* needed to learn. Without addressing the merits of generational theory, I have noticed certain characteristics that differentiate my current law students from ones who have come before. They are "digital natives,"[6] as comfortable with technology as a writing teacher is with the written word. But they crave instant answers, and many are uncomfortable with rather basic critical thinking skills. Thus, modernizing learning objectives has enabled me to better address these students' needs. Moreover, the practice of law has changed over the years, and student needs have changed along with it. Our students' future employers demand we produce "practice-aware" graduates.[7] This necessarily requires a transition from the theoretical to the practical in much of our instruction.[8]

---

4. MaryAnne Nestor & Carl E. Nestor, *Alignment and Backward Design*, YouTube (Nov. 24, 2013), https://www.youtube.com/watch?v=ZTv2HR2ckto&feature=emb_title (based on Grant Wiggins & Jay McTighe, Understanding by Design (2d ed. 2005)); *see also* Meredith Capps et al., Backward Design: A Handy Tool for Remote Teaching,William & Mary Conference for Excellence in Teaching Legal Research & Writing Online, (June 18, 2020) (recording available at: https://scholarship.law.wm.edu/excellence_online_teaching/zoomsessions/june18/1/).

5. Stephen R. Covey, The Seven Habits of Highly Effective People: Powerful Lessons in Personal Change 95 (2d ed. 2004).

6. Lauren A. Newell, *Redefining Attention (and Revamping the Legal Profession?) for the Digital Generation*, 15 Nev. L.J. 754, 794 (2015) (quoting Don Tapscott, Grown Up Digital: How the Net Generation is Changing Your World 116 (2009)); *see also* Kathy Evans, *Are Digital Natives Really Just Digital Labourers? Teens Turning Off Social Media*, Age (Apr. 21, 2016, 5:59 PM), https://www.theage.com.au/national/victoria/are-digital-natives-really-just-digital-labourers-teens-turning-off-social-media-20160419-goa0or.html (noting that "fear has long been a by-product of media usage").

7. I adopted this term from Jay Gary Finkelstein. He writes eloquently about solutions to address the well-documented "need for changing the historical legal curriculum to embody more practical skills, transactional law, and international law." Jay Gary Finkelstein, *Practice in the Academy: Creating "Practice Aware" Law Graduates*, 64 J. Legal Educ. 622, 624 n. 2 (2015) ("I prefer the term 'practice aware' to 'practice ready', which overstates the objective and purpose of law school.").

8. For example, in legal research and writing courses we must prepare students to produce high-quality work in a short period of time. The legal memorandum is no longer the sine qua non of a young lawyer's expertise. Having the ability to produce high quality analysis in a brief email is a much more practical skill. *See* Sheila F. Miller, *Are We Teaching What They Will Use: Surveying Alumni to Assess Whether Skills Teaching Aligns with Alumni Practice*, 32 Miss. C. L. Rev. 419, 434–35 (2014). In first-year contracts classes it is no longer enough for a student to leave law school with a thorough understanding of "contractual issues and the underpinnings of the rationale of contracts." Finkelstein, *supra* note 7, at 624. Now students must also know how to "translate business terms into contractual language that memorializes the agreement of the parties and serves as a roadmap for future operations and collaboration, allocating risk and responsibility." *Id.* (citing Neill J. Dilloff, *Law School Training: Bridging the Gap Between Legal Education and the Practice of Law*, 24 Stan. L. & Pol'y Rev. 425, 426, nn. 1–6 (2013)).

Following the advice of my university's instructional design team, I incorporated this concept of "backward design" to address these deficiencies.[9] In backward design, faculty are encouraged to focus on what students need to know versus what we want to teach.[10] Rather than designing learning activities, building assessments around these activities, and then drawing connections with course objectives—typical "forward design"—backward design counsels that instead we begin by first formulating desired learning objectives.[11] Only after finalizing these objectives should we consider how best to teach and assess them.[12] Therefore, this process forced me not only to reevaluate my learning objectives but also to modernize my learning activities and assessment techniques. As one instructional designer pithily noted, if the objective is to teach the student to bake a flaky pie crust, assigning reading on the history of pie-making and administering a multiple-choice test to assess the student's comprehension of that reading are poor methods to ensure student progress towards the learning objective.[13]

As I embarked on this process, I realized that many of the learning activities I had incorporated for years were no longer effective to ensure student success on assessments, and the resources I was providing my students were out-of-date or certainly sufficiently dated that students might question their efficacy.

As an example, previously in my Lawyering Skills and Strategies course, I focused on preparing a lengthy objective legal memorandum in the fall semester. These days, however, lawyers rarely have the opportunity or budget to prepare such a document. Quick research on a discrete legal issue, fully yet succinctly briefed in an email, is a much more valuable skill.[14] Similarly, from a research perspective, my learning activities focused on finding relevant case law. These days, however, finding relevant case law is rarely a problem. Learning to sort through the firehose of information even the most basic research yields is a much more valuable skill.[15] And finally, because a majority of our students leave law school and pursue a practice more transactional in nature, my past focus on litigation documents—a memo assessing the merits of a client's case, a demand letter, an appellate brief or dispositive motion—did not really prepare students to join the work force.[16] Incorporating new assignments to assess the

---

9. Univ. of Hous. Office of the Provost, A Guide to Best Practices for HyFlex and Online Teaching at UH 10 (2020), https://uh.edu/power-on/teaching/resources-and-support/guide-to-hyflex-and-online-teaching-at-uh-provost.pdf.

10. Nestor & Nestor, *supra* note 4; *see also* Heather L. Reynolds & Katherine Dowell Kearns, *A Planning Tool for Incorporating Backward Design, Active Learning, and Authentic Assessment in the College Classroom*, 65 C. Teaching 17 (2016), https://doi.org/10.1080/87567555.2016.1222575.

11. Capps et al., *supra* note 4.

12. *Id.*

13. Nestor & Nestor, *supra* note 4.

14. *See* LexisNexis, White Paper: Hiring Partners Reveal New Attorney Readiness for Real World Practice 4 (2015), https://www.lexisnexis.com/documents/pdf/20150325064926_large.pdf. *See generally* Jason G. Dykstra, *Beyond the "Practice Ready" Buzz: Sifting Through the Disruption of the Legal Industry to Divine the Skills Needed by New Attorneys*, 11 Drexel L. Rev. 149 (2018).

15. LexisNexis, *supra* note 14, at 4.

16. *Id.*

merits of a contract or teach drafting skills necessary to translate business terms into contractual language will better prepare the students for life after law school.[17]

I suspect this realization will be equally true for doctrinal faculty. Employers' focus on practice-aware graduates, and the American Bar Association's insistence that law schools incorporate experiential learning opportunities,[18] means that all law school faculty must restructure their courses to incorporate skills training and experiential components.[19] And if you accept generational theory, Gen Z students simply learn differently than their predecessors.[20]

This modernization of learning objectives, assessments, and instructional activities is the most unexpected benefit of the transition from ground to cloud and one I will purposefully undertake periodically in the future. That said, while modernization is easy to contemplate, the process is time consuming and overwhelming in scope. I recommend first modernizing learning objectives and then deconstructing the course syllabus into discrete modules. Breaking down the process makes the modernization easier to achieve.

## II. Step 2: Separate the Syllabus into Learning Modules

Some of what I teach naturally lends itself to online instruction. Research and citation skills instruction, for example, is significantly improved when students immediately practice these skills and receive real-time feedback. In contrast, more involved learning objectives may not be suitable for online instruction. Legal analysis, for example, involves both high-level critical thinking and simultaneous application of complicated legal concepts. Students may benefit from online tools that assess their progress in meeting these learning objectives, but they require traditional instruction before these online tools can meaningfully contribute to their success. Thus, to transition from ground to cloud, I first reviewed the course syllabus to identify modules more suited to online instruction. This sorting simplified the modernization process and enabled me to efficiently revamp the syllabus to address changing student needs and

17. *Id.*

18. *See* A.B.A. Sec. Leg. Educ. & Admis. to the Bar, *Standards and Rules of Procedure for Approval of Law Schools*, Standards 303(a)(3) & 304 (2020–21), https://www.americanbar.org/content/dam/aba/administrative/legal_education_and_admissions_to_the_bar/standards/2020-2021/2020-21-aba-standards-and-rules-for-approval-of-law-schools.pdf [hereinafter 2020 ABA Standards].

19. For a meaningful discussion of this up-and-coming issue, see Jay Gary Finkelstein, *supra* note 7, at 626–27 (citing *Course Portfolios*, Educating Tomorrow's Lawyers, http://iaals.du.edu/educating-tomorrows-lawyers/projects (last visited Nov. 1, 2020)). *See also* Adam Lamparello, *Toward a Writing-Centered Legal Education*, 84 Fordham L. Rev. Res Gestae 11 (2015); Dykstra, *supra* note 14; Robert J. Condlin, *Practice Ready Graduates: A Millennialist Fantasy*, 31 Touro L. Rev. 75 (2014).

20. For a thorough discussion of the learning characteristics of Gen Z students, and how they differ from previous generations, *see generally* Graham, *supra* note 3, at 48–71.

employer expectations. My efforts have led to tremendous benefits in the online classroom—benefits I want to retain in the physical classroom.

That said, the sheer number of online learning activities and assessment tools available is overwhelming. Be selective and consider tools most suited to accomplish your needs.[21] Determine whether you need tools to facilitate learning, or those that assess student progress in meeting learning objectives, or both. And once you have isolated your needs, look first to your course textbooks to find useful tools. Publishers have improved e-book offerings to include online learning activities and assessment tools tied directly to each textbook's learning objectives. Thus, these e-book offerings may provide precisely the up-to-date tools you require. If you care to venture further afield, however, consider the following strategies as you select modern learning activities and assessment tools to achieve updated learning objectives.

## III. Step 3: Select Reimagined Learning Activities and Assessment Tools

Backward design counsels that, once we have identified desired learning objectives, we then consider how best to teach and assess them.[22] Technology is ever changing in response to our students' changing needs—after all, today's Gen Z student cohort will one day be replaced by tomorrow's next generation. Certain categories of learning and assessment tools lend themselves well to ensuring student success in any discipline. Others are more targeted to ensuring student success in writing or seminar courses. Select from among the following categories as you reimagine your syllabus to achieve the modernized learning objectives you identify.

### A. POLLING TECHNOLOGY

Many of us have incorporated polling technology for years through the use of classroom clickers. Now, faculty can incorporate not just simple objective polls but a range of interactive technology to bring real-time data into any classroom.[23] The difference between this new polling technology and old-style clickers is faculty's ability to collect not only on-demand objective data, but subjective data as well. For example, one of my favorite techniques in the online classroom is to pose a question to the class using the chat feature of the video-conferencing platform used for class. Students reluctant to verbalize an "out-of-the-box" idea may well do so in writing, and then they will verbally defend their idea once it is publicly challenged. By asking students to briefly

21. I focused my efforts in areas where I had substantially overhauled learning objectives. For me, that was research, citation, and legal analysis in my writing skills courses, and assessment in all of my courses.

22. *See* Capps et al., *supra* note 4.

23. This technology is available to students at little to no cost, through a simple click of their smart phones. My current favorites are Mentimeter and Poll Everywhere. MENTIMETER, https://www.mentimeter.com (last visited Nov. 2, 2020); POLL EVERYWHERE, https://www.polleverywhere.com (last visited Nov. 2, 2020).

respond to a question in a subjective poll, through a word cloud or similar interactive technology, faculty can recreate this low-stress learning and assessment technique in the physical classroom.

In addition, polling technology and directed inquiries offer other tangible benefits to faculty and students. They break up lecture in a way that recaptures student attention, efficiently focuses self-study after class by identifying material that lacks clarity, and sometimes provide much-needed affirmation that students are not alone in their quest to understand a difficult topic. As for me, I find I have a more nuanced understanding of class competencies when I make consistent use of these techniques. Through the information they provide, I am able to tweak my lectures on demand to accommodate each class's needs.

## B. GAME-BASED LEARNING PLATFORMS

Similarly, faculty can incorporate interactive game-based learning in lecture to effectively review dense material.[24] In contrast to traditional Socratic questioning, game-based learning platforms permit students to respond to questions in a low-stress manner, promoting whole class engagement.[25] Researchers note that game-based learning assists students in organizing course content into manageable categories, enabling them to employ a chunking technique useful in processing large amounts of information.[26] Faculty can then tailor subsequent lectures to address identified deficiencies in student comprehension.

## C. ANIMATION AND FLOWCHART SOFTWARE

In addition to targeted review of course materials through game-based learning platforms, faculty may wish to provide a periodic asynchronous review of certain course content. One way to accomplish this is to prepare a daily or weekly summary that students can peruse on their own time—for example, a narrated PowerPoint presentation. But occasionally, alternative methods may better summarize key points. Recently, I prepared an animated summary of restricted hearsay exceptions using an online animation

---

24. Digital game-based learning in higher education is a hot topic, but there is little doubt student engagement is enhanced through the use of digital game-based learning activities when these activities supplement traditional instruction. For a thorough discussion of this issue, see James B. Levy, *Teaching the Digital Caveman: Rethinking the Use of Classroom Technology in Law School*, 19 CHAP. L. REV. 241, 279 (2016) (noting that while new technology may enhance student interest, if it is not tied to a particular learning objective it may actually be counterproductive).

25. Numerous game-based learning platforms are available online, many for little or no cost. *See, e.g.*, KAHOOT!, https://www.kahoot.com (last visited Nov. 2, 2020); PUZZEL, https://www.puzzel.com (last visited Nov. 2, 2020); Quizlet, QUIZLET, https://www.quizlet.com (last visited Nov. 2, 2020); and TriviaMaker, TRIVIAMAKER https://www.triviamaker.com (last visited Nov. 2, 2020).

26. Denise Bord, *Teaching Tips: Enhancing Learning and Exam Preparation*, 21 OBSERVER 1 (Ass'n for Psych. Sci. Jan. 2008), https://www.psychologicalscience.org/observer/enhancing-learning-and-exam-preparation (referencing Michael G. Aamodt, *A closer look at the study session*, 9 TEACHING OF PSYCH. 234–35 (1982), https://doi.org/10.1207/s15328023top0904_17).

tool and shared a flowchart mapping all the hearsay exceptions.[27] My students gave each of these resources rave reviews.[28] Providing something unexpected better captured their attention. And these animated shorts and flowcharts are just that—short. Students view them as an efficient use of their time, yet they offer effective review of class material.

### D. SELF-GRADING ASSESSMENTS

Finally, faculty should regularly employ assessments that permit students to determine, on their own, where their deficiencies are strongest.[29] Even in a traditional course with an issue-spotting essay exam, interim multiple-choice quizzes can allow students to determine what they do not yet know. These can be for a grade or simply for the students' own edification. Either way, they address the ABA's focus on assessing student learning.[30] And they need not involve any extra work on the part of the faculty. Commercial resources offer self-graded quizzes such as these. Check your course textbook or use your school's subscription to services such as The Center for Computer-Assisted Legal Instruction (CALI). Alternatively, make your own self-graded assessments using online quiz makers. These platforms allow faculty to ask questions of students in a self-grading format, but also to provide the students with explanations to guide their studies.[31] Preparing these quizzes may take some work on the front end, but the work is worthwhile. The quizzes are specific to faculty lectures and will remain useful for years to come.

### E. PEER REVIEW SOFTWARE

With regard to those who teach writing or seminar courses, software abounds to assist faculty with the review and grading process. Peer review software, for example, permits faculty to pose specific, targeted questions to guide students as they anonymously review another's work.[32] In so doing, students not only improve their own writing skills but hone reviewing skills they will use in daily practice once they enter the workforce. As many a writing teacher is fond of repeating, there is no good writ-

---

27. For my animated hearsay summary, I used Powtoon, https://powtoon.com (last visited Nov. 2, 2020). The hearsay flowchart is from Margaret Hagan. *See* Open Law Lab Blog (March 2013), https://www.openlawlab.com/wp-content/uploads/2013/03/Hearsay-Exceptions-2013-03-19-10.59.52-842-PM.png.

28. Online animation and flowchart software abounds and much of it is available for free. *See* Katie Wolf, *The 9 Best Animation Software for Beginners and Beyond*, Skillshare.blog (Oct. 23, 2020), https://www.skillshare.com/blog/learn/the-9-best-animation-software-for-beginners-and-beyond; *see also 10 Best Free Flowchart Software for Windows and Mac*, SoftwareTestingHelp Blog (Nov. 13, 2020), https://www.softwaretestinghelp.com/flowchart-software/.

29. Generational theorists note that the Gen Z student cohort, in particular, lacks self-assessment skills. Graham, *supra* note 3, at 58 (citing Ruth Vance & Susan Stuart, *Of Moby Dick and Tartar Sauce: The Academically Underprepared Law Student and the Curse of Overconfidence*, 53 Duq. L. Rev. 133 (2015)).

30. *See* 2020 ABA Standards, *supra* note 18, Standard 314.

31. Students are familiar with the ubiquitous Google form, but countless other platforms and learning management systems facilitate self-graded quizzing, many available for little to no cost.

32. *See, e.g.*, Eli Review, https://elireview.com (last visited Nov. 2, 2020); Peerceptiv, https://peerceptiv.com (last visited Nov. 2, 2020).

ing—only good rewriting.[33] Peer review reinforces this concept in a tangible fashion. Students can see work that misses the mark, analyze how it misses the mark, and then more effectively edit their own work.[34]

### F. ORAL EDITING SOFTWARE

Faculty can also offer students multiple streams of commentary on student work product, employing oral editing software to supplement written commentary.[35] This offers a new twist on the "live grading" conferences many professors have adopted. Rather than *actually* marking up a paper with the student present, faculty can record themselves marking up student work product and talk students through their impressions in real time. In course evaluations, students indicate they favor these recorded comments over traditional ones. They report that they listen to the oral commentary repeatedly yet confess that they seldom read written comments more than once.[36]

## IV. From Ground to Cloud . . . *And Back Again*: What I Will Retain

These are but a few of the learning and assessment tools I adopted to deliver course content once I realigned course learning objectives. This process has revolutionized my effectiveness as a teacher. Following the steps outlined in this chapter, I will continue to reevaluate course content and delivery methods periodically, and I encourage you to do the same. Remember the apocryphal quote attributed variously to Ben Franklin and an ancient Confucian philosopher, "Tell me and I forget. Teach me and I remember. Involve me and I learn."[37]

The unexpected transition from ground to cloud and back again in the Spring and Fall of 2020 involved me in my students' learning in a tangible way. Engaged students learn better and faster, and I owe it to my students to ensure they remain engaged—thereby ensuring their success.

---

33. Many have said this, or a variation, including Judge Louis Brandeis and British poet Robert Graves.

34. Peer review is a touchy subject for many law students, who are especially grade conscious. In my writing courses I assign two projects concurrently, one graded and one ungraded. Students peer review the ungraded assignment. They are then able to translate lessons learned through peer review when they edit their own work on graded assignments.

35. Software that supports oral commentary is plentiful online, much of it available for little or no cost. *See, e.g.*, LOOM, https://www.loom.com (last visited Nov. 2, 2020).

36. That said, if you are a traditionalist and prefer written commentary, I recommend AnnotatePro. This software offers a library of comments for specific assignment categories or enables faculty to enter their own reusable comments to speed the feedback process. It integrates with Microsoft Word, Google Docs, and other web-based applications and makes for a significantly more efficient grading process.

37. Some say this quote instead should be attributed to a Confucian philosopher who lived between 312 and 230 B.C.: "Not having heard something is not as good as having heard it; having heard it is not as good as having seen it; having seen it is not as good as knowing it; knowing it is not as good as putting it into practice." XUNZI, A TRANSLATION AND STUDY OF THE COMPLETE WORKS 135 (John Knoblock transl., Stanford U. Press 1988).

NINE

# Converting a Course to an Asynchronous Format

Kerry Lohmeier*

After reviewing this chapter, readers will be able to:

- Summarize one method for converting a course to an asynchronous format;
- Select and/or produce tools to aid in course conversion;
- Identify tips for converting a course; and
- Decide if designing an asynchronous course is feasible for you and your course.

Asynchronous courses allow flexibility for students and faculty while allowing students to dive deeply into course content at their own pace.[1] I have built and taught two courses using an asynchronous format. The first course was a conversion of a new course,[2] and the second converted a flipped course.[3] Converting a course from fully in-person to fully asynchronous online provides a great opportunity for adding new elements to a course and evaluating how to keep the course relevant for students.[4] This chapter discusses a process and tips to convert a course to an asynchronous format.

* Associate Librarian and Adjunct Professor of Law, University of Utah, S.J. Quinney College of Law. Professor Lohmeier began teaching in 2013 and began teaching online courses in 2020. She has designed and taught asynchronous, flipped, and traditional courses.

1. There may also be opportunities to reach more students. *See, e.g.*, James McGrath & Andrew P. Morriss, *Online Legal Education & Access to Legal Education & the Legal System*, 70 Syracuse L. Rev. 49 (2020).

2. This was a new administrative law course in our Master of Legal Studies program. I worked with UOnline beginning in 2019 to develop the asynchronous version.

3. The in-person flipped course was Legal Research, a required 1L course. In a flipped course, students first engage with new materials outside of the classroom via readings, lecture videos, podcasts, and quizzes. Classroom time is spent on discussion, problem-solving, and other active learning activities that enable students to engage with each other and the instructor as they apply their learning. Tanya M. Marcum & Sandra J. Perry, *Flips and Flops: A New Approach to a Traditional Law Course*, 32 J. Legal Stud. Educ. 255, 256–57 (2015).

4. For an additional perspective on converting a legal research course from synchronous to asynchronous, see Chapter 21: *Designing and Teaching Online Legal Research Skills Courses* by Emily Kline and Megan Austin.

## I. Time Involved in Converting a Course

It is important to plan ahead when converting a course as it is a time-intensive process. You will evaluate materials you already have if you have taught the course before, develop new content, and map the course to ensure you are meeting learning outcomes. You will also walk through a course in student view in the Learning Management System (LMS) to ensure everything is working properly.

Asynchronous courses often present more points of interaction and feedback than synchronous courses. Students work through more learning activities in lieu of class discussion to apply their learning and demonstrate mastery of content. Prompt feedback is necessary to help students move through the course, which requires regular monitoring and participation when you teach the course.

## II. Planning and Mapping the Conversion

Moving a class online provides the opportunity to evaluate learning outcomes and course objectives. Many courses have set outcomes and objectives that tie into the broader curriculum that may not be able to change. What can change is the approach to meeting those requirements. Be creative when thinking of ways to achieve learning outcomes during the design process for the course. You will likely come up with several new activities that fit the curriculum, engage students, and help students apply their learning.

Time spent mapping achievement of outcomes and objectives across the course allows you to tackle the conversion in smaller portions and helps keep the transition focused. There are useful documents to keep your course conversion on track and organized. I used an alignment grid, spreadsheet, and narrative document. I worked with Teaching & Learning Technologies[5] to convert the new course I taught and was provided with a copy of these documents that I could then use to also convert the flipped course.[6] The alignment grid allows you to begin thinking about how the course will meet the outcomes and objectives. The grid was a simple table that allowed me to match objectives to assessments and activities.[7] The narrative document and spread-

5. TEACHING AND LEARNING TECHNOLOGIES, https://tlt.utah.edu/ (last visited Feb. 17, 2021).

6. Before converting a course, you should reach out to your university's teaching and learning center to see if they have templates for you to use. If your institution does not provide templates, you may be able to find sample templates on the internet by searching for "course design template or "course development template."

7. My grid regularly changed as the conversion progressed and I decided different assessments and activities were a better fit for the flow of the course.

sheet are both content maps.[8] The categories on both documents deal with topics taught, objective alignment, and learning activities.[9]

I worked in both content mapping documents initially, but once the topics and objectives were mapped, I preferred working primarily in the narrative document to more fully develop and record my ideas for module content.[10] As course content was developed and then built into the LMS, I would incorporate the information into the spreadsheet. The spreadsheet allowed me to see the entire course at a glance. This was useful for ensuring a variety of learning activities throughout the course, and for balancing the course workload. A balanced workload is important for students, but also for allowing prompt feedback from the professor.

When converting a course, I begin with a topical outline tied to the number of learning modules for the course.[11] Then I link outcomes and objectives for each topic to the modules in my planning documents. If you are converting a course, you have taught before, this stage in the process should move fairly quickly.[12]

For the new course, I created a tentative topic outline that I attached to modules. Then I drafted the module objectives to guide how I planned on teaching each topic. My aim was not perfectly-drafted objectives, as some of the objectives were more guiding notes at this point.[13] Once the topics and module objectives were mapped, I evaluated whether I felt my initial plan would allow students to achieve the overall learning outcomes for the course. This allowed me to make some adjustments to the topics before I spent a lot of time planning module content.[14]

---

8. The narrative document posed questions to help me think about content development. You may find that you only need to use one of the documents to keep your conversion on track. I found both of the documents useful at different points in the process.

9. Examples of the learning activities covered are formative and summative assessments, lectures, readings, and community building.

10. The documents were especially helpful when I needed to put a course conversion on hold. I could use them to quickly see where I was at in the process, and then move on to the next stage of development.

11. In my asynchronous courses and in this chapter, "modules" refers to classes. The number of modules may be different than the number of classes you would have in the same course taught in another format. For example, you may decide to have one module per week for a course that would traditionally meet twice per week in an in-person or synchronous version of the course.

12. When Legal Research was converted to a flipped format those of us who taught the course spent time reviewing the outcomes, objectives, and topics covered in the course. We created our own version of a content map to check for alignment throughout the process. This allowed planning and developing content to move much more quickly for this course conversion.

13. I do fine-tune the objectives later in the process so I can list them at the top of the module in the LMS to guide students as they work through the module.

14. When I looked at the spreadsheet, I could already see that some modules would need too much content (lectures, readings, learning activities) to adequately cover the topics listed. I moved some topics to other modules, made a note that some topics could only be briefly covered, and removed some topics from my map.

## III. Developing Content

When you transition a course, you do not need to get rid of all your materials from a prior version of the course. Mapping out the transition identifies which content can be saved and reused, even if it needs to be repackaged. For me, mapping it out also showed opportunities for thinking about the curriculum differently. This allowed me to incorporate new ideas that achieved the learning outcomes, made the course more engaging, and better fit an asynchronous mode of learning. I began content development for each course by thinking about the summative assessments. I wrote down the topics each assessment should cover and brief ideas about the format for the assessment. This guided the rest of the content development.

### A. SELECTING COURSE READINGS

The first large step I took to develop course content involved selecting course readings. This made it easier to decide which lectures, podcasts, and other materials were needed to prepare students for the learning activities. For the new course I converted, I kept in mind that administrative law is a tough subject for many students. I also considered what uses the masters level students may have for the course in their careers. Consequently, I decided to include several readings that clearly set out the topics covered in select modules. A dual benefit of clear-cut readings was that they provided sufficient time in some modules for drafting assignments and other group activities to enhance learning.[15] I selected a variety of readings from textbooks, law journals, treatises, government agencies, and other reputable sources freely available on the internet. My goal was to provide a variety of perspectives, teach students where they could find reliable sources on agencies, and keep course costs down. This took a significant amount of time as this was a new course; using a textbook to initially convert a course speeds up the process.

The in-person flipped course that was converted did not have very many required readings prior to the conversion. Instead, a number of optional readings supplemented lecture videos. Three professors taught different sections of the asynchronous version of the course. We elected to use a textbook in the newly-converted course to speed up the conversion. Many of the videos we previously developed needed to be redone to keep pace with changes in our available technology and database changes and so were no longer appropriate for the converted course. After researching available textbooks, we decided to use an open-access textbook provided by CALI.

15. For example, one group activity asked students to draft sample regulations that are authorized by a fictional statute I provided so that students could gain a better understanding of what an agency should do when promulgating regulations.

## B. DEVELOPING LECTURES

Once the readings were set, I looked at modules containing similar topics and mapped out the lectures needed to round out content delivery. Initially this meant more lectures than were perhaps warranted in the new course. All lectures were broken down into subtopics that I could record in five to fifteen-minute increments.[16] Shorter lectures were easier for me if a technology issue arose. It also helped with student attention spans. Students then had flexibility to watch a few short videos over the course of a day or several days before diving into learning activities.

For both courses, I looked for lecture materials[17] available that I could use to lighten the workload for converting the course. There were more options available for the flipped legal research course than the other course. Additionally, two other professors converted their sections of Legal Research to an asynchronous format at the same time, so we shared videos we created. This saved a significant amount of time and, as the semester progressed, allowed us to create additional videos that went over assignments students found challenging.

When I added videos to the LMS, I included the video title and length, even if some videos displayed that information within the video, so there was consistency in course design. I provided discussion questions with some lecture videos to guide students through the material. This was useful for the longer, denser lectures in the new administrative law course.

If your university has a teaching and learning center, I recommend reaching out to them about recording lectures. The Teaching & Learning Technologies (TLT) department on my campus provided me with recording equipment, training, and video editing services.[18] If you do not have access to a similar department, other options allow for creating lecture videos that will show both you and the computer screen if you have slides or other information you would like students to view while also being able to see you.[19]

It is important to take a few factors into account when recording lecture videos so that you do not have to record new lectures each year. It is best to leave dates off if you want to reuse the video. Students do not need to know when the video was filmed if the information in the video is still accurate. If you are referring to a change in the law or other significant event, it is best to use the date the change occurred or the event happened. If you say something like "earlier this year" or "last year" you will date the

---

16. My goal was ten minutes or less, but there were a few lectures that went over this.

17. Lectures, podcasts, short, animated videos, demos, etc. that would reinforce or expand upon the readings.

18. I initially was able to use a recording studio with TLT to record lectures. When COVID-19 made that impossible I was given the recording kit to finish the conversion at home. The help from TLT was invaluable in getting high quality lectures I can use for many years.

19. One option is to use your video conferencing software to record a video; another option is to use PowerPoint to record narration over PowerPoint slides.

video. If course modules could be taught in a different order than you have chosen, then you may not want to refer to any prior modules in your videos.[20] This provides the freedom to change the module order or content in the future without having to redo or edit a lot of videos.

## C. DEVELOPING LEARNING ACTIVITIES

Once I tentatively planned the lectures and started developing them, I began considering what I wanted students to do in the module. Classroom discussions that may make up a significant portion of a traditional course are not compatible with an asynchronous course. You can still use the same questions, but the format needs to change.[21] Because the traditional mode of classroom discussion is unavailable, it is important to think of other ways to get students working with course materials.

As you develop activities, keep in mind that you will more than likely need to attach a point value to any activity you want students to complete.[22] To facilitate this, I set a tentative point value for each required learning activity as I developed it. Once the course was fully built and mapped into the spreadsheet, I could see an overview of activities and associated point values. When I neared the end of the conversion, I made adjustments to point values.

More graded activities means more work when the course runs, as each activity will require prompt feedback. Some techniques beyond using technology reduced my time commitment by allowing me to quickly provide written or oral feedback. Putting students in groups for activities was helpful as it greatly reduced the time spent providing feedback. It also benefited students because they built community and worked through more complex course material together.

Prepared sample answers and detailed rubrics take time to develop initially but save time as the course runs. The converted flipped course had weekly practice problems. The weeks we had more challenging practice had either a written sample answer or a video that walked through the research problem. When providing feedback, I was able to provide more minimal individual feedback as I could refer students to specific portions of the sample answer or video. Students were then tasked with comparing their work to the sample and reaching out with any follow-up questions. Detailed rubrics

---

20. The only videos I created that referenced other modules were short introductory videos at the beginning of each module. Each video was a few minutes in length and placed the current module in the context of the course. I can quickly change these as needed going forward.

21. For example, you can assign questions that students simply think about, that they submit a written response to, or that students use to participate in a discussion board.

22. In the first asynchronous course I taught I incorporated ungraded quizzes into several modules. The quizzes checked understanding of main concepts and then had students apply the concepts to hypotheticals. I placed the quizzes in the module under a required activities section and indicated that completing them would prepare students for graded activities. A review of analytics showed me that very few students completed the quizzes. Now I attach a point value to any activity I want students to complete, which was advice I received before beginning my first course conversion but failed to follow.

for both converted courses worked in the same manner. Rubrics provided transparency in grading for students and helped focus their efforts while working through the assessments. The rubrics then allowed me to more quickly provide feedback.

### 1. Using Course Materials You've Already Developed

When I converted the flipped course, the next step in the conversion was looking through all of the materials previously used.[23] A large bank of practice research problems and quizzes that had been tested over many years was available for the asynchronous course. Modifications were made to provide additional instructions on the practice problems and to make the formatting the same across problem sets. Additional quiz questions were developed to ensure coverage of the main concepts in the readings, lectures, and demonstrations. Similar formatting was added to the quizzes for design consistency across activities.

When I started to develop an asynchronous version of the new administrative law course, I also planned to teach the course in person at a later date. I used some of the same discussion questions in both versions of the course. In the asynchronous course, I used some of the discussion questions to create written reflection activities that tied several modules together. I provided other discussion questions as a guide to the reading and lectures in a module. I also modified questions into short diagramming activities of the APA so students could parse the statute before completing more complex activities.

### 2. Developing New Activities

To develop new activities, I brainstormed a list of activities that I either used before, read about, or knew someone else had successfully used in the classroom. Then I researched what others were using in online courses and used materials from a campus faculty boot camp I previously attended to generate a master list of potential activities.[24] I generated a large list of potential activities to use in the new course I transitioned because I was starting from scratch.[25]

After deciding on readings and lectures, I revisited module objectives to keep in mind what I wanted students to do by the end of each module. I often worked on two to three modules simultaneously to ensure I used a variety of learning activities. I

---

23. I had several years' worth of materials used in a traditional and flipped format for this course. Additionally, several other professors teach this course, and we share materials with each other.

24. The materials were a deck of cards with learning activities printed on them. The activities were tied to several Fink's Taxonomy cards. L. DEE FINK, CREATING SIGNIFICANT LEARNING EXPERIENCES: AN INTEGRATED APPROACH TO DESIGNING COLLEGE COURSES (2d ed. 2013).

25. I wanted additional options available in case my creativity decreased as I progressed through the conversion.

consulted my activities list and thought about what a good fit for each module was.[26] When I added a lengthier activity, like drafting sample regulations or a jigsaw group activity,[27] to a module, then I tried to lighten the workload from the activities in surrounding modules.[28]

I used short quizzes in each course to check for a basic understanding of readings and lectures. That was one of the first activities developed in each module if I did not already have a quiz available to use. One column on the spreadsheet I used to convert the courses dealt with interaction between students. I used discussion boards and group work to allow the students to get to know each other, exchange ideas, and work on formative assessments.[29] In the flipped class all professors decided to use a debate platform[30] several times to get students working together to either share research leads, predict the outcome to a problem, or advocate for an assigned side of a research issue.

The flipped course needed very little new content developed beyond the discussion boards. In the flipped class format, a portion of class time was spent demonstrating research databases and processes. To make this portion more interactive in the asynchronous version of the course we created interactive online tutorials[31] over very specific aspects of researching in Lexis, Westlaw, and on other websites that we traditionally emphasized in the classroom. To replicate watching students complete research in the classroom, I had students complete research recordings twice during the semester.[32]

### 3. Materials to Develop as You Regularly Teach the Course

The first time I taught an asynchronous course, I did not think as carefully about the amount of time required for feedback as I should have done. There are some steps you can take to improve efficiency as the course runs. These steps may take a con-

---

26. One thing I considered was the amount of time students would have for activities after completing readings, lectures, podcasts, etc. Other considerations were the complexity of the material, whether a more practical component would benefit the students, and if more engagement between students was needed.

27. Students are in groups and are assigned different topics to explore. Those with the same topic then get together to check their learning via a discussion board before sharing their learning with their assigned group. Students use a short video, handout, or other form of media appropriate for conveying the knowledge.

28. This is where the spreadsheet was particularly useful. There were times when I had too many activities in the module. I ended up removing some activities or moving the activity to an optional category.

29. I used a variety of discussion boards in both courses including an introductions discussion board, ice breakers, muddiest point, responding to set questions, agencies in the news, etc.

30. Kialo Edu, https://www.kialo-edu.com/ (last visited Jan. 8, 2021).

31. Sidecar Learning, https://www.sidecarlearning.com/ (last visited Jan. 8, 2021).

32. Students selected a problem and then recorded their computer screen as they narrated their research process. I provided feedback on their approach to researching the problem. This course will likely revert back to a flipped course once COVID-19 allows us back into the classroom due to current ABA rules. I will continue using the new activities developed for the asynchronous course as they will be a good fit for a flipped format as well.

siderable amount of time to implement but can pay off as you teach the course in subsequent semesters.

If your LMS has a mechanism for automatically providing feedback upon student submission of work, try to use it regularly. I primarily used auto-feedback for quizzes with set answers in both courses. I plan to expand my use of this feature as I teach both courses. In most LMS platforms, you can input many different types of activities as quizzes. In the new course I converted, I built one activity that alternated between asking a graded question and then immediately providing feedback. For example, I asked students multiple-choice questions that went from a basic rule into more complex application questions. I set the quiz to show one question at a time and only allow forward progression through the quiz. I then input the answer as a question worth zero points in the quiz so that every question with a point value was immediately followed by a "question" worth zero points that explained the correct choice. I plan to convert a few more activities into this format for the administrative law course. It has the potential to enhance some of the hypotheticals I used in the course. Students will receive immediate feedback. I will primarily spend time answering follow-up questions and using quiz analytics to see if additional coverage of a topic is necessary.

Going forward, we will build the weekly research problems students complete in the flipped course into our LMS.[33] Then we can attach a sample answer that students will receive upon submitting the problems. This was done for a few complex problem sets throughout the semester, but doing this for all problem sets would save a substantial amount of time.[34] We are also considering modifying some of the problems in each weekly set so that there is only one "best" answer. Those questions could be built using a fill in the blank or similar question type, which would quickly alert students to potential issues with their research.

Another option is to modify or eliminate some of the activities used in the course. For the new administrative law course, I will eliminate some smaller activities that required weekly feedback. Instead, I will develop activities spanning several modules. This will provide students with more time per activity and will space out the feedback for me. I am considering having a final paper or project that serves as the main summative assessment along with a very brief multiple-choice exam. The goal would be to lighten the amount of weekly feedback required throughout the semester while allowing students more choice. Overall, I would like to add more choice into activi-

33. We will build them as quizzes and likely use the option that allows students to upload a file into a quiz answer, but using the essay response for a quiz question would work as well. For the asynchronous course we used the assignment option and uploaded the problems as a word document that students could download to speed up course development.

34. Students received points for completing the work, not for arriving at the correct answer, eliminating the need to assign a grade.

ties, when possible, so students can select an area of interest related to their careers to expand on the required readings and lectures.[35]

A final tip is to add a short video or purpose section to activities. I added one of these elements to several activities I developed. The videos added detail and context to an activity. To create the videos, I thought about the types of questions I would likely get in a live classroom setting about an assignment. Then I addressed those questions in the video. I found the combination of video and thorough instructions worked well. It does add time to the course buildout, so this is something that I primarily used with more complex activities. The purpose section clearly stated how the activity would enhance student learning. It helped me tie materials together and explained to students why they were completing the activity. I plan to add more videos and purpose sections to activities going forward as I noticed a reduction in questions from students with activities containing either of those elements.

## IV. Pacing the Course

Before building the course in the LMS, consider course pacing. You can make all of the course content accessible at the beginning of the course, have content publish as students complete modules, or publish modules on a set schedule. Students often elect to take asynchronous courses for flexibility, so keep that in mind as you make your selection.

The new course I converted ran with a set release schedule for modules. Two modules were released at a time. Due dates for graded learning activities were set every two weeks to match the module publication schedule. The next time this course runs, I anticipate publishing all of the modules at the beginning of the course so that students can access the readings, lectures, and individual learning activities. Group learning activities will be published on a set schedule as the activities build upon each other. This will hopefully allow more flexibility for students.

When the flipped class was converted, modules were given prerequisites and requirements in the LMS to ensure students worked through materials in the correct order. Once a student completed a module the next module opened. To make sure students did not fall behind, they were assigned due dates for required learning activities. Due dates were set on a weekly basis to provide consistency in scheduling for students who chose not to work ahead. The midterm served as a stopping point in the course. Students could not progress beyond module six, the module prior to the midterm, so that the midterm ran the same week for all students. Many students appreciated the flexibility to work ahead at various points in the semester.

35. For example, I would like to provide several case studies covering judicial review of agency action. Students could select a case study of interest to see how judicial review occurred. Depending on the weight of the activity, there may only be questions to answer about the case study or students may also have to apply what they learned to predict the outcome in a similar scenario.

## V. Conclusion

Asynchronous courses provide a wonderful opportunity for faculty and students. Faculty are able to engage with course content in new ways. Students have flexibility to decide when and how often to work with course materials. Planning is key to effectively convert a course into a format that can be used again and again, even while making small adjustments to the course to further learning or take advantage of current events that enhance the curriculum. I hope to have the opportunity to convert additional courses in the future to provide more flexibility for students and to utilize learning pathways for differentiated instruction to help students learn complex material.

TEN

# Team-Based Learning in an Online Teaching Environment

Joy E. Herr-Cardillo*
Melissa H. Weresh**

After reviewing this chapter, readers will:

- Better understand the pedagogy of Team-Based Learning;
- Learn how to incorporate core components of Team-Based Learning into an online Legal Writing curriculum;
- Appreciate how compatible Team-Based Learning is to an online learning environment;
- Learn how Team-Based Learning personalizes the online classroom experience for students; and
- Learn how to leverage other web-based technologies to deliver course content, reinforce critical concepts, and provide students with meaningful assessments.

## I. Why Team-Based Learning Is Particularly Suited to Online Instruction

Team-based learning (TBL) is an instructional method described as a "learner centered teaching strategy designed to promote students true understanding of the sub-

* Associate Professor of Legal Writing & Assistant Clinical Professor of Law, University of Arizona James E. Rogers College of Law. Professor Herr-Cardillo began teaching as an adjunct in 2002 and started full-time in 2017. Since March 2020, all of her instruction has been fully online.

** Dwight D. Opperman Distinguished Professor of Law, Drake University Law School. Professor Weresh began teaching at Drake University Law School in 1997 and has used team-based learning in her classes since 2012. Since March 2020, all of her teaching has been online, with both synchronous and asynchronous instruction.

ject."[1] It is a form of flipped classroom instruction, which simply means the majority of instructional delivery occurs outside of the classroom setting, so that class time can be used for applied learning activities designed to reinforce concepts. The flipped classroom is a "pedagogical approach in which direct instruction moves from the group learning space to the individual learning space, and the resulting group space is transformed into a dynamic, interactive learning environment where the educator guides students as they apply concepts and engage creatively in the subject matter."[2] In this manner, while the TBL instructional method is similar to other approaches in which the professor provides instructional content to students, students are incentivized by the prospect of collaboration to take more responsibility for their own learning.

Specifically, because students are expected to use class time to engage with their peers in interactive learning activities, they are motivated to complete the out-of-class assignments in order to be prepared to interact. In an online teaching environment, the approach ensures that students will be prepared and engaged during synchronous class sessions. By relying on regular interaction with small, permanent team members, the approach also ensures that students have an opportunity to form personal relationships with their peers, even in a virtual environment.

Moreover, the TBL, module-based approach to instruction helps faculty organize material in an efficient and effective manner. The module-based approach encourages deliberate sequencing and delivery of instructional materials and interactive application exercises in an optimal length for online instruction.

## II. Overview of Team-Based Learning

TBL has been adopted across a number of disciplines and has been empirically studied for engagement and efficacy.[3] Researchers have found an increased level of excitement and engagement in TBL classrooms as well as improved performance.[4] Moreover, TBL

1. L. Dee Fink, *Beyond Small Groups: Harnessing the Extraordinary Power of Learning Teams*, *in* TEAM-BASED LEARNING: A TRANSFORMATIVE USE OF SMALL GROUPS IN COLLEGE TEACHING 4 (Larry K. Michaelsen et al. eds., 2004).

2. *Definition of Flipped Learning*, FLIPPED LEARNING NETWORK (Mar. 12, 2014), https://flippedlearning.org/definition-of-flipped-learning/.

3. Georgeanne M. Artz et al., *The Whole is Greater than the Sum: An Empirical Analysis of the Effect of Team Based Learning on Student Achievement*, 60 N. AM. C. TCHR. AGRIC. J. 405 (2016) (empirical study finding a "positive and significant effects [of TBL] on individual exam scores for students at all levels of the ability distribution").

4. JIM SIBLEY & SOPHIE SPIRIDONOFF, INTRODUCTION TO TEAM-BASED LEARNING 4 (2014), https://cdn.ymaws.com/teambasedlearning.site-ym.com/resource/resmgr/Docs/TBL-handout_February_2014_le.pdf. *See also* Anita Sharmaa et al., *Understanding the Early Effects of Team-Based Learning on Student Accountability and Engagement Using a Three Session TBL Pilot*, 9 CURRENTS IN PHARMACY TEACHING & LEARNING 802 (2017) (three-session pilot study finding that "TBL had positive effects on [student] engagement").

facilitates teamwork, cooperation, and other skills that legal employers increasingly demand.[5]

The pedagogy builds upon principles of group learning by emphasizing permanent teams which proceed through sequenced phases of instruction. Important components of a successful team-based learning course include: A) course policy materials to explain and orient students to TBL; B) carefully-sequenced instructional modules; C) strategically-formed, permanent teams; D) readiness assurance process materials; E) application exercises; F) formative assessment, including peer assessment; and G) TBL as a graded component of the course.

## A. COURSE POLICY MATERIALS

Because team-based learning is a novel pedagogical approach, particularly in legal education, it is important to orient students so that they understand that instructional content will be delivered primarily outside class and that, if they fail to complete this content, they will be unprepared to work with their peers during class sessions. Orienting students to TBL is also important because some students are resistant to group work and need to understand how TBL differs from general group work. In an online environment, it is essential that students understand how coursework will be completed.

When introducing TBL, it is important to impress upon students the research-based efficacy of the technique. It is also helpful to remind students that TBL will enhance skills such as teamwork, communication, and collaboration that employers increasingly emphasize as necessary for new lawyers.[6] These are skills that may be hindered in a lecture-based online learning environment but that can be cultivated in an online, interactive TBL environment.

## B. SEQUENCED INSTRUCTION

TBL emphasizes carefully-sequenced instructional modules. Professors are encouraged to divide the course into modules, or units, typically five to seven per semester. For each module, students engage in pre-class preparation through guided readings. Those readings will be followed by an in-class readiness assurance process

5. Judy Curreya et al., *Developing Professional Attributes in Critical Care Nurses Using Team-Based Learning*, 15 Nurse Educ. in Prac. 232 (2015) (asserting that, based on a study of nursing students, "TBL offers real potential for deep learning and provides graduates with capacities for higher level critical thinking, problem solving, and a valuing of team-based solutions in the workforce—all making for more effective team membership and enhanced leadership skills.").

6. *See generally* Alli Gerkman & Logan Cornett, Foundations for Practice: The Whole Lawyer and the Character Quotient (2016), https://iaals.du.edu/sites/default/files/reports/foundations_for_practice_whole_lawyer_character_quotient.pdf (surveying legal employers and finding that competencies such as listening, arriving on time, and treating others with courtesy and respect were necessary for new law graduates).

(RAP), which is then followed by in-class application exercises. Because students will be expected to come to class ready to answer questions about the reading and execute skills based upon the reading, it is important that the professor prepare study guides to focus students' reading on core concepts. Those study guide questions can either be used to simply orient students' focus in out-of-class reading, or the professor can elect to have students submit responses to the questions.[7] In an online environment, the latter may be preferred to ensure engagement with course materials.

### C. PERMANENT, STRATEGICALLY-FORMED TEAMS

Team formation is another essential component of TBL. Teams are formed strategically by the professor rather than self-selected by the students. The professor should attempt to create teams and balance students in terms of year of study, gender, ethnicity, etc. In one of our law school courses, teams are typically formed randomly but may be balanced for certain demographics including, for example, gender, undergraduate degree, etc.[8] Teams consist of five to seven students and are permanent for the course.[9] This permanence ensures that teams will develop the cohesion necessary for success.

### D. READINESS ASSURANCE PROCESS

The RAP is arguably the most beneficial feature of TBL. The RAP is a sequenced instructional phase covering out-of-class preparation, followed by in-class quizzes designed to ensure foundational understanding.

Students are assigned reading outside of class which is focused with the use of study guide questions. Having completed this out-of-class preparation, students are prepared to take a quiz to assess their understanding. Quizzes are multiple-choice. Students first take the closed book quiz individually (the individual readiness assurance quiz or iRAQ), and then take the identical quiz together with their team (the team readiness assurance quiz or tRAQ).[10]

---

7. With respect to the content of study guide questions, see, e.g., Melissa H. Weresh, *Uncommon Results: The Power of Team-Based Learning in the Legal Writing Classroom*, 19 J. LEG. WRITING INST. 49 (2015) (sample study guide questions provided in Appendix 1).

8. In the other author's law school, the Registrar and Assistant Dean of Academic Affairs creates the teams and professors refine for balance. For additional information on forming teams, see *Forming Teams*, LEARN TBL, https://learntbl.ca/team/ (last visited Feb. 6, 2021).

9. In some cases, that means for the entire academic year; in others, it is just for a semester. One author has many of the same students for two semesters and, although the composition of the class changes very slightly in the second semester, endeavors to maintain the consistency of the teams. In the other author's situation, the students stay together, but with a new instructor; nonetheless, the students remain on the same teams. Both approaches prioritize group cohesion in order to help students master increasingly complex concepts.

10. TBL experts may refer to these as quizzes or tests, and therefore may refer to iRAQ and tRAQ for quizzes and iRAT and tRAT for tests. For purposes of consistency, this chapter will use the iRAQ and tRAQ terminology.

In a physical classroom, we typically use Immediate Feedback-Assessment Technique (IF-AT) scratch off style cards for the tRAQ.[11] With IF-ATs, students must come to a consensus as to the possible correct answer. If the agreed-upon answer is incorrect, teams must continue to collaborate to select the appropriate answer. Scores on team quizzes are calculated based upon how many attempts it took the team to arrive at the correct answer. They receive decreasing points for each missed response.

Team quizzes are typically very lively as students reinforce their understanding of critical distinctions between potential responses. In an online environment, we are unable to use IF-AT forms but, as explained in the following section, can nonetheless provide students with the similar experience of continuing to work together until the correct answer is revealed.

During the tRAQ, professors typically circulate between teams, listening to the students negotiate answers, hovering rather than helping. This observation prepares the professor to deliver a wrap-up lecture following the tRAQ. The wrap-up lecture enables the professor to go over the quiz to reinforce critical distinctions between potential responses.

Finally, groups are given the opportunity to appeal if they believe that an incorrect answer they selected arguably corresponds with their pre-reading materials. The appeal must be in writing and must be substantiated by reference to the reading. The opportunity to appeal provides students with a sense of agency over their learning. And the need to substantiate their responses provides yet another opportunity to engage with the material.

## E. APPLICATION EXERCISES

Once students have completed the RAP, they are prepared to proceed to in-class exercises that require them to apply foundational concepts. Application exercises are designed to follow the TBL "4-S" principle, meaning they should be designed around a problem that is *significant* to the course, all teams should work on the *same* problem, the exercise should require teams to make a *specific* choice, and teams should *simultaneously* report their choices on the exercise.[12]

## F. FORMATIVE ASSESSMENT

TBL fosters a tremendous amount of formative assessment. Students receive feedback on their performance during the RAP by receiving a score on their iRAQ, in their interaction with peers during the tRAQ, and in the context of the wrap-up lecture.

11. The IF-AT cards are prepared by Epstein Educational Enterprises. Epstein Educational Enterprises, http://www.epsteineducation.com/home/order/default.aspx. Quiz cards are available in 10, 25, or 50 questions with either 4 or 5 possible responses.

12. Larry K. Michaelsen & Michael Sweet, *The Essential Elements of Team-Based Learning*, 116 New Directions in Teaching & Learning 45–46 (2008).

Feedback on performance is also fostered during application exercises as students work collaboratively to solve problems.

TBL also incorporates peer assessment. Students complete a formative assessment of their teammates at the midterm, providing both a formal "score" of team performance and constructive, written feedback. They also complete a summative assessment of each team member's performance at the end of the course. These two assessment scores are averaged and comprise a portion of the student's final grade.

### G. TBL AS A GRADED COMPONENT OF THE COURSE

Allocating some component of the course grade to TBL incentivizes both individual and team performance. Individual quiz scores, group quiz scores, and an averaged score for the two peer assessments are factored into the final grade.[13] Many students are resistant to group work, fearing that free riders will benefit from the hard work of other students. Allocating a portion of the grade to team performance and peer assessment encourages accountability and reduces the possibility of free riders.

## III. Adapting TBL to the Online Environment

TBL is particularly suited for online instruction, which "emphasizes clear learning goals, interactive feedback, and outcomes-based assessment."[14] TBL is so effective in the online classroom, even those who haven't used TBL in the past should consider using it as a model for designing an online course.

### A. WHAT IS THE SAME?

In light of this compatibility, professors begin by focusing on what aspects of the course remain essentially the same whether delivery is online or in person. As set

---

13. One author allocates fifteen percent of the final grade to TBL, with five percent based on individual quiz score, five percent based on team quiz score, and five percent based on the peer assessment score. The other allocates ten percent of the final grade to TBL, with four percent for each of the individual and team quizzes and two percent based on the peer assessment. As explained on the Team-Based Learning Collaborative website, the graded component of TBL in a course should reflect individual performance, team performance, and peer assessment:

> The individual performance component provides a basis for student accountability to the instructor and to each other. The group performance component provides incentives for the development of group cohesiveness and justifies putting effort into group work. The peer evaluation solves two important motivational problems. One is providing an incentive for individuals to participate in group discussions. The other is removing the students' fear that they will have to choose between getting a low grade on the group assignments and having to "carry" the group work (if other group members fail to do their fair share).

*Answers to FAQs, "How To" Implementation Questions, Question #4*, Team-Based Learning Collaborative, http://www.teambasedlearning.org/answers-to-faqs/#q3_4.

14. Working Group on Distance Learning in Legal Education, Distance Learning in Legal Education: Design, Delivery and Recommended Practices 33 (2015), https://www.cali.org/sites/default/files/WorkingGroupDistanceLearningLegalEducation2015_PDF.pdf [hereinafter "CALI Working Group Report"].

out below, four of the key pillars of TBL overlap with recommendations for effective online instruction: the emphasis on independent learning outside of class; the organization of the curriculum into sequenced modules; the use of frequent assessments to track student progress; and in-class assignments that encourage student engagement.

### 1. The "flipped classroom"

The "flipped classroom" approach requires students to work autonomously outside the classroom, something almost unavoidable in the online environment. Whether the course is delivered synchronously or asynchronously, online instruction by its very nature requires students to learn more independently.[15] Consequently, faculty are encouraged to prepare their students for the different challenges that online instruction poses—in particular, the need for self-direction and self-management.[16] TBL may be uniquely well-suited to facilitating engagement in an online course. In a traditional Socratic course, delivered online, students who are not actively engaged in the dialogue may struggle to stay engaged with the instruction notwithstanding their preparation for class. In contrast, in an online TBL course, in-class engagement and participation is essential for all students, particularly during team activities.

Moreover, transitioning a TBL course online requires little adaptation. The RAP and peer assessment components of TBL incentivize students to complete assigned readings before class. This makes transitioning to an online delivery that much easier because there is no need to adapt the mode of content delivery. Online students are given the same reading assignments as students in in-person classes. And the expectation that students will be working closely with their peers on activities related to the reading makes student preparation and engagement more likely.

### 2. Organization of the curriculum

Course designers for online instruction emphasize the need to organize the curriculum in modules or units to provide clear structure for the students.[17] Course designers recommend a "backward course design" that begins by articulating course learning objectives.[18] Those overall course learning objectives are then used to identify

---

15. *Id.* at 12 ("developments like 'flipping the classroom' take the in person world closer to distance education, and live synchronous learning takes the online world closer to the physical classroom").

16. Kathryn E. Linder, The Blended Course Design Workbook: A Practical Guide 148–56 (2017).

17. Blaine Smith & Cynthia Brame, *Blended and Online Learning*, Vanderbilt Univ. Ctr. For Teaching, https://cft.vanderbilt.edu/guides-sub-pages/blended-and-online-learning/ (last visited Nov. 19, 2020).

18. Grant Wiggins & Jay McTighe, Understanding by Design (2d ed. 2005); *see also* Ryan S. Bowan, *Understanding by Design*, Vanderbilt Univ. Ctr. for Teaching (2017), https://cft.vanderbilt.edu/understanding-by-design/; Linder, *supra* note 16, at 31–37. For an additional discussion of backward design, see Chapter 30: *Backward Design: Course Design for Online Simulation Classes* by Christine Church.

unit or module learning outcomes, which are then "mapped" on a course map that aligns the learning objectives with each unit or module's assignments and activities. The course map establishes a clear pattern of activity and identifies the due dates that guide students' work in the course.[19] It is also effective to design the course so that the class work is broken into "chunks."[20] Approaching course design this way will typically require a lot of front-end work for the professor.

Here again, a TBL course is different than other pedagogical approaches because a TBL course is already organized into sequenced modules or units. Consequently, it adapts easily to the online setting without requiring an extensive overhaul or reorganization of the course materials or progression. Further, the instructional tools for each unit—quizzes followed by application exercises—provide the desired pattern of discrete and predictable activities that the students can anticipate.

### 3. Readiness assurance process

Experts in online instruction also stress the importance of a system of multiple assessments throughout the course.[21] To be effective, online courses should provide both "formative assessments" and "summative assessments."[22] Formative assessments teach course content and also assess student progress whereas summative assessments simply evaluate the student's work.[23]

The RAQs used in TBL are quintessential formative assessments. The quiz questions can be constructed so that they not only test the students' knowledge, but also deliver or reinforce the content that was included in the assigned readings. Particularly in the legal writing context, the questions offer the opportunity to model best practices and challenge the students to recognize them. The individual quiz or iRAQ allows students to assess their own understanding of the materials without outside assistance, and the team quiz or tRAQ that they subsequently take with their team furthers that understanding by requiring them to compare and discuss their individual answers to arrive at group consensus. It is often in the team quizzes that professors observe students fully grasping the concepts covered in the readings, at the same time they are practicing their communication and negotiation skills.

---

19. LINDER, *supra* note 16, at 71–81.

20. Smith & Brame, *supra* note 17. For additional information on "course chunking" see *Instructional Designers' Lens*, CTR. FOR INSTRUCTION & RES. TECH., https://www.unf.edu/cirt/services/id/process_design.aspx (last visited Nov. 19, 2020).

21. CALI Working Group Report, *supra* note 14, at 17.

22. *Id.* at 33–34.

23. *Id.*

### 4. Application exercises

To ensure student engagement, online course designers encourage providing students with active learning activities.[24] One example of an active learning activity is group work.[25] In the online environment, group work provides students with an opportunity to interact with their peers and learn valuable collaboration skills. These types of group activities not only develop important skills that students will need as practicing lawyers but can also provide an experiential learning experience.[26]

The application exercises that are built into the TBL pedagogy are exactly the type of exercises that online course designers recommend. Students apply the concepts covered by the readings and RAQs by completing group assignments. In an online TBL course, students can complete these application exercises in breakout rooms using the shared screen feature, document sharing, or quizzing tools. In fact, in the online version of this activity, the only real difference is the physical location of the students. In an in-person classroom, the students may be sitting around a table, but for many exercises they may all be on their own laptops while they collaborate on a shared document. We have found that in the online version of a TBL course, application exercises function in essentially the same manner except the students work together in a virtual environment.

## B. WHAT IS DIFFERENT?

Given the suitability of the TBL infrastructure to online delivery, there are certainly a few adaptations that help with the transition from an in-person classroom to distance learning, which we turn to now. Some of these changes are not necessary so much as advisable to help students navigate the online environment and to compensate for the loss of the informal communication opportunities that traditional in-person instruction offers.

### 1. Using a learning management system as "home base"

If you haven't already, we encourage you to take the time to fully explore the resources that your LMS offers. Given the new reliance on the course website or LMS, it becomes important to make sure that it captures the flow of the curriculum.[27] For example, each unit or module in the course should have its own LMS module that articulates the learning objectives for that unit, sets out the assigned readings, and

---

24. Linder, *supra* note 16, at 57–70.

25. *Id.*

26. CALI Working Group Report, *supra* note 14, at 13 ("The best distance learning in highly experiential and practice-oriented, just as great in person teaching can be.").

27. John R. Savery, *BE VOCAL: Characteristics of Successful Online Instructors*, 4:2 J. Interactive Online Learning 141, 142 (2005), https://www.ncolr.org/jiol/issues/pdf/4.2.6.pdf.

provides links to any outside resources. As students move through the unit, almost everything they need is either contained on or linked to the LMS module.

For in-person classes meeting in a physical space, the "Study Guide" that helps the students focus their reading might be provided in hard copy and posted to the course LMS. The extent to which students engaged with it was entirely up to them, although our students were informed that the Study Guide focused attention on the concepts that would be addressed in the RAQs. Anecdotally, we knew that most students made use of the study guides, and some of the teams would even meet prior to class to review the Study Guide together.

Online course delivery makes this type of peer pressure and collaboration less likely, so we determined that a bit of structure would better ensure that students completed the assigned readings. In the online format, we divided the study guide questions by units and made completion of each unit's study guide questions an ungraded assignment that students were required to complete before they could take the iRAQ. On the LMS, this type of scaffolding is fairly easy to set up, so for each unit, the students start by downloading the study guide, completing the reading, and then submitting the completed study guide questions. That submission then releases the iRAQ for the unit, which, as discussed in the next section, is a quiz housed on the LMS.

### 2. Readiness assurance process online

In a physical classroom, RAQs are commonly administered in class using paper copies for the iRAQs and scratch-off cards for the tRAQs. Students arrive to class, take the individual quiz on paper, and then move into their groups to retake the same quiz recording their consensus answers on the IF-AT scratch off answer card. Online, this is no longer a viable option.

Because having the students take the iRAQ during a synchronous video session is not an effective use of time, we have the students complete the individual quiz asynchronously before class. Setting up the iRAQ on the LMS is quite simple. Because the quizzes are multiple choice, it is fairly easy to import the questions into an LMS quiz system and designate the correct answer; however, the 2-step readiness assurance process of individual/group quizzes does present some unique challenges. For example, the system only works if students take the iRAQ without learning whether their answers are correct before they meet in class to collectively take the tRAQ. This means setting up the quiz to allow students to take the quiz, have their answers recorded, and still have access their individual quiz during class for the tRAQ without knowing whether their selected answers are correct. It may require some trial-and-error testing to identify the correct settings or, in some cases, identify a "workaround."[28]

28. Arizona's LMS is D2L's Brightspace, which offers quiz settings that allow students to access to view their quizzes after they are submitted without seeing whether their selected answers were correct. Drake used TWEN for their LMS but Blackboard for iRAQs; however, because Blackboard did not allow the students to go back and review their quizzes after they were submitted, students were instructed to make

The greater challenge is administration of the tRAQ in the online classroom. Synchronous class time can be used to have the students complete the group quiz in breakout rooms. Putting teams into the breakout rooms is relatively easy[29] but finding a way for them to check their answers as a group can be a challenge. It is important to have a virtual test environment that obligates teams to continue working toward the correct answer to a question when their initial selection(s) were incorrect. One solution is to mail the IF-AT cards to one member of each group, which only works if the designated team member is sure to attend every class.[30] Cost-effective digital solutions for administering the tRAQ are not readily available, but workarounds can be developed.

As it turned out, one of us was able to use Qualtrics to set up the group quizzes. The link to the Qualtrics quiz was then placed in the LMS for students to activate. This method worked, but the manner in which students worked toward the correct response was a bit glitchy.[31] The other author created a bare-bones class site on Moodle, an open-source LMS[32] with quiz settings that allow the professor to set up the questions so that students are told if their answer is incorrect and informed that they can keep submitting answers until they get the correct one—with a penalty for the incorrect answers.[33]

While the students readily adapted to working in their breakout rooms, figuring out the professor's role while the students are in their rooms can be difficult. In the in-person classroom, while the teams are taking the group quizzes, professors typically walk around the room, surreptitiously listening in on team discussions and debates and taking note of what concepts or questions caused students problems or needed further clarification in a wrap-up lecture. Although Zoom allows the host to move between breakout rooms, that option is much less subtle. In our experience, when a

---

note of their answers so that they could refer to them during the tRAQ. A professor at another institution also using Blackboard, set the value of each question at 0 to prevent students from knowing their score and, through the settings, permitted students to continue to see the quiz and the answers they had selected.

29. Using preassigned breakout groups in Zoom had a bit of a learning curve as we all adjusted to the quirks of the new technology, but once students were in the groups, class ran smoothly.

30. One TBL professor we contacted was unable to get permission from her IT department to use an online solution, so she provided IF-AT cards to at least one member of each team at the beginning of the semester. That student scratches off for the team and then sends a photo of the card once they have completed the tRAQ.

31. In Qualtrics, if an incorrect answer was selected, it disappeared, and students were left with the remaining responses. Once the correct response was selected, teams advanced to the next question. This deprived the teams of being able to continue to see the question and correct answer in order to reflect collaboratively on why the answer was, indeed, correct.

32. Moodle, Moodle.com/about.

33. Notably, Moodle was not the school's official LMS but offered a minimal plan for around $100 per year that was sufficient to create a Moodle course that accommodated all four legal writing courses. Because the sole purpose of the Moodle course was to house the tRAQs, instead of having the individual students create user accounts, the author created generic users—one for each team in each of the four classes—and had a student from each team log on as that user when the teams were in their breakout groups.

professor enters a breakout room to observe, students can become self-conscious and even stop a robust discussion mid-sentence. One technique to diminish this effect is to turn off the professor's video and mute the audio. This makes the professor appear to be more of an "eavesdropper" that silently slips in and out of the room.[34] Alternatively, a professor might make a point to announce her arrival and encourage students to continue their robust discussion.

Students can also be instructed that they can call the professor to their breakout room for technical assistance but not for substantive answers. Nonetheless, this is a helpful option to gauge the timing of tRAQs. Professors are able to broadcast an announcement that the quiz will be ending soon and that teams can summon the professor if they need additional time.

Once the teams complete the group quiz, the professor can close the breakout rooms and complete the short wrap-up lecture in the main room. Of course, identifying what to include in the wrap up is a bit more challenging when the teams are all meeting in separate breakout rooms. In the in-person classroom, it is easier to spot the problem questions by simply observing the teams as the professor moves through the room. The information gleaned from online lurking is a bit more piecemeal. However, in the online setting, it is easy to check the analytics on the individual and team RAQs. Before class begins, the LMS provides quiz results that can be viewed by question, making it easy to spot which questions students struggled with when they took the quiz as individuals. When it comes to the group quizzes, depending on the modality employed, similar information may be readily available while the teams complete the quizzes. Overall, once the technological challenges are resolved, the RAP is as effective online as it is in the physical classroom.

### 3. Modifying in-person classroom application exercises for online

Although many of the application exercises used in the physical classroom already incorporate online tools like shared documents or web-based quizzing and, therefore, transition to the online classroom easily, others require a bit of adapting. For example, many professors use sentence or document "puzzles" to reinforce organizational concepts. For this type of exercise in an in-person class, each team is given an envelope with sentences or paragraphs cut into paper strips. Teams then have to organize the segments into a legal discussion in the correct order. Modifying this assignment before an online course is fairly easy. The document that has the paragraphs or sentences that would otherwise be cut into strips can instead be inserted into a digital document as images so that teams can rearrange them within the document much like puzzle pieces. Typically, the document containing images is easily shared with students as an

34. To further this impression, one author uses a photo where she is peeking around a door as her Zoom profile picture when she is teaching.

attachment to the chat. Once in breakout rooms, one student shares the screen and move pieces of the puzzle with direction from the team. Similar types of exercises can be adapted using online slide tools or discussion boards on the LMS.

Having the teams complete the exercises in their breakout rooms during a synchronous online session works well for completing the task; however, having students simultaneously report their choices can be a challenge in a Zoom classroom. For the puzzle activity described above, this is not a problem. In order to replicate the simultaneously sharing of the group activity, each image is designated with a letter or number. When it becomes time for groups to share their results in the main room, it is easy for a member of the team to share out the order their team chose on the chat. Even so, because some of the exercises require students to apply the concepts by composing a written submission, there isn't always a definitive "choice" to share. Nonetheless, teams can share a document in the main room with the shared screen feature and groups can report out in some other LMS system or forum.

As is no doubt clear from the above discussion, TBL works well in a live, online, synchronous classroom. In that setting, the online experience is very comparable to the in-person classroom. However, even with live, online classes, there are likely to be more asynchronous online components to the course than in an in-person class. For example, students are required to complete their study guides and iRAQs asynchronously before they meet online for the tRAQ. Application exercises are often started in class but completed asynchronously.

While the synchronous class provides the teams with an important social experience, some of that can be replicated in an asynchronous setting. For example, Professor Kenneth Swift has described how he was able to successfully administer online group exercises in an asynchronous online class.[35] His advice is to keep the groups (teams) small (three to four students), set deadlines for initial participation, and allow discussion on a blog or wiki.[36] As he notes, most LMS platforms allow you to create group discussion boards.[37] There are a variety of messaging platforms that teams can use when reaching consensus on the tRAQ answers. Obviously, it will take teams longer overall to complete their group quizzes, but with clear guidance from the professor, and some real-time monitoring to ensure actual discussion before an answer is selected, it is possible to encourage the same problem solving that we see in the synchronous tRAQs.

---

35. Kenneth R. Swift, *The Seven Principles for Good Practice in [Asynchronous Online] Legal Education,* 44 Mitchell Hamline L. Rev. 1, 139 (2018).

36. *Id.* at 139.

37. *Id.*

## C. FINAL THOUGHTS

TBL in an online classroom is just as effective as TBL in the in-person classroom. It requires students to take an active part in learning and provides welcome structure to the course and the class sessions. Moreover, for the students, working together in the breakout rooms fosters peer interaction in a manner that may be unique compared to their other online courses.

ELEVEN

# The Importance of Building Community in Online and Blended Courses

Sophie M. Sparrow*

*The more positive the climate, the more students are likely to learn.*

— Linda B. Nilson & Ludwika A. Goodson[1]

After reading this chapter, readers will be able to:

- Summarize the role of emotion in learning;
- Appreciate the interconnectedness of emotion, learning, and memory in brain networks;
- Recognize the value of social interaction and belonging in learning; and
- Identify the benefits of creating positive learning communities.

Building positive learning communities is important for law students' successful learning.[2] Law teachers face challenges in trying to create those communities without in-person interaction,[3] but we can do it; the chapters that follow enumerate many detailed ways in which law teachers can effectively create constructive and supportive

* Professor of Law, University of New Hampshire Franklin Pierce School of Law. Professor Sparrow has been teaching law students for over twenty-three years. She has been teaching online courses for a year and blended classes and workshops for over three years; she has taught concurrent courses for one year.

1. Linda B. Nilson & Ludwika A. Goodson, Online Teaching at Its Best: Merging Instructional Design with Teaching and Learning Research 8 (2018).

2. *See* Gerald F. Hess, *Heads and Hearts: The Teaching and Learning Environment in Law School*, 52 J. Legal Educ. 75, 87 (2002) (identifying the eight elements of building a constructive law school learning environment: "respect, expectation, support, collaboration, inclusion, engagement, delight, and feedback.... The more elements present, the more likely the environment will be conducive to learning.").

3. Michael Hunter Schwartz, *Towards A Modality-Less Model for Excellence in Law School Teaching*, 70 Syracuse L. Rev. 115, 129–30 (2020).

communities in online and blended courses.[4] Those chapters focus on *how* to create positive learning communities in fully online and blended courses. This chapter instead focuses on *why* it is so important for law teachers to intentionally develop emotionally supportive learning environments in which students can flourish. Based on current research from neuroscience, cognitive psychology, and the scholarship of teaching and learning, this chapter argues that we need to acknowledge and build positive emotional course climates; if we do not, we may deprive our students of significant lasting learning.[5]

## I. The Role of Emotions in Learning

The National Academies of Sciences' recent work, *How People Learn II: Learners, Contexts and Cultures,* underscores the importance of incorporating positive emotion in learning.[6] Synthesizing years of research from the scholarship of teaching and learning, cognitive psychology, and instructional design on learning throughout the life span,[7] the Committee on How People Learn II incorporated social and emotional aspects in their conclusions:

> CONCLUSION 6-1:...Motivation to learn is fostered for learners of all ages when they perceive the school or learning environment is a place where they "belong" and when the environment promotes their sense of agency and purpose.[8]
>
> CONCLUSION 6-2: Educators may support learners' motivation by attending to their engagement, persistence, and performance by...creating an emotionally supportive and nonthreatening learning environment where learners feel safe and valued.[9]
>
> CONCLUSION 7-1: Effective instruction depends on understanding the complex interplay among learners' prior knowledge, experiences, motivations, interests, and language and cognitive skills; educators' own experiences and cultural influences; and the cultural, social, cognitive, and emotional characteristics of the learning environment.[10]

---

4. For an in-depth treatment of how to build community in online courses, see Chapter 12: *How to Build Community for Asynchronous Courses* by Ann Nowak and Chapter 13: *Designing the Course of the Future: How to Build Community in Synchronous Classes* by Eunice Park.

5. *See* Michael Hunter Schwartz, Gerald F. Hess & Sophie M. Sparrow, What the Best Law Teachers Do 35–36 (2013) (defining exceptional learning in law school and describing it as a combination of "exceptional intellectual development and exceptional personal development.")

6. Nat'l Academies of Scis., Eng'g & Med., How People Learn II: Learners, Contexts and Cultures (2018) [hereinafter How People Learn II].

7. *Id.* at 2 (describing reviewing "laboratory-based neuropsychology and cognitive science,...cultural and social psychology, classroom-based education research, and qualitative studies of adult learning and the workplace").

8. *Id.* at 5–6, 133.

9. *Id.* at 6, 133.

10. *Id.* at 6–7.

As the Committee observed, "[p]eople are willing to work harder to learn the content and skills they are emotional about, and they are emotionally interested when the content and skills they are learning seem useful and connected to their motivations and future goals."[11]

Similarly, in their book, *Online Teaching at its Best: Merging Instructional Design with Teaching and Learning Research*, authors Linda B. Nilson and Ludwika A. Goodson synthesized the recent research on learning and arrived at seventeen best practices for teaching that apply across all kinds of teaching; they too include social and emotional aspects of teaching.[12] As the authors note, "we start from the premise that excellent teaching is excellent teaching... whether the environment is classroom based, online, or hybrid.... [b]ecause in terms of the mind, learning is learning."[13] Three of the authors' seventeen best practices focus on the social and emotional aspects of learning—noting the value of teacher enthusiasm, creating a supportive learning environment, and infusing learning with emotions.[14]

Numerous scholars and experts have expounded on the connections between emotions and learning.[15] As Mary Helen Immordino-Yang, a leader in this area, states, we cannot "build memories, engage complex thoughts, or make meaningful decisions without emotion."[16] Emotions, thinking, and learning are interconnected through our brain networks.[17] "Emotions promote thinking which in turn promotes learning...."[18] Citing Immordino-Yang's work, the Committee on How People Learn II points out that

> it is neurobiologically impossible to think deeply about or remember information about which one has had no emotion because the healthy brain does not waste energy processing information that does not matter to the individual. Emotions help learners set goals during learning. They tell the individual experiencing them

---

11. *Id.* at 30 (citations omitted).

12. Nilson & Goodson, *supra* note 1, at 13–14.

13. *Id.* at 1.

14. Among the seventeen best practices identified by the authors are "11. To motivate students, enhance the value of the material by displaying enthusiasm for it.... 12. Create a supportive environment for learning.... 17. Inject emotions into presentations, activities, assignments, and reflections, and help students become more aware of their emotions." *Id.* at 14.

15. *See, e.g.*, Educational Neuroscience: Development Across the Life Span (Michael S. C. Thomas et al. eds., 2020); Mary Helen Immordino-Yang, Emotions, Learning, and the Brain: Exploring the Educational Implications of Affective Neuroscience (2016); Mind, Brain, and Education: Neuroscience Implications for the Classroom (David A. Sousa ed., 2010); Tracey Tokuhama-Espinosa, The New Science of Teaching and Learning: Using the Best of Mind, Brain, and Education Science in the Classroom (2010); *New Directions for Adult and Continuing Education*, *in* The Neuroscience of Adult Learning (Sandra Johnson & Kathleen Taylor eds. 2006).

16. Immordino-Yang, *supra* note 15, at 18.

17. Mary Helen Immordino-Yang & Rebecca J.M. Gotlieb, *Understanding Emotional Thought Can Transform Educators' Understanding of How Students Learn*, *in* Educational Neuroscience: Development Across the Life Span, *supra* note 15, at 244, 248 (citations omitted).

18. *Id.* at 249.

> when to keep working and when to stop, when she is on the right path to solve a problem and when she needs to change course, and what she should remember and what is not important.[19]

As Immordino-Yang elegantly and succinctly summarizes in the title of one of her works, "We Feel, Therefore We Learn."[20] Without emotions, we do not learn as well; our thinking is shallower, we struggle to set effective goals, we remember information less effectively, and we are less equipped to focus on important material and solve problems.[21] "Emotions are, in essence, the rudder that steers thinking."[22]

Focusing on positive emotions and the social component of learning is contrary to the conventional view of thinking, where emotions were believed to interfere with thinking.[23] As the Committee on How People Learn II explains,

> In the past, it was generally assumed that emotion interferes with critical thinking and that knowledge and emotion are separate. However, extensive research now makes clear that the brain networks supporting emotion, learning, and memory are intricately and fundamentally intertwined, even for experts in technical domains such as mathematics. Emotions are an essential and ubiquitous dimension of thought, and emotional processing steers behavior, thought, and learning.[24]

Because emotions play such a large role in thinking and learning, we should try to build communities that foster positive emotional connections between students, between students and teachers, and between students and course material.

Of course, in addition to supporting effective learning, some emotions can also obstruct learning, such as when we face threats, anxiety, and negative stress. "[E]motions like anxiety can undermine learning by causing worry, which depletes cognitive resources and activates brain regions associated with fear and escape rather than with academic thinking."[25] Facing threats, fear, and stress, our brains focus on survival, reducing or impeding our ability to use our prefrontal cortex to engage in higher-order

---

19. How People Learn II, *supra* note 6, at 29–30 (citations omitted).

20. Immordino-Yang, *supra* note 15, at 27.

21. How People Learn II, *supra* note 6, at 29–30 (citations omitted).

22. Mary Helen Immordino-Yang & Antonio R. Damasio, *We Feel, Therefore We Learn: The Relevance of Affective and Social Neuroscience to Education*, *in* Emotions, Learning, and the Brain : Embodied Brains, Social Minds and the Art of Learning, *supra* note 15, at 27, 28; Nilson & Goodson, *supra* note 1, at 90 (stating that "[n]ot only do emotions bring additional neurotransmitters into creating and reinforcing synaptic connections, but they also enhance motivation, which is so important in determining how much effort and persistence students put into their learning.") (citations omitted).

23. How People Learn II, *supra* note 6, at 29 (citations omitted); Immordino-Yang, *supra* note 15, at 70 ("Traditional views of the mind and body, such as that of Descartes, divorced high-level, rational thought from what were thought of as the basal, emotional, instinctual processes of the body.").

24. How People Learn II, *supra* note 6, at 29 (citations omitted).

25. *Id.* at 30 (citations omitted).

thinking.[26] Moreover, even small amounts of stress and perceived dangers—physical or psychological—negatively affect our learning.[27] When we do not create positive learning communities where students feel "psychologically safe" we impede our students' ability to learn.[28] Given the challenge of developing competence in complex legal knowledge, skills, and values, and the significant stress most law students face,[29] it is especially important that we build positive learning communities for law students.

Positive learning communities should not be completely devoid of all stress, however, as some level of good stress, or "eustress" is beneficial to learning.[30] As others have put it, we want to create learning communities with a sense of "'safe emergency'—a state of high attention but without the debilitating anxiety."[31] This state of moderate arousal engages and motivates students more than either too little or too much. When there is no stress, students are less engaged and less motivated to pay attention and learn.[32] As pointed out above, when there is too much stress or anxiety, learning is blocked. The optimal and delicate balance of support and stress is based on biology; "a moderate level of arousal triggers neural plasticity by increasing production of neurotransmitters and neural growth hormones, enhancing neural connections, and cortical reorganization.... [L]earning is enhanced through dopamine, serotonin, norepinephrine, and endogenous endorphin production."[33] We can take advantage of these biological processes to build learning communities in which law students succeed.

## II. Social Interaction and Learning

Positive learning communities have multiple benefits for students enrolled in online and blended law programs. For one thing, communities create social interaction. In in-person law courses and programs, students are constantly and naturally interacting with each other in multiple ways. Students sit next to others in class and hear their

26. See Judy Willis, *The Current Impact of Neuroscience on Teaching and Learning, in* Mind, Brain, and Education: Neuroscience Implications for the Classroom, *supra* note 15, at 45, 49–50, for a description of how the brain filters information into neural networks and processes emotions using the reticular activating system, and James E. Zull, *Key Aspects of How the Brain Learns, in* The Neuroscience of Adult Learning, *supra* note 15, at 3, 3–8, for an overview and foundation about brain structure and cognitive neuroscience.

27. Pat Wolfe, *The Role of Meaning and Emotion in Learning, in* The Neuroscience of Adult Learning, *supra* note 15, at 35, 40.

28. *Id.*

29. *See, e.g.*, Lawrence S. Krieger, *What We're Not Telling Law Students—and Lawyers—That They Really Need to Know: Some Thoughts-in-Action Toward Revitalizing the Profession from Its Roots*, 13 J.L. & Health 1, 3–4 (1998); Nancy J. Soonpaa, *Stress in Law Students: A Comparative Study of First-Year, Second-Year, and Third-Year Students*, 36 Conn. L. Rev. 353, 356–71 (2004).

30. Tokuhama-Espinosa, *supra* note 15, at 37.

31. Louis Cozolino & Susan Sprokay, *Neuroscience and Adult Learning, in* The Neuroscience of Adult Learning, *supra* note 15, at 11, 14.

32. *Id.*

33. *Id.* (citations omitted).

classmates discuss course material with classmates and the teacher. They chat with each other before and after class. They see each other in the hallways and common areas. They may form study groups, participate in social gatherings, play sports together, or share a meal. Many of these same activities and interactions are possible in online environments, but students and teachers have to be more intentional to make them happen; they do not just occur spontaneously through a casual encounter on a stairway or in an elevator. As humans, students need such encounters and interactions with others to thrive.[34] Conversely, lacking such encounters and being physically separated can make them feel isolated, alone, and unconnected.[35]

Educational experts have discussed the importance and impact of social interaction on learning, disputing the traditional focus on individualism and the conception of the isolated thinker.[36]

> The brain is a social organ, and people learn best when they are able to "grow" ideas and "bounce" concepts off of others.... The social nature of learning means that teachers should structure [courses] that encourage social interactions, orchestrating them to encourage maximum participation and thus allow students to construct their own learning.... Students retain more new information and learn better when they engage in social learning.[37]

As the Committee on How People Learn II states, "Individuals' brains are critically shaped by social relationships, and the information they learn through these relationships supports both their emotions and their knowledge about facts, procedures, motivation, and interests."[38] Simply put, we learn more effectively when we interact with others as we learn.[39] When law students hear others' perspectives and discuss differing analyses and legal interpretations, they are more likely to accurately understand and apply legal doctrine and skills. Again, there is a biological basis for the connection between social interaction and learning. When we interact with others, our brains develop greater neural plasticity.[40] When we have greater neural plasticity, our brains create more neuronal networks, leading to greater learning.[41]

---

34. *See* How People Learn II, *supra* note 6, at 29 (discussing institutionalized children's failure to develop biologically, socially, emotionally, and cognitively when lacking positive and stable relationships) (citations omitted).

35. Alfred Rovai, *Building Sense of Community at a Distance,* 3 Int'l Rev. Res. Open & Distance Learning 1, 2 (2002) (citations omitted).

36. Cozolino & Sprokay, *supra* note 31, at 13.

37. Tokuhama-Espinosa, *supra* note 15, at 119–20.

38. How People Learn II, *supra* note 6, at 29 (citations omitted).

39. Rovai, *supra* note 35, at 6.

40. Cozolino & Sprokay, *supra* note 31, at 17–18 (noting that "human brains need social interaction to promote neural plasticity").

41. Sandra Johnson, *The Neuroscience of the Mentor-Learner Relationship, in* Mind, Brain, and Education: Neuroscience Implications for the Classroom, *supra* note 15, at 63, 64.

In addition to fostering social interaction, positive learning communities help students feel like they belong in a law course or program. Synthesizing works addressing the meaning of community, educator Alfred Rovai describes classroom communities as places where students

> will have feelings of belonging and trust. They will believe that they matter to one another and to the group; that they have duties and obligations to each other and to the school; and that they possess a shared faith that members' educational needs will be met through their commitment to shared goals.[42]

When students experience this sense of belonging, they are more likely to be motivated to learn.[43] They are more likely to persist and succeed in their studies.[44] They are less likely to experience stereotype threat[45] or drop out.[46] In addition, students who feel that they belong in an online or blended program may be more likely to be satisfied with their learning experience, feel that they have engaged in significant learning, and believe that they are more engaged in their studies.[47]

Creating positive learning environments and the effective social interaction that builds community and fosters belonging does not just happen on its own. We need to be aware of the importance of emotion in teaching and learning and use it constructively to help online and blended law students succeed. Following best practices in online and blended course and class design means more than having specific learning goals, breaking a course into modules, selecting teaching exercises, choosing course materials, constructing effective assessments, and mastering the necessary technology. We also need to plan how to show our students authentic support, empathy, openness, and caring. Legal educators have observed the positive role that emotions play in helping students learn;[48] now we need to intentionally design welcoming and inclusive learning communities. We need to offer students "a safe haven, emotional attunement, and a scaffold to support the learning process."[49] Distance learning in legal education

---

42. Rovai, *supra* note 35, at 4.

43. How People Learn II, *supra* note 6, at 5–6, 133 (citations omitted).

44. Nilson & Goodson, *supra* note 1, at 121; Rovai, *supra* note 35, at 12.

45. Stereotype threat refers to the concept where members of a negatively stereotyped group perform poorly on an activity because they fear that they will perform according to the negative stereotype. Claude M. Steele & Joshua Aronson, *Stereotype Threat and the Intellectual Test Performance of African Americans*, 69 J. Personality & Soc. Pyschol. 797, 797–98 (1995).

46. Rovai, *supra* note 35, at 3; Xiaojing Liu et al., *Does Sense of Community Matter? An Examination of Participants' Perceptions of Building Learning Communities in Online Courses*, 8 Q. Rev. Distance Educ. 9, 20 (2007).

47. Liu et al., *supra* note 46, at 14, 20.

48. *See, e.g.*, Schwartz, Hess & Sparrow, *supra* note 5, at 48–55 (observing exceptional law teachers' characteristics such as enthusiasm, passion, positivity, and empathy); James B. Levy, *As A Last Resort, Ask the Students: What They Say Makes Someone an Effective Law Teacher*, 58 Me. L. Rev. 49, 56–66 (2006) (noting the important role of teacher "characteristics like warmth, support, and expectations" in positively influencing student learning).

49. Cozolino & Sprokay, *supra* note 31, at 15.

has increased over the past few years and is likely to increase in the coming decades. We owe it to our law students to design, build, and sustain communities where they can thrive, succeed, and graduate to become engaged members of the legal profession. When we apply the community-building approaches detailed in the chapters that follow, we will start doing just that.

TWELVE

# How to Build Community for Asynchronous Courses

Ann Nowak*

After reading this chapter, educators will be able to:

- Incorporate ten easy-to-implement techniques to create community in their asynchronous courses.

I first realized the importance of creating community in asynchronous courses shortly before midnight one Saturday in 2006. I remember the day and time well because I was teaching an asynchronous course while also trying to run my law firm, so my teaching got relegated to late nights and weekends. The house was quiet then, and I could stay up until the wee hours of the morning, working uninterrupted.

Usually, I used this time to read through students' writing, comment on it, and grade it. On this particular night, though, two weeks into the semester, I had no idea that something was about to happen that would change the way I taught forever.

This course was persuasive writing, an entry-level offering in an associate's degree program where all classes were taught asynchronously. As I sat at my kitchen table, alone with my computer, I scrolled through the discussion area in our class site and noticed that one student had just posted a question for her classmates. She asked if anyone knew how to use a semicolon. Other students began responding to her. One by one, they admitted to being confused and were struggling together to figure out what to do with semicolons. I was amazed, but pleased, that this was what they chose to do on a Saturday night.

I knew from my students' short biographies that they were attending college part-time, were in their early twenties, typically had several children, lived in Appalachia, and worked at minimum wage jobs. Most were also the first in their extended family

* Director of the Writing Center, Touro College Jacob D. Fuchsberg Law Center. Professor Nowak began asynchronous teaching in 2006 and synchronous teaching in 2014.

to attend college. Their lives were full, but clearly, they were highly motivated because there they were, late on a Saturday night, trying to learn something that was not even on the syllabus. And they were trying to help each other do it.

For about ten minutes, I watched, fascinated, as they chatted back and forth via posts, trying to sort out how to use this thing called a semicolon. Would they figure it out? They had no idea that I was watching. Finally, when seventeen of my twenty students had joined in the discussion, and they were still struggling, I knew what I had to do.

I jumped in to help.

And then I told them to bear with me for a few minutes while I wrote out what I hoped would be an easy way for them to learn how to use semicolons. A flood of "thank you" posts instantly appeared.

I could have directed them to some website that provided instruction. Or I could have given them the normal explanation about semicolons connecting independent clauses. But I was pretty sure that most of them did not know what "independent clause" meant and were probably too burned out this late on a Saturday night to focus on that kind of explanation.

So, without any time to plan, I delivered an unconventional, spur-of-the-moment explanation involving hoses and hose couplings. Why hoses and hose couplings? I do not know; it popped into my mind and just seemed right. Only later did I realize that this impulsive decision was exactly the kind of thing that helps create community in an asynchronous course. I had made learning vibrant and compelling and tied it to something they could instantly understand and visualize. Further, I had made an effort that showed I cared.

To understand why this class transformation was particularly meaningful, you need to understand that the school at that time did not allow anyone to post photos or videos. We had only our written words, usually not posted in real time. Imagine trying to create community in a class when no one can see what anyone looks like—not even via a photo.

But back to my story. I do not think that I would have created community that quickly if I had used a more traditional approach. I knew that my students lived in Appalachia, so I guessed that they mostly lived in single family houses and drove cars or trucks. I told them to imagine a hose coupling—the thing that attaches two hoses to make one long hose. I told them to imagine that they wanted to wash their vehicle but that there were too many other vehicles in the driveway to be able to bring it close enough to the house to wash it with the hose that was attached to the spigot. I told them to imagine that they also had a hose coupling and an additional section of a hose—a long cut off piece that would enable them to bring water to their vehicle if they could attach it to the hose via the hose coupling. The problem, I said, was that cut off piece did not have threads at the ends because it was only a part of a whole hose. Thus, there was no way to screw it into the hose coupling and, thus, attach that cut off piece to the whole hose.

I then told my students that whole hoses are like whole sentences and that partial hoses are like partial sentences. And I said that just like you cannot attach a partial hose to a whole hose with a hose coupling, you cannot attach a partial sentence to a whole sentence with a sentence coupling—i.e., a semicolon.

I posted this and waited for my students' reactions. Would they think I was crazy? Luckily, they did not. They instantly grasped semicolon use. The visual of the truck, the hose, and the hose coupling made all the difference.

So, also, had my decision to help them out when I saw them struggling late at night. At the time, I did not think that my action was a big deal. But my students thought otherwise. They later told me that what they saw that night was a professor who cared enough to jump in to help when they were struggling—a professor who was willing to be creative and spirited on their behalf.

What was most interesting to me was that when I showed them I cared, they increased their efforts. That night, they did not just say thank you. They began to post sentence after sentence, linking them with semicolons, happily demonstrating a newfound skill.

Why were my students so happy? Because they had mastered a seemingly elusive skill. Why was I happy? Because I learned about the importance of creating community in an asynchronous classroom.

After I accidently stumbled into the realization that students become more interested in, and enthusiastic about, the joy of learning when they are part of a vibrant learning community, I looked for ways to recreate this feeling in all my asynchronous courses. The bottom line was that I needed to figure out ways to make myself seem human and caring, not just about the subject but about helping them master it. And I needed to help them feel like their input mattered to the collective whole—that we were all in it together and that we could all help each other learn.

In this chapter, I am going to explain why creating community in your asynchronous course is vitally important. I am also going to give you ten ways to do this, including short explanations/examples of each. These ten ways are not the only ways. But they are the ways that have worked well for me.

## I. Humanizing Your Approach to Teaching

After my late-night epiphany, I learned that my discovery was supported by the findings of others. That is, professors can facilitate the transformation of their asynchronous classrooms into compelling learning communities by "humanizing" themselves to their students right from the start of the course.[1]

---

1. *See, e.g.*, Michelle Pacansky-Brock, *How to Humanize Your Online Class*, BROCANSKY.COM (Apr. 15, 2015), https://brocansky.com/2015/04/infographic-how-to-humanize-your-online-class.html; Jeffrey R. Young, *How One University Is Working to "Humanize" Online Teaching*, EDSURGE (Mar. 6, 2017), https://www.edsurge.com/news/2017-03-06-how-one-university-is-working-to-humanize-online-teaching; https://onlinenetworkofeducators.org/course-cards/humanizing-online-teaching-learning/.

In the words of Michelle Pacansky-Brock, a nationally renowned educator and writer about best practices for teaching asynchronously, "In our post-COVID age, where online courses are the backbone of instruction, those who possess the knowledge and digital fluency to develop inclusive, asynchronous online learning experiences that are rich with human connection will be not only game-changers but life-changers."[2]

I had taught other asynchronous courses before that fateful night in 2006, but my students had never bonded like this. Even in small classes of about 20 students, posts on discussion boards had felt forced—more like requirements than voluntary and enthusiastic engagement.

After that late-night semicolon party, I doubled down on my efforts to respond to my students' discussion posts and engage them with my own comments. I told them relevant anecdotes from my own life. The more I got involved, the more the students responded—not just to me but to each other.

The key was not just that I made myself available to my students deep into the night; the key was that I cared enough to help them when I did not have to. And that I did it in a fun, creative way that resonated with them. But back then, my students were the ones who started creating the learning community in our classroom. I merely seized the moment and jumped in.

Now, years later, I am the one who creates the learning community in my classroom and invites the students to join me. The key is not to be boring and to be spirited, creative, and invested. If you show your students that you have the desire to make learning interesting, they will almost always meet you halfway. If you hide your joy and seem to forget that your students are actual people with feelings and stresses and desires and fears, you won't connect with them, and you are unlikely to inspire them.

Creating community in an asynchronous course takes energy and creativity. I, personally, think it is harder to teach asynchronously than synchronously because when students can see you in real time and ask you questions in real time—either by voice or by chat—that immediacy bonds you and your students.

About six years after my late-night semicolon party, I experienced firsthand what it was like to be a student in an asynchronous course. MOOCs (Massively Open Online Courses) had recently surfaced on platforms like Coursera. They were asynchronous and free. I enrolled in one and discovered that the professor, rather than teaching solely in writing, recorded instructional videos for students to watch. We then took quizzes and posted our comments on discussion boards. The classes were so big, though, the students' written discussions did not seem very personal or focused. I felt alone as a student in that course, no matter how engaging the professor was.

Years later, I again felt the disconnect of being a student in an asynchronous course when, during the pandemic, my tap dancing teacher discontinued our live Zoom class-

2. Michelle Pacansky-Brock, *Humanizing*, BROCANSKY.COM, https://brocansky.com/humanizing (last visited Feb. 6, 2021).

es and prerecorded them instead. These asynchronous classes were not as compelling even though the teacher and content of the classes were the same. The problem was that students could no longer type questions into the chat for our teacher to answer during class. In the synchronous classes, I felt like I was part of a community, even though I did not "know" the other students. I liked seeing the same people week after week. I felt as though we were connected by a common love of tap dancing and our instructor's style of teaching. In the asynchronous classes, that connection was gone.

Learning can be lonely if you are isolated and cannot connect with your classmates and professor in a meaningful way. As you have read previously in this book, creating community in your classroom is vitally important to help students learn and retain course content and master your learning objectives. To that end, I offer you the following ten tips that have helped me create community during my many years of teaching online.[3]

## II. Ten Tips for Creating Community in Asynchronous Courses

*Tip #1: Develop learning outcomes that sound compelling and relevant to your students' lives.*

Like many of you, I include learning outcomes in my syllabi. In my Law Practice Management course, for example, I state that by the end of the course, students will be able to write a business plan, set up a virtual office, decide what technology they need and why, etc.

It took me years to realize that learning outcomes should not only include hard skills like these but also other essential interpersonal skills—and that continuously talking about these skills helps build community.

For example, by the end of my Law Practice Management course, students who apply themselves will have become better at the skills of public speaking, problem solving and decision making, time management, and negotiating.

But rather than just listing the interpersonal skills in your syllabus, consider adding a sentence for each skill to make it seem compelling and relevant to students. And then discuss these in the first class, either in writing or in a video, to help get buy-in.

Using, as an example, some of the skills from my Law Practice Management course, you could write:

- Public speaking: You will learn to be less fearful, more concise, and more focused when speaking to a group.

3. For an in-depth treatment of how to build community in synchronous online courses, see Chapter 13: *Designing the Course of the Future: How to Build Community in Synchronous Classes* by Eunice Park.

- Problem solving and decision making: You will learn to think outside the box and feel more confident about your decisions.
- Time management: You will learn to budget your time better, so you won't run out of time on projects.
- Negotiating: You will learn the art of giving and taking and knowing where to draw the line in a negotiation.

By adding these simple sentences, you help your students to more easily grasp how they will grow as a result of investing their time in your course.

But how does this relate to building community? You need to circle back each week to the interpersonal-skill learning objectives. Tell students at the beginning of the week which assignments and activities that week will help them with which skill, why, and how. You can either do this in writing or in a video.[4] Then, at the end of the week, ask students to either write in the discussion forum or record a quick video to discuss which skill they worked on with which assignment, what they learned that they might apply elsewhere in their current or future lives, and how they might apply it.

Instead of asking students to post their responses in a discussion for the whole class to see, you can divide the class into small groups and have students post their responses only for group members and ask those students to respond.

*Tip #2: Establish a compelling classroom culture.*

Create a sense of place—a culture—in your course. The human factor is important. The first thing to do is to create a culture of trust. How do you do this? Explain that you want all your students to succeed, that you get no pleasure out of giving low grades. Tell them you expect them to work hard for their grades but that they need to trust that you will help them if they make the effort to be equal partners with you in this journey. What journey? The journey toward self-empowerment through learning.

The first step toward creating a culture in your course is to personalize your asynchronous classroom. This is not hard. Post a short personal bio, but not the stodgy one on your school's faculty webpage. Post one that includes not just degrees and accomplishments but also nonacademic things—like the fact that you have a rescue cat that sits in your lap while you grade, or that you like to tap dance for stress relief after grading. Be creative and a little funny. This makes you seem more approachable, more human. And that human factor is what starts turning your classroom into a community.

*Tip #3: Establish and maintain your lively presence on their discussion boards.*

Make sure you, as the professor, are actively engaged on the class discussion boards. Bring in personal anecdotes where you can. When I teach legal writing, I always tell

4. Weekly videos are discussed in Tip #10.

students that I struggled with it when I was in law school. My students are always amazed that their professor once struggled with the very subject I am teaching. I explain that struggling does not mean you are destined to be bad at something. I explain that I had been used to writing as a journalist before law school and that I had not understood the point of why we needed to use a certain construct for legal writing. And then I tell my students that I am going to explain to them things that I wished someone had explained to me when I was student trying to master legal writing. My students are always grateful for my honesty and caring. And that gratitude helps build community in our classroom.

*Tip #4: Develop a self-assessment questionnaire that piques students' interest.*

This tip grew out of my desperation one summer when I was at an academic conference in Italy and also had to teach the first session of a synchronous course via my laptop in my hotel room. I discovered a day before my class was to begin that the hotel's internet connection was not stable enough to handle a live online class. I panicked. What would I do?

Somehow, I came up with the idea of having my students spend that first class session completing a detailed self-assessment questionnaire that would allow me to get to know them better before we "met" in the next class. Although I did not realize it at the time, this questionnaire would help me create community in my course.

So, I wrote to my students, explained the situation, said that there were no right or wrong answers. I also told them that their answers would not affect their course grade but that not completing and submitting the completed questionnaire would affect the class participation and professionalism portion of their course grade.

To my surprise, this exercise proved to be more enlightening than I ever imagined. In the next class—the live one—I discussed in broad terms what I had learned from their answers and how I would use my new knowledge to empower them toward success in our course and beyond.

Here are some examples:

- I asked, "Do you feel comfortable blowing your own horn? Yes? No? Sometimes? Please pick one and write a one-sentence explanation." Most students answered that they did not feel comfortable doing this because it was "bragging." So, in the next class, I mentioned that most students did not feel comfortable blowing their own horn because it felt like bragging. I explained why it was important to mention your accomplishments when you are in the professional world and how to do it without bragging. For the few students who had said they already felt comfortable with this, I included techniques to help them become even better.
- I asked, "What are your top five strengths? What are your top five weaknesses? List them and write a sentence explaining each one." Numerous students listed time management as a weakness. As a result, I told them that I would develop a

plan to help them and would incorporate it into our class because time management was critical to the practice of law.

And then I told them that these questionnaires helped me to get to know them as people, not just as bodies in my course. I said that I used to be reticent to blow my own horn but that I worked hard to become comfortable with it and why. I also told my students that I, too, had previously struggled with time management. And I explained what I did to overcome it. Only later, wondering if I had overshared, did I realize that I had not. What I had done, instinctively, was bond with my students; I had helped to create community by showing them that I was invested in their success and in helping them succeed.

*Tip #5: Confess (reveal some humanity).*

Do not be afraid to mention your struggles and fears when you were in school. It is not oversharing, and it will not erode boundaries and cause students to lose respect for you. Instead, it helps build that respect because it shows that you are secure enough to show that you understand fear and struggle.

I sometimes tell my students about the long, cold winters when I was a law student huddled over a propane heater because I did not have money to heat the house in which I was living. I tell them about wearing a down jacket and gloves as I typed my law school assignments. And I tell them about the two to three hours that I commuted each way to school, constantly afraid that my car would break down. I tell my students that I know many of them have stresses far worse than this, but that I understand feeling stressed while in law school. Then I tell them that I will do everything I can to make our classes a safe haven, a retreat, a respite from the stresses of life. And I tell them that I will try to make our experience together meaningful to them. And I explain that I do this because when people care about all being together, they lift each other up in a community. Not because they want to help others to get an A. They do it because they like the others and care, and because the others like and care about them. Yes, I actually say all of this. In an asynchronous course, you can say this either in writing or by audio/video recording. But say it. It helps to create community in the classroom.

Here are some more tips about humanizing your course by "confessing":

- Talk about your struggles in law school. Did you have a fear of public speaking? Did you struggle to understand one of the core subjects? Explain how hard you worked to overcome these struggles.
- Talk about a weakness and what you do to overcome it. Pick things to which your students can relate. For example, time management. I tell students that things always took longer than what I expected. So, when I was in law school, I made a time diary and entered everything for a couple of weeks. By doing that,

I got a handle on how long things really took. I also talk about my struggle with procrastination in school, and I teach them a technique that helped me overcome it. The technique is simple: When I want to procrastinate, I set an alarm on my phone for twenty minutes and focus on the task for that time. I have found that I can focus on just about anything if I know that I do not have to do it for more than twenty minutes. As soon as the alarm rings, I get up and do something else for ten minutes. The key is to get up and do something physical—be it walking around, getting a snack, or playing with a pet. I have discovered that the technique does not work as well if I do not get up and do something physical.

- Talk about a mistake you once made and the valuable life lesson you learned from that mistake—lessons you might not have learned otherwise.

*Tip #6: Assign study groups within the class and require reports.*

Although law students often form their own study groups, one excellent way to build community in your course is to assign study groups for the duration of the course. I have found that four or five students per group is ideal. Explain to your students that this will help them get to know others in the course. Also explain that you are going to give the groups prompts to help them think about course material from different perspectives and that learning to think about things from different perspectives is an invaluable skill for problem solving in life.

What are the prompts? They can be anything you want as long as they are open-ended questions that require students to engage in discussions to collectively find answers to the questions. I find that pro/con questions are excellent for this purpose. Typically, I ask students to list ten pros and ten cons and give reasons. The groups must come to consensus on the answers and send them to you.

I require that the groups do this weekly. I also require that students in each group rotate responsibility for sending me the group document. When I have a small class, I require students to meet in groups for forty minutes per week via Zoom. But if you have a large class, or your students live in a wide variety of time zones, you could require your students to meet asynchronously by writing back and forth in a private chat group.

*Tip #7: Develop asynchronous surveys for students to help you to help them.*

I have found that most students feel valued when they say or do something that helps their professor. And helping students to feel valued by their professor helps students to feel as though they are part of something greater than themselves. This is what community is all about.

To that end, I ask students to complete a very short weekly survey and submit it anonymously. Their participation is required. The survey contains the same two questions every week:

1. "What information from our course in the past week was unclear to you? Explain. Please include things that you subsequently figured out either alone or with the help of others. If you figured out things that were unclear, please furnish an explanation that will clarify the information for students in this course now and in future semesters."
2. "What did you read, hear, and/or discuss in this course this week that spurred you to want to know more—either via the receipt of additional information, examples, or both? You must pick something and explain."

I compile highlights of the answers to these questions and post them with my responses.

*Tip #8: Use springboards and make sure you tell students when you do.*

Be prepared to learn from your students' discussion posts and use them as springboards for class discussions. The key is to tell students that you learned from them. Do not assume that this is self-evident to your students. It often is not.

Students love to hear that you learned something from them and that you took the time to explain to the class why this knowledge is important. With law students, you are modeling a skill that is essential for effective lawyering. Tell them this.

The key to being able to do this is to be fluid. You do not need to derail your lesson plan. Be brief. Doing this not only teaches students valuable information, but it teaches them that you value them. It also teaches them that humans can all learn from each other and that it is important to take the time to do that.

*Tip #9: Adopt scripted role-playing simulations with guided debriefings.*

Small group simulations with role playing are a terrific way to build community in in-person and synchronous courses. But can they be done in asynchronous ones? Yes!

Role-playing simulations allow students to step out of themselves and temporarily walk away from their baggage—i.e., their fears, their insecurities, their stresses. This social interaction helps them to feel more relaxed with each other, work toward a goal, and be creative. This builds community in the classroom.

The simulations that have worked best for my classes have been negotiations of various kinds. In an asynchronous class, students can negotiate via posts on a group discussion board or on any chat platform. If your students are in the same time zone, you might want to consider having them negotiate synchronously via Zoom even if your course is asynchronous. But in the end, they have to write up what the group decided and answer guided debriefing questions, including some about the group dynamic.[5]

---

5. *See* LYNNE ADAIR KRAMER & ANN L. NOWAK, THE EXPERIENTIAL GUIDE TO LAW PRACTICE MANAGEMENT: OPENING AND OPERATING YOUR OWN FIRM (Teacher's Manual 2016) (examples of roleplaying simulations and guided debriefing questions).

*Tip #10: Record short welcome and pre-week videos with a twist.*

Consider recording and posting a short, informal welcoming video for students to watch before the first asynchronous class. It should not be longer than three minutes, or you will risk losing your students' attention. Do not make it formal. Formality is distancing, and you are trying to eradicate distance and build community.

In this video, welcome your students, tell them some compelling highlights of your upcoming course, and touch on some of the skills you will help them master during the course.

Then record and post a second video of no more than three minutes in which you tell them why you are excited to be teaching this particular course.

After that, record a short weekly video of no more than three minutes and post it at the beginning of each week to motivate students and let them know what is in store for that week, including the interpersonal skills that you hope they will acquire.

## III. The Bottom Line

As you try to decide which of the above ten tips to implement first, always remember to stop and think about the communities you have been part of in life—your neighborhood, your religious organization, your school, your teams. What did they have in common that made you feel good about being part of them? It all comes down to a sense of belonging, to the human connection, to getting to know people, to having them get to know you, to striving toward common goals, and to working to help each other. Your asynchronous classroom is no different. But you must be active about creating and maintaining that human bond. Otherwise, you and your students will feel like the act of participating is more of a chore than a pleasure.

THIRTEEN

# Designing the Course of the Future: How to Build Community in Synchronous Classes

Eunice Park*

After reviewing this chapter, readers will have tools to:

- Build community between the students and the professor;
- Build community among students; and
- Connect students to the greater law school community.

While the physical classroom allows community to develop as a natural consequence of sharing space in a room, with spontaneous conversations that occur while waiting for class to start or by clustering around a table for a group assignment,[1] building community in the remote world of the online classroom requires intentionality. This chapter focuses on how to build community with intentionality in the synchronous classroom, including the asynchronous coursework that accompanies live class time.[2] Following are eleven tips offered throughout this chapter for building different communities:

**Community Between Students and Professor**

*Tip #1: Post a video or email announcement about yourself.*

*Tip #2: Ask students to share something about themselves with you.*

*Tip #3: Post frequently.*

---

* Associate Professor, Western State College of Law. Professor Park began law teaching in 2000. She has designed and taught synchronous and hybrid courses.

1. Beth McMurtrie, *The New Rules of Engagement?*, CHRONICLE HIGHER EDUC. (Oct. 7, 2020), https://www.chronicle.com/article/the-new-rules-of-engagement?cid2=gen_login_refresh&cid=gen_sign_in.

2. For an in-depth treatment of how to build community in asynchronous courses, see Chapter 12: *How to Build Community for Asynchronous Courses* by Ann Nowak.

*Tip #4: Hold office hours at non-traditional times.*

*Tip #5: Provide frequent feedback.*

**How to Build Community Among Students**

*Tip #6: Have students introduce themselves to the class.*

*Tip #7: Establish rules of electronic communication etiquette.*

*Tip #8: Minimize lecture and provide a variety of ways students can interact with the course.*

*Tip #9: Incorporate technology for creative ways for students to "speak" in class.*

*Tip #10: Enable natural opportunities for student socialization.*

**How to Connect Students to the Greater Law School Community**

*Tip #11: Include other faculty and resources from the greater professional community in your course content.*

## I. "Community": What and Who

What is a "community"? In the classroom, it is a group of individuals who came together because of shared interests or goals, and who feel included and safe in an environment in which knowledge and learning is shared.[3]

Who is doing this sharing? The most obvious answer is that the professor is sharing information with the student, but community-building requires a collaborative culture in which relationships are built not just between the student and the professor but also between the student and other students, and between the student and the greater law school community. Thus, this chapter will present eleven tips for how to build community in the synchronous classroom by structuring the suggestions around each of these three sets of relationships. Certainly, building the relationship among students can also contribute to building the relationship between the students and the professor, or with the greater community. However, by considering discrete sets of human relationships that comprise the classroom, rather than approaching the goal of building community as a monolith, professors will achieve a more thoughtful, deliberate approach to accomplishing this intangible yet critical goal.[4]

3. *Seven Indispensable Strategies to Build Community in Your Online Courses*, MAGNA ONLINE SEMINARS (Jun. 18, 2019), http://seminars.magnaonlinemedia.com/wp-content/uploads/sites/115/2019/06/7-Indispensable-Strategies-handout.pdf.

4. For more on the neuroscience of the importance of community, see Chapter 11: *The Importance of Building Community in Online and Blended Courses* by Sophie M. Sparrow.

## II. How to Build Community Between Students and Professor

### A. WEEK ONE

*Tip #1: Post a video or email announcement about yourself.*

Creating a connection with the students does not need to wait until the first day of live class together. Indeed, the online format creates opportunities to reach out to students in advance. Post a video or email announcement to students prior to the first day. Such an announcement serves two obvious purposes: it welcomes the students to law school and to this class, and it introduces and humanizes yourself. How much and what you wish to share will be a subjective decision that varies depending in part on institutional culture, but in addition to the usual professional background and personal facts, consider including references to any prior online teaching experience to reinforce your familiarity with the platform.

The announcement can also serve a third more subtle purpose. Consider acknowledging the non-traditional classroom format and asserting openly that the coursework will be as challenging and meaningful as ever. Being candid will help gain students' trust of both the professor and the instructional medium and establish a culture of high expectations from the outset. You may also wish to provide links to articles that offer guidance on ways to learn effectively in an online classroom, with practical pointers such as testing out the platform before it is time for class, finding a distraction-free environment, and taking the class as seriously as one held in a law school classroom.[5]

*Tip #2: Ask students to share something about themselves with you.*

Once you have set this groundwork, follow up by asking students to share something about themselves. Show that you are interested in learning who they are. Require that students introduce themselves to you via a brief written assignment, with a specific word limit that is not burdensome. The prompt can be either an open invitation to share something that they would like you to know about them or a more pointed question, like something they learned from current socio-political events likely to be of interest to the students (not necessarily law-related).

Students have sometimes shared personal pieces of history that have given me a context I otherwise would have lacked, enabling me to better understand them not only as law students but as individuals. This introduction also provides some insight into the student's writing ability before the semester begins. Be sure to respond to

5. *E.g.*, Susan Landrum, *A Student Guide to Best Practices for Online Classrooms*, L. Sch. Success Blog (Mar. 18, 2020), https://lawschoolacademicsuccess.com/2020/03/18/a-student-guide-to-best-practices-for-online-classrooms/.

these reflections to acknowledge that you read the piece and appreciate that the student shared this aspect of his or her personal experience with you.

With communication thus established before the first day of class, sometimes the students will re-volunteer an aspect of their personal story later in the semester during office hours—an affirmation of the professor's early interest in learning about their background and of the mutual understanding about part of it.

## B. BEYOND WEEK ONE

*Tip #3: Post frequently.*

Establish a virtual presence. Postings do not need to be limited to assignments and course work. Use the discussion board or announcements feature on your classroom online platform to post material that will be generally interesting or relevant to the students. This could be a news article, a video, cartoon, or upcoming professional event.[6] A bit like a blog, such a feature reinforces to the students your interest in the material and its relevance outside the classroom. It also serves as a reminder of your presence.

Additionally, you can invite students to share an item with you for possible posting to share with the class, if they come across something interesting and relevant. This demonstrates to the students that you value their observations and contributions beyond the formal material. You could also open the post up as an optional discussion board for students to post a comment, enabling another avenue for conversation between yourself and the students (and, indirectly, among the students).

*Tip #4: Hold office hours at non-traditional times.*

Students who are taking online classes may be facing burdens such as taking care of children or parents, using spaces non-conducive to study, or dealing with unsupportive household members. The physical classroom allows students to distance themselves from these burdens in a way that the online classroom does not. However, holding virtual appointments allows for greater flexibility with office hours. While you will still want to have set office hours each week, the ability to hold office hours without requiring a physical location opens up opportunities to accommodate students who may be juggling responsibilities or facing personal challenges. Consider holding office hours evenings, weekends, or early mornings.

---

6. For more on this, *see* Tip #11.

*Tip #5: Provide frequent feedback.*

Not only does feedback provide needed instructional guidance, but it is an important way to relay to students that the professor is engaged.[7] Frequent formative assessments are thus more important than ever in the online environment.

Detailed feedback can be provided using electronic annotation, like the comment feature in Word. Briefer feedback can also be offered in the following ways:

- Immediate in-class feedback on a Google document students worked on together for a group assignment.[8]
- A short, recorded video explanation, instead of an email or other written remarks.
- Comments on a discussion board assignment.

Consider whether, after the conclusion of a particular discussion board, you want to pick a "Most Valuable Discussion Board Post" and email the entire class congratulating that student on his or her participation.[9] This allows you to publicly acknowledge and praise an exceptional contribution, and it will motivate the other students to provide thoughtful posts on the next discussion board assignment.[10]

This leads to our next set of community relationships, among students.

## III. How to Build Community Among Students

### A. WEEK ONE

*Tip #6: Have students introduce themselves to the class.*

In addition to the written assignment in which students introduced themselves to you, provide the students an opportunity to introduce themselves to each other. Unlike the student's introduction to you,[11] the students' introductions to each other can help prompt socialization among themselves. Depending on the size and nature of your class, some options for doing so include the following:

- Require students to post an introduction on the discussion board. Doing so builds in opportunities for students to share their knowledge and experiences,

7. Michele Pistone, *Top 5 Tips for Teaching Law Online*, Ass'n Am. L. Schs. (June 3, 2020), https://ncculaw.zoom.us/webinar/register/WN_KhAhdPXfRIeZbykNHcQMCg.

8. *See* Tip #8 for some assignment ideas.

9. Evie Oregon, How Can Media Richness Theory and Social Presence Theory Improve My Instruction 5 (2019), http://seminars.magnaonlinemedia.com/wp-content/uploads/sites/115/2019/03/Oregon-Media-Richness-20MM-supplemental.pdf.

10. *Id.*

11. *See* Tip #2.

such as a student who might have been in the military or law enforcement, for example.[12] Perhaps the students will even learn of a classmate who is in a different time zone. Be sure to set up your discussion as "threaded," so that students can see and respond to each other's posts. As with the student's introduction to you, provide a limit, such as five to seven sentences, for the length of this introduction.

- Have students post a video introducing themselves. While the advantage is that students can both see and hear each other, a video might be intimidating or too high-stakes for most students as a first social foray. The video could also be something to consider later on in the semester, possibly in connection with an assignment.[13]
- Create a survey or poll that poses some ice-breaker questions, and share the results on the first day of class. This offers a low-pressure way for students to learn some fun facts about each other as a group.

*Tip #7: Establish rules of electronic communication etiquette.*

Either on your syllabus, your online platform, or both, set forth the rules of electronic communication etiquette. Let the students know that you have high standards for their professionalism and conduct toward each other. Consider including the following guidelines for your students:

- Write concisely and professionally. Although emojis can help to convey a warmer tone, avoid relying on emojis in lieu of using careful language.
- Avoid sarcasm, which may not come across as intended in an electronic medium.
- Be respectful, including when disagreeing. Avoid using all capital letters or excessive punctuation.
- Be mindful of cultural differences, as humor and idioms sometimes do not translate well.
- Respect the privacy of others. Do not post a classmate's comment, including, in part or as a paraphrase, in any other forums such as social media.
- Be careful about using language that is not your own. If you want to share something you read somewhere else, include a reference as to where you saw it.

---

12. Brian Udermann, Seven Indispensable Strategies to Build Community in Your Online Courses (2019), http://seminars.magnaonlinemedia.com/wp-content/uploads/sites/115/2019/06/7-Indispensable-Strategies-handout.pdf.

13. *See* Tip #8.

Providing these guidelines for students will foster an environment that balances respect with enthusiastic participation.

## B. BEYOND WEEK ONE

With students now off to a good start, consider next how to continue to foster engagement in the classroom. Students tend to have shorter attention spans online; they can also feel less visible and unengaged.[14] Students' experiences will be enhanced by being able to engage and interact with the course in a variety of ways. Therefore, the effective synchronous classroom will minimize lecture and provide a variety of ways for students to engage and participate as part of the collective community of students in the classroom.[15]

*Tip #8: Minimize lecture and provide a variety of ways students can interact with the course.*

In addition to the many tips already covered, some additional avenues for engagement are provided here. Some of these are traditional law school assignments while others are unique to online learning. The list is organized by asynchronous group, asynchronous independent, and synchronous activities. Depending on the length of class time, the number of students, and the content of a given class, each class session should incorporate multiple of these features.

### 1. Asynchronous group activities

- Collaborative projects.

While students sometimes find group projects stressful, they may welcome some built-in opportunities online to interact with each other outside of class as long as the task is kept simple. Students can produce a shared work product using cloud-based document platforms like Google Docs that allow for simultaneous collaboration in real time or by circulating a file for comments and additions. If the assignment is associated with a handout you have given them, provide a link to the document that students can use to add their work product. This same link can then be used in breakout rooms for synchronous class work, discussed below.

A follow-up idea is to have each group post a video of their group verbally presenting the information to the rest of the class. To add yet another layer to the experience, students could enable online comments to the videos so that other students can respond to the video. Consider providing some guidelines about appropriate comments, such as identifying what they learned from the video or most enjoyed about it.

---

14. Renee Nicole Allen et al., *Recommendations for Online Teaching* (St. John's Legal Studies Research Paper No. 20-0012, July 23, 2020), https://ssrn.com/abstract=3658520.

15. These suggestions will also enhance the student-professor dynamic.

2. Asynchronous independent activities

- Videos.

Consider flipping a classroom by recording a video on lecture material for the students to watch asynchronously before the synchronous class session. Be sure to follow up asynchronous material with some form of an assignment that holds students accountable for watching the video. Possible assignment suggestions include: (1) Quizzes (either separate or embedded in the video); (2) Individual assignments; and (3) Reflections.

3. Synchronous class time

- Breakout sessions.

Divide students into small breakout rooms to conduct a collaborative assignment. The ideal size of the breakout room will vary depending on the nature of the task. Consider also how much time you plan to spend visiting each group and what number of groups is ideal in order to achieve the right balance between spending sufficient time with each group and avoiding down time for the other groups. In general, however, anything larger than five to six students per breakout room tends to make collaboration challenging.

Two structural options exist for the breakout rooms. One is to put students into "clubs" or "study groups" within the classroom, and to work with each other every time. You might designate a name for each group, or even allow students to give themselves a name, to create a sense of camaraderie. You can utilize the name in various ways on handouts and postings throughout the semester. On the other hand, students may enjoy working with different classmates each time and getting to know the other students in the room. Consider which would be more beneficial for your particular group of students. If you do place students in clubs, deliberately structure for diversity, including gender, cultural considerations, age, and other features of students' backgrounds.[16] Insights gained from the students' welcome email to you[17] may come in handy here.

Provide students with clear directions and discrete tasks to conduct in their breakout sessions. If appropriate, provide a link to a Google document in advance to enable collaboration that then can be shared with the rest of the class when everybody reconvenes. You can annotate the document as well, allowing for quick immediate feedback.[18] Screen sharing is also a good option for collaborative work, although this allows only the sharer to edit the document.

---

16. For a further discussion of using teams, see Chapter 10: *Team-Based Learning in an Online Teaching Environment* by Joy E. Herr-Cardillo and Melissa H. Weresh.

17. *See* Tip #2.

18. *See* Tip #5.

- Polls and quizzes.

Class can be opened with a poll asking students substantive questions that can then guide the discussion or content of the class that day. Polls can also be used during class. The poll can either be internal to the video-conferencing platform or an external tool.[19] Quizzes, too, can break up the presentation and reinforce content. Letting students know immediately beforehand that the material will be followed by a brief quiz can enhance attentiveness. Throwing in the occasional "pop quiz" can also enhance general attentiveness because of uncertainty as to when a quiz may make its appearance. Whether or not the quizzes are graded, quizzes can provide a formative assessment of students' general and individual online engagement and understanding of the material, with points missed serving as an effective alert to individual students of any weak points.

- Games.

A variety of free and paid online platforms for games are available and can be adapted to any content.[20]

These activities, asynchronous and synchronous, provide a variety of engaging ways for students to reinforce knowledge, practice skills, or develop a more sophisticated understanding of material.

*Tip #9: Incorporate technology for creative ways for students to "speak" in class.*[21]

Asking students to speak in the synchronous classroom can create some awkwardness since students typically are muted and have to unmute themselves. Although online platforms include features that allow students to ask to be recognized, using diverse techniques to encourage student participation will help.

One way to obtain immediate feedback or answers to simple questions with one or two-word answers is via the "chat" feature. Chat allows all students to type in a quick answer that you and the students also can immediately see rolling in as the answers are entered. This creates a high-speed energetic "conversation" that makes it easier for shy students to play an active role in the classroom.

Another way to engage students is by setting up a slide that poses a question and offers true/false or multiple-choice answers. Have the students pick a stamp or draw

---

19. See the Index of Applications at the end of this book for mentions of other polling platforms like Poll Everywhere.

20. A number of Jeopardy templates are available online such as the one at JeopardyLabs, https://jeopardylabs.com/. Kahoot! is a game-based learning platform that awards points for correct answers to a quiz or puzzle and can be hosted live over video conferencing and is available at https://kahoot.com. Another online study platform that can work well with law school content is Quizlet Live, in which students either compete against each other individually or within a team, with the first to get all questions correct winning the game. It is available at https://quizlet.com.

21. For a discussion of how to engage quiet students, see Chapter 4: *Understanding and Lifting Up Our Quiet Students: Reimagining "Participation" in the Remote Classroom* by Heidi Brown.

using the "annotations" feature to mark their choice. You may choose to put the answer choices in different quadrants on the slide and/or use different colors to set apart spatial sections. Seeing the array of stamps and color choices randomly appear in quick succession on the slide provides a lively visual component to the material that reinforces learning in real time. Like any other group activity, peer pressure can lead students to follow the herd and hesitate to make annotations that differ from ones already made, so mitigate this tendency by offering fewer, rather than many, choices.

Follow up either chat or the annotations with discussion by providing feedback as to the correct answer, if there is one, or asking students to explain why they made their choices.

*Tip #10: Enable natural opportunities for student socialization.*

Allow students to enter the online classroom without the host being present. In the physical classroom, lights are turned on, the PowerPoint is up, and handouts are placed by the door fifteen minutes or so before class starts. Likewise, enabling students to enter the virtual classroom early signals, first of all, that you were previously in the "room" and will be ready to go at class time. It also provides an opportunity for the students to chat with each other before class starts as they naturally would in the physical classroom. Consider featuring a fun poll, photograph, or piece of trivia on the first PowerPoint slide for students to view before class starts to provide a conversation starter.

Playing a soundtrack before class starts can ease the awkwardness and facilitate conversation among those who arrive early. For variety and a little levity, the soundtrack can be adjusted according to the season or the upcoming assignment.

You may also encourage students to come to virtual office hours together if they wish. For many, even office hours in a physical location with professors can be unfamiliar and intimidating, especially for first generation students. Virtual office hours can add another dimension of awkwardness. Some students might appreciate being able to visit office hours with a friend, and they often benefit from hearing each other's questions.

## IV. How to Connect Students to the Greater Law School Community

*Tip #11: Include other faculty and resources from the greater professional community in your course content.*

Students will appreciate feeling connected not just to the professor and the other students in the classroom but also to the larger law school and professional communities. Perhaps your colleagues have produced asynchronous videos that you can incorporate into your materials. Not only is this a way to reduce redundant efforts but students will benefit from the sense of a faculty community collectively supporting their educational experience. Consider also whether former students or alumni can attend your class as a guest speaker and provide study advice, career advice, or real-world perspective. Guests that might not be able to fly in can readily visit online. Also, an online visit by a guest speaker can be easily recorded (with his or her permission), and the video shared with other classes.

Finally, in your frequent online postings, include information whenever possible about networking opportunities, professional websites with career advice, links to writing competitions, and law student podcasts[22] or blogs.[23] These resources will remind students of their connection to a larger community beyond the classroom.

## V. Conclusion

By incorporating these methods into your synchronous class, students will implicitly recognize that you value community. You will foster a sense of belonging within your classroom, the law school, and the community beyond.

---

22. *E.g.*, *ABA for Law Students*, A.B.A., https://abaforlawstudents.com/ (last visited Oct. 26, 2020).

23. *E.g.*, Halle Hara, The Law School Playbook, https://www.lawschoolplaybook.com/ (last visited Nov. 19, 2020).

FOURTEEN

# Effective Collaboration in Online Courses

Darby Dickerson*
Megan Bess**

After reviewing this chapter, readers will be able to:

- Summarize several benefits and challenges of using collaborative work in online courses;
- Select and design an appropriate collaborative assignment for an online course;
- Create groups for a collaborative assignment;
- Predict technology issues associated with the assignment;
- Facilitate a collaborative assignment; and
- Produce a rubric for the assignment.

## I. Benefits and Challenges of Collaborative Work

In law, no one works alone. It's a collaborative endeavor, even for solo practitioners. Lawyers work with clients, co-counsel, opposing counsel, judges, support staff, lay and expert witnesses, consultants, and individuals from other fields, such as doctors, social workers, accountants, and law enforcement.[1] While the legal profession values

* Darby Dickerson is President and Dean of Southwestern School of Law. She has designed and taught online and blended courses since 2019 and is pursuing a Master Online Teacher certificate through the University of Illinois at Springfield.

** Megan Bess is an Assistant Professor and Externship Director at University of Illinois Chicago School of Law. She has designed and taught online and blended courses since 2010.

1. *See generally* SECTION OF LEGAL EDUCATION & ADMISSIONS TO THE BAR, AMERICAN BAR ASSOCIATION, LEGAL EDUCATION AND PROFESSIONAL DEVELOPMENT: AN EDUCATIONAL CONTINUUM 199 (1992); EILEEN SCALLEN ET AL., WORKING TOGETHER IN LAW: TEAMWORK & SMALL GROUP SKILLS FOR LEGAL

collaboration,[2] historically, law schools have emphasized individual and competitive activities and assessments, such as the Socratic Method, 100% final exams, grading curves, writing projects that prohibit collaboration, and advocacy tournaments.[3] Fortunately, law schools are catching up, and more faculty members have started to embrace collaborative learning.[4]

As noted in the chart below, collaborative work, whether on campus or online, can benefit and challenge both students and instructors. Although this chapter provides only a brief overview, we encourage readers to consult the extensive literature on collaborative learning.[5] For online collaboration, instructors should also note that benefits and challenges may vary depending on whether the course format is synchronous, asynchronous, or blended. This chapter presents solutions to many of the noted challenges.

---

PROFESSIONALS 4–6 (2014); Michael I. Meyerson, *Law School Culture and the Lost Art of Collaboration: Why Don't Law Professors Play Well with Others*, 93 NEB. L. REV. 547, 556–62 (2015).

2. *E.g.*, ALLI GERKMAN & LOGAN CORNETT, INSTITUTE FOR THE ADVANCEMENT OF THE AMERICAN LEGAL SYSTEM, FOUNDATIONS FOR PRACTICE: THE WHOLE LAWYER AND THE CHARACTER QUOTIENT 20 (2016) [hereinafter FOUNDATIONS FOR PRACTICE].

3. Meyerson, *supra* note 1, at 553–56; *see* Christine Cerniglia Brown, *The Integrated Curriculum of the Future: Eliminating a Hidden Curriculum to Unveil a New Era of Collaboration, Practical Training, and Interdisciplinary Learning*, 7 ELON L. REV. 167, 169–70 (2015); Dorothy H. Evensen, *To Group or Not to Group: Students' Perceptions of Collaborative Learning Activities in Law School*, 28 S. ILL. U. L.J. 343, 368–76 (2004).

4. *See* Melissa H. Weresh, *Assessment, Collaboration, and Empowerment: Team-Based Learning*, 68 J. LEGAL EDUC. 303, 303–04 (2019); *see also* A.B.A. Sec. Leg. Educ. & Admis. to the Bar, *Standards and Rules of Procedure for Approval of Law Schools*, Interpretation 302-1 (2020–21), https://www.americanbar.org/content/dam/aba/administrative/legal_education_and_admissions_to_the_bar/standards/2020-2021/2020-21-aba-standards-and-rules-for-approval-of-law-schools.pdf. (identifying "collaboration" as a professional skill that may be needed for competency in the legal profession). For a discussion of using Team-Based Learning principles, see Chapter 10: *Team-Based Learning in an Online Teaching Environment* by Joy E. Herr-Cardillo & Melissa H. Weresh.

5. RENA M. PALLOFF & KEITH PRATT, BUILDING ONLINE LEARNING COMMUNITIES 166–92 (2007); Hwa Koh & Jannette R. Hill, *Student Perceptions of Group Work in an Online Course: Benefits and Challenges*, 23 J. DISTANCE EDUC. 69, 70–74 (2009).

## BENEFITS AND CHALLENGES OF COLLABORATIVE WORK[6]

| | Students | Instructors |
|---|---|---|
| BENEFITS | Builds a sense of community and engagement within the course<br>Helps students build professional relationships<br>Increases knowledge acquisition, retention, higher-order problem-solving, and reasoning abilities<br>Helps students hone professional skills such as project management, time management, working cooperatively, delegation, accountability, idea advocacy, expressing disagreement respectfully, principled compromise, setting priorities, and giving and receiving constructive feedback<br>Increases exposure to different perspectives, mindsets, cultures, and working styles<br>Stimulates creativity | Allows for more efficient formative and summative assessment<br>Reduces the number of final assignments to grade<br>Allows instructors to develop more complex and authentic activities<br>Helps when the number of viable projects is limited<br>Promotes variety and creativity |
| CHALLENGES | Coordinating among group members<br>Initial lack of trust among students in a group<br>Free riders, social loafers, dominators, and conflict<br>Groupthink<br>Group hate (dread or fear about working in groups) and student skepticism<br>Technology difficulties | Increased administrative demands (e.g., identifying appropriate topics, forming groups; monitoring groups)<br>Preparing clear and complete instructions<br>Devoting time to teaching process skills, monitoring group work, and coaching teams through challenges and conflict<br>Assessing individual and group effort<br>Assessing teamwork and group dynamics as well as the final product<br>Student pushback and skepticism |

6. This chart was created using the following sources: Heejung An et al., *Teacher Perspectives on Online Collaborative Learning: Factors Perceived as Facilitating and Impeding Successful Group Work*, 8 CONTEMP. ISSUES IN TECH. & TCHR. EDUC. 65 (2008); Alison Burke, *Group Work: How to Use Groups Effectively*, 11 J. EFFECTIVE TEACHING 87, 87–88 (2011) (describing "group hate"); Koh & Hill, *supra* note 5, at 78–88; Weresh, *supra* note 4, at 329–36; *Using Group Projects Effectively*, CARNEGIE MELLON UNIV. EBERLY CTR., https://www.cmu.edu/teaching/designteach/teach/instructionalstrategies/groupprojects/index.html (last visited Oct. 10, 2020); *Benefits of Group Work*, WASH. U. ST. LOUIS, CTR. FOR TEACHING & LEARNING, https://teachingcenter.wustl.edu/resources/teaching-methods/group-work-in-class/benefits-of-group-work/ (last visited Oct. 10, 2020).

## II. Designing Effective Group Work

Principles that cultivate effective group work in traditional classrooms also apply in an online environment. These principles include clearly defining and communicating the course learning objectives and selecting appropriate activities to help students achieve these objectives.[7]

You may determine that students can best meet an objective through a collaborative assignment[8] where they will be accountable as part of a group.[9] To design an appropriate activity, first identify the goals to be achieved by the collaborative activity; ideally, include goals related to students 1) learning content and collaborative skills and 2) developing group processes and a designated work product.[10] Then consider the class, including its size, curriculum level, and student experience.[11] For example, if a course has many students and falls earlier in the curriculum, discussion-based collaboration may be more successful than complex projects.[12] Next, incorporate collaboration to match the level of faculty experience.[13] If incorporating group work into an online course for the first time, start with a few well-planned exercises.[14] Also be flexible about how and when students collaborate, minimizing demands for synchronous activities, specific platforms, and construct-irrelevant factors.[15]

Selecting a collaborative activity that encourages authentic learning will increase engagement and learning.[16] "Authentic learning" focuses on real-world, complex, multidisciplinary problems and their solutions and "intentionally brings into play multiple disciplines," perspectives, working methods, and community.[17] Authentic learning helps students cultivate portable skills such as the judgment to distinguish reliable

---

7. Elizabeth F. Barkley et al., Collaborative Learning Techniques: A Handbook for College Faculty 42 (2014); Michael Hunter Schwartz et. al., Teaching Law by Design: Engaging Students from the Syllabus to the Final Exam 33 (2d ed. 2017).

8. *See* Mark Lieberman, *Online Students Don't Have to Work Solo*, Inside Higher Ed (Apr. 25, 2018), https://www.insidehighered.com/digital-learning/article/2018/04/25/group-projects-online-classes-create-connections-and-challenge.

9. Scallen et al., *supra* note 1, at 7.

10. Karen Swan et al., *Assessment and Collaboration in Online Learning*, 10 J. Asynch. Online Learning Networks 45, 52 (2006).

11. Barkley et al., *supra* note 7, at 57.

12. *Id.*

13. *Id.*; Palloff & Pratt, *supra* note 5, at 29–30.

14. Barkley et al., *supra* note 7, at 57.

15. *Id.*; *UDL and Assessment*, CAST, http://udloncampus.cast.org/page/assessment_udl#.WZuhZoW-cG71 (last visited Oct. 30, 2020) (explaining that construct-irrelevant features can prevent learners and instructors from gaining an accurate picture of students' relevant knowledge and skills; for example, a timed and closed-book Torts examination includes features—such as typing skills and ability to work under pressure—that are not related to students' mastery of Torts content knowledge).

16. *Authentic Assessment*, Ind. Univ. Bloomington Ctr. for Innovative Teaching & Learning, https://citl.indiana.edu/teaching-resources/assessing-student-learning/authentic-assessment/index.html (last visited Oct. 22, 2020).

17. Marilyn Lombardi, *Authentic Learning for the 21st Century: An Overview*, Educause Learning Initiative Paper 1:2007 2 (May 2007), https://www.researchgate.net/profile/Mari-

from unreliable information, patience to follow longer arguments, the ability to apply knowledge in new situations, and the flexibility to work across disciplines.[18] One element of authentic learning is that no individual working alone can achieve success.[19] This strategy—known as positive interdependence—requires that group work must be complex enough for students to perceive that they can succeed only through working together.[20]

In the syllabus, explain the purpose and goals of collaborative work and the relation of group work to course objectives and grading. These explanations will help mitigate students avoiding group work, which happens more frequently in online courses.[21] To increase student buy-in, emphasize the value of the skills developed by collaborative work[22] and highlight the importance legal employers place on collaboration and teamwork[23] by introducing data from employers.[24] Law students will buy into collaboration if they see employers value it.[25]

Tailor group work to the goal of the activity. For example, informal discussion groups are optimal if the goal is for students to brainstorm, review material, or solve hypothetical problems. To ensure that students understand key concepts, each group member should take turns summarizing key information.[26] If the goal is applying or evaluating information, then more involved group activities, such as role play or debating alternative viewpoints, are better.[27]

A sophisticated group project with a deliverable such as a report or presentation requires a more involved process.[28] Consider first assigning a simple exercise to allow groups to become acquainted and develop a process for their workflow.[29] Then devel-

---

lyn_Lombardi/publication/220040581_Authentic_Learning_for_the_21st_Century_An_Overview/links/0f317531744eedf4d1000000.pdf.

18. *Id.*

19. *Id.*

20. David W. Johnson et al., Active Learning: Cooperation in the College Classroom 2:16–17 (1998); *What Are Best Practices for Designing Group Projects?*, Carnegie Mellon Univ. Eberly Ctr., https://www.cmu.edu/teaching/designteach/teach/instructionalstrategies/groupprojects/design.html (last visited Oct. 8, 2020) [hereinafter *Best Practices*].

21. Palloff & Pratt, *supra* note 5, at 19, 24; Swan et al., *supra* note 10, at 51–52.

22. *Best Practices, supra* note 20.

23. Cristina D. Lockwood, *Improving Learning in the Law School Classroom by Encouraging Students to Form Communities of Practice*, 20 Clinical L. Rev. 95, 124 (2013); Sophie Sparrow, *Can They Work Well on a Team? Assessing Students' Collaborative Skills*, 38 Wm. Mitchell L. Rev. 1162, 1166 (2012).

24. *See* Neil W. Hamilton, Roadmap: The Law Student's Guide to Meaningful Employment 25, 27 (2d ed. 2018); Foundations for Practice, *supra* note 2, at 9, 20.

25. Neil Hamilton, *Fostering & Assessing Law Student Teamwork & Team Leadership Skills*, 48 Hofstra L. Rev. 619, 625 (2020).

26. Barkley et al., *supra* note 7, at 45–46.

27. *Id.* at 46.

28. Linda B. Nilson & Ludwika A. Goodson, Online Teaching at its Best: Merging Instructional Design with Teaching & Learning Research 153 (2018).

29. Barkley et al., *supra* note 7, at 57.

op and organize more complex projects into stages, with each stage involving both individual and group work that will allow students to gauge their progress.[30]

As part of the design process, consider the role individual accountability will play and be transparent about how individual and group work will factor into grades. Allowing students to individually demonstrate their knowledge via other assessments, either as part of or in addition to group work, can reduce anxiety about working in groups.[31] Individual quizzes or exams can allow students to demonstrate mastery of key course concepts. Individual reflection on the group process through journals, essays, or discussion board posts can result in deeper connections and more meaningful learning.[32] In some exercises, you can ask each member to note individual contributions through a track-change function.

To improve group performance, instructors must properly orient students about collaborative work.[33] This orientation should:

- acknowledge negative conceptions about group work;[34]
- review skills needed to work collaboratively, including group etiquette, time management, and conflict resolution;[35]
- ensure students understand the necessary technology;[36] and
- share guidelines for successful group interaction.[37]

On this last point, you can create your own guidelines, allow groups to do so, or adopt a middle ground by providing base guidelines for groups to further develop. Sample guidelines could include standards for returning emails, meeting deadlines, honoring individual commitments to the group, and resolving conflict.[38]

Also consider creating a single document or webpage that details all information and instructions related to group work.[39] At a minimum, the document or webpage should include:

30. *Id.*

31. Thomas J. Tomcho & Rob Foels, *Meta-Analysis of Group Learning Activities: Empirically Based Teaching Recommendations*, 39 Teaching Psychol. 159, 162 (2012); *Best Practices*, *supra* note 20.

32. Tomcho & Foels, *supra* note 31, at 162.

33. Elizabeth G. Cohen, *Restructuring the Classroom: Conditions for Productive Small Groups*, 64 Rev. Educ. Res. 1, 26 (1994).

34. *Best Practices*, *supra* note 20.

35. Barkley et al., *supra* note 7, at 66–67; Nilson & Goodson, *supra* note 28, at 156; Swan et al., *supra* note 10, at 52; *Best Practices*, *supra* note 20.

36. Barkley et al., *supra* note 7, at 57.

37. *E.g.*, *Tips for Participating in Group Work & Projects Online*, Drexel Univ. Online, https://www.online.drexel.edu/news/group-tips.aspx (last visited Oct. 19, 2020).

38. Adapted from *Best Practices*, *supra* note 20.

39. Barkley et al., *supra* note 7, at 57.

- the reasons and goals for the assignment and how it relates to the selected learning objective;
- the deliverable;
- any resources (e.g., reading assignments or technology) students need to complete the assignment;
- the type of collaboration expected, permitted, or prohibited;
- a clear description of each step of the activity and whether each step must be completed by an individual or the group;
- the parameters (length, size, and type of submission);
- the deadline and submission instructions;
- that grading criteria for individuals and the group, with reference to a grading rubric; and
- any other expectations or requirements.[40]

For complex assignments, provide guidance about the amount of time each step should take. You may want to note whether revisions will be permitted after the initial submission. For complicated or high-value assignments, piloting the instructions with students at a level similar to your learners is a wise step, as is having another person proofread your final version.

## III. Group Formation

Groups can vary in type, size, duration, and formation procedure. Informal groups can be formed quickly and randomly and are valuable for breaking up longer class sessions and dense material.[41] For example, you can divide students into random groups to work through problems during an online synchronous session. Less planning is needed for this quick and informal group interaction.[42] In contrast, formal groups can achieve more complex goals and often last longer, thus requiring more intentional formation.[43] Base groups, a type of formal group, work on a variety of tasks for a longer period (often an entire term).[44] Choosing one type of group does not preclude using other types.

---

40. Adapted from *How Do I Incorporate Writing Assignments in My Online Class?*, Univ. of Mass. Amherst Ctr. for Teaching & Learning, https://www.umass.edu/ctl/how-do-i-incorporate-writing-assignments-my-online-class (last visited Oct. 19, 2020); *Writing Great Assignment Instructions: Tips for Success*, Univ. of New Eng. Online (Dec. 8, 2016), https://online.une.edu/blog/writing-great-assignment-instructions-tips-success/.

41. Barkley et al., *supra* note 7, at 76.

42. Nilson & Goodson, *supra* note 28, 153.

43. Barkley et al., *supra* note 7, at 57.

44. *Id.*; Karl A. Smith et al., *Pedagogies of Engagement: Classroom-Based Practices*, 94 J. Engineering Educ. 87, 96 (2005).

## A. GROUP SIZE, MEMBERSHIP, AND SELECTION

Group size varies by task and is another factor to consider when designing collaborative work. The goal is to create groups small enough that students can participate yet large enough to have sufficient diversity and resources to accomplish tasks.[45] Large groups can tackle bigger projects but create higher coordination costs.[46] In an online course, groups brainstorming or sharing opinions could include ten or more students.[47] Smaller groups work more efficiently because students can more easily coordinate.[48] For projects and activities that require work product, groups of three to five work best.[49]

Diverse groups expose students to different perspectives. Potential factors to consider include race, ethnicity, culture, native language, socioeconomic, political, and geographic differences.[50] But groups should not be based solely on these characteristics.[51] Other factors to consider include academic background and relevant skills.[52] Ensure a critical mass in every group so members of any category do not find themselves isolated.[53]

Group membership can be random, teacher selected, student selected, or based on a combination approach.[54] Random selection works well for informal groups because it is efficient and perceived as fair by students.[55] Random group assignments are easy to achieve in synchronous online meetings through video-conferencing platforms that allow for random breakout rooms. For non-synchronous random assignments, instructors can number students into groups and inform students of their assignments.

Instructor-determined groups work better for formal groups and promote diversity because you can divide students according to their interests and characteristics.[56] To determine student interests, skills, and schedules, circulate questions or data sheets asking for background and experiences relevant to the course subject and group work.[57] Consider confidentially asking students about their motivation for taking the course, their familiarity with other class members, and their general personality

---

45. BARKLEY ET AL., *supra* note 7, at 77–78.

46. *How Can I Compose Groups?*, CARNEGIE MELLON UNIV. EBERLY CTR., https://www.cmu.edu/teaching/designteach/teach/instructionalstrategies/groupprojects/compose.html (last visited Oct. 8, 2020) [hereinafter *How Can I Compose Groups*].

47. BARKLEY ET AL., *supra* note 7, at 88; SCALLEN ET AL., *supra* note 1, at 58.

48. *How Can I Compose Groups*, *supra* note 46.

49. BARKLEY ET AL., *supra* note 7, at 88.

50. *Id.* at 78.

51. JOHNSON ET AL., *supra* note 20, at 2:9.

52. NILSON & GOODSON, *supra* note 28, at 153.

53. BARKLEY ET AL., *supra* note 7, at 78; *How Can I Compose Groups*, *supra* note 46.

54. BARKLEY ET AL., *supra* note 7, at 78.

55. *Id.* at 79, 84.

56. *Id.* at 82, 84; *How Can I Compose Groups*, *supra* note 46.

57. Adapted from BARKLEY ET AL., *supra* note 7, at 82–83.

traits.[58] Academic achievement can also be a factor, although not at the cost of stymying lower achievers from demonstrating leadership in groups.[59]

A combination approach allows for instructor selection with student input.[60] For example, an instructor could allow students to choose their own groups with articulated constraints (including size and diversity). Or students could be permitted to select a group according to the project topic, with each topic allowing a limited number of spots.[61]

Student-selected groups are not recommended for most activities.[62] Although student selection can increase motivation, students often form homogenous groups based on friendships, thus lessening diversity and undermining learning objectives.[63] Moreover, homogenous groups are more likely to veer off task.[64]

Finally, develop a contingency plan for issues that might arise in group formation.[65] Most experienced teachers try to keep groups together for as long as possible, but there may be instances in which groups are unable to function or membership is depleted to the point that groups must be reformed.[66]

## B. PREPARING GROUPS TO WORK TOGETHER

Introductory activities help groups develop a sense of community and trust and can vary in focus.[67] For simple introductions, group members could interview each other or create group resumes detailing each member's experience.[68] Members could share embarrassing moments involving online communication to lighten the mood and demonstrate how communication in an online course can go wrong.[69] Students could describe their learning style or goals for the course.[70]

Icebreakers can focus on course content and structure. For example, you could present a list of true/false statements about the course for students to answer in groups.[71] Similarly, groups could identify issues the course should address.[72] To emphasize the

---

58. *How Can I Compose Groups*, *supra* note 46.

59. Barkley et al., *supra* note 7, at 78.

60. *How Can I Compose Groups*, *supra* note 46.

61. Barkley et al., *supra* note 7, at 83.

62. *Id.*

63. Barkley et al., *supra* note 7, at 82; Johnson et al., *supra* note 20, at 2:7; *How Can I Compose Groups*, *supra* note 46.

64. Johnson et al., *supra* note 20, at 2:10.

65. *How Can I Compose Groups*, *supra* note 46.

66. Barkley et al., *supra* note 7, at 85; Lieberman, *supra* note 8.

67. Swan et al., *supra* note 10, at 52.

68. Barkley et al., *supra* note 7, at 59, 70.

69. *Id.* at 74.

70. *Id.* at 62.

71. *Id.* at 63.

72. *Id.*

syllabus, students could develop a list of questions about the course and find answers in the syllabus or take a group quiz about the syllabus.[73]

To prepare students for collaborative work, ask groups to answer questions regarding behaviors deemed most and helpful in group settings.[74] Each group could then develop standards for member interaction based on those identified behaviors.[75] You could develop a template about expectations for group work that specific groups could then customize.[76] Groups could also address questions to spark discussion around standards for collaboration, such as:

- Will you have a group leader and/or group roles?
- How will work be distributed?
- How frequently will you communicate and what methods will you use?
- How will the group handle incomplete work?[77]

## IV. Examples of Collaborative Activities

Collaborative work can be simple or complex and can last for part of a class session or online module or for the entire course. Below are examples of collaborative activities that can be integrated into an online course.[78]

| Collaborative Activity | Description |
|---|---|
| Brainstorming | Group discussion to generate ideas and solutions. May be free-flowing or structured, such as a Round Robin session, where you move from one student to the next. |
| Breakout Discussion Groups | Small groups discuss specific issues, brainstorm, or generate ideas or solutions. |

73. *Id.* at 64–65.
74. *Id.* at 66.
75. *Id.* at 67.
76. *Id.* 68–69.
77. Adapted from BARKLEY ET AL., *supra* note 7, at 69; PALLOFF & PRATT, *supra* note 5, at 27–28.
78. BARKLEY ET AL., *supra* note 7, chs. 9–14; Annie Peshkam, *What Your Pre-COVID Course Design Was Missing: 8 Cooperative Learning Practices to Enrich Your Online or Hybrid Classroom*, HARV. BUS. PUBL'G: EDUC. (June 8, 2020), https://hbsp.harvard.edu/inspiring-minds/cooperative-learning-practices; *Online Instructional Activities Index*, UNIV. OF ILL. AT SPRINGFIELD, ION PROF'L ELEARNING PROGRAMS, https://www.uis.edu/ion/resources/instructional-activities-index/ (last visited Oct. 18, 2020); *Active and Collaborative Learning*, UNIV. OF MD. TEACHING & LEARNING TRANSFORMATION CTR. https://tltc.umd.edu/active-and-collaborative-learning (last visited Oct. 18, 2020).

| Collaborative Activity | Description |
|---|---|
| Case Study | A group studies, evaluates, or resolves an actual or hypothetical case. The deliverable might include an oral report, written report, slide deck, or some combination. |
| Collaborative Case Briefing | Students brief an assigned legal case to discuss, prepare their own brief, and then work with others to develop a group brief, or brief a case together. |
| Collaborative Checklist | Students jointly develop a checklist. Examples: A checklist that judicial externs can use to evaluate their social media presence, a proofreading checklist, and a checklist of exceptions to a particular rule. |
| Collaborative Drafting/ Writing | Students draft a legal document or prepare a paper as a group. |
| Debates | Students research an assigned or selected topic, are assigned a position, and then debate other students. Group discussion can follow the debate to deepen learning or analyze student performance. |
| Dialogue Journal | Each student records thoughts in a journal that they exchange with peers for comments and questions. This exercise can help students connect course work to their personal experiences and promote group interaction. |
| Discussion Groups | Students discuss a particular question, case, or concept. This activity has myriad variations. Small groups can report back to a larger group. Consider using specific roles, such as leader (making sure the group is on task), speaker (reports out), recorder (writes the group's ideas), and reflector (manages the group's processes). Discussion questions included in asynchronous modules can help organize or scaffold material. May be coupled with other activities, such as a group checklist or drafting assignment. |
| Document Analysis | Students are given a document—e.g., a contract, set of interrogatories, or statute—to analyze together. |
| Group Reports | A group is assigned a topic to research and report on. |
| Games | Games might include versions of Jeopardy or Family Feud, trivia related to a particular topic, or computerized games developed for your course or subject. |

*Continued*

*Continued*

| Collaborative Activity | Description |
|---|---|
| Jigsaw | A group is assigned a topic on which to become an expert. The group then teaches the material to the rest of the class. The teaching usually is done by having the students redistribute into new groups with one expert from each topic present in each new group. Alternatively, the expert group might be responsible for participating actively while the instructor discusses the material. |
| KWL | K = What you/we know about x; W = What you/we want to know about x; L = What have you/we learned about x. Students are given a topic; as a group, they list what they already know about that topic and what they would like to learn about it. A learning activity is then performed. Following this activity, the group then lists what members have learned. |
| Learning Contracts | Students develop a contract with each other or the instructor about learning goals or processes for the module or course. |
| Online Field Trips and Tours | Visit an online resource, such as a museum or courthouse, or arrange for a live person to take your group on a virtual tour of a particular location. |
| Peer Editing | Students, using a rubric or other guide, review the work of other students. |
| Peer Teaching | A group is assigned a topic to teach to the entire class. |
| Podcasts | A group records a podcast on a topic; when episodes are combined, the class may have its own series. |
| Poll-Group-Repoll | Create and launch a poll designed to produce divergent responses; ask students to discuss their positions in small groups. Relaunch the same poll to see if responses have changed, then discuss any changes. |
| Procedural Demonstrations/ Simulations | Students perform or record themselves performing an assigned task and submit the video for evaluation or discussion. Possible demonstrations include a client interview, an appellate argument, a cross-examination, a title search, or formatting a table of contents in an appellate brief. |

| Collaborative Activity | Description |
|---|---|
| Q&A | Students construct questions for other students to answer. Alternatively, students construct questions for the instructor or a guest expert. Create "learning cells" that will quiz each other throughout the course. |
| Role Playing | Students are assigned specific roles, like plaintiff's counsel, to play in a real or hypothetical situation. |
| Scavenger Hunt | Groups are tasked with using the internet to find information. Scavenger hunts can be a good initial activity for groups to gain trust and learn how to develop processes to work together. |
| Send a Problem | One group tries to solve a particular problem then passes the problem to another group that does the same thing. The final group evaluates the solutions. |
| Think-Pair-Share | Each student thinks about an assigned question and then pairs with another student to compare their responses before sharing with the entire class. |
| Value Line | Each student ranks how they feel about a particular idea; the instructor breaks the students into discussion groups from a mix of the ranks. |
| Wikis | Students work collaboratively to construct a document such as an annotated bibliography or Wikipedia page on a particular subject. |

Some students perceive all group work to be "busy" work. To help overcome this perception, ensure that collaborative activities align with specific learning objectives (as covered in other parts of this chapter). Resources to help align activities with learning objectives include a variety of Bloom's Revised Taxonomy charts that link activities to learning categories.[79]

---

79. *E.g.*, Andrew Churches, Bloom's Digital Taxonomy (2008), https://www.celt.iastate.edu/wp-content/uploads/2020/07/Churches_2008_DigitalBloomsTaxonomyGuide.pdf; Larry Ferlazzo, *The Best Resources for Helping Teachers Use Bloom's Taxonomy in the Classroom* (May 25, 2009), https://larryferlazzo.edublogs.org/2009/05/25/the-best-resources-for-helping-teachers-use-blooms-taxonomy-in-the-classroom/.

## V. Technology

When designing a collaborative exercise, consider what technology students can or may use. Today, the choices are endless; apps to facilitate group work have proliferated.[80] But remember to consider your *whole* class when making these design decisions. Instructors are encouraged to study Universal Design for Learning concepts—which encourage designs to proactively meet the needs of all learners—before implementing group work that requires technology.[81]

Not every student can afford to purchase multiple apps, has a reliable, stable internet connection, or owns a smartphone. An assignment that may seem simple—like having each student make and upload a short video for a group to discuss—may not be feasible for all students. It is also important to select technologies accessible to all learners in the group.[82] For example, a student with low vision may need to use a screen reader to participate.

Other technology-related considerations include:

- **The seamlessness of the student experience.** Multiple systems with multiple logins may frustrate students. Using a university-approved learning management system (LMS) and compatible plug-ins may be the best choices.[83]
- **Training.** Not all students are equally tech-savvy. Accordingly, you may need to find training resources for each tech tool you use. If a high percentage of your students lack comfort with a range of technology, adding tools beyond your institution's LMS and online video-conferencing platform may impede learning. Also master the technology you assign;[84] otherwise, you may lose credibility with your students.
- **FERPA, which requires that certain student records be protected.** Before requiring students to use a particular technology, conduct a FERPA analysis by reviewing both the statute and the terms of use for the platform or app. Most

80. TeachThought Staff, *30 of the Best Digital Collaboration Tools for Students*, TEACHTHOUGHT (Aug. 25, 2020), https://www.teachthought.com/technology/12-tech-tools-for-student-to-student-digital-collaboration/.

81. *The UDL Guidelines*, CAST, http://udlguidelines.cast.org/ (last visited Oct. 23, 2020). For an additional discussion of the UDL Guidelines see Chapter 7: *Using Blended and Online Learning Strategies to Provide Innovative Academic Support to All Students* by Susan Landrum.

82. Tara Bunag, *Empathy and Collaboration: Accessibility in IT*, EDUCAUSE REV. (July 23, 2018), https://er.educause.edu/blogs/2018/7/empathy-and-collaboration-accessibility-in-it; Sheryl Burgstahler, *ADA Compliance for Online Course Design*, EDUCAUSE REV. (Jan. 30, 2017), https://er.educause.edu/articles/2017/1/ada-compliance-for-online-course-design.

83. For a more in-depth discussion of using an LMS platform, see Chapter 16: *A Millennial Law Professor's Guide to Learning Management Systems* by Verónica C. Gonzales-Zamora.

84. Amy M. Johnson et al., *Challenges and Solutions When Using Technologies in the Classroom*, *in* ADAPTIVE EDUCATIONAL TECHNOLOGIES FOR LITERACY INSTRUCTION 13–29 (Scott A. Crossley & Danielle S. McNamara eds. 2016).

university-procured resources comply with FERPA, so sticking to those resources is a safe choice.[85]

- **Other privacy laws and concerns.** Before suggesting or requiring students to use a technology tool, research applicable state and federal privacy laws and review the terms of use to see how the resource uses data provided by users. Most university IT departments evaluate these concerns before purchasing apps, services, and platforms for the campus.

## VI. Facilitating Great Groups

To ensure that students participate actively and constructively in group work,[86] provide a framework for group interactions, give feedback, and anticipate potential problems.[87]

The manner by which you introduce a group activity sets the tone.[88] Ensure students understand how an activity relates to course goals and what actions are expected[89] by providing accurate and thorough written instructions, clearly outlining procedures, and including examples and prompts.[90] Remind students of the rules for group interaction and provide opportunities and mechanisms for them to ask questions.[91]

Monitor groups, but not to the point of stifling their creativity. When groups need assistance, provide support by complimenting their questions and insights and seeking clarification when their concerns are unclear or ill-defined.[92] When groups struggle, provide taskwork assistance (clarify the assignment) and teamwork assistance (assist with behavior).[93]

Help groups when problems arise. First encourage groups to negotiate difficulties on their own.[94] Conflicts will occur and are part of the group process.[95] Jumping in too soon can be counterproductive, as students may miss the opportunity to learn and apply problem-solving skills in a group setting.[96] If a group cannot resolve an issue,

---

85. Alexander R. Schrameyer et al., *Online Student Collaboration and FERPA Considerations*, 60 Tech Trends 540 (2016).

86. Barkley et al., *supra* note 7, at 37.

87. *How Can I Monitor Groups?*, Carnegie Mellon Univ. Eberly Ctr. https://www.cmu.edu/teaching/designteach/teach/instructionalstrategies/groupprojects/monitor.html (last visited Oct. 12, 2020).

88. Barkley et al., *supra* note 7, at 90.

89. *Id.* at 98; Nilson & Goodson, *supra* note 28, at 153.

90. Barkley et al., *supra* note 7, at 99.

91. *Id.* at 99.

92. *Id.* at 92–93.

93. Johnson et al., *supra* note 20, at 2:40.

94. Barkley et al., *supra* note 7, at 119.

95. Janet Weinstein et al., *Teaching Teamwork to Law Students*, 63 J. Legal Educ. 36, 52–53 (2013).

96. Johnson et al., *supra* note 20, at 2:10.

help members identify the problem.[97] If a group struggles to resolve its issue, review strategies for group decision-making, including majority, consensus, and compromise with the group members.[98] As a last resort, you may need to rearrange the groups.[99]

Also determine the best mechanisms—such as online discussion boards or chat—for students to report back regarding their work.[100] Groups can record their ideas via video or audio, and you or other students can respond through collaborative media technology that allows for audio and video comments.[101] For an online alternative to an in-class presentation, groups could present during a synchronous session.[102]

Closure is important for group activity. Help groups synthesize what they learned, but do so with limited substantive input to ensure they are actually learning the course objectives.[103] Instructors should also celebrate success in group work.

Finally, consider seeking student feedback about collaborative work. For example, you might incorporate a formative evaluation at the course midpoint that includes questions about the group work completed to date. You might include questions about specific assignments, questions about peer feedback ("Tell me about receiving feedback from peers" and "Describe your approach to giving feedback to your peers"), or more general questions that could elicit feedback about group work ("If you were redesigning this course to make it a more effective learning experience for you, what two things would you change?" and "What changes are needed in this course to help you improve your learning?").[104]

## VII. Assessment

First, determine whether assessment is necessary. Some informal group activities, such as brainstorming or discussing hypotheticals, may not require assessment. But even if group work is ungraded, provide evaluation and feedback to help ensure students value the assignment.[105]

For group work that will be assessed, decide whether assessment will be formative or summative.[106] While formative assessments may not be graded, they help measure

---

97. BARKLEY ET AL., *supra* note 7, at 120.

98. *Id.*

99. *Id.*; Lieberman, *supra* note 8 (discussing "divorce" from a group).

100. BARKLEY ET AL., *supra* note 7, at 100.

101. *Id.*

102. *Id.*

103. *Id.*

104. *Student Feedback with the Plus/Delta and Critical Incident Questionnaire*, IOWA STATE UNIV. CTR. FOR EXCELLENCE IN LEARNING & TEACHING, https://www.celt.iastate.edu/teaching/assessment-and-evaluation/mid-term-formative-evaluation-using-a-plusdelta-assessment-technique (last visited Oct. 4, 2020).

105. Mark Freeman & Jo McKenzie, *SPARK, a Confidential Web-Based Template for Self and Peer Assessment of Student Teamwork: Benefits of Evaluating Across Different Subjects*, 33 BRITISH J. OF EDUC. TECH. 551, 552 (2002).

106. BARKLEY ET AL., *supra* note 7, at 110.

student progress and provide feedback.[107] Summative assessments are graded and should also include feedback.

## A. GRADING AND EVALUATING PERFORMANCE

Assessing collaboration requires considering student achievement of learning objectives and student participation in group activities.[108] Assessing group work requires considering both the process and products of collaboration.[109] Depending on course objectives, process may be even more important than the final product.[110] To assess process, give students feedback on their cooperative behaviors and ask them to reflect on group interaction and performance. These approaches lead to more cooperative and less competitive behavior within groups.[111] To assess teamwork and provide feedback on cooperative behaviors, assign peer- and self-assessment of individual contributions.[112] Peers are well-positioned to identify each other's levels and degrees of competence.[113] Peer assessment provides valuable feedback for group members and can be factored into grades. Some methods for both peer- and self-assessment include:

- Likert-scales to evaluate each group member's contributions;[114]
- Self- and peer-evaluations completed by each group member;[115]
- Student reports on group interaction and effectiveness;[116] and
- Individual student portfolios to assess individual performance and group contributions (requiring documents or other evidence of group contributions).[117]

Potential questions to use in reflective exercises include:

- How would you rate how well you helped the group?
- What would you do differently next time?
- What did you learn about yourself as a team player?
- What were your most and least successful interactions with your peers?

107. Lori E. Shaw & Victoria L. VanZandt, Student Learning Outcomes & Law School Assessment: A Practical Guide to Measuring Institutional Effectiveness 6–7 (2015).
108. Barkley et al., *supra* note 7, at 120.
109. Swan et al., *supra* note 10, at 46.
110. Barkley et al., *supra* note 7, at 120.
111. Cohen, *supra* note 33, at 26–27.
112. Barkley et al., *supra* note 7, at 106; Freeman & McKenzie, *supra* note 105, at 552–53.
113. Barkley et al., *supra* note 7, at 108; Palloff & Pratt, *supra* note 5, at 48.
114. Swan et al., *supra* note 10, at 53.
115. Barkley et al., *supra* note 7, at 107–08.
116. Swan et al., *supra* note 10, at 52–53.
117. *Id.* at 53.

Invite students to discuss the benefits and challenges of giving peer feedback to prepare them to evaluate each other.[118] For example, prompt students to rely on established guidelines for group interaction in evaluating their peers.[119] Peer evaluation is more impactful if conducted at both the mid-point and end of the term to allow students to progress in their collaborative skills.[120]

Three models are available for assigning grades to collaborative work.[121] First, you can give the group a single grade. If the group produces a single product, all members can receive the same score.[122] This method holds groups accountable but does not consider individual accountability, which can lead to student criticism.[123] Second, you can grade all work individually, which creates accountability and is perceived as fair by students but undermines the importance of group work.[124] And third, you can weigh both individual and group grades.[125] For example, an individual's grade could be a combination of group performance and individual performance. If using this method, you must design an activity that allows you to view individual contributions to the group project.

As noted earlier in the chapter, if group work will factor into course grades, balance the impact by including other assignments based solely on individual work. Consider tools, such as quizzes, that provide students with immediate feedback on individual performance.[126]

## B. RUBRICS

Providing clear criteria by which students will be evaluated helps them to learn more effectively and helps instructors to align evaluation with course goals and learning objectives.[127] Rubrics that contain explicit criteria help students to understand and complete the assignment and help instructors equitably evaluate student work.[128] Rubrics provide transparency about the grading process and assist students in setting goals and priorities.

---

118. *See* Sparrow, *supra* note 23, at 1171–72.

119. *Id.* at 1172.

120. *See id.* at 1171–73; Hamilton, *supra* note 25, at 645.

121. Nilson & Goodson, *supra* note 28, at 55; *Grading Methods for Group Work*, Carnegie Mellon Univ. Eberly Ctr., https://www.cmu.edu/teaching/assessment/assesslearning/groupWorkGradingMethods.html (last visited Oct. 8, 2020) [hereinafter *Grading Methods*].

122. Johnson et al., *supra* note 20, at 8:23.

123. Freeman & McKenzie, *supra* note 105, at 552.

124. *Grading Methods*, *supra* note 121.

125. Barkley et al., *supra* note 7, at 115.

126. *Id.* at 117.

127. Sophie Sparrow, *Describing the Ball: Improve Teaching by Using Rubrics—Explicit Grading Criteria*, 2004 Mich. St. L. Rev. 1, 6, 19–20.

128. *Id.*; Schwartz et al., *supra* note 7, at 178.

To design a rubric, select the activity, such as a debate or discussion forum, you will use to assess student learning.[129] Then develop specific criteria to assess performance or process.[130] These criteria can include behaviors related to group process and product, ranked from most to least important.[131] Rubrics should start with the most important criterion and work down from there, identifying measurements of strength and weakness.[132]

Effective rubrics for group work address specific behaviors.[133] Terms for performance levels include a simple range from poor to excellent[134] or levels of proficiency (e.g., absent, developing, proficient, and exemplary). Rubrics help assign grades if they also include points associated with different performance levels.[135] Sample rubrics follow on the next two pages.

---

129. Johnson et al., *supra* note 20, at 8:25.
130. *Id.*
131. *Id.*
132. *Id.* at 8:24.
133. Swan et al., *supra* note 10, at 48.
134. Johnson et al., *supra* note 20, at 8:24.
135. *See* Sparrow, *supra* note 127, at 9.

## SAMPLE PERFORMANCE RUBRIC[136]

This rubric can be adapted to evaluate both group process and work product.

| | Absent/Poor | Developing/ Fair | Proficient/ Good | Exemplary/ Excellent |
|---|---|---|---|---|
| Criteria 1 | Absence of behaviors and, if applicable, associated points/score | Minimal evidence of behaviors and, if applicable, associated points/score | Sufficient demon-stration of behaviors and, if applicable, associated points/score | Thorough demon-stration of behaviors and, if applicable, associated points/score |
| Process Example: Cooperation with Others | Did not do any work. Did not contrib-ute. Did not work well with others. | Could have shared more of workload. Had difficulty cooperating. Required direction and assistance. | Did own part of workload. Cooperative. Worked well with others. | Did more than oth-ers. Highly productive. Worked extremely well with others. |
| Product Example: Application of research tools to legal question, including tools selected and research steps. | No applica-tion of tools to legal question. | Applied research tools with limitations. Description of application lacks detail. Reasons for selecting spe-cific tools are not clear. | Adequate-ly applied research tools. Description includes suffi-cient detail of research steps. | Accurately and specifi-cally applied research tools. Research steps and reasons for selecting specific tools are clear. |

136. Process example adapted from *Group Work: How to Evaluate It*, CORNELL UNIV. CTR. FOR TEACHING INNOVATION, https://teaching.cornell.edu/resource/group-work-how-evaluate-it (last visited Oct. 10, 2020). Product example adapted from authors' course. For another example of teamwork skills assessment, see Hamilton, *supra* note 25, at 628.

## SAMPLE SELF- AND PEER-EVALUATION RUBRIC[137]

This sample provides a single form for evaluating self and peer performance. A scale of 1–4 could be used for scoring (1=strongly disagree; 2=disagree; 3=agree; 4=strongly agree). Alternatively, students could complete separate evaluations for each group member.

| Criteria | Self | Member 1 | Member 2 | Member 3 |
|---|---|---|---|---|
| Attends group meetings regularly and on time. | | | | |
| Contributes meaningfully to group work. | | | | |
| Prepares work in a quality and timely manner. | | | | |
| Demonstrates a cooperative and supportive attitude and makes efforts to solve problems. | | | | |
| Contributes significantly to the project's success. | | | | |
| TOTALS | | | | |

137. Adapted from *Sample Group Project Tools*, Carnegie Mellon Univ. Eberly Ctr., https://www.cmu.edu/teaching/designteach/design/instructionalstrategies/groupprojects/tools/index.html (adapted from a peer evaluation form developed at Johns Hopkins University (Oct. 2006)) (last visit Oct. 10, 2020) and Nilson & Goodson, *supra* note 28, at 56.

## VIII. Key Takeaways

Group work can help law students develop important professional skills. Keys to developing effective group activities include aligning the activities with course learning objectives; considering the relevant knowledge, skills, values, and processes you will assess and whether you will assess students on an individual, group, or combination basis; and forming diverse groups. You can strengthen student buy-in by explaining the value of group work and providing clear instructions. As groups work together, expect some struggle and do not intervene too quickly. Use technology that all group members can access and that works seamlessly with the course LMS. Finally, provide feedback to students through well-designed rubrics and consider incorporating peer feedback or self-reflection for additional insights.

FIFTEEN

# Using the Community of Inquiry Framework to Make the Most of Assessment in Online Learning

Audrey Fried*

After reviewing this chapter, readers will be able to:

- Describe the Community of Inquiry framework and explain how it can be used to design an online or blended course that promotes deep learning;
- Design an assessment plan that allows faculty to gauge students' learning and provide feedback throughout the course;
- Create collaborative assessments that allow students to build trust and pursue shared goals; and
- Construct assessments that leverage the ease of collaboration and iteration in an online environment to support sustained discourse.

The main purpose of assessments is to provide information about a student's learning.[1] Assessment can be primarily formative, where low- or no-stakes assessment is used to provide feedback to support a student's further learning, or summative, where assessment is used both to provide feedback and to document a student's proficiency at a particular point in time.[2] But assessments can do more than simply evaluate learning. They can help to create a community of inquiry that supports learning as well.

* Audrey Fried advises Osgoode Professional Development on legal curriculum and faculty development. She has a JD, an MA in education focused on online learning, an LLM focused on legal education, and is a doctoral student in education at the University of Toronto. She is the creator of the Redesign for Online course for law faculty at https://www.osgoodepd.ca/upcoming_programs/course-redesign-for-online/.

1. *See* Dianne Conrad and Jason Openo, Assessment Strategies for Online Learning 14 (2018).

2. *See id. See also* David J. Nicol & Debra Macfarlane-Dick, *Formative Assessment and Self-Regulated Learning: A Model and Seven Principles of Good Feedback Practice*, 31:2 Stud. Higher Educ. 199, 199 (2006) ("Formative assessment refers to assessment that is specifically intended to generate feedback on performance to improve and accelerate learning (Sadler, 1998).").

Community of Inquiry (CoI) is a framework for designing and facilitating online or blended courses. Its aim is to create a learning community by focusing on the three elements, called "presences," that overlap to make up the educational experience (see Figure 1 below). The three presences are teaching presence, social presence, and cognitive presence.[3] Teaching presence refers to students' sense that they are being led by an authoritative and supportive instructor. Social presence refers to students' identification with a community of learners pursuing a joint intellectual endeavor. Finally, cognitive presence refers to students' participation in the intellectual work of collaborative knowledge construction within the learning community and supported by the instructor.

FIGURE 1: THE COMMUNITY OF INQUIRY MODEL (COI)

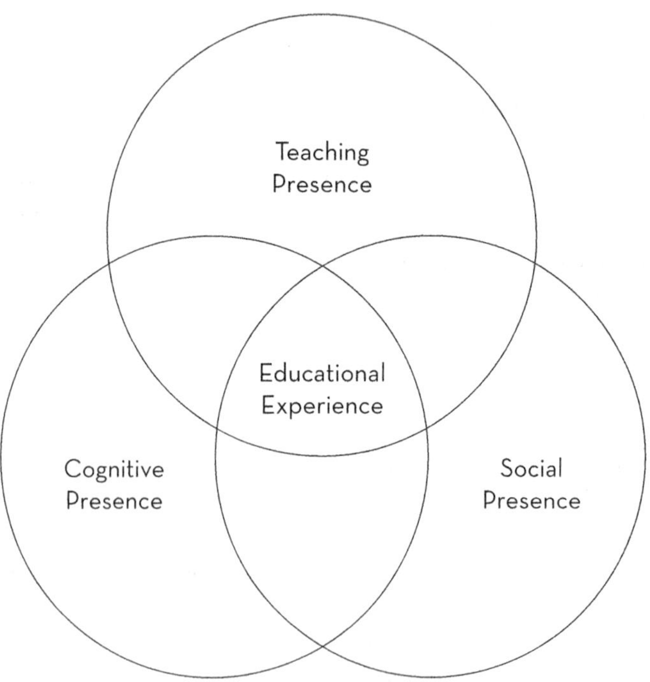


The CoI model is particularly well-suited to law teaching because it aims to create a learning community where "students listen to one another with respect, build on one another's ideas, challenge one another to supply reasons for otherwise unsupported opinions, assist each other in drawing inferences from what has been said, and seek

3. D. Randy Garrison et al., *Critical Inquiry in a Text-Based Environment: Computer Conferencing in Higher Education*, 2 Internet & Higher Educ. 1 (2000).

to identify one another's assumptions."[4] Assessments can be used in a variety of ways to support the three presences, contributing to the development of a community of inquiry and the deep learning that emerges from it.[5]

## I. Teaching Presence

Teaching presence is generated by the active engagement of an authoritative and supportive instructor, through both the design and facilitation of a course. It is a "unifying force [that] brings together the social and cognitive processes" of the community of inquiry.[6] One of the most important and difficult aspects of teaching presence in an online course is communicating with students about their learning on an ongoing basis.[7] When classes are held in person, some of this communication takes place in class. Instructors read the non-verbal cues of students, gauging their level of confusion, their level of interest, or their level of discomfort. This information helps faculty determine whether to review a concept, delve more deeply into it, or address a difficult or controversial issue. When done well, this type of communication enables faculty to be responsive in a way that not only improves learning but also conveys to students that the faculty member cares about their learning. This strengthens the faculty-student relationship and increases both faculty and student satisfaction.[8] Because nonverbal cues are diminished online, instructors must take a more deliberate approach. This is where assessment can help.

In fact, assessment is most obviously linked to this aspect of teaching presence. Assessments, by their nature, give instructors information about their students' learning and provide opportunities for the instructor to use that information to make subsequent teaching decisions. As Nicol explains, "[f]requent assessment tasks, especially diagnostic [or formative] tests, can help teachers generate cumulative information

---

4. Norman D. Vaughan et al., Teaching in Blended Learning Environments: Creating and Sustaining Communities of Inquiry 11 (2013) (quoting Matthew Lipman, Thinking in Education 20 (2003)).

5. *See, e.g.*, D. Randy Garrison & Martha Cleveland-Innes, *Facilitating Cognitive Presence in Online Learning: Interaction is not Enough*, 19:3 Am. J. Distance Educ. 133, 141 (2005) (finding that participants in a course "specifically designed to encourage deep approaches to learning through focused critical discourse . . . showed a significant shift to a deep [as opposed to a surface or achievement-oriented] approach to learning").

6. Vaughan et al., *supra* note 4, at 12.

7. *See* Joanna C. Dunlap & Patrick R. Lowenthal, *The Power of Presence: Our Quest for the Right Mix of Social Presence in Online Courses*, *in* Real Life Distance Education: Case Studies in Practice 1 (Anthony A. Piña & Al. P. Mizell eds., 2013), https://www.researchgate.net/publication/265375908_The_power_of_presence_Our_quest_for_the_right_mix_of_social_presence_in_online_courses#fullTextFileContent (explaining that although "connections students have with their teacher and with each other" are "[a]t the heart" of "engaging, memorable, and impactful learning experiences," students "often complain about feeling like their professor is absent from the course").

8. *See* Anthony G. Picciano, *Beyond Student Perceptions: Issues of Interaction, Presence, and Performance in an Online Course*, 6:1 J. Asynchronous Learning Networks 21, 22–23 (2002) (reviewing research that "both students and faculty typically report increased satisfaction in online courses depending on the quality and quantity of interactions").

about students' levels of understanding and skill, so that they can adapt their teaching accordingly."[9] They also give instructors the opportunity to reach out to individual students who may be struggling. In this way, assessment, especially formative assessment, can play a crucial role in creating teaching presence.

However, it is important to design assessments that do not unduly expand the workload of either students or faculty. There are several ways to do this. Most simply, instructors can break existing large assessments into smaller assessments and distribute them throughout the term so that students receive feedback earlier and instructors are able to get a sense of students' learning throughout the term. For example, a midterm exam could be broken into two or more low-stakes quizzes, a final exam could be shortened and one or more of the questions could be used as a formative test or assignment earlier in the term, a series of shorter papers could be offered in place of a long paper, or paper proposals and annotated bibliographies for a final paper could be assigned early in the term. In each of these scenarios, instructors can use a rubric to provide efficient and high-quality feedback.

Another possible approach is for faculty to assign multiple mini-assessments that function as check-ins on student learning. These mini-assessments can be graded for completion and simply be credited towards participation with global feedback given to the class as needed. Such mini-assignments might include one-minute or one-page papers that summarize, synthesize, or reflect on a class discussion or set of readings,[10] the submission of questions for class discussion, or short online quizzes to check for understanding, gauge opinion, or collect suggestions or feedback for future classes or activities. By asking students to complete these mini-assessments using an online form or through the course website, instructors can easily review all the assessments in one place, identifying students who are struggling or common areas of confusion to guide their teaching even in the absence of the non-verbal indications they might have gotten in a live class.

Instructors may also choose to divide the class into groups and assign mini-assessments to different groups on a rotating basis so that only a subset of students completes each assessment. Alternatively, instructors may require students to participate in a minimum number of weekly assignments throughout the term. For example, students may be asked to complete short reflections on at least six of twelve classes. Again, this reduces the number of students who complete each assessment. Finally,

---

9. David J. Nicol & Debra Macfarlane-Dick, *Formative Assessment and Self-Regulated Learning: A Model and Seven Principles of Good Feedback Practice*, 31:2 Stud. Higher Educ. 199, 214 (2006).

10. *See, e.g.*, *id.* (reviewing research by Angelo and Cross that showed that "teachers can gain regular feedback information about student learning within large classes by using variants of the one-minute paper" asking questions such as "What was the most important argument in this lecture? What question remains uppermost in your mind now at the end of this teaching session?" and pointing out that in addition to "giving feedback to the teacher, one-minute papers can also be used to provide feedback to the student" by "replay[ing] some of the student responses... at the next teaching session" to "allow[] teachers and students to share, on a regular basis, their conceptions about both the goals and processes of learning.").

students may be assigned to complete mini-assessments in groups or with a partner, reducing the burden on each student and the number of assessments that the instructor must review. These approaches reduce the workload for both students and faculty while allowing faculty to gain a sense of students' learning. With fewer assessments to review, instructors may choose to provide individual feedback in addition to global feedback.

Another option is for faculty to assess students' learning in real time during synchronous online classes. One way to do this is to use electronic polling (audience response systems) in class. Instructors might ask questions that check for understanding, gauge opinion, or directly ask students to rate their level of confusion or interest. Instructors should count participation in these polls towards class participation rather than tracking them for accuracy. This will encourage students to participate without fear that they will make a mistake. Instructors might also assess students in real time by assigning them to participate in simulations, debates, or other types of performance-based assessments. Depending on the degree of preparation expected, performance-based assessments can be either graded or counted towards participation.

Any combination of these approaches will provide faculty with rich information about students' learning, bolstering teaching presence and enhancing the learning experience of students. In addition, using assessments throughout the term will likely help students engage more deeply in the course by providing a structure for class preparation and post-class reflection, as well as providing feedback to support learning. With careful design, this can be accomplished without overwhelming either students or faculty.

## II. Social Presence

Assessments can also play a role in fostering social presence, or the presence of a community of learners focused on pursuing a joint intellectual endeavor. In a course with strong social presence, students "identify with the interests of the community... communicate purposefully in a trusting environment, and develop inter-personal relationships by... projecting their individual personalities."[11] Social presence creates the foundation that enables "learners to express themselves freely, engage in group discussions, and develop a sense of belonging to the group and its academic goals."[12] In other words, social presence is a necessary complement to the collaborative knowledge construction that is the heart of cognitive presence.

Like teaching presence, social presence can be more difficult to create online. Social presence depends on "learners gain[ing] a sense of being connected to, and

11. Norman Vaughan, *Community of Inquiry Framework, Digital Technologies, and Student Assessment in Higher Education*, *in* EDUCATIONAL COMMUNITIES OF INQUIRY: THEORETICAL FRAMEWORK, RESEARCH AND PRACTICE 335 (Zehra Akyol & D. Randy Garrison eds., 2013).

12. Susi Peacock & John Cowan, *From Presences to Linked Influences Within Communities of Inquiry*, 17:5 INT'L REV. RES. OPEN & DISTRIBUTED LEARNING 267, 271 (2016).

engaging with, other sentient beings who have a history, emotions, and a genuine concern for others in the community."[13] This is easier to accomplish in person because the non-verbal information conveyed in person is so much richer.[14] There are also more opportunities in person for students to have the kind of brief, casual interactions with peers that build familiarity and form the basis of trust. Students often chat with the person sitting next to them or while waiting for the classroom doors to open. While instructors can help students get to know each other online by assigning written or video introductions as well as building in time for informal conversations, something more is needed to help develop the trust and interpersonal relationships that are essential to the next phase of the development of social presence—the emergence of shared intellectual goals and purpose. It is at this stage that assessments can make a contribution.

Assessments can both structure and provide motivation for collaborative learning. For example, instructors can assign students to work together to solve a problem, complete a project, or to engage in collaborative knowledge building through academic discourse.[15] As I discuss further in the section on cognitive presence below, the online environment can be especially conducive to this type of assignment. Students can work on projects or problems using shared documents, websites, databases or other digital artifacts. They can share ideas by collaboratively annotating a document or contributing to a shared repository or list. And they can engage in rich, thoughtful academic discourse through online discussion forums. Another approach is to assign individual assessments that are then peer reviewed. In addition to providing a valuable opportunity for students to work together, when appropriately scaffolded, formative peer review can provide additional feedback for students, expose students to a variety of approaches to an assignment, and help students develop the capacity to assess their own work.[16] Digital tools can facilitate peer review by allowing students to easily annotate and provide comments on the work of others. In these ways, assessment can

---

13. *Id.*

14. *See* Jered Borup et al., *Improving Online Social Presence Through Asynchronous Video*, 15 INTERNET & HIGHER EDUC. 195, 195 (2012) (explaining that "absence of visual conversational cues can make it more difficult" to establish social presence).

15. *See, e.g.*, Carl Bereiter & Marlene Scardamalia, *Commentary on Part I: Process and Product in Problem-Based Learning (PBL) Research*, *in* PROBLEM-BASED LEARNING: A RESEARCH PERSPECTIVE ON LEARNING INTERACTIONS 186 (Dorothy H. Evensen et al. eds., 2000) (distinguishing between problem-based learning, where the goal is to solve a problem, and knowledge building, where the goal is to improve the "state of collective knowledge").

16. *See* Lucy Yeatman & Louise Hewitt, *Feedback: a Reflection on the Use of Nicol and Macfarlane-Dick's Feedback Principles to Engage Learners*, LAW TCHR. 1, 10 (2020) ("Sadler regards peer review as an essential mechanism for exposing students to a sufficient amount of work so as to enable them to develop the type of holistic and complex appraisal needed to form a judgement on the quality of the work. Peer review can help students to internalise and make sense of the marking criteria."). *See also* David Nicol, *From Monologue to Dialogue: Improving Written Feedback Processes in Mass Higher Education*, 35:5 ASSESSMENT & EVALUATION HIGHER EDUC. 501, 509 (2010) ("Having experience in [the] role [of assessor] is important if students are to develop the ability to evaluate their own work and to acquire the skills needed for life beyond the university.").

be used to support social presence by providing students with opportunities to build trust and work together towards shared goals.

## III. Cognitive Presence

Cognitive presence focuses on the intellectual activity in a course from the perspective that learning is fundamentally a social process. The essence of cognitive presence is collaborative knowledge construction, in which students create shared meaning through sustained discourse and reflection.[17] Cognitive presence "include[es] a broad range of cognitive activities involving critical thinking, together with related processes such as reasoning, evaluation, judgment, creativity, reflection, imagination, and deliberation."[18] Social and teaching presence support these activities by creating the necessary learning community and guiding student learning. Well-designed assessments can contribute to cognitive presence because, as Cleveland-Innes and Wilton explain, "we know from the literature on deep learning that… [a]ssessing learning through activities involving application, problem solving and creativity fosters deep, meaningful learning."[19]

Assessments of this kind are most effective when they are designed as learning activities embedded in the course's learning community. Students can work together on authentic tasks,[20] such as providing advice, creating a legal resource, or solving a legal or policy problem. These kinds of assessments can be especially powerful when they make use of the affordances[21] of online learning. For example, online discussion, collaborative annotation, and collaborative documents provide shared spaces and the flexibility of asynchronous interactions. Digital spaces also make it easy to share thoughts, learning artifacts, or other work products with peers, experts, or community organizations, and then to revise and improve them. By leveraging the relative ease of collaboration and iteration online, instructors can ensure that assessment activities foster the sustained reflection and critical discourse that students need for deep learning.

One example of this kind of assessment is described in Nolfi's paper on online case-based discussions, which revolve around a case study, or "description of a real-life

17. *See* VAUGHAN ET AL., *supra* note 4, at 11–12 (quoting Garrison et al., *supra* note 3, at 11).

18. Peacock & Cowan, *supra* note 12, at 270.

19. MARTHA CLEVELAND-INNES & DAN WILTON, GUIDE TO BLENDED LEARNING 34 (2018).

20. Authentic assessments focus on solving real-world problems rather than made-for-school problems. For example, in a privacy law class, an authentic assessment might ask students to write a policy proposal to address a genuine privacy problem rather than asking them analyze the implications of a fictional privacy problem. To write the policy proposal, students will have to gather information about the problem and generate a proposal. In contrast, the fictional problem will likely include all the information needed to reach a single correct answer.

21. "Affordances" are the properties of the medium that "determine… how it could possibly be used." Grainne Conole & Martin Dyke, *What are the Affordances of Information and Communication Technologies?*, 12:2 ALT-J, RSCH. LEARNING TECH. 113, 115 (2004). In this case, the properties of online learning technologies facilitate easy collaboration and iteration.

situation where individuals or an organization are faced with a problem or challenge that requires some form of decision-making to resolve."[22] Case studies "allow[] adult learners to employ a range of cognitive skills including problem solving, critical-reasoning, and analytical skills,"[23] particularly when the case involves "ill-structured problems... [which] may have unclear goals and incomplete information."[24] This type of assessment is "ideal... for students to develop and enhance their critical and reflective thinking skills."[25] As Nolfi explains, "[t]he collaborative social space of the [online case-based discussion] encourages in-depth analysis of a problem whereby students consider each other's perspectives and experiences and how they may or may not align with their own."[26] In addition, "[t]he asynchronous nature of the discussion... enables students to consider their contributions in a more deliberate and thoughtful way as the time constraints may be minimal."[27] Assessments such as this promote cognitive presence by engaging students in collaborative, complex tasks that require sustained critical discourse and foster deep learning.

## IV. Conclusion

By designing assessments guided by the CoI framework, instructors can go beyond using assessments as one-off, stand-alone evaluations, instead ensuring that assessments contribute to the development of a vibrant learning community that supports deep learning. Assessments have the potential to contribute to each of the three presences identified by the CoI model. Formative assessments should be used throughout a course to strengthen teaching presence by ensuring that instructors have a good sense of students' learning so that they can adjust their teaching as needed and provide support to students who are struggling. Wherever possible, collaborative assignments and peer review should be used to foster social presence by providing students with opportunities to build trust and pursue shared learning goals. Finally, assessments should be designed to contribute to cognitive presence by leveraging the affordances of online learning to facilitate iterative, collaborative work on authentic tasks that engage students in sustained critical discourse. When used in these ways, assessment can become a powerful tool that supports learning rather than simply evaluating it.

---

22. Tricia S. Nolfi, *Promoting Reflective Thinking in Adult Learners: The Online Case-Based Discussion*, *in* Handbook of Online Discussion-Based Teaching Methods 2 (Lesley Wilton & Clare Brett eds., 2020).

23. *Id.* at 6.

24. *Id.* at 3.

25. *Id.* at 5.

26. *Id.* at 10.

27. *Id.*

SIXTEEN

# A Millennial Law Professor's Guide to Learning Management Systems

Verónica C. Gonzales-Zamora*

After reviewing the chapter on Learning Management Systems (LMS), readers will be able to:

- Identify the different types of LMS platforms and toolsets available for online or remote learning;
- Understand the full range of benefits that LMS platforms and toolsets provide for both educators and students;
- Evaluate the major advantages and disadvantages of the three main type of LMS platforms; and
- Compare and contrast features of LMS platforms and toolsets in order to choose and design one that centers student experience and incorporates course learning objectives.

Legal education technology must be a deliberate pedagogical decision that not only considers the student perspective but is designed around it[1] in consultation with

* Assistant Professor of Law, University of New Mexico School of Law. Professor Gonzales-Zamora began teaching civil procedure, ethics, poverty law, and appellate decision-making in 2019 and began teaching those same courses online in 2020.

1. *See, e.g.*, Amy L. Ostrom et al., *Leveraging Service Blueprint to Rethink Higher Education: When Students Become "Valued Customers", Everybody Wins,* Ctr. For Am. Progress (2011), https://www.americanprogress.org/issues/economy/reports/2011/10/31/10512/leveraging-service-blueprinting-to-rethink-higher-education/ ("We believe service blueprinting can help university leaders and employees redesign, reinvent, and reimagine their educational offerings and service processes from the student's point of view. There are many grant-funded initiatives focused on improving higher education, but it is important to ask whether the changes proposed will improve or worsen the student experience and outcomes."). *See generally* Tanina Rostain et al., *Thinking Like a Lawyer, Designing Like an Architect: Preparing Students for the 21st Century Practice*, 88(3) Chicago Kent L. Rev. 743, 751–52 (2013), https://scholarship.kentlaw.iit.edu/cklawreview/vol88/iss3/5 (explaining the pedagogical value of designing apps in law school

the program and course objectives and outcomes. This is particularly true given that thirty-eight states expressly advise lawyers to "keep abreast of changes in the law and its practice, including the benefits and risks associated with relevant technology" in the official comment 8 to Model Rule of Professional Conduct 1.1.[2] Incorporating a Learning Management System (LMS) is one way a professor can enhance efficiency while also training students to narrow the justice gap through technology.[3]

In this chapter, I approach the challenge of choosing and designing a student-centered LMS from the lens of a woman of color who is also a tech-savvy millennial[4] (or as my colleagues often say "technologically literate") in ways similar to many law students who comprise student bodies generally more diverse and more tech-savvy than their law school faculties. In Part I of this essay, I offer a broad yet concise definition of LMS. In Part II, I briefly summarize the benefits of incorporating an LMS into law teaching and the current prevalence in law and undergraduate teaching. In Part III, I provide strategies for focusing on student-centered design of an LMS. Following the text, I provide a table describing four major LMS platforms and toolsets and comparing the major features of each.

## I. What Is an LMS?

An LMS, in essence, facilitates teaching and learning by providing professors the ability to organize and share information, and to provide access to online learning services.[5] The Center for Computer-Assisted Legal Instruction (CALI), the research authority on computer-mediated legal education tools that increase access to justice, defines an LMS as a "proprietary or open-source learning management system [that] collect[s] online teaching tools in one place; some schools collect individual tools and assemble their own technology teaching toolset."[6] Like all course materi-

---

by anticipating the questions and concerns of users, "an imaginative exercise requiring [law students] to put themselves in a typical user's shoes"); Lorne Sossin, *Designing Administrative Justice*, 34 Windsor Y.B. Access Just. 87 (2017), https://digitalcommons.osgoode.yorku.ca/scholarly_works/2733/ (applying design thinking in the context of establishment of new tribunals and reform of current tribunals in Canada).

2. *See* Robert Ambrogi, *38 States Have Adopted the Duty of Technology Competence*, Lawsitesblog.com, https://www.lawsitesblog.com/tech-competence (last visited Jan. 11, 2021).

3. James E. Cabral, *Using Technology to Enhance Access to* Justice, 26 Harv. J. L. & Tech. 241, 315 (2012).

4. *See* Verónica Gonzales-Zamora, *Get in Good Trouble: A Collection of Essays by Millennial Law Scholars*, 69(2) J. Legal Educ. 9 (Spring 2020).

5. Morten F. Paulsen, *Online Education Systems: Discussion and Definition of Terms*, NKI Distance Education, (July 2002), https://www.porto.ucp.pt/open/curso/modulos/doc/Definition%20of%20Terms.pdf.

6. Working Grp on Distance Learning in Legal Educ., Distance Learning in Legal Education: Design, Delivery and Recommended Practices 21 (2015), http://www.wgdlle.org/files/2015/12/WorkingGroupDistanceLearningLegalEducation2015_PDF.pdf (last visited Nov. 9, 2020). The text provides the following examples of proprietary or open source LMS—Blackboard, Moodle, Brightspace, Canvas, and Sakai—as distinguishable from existing resources being used to bridge online learning such as CALI's Classcaster or Westlaw's TWEN system. *Id.*

als, the LMS tool is within a professor's academic freedom,[7] thus offering a myriad of variations that can be customized based on the specific student needs and objectives of a particular course.[8]

Presently, three main types of LMS are available: (1) proprietary, (2) open-source, and (3) cloud-based.[9] First, propriety LMS platforms have been licensed by developers with the goal of producing profits.[10] These systems normally include ongoing support for customers.[11] However, these types of LMS platforms are expensive, less adaptable to changes in course objectives or student needs, and run the risk of being discontinued due to their non-public coding source.[12] Examples of proprietary LMS platforms are Blackboard, TWEN, and Lexis Classroom.[13]

Open-source LMS platforms are those for which the source code is publicly available. These LMS platforms are relatively inexpensive to use.[14] Despite being cost effective, the open-source LMS platforms are still innovative because open-source coding encourages ongoing innovation and adaptability by the public.[15] They are considered more secure than cloud-based programs.[16] On the other hand, open-source LMS platforms lack ongoing customer service support, rely heavily on potentially inexperienced online communities for user support, and provide little accountability or

---

7. According to W. Warren H. Binford, "legal educators must provide leadership and vision, partnering with publishers and software programmers and developers to ensure our students receive the best legal education possible in the Digital Age. If we do not, commercial enterprises will simply dictate our teaching resources and methods and, in the process, perhaps our obsolescence." W. Warren H. Binford, *Envisioning a Twenty-First Century Legal Education*, 43 J. L. & Pol'y 157, 158 (2013).

8. *See also* Shane Gallagher, *Assessing SCORM 2004 for its Affordances in Facilitating a Simulation as a Pedagogical Model* (2007) (Ph.D. dissertation, George Mason University), https://search.proquest.com/openview/0c0b3cb9db70880a2f614e518d5ff14a/1?pq-origsite=gscholar&cbl=18750&diss=y; Paris Avgerious et al., *Towards a Pattern Language for Learning Management Systems*, 6 J. Educ. Tech. & Soc'y 11 (2003).

9. Ctr Educ. Innovation, Trends and the Future of Learning Management Systems (LMSs) in Higher Education 2 (2019), https://operationaltraining.files.wordpress.com/2019/07/cei-report-trends-and-the-future-of-learning-management-systems-in-higher-education.pdf [hereinafter Trends and Future of LMS].

10. *Id.*

11. *Id.*

12. *Id.*

13. *Id.* at 3.

14. *Id.*

15. *Id.*

16. *Id.*

professional tech support if something goes wrong.[17] Examples of open-source LMS platforms are Moodle, Canvas, and Open edx.[18]

Cloud-based LMS platforms, currently trending in the eLearning industry, are known for their flexibility and ease of use.[19] They are also popular for their low-cost, diverse, personalized tools.[20] Other benefits include reduced need for physical space to house office and equipment, reduced software maintenance time and expense, and ability to scale up or down quickly based on demand.[21] The ease of use is high given student and professor pre-existing familiarity with cloud-based products[22] such as Dropbox, Office 365, and Adobe Creative Cloud. One of the most useful features is mobile access.[23] Although popular, one of the drawbacks of cloud-based LMS platforms is that security can be less robust for some LMS programs.[24]

## II. Benefits of an LMS

Generally, LMS platforms provide or attempt to provide several tools in one platform for the ease and convenience of both the learner and the instructor. I have distilled the benefits to four main categories of particular interest to law professors. First, most LMS platforms can make course prep more efficient and less time-consuming for professors.[25] Although some professors may spend significant time setting up an LMS initially, the LMS becomes a repository for content that can be used over and over again, across semesters or across sections, while still being flexible so that materials, links, and content can be updated easily. Having a centralized location for course information reduces the amount of time the professor repeats deadlines or other "housekeeping" information. It also reduces time spent uploading and distributing information

---

17. *Id.* Although Canvas is an open-source, cloud-based LMS, it can be maintained and hosted by a professional support company such as Instructure. This arrangement, called a SaaS (software as a service) program, allows a Canvas user to pay for one of four tiers of helpdesk support. *See Support Terms*, INSTRUCTURE, https://www.instructure.com/canvas/support-terms (last visited Jan. 11, 2021). For additional information about SaaS, PaaS (platform as a service), and IaaS (infrastructure as a service), see Stamatia Bibi et al., *P. Business Application Acquisition: On-Premise or SaaS-Based Solutions?*, 29 IEEE SOFTWARE MAGAZINE 86–93 (May/June 2012), https://www.researchgate.net/publication/232657399_Business_Application_Acquisition_On-Premise_or_SaaS-Based_Solutions.

18. TRENDS AND FUTURE OF LMS, *supra* note 9, at 3.

19. *Id.* at 4.

20. *Id.*

21. Mark Rhyman, *Five Reasons Why Switching to SaaS Will Be the Best Investment You Make This Year*, FORBES TECH. COUNCIL (May 15, 2017), https://www.thomabravo.com/.

22. TRENDS AND FUTURE OF LMS, *supra* note 9, at 4.

23. *Id. See also* Education Statistics, EDUCATIONDATA.ORG (2017), https://educationdata.org/online-education-statistics (noting that at least 79% of graduate and undergraduate students surveyed completed at least some online coursework on their mobile devices in 2017).

24. TRENDS AND FUTURE OF LMS, *supra* note 9, at 4. For a more comprehensive list of LMS programs and other types of systems such as Classroom Management Systems (CMS), see PETER BERKING & SHANE GALLGHER, CHOOSING A LEARNING MANAGEMENT SYSTEM—ADVANCED DISTRIBUTED LEARNING INITIATIVE 1, 135–43 (2016).

25. TRENDS AND FUTURE OF LMS, *supra* note 9, at 10 (listing benefits of LMS, including saving professor cost and time by one third, or increasing student achievement by one third).

by email, sending large files in multiple emails (such as links to class recordings), and, possibly, even lecturing from semester to semester.

Second, some LMS platforms may make online, in-person, and blended learning more accessible, particularly for the asynchronous portions of the course.[26] Learning materials, live lectures, and assignments can all be delivered to a student at any time and any location as long as the student has a high-speed internet connection.[27] The LMS can link to live or recorded content such as a video conference link, recording of a previous live meeting, or a pre-recorded video or supplemental materials (e.g., podcasts, slides, documents, and videos), [28] which are then accessible by the student at their convenience. The flexibility of these features allows for students with unexpected illnesses or childcare emergencies to continue learning without interruption. LMS platforms also have potential to create more accessible learning for the many students who do not reside in an urban area with a law school or who do reside in an area with too few lawyers or underrepresented populations.[29] These students may want to attend law school but may not be interested in uprooting to do so.[30] It may also make learning more accessible for students in need of flexible schedules to allow for full-time work, particularly for undocumented students who may not be eligible for typical student financial aid programs. What once prevented these students from accessing law school remotely—the clumsiness of slow internet, switching between multiple platforms, managing real-time communication and internet communication, and minimizing isolation and anonymity[31]—are now manageable through a centralized LMS.

Third, some LMS platforms allow professors to assess students, provide feedback, and easily see which students may need help acquiring specific skills or more engagement by the professor.[32] Many LMS platforms do this through the assessment and grading functions or through learning analytics which track how often and for how

---

26. Yvonne M. Dutton et al., *Assessing Online Learning in Law Schools: Students Say Online Classes Deliver*, 96 Denv. L. Rev. 493, 511 (2019).

27. *See* Berking & Gallagher, *supra* note 24, at 10.

28. *See, e.g.*, Ellen S. Podgor, *Teaching a Live Synchronous Distance Learning Course: A Student-Focused Approach*, 2006 U. Ill. J.L. Tech. & Pol'y 263, 270 (2006).

29. James McGrath & Andrew P. Morriss, *Online Legal Education & Access to Legal Education & the Legal System*, 70 Syracuse L. Rev. 49, 52 (2020) (noting that instructors should be mindful of barriers to broadband service and access to hardware for online learners). *See also* Catherine J.K. Sandoval et al., *Legal Education in the Era of COVID-19: Putting Health, Safety and Equity First*, 61 Santa Clara L. Rev. (forthcoming Spring 2021), https://ssrn.com/abstract=3660221.

30. *See* McGrath & Morriss, *supra* note 29; *see also* Sandoval et al., *supra* note 29.

31. Tahirih Lee, *Technology-Based Learning: A Transnational Experiment*, 64 J. L. Educ. 455, 470–71 (2015), https://www.jstor.org/stable/24716687 ("Distance learning programs are part of this problematic use of technology.... The more you attempt to make these courses more interactive by recreating as much as possible a live classroom experience, linking students and teachers live by either video teleconferencing or discussion boards, the more you slow down the delivery of the material."); *see also* Daniel C. Powell, *Five Recommendations to Law Schools Offering Legal Instruction over the Internet*, 11 J. Tech. L. & Pol'y 285, 298 (2006) ("The problem with web-conferencing is that the software design and the traffic on the common Internet make it too difficult for instructors and students to both communicate in actual time and to move between supporting documents.").

32. Binford, *supra* note 7, at 176–77 (discussing use of technology for remediation).

long students are engaging with specific activities or with the platform as a whole. Assessments can often be automated to be delivered, scored, recorded, and analyzed without professor intervention, and the professor can easily pinpoint which students earned the lowest scores.[33] Professors can also automate gentle reminder emails to students who have not turned in a particular assignment. Importantly, the assessment feature supports law schools in complying with ABA Standard 314 which requires formative and summative assessment methods to measure and improve student learning and provide meaningful feedback to students about their learning.[34]

Finally, the LMS platform can help prepare law students for obtaining and maintaining competence in using technology in law practice. Law schools are often criticized for not preparing students for the rigor of law practice.[35] Using an LMS can prepare students for using digital platforms to communicate with clients and colleagues, store information, share cloud-based information, and argue virtually.[36] Students well-versed in LMS platforms are also more prepared to use interactive websites such as e-filing systems, mobile tools for researching rules or cases when away from the physical library,[37] and online dispute resolution tools.[38] I teach ethics and professionalism, and I am often surprised that most students by their third year have yet to discuss how to properly safeguard and retain client data, or manage costs and fees for private legal research tools to comply with reasonable fee requirements, or use encrypted email communication to protect confidentiality of important information—all hot topics in law practice right now. Using an LMS helps professors teach technology competence and professionalism earlier in law school and prepare students for the new wave of technology tools available to support law practice and legal aid services.

---

33. *See* BERKING & GALLAGHER, *supra* note 24, at 10.

34. A.B.A. Sec. Leg. Educ. & Admis. to the Bar, *Standards and Rules of Procedure for Approval of Law Schools*, Standard 314, at 24 (2020–21), https://www.americanbar.org/content/dam/aba/administrative/legal_education_and_admissions_to_the_bar/standards/2020-2021/2020-21-aba-standards-and-rules-for-approval-of-law-schools.pdf.

35. *See, e.g.*, David Segal, *What They Don't Teach Law Students: Lawyering*, N.Y. TIMES (Nov. 19, 2011), https://www.nytimes.com/2011/11/20/business/after-law-school-associates-learn-to-be-lawyers.html.

36. Sandoval et al., *supra* note 29, at 69. I attended two webinars during the summer of 2020 that shed light on the technology changes and shifts in the courts resulting from the pandemic, and for which law students must be prepared: (1) ABA, *COVID-19 and Safe Access to the Courts: Strategies and Future Planning* (Mar. 24, 2020), https://www.americanbar.org/events-cle/ecd/ondemand/398703075/; and (2) National Judicial College, *Dean Erwin Chemerinsky—A Constitutional Examination of the COVID-19 Pandemic With Chief Justice George Draper of the Missouri Supreme Court, and Justice Sabrina McKenna of the Hawai'i Supreme Court* (Apr. 14, 2020), https://judges.webex.com/judges/lsr.php?RCID=a2cf3763ae81436b842df4350b1ab332.

37. *See generally* Cabral, *supra* note 3, at 246–56 (web-based legal services), 267–78 (mobile strategies), 278–92 (describing e-filing and electronic settlement facilitation).

38. The New Mexico Supreme Court recently authorized an Online Dispute Resolution Pilot Project that offers a free, convenient, online mediation of small claims disputes via an online tool available at https://newmexicocourtsdmd.modria.com/. *See In the Matter of the Expansion of the Online Dispute Resolution Pilot Project for New Mexico State Courts*, No. 20-8500-036 (Sept. 2, 2020), https://adr.nmcourts.gov/uploads/files/ODR/Order%20No_%2020-8500-036%20(Expanding%20and%20Revising%20ODR%20Pilot%20Program%209-2-20).pdf (last visited Jan. 11, 2021).

In 2010, thirty-seven law schools offered synchronous courses, and forty law schools offered asynchronous courses.[39] That number was trending upward until the height of the pandemic when nearly all law schools offered some form of distance learning.[40] The trend in undergraduate coursework is also toward increasing online education. For example, in 2019, 46% of faculty reported teaching an online course for credit (compared to 39% in 2016).[41] In 2019, 38% of faculty members used a blended course format including in-person and online learning.[42] Because it is important to build on existing student skill sets, faculty should also consider the trends and patterns of undergraduate distance or online or remote degree programs in the United States.

An informal poll by CALI during the summer of 2020 revealed that most of the faculty who attended the CALI training on online teaching used an LMS program (see below chart).[43] The vast majority use TWEN, Canvas, or Blackboard. Many law professors use something other than the LMS offered by their respective law school.

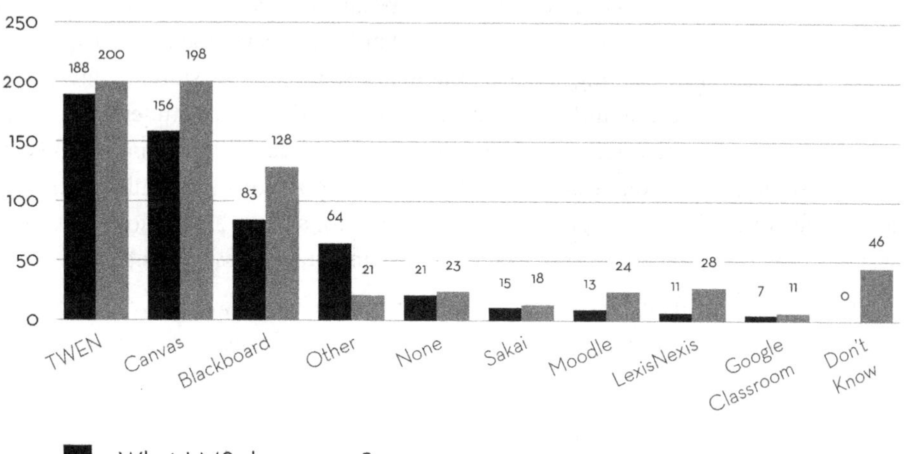


39. Gerald F. Hess, *Blended Courses in Law School: The Best of Online and Face-to-Face Learning?*, 45 McGeorge L. Rev. 51, 52 (2013).

40. A.B.A. Sec. Leg. Educ. & Admis. to the Bar, *Report to the House of Delegates: Resolution 111E*, at 5–6 (2018). Standard 306 was amended in 2018 and then temporarily relaxed during the 2020–2021 global pandemic but there is no indication that the relaxed standards will continue once the circumstances of the pandemic are no longer present.

41. *Online Education Statistics*, EducationData.org (2019), https://educationdata.org/online-education-statistics (last visited Jan.11, 2021).

42. *Id.*

43. *See Preparing for the Future of Legal Education—Online Teaching Tips & Techniques*, CALI (June 9, 2020), https://onlineteaching.classcaster.net/ (last visited Nov. 9, 2020).

For professors interested in building on existing skillsets of law students coming out of undergraduate studies, it is helpful to know the top three LMS programs used in higher education institutions in the United States. As of Fall 2020, the top three LMS used in higher education were Instructure Canvas (36.7%), legacy Blackboard Learn (26.8%), and Moodle (16.2%).[44] Additional information is needed, however, regarding professor and student satisfaction, patterns of particular tools for particular types of courses (such as didactic vs. seminar), and patterns across different schools (small vs. large, for instance). With this data, professors will continue to improve student-centered LMS platforms for each of their courses.

## III. Prioritizing Student-Centered Features for an LMS Companion to Law School Course

Student-centered pedagogy and course design consider student needs, pre-existing skills, and course objectives.[45] Students likely expect student-centered design of LMS platforms, given the billions of dollars invested in designing a seamless and "user-friendly" flow on social media platforms, retail tools, and thousands of apps in almost every other part of their personal lives. For example, in assessing the quality of asynchronous online teaching and learning in law schools using student perceptions, Professor Yvonne Dutton and her colleagues concluded that law students appreciate organization of the material and assignments, and consider a course high quality if it engages students with course content and provides opportunity for regular assessment and professor feedback.[46] A professor should thus consider which platforms or software or toolset will facilitate organization, engagement, and assessment.

Professors may also learn from access to justice scholars who have studied "human-centered,"[47] or "user-centered,"[48] or so-called "user-friendly" design in the con-

---

44. *8th Annual LMS Data Update*, EDUTECHNICA.COM (Dec. 9, 2020), https://edutechnica.com/2020/12/09/8th-annual-lms-data-update/.

45. *See* Tim Brown, *Design Thinking*, HARV. BUS. REV. 84 (June 2008), https://hbr.org/2008/06/design-thinking (providing a description of design thinking, a methodology that centers around what people want and need instead of simply making a product more attractive looking).

46. Dutton et al., *supra* note 26, at 497.

47. *See, e.g.*, Margaret D. Hagan, *A Human-Centered Design Approach to Access to Justice: Generating New Prototypes and Hypotheses for Intervention to Make Courts User-Friendly*, 6 IND. J. L. & SOC. EQUAL. 199 (2018), https://www.repository.law.indiana.edu/ijlse/vol6/iss2/2; Dan Jackson, *Human-Centered Legal Tech: Integrating Design in Legal Education*, 50 L. TCHR. 82 (2016), https://papers.ssrn.com/sol3/papers.cfm?abstract_id=2767486#.

48. *See, e.g.*, W. David Ball, *Redesigning Sentencing*, 46 MCGEORGE L. REV. 817 (2014), http://heinonline.org/HOL/Page?handle=hein.journals/mcglr46&div=50&g_sent=1&collection=journals; Leo G. Anthopoulos et al., *Applying participatory design and collaboration in digital public services for discovering and redesigning eGovernment services*, 24 GOV'T INFO. Q. 2 (2007), http://uxconsult.com/wp-content/uploads/2013/03/Applying-participatory-design-and-collaboration-in-digital-public-services-for-discovering-and-re-designing-e-Government-services.pdf.

text of law.[49] For example, a design textbook notes that "a well-designed system or object must be easy to learn, effective to use and provide an enjoyable experience."[50] By incorporating design-think principles from access to justice technology communities, the student interaction with an LMS itself becomes a part of the pedagogy by increasing student literacy in user-centered systems.[51] Law students can then enter practice already having engaged with technological systems that are user-centered and can apply that first-hand knowledge to improve and create systems that are more accessible to and easier for users seeking access to justice.[52]

Professors should prioritize consideration of how LMS features can be incorporated to meet course objectives. In other words, there is no one-size-fits-all LMS. Different instructors and courses will have different priorities to consider when selecting an LMS.[53] For example, if collaborative work is important in a course that requires peer problem-solving or team-based learning, the professor will want to seek out tools and/or LMS features that support collaborative engagement such as group grading. If a professor wishes to rely heavily on formative and summative assessments to track student progress, that professor will want to select an LMS with a quizzing or assessment feature. Then a comparison of other secondarily important features, such as cost, industry, or ease of use for professor, can help narrow the choices for an LMS.

In determining what is the most effective and efficient learning or content delivery method to meet course objectives, law school faculty should also consider the latest pedagogical research. For example, in a special report recently published by Scientific American Mind, the authors "reviewed more than 700 scientific articles discussing 10 common learning techniques."[54] They concluded that the most ineffective and inefficient study methods were highlighting and rereading, two study methods that are widely encouraged and practiced in legal education. As for the two methods that appeared to yield the highest dividends, the report focused on self-testing and distributed practice (also known as spaced learning),[55] a method which is infrequently

---

49. *See, e.g.*, John A. Clarke & Bryan D. Borys, *Usability is Free: Improving Efficiency by Making the Court More User-Friendly*, *in* Future Trends in State Courts (2011), https://ncsc.contentdm.oclc.org/digital/collection/ctadmin/id/1844/; Ginnifer L. Mastarone & Susan Feinberg, *Access to Legal Services: Organizing Better Selfhelp Systems*, Professional Communication Conference (2007), https://ieeexplore.ieee.org/abstract/document/4464041.

50. Rostain et al., *supra* note 1, at 755.

51. Paul Lippe, *Do Lawyers Have the 'Design Mojo' Needed to Rethink the Delivery of Legal Services?* A.B.A.J. (Dec. 2013), http://www.abajournal.com/legalrebels/article/legal_by_design.

52. Nisha Francine Rajoo, *Law by Design: What the Legal Profession Can Learn from Design Thinking*, L. Gazette (Dec. 2019), https://lawgazette.com.sg/practice/practice-matters/law-by-design-thinking/ (summarizing design thinking principles used by Stanford's Legal Design Lab and describing practical applications in trial advocacy, firm processes, and legal service delivery).

53. Binford, *supra* note 7, at 161.

54. John Dunlosky et al., *What Works, What Doesn't*, Sci. Am. Mind, Sept.–Oct. 2013, at 47–53.

55. *Id.*

used in most law school classrooms.[56] A professor might consider how to incorporate self-testing and spaced learning into the classroom using LMS features such as ungraded quizzes or practice quizzes, or modules to organize recapitulations.[57]

Generally, the LMS functions that facilitate teaching-learning include some type of protection from unauthorized use; a centralized and organized system; and ability to upload and deliver materials to students, keep track of students' performance, administer quizzes, set up discussion fora, conduct surveys, track participation, administer assessments, and more to facilitate the online learning experience. Other scholars suggest that a successful LMS should support the development and execution of four main basic tasks, via a friendly and uniform user-interface: (1) information distribution; (2) learning material management; (3) multiple communication facilities; and (4) class management.[58] But it can be difficult to know which features a particular LMS has. The chart at the end of this chapter compares features of the commonly used toolsets and LMS programs in legal education. Although this compilation is neither comprehensive nor exhaustive, it provides a starting point.[59]

Additional research questions about LMS platforms should be explored. First, more data is needed about the user experience for students. Lack of data is the largest barrier to student-centered design. Until then, informal methods of information gathering such as through a teaching assistant, students themselves, a mid-semester or end-of-semester survey, or teaching evaluations may provide useful information about the student experience with the chosen LMS. It is important to hear from students who traditionally experience more barriers to success in law school such as first-generation students, non-traditional students who may be less tech-savvy, BIPOC students, and students from rural communities with little to no access to reliable high-speed internet.

Second, it should be noted that technology should not be accepted wholesale, particularly if it is offered free of cost. For instance, additional research is needed regarding privacy concerns related to viewing a public Google site with the Google Analytics feature enabled, such as the use of cookies or other location tracking tools. Professors should consult with their IT departments to ensure a particular tool is not violating Family Education Privacy Rights Act (FERPA),[60] or other data regulation.

---

56. Brian Sites, *Learning Theory and the Law: Spaced Retrieval and the Law School Curriculum*, 43 L. & Psychol. Rev. 99, 100–01 (2018–19).

57. For guidance in collecting and reporting data to assess online learning, see Chapter 19: *Using Scientific Methods for Evidence-Based Decision Making in Designing, Evaluating, and Assessing Digital Learning in the Legal Academy* by Victoria Sutton.

58. M. Parkes et al., *Student preparedness for university e-learning environments,* 25 Internet & Higher Educ. 1–10, 13 (2014), https://www.sciencedirect.com/science/article/abs/pii/S1096751614000724; *see also* Colin McCormack & David Jones, Building a Web-based Education System (1997).

59. For more detailed features list and sample rubrics, see Berking & Gallagher, *supra* note 24, at 128–30, 133–35.

60. 20 U.S.C. § 1232(g).

Third, it is not clear who or what owns the content and/or course design once it is entered into the LMS—either the school, the LMS, the professor, or some combination thereof. Fourth, additional research is also needed about compliance with federal laws and regulations protecting people with disabilities from discrimination and the availability of various accessibility tools for all populations, especially those who are differently abled. Finally, additional research is needed about the business practices of the corporate LMS programs. For example, whether they work toward and support racial equity, social justice, clean energy, sustainable sources, and fair labor practices may affect the value assessment.

## IV. Conclusion

Selecting a student-centered LMS or toolset can be time-consuming and confusing. But it can save valuable preparation, communication, and review time in the future. It can also help professors see which students need help more easily and sooner than the final exam. LMS platforms help professors and students stay organized, particularly when teaching and learning must be flexible to the circumstances of the pandemic. Each LMS and toolset offers different features with advantages and disadvantages but focusing on student needs and course objectives can help law professors make the right selection. More importantly it can spark the innovation legal education needs to keep up with innovations in students' everyday lives, law practice, and access to justice.

TABLE COMPARING FEATURES OF FOUR MAJOR LMS AND TOOLSETS

| | TWEN (Westlaw)[61] | Blackboard Learn[62] | Google Sites[63] | Lexis Classroom/ Canvas[64] |
|---|---|---|---|---|
| SUSTAINABILITY & ACCESSIBILITY | • Proprietary<br>• TA access<br>• Share documents<br>• Stay organized | • Proprietary<br>• TA access<br>• Deliver course content<br>• Measure student effort | • Cloud-Based<br>• TA access<br>• DIY website (drag-n-drop)<br>• Share information<br>• Stay organized<br>• Quiz students | • Open-Source (Canvas)<br>• TA access<br>• Deliver course content<br>• Communicate with students<br>• Discussion forum<br>• Assignment submissions |
| INTEGRATED & CENTRALIZED APPLICATIONS OR TOOLS | • Module layout<br>• Assignment submission | • Module layout<br>• Assignment submission<br>• Calendar<br>• Third-party video record | • DIY design layout<br>• Google forms to accept assignments<br>• Google Calendar<br>• YouTube for video record<br>• Announcements area on site | • Module layout<br>• Assignments accepted & tied to gradebook<br>• Integrated calendar<br>• Third-party video record<br>• Student notified of announcements |
| ACCESS & PRIVACY | • Access tied to school email<br>• Likely FERPA compliant<br>• Very easy to use & design | • Access tied to school email<br>• Likely FERPA compliant<br>• Somewhat easy to use<br>• Somewhat easy to design | • Professor controls access<br>• Private website —no login<br>• Very easy to use<br>• Somewhat difficult to design<br>• Mobile access | • Access tied to school email<br>• Likely FERPA compliant<br>• Somewhat difficult to use<br>• Difficult to design<br>• Mobile access |

61. "The West Education Network (TWEN by Westlaw) is an online extension course of the law school classroom. Faculty can create TWEN course sites, share information, and stay organized." *Students Guide to TWEN*, Westlaw.com (2010), http://lscontent.westlaw.com/images/content/TWENStudGuide10.pdf (last visited Nov. 10, 2020). *See also Administrators Guide to TWEN*, Westlaw.com, https://lscontent.westlaw.com/images/content/documentation/AdminTWENGuide2013.pdf (last visited Nov. 9, 2020). I consider TWEN even though it is a tool and not technically an LMS because it is one of the most popular tools used by law faculty according to CALI's unofficial live polling. *See* CALI, *supra* note 43.

62. "Blackboard is a course management system that is used both as a primary method to deliver course content and to measure students' effort." Michael F. Spivey & Jeffrey J. McMillan, *Using the Blackboard Course Management System To Analyze Student Effort and Performance*, 39 J. Fin. Educ. 19 (2013). *See*

| TWEN (Westlaw) | Blackboard Learn | Google Sites | Lexis Classroom/ Canvas | |
|---|---|---|---|---|
| • Upload PowerPoints<br>• Storage varies by school | • Upload powerpoints<br>• Share external links<br>• School determines storage quota per student & faculty | • Upload PowerPoints & edit in google slides<br>• Share external links<br>• Share internal docs<br>• Includes 10 GB storage with option to buy more google drive | • Upload PowerPoints<br>• Share external links<br>• Share internal docs<br>• Includes 10 MB storage with option to buy more | STORING & SHARING INFORMATION |
| • Emails updates to students<br>• LiveChat feature | • Send-only emails<br>• Discussion forum<br>• Third-party video conference (Zoom) | • Gmail for email<br>• Google Forms for surveys<br>• Google Meets for video conference<br>• Collaboration with Google Docs, Slides, Sheets | • Integrated inbox<br>• Discussion board<br>• Third-party video conference (Skype)<br>• Peer review of assignments | COMMUNICATION & COLLABORATION |
| • None | • Quizzes<br>• Gradebook<br>• Some learner analytics | • Google Forms for quizzes<br>• Google Spreadsheets helps track grades<br>• Google Slides extension for polling (Poll Everywhere) | • Quizzes with answer explanations<br>• Robust gradebook allows feedback<br>• Grading rubric for any or all assignments<br>• Learner analytics | ASSESSMENT & PERFORMANCE TRACKING |

*also Black Board Administrator's Guide*, https://help.blackboard.com/Learn/Administrator/Hosting/Get_to_Know_Blackboard_Learn (last visited Nov. 9, 2020).

63. "Google Sites is a website building platform from google. It allows you to create a website without having to know to code it yourself." Daniel Nations, *What Is Google Sites and Why Use It?*, Lifewire.com (Feb. 24, 2020), https://www.lifewire.com/what-is-google-sites-and-why-use-it-3486337. *See also Google Workspace Learning Center*, Google.com, https://support.google.com/a/users/answer/9282722?visit_id=637405808250701196-1314887541&hl=en&rd=1 (last visited Nov. 9, 2020).

64. "Lexis Classroom [Canvas]... allows professors to access, posts, and manage class material in one place. Lexis Classroom also allows communication with students more efficiently through inbox messaging, discussion forums, assignment submissions, and other features." *Lexis Classroom Instructor Training Guide*, LexisNexis.com, https://www.lexisnexis.com/supp/lawschool/resources/faculty/lexis-classroom-user-guide.pdf (last visited Jan. 11, 2021).

SEVENTEEN

# Breaking Open the Classroom to Close the "Skills Gap"

Anita M. Singh*

*"For the things we have to learn before we can do them, we learn by doing them."*

—Aristotle

After reviewing this chapter,[1] readers will be able to:

- Understand why teaching online may help close students' practical "skills gap";
- Leverage the concept of "virtual intelligence" in their course planning;
- Design courses that immerse students in an environment more closely resembling the environments in which they will ultimately practice; and
- Present students with opportunities to challenge themselves in new ways to better develop the skills legal employers are most looking for.

As the old adage goes, law school teaches students to think like lawyers. Of course, we should not sell ourselves so short—we also teach students to write like lawyers, to research like lawyers, and to speak like lawyers. We help them become ethical and principled advocates, logical problem-solvers, and rigorous analysts.

But even with all of this, is it possible we have been derelict in one of our most critical duties? We have been teaching students how to lawyer. But have we really been teaching them how to *be* lawyers?

---

* Associate Director of Fundamentals of Lawyering and Associate Professor of Legal Research and Writing, The George Washington University Law School. Professor Singh began law teaching in 2009 and began teaching courses online in 2020.

1. This chapter excerpts, adapts, and expands upon my forthcoming piece, Anita M. Singh, *From Crisis Springs Opportunity: Using Virtual Learning to Develop More Effective Lawyers*, St. Louis U.L.J (forthcoming).

According to a key constituent, the answer is a resounding "no." In 2015, a survey of 300 hiring partners and senior associates who supervise new attorneys, representing varied practice areas from small to large U.S. law firms, revealed a full 95% said "recently graduated law students lack key practical skills at the time of hiring."[2] In another survey the same year, a related, and more disturbing issue surfaced. Although most practicing attorneys working with recent law school graduates found them ill-prepared for practice, 3L law students were woefully unaware of this, with nearly the same percentage stating that they believed they possessed "sufficient practice skills."[3] Want to know what is even more fascinating? Law school faculty members were split down the middle—with just under half thinking that new attorneys are equipped to do their jobs after graduation.[4]

*Fewer than half.*

Taken to its logical conclusion, that means many, if not most, of us think that the way we teach today is an imperfect fit for staffing the future of the legal profession. We believe we could do more, and that we could do it better.

As a full-time professor of a course called Fundamentals of Lawyering, I agree, and I see the opportunity to begin filling in these gaps from day one. By moving beyond the physical classroom, we have tremendous opportunities to do more than teach students *what* they will need to do as lawyers by teaching them *how* to do those things. Because even though "law schools are not alone in their responsibility for today's challenges, nor are they alone in their responsibility to address them,"[5] we can do more to bear our portion of the responsibility.

This chapter outlines the various manifestations of the skills gap, focusing on a suite of characteristics that transcend traditional lecture or assignment and thus may be most easily tackled by breaking open the physical classroom as we know it. It also explains the overlap between these characteristics and a concept known as "virtual intelligence" to explore why leveraging technology may provide the ideal opportunity to immerse students in experiences that will help them grow in these less tangible areas. It concludes with five structural elements to consider when designing law school courses to capture these skills.

---

2. LexisNexis, White Paper: Hiring Partners Reveal New Attorney Readiness for Real World Practice 1 (2015), https://www.lexisnexis.com/documents/pdf/20150325064926_large.pdf.

3. *New Lawyers Believe They are Ready for the Job; Practicing Attorneys Disagree According to First-Ever State of the Legal Field Study*, BARBRI Group (Mar. 5, 2015), https://www.thebarbrigroup.com/new-lawyers-believe-they-are-ready-for-the-job-practicing-attorneys-disagree-according-to-first-ever-state-of-the-legal-field-study/.

4. *Id.*

5. Alli Gerkman & Zachariah DeMeola, *Foundations for Practice: The "Whole Lawyer" and the Path to Competency for New Lawyers*, 87 B. Examiner 17, 25 (2018), https://www.ncbex.org/pdfviewer/?file=%2Fassets%2Fmedia_files%2FBar-Examiner%2Farticles%2F2018%2FBE-870218-Gerkman-DeMeola.pdf.

## I. Rethinking the Skills Gap

I am not the first to say that today's law graduates may know very well what they are supposed to do as a lawyer but not how to do it effectively. Surveys show this problem manifests in several ways. Some show students are ill-prepared in particular technical legal skills, like drafting pleadings, writing jury instructions, structuring transactions, and conducting due diligence.[6] Yet others show that students' deficits are more intangible and, in many ways, more interesting.

As one example, the Institute for the Advancement of the American Legal System surveyed more than 24,000 lawyers to learn what "foundations" entry-level lawyers needed to succeed in law practice. Neither legal knowledge nor traditional legal skills appeared in the top ten.[7] In fact, only research, writing, and speaking cracked the top twenty.

The top two "foundations" were the ability to keep information confidential and punctuality. Foundations ranked sixth through eighth covered listening attentively, being responsive, and being diligent. And paying attention to detail was number ten. Essentially, the entire top ten list was a mix of non-legal professional skills and what the survey designers refer to as "characteristics"—things like integrity, common sense, and intelligence.[8]

Teaching in a way that will have a meaningful impact on these characteristics can be challenging. For example, Shultz and Zedeck identify "conflict resolution" as a category of skills critical to lawyer effectiveness. But within that category lies both negotiation (a traditional "skill" that students can practice) and the ability to see the world through the eyes of others (something far less tangible). The former is easy to assign. It can be explained through lecture, practiced through classroom exercises, and tested through simulation. The latter, on the other hand, cannot. It transcends any particular project, paper, simulation, or lecture. A professor cannot create a single exercise in the traditional sense to capture this characteristic, or at least doing so would not be the most effective way to improve students' skills in these areas.

---

6. *See, e.g.*, LexisNexis, *supra* note 2, at 3.

7. *See generally* Gerkman & De Meola, *supra* note 5.

8. These same skills also appear in Professors Marjorie M. Shultz and Sheldon Zedeck's extensive and groundbreaking research into lawyer effectiveness. *See* Marjorie M. Shultz & Sheldon Zedeck, *Predicting Lawyer Effectiveness: Broadening the Basis for Law School Admission Decisions*, 36 L. & Soc. Inquiry 620, 629 (2011). Their work was not designed with curricular innovation in mind; rather, they designed their study to assist with admissions decisions—both to help diversify the incoming classes in law schools, and to revise the LSAT. Shultz and Zedeck identified twenty-six factors that make lawyers effective. Their list shares two key characteristics with many others—first, it recognized the importance of writing well, being diligent, working hard, and being responsive. And second, it recognized that these skills fall into several categories, which can be largely divided by function—*e.g.*, research and information gathering, communications, planning and organizing, and conflict resolution.

To best think about how to tackle these skills within (or outside of) a classroom, I have found it helps to think of the many factors that comprise effectiveness in three clusters:[9]

1. Intellect and Cognitive Capacity;
2. Technical and Practical Skills (Legal and Professional); and
3. Elements of Professionalism that Transcend Assignment.

Assuming the first is immutable, and the second is the traditional focus of legal pedagogy (and thus an area where how to teach the necessary skills is more obvious), I have spent my time thinking about the third. Lecture, doctrinal classes, and skills classes exist on topics in this third category. However, for students to truly understand how to develop in these areas, reading, writing, and talking about them are not enough. The challenges that build strength in these areas must be *experienced.*

So how can we create those experiences? We need to think more about the structural elements of our courses, rather than the substantive ones. Outside of a true simulation, can we really teach law students to pay attention to detail? To be on time? To own their mistakes and accept responsibility? To be confident in their choices and willing to defend them?

Yes. And the answer is just outside the bounds of the physical classroom.

## II. The Curious Case of the Classroom

The start of a new semester is always full of excitement—rows upon rows of law students sitting in large lecture hall, waiting to be called upon. To absorb lectures, to engage in enriching and intellectually stimulating dialogues and colloquies, or to discuss challenging issues with their colleagues and their peers.

Perhaps early on, students have anxiety about the law school experience. But soon enough, they understand the routine. They attend classes at a prescheduled time, covering predetermined topics listed clearly on a predesigned syllabus, and then they return to their homes. They study. They read. They outline. Rinse and repeat. It is a predictable rhythm, a comforting (even if rigorous) pace.

But when these students enter an office, everything changes. Gone are the predictable schedules, the carefully laid out instructions, the concretely demarcated tasks, the physically co-located colleagues and peers, and all the knowns. In their place are teams scattered across the globe, living in different time zones, embracing multiple modes of communication, and working with imperfect or impartial information, less guid-

9. These categories, a kind of hybrid of the eight Shultz and Zedeck umbrellas and the categories created by the Institute for the Advancement of the American Legal System, organize lawyer effectiveness factors so that we may focus in on our areas of strength and greatest opportunity. These categories rely upon commonalities among what the factors are and how they can be taught. *See generally* Gerkman & De Meola, *supra* note 5.

ance, and more autonomy. The intern or attorney, unlike the student, is pulled into last-minute meetings, given unforeseen new assignments without samples to guide them, asked to juggle things they never saw coming, and thrown into situations where they need to rely on new resources and new colleagues.

For better or worse, things are no longer confined to neat, pre-defined blocks. Projects and deadlines collide with other projects and deadlines. Work bleeds into home life, and attorneys are asked to exercise expert judgment and professionalism.

We have long wondered why there is such a skills gap between law school and newly minted lawyers. But the answer stares us straight in the face. These professional skills can only be developed in a professional environment. But outside of clinics and simulations, the physical classrooms of law schools could not resemble an office less.

In the wake of the COVID-19 pandemic, with more and more people working remotely for the foreseeable future (including long post-pandemic[10]), lack of realism has become even more true. With new learning modalities and flexibilities, however, never has there been such an opportunity to make the law school classroom better resemble an office.

## III. The Case for Focusing on Virtual Intelligence

By going beyond the physical classroom and leveraging remote learning opportunities, we can promote "virtual intelligence" through immersion. And we can do it in any course in any subject, to help students refine their professionalism skills and become more practice ready. In fact, we can do it without changing a thing about the substance of our courses—it will simply, by virtue of structure, happen seamlessly in the background.

What exactly is virtual intelligence? At its simplest, it is a suite of skills and behaviors that help build trust and improve performance when we interact with others remotely.[11] This is particularly important because the gap between the working environment and the physical classroom has only widened in recent months. Post-pandemic, surveys reveal that as many as one in five workers could be entirely remote after the pandemic.[12] But before I go further, I should be clear—virtual intelligence is

---

10. *See* Olga Khazan, *Work from Home is Here to Stay*, ATLANTIC (May 4, 2020), https://www.theatlantic.com/health/archive/2020/05/work-from-home-pandemic/611098/.

11. *See* Barbara Z. Larson & Erin E. Makarius, *The Virtual Work Skills You Need—Even If You Never Work Remotely*, HARV. BUS. REV. (Oct. 5, 2018), https://hbr.org/2018/10/the-virtual-work-skills-you-need-even-if-you-never-work-remotely ("Research consistently indicates that virtual work skills—such as the ability to proactively manage media-based interactions, to establish communication norms, to build social rapport with colleagues, and to demonstrate cooperation—enhance trust within teams and increase performance.").

12. *See* Derek Thompson, *The Workforce Is About to Change Dramatically*, ATLANTIC (Aug. 6, 2020), https://www.theatlantic.com/ideas/archive/2020/08/just-small-shift-remote-work-could-change-everything/614980/.

a critical skill for our students to learn, regardless of whether their schooling or future employment remains remote or virtual in the future.

Virtual work—defined broadly—is ubiquitous. Even when lawyers report in person to their offices, it is integrated into day-to-day communications with everyone from co-workers working across the globe to colleagues down the hall. Even a few years ago, "people tend[ed] to significantly underestimate the proportion of their work that is virtual, largely because they believe[d] virtual work occurs outside the office."[13] In reality, our high-tech, global, interconnected world calls on all of us to be virtually intelligent—capable of reliably building trust, effectively communicating, and working in ways that were not contemplated even five or ten years ago. Today's attorneys are video conferencing with clients half a world away, texting with colleagues in their office, and presenting to their supervisors via a shared screen—sometimes all at once.

By focusing on ways to promote virtual intelligence, we can simultaneously enhance more "ordinary" professionalism skills. Four key skills support virtual intelligence: establishing behavioral guidelines, developing trust, coordinating information, and using media.[14] And although the authors suggest that virtual work requires "a different set of social and interpersonal skills and behaviors than face-to-face work,"[15] in my mind, it is more a matter of degree than difference.

These key virtual intelligence skills overlap significantly with the same lawyer effectiveness factors that transcend assignment. Essentially, by moving some or all class interactions outside of the physical classroom, students are forced to develop enhanced skills and behaviors in the areas employers routinely cite as most valuable, yet least developed, in law graduates—things like diligence, flexibility, active listening, relationship building, attention to detail, and executive functioning, among many others. When interacting virtually, "social interactions—including etiquette, cooperation, conflict management styles, and other interactional behaviors—must be made *more explicit* than they would in a comparable face-to-face interaction."[16]

Thus, breaking out of the classroom is a kind of forcing function for both faculty and students. Succeeding in law school virtually will require virtual intelligence. And virtual intelligence, in turn, requires individuals to engage expertly in, among other things: traditional project management tasks like setting goals, deliverables, and milestones, and meeting deadlines; conventional social engagement like demonstrating enthusiasm and developing ways to overcome communications hurdles[17]—technical or otherwise; and taking actions to earn both "ability-based trust, such as demonstrat-

13. Larson & Makarius, *supra* note 11.

14. Barbara Z. Larson & Erin E. Makarius, *Changing the Perspective of Virtual Work: Building Virtual Intelligence at the Individual Level*, 31 Acad. Mgmt. Perspectives 159, 161–64 (2017).

15. Larson & Makarius, *supra* note 11.

16. Larson & Makarius, *supra* note 14, at 161 (emphasis added).

17. *Id.*

ing competence on tasks and highlighting skills,"[18] and "relational trust from others through active participation and timely responses, in-depth feedback, open communication, delivering agreed results, and cooperative behavior."[19]

In sum, virtual delivery will enhance our ability to teach fundamental professional skills—because their significance, and the challenge of their mastery, are heightened in a virtual environment. And there is no better way to teach virtual intelligence than virtually. Online or partially online courses, and the challenges inherent in virtual interactions, provide an ideal environment to create immersive working conditions in which students are required to be more autonomous and self-directed—more virtually intelligent and more practically effective.

## IV. Not Every Course Can Be a Simulation—Or Can It?

I have given much thought to whether we can simulate the working world through the structure—not the content or categorization—of our traditional courses. And I believe not only that we can, but that we can do even more effectively when we move interactions online.

Virtual classes, or classes with at least some number of virtual interactions, by their nature require clear expectation management, deadlines, division of labor, autonomy, and resourcefulness. They require that students become experts at giving and receiving feedback and learn to gain trust in an environment where ordinary social graces may no longer carry the day—because "judgment of ability is a more salient factor in building trust when interactions are mostly virtual, as the other kinds of cues needed for assessing benevolence and integrity are more difficult to obtain."[20]

Knowing that, we must capitalize on the challenges inherent in virtual learning to enhance our students' ability to excel in both in-person and remote interactions in the office of the future. To successfully teach virtual intelligence, and thereby improve students' skills in the areas of greatest need—those that we have historically struggled to teach because they transcend assignment or lecture—will require deliberate and strategic course planning. In particular, faculty should integrate five elements into their course design, regardless of subject:

A. Acknowledgement of the challenges inherent in the virtual environment, the existence of a practice skills gap, and the relationship between the two;

B. Clear expectations and rules of engagement;

---

18. *Id.*

19. *Id.*

20. Maria Yakovleva et al., *Why Do We Trust? Moving Beyond Individual to Dyadic Perceptions*, 95 J. Applied Psych. 79, 86 (2010).

C. Strategic opportunities for students to learn from their mistakes in critical effectiveness areas;

D. Opportunities for unsupervised peer interactions; and

E. Planned unpredictability.

The utility of this approach is not limited to virtual interactions; however, the first two considerations are particularly critical to setting the scene and earning trust in a virtual environment, while the last three are structural elements that work particularly well in virtual environments.

## A. STEP ONE: ACKNOWLEDGE THE CHALLENGES OF THE VIRTUAL ENVIRONMENT

In an online environment, trust is critical.[21] Given the challenges of law school, and the power dynamics between professor and student, it is particularly important to acknowledge that potential issues could arise when interacting virtually; the experience will be imperfect. With increased social distance comes an increased chance for miscommunication and lack of connection, and with increased use of technology comes an increased chance of technology or user error. At the same time, this is also the time to expressly discuss with students the value of becoming virtually intelligent.

This acknowledgement should be both written—in the form of an express statement in course syllabi and policies—and discussed live on day one. The precise wording is not important—what matters is that you own issues before they happen. Students need to know that when operating outside of a physical classroom, they are in a less controlled environment, meaning that things will happen—network connectivity will go down, someone will forget to mute themselves, calendar invites will omit the meeting links, and more fundamentally, people may have difficulty truly connecting with each other. But all of this is expected and acceptable, and, in fact, working through those challenges has tremendous value. In other words, acknowledging at the outset both that the experience will be imperfect and that the imperfection is among the most valuable parts of your course will go a long way toward setting the stage for success.

## B. STEP TWO: SET CLEAR EXPECTATIONS AND RULES OF ENGAGEMENT

One of the key components of virtual intelligence is establishing behavioral guidelines—related both to social relationships and task interactions.[22] This is critical in the workplace, and critical in the classroom, physical, virtual, or mixed.

---

21. Larson & Makarius, *supra* note 14.

22. *Id.* at 161.

Here, we must lead by example. Of course, some of the code of conduct seems obvious—e.g., do not expose yourself on a video conference—however, recent experience suggests even the most obvious may be worth reiterating.[23] And even more important are the less obvious things to establish, including:

- Communication Response Timelines: How quickly will you respond out of class, and how quickly do you expect students to respond to you? If a student cannot meet your response timeline, do you expect a response asking for more time?
- Work Hours: Are there any hours in which you will be "offline"?
- Modes of Communication:
  - Are you open to students "chatting" during a lecture session?
  - What is your preferred mode of communication when not in class (text, chat, email, phone call, video conference)?
- Pace and Style of Communication:
  - How, when, and what can they expect to hear from you regularly? Will you email them summaries of work weekly? Are you using a liquid syllabus? Do you have a website or bulletin board? Pick a strategy and stick with it.
- Virtual Classroom Etiquette: Do you expect students to mute themselves during lecture? Do you prefer cameras to be on? When working on collaborative documents, would you like them emailed or sent via a shared drive link? When using shared drives, how do you plan to ensure version control and document integrity?

And remember to communicate this outright—delivering results and timely responses are two key components of earning trust when working virtually.[24]

This is what they will need to do forever, and they can start right away. Then, when there are small failures, you can point to this to remind them of why those little things matter.

By establishing clear expectations, responsibilities, roles, and rules, and by following them yourself, you are setting the stage for a successful virtual working relationship but also planting the seed for students to engage in successful project management down the road.

---

23. During the COVID-19 pandemic quarantine, countless stories of employees engaging in inappropriate conduct on videoconferences—intentionally and unintentionally—emerged. *See* Joyce E.A. Russell, *The Dos and Don'ts of Video Meetings*, Forbes (Mar. 28, 2020), https://www.forbes.com/sites/joyceearussell/2020/03/28/so-now-youre-in-video-meetings-the-dos-and-donts/#36feda4112b0.

24. Larson & Makarius, *supra* note 14, at 161.

### C. STEP THREE: OPPORTUNITIES TO LEARN THROUGH ERROR

Once the ground rules have been established, the fun begins—finding ways to simulate failure in a safe way. Provide opportunities for students to make mistakes early and often—but not in terms of demonstrating substantive knowledge; rather, in terms of process, common sense, or following instructions. This step is critical because may believe that "we learn much more from failure than we do from success," particularly where we take personal ownership.[25]

Before discussing specific examples of how to do this, I should emphasize that this must be done with great care, and only after you have gained the trust of your class through acknowledging the value of imperfection, setting clear expectations and delivering upon them, and demonstrating a true investment in every student's long-term success. Before even attempting to set students up to potentially make the kind of mistakes they could make in a practice environment, a professor must 1) emphasize that particular these types of mistakes, when made in law school, are safe (and free of practical consequence); 2) expressly discuss with students the value of facing potential practical pitfalls while still in law school; and 3) "create a shared understanding, or framing, around the types of failures that employees can expect to happen at work; and reward the messenger who brings up bad news."[26]

Creating a "culture of psychological safety"[27] around failure and error can be challenging, but in the business world, when failure is assessed in a non-punitive way, it turns out that both those responsible and others around them learn—directly and vicariously, respectively.

I have a few favorite examples of how I have done this in my own legal writing class, which I have written about before.[28] Some of these examples are drawn from in-person classes, but the challenges students face when operating in a remote or virtual environment provide even greater opportunity to use this tactic.

For one, early in the semester, I provide clear requirements regarding email subject lines and formats for all assignment submissions. I tell them precisely why—that I create inbox rules to route their submissions to a folder in my email account. I also told them that failure to comply with the rule would result in their submission being skipped by my email service, and that would result in a penalty for non-submission (on minor assignments), though I would still give feedback (at least the first time).

---

25. *See* Gretchen Gavett, *When We Learn from Failure (and When We Don't)*, HARV. BUS. REV. (May 28, 2014), https://hbr.org/2014/05/when-we-learn-from-failure-and-when-we-dont (quoting A.G. Lafley).

26. *Id.*

27. *Id.*

28. I wrote about the following examples in Singh, *supra* note 1.

On the first few assignments in the fall, multiple students failed to follow these instructions. By mid-semester, I had 100% compliance. By December, when I failed to provide instructions, the class respectfully pointed out my error and asked me for them. The students had moved from learning to comply with instructions to learning to point out respectfully when I had not complied with them.

In my courses, we do this over and over again—not merely in exploring technical skills, but in real world, practical issues (often using virtual delivery mechanisms). This is never through a formal lesson and always in the background.

Another example—after setting a quick baseline for attention to detail by deliberately leaving attachments off an email and seeing how many students noticed and how they raised it (they all did), I introduced a more "lawyerly" test. Within the files I provided my students for their first written assignment was an email from a landlord to a tenant alleging lease violations, along with notice to vacate within 30 days, dated September 23, 2019.

Our course's next assignment was a supervisor email. I asked the students to email me, as their supervisor, by October 13, 2019, with the high points of their preliminary legal analysis and any anticipated issues, concerns, or things I need to be aware of that might crop up within the next two weeks. Based on my students' universal recognition of missing email attachments, I expected at least a sizable portion of the class would flag that our client would be forced to vacate their property within the next two weeks if we did not request an extension from the landlord or provide evidence that we had cured the breach.

To my surprise, not a single one did.

When asked, my students said they did not miss the issue because they had assumed we were writing on a fictional timeline—they knew we were not. They missed the issue because they missed the letter's date entirely, or they failed to take the time to calculate the date on which the client would be required to vacate.

Next up on our syllabus was a client letter. Knowing I was going to try this experiment, I had planned two different versions to follow—and I was prepared to let students in the same class write different assignments based on whether they individually had spotted the issue. In one, the student would simply have to provide a client update on timing for the legal analysis in light of the extension they requested. In the other, the student would have to take responsibility for the oversight, extend apologies, and present an action plan. I told my students that their assignment would have been shorter and easier had they identified the issue in the first instance, and they understood why it was not.

In short, I gave my students a chance to fail, and then I attempted to tie it to real-world (but not law school) consequences—in particular by demonstrating how much more (and more difficult) work could be created (for them) by this kind of oversight.

Having prepped them, I tried again.

Within another set of documents on the same assignment, in a consecutively paginated file, where each page stood alone (in other words, no sentence or section bled from one page to the next), I simply removed page 4, which contained a critical email from the client to the landlord. Reading along, no content was obviously missing, and there was nothing to indicate that the students needed additional information; however, the pagination of the file, with no blank pages, was very clear—1, 2, 3, 5, 6, 7, 8. Administrative issues like this happened regularly when I was in practice.

Surely, now that they were wise to my games, I would be flooded with questions about this, right? No.

Among all my law students presented with the record, not one flagged the missing page 4. In fact, after two weeks had passed, when I flagged the omission for them, all but one said they did not even notice it. The one who reported that he had noticed said he thought it was a typo and did not want to raise it to me.

This works in any class.

Request that students bring something to a lecture session—it does not matter what it is. It could be the casebook supplement or a hat. Ask them to hold it up. A colleague and I were lamenting the professionalism of students recently, and I shared the types of exercises I use to test following instructions. The next day, he ran an experiment, asking students in a large doctrinal class to bring the case book supplement to class. Upon arrival, he asked students to raise their supplement if they brought it. He told me he also found that fewer than 50% had done so. Following his experiment, I asked my students how things were going—and they said good, but reported that their "whole class was chastised by [this professor]." When I asked why, they said "for the same reason you did—we did not do what he asked, and it was something easy." It stuck with them.

You can just as easily ask them to do something for a virtual class—change their screen name for a virtual lecture, text you something, or save a document to a shared drive. Simple is fine—you will be surprised how many students will not follow simple instructions the first few times. And these failures need not be attached to points or grades; in fact, I find they are most successful when they are targeted instead at student's own desire to succeed, and to learn what it takes to be an effective lawyer. Rather than creating external pressure or consequence, the idea is to nurture *internal accountability*. If done right, these small, nearly cost-free failures yield big teaching gains and provide an easy fix for a problem that has persisted for far too long.

## D. STEP FOUR: UNSTRUCTURED PEER ENGAGEMENT

We know that students' virtual attention spans will be short, so by allowing for more interactions to take place asynchronously in smaller chunks with smaller cohorts, we can address that issue and also give our students more independence and more freedom than ever before. Exercises that we might have previously used with students sitting in a classroom, on a clock, with us hovering nearby, should now be self-scheduled, done with impartial information that requires resourcefulness, and in breakout groups with their peers that require expert negotiation, conflict resolution, and interpersonal skills. When they run into speedbumps in these independent engagements, we can test how they persevere. What do they report back? What do they resolve themselves? When do they think they may give up? Less work directly under our watchful eyes empowers students to take control of their own education.

By breaking out of the physical classroom and asking for more asynchronous, small group virtual work, you can also test students' ability to coordinate information: "successful virtual workers coordinate information to make sure that everyone with whom they interact has the same information (e.g., ensuring that information is evenly distributed and that technical problems don't get in the way of the message) and is interpreting it in a consistent manner."[29]

Give one student a piece of information and ask them to share it with others in preparation for your next lecture—do they do so? Give another student a slightly different piece of information and ask them also to share it with others in the same small group or class. How do they come to you to clarify the inconsistency—or do they at all? Ask students to share your instructions or your feedback on their work with their peers. Do they do it? Is it clear? The idea is not to withhold information from anyone, but to test their ability to handle teamwork and ambiguity. Ultimately, you as the professor will share the information, instructions, or feedback with everyone (and will do so well before they need it). But first, you have an opportunity to teach them critical skills they will need when working with busy supervisors or teams spread across the globe.

What kinds of exercises work for this? Peer reviews of written work. Group oral presentations. Collaboration on document or a response to professor questions. In other words, the sky is the limit, but the beauty of going beyond the physical classroom is that we can create a controlled experiment in what seems like an uncontrolled environment.

## E. STEP FIVE: PLANNED UNPREDICTABILITY

This final step is perhaps the most important, and the most fun. Breaking out of the physical classroom means we can break free from predictable, time-and-space-bound interactions and allow students to navigate challenges like scheduling and negotiating with others. In fact, perhaps "class time" does not (or should not) exist—it is a continuum. Just like work no longer stops at the office door, creating unpredictability allows us to ask our students to set their own boundaries, be self-disciplined, and manage their work like a professional. They will need to be flexible and adaptable, comfortable with ambiguity and uncertainty, and resilient.

---

29. Larson & Makarius, *supra* note 14, at 161.

This is where we can really emulate the office. In every course, this may take a different form, but the result is the same. Students should become comfortable that the sands may shift under their feet. This can be accomplished in three principal ways: first, we can change logistics; second, we can change substance; and third, we can change mode of communication.

In terms of logistics, this is simple enough—reschedule deadlines, change reading assignments, or change the order of written work. When done well, student evaluations reveal they appreciate this, as when you have trust and have set expectations, they understand that this realism promotes greater flexibility and tests their ability to prioritize. To ensure success, professors should make reasonable changes, communicate the changes with empathy and clarity, and allow for students to engage in professional communication where they believe that the modifications are unreasonable or unclear. On this last point, if you explain how the work they have already done will further the new approach and how learning to pivot to address emerging issues is realistic, I have found that students are excited to shake things up.

In terms of substance, change the facts students are thinking about. Maybe withhold a fact or insert an intervening act? If you have the trust of your students, this will not seem like hiding the ball; fail to get that trust early on, and this will not work.

Concretely, how do you break out of the physical class? As just one example, the afternoon before an evening deadline, or a few hours before class, send them a "voicemail" asking them not to submit yet or to be prepared to discuss because there is new information.

As for the final tactic—changing a mode of communication, after completing written work product, you could tell them they will have to convert their analysis to a PowerPoint to share with the class via a video conference. Or rather than preparing to answer questions in class as originally described, they will need to record a video summary with a partner virtually and upload it for the class to review for later discussion.

Remember—and remind your students, the stakes in law school are low. But these scenarios are real and will prepare them for the higher-stakes office environment.

## V. Conclusion

In sum, by moving beyond the physical classroom, students will have the opportunity to work with their colleagues and their professors in ways that challenge them to develop the skills they will need in the workforce, and professors have the opportunity to structure courses in a way that will promote the learning of virtual intelligence, thereby developing more effective lawyers.

EIGHTEEN

# Transforming Your Physical Space into an Online Space

Antonia Alice Badway Miceli*

After reviewing this chapter, readers will be able to:

- Conduct a complete inventory of resources available in their physical space that need to be adapted for an online format;
- Select an online platform that is capable of providing those resources online;
- Make a plan for transforming their physical space into an online space;
- Advise students on how to create a safe, dedicated physical learning environment for law school studies and bar exam preparation;
- Advise students on how to create a schedule that allows for appropriate law school study, time to refresh, and self-care; and
- Advise students on strategies to stay actively engaged in both synchronous and asynchronous online classes.

Shifting from an in-person delivery of an academic support and bar examination preparation program to an online model brings new opportunities—new ways of providing student support, developing relationships with colleagues and students, expanding access to your program, and improving efficiency within your program. However, this shift also requires that you determine how best to deliver personal interactions with students and with your fellow faculty and staff members. Moreover, you have to find digital mechanisms to deliver the supplements, handouts, and other common information that are readily at the fingertips of your students when they visit a physical space within the law school.

* J.D., M.P.H. Professor, Director of Academic Support and Bar Examination Preparation, Saint Louis University School of Law. Professor Miceli began law teaching in 2011 and began teaching courses and workshops online in 2020. She has designed and taught synchronous and blended courses and workshops.

This chapter provides concrete steps for faculty and staff to take when shifting academic support and bar support programs from a physical space to an online environment.[1] It also provides recommendations for guiding students in making their successful shift from the physical classroom to an online learning environment in any course.

## I. Making a Successful Transition to the Online Environment—A Guide for Faculty and Staff

### A. STEP ONE: TAKE AN INVENTORY OF YOUR CURRENT PHYSICAL RESOURCES

For faculty and staff, the first step in translating physical space into an online presence is to identify what your physical space entails, both for you and your students. Depending on your program, physical space can range from a single person's office to an entire suite of offices and library shelves.

#### 1. In-person classes and meetings

Perhaps the most common resource provided in your physical space is the opportunity to meet with you in-person. These in-person meetings take a variety of forms. You may teach a class to a group of students, possibly arriving early and staying after to meet with students and answer questions. You may hold drop-in office hours where you leave your office door open. You may hold confidential appointments, where the door needs to be shut, to protect the confidential nature of information shared within the meeting, or to allow the student to be vulnerable and express emotions about their law school experience. Identifying *all* of the different types of in-person interactions is essential to evaluating platform options for providing these interactions online.[2]

---

1. For an additional discussion of moving an Academic Support Program online, see Chapter 7: *Using Blended and Online Learning Strategies to Provide Innovative Academic Support to All Students* by Susan Landrum.

2. In conducting our own inventory, we identified a variety of in-person interactions between our academic support and bar examination preparation faculty and our students. First, we offer academic support classes, information sessions, and workshops. We also conduct private, sensitive closed-door meetings between faculty and individual students and alumni regarding academic concerns or bar exam applications. We also have casual conversations with groups of students who stopped into our office space to say hello and grab a treat, which often develop into unofficial advising sessions. Lastly, our upper-division student fellows hold office hours with students, so they also need an online presence for their own student support activities, as well as for our meetings with them.

### 2. Books, printed materials, and other common information resources

Beyond in-person meetings, the next most common resource in the physical space is access to supplemental materials for students, faculty, and staff.[3] These materials may include traditional study aid books, as well as physical handouts that need to be converted into an electronic format and moved online.[4] You may also identify other common information resources that may be more efficiently provided online, such as frequently asked questions from students.[5]

## B. STEP TWO: IDENTIFY A CAPABLE PLATFORM TO UTILIZE

### 1. In-person classes and meetings

In-person classes and meetings are typically the easiest piece of the puzzle to shift online because of the adoption of online meeting platforms. Online meeting platforms may be used for online synchronous instruction, as well as to provide online office hours.

The first step in making the transition to online teaching and meetings is to create a physical teaching space in which to meet online. Just as I advise students later in this chapter, it is important for faculty and staff to identify a quiet and low-traffic area to dedicate to online interactions. A simple white sheet, or an inexpensive green screen purchased online, can be hung behind your workspace to cover up a cluttered wall of books or other life objects, removing distracting elements from your background. Using a combination of floor and reading lamps allows you to project light off both the ceiling and the wall, giving you adjustable lighting options depending on the weather outside and the time of day. With your teaching environment in place, invest in a stable internet connection, a webcam with sufficiently high resolution, and high-quality noise-canceling headphones with a microphone.

Assuming that the audience also has a stable internet connection and compatible hardware, classroom content can be presented in the same manner as in the traditional classroom, using a presentation slide deck with a shared screen or by writing on a physical or virtual white board that students can see on their screen. Screen sharing functions also allow students to share their own documents so you can review the document together, whether as part of a classroom exercise or in office hours. Most

3. In addition to our library of supplements, our physical space contained copies of commercial bar review materials so students could compare courses when making their bar preparation course selection.

4. Our physical space housed many printed handouts on topics ranging from course selection that maximizes bar exam preparedness to selecting supplements based on individual learning styles. We converted these into accessible online formats and added them to our online landing page.

5. Once we identified the many in-person communications that needed to be relocated into the online space, we also identified some common questions and answers raised to the faculty or upper-division fellows on a regular basis, which could be added to our online space.

important to office hours, online meetings allow you to maintain eye contact with the student, so the student knows that you are focused on their personal advising session.

In your physical space, students are able to wait outside of your office for their turn to meet with you, maintaining the privacy of the student currently within your office. To maintain that same level of privacy in your online office hours, be sure to enable the waiting room function on your online meeting platform. The waiting room function allows you to admit individuals to your online office one at a time, or in groups, and also allows you to keep track of how many students are waiting for you "outside" of your online office. Just as you hold regular office hours in your physical space that repeat each week, you can create recurring links to your online office hours. Alternatively, online scheduling tools are available that allow students to self-schedule meetings with you and receive an automatic invitation to the online meeting in response.

### 2. Books, printed materials, and other common information resources

Creating an online landing page for your online presence is essential for maintaining a central repository of information for your students, much like they would have in your physical space. Students often have some basic familiarity with the school's learning management software (LMS) from prior coursework, making the LMS an ideal location for your landing page.[6] As you design your landing page, be sure to make it user-friendly.[7] For example, you can use your online landing page to provide easy access to links for your office hours and online programming. Keep your audience and the purpose of each section of your online space in mind as you connect it into your online landing page.[8] And be thoughtful in how you organize your online space by breaking sections up by class year, or topic, tailoring it to specific areas of

6. Given the choice between two available LMS options, we ultimately selected an LMS that allowed for more visual elements to be incorporated into the design, which helps us to maintain the welcoming and accessible nature of our physical space within the new online model. We provide photos of ourselves and our upper-division student fellows next to links to our online office hours. We also provide photos of various supplements, to help students identify titles they had previously used and liked in our library, and perhaps could not remember by name, but could remember by appearance. Similarly, we convert flyers and other printed material from commercial bar review providers into graphics that we post to our virtual landing page, as well as provide their representatives' contact information and direct links to their websites. Despite coming into this process with a basic understanding of how to create an LMS course page, making the shift to an online program is neither fast nor easy. We gleaned many useful tricks and recommendations on how to present our information from public social media pedagogy groups. YouTube tutorials were also helpful.

7. For a more in-depth treatment of choosing and using an LMS, see Chapter 16: *A Millennial Law Professor's Guide to Learning Management Systems* by Verónica C. Gonzales-Zamora.

8. We broke our landing page into a series of different tabs, each covering one of the purposes for which a student came into our physical space. Our tabs are based on class year (1L, 2L, 3L/4L), as well as based on topic (MPRE, Bar Exam, Online Supplements, etc.). And, because the most common reason a student enters our physical space is to meet with a faculty member or upper-division fellow, we include our online office hour links directly on the main landing page.

student support.[9] Embrace this opportunity to create a more personalized experience for your students!

Building out your online presence also allows you to broaden your accessibility focus beyond traditional academic accommodation concerns to include technological, time, and space concerns.[10] Thinking outside the box about what materials and programming can become "on demand" expands access to your program to *all* students and frees up your time to grow your program in new and exciting ways.

First, explore new ways to connect your students directly to online versions of the books and supplemental materials that are available in your physical space. Start with your own school's law library to determine the full extent of online study aids available through your law library's subscriptions. For those materials that are only available in your physical space, you can create an easy and affordable digital method of checking those materials in and out, allowing you and your students to monitor the inventory of those materials from outside of the building.[11]

Second, collect and organize recordings of your past programs to post online for students to view on demand. Next, convert your tangible materials, such as handouts, into electronic form to post to your online space.[12] Make all of this an ongoing process whereby you grow and refine your collection of online materials over time, keeping material relevant and accurate.

---

9. While our physical space provides supplements and study aids which were organized by class year, our online space also allows us to organize our other resources by class year. For example, the Missouri Board of Law Examiners provides for an early character and fitness review for 1Ls that results in both an early character and fitness determination, but also money savings on an eventual bar exam application. Our online space allows us to provide students with electronic resources on this topic, including web links and an information session recording, under the 1L tab of the online space, whereas in our physical space we have to depend on person-to-person communication of this information. We are similarly able to post the recording of our Multistate Professional Responsibility Exam (MPRE) information session to the 2L and 3L/4L tabs, as well as to a new MPRE tab, so 1Ls were not left to wonder whether the information was relevant to them.

10. In addition to the resources that we make available in our physical space, our online space allows us to post a calendar of ongoing programming, provide links to the Center for Computer-Assisted Legal Instruction (CALI) academic success lessons, link directly to online study aids available through our library, provide asynchronous modules on general academic support and bar exam preparation topics for students to access year-round, provide customizable study schedules and exam schedules for students to download, and link directly to other information on the law school website, such as the 1L exam schedule and registration information.

11. We moved our borrowing procedure for supplements from a physical card catalog to an online form, which is accessed either by clicking on a web link housed in the supplements section of our online space or by scanning a QR code that we created so students could point their cell phone's camera at a flyer in our physical space to be directly routed to the online form. The online form populates a shared online spreadsheet so we can monitor inventory and due dates and contact students with overdue books via email.

12. Because we could no longer host a Bar Prep Fair helping to connect our students to the commercial bar exam preparation vendors, information about the different bar review courses became another essential resource to move online. In addition to converting our own handouts to electronic formats, we keep in contact with the corporate representatives of these companies to collect their marketing materials and make them available to our students under the bar preparation section of our online space.

While shifting your physical space to an online space takes time, the beauty of this work is that so much of it can be front loaded during the design phase. Allow yourself the time to create the first version of your online space, as well as time to have a select group of students and colleagues test this version so that you can make additions and refinements to it before rolling out your updated version to the public.[13] Your efforts to both thoughtfully design and refine your online space will result in a self-directed tool for students to support their own studies.

## II. Prioritizing Learning in an Online Space— A Guide for Your Students

### A. STEP ONE: CREATE A SAFE LEARNING ENVIRONMENT

When shifting from the physical classroom to an online learning environment, the most immediate concern for students is to create a safe physical learning environment that they can designate for their law school studies. This dedicated space is important for mental health, focus, and productivity and allows the student to physically separate law school from their home life, even when these both take place in close proximity. The smallest physical changes can make a difference. For instance, if a student must use their dining room table for both study and meals, they should consider sitting in different chairs or sitting at different spots at the table while they study than when they eat.

In selecting this dedicated study space, students should try to identify a well-lit and low-traffic space in which to work. If they share that physical space with others, the student should try to set boundaries around their workspace, whether with a door, or by using a room divider or screen. It is important that the student remind family and friends that they are still in law school, even if they are physically at home. The student might consider hanging a sign on their door and directly asking others not to disturb their studies during defined times each day, or at a minimum, when a "Do Not Disturb" sign is posted.

Once the student has identified a dedicated workspace, it is imperative that they minimize environmental distractions within that space. In the physical law school classroom, there are very few environmental distractions, other than perhaps the laptop screens of peers and the occasional accidental ring of a cell phone. Conversely, because it is unlikely that a student's designated workspace for online learning was initially designed for study and focus, it is likely to be filled with potential environmental

13. Over the course a summer, our team gathered tips on how to set up Blackboard sites to be visually appealing, we practiced sharing screens on Zoom with each other and our upper-division fellows so we could move side-by-side work to an online format, and we explored the full extent of online study aids in our law library's subscriptions. We allowed for some additions and refinements to the online space during the first few weeks of the fall semester, as we identified information that was either not contained on the online space or was proving difficult for students to locate within the site.

distractions. To assess and remediate these distractions, the student should consider what they can see and hear from their workspace.

Some aspects of the study environment are within the student's control, and these are typically the easiest to fix. First, the student should avoid choosing a workspace that is too comfortable, such as a couch or bed. These locations are too relaxing for active learning and will make it harder for the student to separate their study and home environments once the study day is complete. Instead, the student should try to replicate the law school classroom environment with a table and chair, and build in intentional breaks to stretch and move around, like they would have in moving between classes in the law school building.

Next, the student should be sure to avoid clutter and work to keep their workspace neat and tidy, limiting the items in their workspace to only those items needed during a specific study session. This will allow the student to focus on the task at hand. They must also minimize digital environmental distractions by putting their cell phone away, silencing notifications on both their phone and computer, and blocking frequently visited websites by using one of the many available website blocker tools. By cutting off their access to these digital distractions, the student removes the need to rely on their own willpower to resist the digital siren's call. Instead, the student may build digital breaks into their daily schedule, during which time they can allow themselves access to checking those devices and websites.

Students must also work to minimize internal distractions. A great tool to avoid letting their mind wander to other life tasks is to keep a notebook and pen readily available, where they can write down random thoughts that pop into their mind during a study session. By acknowledging these random thoughts and writing them down, the student can allow themselves to set such thoughts aside for the time being and commit to dealing with them later after the study session is completed.

Another useful mechanism for minimizing internal distractions is by harnessing the power of accountability. The student can create an online peer-study group, or use websites that utilize the buddy system to create short sessions of intense and distraction-free work, followed by a break, and then another short session of intense and distraction-free work. Harnessing the power of an accountability partner can reduce a student's level of internal distraction and increase their study efficiency.

Lastly, students should create a fully stocked learning environment. They should collect the necessary supplies, including water and healthy snacks, pens and pencils, tissues, etc., *before* beginning their study session. By keeping supplies readily on hand, they remove the need to take a study break to go hunting for these items, and instead can spend that time focused on their studies.

While many aspects of the study environment are within a student's control and can be prepared in advance, others may require strategies that *reduce*, rather than eliminate, distractions. For example, if the only available workspace is heavily trafficked, or is commonly associated with other activities like meals or watching the television, the student can utilize a room divider or curtain to block their line of sight and help reduce visual distractions. Additionally, if the available workspace is noisy, the student can reduce noise distractions by using noise-canceling headphones while they study.

The key to creating a safe and dedicated learning environment is for the student to take a full inventory of their planned study environment so they can prepare well in advance of its first use.

## B. STEP TWO: MANAGE TIME WISELY

While it may seem like a shift to online learning will free up time and make it easier to study for law school, how students manage this newfound freedom is extremely important for efficient and effective study. In reality, the only real thing that changes when a student shifts to online learning is that they no longer have a commute to the physical law school building. The added environmental distractions with the shift online create an even greater need for students to design a "normal" routine that they can stick to, so they don't try and squeeze in extra episode of the new Netflix show they have been binge watching and instead stay motivated and engaged in the law school experience.

First, a student should create a weekly schedule that includes time blocks for class preparation, class attendance and/or participation, and post-class synthesis of materials. The student should identify the times of the day when they are at their best and designate that time for law school study. By scheduling discrete blocks of time when they intend to study each day, the student allows themself to create a cushion between their "school" self and their "home" self.

Next, remind the student to schedule breaks. In the physical law school building, the student would have changed rooms between classes, allowing the opportunity to stand up, stretch their legs, use the restroom, and refill their water bottle. Now that the student is online, they should consider using a timer to track their designated study time and build in refreshment periods between study sessions. The student should use those transitions to stand up and stretch, talk a short walk outside, or engage in some other physical activity. Pausing to refresh will help them remain focused throughout the day.

It is also important to remind the student that this schedule need not be set in stone. Just as they would revise any written work product, they should revise their schedule as needed. The student should keep track of how long their study tasks take and note the distractions that interrupted their study so that they can eliminate those distractions moving forward.

Finally, it is important that the student not automatically recategorize their newly found free time resulting from the elimination of their commute as additional study time. The time the student saves from commuting back and forth to class should not be added to their study day but should instead be taken as free time to engage in self-care and offset the added stress that comes with online learning.

## C. STEP THREE: STAY ACTIVELY ENGAGED IN ONLINE COURSES

Whether enrolled in a synchronous, asynchronous, or blended law school class, it is imperative that students actively engage in online courses in the same, or similar, manner that they would were they in the physical law school classroom.

### 1. Synchronous online classes

A key difference between an in-person class and a synchronous law school class taught online is the background environment a student presents to professor and peers. In addition to the earlier considerations in designing a designated learning space, the student needs to consider what their professor and peers will be able to see and hear of both the student and the student's environment during class. First, the student might consider sitting with a blank wall or solid colored sheet behind them, creating a background that is both appropriate for class and also maintains the student's privacy. Next, the student should consider their space's lighting. Ideally, the student should be seen, but without a glare, so the student should consider arranging themself or their lighting source so that the lighting source is in front of them and a bit off to the side. And when in doubt, the student can perform an internet search on "How to look your best in online meetings" for a plethora of articles and videos laying out step-by-step instructions on maximizing how one looks and sounds online.

Additionally, the student should ensure that they are presenting themself in a way that is professional when communicating with their professor and peers, considering their appearance just as they might when going to the physical law school building, even if they only need to focus on what they are wearing from the waist up. It is important to remember that the student is developing professional relationships with both professors and peers. These individuals will serve as references for the student when they apply for employment and the bar exam and will likely form the basis of their smaller circle within the legal community when they step out into the profession.

Part of the student presenting themself in a professional manner is by remembering to minimize background noise when speaking during class and keeping themself muted when they are not talking. The student should also minimize their digital distractions just as they would have in the physical classroom. A good rule of thumb is that if the student wouldn't have it turned on or open during class in the physical classroom, they shouldn't have it available to themself during the online class. Instead, they should use this as an opportunity to really engage with their professor and peers, just as they would in the physical classroom.

While the student's environment and mode of class participation may change when shifting online, their class preparation and in-class note taking should not change. The student should prepare their mind for class just as they would before class in a physical classroom: reviewing their reading notes, looking at where they are in the syllabus to situate themself in the big picture of the course, and formulating questions during their reading and make predictions about why the professor assigned the reading for today's class so that they can check those predictions during class, thereby keeping themself more engaged during class. During a synchronous class, the student should take notes just as they would in the physical classroom. If the student's law school utilizes an online meeting platform that provides an option to focus solely on the person speaking, the student should set their view that mode to reduce the distraction of seeing their peers' faces and actions. It can be tempting to rely on class recordings, but remind the student that they likely won't have time to re-watch many class videos, so they should take notes just as they would have in the physical classroom where class wasn't always recorded. They might also consider trading notes with a peer or study group to create an accountability system.

Finally, the student should show up early for class, stay late, and take advantage of their professor's office hours! Just because there is not a physical space in which to congregate before and after class does not mean the student cannot use that time to build relationships with their professors and peers. The student might consider setting up an online meeting with their study group before class to help them review the material and prepare for the upcoming class session. This will help the student stay connected with both the material and other students. During class, the student should keep a running list of questions so they can follow-up after class with their professor or peers, particularly if their professor "lingers" in the online classroom to answer questions. Lastly, the student should attend their professor's office hours, whether prearranged or by appointment, which will allow the student both to ask their questions and further develop a relationship with their professor.

### 2. Asynchronous online classes

While the synchronous online class more closely resembles a traditional law school class, taking place in real time and allowing for the infamous cold calling interaction between professor and student, asynchronous online classes deviate from what students traditionally experience in law school. Rather than reading and class attendance taking up the majority of the student's time, they are likely faced with prerecorded lectures and assignments, which may include discussion board posts and responses and online formative assessment quizzes.

The first, and most important step, is for the student to familiarize themself with the technology that will be used in their class. Even if they have taken online courses prior to law school, they may not have experience with their law school's specific LMS or online meeting platform. Because the student's ability to access course materials and submit assignments will be 100% dependent upon their grasp of these programs, it is imperative that they take the time to explore them prior to the beginning of the first week of class and reach out to their school information technology support if they run into any issues.

Next, the student should review the syllabus to ensure that they understand when course materials will be released each week and when submissions are due. The student should take time to add these release dates and deadlines to their weekly schedule, and plan when they will watch prerecorded lectures. By intentionally adding these items to their weekly schedule, the student will be able to keep in mind when they are at their best during the day and optimize their ability to take in the information presented.

The remaining steps may sound familiar to the student's "old" law school life. First, just as in the physical classroom, the student should try to actively engage with the material, not just sit back and passively watch the recording. They should take notes like they would in class, but then take advantage of the online platform and hit pause to write down any lingering questions and points of confusion. A further benefit of prerecorded lectures is that the student is able to rewind and re-watch a section right away to clear up a concept or confirm their confusion so they can reach out to their professor or peers with questions. The student should also consider watching the lecture in chunks no longer than 20 minutes at a time, the average attention span for adults. However, they will need to allot more time for watching lectures than the actual run time of the recording itself in order to allow for them to actively engage in this manner.

Next, the student should synthesize each week's materials by asking themself what the big picture takeaway from this week's lecture and assignments was, and consider how this week's materials fit into what they have learned in the course. This is a great opportunity to utilize study partners or groups to compare the student's synthesized notes and make sure they didn't miss anything. This is also a chance for the student to utilize their professor's office hours, which may be their only real opportunity to interact face-to-face with their professor in an asynchronous class.

## III. Conclusion

While the move online may present some challenges, it also is an opportunity for law school faculty, staff and students to strengthen their existing programs and study methods, as well as to identify new opportunities for connection and accountability. We should all view this experience through the lens of personal growth, confident that the time and effort invested will result in long-lasting change that will create stronger, and more adaptable, legal professionals moving forward.

NINETEEN

# Using Scientific Methods for Evidence-Based Decision Making in Designing, Evaluating, and Assessing Digital Learning in the Legal Academy

Victoria Sutton*

After reading this chapter, readers will be able to:

- Summarize student perceptions about online learning during the pandemic from several studies;
- Design an appropriate research survey for your an online course;
- Develop a checklist to ensure you have met human subject testing requirements for your institution before you begin your study;
- Produce an analysis of your results; and
- Communicate the value and use of evidence-based decision making in legal education.

A Wolters Kluwer report, *The Leading Edge Report,* in a survey of forty law schools, conducted May 2014, found that there was a general "wide-scale perception that online education is worth less than on-campus education."[1] There is also confusion among the state bars about online education. Not all state bars accept the same number of

---

* Victoria Sutton, MPA, PhD, JD, is the Horn Distinguished Professor at Texas Tech University, School of Law. Prof. Sutton began law teaching in a tenure-track position in 1999 and began teaching courses online in 2012. She has designed and taught synchronous, asynchronous, and hybrid courses.

1. Wolters Kluwer, Legal Education Leading Edge Report, 2015 Edition 19 (2015). Figure 4. Response to the question: "Many law schools are considering expanding the number of online course options their students have access to. Such online courses would involve students meeting faculty 'virtually' at specified times for discussions of study materials, accessing pre-recorded lectures, and downloading assignments and papers online. Which statement best describes your law school's plans for including online courses in its curriculum?" The survey was conducted in May 2014 and was completed by 40 respondents. Of these, 36 answered this question: 19% answered "We do not plan to offer"; 67% the majority, answered, "We plan to move cautiously"; and only 14% responded, "We plan to be aggressive."

online hours, although the ABA has a standard for the maximum number of online hours.[2] Recently the New York Bar was at the center of the controversy where more than one law school in New York moved forward with offering a blended online legal education.[3] Whether all law schools' graduates would be able to sit for the New York bar exam remained in question while the law schools worked with their state bar.[4]

Until August 2020, the American Bar Association expected more from online courses than traditional courses. In a separate standard, ABA Standard 306, specifically for online courses, the ABA required demonstration of meaningful engagement with the student where that was not required in a traditional law course.[5] The ABA also required some evidence that the person doing the work was the person enrolled in the course.[6] No such demands were made for in person courses. Work being done out of class could just as easily be done by someone not enrolled in the traditional law course, as in an online course.

Then the pandemic-caused shift to online education triggered an unprecedented change in course delivery for all schools, with a movement to one hundred percent online courses in the spring of 2020. With so many faculty unprepared for online legal education, the quality of this online delivery was low according to the surveys that were administered to undergraduate students.[7] In a survey among 1,500 students at Arizona State University, the researchers identified an unanticipated result that students are 4 percentage points less likely to enroll in an online class given their experience with online instruction due to the pandemic.[8] They also cited to surveys at different universities in Washington and New York with similar findings, i.e., "75% of students are unhappy with the quality of their classes after moving to online learning due to COVID-19."[9] In the only published survey done among law students during the COVID-19 transition, a little more than one-third (35%) of students said the COVID-19 transition experience made them less inclined to take online courses and

---

2. A.B.A. Sec. Leg. Educ. & Admis. to the Bar, *Standards and Rules of Procedure* for *Approval* of *Law Schools*, Standard 311(a), (e), at 23 (2020–21), https://www.americanbar.org/content/dam/aba/administrative/legal_education_and_admissions_to_the_bar/standards/2020-2021/2020-21-aba-standards-and-rules-for-approval-of-law-schools.pdf [hereinafter 2020 ABA Standards].

3. Mark Lieberman, *States Limit Spread of Online Legal Education*, Inside Higher Ed. (Jan. 23, 2019), https://www.insidehighered.com/digital-learning/article/2019/01/23/new-york-maintains-restrictions-around-online-programs-amid.

4. *Id.*

5. A.B.A. Sec. Leg. Educ. & Admis. to the Bar, *Standards and Rules of Procedure* for *Approval of Law Schools*, Standard 306(e), at 19 (2017–18), https://www.americanbar.org/content/dam/aba/publications/misc/legal_education/Standards/2017-2018ABAStandardsforApprovalofLawSchools/2017_2018_aba_standards_rules_approval_law_schools_final.authcheckdam.pdf [hereinafter 2017 ABA Standards].

6. 2020 ABA Standards, *supra* note 2, Standard 511. (formerly 2017 ABA Standard 306(f)).

7. Esteban M. Aucejo et al., *The Impact of COVID-19 on Student Experiences and Expectations: Evidence from a Survey* (National Bureau of Economic Research Working Papers Series No. 27392, June 2020), https://www.nber.org/papers/w27392.

8. *Id.* at 8.

9. *Id.* at n.8.

about one-fifth of those said it was a bad experience they would not want to repeat in law school.[10]

Online learning is continuing to go through transformations during each phase of the pandemic, and it is unlikely that the pandemic will leave us where it found us. Online learning has made an indelible mark on legal education and it is likely going to continue to expand as a platform. Faculty have responded from two schools of thought. Despite the emergency transition, many law professors have risen to the challenge and taken the opportunity to improve their teaching and online skills, and some will choose to continue to teach online once we are in the post-pandemic recovery phase. Many law professors seem to hope this will just go away and plan a return to pre-pandemic practices in the post-pandemic phase, as they deride any talk that online learning could offer new pedagogical opportunities for teaching law.

Given these tensions, it is clear that more than ever, law schools need good data for decision making about online legal education. But evidence-based decision making has yet to reach the legal academy in other than two important measures: marketing and bar passage rate, those often overlapping. So empirical research has been focused on marketing which is of utmost importance to law schools;[11] as well as data collection on bar passage rate. This also includes data related to data collected for the all-important benchmark of the U.S. News and World Report ranking of law schools each year. Any other type of decision making, including decisions about online learning, has been decided by relying on opinion. "The loudest voice in the room" has literally been the way that legal education decisions have been made. (Visit any faculty meeting at a law school if you have any doubt of this.)

## I. Evidence-based Decision Making as a Tool for Legal Education

Evidence-based decision making is simply using quality data and research to make decisions, rather than relying purely on opinion-based decision making. Opinion could be based on decades of experience in law teaching, reputation of the school, interests of the faculty, and technological resources. All of these are valid considerations. However, opinions concerning the value of online learning in law, the effectiveness of online learning, or such things as getting to know your students enough to be able to advise them and teach them are all factors that can be measured quantitatively. That kind of critical information should not be reduced to "what I have heard is . . ." for decision making that affects the future of your law school.

---

10. Victoria Sutton, *Law Student Attitudes about their Experience in the COVID-19 Transition to Online Learning* (July 31, 2020) (unpublished manuscript) (on file with the author), https://ssrn.com/abstract=3665712.

11. *See generally* Christopher Ryan, *Analyzing Law School Choice*, 2020 U. Ill. L. Rev. 583 (2020).

Another important reason to use evidence-based decision making is to invest resources wisely in programs and processes that are effective for student learning. For example, a law school may be surprised that no improvement was made in bar passage rate after investing resources in an online bar preparation course. Only later, you might discover that, if you had surveyed the students about their opportunities and obstacles, you might have found that 60% of them had little or no internet access during the critical two months before the bar examination and, therefore, could not utilize the pricey bar preparation investment.[12]

Evidence-based education is used extensively in medical education as well as other areas of practice, very effectively. In federal education policy and law, there are statutory requirements to create an environment for evidence-based education.[13] The Wing Institute, a non-profit organization dedicated to evidence-based decision making in education, identifies three critical legal mandates for using evidence-based decision making:

- The Every Student Succeeds Act (ESSA) contains over 100 references to using evidence from "scientifically-based research" contains over 100 references to using evidence from "scientifically-based research";
- The Education Sciences Reform Act (ESRA) of 2002 was enacted "to provide for improvement of Federal education research, statistics, evaluation, information, and dissemination." ESRA established the Institute of Education Sciences (IES) within the Department of Education; and
- The Individuals with Disabilities Education Act (IDEA) requires schools to use "effective research-based" programs.[14]

The use of evidence-based decision making for business is firmly established as critical to management. The International Standards Organization has set a standard for evidence-based decision making, which is one of the seven principles for a quality management system (QMS) in the business sector. This standard, ISO 9001:2015,[15] requires review of systems based on data, continuation of monitoring processes, and quality data collection for that purpose.[16] This would be an excellent principle for legal education to consider as a process.

---

12. *See* Kim Schildkamp, *Data-Based Decision-Making for School Improvement: Research Insights and Gaps*, 61:3 Educ. Res. 257 (2019).

13. *Evidence-Based Education*, The Wing Inst., https://www.winginstitute.org/evidence-based-education-overview (last visited Nov. 19, 2020).

14. *Id.*

15. ISO 9001:2015 is an internationally recognized standard for creating, implementing, and maintaining a Quality Management System for a company.

16. Mark Hammer, *Seven Quality Management Principles behind ISO 9001 Requirements*, 9001 Acad. (Feb. 4, 2014), https://advisera.com/9001academy/blog/2014/02/04/seven-quality-management-principles-behind-iso9001-requirements/.

One of the problems that has been cited as to why evidence-based decision making is not used more often in the broad field of education is the complaint that not enough is available, and there is no culture of using evidence-based decision making to make decisions in education.[17] So the need to develop a body of research and a process and culture of collection of data in legal education is important. It is now particularly important to measure the effectiveness and the environment for online legal education. The context of the pandemic transition makes the need more immediate.

## II. Developing a Culture of Research in Legal Education

There is a need to develop a body of research for online legal education from which law schools can draw quality data for evidence-based decision making. This was never more clear to me than when preparing for teaching online in 2016. As a scientist (as well as a lawyer) who has done research, I first looked for existing research to give me more insight into how to design and teach law online. There was a significant amount of research on online teaching in undergraduate and other graduate education, but nothing published on teaching law online. It is no surprise then, that in the complete void of research, truisms were just repeated that online education does not work for teaching the law.

Because of the complete lack of published research, I read what I could from existing research for online teaching for undergraduates. For example, video lectures should be no more than five to seven minutes long for teaching online. I also sought out others who had taught law online, but the oversight from the ABA and the competitive nature of law schools prevented this free exchange of scientific information.

I next designed my course as close to the Socratic method as possible online, and at the same time, designed a survey tool to measure and assess the effectiveness of teaching law online. So, in 2016, I would begin to build a body of research in the field of legal education, and I would have to write the first article.[18]

Currently, I am pleased to observe that the body of scientific research about measurements of legal education online is growing, but too slowly. More faculty should be doing their own surveys for publication and, if necessary, teaming with another faculty member from colleges of statistics or education where these types of analyses are part of their body of research. The culture of doing research is also important to build by asking questions about your course effectiveness as you are building it and by thinking about how to measure the success of your teaching tools. Grades are good indicators, but they do not always demonstrate effectiveness.

---

17. *Evidence-Based Education*, *supra* note 13.

18. *See* Victoria Sutton, *Asynchronous, E-Learning in Legal Education: A Comparative Study* (August 5, 2016) (unpublished manuscript) (on file with the author), https://ssrn.com/abstract=2819034.

We are designing and teaching online courses on the bleeding edge of legal education due to the pandemic transitions, so we are in a unique position to think and know what should be evaluated.

## III. The Legal Professoriate is Building a Body of Research on Online Legal Education

What is different between publishing scientific research and legal scholarship?

There is a difference. In legal scholarship, we strive to develop original thinking, analysis and observation about an old case, or about a new one. We neither have to reconcile our analyses with previous published articles written on the same subject nor do we have to explain why we are deviating from previous observations.

However, in scientific research, it is imperative to understand the field enough to be able to identify supporting research and to build your research as the next logical step from that research. A literature search must be done in similar scientific research, and researchers must cite all previous research that is in that line of research. It must be explained carefully if your research or methods deviate from that practiced and accepted in the field of science. Those explanations are quantitative and qualitative descriptions of the foundational research. At this point, in our building of the body of scientific research, almost all research is new and novel with very little to build upon. However, you still must find previous research from other fields to bridge the scientific underpinnings so important to the culture of the science. We, the legal academy, must learn the scientific process of building research on previous research to make this research valid, relevant, and useful.

It must become important to ask questions about whether programs, curriculum changes, or course-delivery methods are actually effective. The art of inquiry is then to design questions to get at the answers to your effectiveness questions. This process is not too unlike developing questions for a deposition or drafting interrogatories, so law professors will have a natural talent for this kind of inquiry.

Let us consider how you might start. You have designed a new online course, and you would like to use several formative assessments throughout the course, as well as the traditional final examination. So, for example, as you design the course, you might develop survey questions for the students in your course about how effective they thought formative assessment "x" was in the course. That is a very direct question. To test that you are getting an accurate answer and the student is not simply anticipating the answer you want to draw from them, you might include a ranking question to list the formative assessments in the order of their effectiveness. The student may have responded that the tool was very effective, but in the ranking you may find it was the least effective of other formative assessments, for example. A third question about how satisfied are they with taking this course online could be asked using a Likert scale (e.g., ranking 1 to 5, least to greatest) giving you a third data point for that respondent about factors that could influence their responses. If you triangulate those three responses from that student you will see if the results of your formative assessment "x" may have been ranked low, or found ineffective by those who simply disliked having courses online. With that information you may decide to separate the responses and view only those who ranked their satisfaction with taking a course online as a 3 and above, to eliminate the influence of generally disliking online learning to better assess your formative assessment tool.

One of the questions that proved very discriminating in my survey during the pandemic transition in April 2020 was whether the student thought too much or too little was being done by the government and the university in response to the pandemic. Correlating these responses with the responses from the question as to whether the student thought they were getting progressively better during the semester with online learning, a large percentage of the students who said online learning was not getting better for them over time, also thought too much was being done by the government and the university in response to the pandemic.[19] This helped identify a substantial factor that influenced whether they felt online learning was not getting better over time.

## IV. The Research Process—Research Design

How do you build this body of research? You have designed your course, and so you are in the research design phase as you develop your first draft of questions that test what you want to assess about your course. Research designs fall into two categories: experimental and quasi-experimental. Both types are valid research designs but require knowing how to analyze each type.[20]

As you continue with the research design phase, you will also need to identify who you will survey. In this case, you will be surveying all the members of your course, and that number is designated as "n." So your n = the number of students in your course.

The research design that we have discussed so far is a simple case study where you are using one case—your course in one semester—to make observations. You may want to go further with your research and plan for more observations.

For example, thinking about the long term for your research design, you may want to continue this survey from year to year in the same course and compare the results. You would then have a "time-series"[21] where you keep all of the other factors the same except time. Then you can make a valid comparison over time. You can determine how students change or if they change over time. However, you may want to alter your

19. Sutton, *supra* note 10.

20. *See* Donald T. Campbell & Julian C. Stanley, Experimental and Quasi-Experimental Designs for Research (1963). This is the classic reference for research design in social sciences, and the designs discussed in this section are from this source.

21. A time-series design is intended to demonstrate trends or changes over time. Unlike the interrupted time-series design, its purpose is not to examine the impact of an intervention, but simply to explore and describe changes.

course assessments after learning from the first survey analysis (the intervention) and then plan to test the revised course assessments the next year to see how they compare. This research design is often categorized as a quasi-experimental design because they may have smaller sample sizes and have other factors that may affect the outcome, like the change in the course from year to year. This would be a comparative design where you compare "like" groups. This is also considered a valid research design as long as you explain in your qualitative analysis how the changes in your course assessments affected the outcome.

Another research design you might like to use is the pre-test, post-test design. Law professors may already use a similar method to ask students questions that foreshadow the questions that will be answered during the course. You might want to use this for a substantive analysis of what they have learned in the course, or you might want to use it to measure perception of how they considered online learning before and then at the end of your course, for example. In the analysis, the qualitative explanations about what changed and even additional comments in the survey tool to explain their responses can be used.

You may want to use the case study and leave open the possibility of a time-series to do the survey again next year. Keep in mind, you will have to notify your university's Institutional Review Board (IRB) for any subsequent uses of the survey.

### RESEARCH DESIGNS

| Experimental | Quasi-Experimental |
|---|---|
| • Case Study (qualitative description)<br>• Time Series (changes over time) | • Post-test only, pre-post (improvements from intervention)<br>• Comparison groups (compare like groups)<br>• Explanatory Case Study (evaluate progress and explore contributions to success or failure) |

## V. The Research Process—The Survey Period

You will likely wait until the end of the semester and after the final examination to send your survey. It is not considered unethical to offer a small reward for completing a survey like a $5 gift card. However, it is not necessary to offer anything except a thank you.

At the beginning of the semester you will want to contact your university's IRB to notify them that you plan to do research involving human subjects. Any research involving human subjects must be reviewed by the IRB to not only comply with federal regulations but also to be published. You will not be able to publish your research in a reputable journal if you do not obtain clearance from your IRB for your research. That said, it is likely that this will be considered low risk to the human subjects and you will be able to proceed. Note that your research is not "approved" it is simply cleared to move forward.

To summarize, your research process steps include: your research design; your survey questions; and your identification and selection of your sample. Now you are prepared for the survey at the end of the semester. You must document well the conduct of the survey and the dates when students are surveyed. In survey methodology, you should set up your survey so that you can follow up once or twice with students who have not responded.

## A. THE RESEARCH PROCESS—ANALYSIS

The analysis part of your research should be both quantitative and qualitative. Quantitative analysis would include statistical analysis that might use regression analysis and any correlations among factors that you make. This part may require the assistance of a co-researcher or assistant who is skilled in statistical analysis. Here, you would use objective measures in your data to make observations about causation, explain confounding variables, and explain any threats to internal validity. This means that you need to identify anything that would affect the results and explain it, using the data. For example, if during the semester, a complete shutdown due to pandemic measures interrupted the course in some way, you would need to explain how or if this affected the results in the survey by using the data.

Confounding variables are important to examine. A confounding variable is a "third variable," or variables that the researcher failed to control or eliminate, damaging the internal validity of an experiment. For example, assume you are using the final examination scores as a measure of the course success in learning. But you think final examination scores are affected by hours of sleep, and the biggest university sports event of the year was the night before your final examination. In that case, you may want to survey the students about how many hours of sleep they had the night before the final examination because that might affect your use of exam scores as a measure, threatening the internal validity of that research. If you find that the number of hours correlates positively with the exam grades—that is, the more sleep (up to 8 hours) that students had the night before the exam, the higher the exam grade—you will have data points that are not in a perfect line. However, the closer these fall into a perfect correlation, the more you can conclude sleep was a confounding factor. Another example of a possible confounding factor might be the number of hours studying for the exam. That might not be accounted for in your use of exams as a measure, and you would want to survey students to eliminate that factor as a confounding factor to the validity of using exam scores as a measure of successful online learning.

This part of the analysis also requires understanding the effect of the number of respondents in your survey and whether you can draw any statistically significant conclusions from your survey. Typically, you need large sample sizes to find statistically significant conclusions, but there are techniques for small sample sizes. Statistically significant conclusions are stated with a confidence level[22]—that is, at what confidence level can I make these statistically significant conclusions? A confidence level of 95% is typically considered a reliable conclusion, but you can certainly discuss any findings at any level but without relying on them as conclusive.

In the qualitative part of your analysis, you will be able to use narrative to explain your findings. Normally, with your small sample sizes, you will not be able to make more than observations about percentages in responses. Here, you will have an opportunity to explain your findings in a narrative form in the qualitative part of your analysis. You will want to explain any "causation," which has a similar meaning in law as it does in statistics, and the causation can be explained qualitatively. For example, you might conclude that responses that 40% of students had unreliable internet would likely contribute to the cause of how they felt about online learning. Be wary of "false correlations," which correlate two factors that make it seem like one caused the other factor to occur. The classic example of a false correlation is to look at the number of storks born in Germany and the number of babies born in Germany. The number of both rise in the spring together, suggesting the theory about storks delivering babies is true! Take care to question your own conclusions about correlations when they have no other reason to be true other than they happen to correlate.

Confounding variables are another reason to ask demographic questions at the beginning or end of each survey. Questions about gender, year in law school, and age are all important categories that can help identify threats to internal validity. For example, if you find that 10% of your students have childcare duties and you use the gender data to correlate with that question, you may find that 90% of those students with childcare duties identify as female. That would be part of your qualitative analysis and perhaps recommendations.

## B. RESEARCH DESIGN—CONCLUSIONS AND RECOMMENDATIONS

Just like any article, research needs conclusions. You may also feel strongly about recommendations and that is appropriate for a research article. Your conclusions should stay closely with the data and qualitative analysis that you made based on your data collection and analysis. Any explanations for confounding variables that were considered to ensure internal validity of your research should also be mentioned.

---

22. The confidence level tells you how sure you can be. It is expressed as a percentage and represents how often the true percentage of the population who would pick an answer lies within the confidence interval. The 95% and the 99% confidence levels mean you can predict this will be the outcome at a 95% or 99% level, respectively.

Finally, making recommendations in the context of online learning is certainly important and it will likely help your readers.

Publication of your research may be challenging since our journals are designed for law review-type articles. Even the flagship journal of the legal academy has failed to recognize the important of empirical research about online learning and for all of its notice of a peer-review process, it actually lacks any peer-reviewers for empirical research and has not attempted to find them when they needed them. So there is a need for a journal in the legal academy to be a depository for this kind of research, or continue to use SSRN as a place where research that is immediately important can be made available in a fraction of the time of a journal publication. This research is in the category of legal education and is frequently read and downloaded. In the first few months of making my research on law students' attitudes about online learning during the COVID-19 transition, it was a top ten download in that category for weeks. Having your research read and hopefully used should begin to take on significance for academic publication in law schools.

## VI. Conclusion

Please do research. Designing research that is publishable is important to build a body of research so that evidence-based decision making can be part of the better use of resources for law schools. The pandemic has presented unprecedented opportunities to do research on teaching law online, and it should be a springboard to continue doing research in a post-pandemic world. It is important that you share your valuable insights from your teaching and observations that can be quantified to demonstrate or test effectiveness to add to the body of research. Please be mindful of the need to build on previous research and remember to cite to the few foundational research articles that have been published on online legal education. It is not just a citation credit for the authors but enhances your own research as scientific research. When we create this culture of research and using that research as evidence-based decision making, only then will we replace the loudest voice in the room with reasoned scientific analysis in evidence-based decision making.

SECTION THREE

# The First Year Curriculum

TWENTY

# A Whole New Meaning to Cybercrimes: Teaching Criminal Law and Procedure in an Online Learning Environment

Tonya Krause-Phelan*

This chapter will provide professors with:

- A brief description of active learning and its importance in legal education;
- A brief distinction between synchronous and asynchronous course content;
- A summary of several science-based teaching techniques and learning concepts that can be integrated and implemented effectively into online Criminal Law and Procedure courses;
- Course design overviews for both Criminal Law and Procedure that break the course content into asynchronous, synchronous, and assessment categories; and
- Examples of active learning exercises and activities that use scientifically-backed teaching techniques and learning strategies.

On the one hand, most Criminal Law and Procedure professors[1] consider themselves fortunate to teach courses that cover inherently interesting topics. Most students have been exposed to the subject matter before attending law school, which enhances classroom discussions. On the other hand, students often mistake their level of interest and familiarity with the subjects as having knowledge, understanding, and mastery of the material.

To combat the students' false sense of security and to ensure that students engage in a way that allows them to learn the material, Criminal Law and Procedure professors

* Professor, Western Michigan University—Cooley Law School. Professor Krause-Phelan began law teaching in 2005. She began teaching courses synchronously and asynchronously online in 2014.

1. I am assuming two separate, required courses.

have long incorporated supplemental sources such as movies, literature, song lyrics, music videos, instructional videos, and various legal documents into their course design. Similarly, professors have historically used role-playing, mock trial, and advocacy exercises to help students synthesize the course content and apply the material in a way that fosters more in-depth learning. These types of auxiliary teaching aids provide students with an active learning platform. Active learning helps students use the substantive material they are learning in a practical way.

Having practiced as a criminal defense lawyer before becoming a professor, I instinctively included these types of activities in my course design. Once a professor, I quickly learned that I needed to be concerned not just with my teaching techniques but also with my students' learning. As a result, I began to learn about learning. In doing so, I refined my use of active learning techniques and began to intentionally integrate scientifically-backed teaching techniques and learning strategies into my course design. Many of these techniques and exercises were originally designed for the physical classroom. As learning management systems (LMS) and technology improved, I modified many of these activities for online use.

As law schools move more courses outside the physical classroom, professors are exploring effective ways to deliver legal education in the non-physical learning environment.

With some planning, deliberate course design, and integration of innovative teaching techniques and strategies, professors can provide a creative and effective online learning environment.

## I. Preliminary Considerations for Online Course Design

For both Criminal Law and Procedure, the course design concepts discussed in this chapter are based on a fourteen-week term, with exams administered in the fifteenth week.[2] Active learning as well as scientifically-backed teaching techniques and learning strategies are integrated into each week's asynchronous and synchronous material.

### A. ACTIVE LEARNING: AN ESSENTIAL BUILDING BLOCK

Active learning lies at the core of the course overviews and summaries discussed in this chapter. Gerry Hess, a leader in modern legal education and former director of the Institute for Law Teaching and Learning, defines active learning "[a]s anything

2. Each of the fourteen classes are taught once per week in three-hour blocks, with a ten-minute break after each fifty minutes of instruction. Per ABA Standard 310, it is expected that students will do two hours of work outside the classroom for every credit hour. A.B.A. Sec. Leg. Educ. & Admis. to the Bar, *Standards and Rules of Procedure* for *Approval* of *Law Schools*, Standard 310 (2020–21), https://www.americanbar.org/content/dam/aba/administrative/legal_education_and_admissions_to_the_bar/standards/2020-2021/2020-21-aba-standards-and-rules-for-approval-of-law-schools.pdf.

beyond listening to lecture."[3] Proven benefits of active learning include providing increased opportunities for students to develop and improve skills, fostering students' higher-order thinking, engaging students in activities and exercises, and providing opportunities for students to explore their own attitudes and values.[4]

According to research, "active learning methods are especially effective for student learning when compared to classes that primarily consist of lecturing."[5] In other words, active learning provides opportunities for students to *do something* with the learning material rather than passively *listen to something* about the learning material. When engaged in active learning, students *use* the information to solve problems.[6]

Active learning also allows course content to be broken up into smaller, digestible segments. When active learning exercises are interwoven into the course design, students use, apply, and reflect on what they are learning as they are learning it. These real-time active learning opportunities lead to deeper learning[7] as well as deeper retention of the material.[8]

In the traditional in-person classroom, many opportunities exist for active learning, such as small group exercises, mock trials, motions and other advocacy exercises, document preparation, and assessments. These all immerse students in active learning. Most of these activities can easily be conducted online as well. Keeping students engaged with active learning is even more important in an entirely online setting when students can turn off their cameras and disengage, encounter environmental distractors, or struggle with service accessibility.

Integrating active learning opportunities into the online setting will necessarily revolve around the Learning Management System (LMS) and audio-visual conferencing platforms. Many common audio-visual conferencing platforms provide a live-streaming chat function that runs on the side or bottom of the screen throughout the entire meeting. Students can comment, ask questions, or answer questions posed by the professor in real time. While it can be challenging to monitor the chat box while also trying to conduct class and share other course content, professors can maximize the benefits of this tool by tasking their teaching assistants, or a student if a teaching assistant is unavailable, to serve as the chat moderator. This tool is also particularly effective to conduct a quick, informal polls.

---

3. Kenneth R. Swift, *The Seven Principles for Good Practice [Asynchronous Online] Legal Education*, 44 Mitchell Hamline L. Rev. 105, 114 (2018) (citing Gerald F. Hess, *Principle 3: Good Practice Encourages Active Learning*, J. Leg. Educ. 401 (1999)).

4. Hess, *supra* note 3 (citing Michael P. Ryan & Gretchen G. Martens, Planning a College Course: A Guidebook for the Graduate Teaching Assistant 2 (1989)).

5. *Active Learning*, Center for Teaching Innovation, Cornell University, https://teaching.cornell.edu/teaching-resources/engaging-students/active-learning (last visited Nov. 19, 2020).

6. Paul L. Caron & Rafael Gely, *Taking Back the Law School Classroom: Using Technology to Foster Active Student Learning*, 54 J. Leg. Educ. 551, 552–53 (2004).

7. Hess, *supra* note 3, at 402 (citing William M. Timpson & Paul Bendel-Simso, Concepts and Choices for Teachers: Meeting Challenges in Higher Education 101–02, 110 (1996)).

8. *Id.*

These audio-visual platforms also provide the ability to create and host breakout rooms where students can engage in small group exercises. Breakout room functions are particularly efficient and allow professors, with a few keystrokes, to divide the class into a set number of groups, monitor each breakout room, and automatically bring students back to the main classroom when students finish the exercise. In the event the platform available to the professor does not host breakout rooms, setting up individual meetings through the institution's portal or calendaring systems for each group might serve as a suitable alternative.

## B. SYNCHRONOUS AND ASYNCHRONOUS COURSE CONTENT

Online classes provide students with learning material in two basic forms: asynchronous and synchronous content. These two forms are similar in that both are offered online and students can access the course content from anywhere. However, there are some important differences between the two formats to keep in mind when designing your online course.[9]

Asynchronous course content gives students material they can access and complete on their own time and in their own space. The instructor sets parameters regarding what the student is expected to do with the material and when they are expected to complete assigned tasks.[10] Synchronous material, on the other hand, involves classes that occur at set times. Synchronous courses involve the students and the teacher being in the same place at the same time, whether in a physical classroom or a virtual classroom.[11]

Starting with asynchronous material, instructors can use this format to enhance students' understanding of the assigned material *before* meeting in the synchronous setting. Common ways to provide asynchronous material prior to class include flipped recordings, presentation slides,[12] guided questions or worksheets, discussions board prompts, and short low-to-no stake assessments. While no set rule exists regarding when asynchronous material should be posted, it is better to give students access to the material with as much time as possible prior to the class in which the content will be used. Doing so promotes student accountability and student learning.[13]

Traditional reading assignments will remain a bedrock feature of law school course design. In addition to the parameters of ABA Standard 310, professors are encour-

---

9. *See generally* Michele Pistone, *Law Schools And Technology: Where We Are and Where We Are Heading*, 64 J. Leg. Educ. 586 (2015).

10. *Id.* at 593–94.

11. *Id.* at 594–95.

12. In addition to PowerPoint, other presentation slides that work well are Google Slides, Keynote, and Prezi. For other available slide presentation options, see *6 Alternative Presentation Tools Better Than PowerPoint*, TecInteractive, https://www.tecinteractive.co.uk/presentation-tools-better-than-powerpoint/ (last visited: November 17, 2020).

13. Many law students are highly scheduled and plan their study time accordingly. Giving students ample time to schedule and complete the asynchronous course material is vital to their preparation, learning, and overall success.

aged, however, to pay attention to the amount of reading assigned per week, particularly in light of any additional material, assignments, and assessments the professor builds into the course.[14]

Synchronous instruction takes on a new meaning in the online setting. Although not in the same physical space, students and professors, through the magic of technology and the internet, are connected in the same virtual room. Many of the teaching techniques and active learning strategies used in a physical classroom can be incorporated into a synchronous course, although they might need to be sightly tweaked to accommodate the online learning format. The same is true for asynchronous content.

### 1. Flipped classrooms and lectures

Generally speaking, asynchronous classrooms place emphasis on student learning instead of the professor's teaching.[15] Flipped learning is essentially active, student-centered learning.[16] The overarching purpose of this type of asynchronous material, therefore, is to facilitate active learning. When students have actively engaged with the material prior to the synchronous class, the professor and students can engage in activities that allow students to use, apply, and reflect on the material.[17]

One way to flip a classroom is to create pre-recorded lectures that students access and review online in their own time and space. While there is no universal template, there are a few practical considerations to keep in mind. First, flipped lectures should be relatively short, between five to fifteen minutes.[18] They should provide enough information to introduce topics, breakdown difficult subjects, or provide students with suggestions on how to dissect and process the material. Second, if a topic is particularly dense or difficult, consider dividing the material into a series of shorter recordings. Third, break up the pre-recorded lectures with active learning exercises such as writing prompts or short quizzes. Fourth, use the asynchronous content to lay a foundation for the activities scheduled for the synchronous portion of class, whenever

---

14. Avoid the temptation to "pile on" asynchronous content and assessments just because the technology is available to do so. If students' coursework is entirely online and other instructors are incorporating asynchronous material as well, the student can quickly become overloaded. If the student perceives the asynchronous material is busy work, instead of a valuable learning tool, students become overwhelmed and disengage from learning.

15. *See generally* Perry Binder, *Flipping a Law Class Session: Creating Effective Online Content and Real Word In-class Team Modules*, 17 Atlantic L.J. 34 (2015).

16. *See generally* Jennifer Rosa, *Flipped Learning: Promoting Collaboration, Cooperation and Civility*, 96 Mich. Bar.J., Oct. 2017, at 56.

17. Binder, *supra* note 15, at 41.

18. *See generally Best Practices for the Flipped Classroom*, Hanover Research Insights Blog (Oct. 15, 2013), https://www.hanoverresearch.com/insights-blog/best-practices-for-the-flipped-classroom/ (last visited Jan. 31, 2021). *See also Flip Like an Expert—Best Practices for Successful Flipped Classrooms (Part 1—Content)*, Flip Learning, https://flippedlearning.org/syndicated/flip-like-expert-best-practices-successful-flipped-classrooms-part-1-content/ (last visited Jan. 31, 2021).

possible and practical.[19] Finally, have a stated pedagogical purpose for the asynchronous material; otherwise, students will perceive that they are being given "busy work."

Several forms of tools are available to create asynchronous course content. Creativity, the LMS, and available resources are the only limitations. Recordings, presentation slides, discussion boards, and various active exercises are the most common examples of rich, vibrant asynchronous content

#### *a. Recording tools*

Recording tools, whether external or embedded within the LMS platform, allow instructors and students to actively collaborate through video and audio media. Content can be uploaded, created, edited, and managed via audio and video files within the LMS. Most LMS platforms allow instructors to use existing files or to create new ones.[20]

#### *b. Presentation slides*

At every level, presentation slides have become a staple of modern education. Slide decks allow professors to prepare visual prompts, brief summaries of topics, or directions for group activity. While there is no universal template, there are several considerations for creating and using slides in an entirely online format. While many instructors use presentation slides as the backdrop for their pre-recorded asynchronous content, just narrating over existing presentation slides will likely be ineffective.[21] Instead, presentation slides should have minimal wording, the wording should be limited to take-aways, and the images should be crisp and compatible with the material. Any animation should convey visual information but not distract from it. In the online format, presentation slides should be more like a storyboard than a bullet point outline.[22]

Many LMS platforms permit instructors to embed content into their recordings. Inserting active learning tools into the flipped lecture can be very effective. For example, insert a true/false or multiple-choice question immediately following an explanation of a topic. Other examples include linking to corresponding legal documents like a criminal complaint, indictment, or an affidavit and search warrant. Another example is to cue the students to pause the recording and jot down comments, answers, or

---

19. For additional treatment of using a flipped classroom strategy, see Chapter 10: *Team-Based Learning in an Online Teaching Environment* by Joy E. Herr-Cardillo and Melissa H. Weresh.

20. Flip Learning, *supra* note 18. Other communication tools exist that can be used for recording content, including Panopto, YouTube, and Google Drive to name just a few.

21. Emily A. Moore, *Adapting PowerPoint Lectures for Online Delivery: Best Practices*, Faculty Focus (Jan. 7, 2013) (last visited Nov.16, 2020).

22. *Id.*

questions. This breaks the content up into manageable units, and it allows students to see if they understand what they have just heard.[23]

### c. *Discussion boards*

Recognizing that students learn from talking about the subject matter with other students, discussion boards are effective learning tools. Most students are familiar with using discussion boards. However, there seems to be growing consensus that professors and students are fatigued by discussion boards.[24] As a result, professors are encouraged not to create a discussion board just for the sake of having one; discussion boards must be meaningful and further the student's knowledge on any given subject matter.[25]

To be meaningful, discussion boards should encourage communication between the students; this is particularly important when the entire class is online. One way to encourage communication and collaboration is to keep professor prompts to a minimum, ask open-ended questions that encourage discussion, and consider not imposing immediate deadlines, instead give students time to think about their responses.[26] Professors are encouraged to participate to ensure students are engaging in meaningful dialogue. By monitoring student responses, professors know who has not responded, submitted non-responsive posts, or furthered the prompted discussion. Professors can demonstrate this "visible listening" by reaching out to the students to give feedback and encouragement.[27]

## II. Course Design Considerations: Incorporating Science-Backed Teaching Techniques and Supporting Student Learning

In addition to the basic and technological logistics, consider how to incorporate effective, science-backed teaching techniques and learning strategies into online course design. Cognitive psychologists continue to study and understand how the mind works.[28] As research and understanding continues to grow in these areas, educators can take advantage of that information to shape educational endeavors.[29]

---

23. *Id.*

24. Mark Lieberman, *Discussion Boards: Valuable? Overused? Discuss.*, Inside Higher Ed. (March 27, 2019), https://www.insidehighered.com/digital-learning/article/2019/03/27/new-approaches-discussion-boards-aim-dynamic-online-learning.

25. *Id.*

26. *Id.*

27. *Id.*

28. Peter C. Brown & Henry L. Roediger III, Make It Stick: The Science of Successful Learning 8 (2014).

29. *Id.*

Several science-backed teaching techniques and learning strategies lend themselves well to the study of Criminal Law and Procedure. Those techniques and strategies are spaced retrieval, elaboration, skills exercises, assessment, reflection, and meaningful feedback.

## A. SPACED REPETITION, SPACED RETRIEVAL, AND ASSESSMENTS

The concept of spaced retrieval combines two learning theories: spaced repetition and retrieval theory.[30] By spacing out studying over time, the student's ability to retain the material is enhanced.[31] By providing students with opportunities to retrieve information over set periods of time, students develop more durable retention.[32] Spaced *repetition* relates to the presentation of material and particular study strategies; spaced *retrieval* focuses on assessing how and what the student is learning. Assessment is at the core of spaced retrieval.[33]

Spaced repetition and retrieval are important because they interrupt forgetting.[34] While it seems counterintuitive, "[f]orgetting is critical to the learning of new skills *and* to the preservation and reacquisition of old ones."[35] "Using memory changes memory—and for the better. Forgetting enables and deepens learning, by filtering out distracting information *and* by allowing some breakdown that, after reuse, drives retrieval and storage strength higher than they were originally."[36] Students must forget to remember and remembering helps to learn.

Assessments are the most common and effective way to implement spaced repetition and spaced retrieval. Commonly referred to as the "testing effect," spaced retrieval forces students to interrupt forgetting. By retrieving what students learned, students can readily determine what they know and what they do not. Because retrieving the memory connects the information to something the learner already knows, the learner has an easier time recalling information at the next attempted retrieval.[37] In the online format, embedding quizzes into asynchronous material, giving spot quizzes during synchronous instruction, and performing active learning exercises without notes are valuable ways to implement informal assessment. Graded assessments continue to serve as a valuable tool in addressing spaced repetition and retrieval.

---

30. Brian Sites, *Learning Theory and The Law: Spaced Retrieval and the Law School Curriculum*, 43 L. & Psych. Rev. 99, 104 (2018).

31. *Id.* at 101.

32. *Id.*

33. *Id.* at 107.

34. Brown & Roediger, *supra* note 28, at 20.

35. Benedict Carey, The Surprising Truth About How We Learn and Why It Happens 40 (2015).

36. *Id.* at 40, 41.

37. *See generally* Brown & Roediger, *supra* note 28, at 19, 20.

In the online format, LMS platforms provide assessment features. For example, professors can input formal or informal assessments into the course page. Many LMS assessment features allow the professor to create or upload grading rubrics, insert comments, or comment directly into student assessments. Many LMS assessment features also support multiple-choice questions, short answer, and essay questions. They also provide automatic grading and analytics to help professors gauge student progress.[38]

Next to assessments, flashcards are probably the most recognized way to perform spaced repetition and retrieval. To use flashcards effectively,[39] repetition must be strategically timed and spaced.[40] Criminal Law is well-suited to the use of flashcards given the number of crimes (and their corresponding elements), defenses, and rules the students must memorize. In the online format, flashcards can be created by either the professor or the student using a blank template on a slide deck app. The first slide presents the prompt, and the second slide presents the answer. When students access the flashcards in the slide deck via their laptops or mobile devices, they can swipe through the slide deck just as if they were flipping through a hard set of flashcards.[41]

## B. ELABORATION

Elaboration is the process of finding additional layers of meaning in new materials.[42] Elaboration allows students to master new material by increasing the mental cues associated with the topic and improves the ability to recall the information at a later time.[43]

One way to effectively use elaboration is to have students use metaphors or to create a visual image for the material.[44] In Criminal Law, for example, after watching a lawyer use a metaphor to explain the concept of reasonable doubt in an instructional advocacy video, students work to create their own metaphor to describe a reasonable doubt. Flowchart exercises are an effective elaboration technique for Criminal Procedure students to use as they navigate Fourth Amendment search and seizure law and the various exceptions to the warrant requirement.

---

38. *Id.*

39. See *id.* at 64 for an explanation of the proper way to implement spaced repletion and spaced retrieval when using flashcards. Students fall into the familiarity trap and passive learning if they fail to use the flashcards properly.

40. *Id.*

41. Gabriel H. Teninbaum, *Spaced Repetition: A Method for Learning More Law in Less Time*, 17 J. HIGH TECH. L. 273 (2017). For a very brief description of using flashcards in the law school setting, see NELSON P. MILLER, THE ART AND SCIENCE OF LAW INSTRUCTION: DAILY MESSAGES JOURNALING A LAW FACULTY'S YEAR 11–12 (2020).

42. BROWN & ROEDIGER, *supra* note 28, at 206–07.

43. *Id.*

44. *Id.*

### C. INTERLEAVING

Interleaving requires students to study multiple topics at one time as opposed to blocked practice where students study one topic thoroughly before they study the next topic.[45] For example, in Criminal Law, during the two-week unit covering inchoate crimes, students participate in several exercises requiring them to navigate between the four different crimes when analyzing group criminal activity.

### D. SKILLS-BASED EXERCISES AND ACTIVITIES

Skills-based exercises are the epitome of active learning. There are numerous, skills-based exercises and activities that work well in online courses. In Criminal Law, litigation-based exercises are especially instructive. For example, mock sentence hearings, motion arguments, and closing arguments lend opportunities for students to use what they are learning. Preparing legal documents like proposed jury instructions, criminal complaints, verdict forms, and affirmative defense pleadings afford students the ability to write about what they are learning. Similarly, in Criminal Procedure, litigation-based activities like mock motions to suppress, identification procedures (photo lineups), and applications for search warrants serve to actively engage the students in the material.

### E. REFLECTION

Reflection combines retrieval and elaboration.[46] Using reflection, students answer questions like, "What happened? What did I do? How did it work out?"[47] and elaborate by answering questions like, "What will I do differently next time?"[48] Professors can nudge students' reflections with specific prompts geared toward the particular topic. Because reflection triggers several cognitive functions and learning strategies, it *can* lead to better learning.[49]

Reflection can be used to promote learning in Criminal Law and Procedure classes, especially after assessments and skills-based exercises. Whenever students have engaged in an active learning or skills-based exercise, writing out answers to reflection questions serves as a meaningful chance for students to think about what they learned. Answers to these questions provide important information to both the instructor and the learner. The professor can gauge whether any adjustments should be made to the instructional delivery, and the learner can evaluate what to do differently. In other words, the answers to the reflection question lead to feedback.

---

45. *Id.* at 206.
46. Brown & Roediger, *supra* note 28, at 66.
47. *Id.*
48. *Id.*
49. *Id.*

### F. FEEDBACK

Feedback is a way of delivering evaluative and corrective information about what the student learned. Generally, feedback should be promptly given; although delayed feedback is appropriate for longer projects.[50] Although it sounds simple, three important questions must be posed and answered to make the feedback meaningful: 1) What are the professor's goals regarding student performance? 2) What progress is the student making toward the goal? 3) What activities must the student undertake to make better progress toward the ideal performance?[51] "Effective feedback engages students in active learning ... [by helping] them learn the concept, self-monitor [to] assess[] their understanding, and build self-motivation."[52]

## III. Putting It All Together

The online course design for Criminal Law encompasses three main components: asynchronous content, synchronous content, and assessments. My primary, overarching goals for all three components of course design are student engagement and active learning. The material I use for each component varies slightly from week to week, depending on the subject matter, the type of available content, and the complexity of the concepts. Below is a summary of the asynchronous, synchronous, and assessment content I have incorporated into the Criminal Law classes I have taught in an online format.

### A. PART ONE: CRIMINAL LAW—CONNECTING CRIMES IN AN ONLINE CLASSROOM

#### 1. Asynchronous content

The asynchronous portion of class requires students to engage with the material prior to the scheduled class in which the subject matter will be discussed. In addition to the reading assignment, I post flipped recordings and presentation slides for each weeks' subject matter. I often embed multiple-choice questions or guided questions within the flipped recording. I also provide links to outside videos, statutes, jury instructions, and other resources, such as news articles, standardized forms, pleadings, and case law not included in the course text. Frequently I post discussion board prompts within the LMS. Whatever type of asynchronous content I use, it is designed to get students thinking about the material and using it in a meaningful way *prior* to class.[53]

---

50. Terri LeClercq, *Principle 4: Good Practice Gives Prompt Feedback*, 49 J. Legal Educ. 418, 421 (1999).

51. Elizabeth M. Bloom, *A Law School Game Changer: (Trans)Formative Feedback*, 41 Ohio N.U.L. Rev. 227, 233–34 (2015).

52. *Id.*

53. For additional treatment of pre-class assessment, see Chapter 24: *Teaching Civil Procedure Online with Formative Assessment* by Cynthia Ho.

**Current events and news articles.** I embed some type of current event or news article into most of the weekly asynchronous content. For example, when covering theories of punishment and sentencing, I embed links to recent news articles concerning noteworthy, creative, or outrageous judicially imposed sentences.[54] Depending on the type of sentence highlighted in the news article, discussion board prompts allow students to apply punishment theories and goals of sentencing to current fact patterns.

Embedding links to recent news articles about individuals charged with Felony Murder is also helpful in assisting students to distinguish between Felony Murder and other forms of homicide, which helps to emphasize how the definition of crimes and the available evidence impact prosecutors' charging decisions. A news article about a successful "sleepwalking defense" prompts lively application on the discussion board about what otherwise appears to be a shocking defense.[55] Newsclips or news videos about controversial charging decisions in homicide cases where self-defense or "stand your ground" issues were raised set the stage for robust discussion, debate, and application of homicide and self-defense laws.

**Videos and metaphors.** When teaching basic tenets of criminal law, I provide students with links to the federal and state jury instructions setting forth the elements of a crime, burden of proof, proof beyond a reasonable doubt, presumption of innocence, and types of evidence. I also give students a link to an advocacy video showing a lawyer articulate a reasonable doubt metaphor.[56] This video becomes the basis of a short, reflection, and informal assessment—described below—giving students the opportunity to articulate what reasonable doubt means.

**Statutes and Jury Instructions.** During the Rape and Criminal Sexual Conduct unit, in addition to posting a state criminal sexual conduct statute,[57] I provide students with an article on reading, interpreting, and understanding statutes. I also provide students with a news article regarding a high-profile defendant and the application of the rape shield statute to his case.[58]

Speaking of jury instructions, I embed or post jury instructions in the asynchronous content, along with the relevant statutes, for nearly every crime and defense covered in the course syllabus. The jury instructions and statutes often serve as the basis for an informal assessment, group exercise, or individual writing exercise.

---

54. *See* Alex Horton, *Two Men Lied About Being Veterans. The Judge's Sentence: Wear Signs Saying 'I Am A Liar.'*, Wash. Post (Aug. 27, 2019), https://www.washingtonpost.com/national-security/2019/08/26/two-men-lied-about-being-veterans-judges-sentence-wear-signs-saying-i-am-liar/?noredirect=on.

55. *See* Wayne K. Roustan, *Sleepwalking Used As Legitimate Criminal Defense*, SunSentinel (May 20, 2012), https://www.sun-sentinel.com/news/fl-xpm-2012-05-20-fl-sleepwalking-crimes-20120520-story.html.

56. George McCranie, *In a Criminal Trial—What Does Beyond a Reasonable Doubt Mean?*, YouTube (Oct. 5, 2019), https://www.youtube.com/watch?v=joLEkzsSUmA&t=341s.

57. Mich. Comp. Laws §§ 750.520a–750.520e.

58. Kirk Johnson, *Rape Shield Law Will Be Applied in Bryant Case, Judge Says*, N.Y. Times (June 11, 2004), https://www.nytimes.com/2004/06/11/us/rape-shield-law-will-be-applied-in-bryant-case-judge-says.html.

**Court forms and standardized templates.** Using standardized templates in asynchronous content is another useful teaching technique and learning tool. For example, I embed a blank, standardized criminal complaint template to help students understand the importance of statutory language, elements, and drafting the official charging document.[59] Standardized forms are also useful in preparing defense-related documents such as the Evaluation Order Relative to Criminal Responsibility necessary for a possible insanity defense.[60]

**Documents and pleadings.** Using documents and pleadings from actual court filings in criminal case is invaluable; they can serve as examples of best practice or examples of mistakes. As a case in point, I will provide an example of a federal conspiracy indictment[61] to create a guided exercise that requires students to identify the elements of conspiracy, identify the roles of multiple defendants, and apply and discuss the *Pinkerton* rule.[62]

**Discussion board prompts.** Students also receive discussion board prompts throughout the term. Some recent examples include commenting on sentences imposed in recent cases, the homicide charges filed in police killing cases, controversial defense of habitation/self-defense cases, dog mauling homicides, infant deaths in hot car cases, just to name a few. Students are required to post responses before class.[63]

### 2. Synchronous content

The course design for my Criminal Law course is typically broken into three hourly segments. The first hour of class begins with an interactive,[64] short (approximately ten to fifteen minutes) review of the previous week's material. This "loopback" review is comprised of short questions designed to highlight the major concepts, rules, and elements covered in the previous week's class.

---

59. State Court Administrative Office, *SCAO-Approved Court Forms, Felony Set: Felony Information, Felony Complaint, and Felony Warrant*, Mich. Cts., https://courts.michigan.gov/Administration/SCAO/Forms/courtforms/mc200.pdf (last visited Feb. 5, 2021).

60. State Court Administrative Office, *SCAO-Approved Court Forms, Order for Evaluation Relative to Criminal Responsibility*, Mich. Cts., https://courts.michigan.gov/Administration/SCAO/Forms/courtforms/mc206.pdf (last visited Feb. 5, 2021).

61. Indictment, U.S. v. Edwards (No. 1:11CR161–1), https://www.justice.gov/sites/default/files/opa/legacy/2011/06/03/edwards-indictment.pdf.

62. Pinkerton v. United States, 328 U.S. 640 (1946).

63. The discussion board prompt is based on the shooting death of Renisha McBride. *See generally Renisha McBride, Detroit woman, shot to death while seeking help after a car accident, family says*, CBS News (Nov. 8, 2013, 8:51 AM), https://www.cbsnews.com/news/renisha-mcbride-detroit-woman-shot-to-death-while-seeking-help-after-a-car-accident-family-says/; *Murder of Renisha McBride*, Wikipedia, https://en.wikipedia.org/wiki/Murder_of_Renisha_McBride (last visited Feb. 27, 2021). Professors are encouraged to modify the facts of the case as needed to accomplish the desired learning outcomes.

64. In this context, interactive means all students are expected to answer the review questions I ask. In the online environment, the chat function provides a quiet, non-disruptive way to conduct this type of "loopback" review.

**Polling.** From there, using the polling feature within the LMS, I pose a few questions designed to gauge how much of the asynchronous material the students absorbed, which informs me about which areas I might need to provide additional instruction. The polling inquiries also allow me to get a sense of how deeply the students interacted with the asynchronous material and to let the students know that I am monitoring their involvement with the asynchronous material.[65]

**Case Method and Socratic Variations.** From there, I pivot to covering the assigned cases and reading material. Although the Socratic method is often criticized for not being the most productive teaching technique and learning tool, it does have an important connection to legal practice.[66] Consequently, I make an effort to maximize its efficacy with some "fun" modifications. The first variation I call "Rapid-Fire" Socratic. This variation involves all students being "on call" to answer questions. As I pose each question, I call on a different student to answer the question. This variation requires everyone to be focused on the discussion and to actively listen not only to the questions I ask, but to listen to the answer their classmates provide. The second variation I call "Stop-and-Go" Socratic. This Socratic variation starts by questioning one reciting student. From there, I call on other students to respond to the answers given by the reciting student or to respond to hypotheticals based on the reciting student's answer. "Stop-and-Go" ends with asking the original reciting student wrap-up questions designed to conclude the point.

Depending on the length of time necessary to cover the assigned cases, the final one or two hours of class are dedicated to active learning exercises. Ideally, the active learning exercises should incorporate one or more of the scientifically backed teaching techniques and learning strategies.

**Breakout Groups.** Many of the active learning exercises I integrate into class are facilitated through the use of breakout groups, which I use from the very first week of class.[67] For example, in the first week of Criminal Law, students learn the theories of punishment and the goals of sentencing. Dividing the class into groups, students, using the federal sentencing statute,[68] must answer guided questions to identify and label the sentencing theories and goals represented in the statute. After the groups finish answering the guided questions, I assign a fact pattern and guided questions instructing students to prepare for a mock sentence hearing. The students are divided into prosecution and defense groups and are allotted approximately twenty minutes to craft their sentencing arguments. Students return to the main classroom to present

65. For additional information on polling and polling software, see Chapter 8: *From Ground to Cloud and Back Again: Modern Tactics to Improve Your Teaching* by Katherine Brem.

66. *See, e.g.*, Jamie R. Abrams, *Reframing the Socratic Method*, 64 J. Legal Educ. 562 (2015); Donald G. Marshall, *Socratic Method and the Irreducible Core of Legal Education*, 90 Minn. L. Rev. 1 (2005).

67. For a more in-depth treatment of breakout rooms specifically and collaborative learning generally, see Chapter 14: *Effective Collaboration in Online Courses* by Darby Dickerson and Megan Bess.

68. 18 U.S.C. § 3553.

their sentencing arguments. Afterward, using guided questions, students give feedback to one another's presentations.

Breakout groups work well for other types of active learning exercises. To introduce students to statutory interpretation and writing jury instructions, groups receive a particular state's murder statute and directions to write an appropriate jury instruction using the example previously provided. For the second exercise, I provide groups with a fact pattern, directions, and guided questions to conduct a motion for proposed jury instructions. I designate students as prosecutors or defense attorneys and allot twenty minutes for students to develop their respective arguments. Afterward, students present their jury instruction arguments. Using guided questions and a rubric, students provide peer feedback.

For some active learning exercises, the breakout groups are the second portion of the exercise, not the first (i.e., solving the problem together). When exploring modern felony murder, students often struggle with understanding that jurisdictions define and apply the felony murder rule differently. To help students understand and apply these concepts, I provide students with a worksheet with two to four fact patterns, based on the assigned reading. For each fact pattern, students must analyze, using different jurisdictional tests than the one presented in the assigned case, whether the defendant could be charged and convicted of felony murder. After working individually, I send the students off in groups to breakout rooms. While students are in the breakout rooms, I circulate among each room to answer questions and to ensure students are progressing through the exercise. Most conferencing platforms allow students to send questions to the professor as well.

Students are given approximately fifteen minutes to reach group consensus on the correct answers. Back in the main classroom, each group reports their answers. I provide feedback. A similar exercise can be used for attempted crimes. In breakout groups, students examine one of the assigned cases using a different jurisdiction's test than the one analyzed in the assigned case. The group must prepare a written analysis using the new test. The second exercise requires each group to analyze a new fact pattern and prepare a criminal complaint. This exercise provides students the opportunity to examine and review the elements of the target crime as well as the inchoate crime.[69]

**Skills-based Exercises.** Online breakout groups are effective for skills-based exercises as well. For instance, using an assigned case, students receive instructions and a rubric for preparing, conducting, and deliberating mock closing arguments. I divide students into a prosecution team (one or two students) and a defense team (one or two students). The teams have twenty to thirty minutes to prepare a closing argument.

69. If time runs out (and most likely it will) and the groups cannot report back to the class, direct them to submit their written responses and then post them on the course LMS for everyone to review. Or the professor can hold it over and use it as a loopback/review at the top of the next class. I prefer the latter; it requires the students to review the material before attending the subsequent class.

Meanwhile, back in the main virtual classroom, the remaining students are assigned roles as jurors, prosecution analysts, defense analysts, or jury analysts; they receive instructions about their roles.

Students conduct the mock closing argument to the assigned jury during the third hour of class. After the closing arguments, the jurors deliberate based only on the facts presented by the student-lawyers, not what they remember from their prior reading of the case. The entire class watches the jury deliberate. After the jury reaches a verdict, the student-analysts provide feedback. The professor also provides feedback. Having received guided questions to assist them, students must prepare a one or two-page reflection describing how their understanding of the material improved based on the exercise.

Later in the term, during the justification defense unit, I incorporate a second advocacy, skills-based exercise. This second closing argument exercise involves a murder case that raises a self-defense issue. Four students (two prosecutors and two defense lawyers) who volunteered the previous week are given fact pattern from which to prepare closing arguments; they have an entire week to prepare their respective closing arguments based on a hypothetical case and Michigan law. At the beginning of the next class, the four lawyers proceed to separate breakout rooms where they review their closing arguments. Meanwhile, in the main classroom, I divide the remaining students into the following groups: jurors, prosecution analysts, defense analysts, or jury analysts. I instruct the groups and give them guided questions to use during the exercise.

After the prosecution and defense students present their closing arguments, the jury deliberates in front of the entire class, using only the closing arguments and the professor's jury instructions. After the jury reaches its verdict, the analysts provide peer review, using the professor's guided questions. After the exercise, all students must prepare a written reflection using guided questions.

Finally, breakout groups can also be an effective tool for conducting deductive reasoning exercises. For instance, in Week Five, to prepare for the upcoming midterm, I use breakout groups to allows students the opportunity to work through practice multiple-choice questions. Each group must analyze one to three multiple-choice questions. Working together, they must select the correct answer and be prepared to justify their choice as well as explain why the other answers were incorrect. Back in the main classroom, each group presents their answers and explanations.

**Group Activities and Class Exercises.** Not all group activity has to be in the form of breakout groups. Instead, sometimes the entire class can participate in an activity *en masse*. One example that works well is what I call "Red Light, Yellow Light, Green Light." In this exercise, the students use three ordinary objects from home, (one red, one yellow, and one green). I present a hypothetical, fact by fact. With each fact, the students hold up one of the objects to identify the defendant's conduct. Green represents no conduct or mere preparation to act. Yellow represents conduct, but not enough yet to be considered an attempted crime. Red represents an attempted crime.[70]

Similarly, a "continuum" exercise works particularly well to help students understand and "quantify" the *actus reus* elements of modern attempted crimes. In this exercise, students interactively explore each assigned case's facts. At the end of each case, using the meeting platform's whiteboard, the class collectively agrees where to place a particular jurisdiction's attempt *actus reus* element on a continuum with mere preparation at one end and a completed attempt at the other end.

**Individual and Miscellaneous Review Exercises.** During the two-week unit covering inchoate crimes, students are often frustrated with determining the criminal culpability of individuals in group criminality or attempted crimes. At the end of this unit, using a guided worksheet, students must apply conspiracy law to the attempt and solicitation cases from the previous week's material. This exercise forces students to use previously learned material in the context of a new set of facts; it also provides a platform to discuss the importance of ethics and competence related to a prosecutor's charging decision.

Other exercises that work well for individual guided worksheets (but can be used in breakout group exercises) are doing a *Morissette* strict liability analysis of a modern statute.[71] A similar individual exercise involves providing students with a hypothetical case, jury instructions, and a guided worksheet to determine the applicability of the mistake of law defense.

**Engaging Reviews.** In addition to the built-in "loopback" reviews I conduct at the beginning of each class, there are several points throughout the term where fun but meaningful review can be injected into the course content. One example that most students seem to enjoy is watching a portion of a music video that depicts a homicide involving facts that might trigger self-defense or heat of passion claims.[72] Following the music video, the class discusses. Students participate in an overarching group review of murder, manslaughter, and self-defense.

The final class of the term is slated as a cumulative, substantive review. Instead of trying to do a week by week summary and review of every topic covered throughout the term, I provide students with a series of multiple-choice questions, short answer questions, and example/non-example exercises to review and complete before class. Students discuss and ask questions about those exercises during class.

---

70. Although these exercises sound elementary, students LOVE them! Most students express that these two exercises help them visualize the amount of conduct necessary to prove an attempted crime in a particular jurisdiction.

71. Morissette v. United States, 342 U.S. 246 (1952); MICH. COMP. LAWS § 750.317a.

72. Maroon 5, *Wake Up Call (Official Video)*, YOUTUBE, https://www.youtube.com/watch?v=dkQ0O-J5Byls. I warn students before they watch the video that it depicts sexual overtones and the objectification of women. In the online setting, I have students turn off their audio and video, watch the video on their own, and then return to class. This avoids any problems with connectivity or bandwidth issues.

### 3. Assessments

**Informal Assessments and Exercises.** Informal assessment is incorporated every week, often in both the asynchronous and synchronous class segments. This includes the multiple-choice and short answer prompts embedded into the asynchronous recordings. Why? Because the students are being asked an analytical question about the material and they receive immediate feedback regarding the correct answer.

Similarly, when students create and present their own metaphor to explain the concept of reasonable doubt, they receive professor feedback, as is the case with all of the in-class and group exercises.

Several times throughout the term, students go offscreen to take a short, non-graded, multiple-choice assessment. Students receive immediate feedback and explanations for the answer choices upon submission.

**Formal Assessments.** The first formal, graded assessment I assign is a mandatory essay question at the end of the homicide unit. The assessment is administered through the course LMS. The grading rubric is input directly into the LMS grading tool, which allows me to give direct, individualized feedback within both the student's written answer and within the rubric.

The second formal assessment is the midterm. This assessment consists of twenty multiple-choice questions covering the course content from the first five weeks and is posted on the LMS course page.

The third formal, graded assessment is another essay question administered two-thirds of the way through the semester using the course LMS.

The fourth formal, graded assessment is a mini-exam consisting of five multiple-choice questions and one short essay under timed conditions. Like the midterm, the mini-exam is posted on the LMS course page and students take it during the schedule class time.

The cumulative final exam is the last formal assessment of the term. Worth fifty percent, the final exam consists of multiple-choice questions and one to three essay questions.

## B. PART TWO: CRIMINAL PROCEDURE—PLUGGING INTO POLICE, PROCESS, AND PROTECTING RIGHTS

The course format for my online Criminal Procedure class parallels the structure I use in Criminal Law class, encompassing the same three main components: asynchronous content, synchronous content, and assessments. As with Criminal Law, my overarching goals for all three components of course design are student engagement and active learning. In Criminal Procedure, I incorporate advanced advocacy skills exercises. The material I use for each component varies slightly from week to week depending on the subject matter, the type of available content, and the complexity of the concepts. Below is a summary of the asynchronous, synchronous, and assessment content I have incorporated into the online Criminal Procedure classes.

### 1. Asynchronous content

Like my course design for Criminal Law, I provide a fair amount of asynchronous material. Most notably, most weeks include an asynchronous recording in addition to the reading assignment. The recordings are designed to familiarize the students with the material, highlight notable points, or explain difficult concepts. Within these recordings, I embed standard court forms such as complaints, warrants, and verdict forms.[73] Additional asynchronous material includes graphics,[74] legal documents (including indictments, motions to suppress, plea bargains, immunity grants, *Miranda* warnings, photo identification forms, waiver forms), rules of criminal procedure, writing prompts, and multiple-choice questions. Almost all of the material I post in the asynchronous modules serves as a basis for individual or group learning exercises.

**Discussion Board Prompts.** As in Criminal Law, I also prompt discussion board topics. For example, I direct students to watch a music video and provide a prompt for them to respond to the course discussion board regarding basic concepts of constitutional criminal procedure.[75] Another example of a discussion board post that prompted robust discussion dealt with the execution of search warrants in the context of the Breonna Taylor case.[76]

**Instructional videos.** To begin preparing for the Motion to Suppress exercises that take place in Weeks Six and Seven, I prepare an asynchronous recording on motion advocacy, which is linked to other instructional videos,[77] guided questions, and oral advocacy checklists.

Another useful video that I include in the asynchronous portion of class is the Think LegalEase video[78] that provides an animated overview of *Terry v. Ohio* and its progeny. During the Double Jeopardy unit, I direct students to watch a movie clip and provide a prompt for them to respond to the course Discussion page; it also serves as the basis for a guided worksheet exercise.[79]

---

73. *See generally* State Courts Administrative Office, *SCAO approved court forms*, Mich. Cts., https://courts.michigan.gov/administration/scao/forms/pages/default.aspx (last visited Nov. 21, 2020).

74. For an example, see *Criminal Justice System Flowchart*, Bureau of Just. Stat., https://www.bjs.gov/content/largechart.cfm (last visited Nov. 21, 2020).

75. I ask students to post a response to the following prompt: Describe how the lyrics of Springsteen's *A Long Walk Home* serve as a metaphor for constitutional criminal procedure. *See* Bruce Springsteen, *Long Walk Home (Official Video)*, YouTube (Oct. 2, 2009) (time marker 2:57–3:11), https://www.youtube.com/watch?v=iywFZqtPlhU.

76. *See generally Shooting of Breonna Taylor*, Wikipedia, https://en.wikipedia.org/wiki/Shooting_of_Breonna_Taylor; *see also* Search Warrant (No. 20-1371), https://reason.com/wp-content/uploads/2020/06/Breonna-Taylor-search-warrants.pdf.

77. For example, Michael Tigar, *12 Tips for Appellate Advocacy*, Duke University College of Law, YouTube (Oct. 27, 2011), https://www.youtube.com/watch?v=BCj5ogtf2uo, and *Tips for Oral Arguments*, YouTube (July 23, 2015), https://www.youtube.com/watch?v=JzKExC2MJsQ.

78. Think Legalease, *Terry v. Ohio (Stop & Frisk)—Landmark Cases—Episode #12*, YouTube (August 13, 2016), https://www.youtube.com/watch?v=0XynN0EAj8M.

79. Movieclips, *Double Jeopardy (3/9) Movie CLIP—Double Jeopardy (1999) HD*, YouTube (May 23, 2012), https://www.youtube.com/watch?v=HGdt0QR55Ko&t=25s.

### 2. Synchronous content

Just as in Criminal Law, my Criminal Procedure class is broken into three-hour segments. The first hour typically begins with some form of polling, often using the polling function on the LMS. In the first week of the term, I poll the students asking them to use three words to describe their opinion of the criminal justice system via an interactive presentation software.[80] As the students enter their answers, they are recorded in real time, forming a word cloud, and are displayed on my shared screen.

**Case Method and Socratic Variations.** In addition to the variations of Socratic instruction I use in my Criminal Law course, I also use the "Resident Expert" method. I assign one to two students (depending on the size of the class) the responsibility of Socratic presentation for landmark and seminal cases. The resident experts' responsibility includes not only reading the unedited case, but they are responsible for answering questions about the case, hypotheticals about applying the law of the case, and distinguishing the case from the other assigned cases. Typically, I interject the "Stop and Go" variation with the "Resident Expert" variation to keep everyone engaged. Students turn to the assigned cases in the remaining time and respond to rapid-fire Socratic questions.

**Breakout Groups.** Many of the active learning exercises I do are implemented through breakout groups. Designed to get students thinking about the relationship between the Fourth Amendment, the definition of search, and the impact of technology, one breakout group exercise I have used involves dividing students into a prosecution team and a civil rights team. The groups are tasked with preparing an advisory opinion on whether a new piece of technology acquired by a local department can be used without violating the Fourth Amendment. After fifteen to twenty minutes, students present their opinions to the class. I provide feedback.

Another effective breakout group exercise involves an affidavit for search warrant, a search warrant, and a return and tabulation form that I posted with the asynchronous material for that week's class. Students move to breakout groups where they are given an actual affidavit and search warrant from a closed criminal case.[81] Groups have approximately twenty minutes to draw a visual representation of the evidence the police

80. *See generally* Mentimeter, https://www.mentimeter.com/. Mentimeter is a tool that uses live quizzes, word clouds, Q&As to build interactive real-time polls. In this particular poll, I used the word cloud function. I save the word cloud and post it to the course LMS page. During the last class, we do the same poll to see if opinions have changed in light of what they learned throughout the term.

81. Professors can acquire affidavits and search warrants relatively easily online. *See, e.g.*, Search Warrant (No. 20-1371), https://reason.com/wp-content/uploads/2020/06/Breonna-Taylor-search-warrants.pdf.

Friends, colleagues, former students, and other contacts can be good sources to acquire a real-life affidavits and search warrants. Students are often shocked at how little evidence is needed to establish probable cause so it is definitely worth the effort to find these examples.

officer used to establish probable cause;[82] the group also must analyze whether the magistrate should have authorized the warrant.

The groups then return to the main classroom to report their conclusions, and I provide feedback.

During the Interrogation unit, I form breakout groups and provide the groups with links to interrogation videos. Using the guided questions I provided, students must analyze and determine whether there any legal challenges that can be raised to the manner in which the government conducted the interrogation. Students are brought back into the main classroom to present their analysis and conclusions; their respective conclusions must be supported by pointing to specific timestamps in the video.

**Skills-Based Exercises.** In my Criminal Procedure class, students conduct two motion to suppress arguments, one during the Fourth Amendment unit and one during the Interrogation unit. Each student has the opportunity to play the role of prosecution and defense (if the student was a prosecutor in the first exercise, they play the role of defense counsel in the second exercise).

I provide students with their assigned case file, their roles and pairings for arguments, their assigned roles as judges for other students' arguments, and a grading rubric.

I base the motion to suppress exercise on state court or federal circuit court cases. In selecting the cases for the exercises, I choose cases that present at least two issues aligning with course content; I choose cases that provide access to the party briefs as well as the court opinion. Students are paired and each must argue one of the issues. Each side has fifteen minutes for argument, the movant is given one minute for rebuttal.

Students scheduled to argue during the Fourth Amendment motion to suppress exercise must serve as judges for interrogation motion to suppress exercise and vice versa. Students serving as judges are expected to have read the cases and briefs, and they are required to ask questions during the arguments. After each argument concludes, I provide feedback and quickly review the substantive topics covered in that particular argument. Students must write a brief reflection, whether litigant or judge, answering guided questions about what they learned from the experience.

When conducting the motion to suppress exercises for the Interrogation unit, the assignments, roles, and responsibilities are the same as the Fourth Amendment exercise with one exception. This time, students are given hypothetical cases and must use the cases learned in class to construct their suppression arguments. Using guided questions, students must write a reflective piece for this assignment, as well.

---

82. The goal of students drawing a visual representation of the affiant's supporting evidence is to understand that connecting pieces of circumstantial evidence is often how law enforcement establishes probable cause.

**Group Activities and Class Exercises.** After showing the entire class a photo line-up, I give students an identification procedure witness form; they complete the form just as a witness would in real life. After everyone fills out the form, I conduct the photo ID again. Students are given the opportunity to change their selection. I provide feedback regarding the results of the identification procedure in the context of current identification law and practical experience.

During two to three of the classes covering the Fourth Amendment, I reserve fifteen to twenty minutes at the end of class for students to move to breakout groups and work on their Fourth Amendment flowcharts. I bring students back to the main classroom the last few minutes of class; students' flowcharts must show progress.

**Individual and Miscellaneous Review Exercises.** At several points throughout the term, I provide several opportunities for individual exercises, usually in the form of a guided worksheet. Topics for which guided worksheets are particularly effective are defining searches, recognizing exceptions to the warrant requirement, authorizing a search or arrest warrant, interrogation and confession issues, self-representation and guilty pleas, and double jeopardy.

**Engaging Reviews.** Just as in Criminal Law, Week Fourteen is slated as a cumulative, substantive review, I do not conduct a week by week summary. Instead, I provide students with a series of multiple-choice questions, short answer questions, and example/non-example exercises to review and complete before class. During the synchronous portion of class, I have found that infographics, visual cues, and processing-style exercises, such as flowcharts, work best for reviewing this course content. Students discuss and ask questions about those exercises during the final class.

### 3. Assessments

**Informal Assessments.** Informal assessment is incorporated every week, oftentimes in both the asynchronous and synchronous segments of the class. This includes the embedded multiple-choice and short answer prompts embedded into the asynchronous flipped recordings.

Several times throughout the term, students go offscreen to take a short, non-graded multiple-choice assessment. Students receive immediate feedback and explanations for the answer choices upon submission.

And finally, almost all group activities, breakout group exercises, and individual exercises are followed up with reflection by the student and feedback by the professor.

**Formal Assessments.** The first and fourth formal graded assessments are essay assignments administered through the LMS. The grading rubric is input directly into LMS's grading tool, which allows for direct, individualized feedback both in the student's answer and in the rubric for that student. The second and fifth formal assessments occur with the Fourth Amendment Motion to Suppress exercises.

The third formal assessment is the Fourth Amendment midterm and is administered as a multiple-choice exam through the course LMS.

The cumulative final exam is the last formal assessment of the term. Worth fifty percent, the final exam consists of multiple-choice questions and one to three essay questions.

## IV. Conclusion

Moving courses to an online format might involve a steep learning curve and a involve a large initial time investment. But with patience and perseverance, converting course content to the online format is well worth the time and energy. By building the course structure around asynchronous, synchronous, and assessment material, professors can connect students to a vast wealth of information and learning material through the magic of the internet. By accessing, using, and working with the asynchronous material prior to class, professors have more time to implement active learning exercises, tools, and strategies during the synchronous segment of class. Further, the online class setting through a nimble LMS also makes it easier for professors to integrate science-backed teaching techniques and learning strategies into the course design.

TWENTY-ONE

# Designing and Teaching Online Legal Research Skills Courses

Megan Austin*
Emily Kline**

After reviewing this chapter, readers will be able to:

- Engage in learner-centered online course design and teaching;
- Integrate principles of backward design and Universal Design for Learning (UDL) in course design and instruction;
- Develop ideas for learning objectives, course activities, and assessments to promote student engagement and collaboration;
- Implement an online flipped classroom;
- Design flipped classroom exercises using synchronous and asynchronous tools to teach core concepts, research design, and research skills; and
- Create synchronous and asynchronous activities and assessments.

Legal education is in a time of self-reflection and self-assessment. To help students develop into effective legal professionals, educators are using learning theory to inspire and underpin new instructional approaches to teach more inclusively and actively engage law students in learning professional skills.

In this chapter, we describe instructional approaches to two different online skills courses: a flipped classroom legal research skills course and a fully asynchronous advanced legal research course. Our focus is practical; we discuss course design, assess-

* Law Instruction Librarian and Professor of Practice, University of Oregon School of Law. Professor Austin began teaching legal writing in 1994 and legal research in 2012. She has taught legal research in online synchronous and asynchronous formats since August 2019.

** Assistant Clinical Professor of Law, Rutgers Law School. Professor Kline began teaching law in 2001. She has taught Legal Research and Writing in an entirely synchronous format since March 2020.

ments, activities and assignments, and technologies. Our practices, however, are rooted in constructivist learning theory and learner-centered teaching. The first section briefly introduces constructivist learning theory and learner-centered instruction, with special attention to collaborative learning, The second section describes the design and delivery of a synchronous online flipped legal research course.[1] The final section discusses designing and teaching a completely asynchronous advanced legal research course.

## I. Learning Theory for Legal Education and Online Education

Recently law schools have increased experiential opportunities and focused on implementing learning outcomes and assessments. However, no single unified learning theory underlies legal education.[2]

Constructivism as a learning theory focuses on students building knowledge based on their prior experiences, giving them a role in their own learning, and encouraging collaboration and self-reflection.[3] Constructivist learning theory underlies student-centered teaching methods, which contrast with traditional teaching approaches where knowledge is transferred from the teacher to be passively received by the student. The role of the teacher using constructivist, learner-centered approach is to create a collaborative, problem-solving environment where students become active participants in their learning.[4]

In learner-centered instruction, the focus is not on what instructors are going to present/lecture but rather on what and how students will learn. The main practices in learner-centered instruction are connecting learning to real life experiences; being transparent about the purpose and relevancy of the activities and assessments in relation to personal, academic and professional goals; creating a social context for and engaging in collaborative learning; and emphasizing active student engagement rather than just passive listening.[5]

---

1. For a discussion of using team-based learning principles to guide flipped classroom design, see Chapter 10: *Team-Based Learning in an Online Teaching Environment* by Joy E. Herr-Cardillo and Melissa H. Weresh.

2. For discussions of learning theory in legal education, see, e.g., Rebecca Flanagan, *Anthrogogy: Towards Inclusive Law School Learning,* 19 Conn. Pub. Int. L.J. 93 (2019); Gerald F. Hess, *Collaborative Course Design: Not My Course, Not Their Course, but Our Course,* 47 Washburn L.J. 367 (2007); Michael Hunter Schwartz, *Teaching Law by Design: How Learning Theory and Instructional Design Can Inform and Reform Law Teaching,* 38 San Diego L. Rev. 347, 380–82 (2001).

3. Peter C. Honebein, *Seven Goals for Constructivist Learning Environments, in* Constructivist Learning Environments: Case Studies in Instructional Design 11–12 (Brent G. Wilson ed., 1996); Schwartz, *supra* note 2, at 380–81.

4. Saul McLeod, *Constructivism as a theory for teaching and learning,* Simply Psychology (July 17, 2019), https://www.simplypsychology.org/constructivism.html.

5. Mary Ellen Weimer, Learner-Centered Teaching Five Key Changes to Practice 15 (2013); Phyllis Blumberg, *How Critical Reflection Benefits Faculty as They Implement Learner-Centered Teaching,* 144 New Directions for Teaching & Learn. 87, 88–89 (2015).

The learner-centered approach encourages collaborative problem solving through discourse with the professor acting as a facilitator and co-collaborator.[6] The value of collaborative learning has been well-documented and is two-fold.[7] First, collaborative learning has been shown to more effectively increase student knowledge and achievement.[8] Second, collaborative learning teaches students the skill of collaboration itself—which has been documented as one the more important lawyering skills for practicing attorneys.[9]

Implementing a collaborative, learner-centered instructional approach requires skills in course design because the approach is less rehearsed, more spontaneous, and attentive to a variety of student backgrounds.[10]

The critical practice of instructional design combines the constructivist, learner-centered theoretical foundation with the process of creating engaging learning experiences.[11] Whole books have been written on online course design,[12] so an exhaustive explanation of design models is beyond the scope of this chapter.[13] Most instructional design involves analyzing the instruction context, the learners, and learning tasks; creating assessments; determining instructional strategies, and evaluating instruction.[14] Experienced and effective online course instructors consistently

---

6. Anthony G. Picciano, *Theories and Frameworks for Online Education: Seeking an Integrated Model*, 21 Online Learn. J. 166, 176 (2017), https://files.eric.ed.gov/fulltext/EJ1154117.pdf.

7. For an in-depth treatment of integrating collaborative learning in your course, see Chapter 14: *Effective Collaboration in Online Courses* by Darby Dickerson and Megan Bess.

8. Elizabeth L. Inglehart et al., *From Cooperative Learning to Collaborative Writing in the Legal Writing Classroom*, 9 J. Legal Writing Inst. 185, 187 (2003) ("Hundreds of studies document the benefits that accrue from using cooperative and collaborative learning and trace that use back several centuries.").

9. Alli Gerkman & Logan Cornett, University of Denver AALS Study: Educating Tomorrow's Lawyers (2015), https://iaals.du.edu/publications/foundations-practice-whole-lawyer-and-character-quotient [hereinafter Denver Study].

10. Weimer, *supra* note 5, at 12, 63.

11. Marina Arshavskiy, Instructional Design for ELearning: Essential Guide to Creating Successful eLearning Courses 9; Robert John Ceglie & Ginger C. Black, *Lessons from the Other Side of the Computer: Student Perceptions of Effective Online Instruction*, *in* Handbook of Research on Developing Engaging Online Courses (Amy W. Thornburg et al. eds., 2020).

12. *See, e.g.*, Jennifer Camero, Teaching Law Online (2015); Susan Schor Ko, Teaching Online: A Practical Guide (2017); Best Practices in Online Teaching and Learning Across Academic Disciplines (Ross Alexander, ed., 2017); Shalin Hai-Jew, Form, Function and Style in Instructional Design: Emerging Research and Opportunities (2020).

13. For an overview of course design, see Chapter 8: *From Ground to Cloud and Back Again: Modern Tactics to Improve Your Teaching* by Katherine Brem and Chapter 9: *Converting a Course to an Asynchronous Format* by Kerry Lohmeier.

14. Schwartz, *supra* note 2, at 383. *See also* Lisa E. Gurley, *Educator's Preparation to Teach, Perceived Teaching Presence, and Perceived Teaching Presence Behaviors in Blended and Online Learning Environments*, 22 Online Learning J. 197, 198 (2018).

use a systematic course design process and backward design,[15] consider learner needs, and design learner interaction during the design process.[16]

The following examples of a synchronous online flipped course and a completely asynchronous course incorporate a collaborative, learner-centered approach in their design and delivery.

## II. Designing and Teaching a Fully-Online Flipped Classroom Research Skills Course

The online flipped course approach marries asynchronous and synchronous teaching methods to encourage collaboration, student engagement, and consistent professor-student and student-student contact. When designing this online course for delivery using the flipped course model, I focused on strategies that enabled students to become invested in the research process, to work on projects that reflected "real" lawyering work, to connect research skills to lawyering skills, and to engage in collaborative learning. Below, I will address the benefits of the online flipped course model, as well as considerations in developing an effective research assignment, collaborative approaches for teaching core concepts, research design, and research skills in the flipped course, and suggestions for both synchronous and asynchronous assessments. The approaches I discuss below can be integrated into a beginning or advanced legal research course, a first-year legal research and writing course or an upper-level skills class with a research and writing component.

### A. THE ONLINE FLIPPED COURSE

The flipped course and its tools are well-suited to an online environment. The flipped model has been found to be especially effective in teaching legal research skills.[17] Learning to be an efficient and thorough researcher takes hours of practice. The flipped course model, where the basic finding skills are taught outside of scheduled class, allows students to have more time in class to practice their skills in an engaging and collaborative learning environment.[18]

In the online flipped course, I produce asynchronous materials using video, narrated PowerPoint, audio-recorded lecture, and reading materials. Students benefit from receiving the technical aspects of the research process asynchronously because it allows students to go back to the material as often as needed. The asynchronous

---

15. For a detailed discussion of using backward design to re-design a course, see Chapter 30: *Backward Design: Course Design for Online Simulation Classes* by Christine Church.

16. Florence Martin et al., *Award-winning faculty online teaching practices: Course design, assessment and evaluation, and facilitation*, 42 INTERNET & HIGHER ED. 34, 38.

17. Laurel E. Davis et al., *Teaching Advanced Legal Research in a Flipped Classroom*, 22 PERSPECTIVES: TEACHING LEGAL RES. & WRITING 13, 16 (2013).

18. *Id.*

lessons can also provide links to additional reading and resources, allowing students to expand and reinforce their learning.

The asynchronous portion of the class also allows students to collaborate on documents and receive quick responses on their work from me and from other students. Students can upload assignments such as research logs, journals, or charts to the learning management system (LMS) or share via cloud-based documents. Students can then collaborate on these documents in real time or at their convenience, adding content, questions, and analysis. If students want to raise a question with me or the group, these questions can be easily added to the document, with the opportunity for me or the other students to respond quickly in between scheduled class sessions.

In the synchronous portion of the class, students engage in experiential learning where I act as a facilitator and guide. The in-class hands-on activities provide the opportunity for research skills acquisition while I monitor and provide guidance. The guidance I provide during the synchronous portion of the class is integral to helping students grasp how legal research skills are fundamentally interconnected with issue spotting, legal analysis, synthesis of information, and application of law to facts. Guided research activities allow me to help students master these interconnections as they move through research design and implementation.[19]

I hold some synchronous class time with the entire class, but I strive to do as much as possible of the synchronous class in small groups of no more than five students in either separately-scheduled sessions or in breakout rooms. If I schedule breakout rooms, students have the full class period to work together, and I can visit multiple rooms providing guidance where needed. If I schedule shorter synchronous class blocks for each group, I can spend more focused time with a smaller group of students.

### 1. Creating a comprehensive assignment

Creating a comprehensive research assignment that covers the entire semester is integral to teaching core concepts, legal research design, and research skills. I upload the research assignment as a PDF file to the LMS early in the course so that students become familiar with the assignment even before I require them to develop a research design and research the legal issues.

I create my assignments to mimic law practice, both in the types of documents that comprise the assignment and the legal questions students must research. I create assignments that rely on documents that would typically be present in a case file, like a client interview, pleadings, a police report, deposition testimony, or other investiga-

19. Sarah Valentine, *Legal Research as a Fundamental Skill: A Lifeboat for Students and Law Schools*, 39 U. Balt. L. Rev. 173, 200 (2010).

tion documents.[20] This ensures that students will be exposed to the types of litigation documents they will see in practice. I also create open-ended assignments that mimic legal issues that a first-year lawyer may be asked to investigate, which promotes the student's ability to spot legal theories and solutions applicable to a client's case. [21]

The complexity and structure of the open-ended assignments can vary depending upon the level of the class. In a first-year legal research and writing course, the assignments can be more directed: the client file might indicate that there is a "burglary charge" or an "intentional torts" claim, allowing the students room to focus on the level of burglary at issue or the type of intentional tort. Advanced research or skills courses could give students less information about the type of claim or area of the law. For example, based upon the facts, students may recognize that an employee had a workplace related dispute but would have to determine whether the issues involved statutory state or federal employment law claims and/or torts claims, etc.

### 2. Using the online flipped course to teach core concepts

Early in the course, I use the open-ended assignment to introduce or reinforce core concepts such as jurisdiction, hierarchy of the courts, weight of precedent, and types of sources. I also use the assignment to focus on basic analytic concepts that students must understand prior to beginning the research process—for example, how to recognize a legally relevant fact or the difference between fact and argument. I present the basic concepts in readings, narrated PowerPoints, or asynchronous videos. I then conduct synchronous classes to reinforce the concepts contained in the asynchronous materials, building off the facts and legal issues presented in the assignment.

In our synchronous class on core concepts, I rely heavily on the poll and chat features. These features of the online class platform are very effective at engaging students in the learning process, avoiding the "lecture" approach to presenting the material, and assessing the students' level of comprehension.

For example, when covering the role of precedent and binding and persuasive authority, I create an anonymous multiple-choice poll that asks students to determine which courts would be binding on the legal issue in our assignment and which would be merely persuasive. Polls can similarly be developed to address questions involving whether certain law that governs the assignment is common or statutory law and to determine whether students can distinguish primary law from secondary sources. I also create polls that address core analytic understanding. For example, in one poll, I ask students, "Is this a fact?" I then use both objective facts from the complaint as

---

20. Kristin B. Gerdy, *Teacher, Coach, Cheerleader, and Judge: Promoting Learning Through Learner-Centered Assessment*, 94 LAW LIBR. J. 59 (2002)

21. Ellie Margolis & Susan L. DeJarnatt, *Moving Beyond Product to Process: Building a Better LRW Program*, 46 SANTA CLARA L. REV. 93, 112–13 (2005).

well as allegations or statements that contain speculation and ask students to identify which statements qualify as "fact."[22]

After students complete the polls, I share the answers with the class. Sharing the answers works well to allay students' fears that they are the only ones who do not know the answers—I find that even with questions that I believe would be "easy," students are surprisingly mixed in their response. I then ask students to volunteer to discuss their answers for each of the questions. We discuss the answers as a class, engaging in a back and forth with me as the facilitator and the students as active participants in the learning process.

The chat function can be used to encourage participation and active learning in similar ways. While polls have the advantage of anonymity, which can encourage students who lack confidence to participate more readily, the chat feature can elicit more detailed responses from students. For example, I ask students to list in the chat one or two sources that would be binding on our assignment research and one or two that might be persuasive. I ask students to list the types of primary sources that might be binding (case law, statutes, constitutions) and secondary sources that could be helpful (law reviews, ALR's, treatises, etc.). Finally, I ask students to list one statement from the complaint or other case document that is an objective fact, and one that is an allegation or argument. I then call on students to expand on their answers, delving deeper into their understanding of the core concepts.

### 3. Using the online flipped course to teach research design

Teaching students to design a research plan prior to jumping in and searching for authority is a key lawyering skill[23] and saves time and effort. Amy Sloan, in *Basic Legal Research; Tools and Strategies*, outlines the process of developing a "coherent and effective research design" as: "(1) obtaining preliminary information about the problem; and (2) writing out a plan to follow."[24] Researching is more efficient, accurate, and complete when the researcher begins with a research plan. The perennial question that law students often struggle with—when do I stop researching—will be more easily resolved where the researcher has a comprehensive plan and follows it.

To teach research design under the flipped course model, I begin with asynchronous lectures, PowerPoints, or videos on the essentials of developing a research plan. In the asynchronous material, I teach students that when developing a research plan, they must identify: the issues in the case, including client goals; the areas of the law that may be implicated; jurisdictional questions, including whether federal, state, or local laws apply; and key facts. In addition, I instruct students to identify the sources

---

22. I am grateful for the help of my colleague, Amy Soled, an Associate Clinical Professor at Rutgers, who suggested ideas for these poll questions.

23. The Task Force on Law Sch. & the Profession, Am. Bar Assoc., Legal Education and Professional Development: An Educational Continuum (1992).

24. Amy E. Sloan, Basic Legal Research Tools and Strategies 299 (7th ed. 2018).

they plan to research. Depending upon the complexity of the course or assignment, students should consider sources such as case law, statutory codes, treatises, law reviews, practice guides, jury instructions, regulatory codes, legislative histories, etc.

The experiential learning process of developing an effective research design plan from the client file occurs in the synchronous class. In breakout rooms of five students maximum, I facilitate each group's efforts, answering student questions and guiding students as they bounce ideas and suggestions off me and the other group members. Students should work collaboratively to issue spot the client's legal claims and liabilities, determine which laws apply to those claims, understand which key facts within the file may aid in the development of search terms once the research process begins, and catalog and rank the sources that would be most useful in which to begin the research. When a group starts going down an incorrect path, I guide the students in a different direction. Where the group is successful, I encourage the process that the group used, reinforcing effective collaborative methods.

I also hold large class blocks during which the groups return to the classroom to report on their recommendations. Having participated and guided each group in their design plan, I can easily organize the discussion around successful techniques that the group used as well as discussing paths that led to less successful outcomes.

### 4. Using the online flipped course to teach research skills and design implementation

Conducting legal research is a lawyering skill requiring students to not only have the ability to locate sources but also to understand the relevance of those sources, use those sources to craft and support arguments that resolve the legal issues, and to modify initial research strategies as necessary. The AALL's Principles and Standards calls for lawyers to "understand research as a recursive process;" to reflect on the "successes and failures of prior strategies for integrating new information into the analysis;" and to "recognize when specific questions within the larger research problem have not been answered."[25]

As when teaching research design, I start with asynchronous tools to teach basic or advanced research skills. I focus my lessons on how and when to research different types of source material, including common law, statutory law, and secondary sources. I instruct students on how to perform natural language and terms and connectors searches, citator searches, and headnote searches. I also instruct students to cite check their cases and statutes to make sure they are still good law.[26]

---

25. Am. Ass'n L. Librs., Principles and Standards for Legal Research Competency (2013) [hereinafter Principles & Standards].

26. Basic and advanced training with services such as Westlaw and Lexis should be facilitated at this stage and can be taught in a synchronous format by the account representatives.

During synchronous class time, I act as a facilitator to help students implement their design plan and develop efficient and thorough research skills. Using the assignment and the design strategy initially developed by the student groups, I facilitate continued small group work in either breakout rooms or small group sessions. Westlaw, Lexis, or other databases can be viewed with the student group in real time via screen sharing either by me or by a group member. We work collaboratively on developing the following research skills:

1. Understanding Natural Language versus Terms and Connectors or Boolean Searching: While natural language searching is most intuitive, Boolean searching will often yield much more efficient results. If students begin with a natural language search that results in an overwhelming number of cases, I direct them to utilize Boolean searching methods to narrow the scope.
2. Understanding Citator Searching Techniques: Starting with a helpful case that the students have already found, I encourage students to use the Westlaw Topic and Key Number system or the Lexis Headnotes and Topic searches. I act as facilitator as the student group tries different key number or topic searches and evaluates their success.
3. Learning to Use Statutory Annotations and Notes of Decisions: I help students gain familiarity with researching statutory subsections, legislative history, and related law. I can guide students to find statutes using the History and Case Notes' Table of Contents. We can compare the efficiency of using the Case Notes to natural language, Boolean, and citator searching for case law.
4. Understanding the Interplay Between State and Federal Law: I can assess whether students are focusing on the appropriate jurisdiction and are considering alternate jurisdictions to research where necessary. For instance, students may easily find a federal statute, but not consider whether there is similar state legislation. Students may thus have questions as to when to research state law versus federal law, why some federal cases analyze state law claims and vice versa, and whether a plaintiff can bring a claim under both federal and state law. Acting as a facilitator in real time during the research process allows me to answer important questions as students develop them.
5. Learning to Search Alternative Databases: With a more advanced research project, I monitor which databases students are searching, suggesting alternative searches where necessary. I provide commentary on whether and how they are accessing free online databases, like court websites, the Caselaw Access Project website, or Findlaw, and whether they are choosing secondary sources versus primary sources. I can also suggest types of sources that students may be unfamiliar with—including dockets, or secondary materials such as practice forms, court rules, or briefs. As I act as the facilitator and suggest different research sources in real time, the students gain familiarity with multiple databases, sources, and methods that they may otherwise not use if researching individually on their own time.

After working on these research skills in small groups or breakout rooms, I can unite the student groups in the classroom to review and present research methods. This can be an effective way for the class as a whole to collaborate and learn from each other. Each group can share their research methods and processes with a focus on which methods were most successful, resulting in a targeted list of relevant sources, and which methods were least helpful, resulting in too broad a list of sources or sources that were off-topic.

### 5. Research synthesis, evaluation, and assessment

Teaching should be viewed as a continuous process of learning and assessing that learning.[27] Intertwining assessments with the learning process enables students to learn and improve during their engagement with the research assignment rather than simply by receiving instructions on what they did wrong after the assignment is over. This allows students to pivot immediately to use new skills and understandings "in process," which results in greater student engagement and acquisition of skills. Further, assessments should be structured to focus on connecting research results to the lawyering process and synthesizing research results in order to move forward with litigating the case.

I assess students' performance on research design through the requirement that each group produce a research log. The research log documents the group's research design strategy ensuring that students are developing a comprehensive plan. This log can be shared between me and the group members through a cloud document and/or uploaded for easy access onto the course's LMS. This document can then be revised, edited, and responded to asynchronously in between class sessions. The research log may require students to set out an initial issue statement, a list of potential search terms, relevant jurisdictions to search, and an outline and hierarchical list of sources that the researchers plan to consult.

There are several ways in which I assess student performance on research skills. Facilitating a synchronous class session where each student group presents research findings to the class is an effective way to assess whether students have found relevant sources and to reinforce that research is a connected process. Rather than sharing all of the sources that each group found, each student group can be asked to choose one or two sources that the group feels are particularly relevant to the assignment. The group can then be asked to prepare to answer a variety of questions about the source(s). For example, the group may be asked to discuss: (1) how they found the source, (2) the facts, holding, and rules from the source that directly bear on one of the issues in the assignment, and (3) how the facts of the precedent case compare to the facts of their own case. With an advanced course, student groups can be asked to evaluate: (1) the strengths and weaknesses of the source, (2) how the case might be useful to each party based upon a narrowing or broadening of the holding, and (3) how the facts of the case could work both in favor of or against the party they represent

27. Gerdy, *supra* note 20, at 46.

in the assignment. If the case leaves certain questions unanswered, the group can be pushed to articulate what these questions may be and to formulate further research questions where necessary.

By finding a source and discussing its connection to the assignment, students understand research as an analytic process rather than a mechanical task. They learn that effective research is necessarily interconnected to case synthesis, legal analysis, and advocacy. By requiring students to articulate how they located sources and how those sources relate to the client's claim, I can assess whether students understand basic and advanced finding skills, how their sources relate to the legal claims and facts of the assignment, how these sources can be synthesized with other relevant sources, and finally, how these sources can be used to advocate on behalf of the client.

Another form of assessment is to require each group to create a research chart. Charts are an effective assessment tool because they allow me to see whether the students have focused their research on the proper issues and have found the universe of relevant sources. It also allows me to see if they are synthesizing the sources to answer the research question. At the same time, charts encourage students to see the connections between the sources they have found and to spot holes in their research.

The chart can be organized by the elements or factors of the claim and may require students to list relevant statutory sections, the facts and holdings of relevant cases, and how the facts of each case relates back to the elements of the claims. The chart can be uploaded to the LMS allowing for easy access by me and the group members. Students can regularly update the chart as needed throughout the research process. Where students have questions or comments, they can use verbal comment technology, or provide written comments on cloud-based documents. I and other group members can respond to these comments and questions asynchronously in between synchronous class time.

Finally, I assess students' research through the requirement that the groups create a research journal. In the research journal, I ask students to reflect on the research process and detail how and why they gathered various sources of legal authority. The research journal requires students to perform a critical evaluation of the authority they found, rather than merely listing their final sources. As with the research log and the research chart, the journal should be a collaborative group document that can be accessed online or uploaded onto the LMS.

## III. Designing and Teaching an Asynchronous Advanced Legal Research Course

This section describes a fully asynchronous online advanced legal research course that is based on a learner-centered teaching approach. This approach connects learning to practical experience, clearly articulates the purpose and relevancy of activities and assessments in relation to students' academic and professional goals, encourages active student engagement, and creates a collaborative context for learning. For the course design process, I used backward design and integrated principles of Universal Design for Learning (UDL) to make the course as inclusive as possible.[28] This section outlines the backward course design process and principles of Universal Design for Learning, and describes specific design and teaching decisions in the advanced legal research course.

### A. THE COURSE DESIGN PROCESS: USING BACKWARD DESIGN AND UNIVERSAL DESIGN FOR LEARNING

I had taught advanced legal research for many years in person and knew that I could not simply transfer an in-person class into an LMS to deliver remotely. Online courses can isolate and disorient students,[29] so course planning for a fully asynchronous course requires special attention to establishing a community of learners, engaging every student, as well as developing a strong and consistent instructor presence.[30] I engaged in an analytical course design process to develop a course that would promote engaged, hands-on, collaborative learning of an important professional skill.

Based on various course design models, my design process involves analyzing and defining students' needs and the context of the course, then using backward design to develop learning outcomes or goals, create assessments, and construct learning activities that are directly aligned with those learning goals.[31]

The backward design begins with the end result of the instruction, or determining what the students should know or be able to do at the end of the course or session (learning outcomes).[32] Determining the desired outcomes and corresponding assessments, learning materials, and activities requires analysis of the students and what they need to know. Not all law students are the same, so the process of "analyzing the student" is complex. The course design, therefore, needs to recognize and support the diversity of experiences that students bring to their legal education.[33]

In addition to considering the individuality of law students and their varied professional and educational backgrounds, course design needs to account for the reasons why students are taking an advanced (elective) research course. Law students will enter a profession where employers will expect them to be prepared with solid research, writing, and communication skills. The goals of a legal research course need to emphasize repeated practice finding resources, using multiple databases and free sources,

---

28. For an additional discussion on UDL, see Chapter 7: *Using Blended and Online Learning Strategies to Provide Innovative Academic Support to All Students* by Susan Landrum.

29. Martin, *supra* note 16, at 36. For an in-depth treatment of how to build community in an asynchronous course, see Chapter 12: *How to Build Community for Asynchronous Courses* by Ann Nowak.

30. Martin, *supra* note 16, at 36. For a more in-depth discussion of the importance of community for learning, see Chapter 11: *The Importance of Building Community in Online and Blended Courses* by Sophie Sparrow.

31. Martin, *supra* note 16, at 40.

32. *Id.*

33. Rebecca Flanagan, *Anthrogogy: Towards Inclusive Law School Learning*, 19 CONN. PUB. INT. L.J. 93, 98 (2019).

as well as communicating effectively about the legal research process, the sources of law, and the information the sources provide.

Another consideration in course design is inclusivity. Because law students come from such diverse backgrounds and experiences, course design should be guided by principles of Universal Design for Learning (UDL).[34] In teaching and learning, UDL proactively designs learning to be accessible for all students, no matter their backgrounds, or diverse abilities, so that activities, exercises, content, and assessments do not have to be retrofitted to comply with legal requirements for accommodation.[35]

Based on neurological science, UDL guidelines provide a framework for effective engagement, participation, and learning for all students.[36] According to those guidelines, the course design should consider the affective network, the recognition network, and the strategic network.[37]

The affective learning network concerns student engagement, motivation, and persistence. To address the affective learning network, course instructors need to create strategies for igniting students' curiosity and interest, as well as keeping them interested and motivated, such as tying assignments to actual practice scenarios and skills.

The recognition network concerns the different ways in which learners take in information. To address the recognition network, instructors need to employ a variety of inputs, to provide options for perception and comprehension.[38] For example, instead of using only lecture to present content, an instructor uses a combination of video, demonstration, reading assignments, small group discussions, and hands-on exercises to allow students to interact with the course content in multiple ways.

The strategic network concerns how students demonstrate mastery of what they have learned.[39] Different students express themselves more effectively in one medium or another. Therefore, instructors provide multiple options for students to demonstrate that they have learned the material, such as writing an email to a supervisor, recording a video, leading a simulated research conference, or creating a visual research log.

Asynchronous courses promote principles of inclusivity through UDL by offering students flexibility in interacting with course content in a variety of formats. First, in an asynchronous environment, students can choose when and where to work on

34. *Id.* at 129; *see also* Dyane L. O'Leary, *Flipped out, Plugged in, and Wired up: Fostering Success for Students with ADHD in the New Digital Law School*, 45 Cap. U. L. Rev. 289, 326 (2016); Kathleen A. Booth & Marla J. Lohmann, *Using Universal Design for Learning (UDL) for Optimal Student Engagement in the Online College Classroom*, *in* Handbook of Research on Developing Effective Online Courses (Amy W. Thornburg et al. eds., 2020) (for a general discussion on UDL in online courses).

35. Flanagan, *supra* note 33, at 130.

36. *About Universal Design for Learning*, Cast, https://www.cast.org/impact/universal-design-for-learning-udl (last visited Feb. 8, 2021).

37. *The UDL Guidelines*, Cast, http://udlguidelines.cast.org (last visited Feb. 8, 2021).

38. *Id.*

39. *Id.*

course materials. Second, asynchronous courses routinely use captioned videos to deliver content, allowing students to watch or listen to the content multiple times to comprehend and apply the course concepts. Finally, asynchronous courses use discussion forums that encourage student interaction and collaboration, while providing students with the lead time they need to formulate and reflect on their responses.

## B. AN EXAMPLE OF DESIGN AND DELIVERY OF ASYNCHRONOUS ADVANCED LEGAL RESEARCH

This section outlines and explains the design and delivery of an asynchronous online advanced legal research course.

### 1. Analysis of the learners

Students taking the course are second or third-year law students who enjoy legal research or recognize that they need more practice. Most of the students come with basic legal research skills focused mainly on foundational proficiency in using Westlaw or Lexis.

Responses to a "research self-assessment survey" that I provide to students indicate that most students feel comfortable with finding statutes and cases using natural language searching, as well as a few types of secondary sources on the major research platforms. Many students admit that they lack confidence with Boolean searching, using indexes or other tools to find resources, and any kind of research involving administrative law or legislative history. Most say that they are inefficient or slow. Students often observe that a summer internship exposed weaknesses and lack of knowledge that they were unaware of previously. This valuable information forms the basis for creating the learning outcomes for the course.

### 2. Learning outcomes/goals

The design of advanced legal research is based on the principle that law students should practice how to conduct legal research in a simulated practice environment. Therefore, I drafted learning outcomes that emphasize skills that lawyers need in practice: analyzing facts, planning research, engaging in critical reading, searching for and finding sources, evaluating sources, communicating research findings to colleagues, and critically reflecting on their research. The learning outcomes create space for the important skill of collaboration by emphasizing communication of legal information to colleagues.

The core course material consists of a client file containing minimal facts, and setting out several questions posed by the simulated client. Students are conducting research to prepare for a meeting with the client. The scenario requires research in state and federal jurisdictions on enacted law, case law, administrative law, and legislative history, as well as practice-oriented materials and ethical rules.

### 3. Assessments or other evidence of accomplishing learning outcomes

Design for an online course, just like design for an in-person course, requires formative and summative assessments as evidence of achieving the learning goals or outcomes.[40]

Assessments need to align with the learning goals or outcomes. For example, a multiple-choice test on terminology and different types of sources of law does not assess whether a student can evaluate a set of facts and find relevant legal information using research tools. Such a test would not be aligned with the learning outcomes. Students might fail to see the relevance of the test to the development of their practice skills, and as a consequence, determine that they are engaged in "busy work," thereby becoming disengaged from the course. As noted above, students will more likely maintain attention and enthusiasm for tasks that are authentic—meaning connected to real-life legal practice.

Also, instructors should provide substantive, meaningful feedback to students, rather than just assign a grade on assessments.[41] Students will not be able to determine skills that are lacking, strategies they could improve, or more effectively navigation of research platforms, if they receive only a grade on an assignment or project.

In the advanced legal research course, students complete weekly journal entries as formative assessments that explain the research they have conducted during the week and reflect on their progress as researchers. Students are prompted to reflect on new resources or new ways of searching, problems or challenges they encountered or solved, and how they collaborated with other students.

Another formative assessment requires students to design a research log, chart, or other document that tracks and organizes their research results. Students have commented that this project is useful and relevant to not only their academic goals but also their professional externships or paid work.

In addition, students lead a "research conference" as a role play via video-conferencing. A student or small group of students meets with a "supervisor" to explain their progress on the client's problem. The students get real-time feedback from the instructor and other students via comments and questions, and they receive formalized feedback through instructor comments after the conference. The conference highlights gaps in their knowledge or research process, which they can remedy before a higher-stakes project is due.

---

40. For additional ideas for formative and summative assessment as well as using assessment data to assess learning outcomes, see Chapter 24: *Teaching Civil Procedure Online with Active Learning* by Cynthia Ho.

41. Charity L.B. Jennings, *Enhancing Social Presence in Online Courses: Facilitation Strategies and Best Practices* 259, *in* HANDBOOK OF RESEARCH ON DEVELOPING EFFECTIVE ONLINE COURSES (Amy W. Thornburg et al. eds., 2020) (discussion of feedback as important in enhancing social presence in online courses).

The summative assessment requires students to document, explain, and synthesize all of their research and communicate it to a supervisor or colleague. Students can choose from a variety of formats for the project including a research memorandum, a website, a video, or an extensive graphic, to name a few options. The final project also requires students to reflect on their stated research goals from the beginning of the course and their progress toward meeting those goals.

### 4. Learning Activities

Online courses, with their technology-rich environment, facilitate creative and varied activities, experiences, and course materials. Also, skills courses like advanced legal research lend themselves to students actively practicing that skill rather than listening passively to a lecture, or reading about sources of law and research platforms. Important considerations for designing course materials and activities are (1) directly aligning them with the learning outcomes and assessments, (2) encouraging collaboration and cooperation among students, and (3) providing a variety of activities integrating principles of Universal Design for Learning.

In advanced legal research, I set up the LMS with weekly modules that follow a similar structure from week to week. Students engage in multiple types of activities each week: a video explaining sources of law and leading students in an interactive demonstration of the research process on various platforms; textbook readings introducing or clarifying terminology or types of resources; a student-led small-group discussion on the progress of their research; an optional online drop-in session for discussion and collaboration with students and the instructor; and a weekly journal entry documenting their research work and reflecting on their research goals. The weekly activities, in total, allow for both active and passive independent work on research, collaboration with classmates, feedback from the instructor, and reflection.

The weekly modules are consistent in form, substance, and due dates. Discussion posts and responses are due on the same days each week. The online drop-in meeting is held at that same time each week; journal entries or projects are due on the same days and times each week so that students can establish a routine and schedule for the course.

### 5. Developing a learning community and instructor presence

One of the biggest challenges in online learning is ensuring students engage with the course and stay engaged, rather than feeling isolated, confused, or lost. Developing a learning community that supports sustained connection to the course begins in the design phase and continues throughout delivery of the course.

Constructivist learning theory, as well as a learner-centered approach, values the social aspect of learning. So too, in online learning, building relationships and a community is crucial.[42] Therefore, the role of the instructor in online learning is very

42. Martin, *supra* note 16, at 79.

different from being an authority figure behind a podium. The role of the online instructor is to develop an active and reliable presence and engage learners by creating a classroom community, engaging in consistent and frequent communication, and providing individualized and substantive feedback.[43]

I create a module for the first week that includes an introductory video demonstrating navigation of the LMS, course materials, and the online textbook.[44] I share my background in practicing law and teaching, and my hobbies. Finally, I give students a list of what they should be doing for the week. Often students are overwhelmed in the first week of classes, so I find that a short bullet-point list often gives them some feeling of control and manageable goals. I also create a discussion forum for the whole class so they can introduce themselves to foster an environment of collegiality.

In subsequent weeks, students are divided into smaller discussion/collaboration groups to engage in conversations about resources, research process, or challenges in finding the information. The smaller groups encourage more familiarity and a conversational rapport so they feel comfortable learning from each other. In the past, I have authored the weekly discussion prompts on substantive topics connected to the research problem. However, I found that student responses to my prompts seemed forced, perhaps not meeting the goal of authentic interaction and collaboration. As a result, I currently designate a discussion leader in each group to create the prompt or question for the week. Surprisingly, I have seen no resistance to this format. Students create interesting questions that are immediately relevant to the research they are doing for the week; the other group members respond with suggestions of resources they found or a strategy they used. The discussions are productive and professional. I monitor the discussions and try to strike a balance of responding or providing guidance if a student has a question, but not interfering in vibrant student exchanges.

Equally important as student-to-student interaction is the interaction between instructor and student, which needs to be varied in form and formality, as well as continuous, constructive, and timely.[45] Students value quick and substantive feedback.[46] To be present for students and keep them engaged with our class, I respond to student emails within twelve hours maximum, but mostly within two hours. I also send an announcement at the start of each week that summarizes the weekly agenda and reminds students of due dates. For students' weekly journal assignments, I provide individual comments within forty-eight hours. The quick response time allows them to

---

43. *Id.*

44. I use Kent C. Olson, Principles of Legal Research (2015), which is available online to law students as part of their West Academic subscription.

45. Dixie F. Abernathy & Amy Wooten Thornburg, *Theory and Application in the Design and Delivery of Engaging Online Courses: Four Key Principles That Drive Student and Instructor Engagement and Success*, 253–54, *in* Handbook of Research on Developing Effective Online Courses (Amy W. Thornburg et al. eds., 2020).

46. In response to questionnaires I provide to students at the beginning of a course, students consistently state that they want quick, individualized feedback on their work.

investigate missing resources, or apply those comments to their work for the following week. The weekly substantive comments also allow them to address inaccuracies or omissions before they are graded on a more high-stakes project.

Weekly videos provide another avenue to interact and connect with students. The videos address questions that came up the previous week in discussions or in students' individual research journals. The videos demonstrate navigation of research platforms and remind students of their research goals for the week and any upcoming deadlines. By seeing me and hearing my voice, students maintain that connection with the class community and the material.

Finally, because some students learn better if they are talking directly to the instructor, I hold weekly video conference drop-in sessions for students to ask questions or work through a problem. These sessions are optional for most weeks, with one required session toward the end of the course to simulate talking to a supervisor or colleague about their research process and results.

## IV. Conclusion

Law students frequently comment that they lack confidence in their legal research skills and that they perceive legal research to be among the most important skills they need to learn in law school. These sentiments are echoed by legal employers who rank research as one of the most essential practice-ready skills for new lawyers and, yet, indicate high levels of dissatisfaction with the researching abilities of new law school graduates. Online platforms open the door to new creative approaches to help cure the deficits in our law students' research skills and to produce practice ready graduates. Both synchronous and asynchronous online courses provide the opportunity for active engagement, collaboration, and simulated realistic practice of research skills. To meet the challenges of the online environment, which can be disorienting and isolating for some students, instructors should engage in intentional course design by identifying learning outcomes, implementing a variety of course activities and assessments, and providing extensive feedback. Harnessing online technologies with purpose and thought can both revolutionize the legal research classroom to produce more competent lawyers and help students develop the communication, collaboration, and technological skills that will prepare them for professional practice.

TWENTY-TWO

# Flexing Your Muscles: Using Backward Design to Create a Property Course That Can Be Taught in Multiple Modes

Kimberly E. O'Leary*

After reviewing this chapter, readers will be able to:

- Create a course using backward design;
- Compare different modes of instruction relative to the elements of backward design;
- Choose appropriate teaching methods depending on the mode of instruction; and
- Adapt a course from one mode to the other with minimal additional effort.

This chapter examines how to design a Property course to be taught in different modes. The teaching modes are described in the chart in Part I below. Using backward design, a teacher can teach the same course in any of these modes without significant additional work.[1] Once the right teaching tools are in place, the course can be adapted to any desired teaching mode. This chapter will also discuss strengths and weaknesses of each mode of instruction.

I teach the second half of a six-credit Property Law course. Property I introduces students to foundational concepts: personal property rights (capture, finders, gifts); adverse possession; the estate system, including all estates except leasehold estates; basic

---

* Professor of Law, WMU-Cooley Law School. Professor O'Leary began law teaching in 1988 and began teaching courses online in 2017. She has designed and taught courses in traditional and online formats, using synchronous and asynchronous components.

1. For a more in-depth treatment on backward design, see Chapter 8: *From Ground to Cloud and Back Again: Modern Tactics to Improve Your Teaching* by Katherine Brem, and Chapter 30: *Backward Design: Course Design for Online Simulation Classes* by Christine Church.

concepts related to title and residential real estate transactions; and mortgages. Property II—the course I teach—includes leasehold estates and land use controls (including nuisance, servitudes, zoning, eminent domain, and implicit takings). I use a standard Property Law textbook.[2] This chapter will use Property II as an example of the adaptation process. I have taught Property in traditional, online synchronous, and blended modes.

## I. Defining the Teaching Modes

### THE FOUR MODES OF INSTRUCTION

| Mode of Instruction | Traditional | Online Synchronous | Asynchchronous | Blended |
|---|---|---|---|---|
| Location of synchronous classes | 100% on-site, in-person classes | All synchronous classes are online, but some weeks may be taught asynchronously | No synchronous classes | Some classes are in-person, some are online, and some might be asynchronous |
| Location of course materials | LMS[3] with option for print texts and handouts | LMS with option for a print text | LMS with option for a print text | LMS with option for print texts and handouts. |
| Location of out-of-class activities | LMS repository for syllabus (reading assignments, other tasks), quizzes, practice problems. Might have some paper handouts. | LMS repository for syllabus (reading assignments, other tasks), quizzes, practice problems. All handouts must be posted on LMS. | LMS repository for syllabus (reading assignments, other tasks), quizzes, practice problems. All handouts must be posted on LMS. | LMS repository for syllabus (reading assignments, other tasks), quizzes, practice problems. All handouts should be posted on LMS but might have some paper handouts. |
| Method of in-class activities | Socratic method, small-group activities, polls, cards, presentations, admission or exit tickets, flip charts, etc. Can be electronic or paper. | Breakout groups, online platforms for spreadsheets, docs, quizzes or polls, presentations, and cold calls. | n/a | All synchronous activities in this row are available |
| Assignment submission | Physically hand in papers, use drop box, or upload to LMS | LMS | LMS | Physically hand in papers, use drop box, or upload to LMS |

2. JESSE DUKEMINIER ET AL., PROPERTY (9th ed. 2017).
3. I use the Canvas learning management system (LMS).

| Mode of Instruction | Traditional | Online Synchronous | Asynchchronous | Blended |
|---|---|---|---|---|
| Exam/Quiz submission | Physically-proc-tored exam in class, or LMS with cheating prevention measures:<br>• proctor software,<br>• open book,<br>• collaborative,<br>• relying on Hon-or Code, or<br>• timed exams | LMS with cheating prevention mea-sures:<br>• proctor software,<br>• open book,<br>• collaborative,<br>• relying on Hon-or Code, or<br>• timed exams | LMS with cheating prevention mea-sures:<br>• proctor software,<br>• open book,<br>• collaborative,<br>• relying on Hon-or Code, or<br>• timed exams | All options in this row are available |
| Professor "lecture" | Lecture in class and/or post videos on LMS | Lecture in class and/or post videos on LMS | Post videos on LMS | Lecture in class and/or post videos on LMS |
| Discussion | • In-class discus-sion (all or small groups)<br>• Discussion board prompts on LMS<br>• Outside projects requiring collab-oration | • In-class discus-sion (all or small groups)<br>• Discussion board prompts on LMS<br>• Outside projects requiring collab-oration | Discussion board prompts or outside projects requiring collaboration | All options in this row are available |

## II. Backward Design in a Property Course

Backward design is building a course by starting with course objectives ("when students complete the course, they will be able to do x"). Backward design is a good way to design any course, regardless of teaching mode. To do this:

1. Identify learning objectives for the course;
2. Determine how you will assess whether students (a) understand the concepts and skills in the learning objectives during the course and (b) meet those objectives when they complete the course;
3. Identify the resources you will provide to help students achieve the objectives; and
4. Create learning opportunities to help students achieve the objectives.

The first and third steps usually look the same, no matter what mode you are teaching in. The second and fourth concepts vary, depending on the teaching mode.

## A. LEARNING OBJECTIVES

Learning objectives should be short and concise statements, using active verbs to describe what students should be able to do after they complete the course. At my law school, full-time faculty in each department (in my case, the Property department) collaboratively developed learning objectives for each required course. These are the learning objectives we developed for Property II[4]:

---

After completing the Property II course, students should be able to:

1. Identify, define, analyze, and evaluate the law relating to:
    - landlord-tenant relations, including the creation and termination of leasehold estates;
    - the requirements of federal fair housing legislation;
    - the transfer of possessory rights by assignment and sublease;
    - default by tenants and corresponding landlord remedies, and landlord duties of repair and maintenance of premises;
    - servitudes, including the creation, scope, assignment, and termination of easements, real covenants, and equitable servitudes;
    - the common law tort doctrine of nuisance and its commonly available remedies; and
    - government regulation of land use, including legal constraints governing the design, implementation, and enforcement of zoning ordinances, the Fifth Amendment power of eminent domain, and when regulation might constitute an implicit taking requiring just compensation.
2. Differentiate between majority and minority U.S. jurisdictions when rules are different.

---

Notice that these objectives contain both a skills dimension and a knowledge dimension. The skills are to identify, define, analyze, and evaluate certain doctrine, and to differentiate jurisdictional differences. The knowledge dimension is the doctrine the students are learning.

## B. ASSESSMENT

Once you set course objectives, outline how you will assess the students. Assessments are one of two types: formative or summative. Formative assessments are designed to determine whether students understand concepts and skills while the course is proceeding and to give feedback so students can improve and master the material. Students improve when they can see for themselves what they are doing well and

---

4. Email from Property Department Chair David Finnegan to Kim O'Leary, Aug. 16, 2020. Shared with permission.

what they are misunderstanding or doing poorly ("metacognition"), and students who think this way retain learned concepts longer than students who do not.

Summative assessments are a form of benchmarking: did the student demonstrate the skills and the knowledge expected of them? In backward design, one typically starts with the summative assessments and works back toward formative assessments, because summative assessments typically occur at the end of the course (and this is *backward* design).

In a Property course, and most core courses in law school, the primary summative assessment is a final examination. However, a teacher might choose to have shorter summative assessments related to particular material throughout the course. Formative assessments—some graded, some ungraded—provide multiple opportunities for student metacognition. In my Property course, student grades are based on points, and students earn points by submitting formative and summative graded assessments. I also assess in other ungraded ways throughout the course.

The benchmark, ***summative*** assessments in my course break down as follows:

- A final exam consisting of essays, worth forty-five percent of the grade; this exam assesses a student's ability to identify, define, analyze, and evaluate assignment and sublease of leasehold estates, servitudes, and government land-use regulation, differentiating majority and minority rules.
- A required opinion letter worth ten percent of the grade; this assignment assesses a student's ability to identify, define, analyze, and evaluate nuisance law and its remedies, differentiating majority and minority law. It additionally requires students to think in a client-centered manner and write to a lay audience.
- A midterm essay exam worth fifteen percent of the grade; the midterm assesses a student's ability to identify, define, analyze, and evaluate all of the doctrines associated with leasehold estates, except assignment and sublease, differentiating majority and minority law. The midterm is also a formative assessment as to the skills involved (ability to identify, define, analyze, and evaluate doctrine) in preparation for the final examination—where the students will have to demonstrate those same skills.

The graded ***formative*** assessments include:

- Weekly online discussion posts, worth very low points each week. But, collectively the discussion posts plus a quiz offered in an asynchronous week are worth five percent of the grade. Requiring students to post answers to weekly questions helps students to process what they have learned from the resources (reading assignments and videos); to help them think about the concepts before classroom sessions or asynchronous work; and to help me see, broadly, which concepts are well-understood and which are not. I can adjust what I cover in classroom sessions or videos based on their responses. The scores are based on good-faith effort.

- The quiz in an asynchronous week combines with the discussion posts for five percent of the grades. In that quiz, students are required to apply several "implicit takings" tests to one set of facts. This quiz allows me to check students' understanding of a difficult concept and provide feedback.
- A practice essay, followed by required peer-editing, the week before the midterm, worth five percent of the grade.[5] This assignment helps students achieve metacognition of the skills dimension (identify, define, analyze, and evaluate)—and of the knowledge dimension (leasehold estates). Peer-grading two of their classmates' practice exams gives them valuable insight into what I look for when I grade their midterms, and it helps them internalize the process steps.
- Two online bar-style multiple-choice tests, worth a total of twenty percent of the grade. This assignment is collaborative and open book, and students have three weeks to complete each test; however, once they have submitted it, each student is required to analyze all incorrect responses using a self-analysis chart. This helps students to learn detailed doctrinal points. Since it covers all the doctrine in the course, it requires students to revisit previously learned material (spaced repetition). It helps them to identify problems with the process skills related to bar-style multiple-choice (metacognition). And the results provide data to help me understand student weaknesses.

In all teaching modes, my graded assessments have mostly the same structure. The real difference is the level of security provided for summative assessments. For teaching modes where students physically take exams on-site (traditional and blended), I typically give the two summative exams (midterm and final) on site and proctored. All other assessments are online, whether the class is in "traditional" mode or not. Thus, the only assessments I need to adapt are the summative assessments.

Summative assessments differ from mode-to-mode in several ways:

**Timed exams:** When I teach in-person, students' exams are strictly timed. But timed exams are challenging for students online. Not all students can afford premium internet service. Even when their internet is good, it may be compromised during certain times of the day because of heavier use in their area. Students in rural areas or near geographic features that block signals may experience frequent problems. Students' housemates may also use computers and the internet. Noise can be unpredictable and outside a student's control.[6] Some students have caregiver responsibilities, especially

5. I use my LMS to set up the peer-edit assignment. I then record video instructing the students how to use my grading rubric for the peer-editing portion of the assignment.

6. For example, during an exam conference with a student, we were frequently interrupted by the sound of a drill. The student's landlord was repairing the apartment above his. After a half-dozen interruptions, we agreed to reschedule the meeting. If this had been a timed exam, the student's concentration would have been constantly disrupted.

during pandemic conditions. Even if nobody in the household is sick, students may have to care for toddlers, elders, or others—sometimes unexpectedly.

***Bottom line:*** When I offer an exam online, I give students a window of 24–48 hours to take the exam. I allow them to start, pause, and come back without penalty. Though this could lead to cheating, if the exam primarily tests the ability to analyze novel situations, it does not appear—anecdotally at least—to result in more Honor Code incidents than one would expect in an in-person class.

**Proctored exams:** For online exams, lock-down browsers and camera monitors can be problematic. When I first heard about them, I was excited and hopeful that online exams could replicate on-site exams. But in our limited tests, lock-down browsers have not been reliable, have produced some computer problems for students (such as overheating), and create extra stress. Cameras recording students who live in small spaces—especially with others—cause privacy concerns. Some students of color state they must shine a bright light directly onto their faces. The programs can also be subject to software glitches and attacks.[7]

***Bottom line:*** Instead of using security software, I tailor the exam to the conditions. Before any institution uses security software, it should test rigorously to ensure fairness to students. This software might be more viable if used during more normal, less stressful conditions than a pandemic.

**Exam structure:** Short, targeted questions, added to one of my typical "thick" multi-issue questions, effectively evaluate what students know and can do. In a timed, on-site exam, students focus for a limited time in quiet conditions. They can jot down notes and write on the exam paper. Online tests disadvantage students who don't have a printer, spacious desk, or who experience interruptions. And, ironically, open-book exams can disadvantage students because so much information can cause them to lose focus. But you can create short and focused questions that are also effective.

Regardless of teaching mode, my midterm is one multi-issue essay. But even though students have more time online (the 24-hour window), the quality of the answers hasn't really changed. I alter the final exam, however, for an online synchronous course. In traditional mode, I typically had three multi-issue essay questions. I sometimes included some "short-answer" questions, testing students' memory of elements and rules. These closed-book exams lasted 165 minutes. In the online synchronous and asynchronous settings, I have one multi-issue essay, followed by three or four single-issue focused questions that test difficult material. Students have no wiggle room.

I caution students to use their own words when formulating rules rather than copying and pasting rules from outlines, slides, and the internet. Given my ground rules,

---

7. In 2020, there were numerous software problems encountered by bar examination test-takers that used lockdown features. *See, e.g.*, Jack Evans, *The Florida Bar exam software crashes, freezes and can lead to hacks, examinees say*, Tampa Bay Times, August 13, 2020, *available at* https://www.msn.com/en-us/news/us/the-florida-bar-exam-software-crashes-freezes-and-can-lead-to-hacks-examinees-say/ar-BB17Vog5 (last accessed Feb. 10, 2021).

copying and pasting rules is not cheating; however, it makes for inelegant statements that do not precisely apply to my facts, which lowers their grades. I never put "list the elements" short-answer questions on online exams. Students can look those up online or in their notes, rendering those questions useless.

***Bottom line:*** Think about how to ask the right questions when giving an open-book, online summative exam. You can devise an open-book test that is challenging and requires students to demonstrate knowledge and skills.

As for the rest of my assessments—the formative ones—teaching mode makes no difference. Even before we went online, for example, both traditional students and blended course students had a weekly discussion question on the LMS. One practice essay with peer edits was entirely asynchronous, even for my in-person class. And lecture or demonstration videos are effective in online and in-person courses. Drawing on learning theory suggesting that students learn more when collaborating with each other, I offer collaborative quizzes in both online and in-person courses.[8] Creating this material takes time, but it can be reused every term and does not have to be created all at once.

***Bottom line:*** You can use online assessments in all courses very successfully.

## C. RESOURCES

The next step in backward design is providing resources to assist learning. Resources do not need to change for each teaching mode. My resources are more attuned to the digital course platform (e.g., more videos), but they are equally valuable for traditional teaching mode.

***Textbook(s).*** The primary resource for my students in Property II is the book. Just as in a traditional course, each week, I assign the chapters that correspond to the doctrine I am covering in the course. The assignments are posted on the LMS, using the "interactive" syllabus feature and weekly modules.

***Videos.*** The key addition since moving online has been using more video. Before moving courses online, I had some video components: review videos and asynchronous modules that incorporated videos. After we moved online, I added two new types: "how to approach the reading" videos and "going through practice exam" videos.

8. Student collaboration in an entirely online environment is more challenging than courses where there is some in-person participation. Students have to actively seek one another out. I discuss this issue with my students, suggesting they reach out. In one course, students created a group in the LMS and arranged to meet there to work on the collaborative quiz. I also use teaching assistants, who reach out to students and encourage group sessions. My teaching assistants are not allowed to collaborate with enrolled students on the graded collaborative quizzes, but they form groups early on that can then serve as a springboard for collaboration.

Videos enhance every teaching mode. For synchronous classes, class time is spent on interactive application rather than lecture. For completely asynchronous classes, videos present material with some sense of faculty presence. The big downside to videos is when professors require so many videos that the amount of work is unfair, so students lack time to prepare for other courses or to synthesize their learning. To ameliorate that problem, make some videos optional, or reduce synchronous class time to accommodate the video time. ABA rules require at least three hours of work per week for each credit hour. That usually means two hours of asynchronous work for one hour of synchronous work. But if the class is asynchronous, this would mean three hours of asynchronous work per credit for that week.

*Review videos.* These videos summarize key concepts from a unit after we cover it in class.

*Preview videos.* Some professors create preview (before class) videos that are essentially doctrinal lectures. Adapting a suggestion from a colleague, I instead create preview videos that show what students should be looking for in the reading. For example, I might say, "When you begin the unit on easements, note the several ways to create them. First, understand the elements necessary to create an express easement before tackling the other ways of creating easements." Or I might say, "For leasehold estates, think about what rights go with the estate. What is the tenant entitled to? What rights does the landlord keep?"[9] This type of video is helpful in any teaching mode.

*Embedded quizzes in videos.* Another tool is embedding quizzes in videos. It involves periodically pausing the video and inserting a question that students must answer before the video continues. There are many tools that have embed features.[10] Embedded quizzes offer several benefits. First, if your video is over ten minutes, the quiz breaks up the video, giving students time to process the material. Second, students can test whether they have understood a just-explored concept (metacognition). Third, by sprinkling in quiz questions, you can track whether students have watched the whole video. Embedded quizzes can be used with any teaching mode, but they are especially important when the unit is entirely asynchronous. Students can pause frequently to process material and check their understanding as they go.

*Videos from outside sources.* You can upload videos from a lot of sources on the internet.[11] Make sure that using the video falls within the fair use doctrine or pay for the right to post it.

*Videos where I discuss my thought processes.* I have videos in which I explain my thought processes. For example, I may explain how I would approach a sample exam essay, including showing how I would draw pictures of the land parcels described

9. I created one short video that I post in the first week of class, based on Tim Iglesias's article, *A Novel Tool for Teaching Property: Starting with the Questions*, 20 Chap. L. Rev. 321 (2017).

10. I use the embed feature in the Canvas LMS "Studio," but I could also use Panopto or WebEx. I am sure there are other tools available.

11. I have used portions of videos from Quimbee, YouTube, and National Public Radio.

in the facts. Students find these videos enormously helpful for exam prep, they can watch them as many times as they want, and it takes zero class time. I have videos that explain why they should self-examine how they got multiple-choice questions wrong. I have videos that explain how to use my grading rubric for the peer-edit assignment. Anything that helps them to see what is obvious to us helps them. These videos are posted to the LMS for all teaching modes.[12]

Keep in mind some best practices when making videos. First, research indicates that videos should be somewhere between six and fifteen minutes.[13] This is challenging for law professors, who have trouble believing that there is anything worth saying in under fifteen minutes. My advice: think about smaller chunks of information and make several shorter videos. If you just can't seem to make them short, consider embedding questions to break the videos up. Second, videos should have captioning. This is of obvious benefit to students with hearing issues, but it also helps students who have some types of learning disabilities, or who for another reason have trouble tracking or understanding what you are saying. There are many free captioning tools available. I use the tool that comes with Canvas Studio. It automatically generates the text, and you can easily edit for accuracy. The shorter your video, the less time this takes. Third, students find it helpful when you post any documents or other visual aids you use in the video, so they can download them and take notes.

***Additional resources.*** I also use various study aids, such as flow charts or sample documents, that can be uploaded to the LMS. You can build your library of study aids over time. Because these resources are posted on the LMS, they are equally available no matter what mode of teaching is used. However, the purely asynchronous mode would require more care in how online resources are sequenced. This is because in synchronous classes, teachers provide context for how students access learning resources through regular inter-personal contact. In an asynchronous course, the teacher's way of guiding a student is entirely within the LMS. Therefore, the materials must clearly guide the student in the order the teacher wants the student to pursue.

## D. LEARNING OPPORTUNITIES AND ACTIVITIES

The final step in backward design is developing learning opportunities and activities for your students. Of course, students are learning through the assessments and resources described above. But I think of learning activities as two other types: class activities (synchronous or asynchronous) and optional activities posted on your LMS.

---

12. Legal Educators who research bar passage and academic support advocate explaining more of what we think of as intuitive. *See, e.g.*, Suzanne Darrow-Kleinhaus, *Incorporating Bar Pass Strategies into Routine Teaching Practices,* 37 Gonz. L. Rev. 17, 20 (2002) ("We must not wait for students to make the connection between the cases they read for class discussion and how an attorney actually uses such cases to solve client problems; we must tell them.").

13. *See, e.g.*, Barbra Burch, *Video Length in Online Courses: What the Research Says,* Quality Matters, https://www.qualitymatters.org/qa-resources/resource-center/articles-resources/research-video-length (last accessed Feb. 10, 2021).

In all teaching modes, I try to provide resources for students to understand the material while freeing as much time as possible for interactive class activities. One teaching goal is to integrate skills with doctrine, and another is to provide as many opportunities as possible for students to actively engage with material in ways that are likely to improve long-term learning.[14] So I assign the following activities:

**Weekly discussion posts.** As explained in the assessment section, students post answers to weekly discussion questions before class. I do not respond to every post; instead, I look for trends. During class, I frequently refer to student posts—to reinforce concepts they understood, to correct concepts they misunderstood, and to pick up on interesting conversations. This simple technique ties digital resources to classroom conversation. It works in synchronous class sessions in any mode. For asynchronous units, I replicate it by diligently responding to discussion posts directly on the thread.

**Workbook exercises.** My law school has worked closely with the Instructional Design and Management Research Lab headed by Dr. Douglas Johnson at Western Michigan University. Based on several years of collaborative work—most notably between Dr. Johnson and Dean Emeritus Nelson P. Miller—specific activities have been identified that help law students learn analytical skills needed in core courses such as Property.[15] These include:

- Issue-spotting exercises (e.g., give students short scenarios; then ask what type of property interests are involved);
- Factors-practice exercises (e.g., give students factors that affect a claim by a party, followed by facts; then ask which party the facts help, and which factor the facts prove);
- Examples/non-examples (e.g., after introducing a concept, give students short scenarios; then ask whether each scenario is an example or a non-example of the concept);
- Comprehensiveness exercises (e.g., give students a short statement, then prompt them to add information to complete the concept);
- Discrimination exercises (e.g., give students rule statements, then ask whether they over-generalize, under-generalize, or misconceive the rule);
- Definitions (e.g., have students define concepts in their own words);
- Problem-solving exercises (e.g., give students a client's fact pattern, then describe the client's questions; ask students to answer them).

---

14. For a complete discussion of my teaching goals, see Kim O'Leary et al., Improving Student Learning In The Doctrinal Law School Classroom (2020). *See also* Peter C. Brown & Henry L. Roediger III, Make It Stick: The Science of Successful Learning 3 (2014).

15. Dean Miller and I created a workbook for Property II. *See* Kim O'Leary & Nelson P. Miller, Property Law II Workbook: A Behavioral Approach to Learning (2019). The workbook contains all the exercises I use in class, plus additional exercises students can work on outside of class. I post a PDF of the document on Canvas, but some students prefer to buy the book and hand-write on the worksheets.

These exercises are designed for pairs or small groups to complete during class. In the in-person classroom, I give groups fifteen to twenty minutes to talk through the exercises or write on flip charts. I monitor how they are progressing and answer questions from the groups. These exercises help students apply the concepts, and they lead to excellent questions when students find gaps in understanding. Students also benefit from peer-to-peer learning. I instruct them to put everything away and work out the answers by talking, which encourages memory retrieval and learning from mistakes. Afterward, the whole class debriefs and discusses problem areas.

In switching to online teaching, small-group work is different. In in-person classes, having students physically get up and move around creates learning benefits. I often have student groups outline on large flip chart papers around the room and move around the room to discuss the problem. I also walk between the groups and listen in, guiding as I deem it is needed. Online, I can create breakout groups, and students can talk with one another. But listening in is harder because when I join a group, I interrupt them. So, I adjust the nature of my guidance, tending to give online small groups more time, and joining each group at least once to see where they need help.[16]

**Small-group case analysis.** Because of my skills background, I have never been comfortable with the Socratic method. My students spend more time doing application exercises than in-depth case analysis. But when I want to focus the class on a case in an in-depth manner, I usually divide the class into groups, asking each group to focus on a different question related to the case, and then they report back to the larger group to clarify the issues. In synchronous online classes, this did not work very well. Cases are too complex to be worked on in the groups without any monitoring and, as I explained above, monitoring does not work as well when you interrupt the group to join it. Having students use a common cloud document is also not very effective, as some students participated and others did not.

A spreadsheet works best for my students. I create a spreadsheet in advance with the case name and questions I want the students to answer. I put the groups in the rows and the questions in the columns, leaving spaces between group rows and columns. I send students into small groups online and give them a link to the spreadsheet.[17] The groups grapple with the questions and put the information in the spreadsheet. I monitor their progress by opening their shared document on my own screen. I can pose questions in the white space next to their answers, and they can think more about their answer and revise. The entire class can see everyone's responses and my questions. This replicates the feel of my walking between groups. The process looks something like this:

16. For a more in-depth treatment of collaborative learning generally, see Chapter 14: *Effective Collaboration in Online Courses* by Darby Dickerson and Megan Bess.

17. Make sure you give students edit permission in advance. If you do not, they will not be able to write on the spreadsheet.

| | What are the key timeline facts for the properties? | *Professor questions* | What are the elements of easement by necessity, and how do they apply to the facts of this case? | *Professor questions* | What are the elements of easement by prescription, and how do they apply to the facts of this case? |
|---|---|---|---|---|---|
| Group 1 (start with key timeline then easement by necessity) | Hill to Rosier, 100 acres in 1896 Hill to Othen, 60 acres in 1897 Hill 16.31 acres to Rosier & 53 to Othen in 1899 | *Who bought the property when?* | 1) must be strict necessity to get to the property, not mere convenience 2) unity of ownership of the dominant & servient estate 3) existed at the time of the severance of the two estates. In this case, the easement was not present in the deed conveyed in Feb of 1897, so it doesn't meet the elements of necessity | | |
| Group 2 (start with key timeline then easement by prior existing use) | Hill conveys 100 acres 8/26/1896; 50 acres 1897 to 1904; Jan 26, 1899 Hill conveys 53 acres to Othen and 16.31 acres to Rosier in 1924 | *What was the length of time it was used and by whom?* | | *Can you apply the facts not just list the element?* | **Replaced:** "1. One routinely trespasses (as if the fact herein. 2. The Trespassing has occurred for a long time (as is the fact here) – they used the land for a long time 3. Open – the owner could see them coming and going, it was open. 4. Notorious – it was known widely and was unfavorable 5. Adverse – the trespassing was permitted (ELEMENT FAILS!) 6. Continuous – this wen ton without end 7. True owner knew about it and did nothing, the owner did not say stop, but instead just built a levy. |

In asynchronous mode, you can approximate this in a different way. In one asynchronous week, students review a series of cases and some videos on implicit takings. Then they take a quiz in which they discuss how they would approach the same facts using five different cases. Because it is an asynchronous week, we don't have the three-hour class, so I have time to provide individual feedback. Because the questions are so targeted, it is much faster than grading a regular essay.

**Class discussion.** In an in-person classroom, discussing a topic with the entire class works well. You can "read the room"—nodding and prodding and getting full participation. You can easily see questions, and students respond to each other. In a synchronous online class, it is harder to see faces or "read the room." However, using chat during a discussion can elicit contributions from students who rarely participate in an in-person classroom. On balance, though, class discussion is less animated online. In asynchronous mode, a discussion forum allows some class discussion. Include incentives to get students to interact in a meaningful way by assigning points based on the quality of their interaction. I don't usually use discussion posts that way because I don't teach entirely asynchronous courses. But if I did, I would strongly encourage back-and-forth discussion. When the backward design process is complete some of the weeks look like this:

| Week | Learning outcome for the course | K, S, E? | Learning Activities | Procedures for evaluation of student learning (assessment) | Resources for student (books, posted on Canvas, etc.) |
|---|---|---|---|---|---|
| | *. . . at the end of this course, students will be able to* | | | *. . . as evidenced by . . .* | |
| Weeks 1–14 | Identify, define, analyze and evaluate the law | S | Asynchronous practice essay & peer review assignment (wk. 6); asynchronous quiz on implicit takes (wk. 12) asynchronous unit (wk. 14) videos on practice essays, practice quizzes, metagocnition video | Midterm and final exams | Grading rubrics; video on how to approach essays, how to grade using my rubric, preview videos "what to look for in this week's readings", self-analysis grid for M-C quizzes, sample opinion letters |
| Week 4 | The common law tort doctrine of nuisance, and its commonly available remedies | K, E | Week 4 discussion post; videos (use in class), workbook exercises, polls, simulated client interview video, Google sheets/small group analysis, end of class poll | Opinion letter assignment, M-C tests | Video: how to approach nuisance law; book, pp 731–60, chart on nuisance law, workbook Chapter 4, PPT Week 4, discussion post |
| Weeks 5, 7, 8, 9 | Servitudes, including the creation, scope, termination of easements, real covenants & equitable servitudes | K | Weeks 5 & 8 discussion posts, workbook exercises, creation of easements poll, Google sheets/ small group case questions, video on Redlining | Final exam, M-C tests | Preview videos on servitudes, Book, pp 761–99 (Wk. 5), 799–834 (Wk. 7), 835–94 (Wk. 8, creation of easements flowchart, PPTs Weeks 5, 7, 8, 9, review videos, posted files examples of easements and restrictive covenants in deeds |

## III. Conclusion

Backward course design allows a single course to be taught in multiple teaching modes. Regardless of teaching mode, course outcomes and resources such as the book and videos can be the same. But assessing students and engaging them in learning activities will change. In-person classes offer more opportunities for "reading" a room and transitioning activities in a more natural way. Students can move about, which enhances learning and forestalls boredom. On the other hand, online classes offer more opportunities to hold every student accountable. Students can be given structured assignments that require full participation and feedback. Chat features can solicit participation from reticent students.

My favorite teaching mode is the blended because I can use the best of all modes. Regardless of the mode of instruction, law professors should make full use of a digital "hub" for each course, containing resources, practice tests, videos, and other learning tools. Once those tools are developed, adapting from one mode to another is relatively painless.

TWENTY-THREE

# Thrive, Strive or Just Survive: Contracts Beyond the Physical Classroom

Amy C. Bushaw*

After reviewing this chapter, in the context of Contracts, you will be able to:

- Incrementally add online elements to a large-enrollment, required course;
- Select and design online elements to support student well-being;
- Implement online elements to enhance student autonomy;
- Craft online activities to amplify students' individual perspectives, values, and interests;
- Enliven recorded content to engage students and establish connections to their past experiences and professional futures; and
- Choose appropriate online content and activities to help students build a sense of professional competence and community.

This chapter reflects on the pursuit of online strategies in the first-year Contracts course, with a focus on strategies to support law students' well-being. For practical or pedagogical reasons, you may be planning a Contracts course that is fully or partially online. Some of you may be undertaking thorough redesign; others may contemplate incremental change. In this chapter I illustrate how the overarching objective of fostering law student well-being might inform course design. Whatever your reasons for moving online, if you are judicious about your choice of technologies and thoughtful about how you use them, you may discover new ways to enable your students to thrive.

* Professor, Lewis & Clark Law School. Professor Bushaw began law teaching in 1992 and first added rudimentary online elements to her courses in 2000 while teaching abroad. Since then, she incrementally added and refined asynchronous online elements to her in-person classes. She first taught synchronously online in 2020.

I begin with a brief primer on some of the dimensions of law student well-being. I provide illustrations of how online components of course design might attend to each of these dimensions. I follow this general discussion with some specific examples of online content, group exercises, and other activities and explain the functions they might play in a typical Contracts course. These elements contribute to learning outcomes specific to Contracts, but also nurture attitudes, habits, and skills that support the students' long-term well-being.

If Contracts is not your field, if you seek to prioritize different goals for your course than I do for mine, or if the way you plan to deliver your course varies from my experience, I remain hopeful you will find something in this chapter that you can translate to your own circumstances.

## I. Contracts and the Dimensions of Law Student Well-Being

There is reason to be concerned about the well-being of our students.[1] A national task force on lawyer well-being recently detailed alarming rates of distress among lawyers and law students, and urged immediate and broad-based action.[2] The report came on the heels of decades of research on the well-being of law students and lawyers, some of which identified ways in which law schools have fallen short in fostering the attitudes, habits, and skills that would allow students to thrive.[3] A number of schools and individual members of the faculty and staff have heard the calls to action, and have instituted well-being programming in the first year of law school and beyond.

Contracts courses can supplement broader institutional well-being resources and initiatives. Contracts is mandatory at most schools and, at some, spans the entire first year. Professors who teach these courses have an opportunity to develop strong relationships with a broad swath of students at the very beginning of their law school careers. Contracts is also a topic that intersects with a range of life experiences and crops up in many if not most practice areas. Although students may not think of it at first, with some guidance, most can find something in the subject matter that resonates with their lived backgrounds or future aspirations. Contracts professors can consider how to tailor the learning experience to reinforce attitudes that will support the students' well-being while in law school but also allow them to imagine a professional life in which they will thrive. Course activities also can give students an opportunity

---

1. For an additional discussion of student well-being, see Chapter 5: *Integrating Digital Wellness into Online Education* by N.E. Millar.

2. Nat'l Task Force on Lawyer Well-Being, The Path to Lawyer Well-Being: Practical Recommendations for Positive Change (2017), https://www.americanbar.org/content/dam/aba/images/abanews/ThePathToLawyerWellBeingReportRevFINAL.pdf.

3. For a brief summary of some of the literature, see Amy C. Bushaw, *Humanizing the Delivery of Legal Education*, *in* Building on Best Practices: Transforming Legal Education in a Changing World 73 (Deborah Maranville et al. eds., 2015).

to develop habits and skills that are relevant not only in the law school context but to their practices beyond law school as well.

Because Contracts courses often have large enrollments, the logistics of attending to the needs of individual students while engaging the class as a whole can prove challenging. Further, some professors feel pressure to achieve sufficient doctrinal and analytical coverage in the available time, especially since the course is a foundational one. To professors who teach the course in one semester rather than two, this pressure may be acute. Contracts professors may run a very tight ship in the physical classroom. They may conclude that further adapting their course content and teaching methods to address law student well-being directly is a luxury they cannot afford. In contrast, Contracts professors who are migrating to classes that are fully online may struggle to capture the personal connections they have been able to forge in the physical classroom. They may be looking for new ways to create an effective and welcoming classroom presence.

Whatever the context, the addition or adaptation of online elements may allow Contracts professors to attend to law student well-being without sacrificing other important pedagogical goals. Although the use of online tools in Contracts is not the only curricular avenue to support the well-being of law students, small and incremental enhancements carry the potential for wide-ranging and lasting impact.

The well-being literature is now rich and varied and contains significant prescriptions for legal education.[4] Some authors identify practices that undercut student well-being,[5] while others emphasize techniques to enhance enthusiasm,[6] nurture satisfaction,[7] and support the development of professional identity.[8] Drawing from this literature, I chose four lodestars to help guide my course design generally: autonomy, intrinsic values, competence, and connection.[9] Specifically, I believe it is

---

4. *Id.* For a more thorough treatment of the well-being literature, as well as its application to law practice and legal education, see NANCY LEVIT & DOUGLAS O. LINDER, THE HAPPY LAWYER: MAKING A GOOD LIFE IN THE LAW (2010).

5. Todd David Peterson & Elizabeth Waters Peterson, *Stemming the Tide of Law Student Depression: What Law Schools Need to Learn from the Science of Positive Psychology*, 9 YALE J. HEALTH POL'Y, L. & ETHICS 357, 375 (2009) (surveying various critiques of legal education and its contributions to law student distress).

6. *See, e.g.*, Emily Zimmerman, *An Interdisciplinary Framework for Understanding and Cultivating Law Student Enthusiasm*, 58 DEPAUL L. REV. 851 (2009).

7. *See, e.g.*, Debra S. Austin, *Positive Legal Education: Flourishing Law Students and Thriving Law Schools*, 77 MD. L. REV. 649 (2018).

8. *See, e.g.*, Neil W. Hamilton et al., *Empirical Evidence that Legal Education Can Foster Student Professionalism/Professional Formation to Become an Effective Lawyer*, 10 U. ST. THOMAS L.J. 11 (2012) (exploring the role of legal education in the development of values and ethical identity formation).

9. The influential work of Lawrence S. Krieger and Kennon M. Sheldon, as well as my understanding of the self-determination theory on which it draws, strongly influenced my choice of lodestars. For a general description of self-determination theory and a summary of some of this work, see Lawrence S. Krieger, *The Most Ethical of People, the Least Ethical of People: Proposing Self-Determination Theory to Measure Professional Character Formation*, 8 U. ST. THOMAS L.J. 168 (2011). *See generally* Johnmarshall Reeve, *Self-Determination Theory Applied to Educational Settings*, *in* HANDBOOK OF SELF-DETERMINATION

possible—and perhaps more importantly, practical—to craft online learning activities to support autonomy, amplify intrinsic values, foster a sense of professional competence, and contribute to a feeling of community in the context of the first-year Contracts course.

I discuss each of these factors in turn, and provide examples of how each might inform the use of online elements in a Contracts course. In the examples, I highlight methods to deliver content, facilitate group exercises, and provide individualized learning experiences beyond the physical classroom.

## A. AUTONOMY

Authors posit a strong correlation between a sense of autonomy and self-reported well-being.[10] Those who feel they have the flexibility to direct their efforts to activities that they deem enjoyable, important, or valuable report higher levels of satisfaction in their studies and work. Most students do not choose to study Contracts—instead, it is required. Some may come to the subject with a pre-existing passion or interest, but many do not. Within this mandated structure, professors who seek to support students' sense of autonomy provide students with meaningful choices regarding the progress of their learning.

Online tools allow greater flexibility in the timing and mode of the delivery of instructional content than the traditional classroom. This flexibility may help professors tame some of the logistical challenges inherent in supporting the students' autonomy in a large-enrollment, foundational course. A professor can "flip" the classroom to deliver instructional materials according to the students' schedule and reserve synchronous meetings for discussion or other interactive pursuits. Professors can develop or access online exercises or other forms of formative assessment, and students can decide when, if, and how such activities might contribute to their learning. Professors can encourage students to reflect on their own progress and to communicate what concepts or skills give them difficulty, and craft online learning activities to respond to the students' felt needs. Although the creation or selection of these tools requires a significant up-front investment of time, a professor who uses them as an adjunct to more traditional teaching methods can choose to implement them gradually over a few terms or even years.

---

RESEARCH 183 (Edward L. Deci & Richard M. Ryan eds., 2002); Richard M. Ryan & Edward L. Deci, *Self-Determination Theory and the Facilitation of Intrinsic Motivation, Social Development, and Well-Being*, 55 AM. PSYCHOLOGIST 68 (2000).

10. *See* Reeve, *supra* note 9, at 186 (describing how students benefit from autonomy-supportive teaching behavior); Kennon M. Sheldon & Lawrence S. Krieger, *Understanding the Negative Effects of Legal Education on Law Students: A Longitudinal Test of Self-Determination Theory*, 33 PERSONALITY & SOC. PSYCHOL. BULL. 883, 893 (2007) (discussing data that shows a correlation between perceived autonomy support and subjective well-being among law students); Lawrence S. Krieger & Kennon M. Sheldon, *What Makes Lawyers Happy?: A Data-Driven Prescription to Redefine Professional Success*, 83 GEO. WASH. L. REV. 554, 582 (2015) (discussing data that shows a correlation between perceived autonomy support and professional satisfaction) [hereinafter Krieger & Sheldon, *Data-Driven Prescription*].

In the traditional Contracts course, a professor might ask students to read a text in advance of class and, during class time, engage in lecture, dialogue, or discussion. As a simple first step, professors might record a lecture they would otherwise give in class and provide students access to it in advance. This small change enhances the students' autonomy to control their schedules. The professor could even provide the lecture in multiple formats: a video recording, an audio recording, and a transcript. This allows students to choose the format that works best for their circumstances and learning style. Later, some students might find the recordings to be a useful means to review the topic as they refine their notes or prepare for an exam. Contracts students regularly tell me that the first few weeks (if not months) of the course go by in a fog, and they wish they had the opportunity to go back and attend the early classes with the experience they have gained from the later classes. Short, crisp recordings that introduce a topic or summarize a body of material could prove very useful, whether students access them in advance or as a means of review.

Online exercises can help students engage actively with the course content on their own terms and according to their schedules. Although they differ in their capabilities and flexibility, many learning management systems allow for online quizzing or other assignments. Increasingly, legal publishers provide online self-assessment tools that students can access, either as an adjunct to a text or as a stand-alone service. Contracts professors who include a significant virtual element in their courses likely will rely heavily on some of these tools. With small adjustments or enhancements, professors can also adapt their design to help foster law student autonomy.

Suppose, for instance, that a professor asked students to complete online exercises for each class session or unit. A professor could maximize the students' autonomy by making the exercises entirely optional and bill them as an opportunity to build skills and get feedback. A professor who felt that the exercises directly contributed to course goals might give the students credit for completing the exercises, but not necessarily grade them from a qualitative standpoint. This approach could emphasize that the exercises are opportunities to practice, and that students should not expect to be perfect the first time they encounter new information or attempt to use new skills. Especially if the professor built feedback into the exercises (something that can be automated with many learning management systems), the professor could encourage students to revisit the exercises periodically to review concepts or merely observe how their understanding and skills have grown. A small incentive for completing the exercises on a timely basis might be enough to encourage the students to engage, while still allowing that building professional competence is a process. Even if completion of the exercises was a graded component of a course, the professor could still build in some measure of autonomy by giving the students some choices about when or how to complete them.[11]

11. For instance, a professor might say "I recommend you complete this exercise before class as part of your preparation, but you will still get credit for it if you complete it by the end of the weekend if you choose instead to use it as a tool to review our class discussions."

Of course, students attend law school to gain professional knowledge, skills, and values that they do not already have. Professors should exercise their judgment to create structures that enable students to achieve appropriate learning objectives. Too much autonomy—whether within the physical classroom or beyond it—may prove chaotic, overwhelming, and counterproductive for the students' learning. Judicious use of online learning management systems can present choices to students in an organized, consistent, and transparent way. Careful design can reduce the burdens on the professor and automate tracking of student paths, responding to student needs, and providing appropriate feedback.

## B. INTRINSIC VALUES

Autonomy is particularly powerful when one exercises that autonomy in the pursuit of meaningful goals. Psychologists posit a strong correlation between well-being and the pursuit of intrinsic values, and data in the legal context support this correlation.[12] Those who see their work as meaningful, valuable, or enjoyable tend to find it satisfactory as well. Those who pursue tasks to seek the approval of others, to amass power or prestige, or because they feel they must, may experience ambivalence or even dissatisfaction with their pursuits. Translated into the law school context, we can expect that students who undertake learning activities because they find them enjoyable or because they are developing an interest or passion in the subject matter will experience their education differently than those who study because they feel they must to gain the approval of their classmates or professors, achieve good grades, or obtain a prestigious job. The same goes for lawyers: if they see their intrinsic values reflected in the work that they do, they tend to report that their professional lives have meaning and contribute to their well-being.[13]

The factors that lead a person to pursue extrinsic goals rather than intrinsic ones may be complex and to some degree immutable. A few empirical studies document a profound shift among law students towards a more extrinsic orientation, particularly over their first year.[14] The shift was correlated with a sharp decline in the students' reported well-being.[15] These effects continued into the second and third years of legal study.[16] Professors who seek to counteract these effects may create early and regular opportuni-

---

12. *See* Krieger & Sheldon, *Data-Driven Prescription, supra* note 10, at 581–83 (stating in their study their "hypotheses regarding the primacy for lawyer well-being of intrinsic over extrinsic values, and of actions over aspirations, were both supported by the data" and such factors more strongly predicted lawyer well-being than any of the "external 'grades and money' factors").

13. *Id.*

14. Kennon M. Sheldon & Lawrence S. Krieger, *Does Legal Education Have Undermining Effects on Law Students? Evaluating Changes in Motivation, Values, and Well-Being*, 22 Behav. Sci. & L. 261, 280–81 (2004) (detailing the results of studies at two law schools showing reports of subjective well-being plummeting over the first year of law school, as correlated with sample-wide decreases in intrinsic motivation).

15. *Id.*

16. *Id.*

ties for the students to reflect on the substance of what they are learning, and to muse about how it relates to their individual life experiences and future aspirations. Depending on how professors structure activities, an online environment can provide a private, individual space for students to observe how law school is affecting them and consider how they might use their legal training to affect the world. If students build habits of attention and reflection—without any need to absorb specific information or create a specific work product—they might find it easier to discover how Contracts intersects with things that are important to them. The same habits of attention and reflection, carried into their future professional lives, likely will serve them well.

The importance of creating an inclusive learning environment may seem self-evident to professors. Yet most of us recognize that it is far too easy for students in large classes to sink into relative invisibility, even if brief moments of public performance (or dare I say terror) sometimes punctuate that invisibility. Online tools can facilitate the integration of many perspectives and values, even in a large class. In a synchronous session, a professor could use online polling tools to solicit opinions and impressions to gauge the mood of the virtual room or to illustrate a range of perspectives. For instance, whenever a question came up about what was "reasonable" in the context of contracts doctrine, a professor could poll the students to find where the weight of opinion rested. A simple exercise like this could also illustrate that individual perspectives and life experiences remain relevant to contract law, especially when it comes to questions of fact.

A professor periodically could invite students to reflect more deeply on specific questions. Depending on the topic, the professor could ask them to post their answers to a discussion board, an online diary, or some other format for the professor's eyes only. For instance, a professor might ask the students to describe something they have experienced or that they care about, and to muse about how contract law might be relevant to that experience or passion. Alternatively, a professor might ask students to identify a case in their readings to date that inspired a strong emotional reaction, and to describe what it was about the case that struck a chord. These types of exercises are useful if they encourage students to reflect on their intrinsic values and how they relate to Contracts. The online format encourages every single student to attend to individual experiences, perspectives and reactions. Further, the professor gains a fuller picture of who the students are and how they are experiencing Contracts, information that may prove valuable as the professor seeks to engage each of them as the course proceeds.

Although contracts issues permeate daily life and span most practice areas and contexts, students may not come to law school with a specific interest in the subject matter. Successful teachers often exhibit the kind of enthusiasm and passion for their subject that is contagious.[17] Professors who rely extensively on online teaching meth-

---

17. Michael Hunter Schwartz et al., What the Best Law Teachers Do 192 (2013) (describing the energy and enthusiasm of professors included in their study).

ods and learning activities may need to develop new and more explicit ways to communicate their own love of the subject. Professors who seek to add online components to a traditional Contracts classroom might choose some for the specific purpose of engaging the students' individual passions and interests, again something that might be challenging to achieve in a large group setting.

Professors who teach from the physical classroom may have already taken steps in this direction. Many of us have gathered a cache of visual or audio materials we use to enliven the physical classroom. Most of them migrate easily to the online environment. For instance, many students find the treatment of standard terms fascinating, particularly in the consumer context. They come to Contracts curious about how the law treats such terms, and whether consumers will be subject to them even if they don't read them or understand them. Some cartoons and videos highlight the real or perceived hazards consumers face when they manifest assent to standard terms.[18] As a precursor to reading relevant cases, a professor could ask students to view cartoons or watch a video, and then reflect on how they think the law *should* deal with standard terms in this context. Students could note their reflections in an online diary or submit them online as an "entrance ticket" to a synchronous discussion or other course activity. The students may understand the relevant issues and the way that some courts have dealt with them from reading the cases alone. The addition of cartoons or videos not only entertains, but when coupled with thoughtful prompts for reflection also helps to highlight the connections between the subject matter and the students' lived experience. These connections may prove as effective in framing the issues and introducing the topic as any lecture—online or otherwise—would be.

Virtual tools may lack the easy personal touch to which we have become accustomed in the physical environment. With foresight, however, a professor may be able to use the flexibility of some platforms to allow students to tailor content and learning activities to their specific curiosity about Contracts without compromising their ability to attain the overarching learning objectives of the course.

## C. COMPETENCE

People may find it difficult to persist in challenging tasks if they feel they neither have nor can acquire the information or skills they need to achieve their important goals. To enhance students' learning, writers have emphasized the importance of con-

18. Copyright restrictions may limit the ability to post print materials online freely but, often with some direction, the students can access relevant cartoons on their own or find ones that are new to the professor. In the instructions for the exercise, for instance, the professor might state "you may have seen cartoons or other humorous materials satirizing the use of standard terms in consumer transactions. If you have not seen the Bill Gates' Towel Boy series from the Dilbert comic strip, for instance, you might see if you can track it down and take a look." YouTube.com is a fertile source of relevant video content. *See, e.g.*, Jena Kingsley, *Terms and Conditions Social Experiment/Prank*, YouTube (Dec. 1, 2015), https://www.youtube.com/watch?v=xZGh9bHmvRg. As far as I understand, there are fewer copyright issues associated with sharing links or videos from such freely available sources.

sistent and appropriate formative assessment, as well as other measures to foster a growth mindset among students.[19] The well-being literature sometimes refers to the importance of a sense of competence: the attitude that any shortcomings in knowledge and skill are temporary, and the belief that with incremental improvement, one can gain the tools one needs to succeed.[20]

Many Contracts lawyers operate in the virtual environment. They communicate with clients through email and other messaging systems, they negotiate documents through online platforms, and they settle disputes through online proceedings. Thriving online may itself be a critical professional skill. Learning activities that help the students envision how the content of what they are learning is relevant to their futures may build their sense of competence; so too may the mode by which they learn it. Online components in Contracts can build students' confidence in their own ability to learn. They can also help students connect their learning to their overall educational goals and professional futures.

Even minor roadblocks can impede a student's sense of confidence. At the outset of a Contracts course, a professor could include a simple exercise to encourage students to communicate when they confront challenges, and to create a mutually supportive environment. As the first online exercise of the year, for example, a professor might include a simple yes or no question to indicate whether students have used the relevant learning management system before. In automated feedback based on the answer the student gives, the professor might invite suggestions for improvement and guide students to resources that could help them resolve any issues.[21] The answers to the question would give professors an easy way to identify any students who may be having difficulty accessing the technology before those difficulties became intractable. Of course, it would be possible (and perhaps advisable) to put any information the students need into a syllabus or other materials containing basic information about the course. But through the simple addition of a question that would take no more than a few minutes to locate and answer, the professor ensures that the student has the relevant information at the time it is most likely to be helpful, and opens channels for mutual support going forward.

---

19. *See, e.g.*, Kaci Bishop, *Framing Failure in the Legal Classroom: Techniques for Encouraging Growth and Resilience*, 70 Ark. L. Rev. 959, 985–87 (2018) (discussing the potential of formative assessment to help students overcome a fixed mindset and fear of failure).

20. Reeve, *supra* note 9, at 186–88 (discussing the role of competence in self-determination theory).

21. For instance, if the student answers "yes," the feedback might be "Wonderful. If you want a quick refresher, there are some useful resources at [support website for LMS]. I'm relatively new to [name of LMS] myself and have found answers to many of my questions there. If you have any thoughts about how the operation of the site might be improved, I'd love to hear them." If the student answers "no," the feedback might be "I'm relatively new to [name of LMS] myself. Students have told me it's a little tricky to use at first, but as you grow familiar with it you may find it to be a powerful tool. If you do encounter any challenges with it, there are some helpful videos and other resources available at [support website for LMS]. Of course, please also let me know if you have any questions about how it operates, and we can work through any difficulties together."

Not all students experience law school the same way. Some professors may wish to address directly the fact that some students struggle with depression, confront significant anxiety, or otherwise doubt their own ability to master their studies. Yet it may be awkward and counterproductive to initiate a discussion about such things in a large group setting. Online activities and resources may provide a mechanism to introduce potentially sensitive and painful topics.

Some Contracts professors, for instance, start their courses with a brief introduction to contract remedies. Many casebooks include, or at least refer, to the classic case of *Hawkins v. McGee*.[22] This case, in which the court discusses the appropriate measure of damages for a botched skin graft, is perhaps most famous for its role as fodder for Professor Kingsfield's brutal Socratic dialogue in the movie *The Paper Chase* (1973) (and after that, the television series). As part of their course activities, students could view an online clip of the dialogue at their leisure, and then answer a few substantive questions about the case, Professor Kingsfield's inquiries, or the hapless student's responses. Not only might this be an engaging way to introduce the relevant legal concepts, it also could provide an opening to address the topic of law school anxiety.

Without taking up class time, a professor could introduce the students to some of the attitudes and skills that will help them safeguard their own well-being and serve values that are important to them. Professors, for instance, could ask students to reflect on how law school has affected their confidence, and post their thoughts to an online diary. The professor also might share some resources that students could peruse at their leisure, such as techniques students can use to enhance their learning in a classroom where the Socratic method is the dominant pedagogy. Alternatively, a professor might refer students to some resources on overcoming anxiety about speaking in class[23] or other aspects of the law school experience. Certainly, this might be a good opportunity to provide some information about how to access mental health counseling and other relevant resources on campus. Not all students will need this information, but the mere fact that the professor feels it is appropriate to raise such topics may reassure some who are experiencing distress and may cause some to seek support.

Online exercises could also reinforce students' confidence about the subject matter. For instance, an exercise could relate to Contracts topics that students typically find challenging, and could have the subsidiary purpose to reassure students about the difficulty of the task they have just completed. Suppose, after an online exercise designed to illustrate the intricacies of UCC 2-207, a professor asked students to report on their level of comfort with the material, and invited suggestions for additional activities or materials that might help the students attain mastery.[24] This exercise would

22. 146 A. 641 (N.H. 1929).

23. *See, e.g.*, Heidi K. Brown, *The "Silent but Gifted" Law Student: Transforming Anxious Public Speakers into Well-Rounded Advocates*, 18 Legal Writing: J. Legal Writing Inst. 291 (2012).

24. The prompt might read something like this: "UCC 2-207 is the first complex statutory provision we have encountered in this course. Most students (not to mention professors and lawyers) find it challenging to interpret and apply. Now that we've spent some time working with it, I expect you're becoming

communicate concern about the students' level of confidence, and would be particularly powerful if the professor followed up by facilitating the students' suggestions (for instance by providing an optional synchronous session or additional explanatory materials online). Other questions could seek to discover the students' level of confidence on more general legal analysis skills, and offer additional on-demand resources for those who would welcome them.[25]

Online content and activities can also help to illuminate the intersections among first-year courses. Even if Contracts is not a student's primary area of interest, the student may come to realize that the first-year courses complement each other and provide a broad-based foundation for many ways of thinking and practicing. Professors could reach out to colleagues who teach other first-year courses, and ask them to collaborate in developing some limited online materials to illuminate the interconnections among subjects. If the logistics of inviting a colleague to the physical classroom for a ten-minute discussion are overwhelming, a short interview, recorded and edited for posterity, might not require the same coordination or investment of time. Many modern contracts cases, for instance, involve the enforcement of arbitration agreements or forum selection clauses. A brief discussion with an expert in Alternative Dispute Resolution or a Civil Procedure colleague might illuminate the practical effects as well as the perceived benefits or hazards of such clauses. Or a Torts colleague could provide some perspectives on why the theoretical status of promissory estoppel—tort, contract, or something else—might matter. Discussions like these could help students appreciate how Contracts fits into the broader framework of the law, while also sending the message that not everyone needs to be an expert in everything.

More generally, professors who seek to increase their students' sense of competence may craft the virtual components of their course to reinforce the connections among what the students are learning and what they will do as lawyers. Guests from the world of practice can be a source of information and inspiration, but sometimes the logistics of inviting a guest to the physical classroom can be difficult. Guests who have limited availability might be free to participate in a short virtual question and answer session even if their schedules didn't permit an in-person visit. Some might be willing

---

comfortable with it in some of its details, but may need further practice and review to fully master it. Is there anything about this provision that is causing you particular confusion, and if so, do you have any suggestions about what might help resolve that confusion?"

25. For instance, a professor might provide a series of multiple-choice questions for students to use in self-assessment on specific topics. Depending on the subtlety of the questions, wrong answers might inspire a crisis in confidence among the students. To reassure the students about the function of the questions and to help them address any deficiencies they might identify in their skills, the professor might include a final yes or no question to ask whether they would find an optional session on multiple choice skills to be useful. If there is enough interest, the professor could schedule a video conference for those students who would like to attend, and record the session for those students who would like to view it at their leisure. The professor could also offer to meet individually with students who find the multiple-choice format to be particularly intimidating or challenging.

to record a brief interview in circumstances where the needs of course coverage didn't justify a longer guest appearance.

After reading a case involving the interpretation of difficult contract language, for instance, students might watch a video where an experienced lawyer attempts to interpret the language at issue or maybe "marks it up" to better express one of the parties' articulated goals. The lawyer might explain how contract negotiations typically proceed, and in particular, what online tools the lawyer uses to communicate with clients or with other lawyers. The video could be coupled with a learning activity that asks the students to reflect on the content of the video, to discuss it with others on a group discussion board, or to post comments to the "marked up" draft to reflect the other party's likely concerns. Activities such as these could help students envision how the disputes they encounter in cases come to be, and how the things they are learning in Contracts might translate to their future lives as lawyers.

## D. CONNECTION

Many of us talk about the personality or culture of our schools with pride, and boast about the strength of our community. We suggest a sense of community is conducive to learning; psychologists see a sense of community as a component of well-being and satisfaction as well.[26] We can expect that law students will not only learn better but will in fact feel better about themselves and their lives if they feel connected to people who support them and wish them well.

The first year of law school can forge friendships and professional relationships that may last for decades. It can also be a time that isolates and alienates law students from people who care about them. An online learning environment poses particular challenges for the student who feels a lack of human connection. So too, perhaps, does legal practice in an increasingly virtual world.

The larger the class, the more challenging it can be to facilitate interactions that are professional, yet authentic and personal. Contracts professors might craft online activities that communicate an interest in the students as individuals and allow them to learn more about each other. To the extent these activities result in stored content, the professor will have an archive of details about the students that can inform how the professor interacts with the students and encourages the students to feel connected to others. If a topic comes up in the course that is particularly relevant to a student's background or interests, the professor who takes note can highlight that fact.

---

26. A number of other chapters include more extensive discussions of the value of community and connection in the law school generally and describe specific strategies for the online context. See Chapter 11: *The Importance of Building Community in Online and Blended Courses* by Sophie Sparrow, Chapter 12: *How to Build Community for Asynchronous Courses* by Ann Nowak, and Chapter 13: *Designing the Course of the Future: How to Build Community in Synchronous Classes* by Eunice Park. Here I focus on the particular challenges of a large enrollment, required course like Contracts.

Professors can also create online structures to facilitate a professional sense of community among the students. First-year Contracts students who do not have an opportunity to interact in person with their classmates may find it difficult to forge a peer group that allows for supportive and meaningful connections. Professors can facilitate this effort by building in easy mechanisms for the students to communicate with each other. Many learning management systems allow for group discussion boards, group chats, and group assignments. Video-conferencing tools allow students to meet in small groups (within a synchronous class session or otherwise), even if they aren't in the same space. In structuring the use of these mechanisms as part of ongoing class activities, professors can be attentive to how to use them to best support a sense of community as well as contribute to the learning objectives of the course.

If a professor divided the class up into law firms, group exercises could foreshadow the type of collaboration that arises in practice settings. The professor could note at an early stage of the course that one of the functions of the law firm is to provide a ready-made professional sounding board and support system for every student.[27] If the professor built in periodic opportunities for the law firms to communicate online outside scheduled class time, the continuing relationship among the students could help foster a sense of connection and belonging in a professional context.

A few early online exercises could have the object of setting a constructive and mutually supportive tone within the law firms. The very first exercise might ask students to post something about themselves to the law firm discussion board.[28] This exercise could allow the students to start to identify with their colleagues and form a cohesive group within the larger class. Although it would be possible to do a similar exercise with the class as a whole, communication within a smaller group may seem safer and might reduce the pressure to conform to preconceived norms. It also increases the chances that the students will read, remember and respond to each other's posts. If the professor also is a member of the group (with, of course, appropriate disclosure of that fact), the professor can learn things about individual students that permit the professor to speak to their interests and passions as the course proceeds.

---

27. In explaining the purpose of the law firms to the students, a professor might note something like this: "Law is a profoundly social enterprise. The practice of law is all about working with people, and avoiding, mitigating, or solving their problems. Once you become a lawyer, you will be working closely with other lawyers and with your clients. There is no need to fly solo in law school. In fact, it is helpful to start practicing and refining your communication and collaboration skills from the get go. In the interests of encouraging that, I want you to feel that you always have someone pulling for you and supporting you in this class. To that end, I will be dividing you up into law firms so you will have your own set of Contracts colleagues for the duration."

28. A possible prompt might read: "Please post a short introduction. You don't have to follow any specific format—you could tell your firm a few choice bits about your background, your interests, or perhaps your hopes for the future—anything that you think will help your colleagues get to know you. You may also post a picture of yourself, your family, your pet or your favorite place in nature. Within the bounds of professionalism, the only limits are your creativity."

The professor might design the first few substantive law firm exercises to highlight the importance of varied voices. Students come to Contracts with different levels of interest, experience, and skill. Some students may have enrolled in law school to study environmental law or in hopes of becoming a diplomat—they may question what they have to contribute to group discussions. Some may have a great deal of business experience or even specific contracting experience, and may wonder what they can learn from classmates who do not have that background or exposure. One way to build a collaborative atmosphere is to draw out the importance of multiple perspectives in the study and practice of contract law. A simple issue-spotting exercise, for instance, might serve this purpose. As the course progresses, the professor could increase the substantive content of the group exercises, and rely on peer feedback to encourage students to learn from each other.

## II. Use of Well-Being as a Lens in Course Design

Our faculty has identified a common set of learning outcomes for the first-year Contracts course. By way of example, I choose a few (out of many) to illustrate how well-being might serve as a lens to envision possible online learning activities to foster the chosen outcome. In each case, I provide examples of content delivery and exercises that might occur beyond the physical classroom but nonetheless contribute to the desired outcome. I highlight how each might support student autonomy, emphasize an orientation towards intrinsic values, encourage a sense of professional competence, or forge human connection and a supportive community.

*Learning outcome: Demonstrate, at a level appropriate to one year's study of the principles of Contract law, a basic ability to determine whether a contract is governed by Article 2 of the Uniform Commercial Code or by the common law, and articulate how these two bodies of law interact.*

Not all Contracts courses include an introduction to UCC Article 2. For those that do, the students may encounter UCC Article 2 very early in the first semester, sometimes during the first or second week. Sometimes the students' first opportunity to contrast common law principles with analogous rules under the UCC does not arise until several weeks later. Accordingly, it is helpful at the outset to provide the basics of the doctrine in a clear, logical way so students will have the foundation to approach more subtle issues as the course proceeds. If a professor provides a short recorded lecture, reading, or visual representation of the basic concepts, students who are not yet ready to absorb them at the beginning of the course can return to the materials when the topics come up again. By directing the students to the materials a few weeks after first presenting them and suggesting the value of review, professors could emphasize how the students' ability to absorb and synthesize concepts had grown over a short period of time. A short statement to this effect could help to reinforce a growth mindset among the students and develop a sense of increasing professional competence.

Some professors wish to go beyond the basics, and introduce students to some of the more subtle aspects of when UCC Article 2 might apply to a transaction. For instance, some professors might assign cases that apply the predominant purpose test to determine if a transaction that involves both the sale of goods and the provision of services should be governed by UCC Article 2. Others might address the controversial treatment of software licensing agreements and other similar transactions as within the scope of UCC Article 2. These scope questions may well arise before the students have a sense for why the answers to the questions matter.

The scope of UCC Article 2 may seem a technical, arcane topic, but it implicates issues that often prove inherently interesting to students. They wonder why a seller of goods, for instance, might be strictly responsible for the quality of those goods while someone who provides a service that incidentally involves the exact same goods might not. Although it might be premature for students to contrast the implied warranty of merchantability with a negligence-based standard, it probably is not premature to ask them to muse about the circumstances under which someone who provides something for a price should be responsible for the ultimate quality of whatever the other party receives. In a low-stakes online exercise, a professor could ask students to detail experiences they might have had in which they were disappointed with the quality of what they might have received, and what their expectations were about who was responsible for making things right. The students might note their reflections in an online diary or perhaps post them to a group or class discussion board. A small exercise like this might help reinforce the notion that the students' lived experiences matter, and in fact are highly relevant to contract law.

Alternatively, students tend to be very familiar with software transactions and may be very interested in how those terms they "agree" to every time they update an app bind them. Yet they likely don't know if or why it matters whether UCC Article 2 applies to these transactions. A professor could ask students to reflect on the last time they were asked to "agree" to such terms, whether there was any physical object associated with the transaction at issue, and whether or why the answer to that question might matter. Again, such a low-stakes exercise allows students to bring personal experiences into the classroom, and helps to stoke curiosity about if and how the law intersects with such experiences.

*Learning outcome: Demonstrate, at a level appropriate to one year's study of the law, a basic ability to apply legal rules articulated in a court opinion to similar but not identical cases or situations.*

Professors may ultimately want their students to be able to demonstrate their mastery of this outcome through written analysis. Since the topic of the scope of UCC Article 2 comes so early in the course yet presents a certain level of ambiguity and complexity, it might provide an excellent opportunity for students to take their first stab at written analysis in the Contracts context. The professor could provide a short video or handout explaining what goes into a strong written analysis, including a discussion of the importance of analogizing and distinguishing cases from related fact patterns. Many texts and other resources contain simple problems that pose scope issues (or perhaps several), or the professor could create one. As an online exercise, the professor could instruct the students to set aside a short amount of time to attempt a written analysis of the problem in light of the cases the students have just read. To keep the stakes low, the professor might remind the students that this is just a first attempt, and encourage them to take any suggested time limitations seriously. The primary goal might be to send the message that written analysis (especially under time pressure) is a skill that takes time to develop and is worthy of practice.

*Learning outcome: Demonstrate, at a level appropriate to one year's study of the law, a basic ability to distinguish when an issue is reasonably debatable, and use appropriate techniques to address uncertainty in the law.*

It may prove premature for the professor to provide individualized feedback to an early exercise like the one described above. Instead, the professor might encourage students to discuss the exercise with the other members of their law firms via video-conference or on a group discussion board, with an eye towards sussing out the full universe of questions that the members of the firm thought worthy of consideration. Especially if the problem presents several issues but even if it does not, students likely will take different approaches to it. If a student's answer differs from that of other students, the temptation may be to assume that the student is on the wrong track. As often as not, there is something of value in most approaches, and exercises like this one can introduce students to the notion that an authentic legal issue does not admit to a single correct answer. An ability to view a fact pattern from varying perspectives can illuminate issues a student might not otherwise spot. A collaborative brainstorming session can emphasize the value of working with others to expand one's view.

To bring home the point that a thorough written analysis considers a variety of approaches to uncertain issues, a professor could follow up on group work by providing a model analysis. The professor could emphasize that law students who are a few weeks into their first semester should not expect to be able to write a thorough analysis at this stage of their study, but with practice they should see their skills develop relatively quickly. Further, if the professor coupled the model analysis with an explanation for why this kind of thorough written analysis is relevant to a lawyer's work, the professor could connect what the students are learning with what they eventually hope to do.

As the course progressed, the professor could repeat the exercise with problems of increasing levels of subtlety or complexity. After a few repetitions of the issue spotting exercises, the professor may wish to advance to an exercise that focuses on the prioritization of issues and the development of a thorough analysis of the most important among them. One way to do this would be to assign a problem that implicates a number of issues from the course to date. For instance, by the time students are nearing the end of their study of offer and acceptance, they may be ready to integrate the various legal principles they have learned into a more comprehensive analysis. A possible problem might pose a series of communications or performances that arguably constitute offers, counteroffers, rejections, revocations and/or acceptances. The professor could post the problem online, encourage the students to collaborate with their law firm colleagues to develop a thorough issue outline, then ask the students to complete another written analysis based on the collaborative outline. Again, the professor could recommend fairly tight time constraints to emphasize the low-stakes nature of the exercise. After the students turn in their written analyses, the professor could make available a rubric granting points based on the relative importance of the various issues implicated by the problem, and ask that the students swap their analyses within their firms and score each other's work in accordance with the rubric. The professor could emphasize the educational merit of getting peer feedback as well as giving it. To cap off the series of exercises, the professor could ask the students to reflect in an online journal about what they learned about themselves, their colleagues, contract law or written analysis.

At many schools, there are Legal Writing classes that focus directly on written analysis skills and many of them may include exercises like the ones I describe here. Even if they are not the central focus of the Contracts course, small, low-stakes exercises give the students an opportunity to practice what they are learning elsewhere and help them transfer their learning from one context to the next. Although their primary object may be to reinforce Contracts doctrine and related legal analysis skills, with careful design such exercises also can help to support law student well-being.

*Learning outcome: Demonstrate, at a level appropriate to one year's study of the principles of Contract law, a basic ability to recognize which contracts are subject to the statute of frauds and determine if the requirements of the statute have been satisfied.*

I close with an example of how principles of well-being might shape the online methods a professor could use to teach specific elements of Contracts doctrine. Many laypeople share the belief that contracts must be in writing to be enforceable. They assume the contract is the writing and the writing is the contract. Although they are often several weeks (if not months) into their study by the time they confront the statute of frauds, many students continue to conflate the notion of a contract from a legal point of view with the written document that parties sometimes use to memorialize the terms of their agreement. The topic of the statute of frauds can bring this confusion into sharp relief.

To dispel this confusion, professors might want to emphasize that the statute of frauds is, in most states, just what it says it is—a statute. The question of whether a particular legal relationship is subject to the statute of frauds is answered differently, depending on which statute of frauds is at issue. The more students can separate the issue of whether the parties have entered into a contract generally from the more specific issue of whether a statute of frauds applies and if so, what it requires, the more likely they will be able to place the statute of frauds into its appropriate frame. This is an area where I have observed that a few tailored online exercises can lead to the sort of "aha" moment that allows students to challenge their preconceived notions of the relationship between contracts and signed writings.

Many texts introduce the notion of the statute of frauds with some description of the 1677 English statute for the prevention of frauds and perjuries and the general categories of contracts to which it applied. To emphasize that modern statutes of frauds jump off of, but are not identical to, the 1677 statute, a professor could post links to a sampling of state statutes and ask the students to choose one. Maybe students could choose a statute from a place they have lived or would like to visit, or perhaps they could choose a statute from a state that they predict might take an eccentric approach to contract law. The student could then browse the language of the statute and compare it to the general description in the text. A quick examination might reveal whether the state statute they chose generally followed the structure of the 1677 statute, or whether some categories in the original statute no longer appeared. In some cases, students may discover that new categories of contracts have been swept into the scope of the state statute of frauds, including for instance promises to cure a medical condition,[29] commitments to lend money,[30] or even promises to renew a newspaper subscription.[31] (If a professor knew that a student had experience in medicine, banking, or elder care, the professor might even direct that student's attention to the relevant state statute.) The students could reflect on what they found and what they think it means in an online diary, or they could report the results of their research to their law firm colleagues. An exercise like this one allows the students to pursue something that catches their attention, to share their discoveries with their colleagues, and to see how the law is both durable and evolves in response to political interests.

Much as the coverage of the statute of frauds can be mysterious, so too can the consequences of applying it. Some students conclude that if a statute of frauds applies and is satisfied, it follows that a contract exists (which is not necessarily the case). Other students question what the consequences are if the statute of frauds does not apply, or if it applies, if it is not satisfied. Sometimes these confusions resolve when students understand how statute of frauds questions arise in litigation, and how courts resolve them. Professors who wanted to explicitly draw in the procedural aspects of a statute of frauds defense might call on a Civil Procedure colleague to engage in a recorded dialogue. The Civil Procedure colleague could help walk through when and how a statute of frauds defense might arise in a Contracts lawsuit, at what stage the court

29. *See, e.g.*, OHIO REV. CODE ANN. § 1335.05 (Baldwin, Westlaw through Files 95, 97 through 107, and 109 through 115 of the 133rd Gen. Assemb. (2019–2020)).

30. *See, e.g.*, ARK. CODE. ANN. § 4-59-101 (West, Westlaw through acts effective Feb. 2, 2021 in the 2021 Reg. Sess. of the 93rd Ark. Gen. Assemb.).

31. *See, e.g.*, FLA. STAT. ANN. §§ 725.01, 725.03 (West, Westlaw through the 2020 Second Reg. Sess. of the 26th Legis.).

would typically address that defense, and what the respective consequences would be if the defense was successful or unsuccessful. If the Civil Procedure colleague shares the same students, it might be possible to highlight some connections between this discussion and what the students are learning in their Civil Procedure class. Students could take away some real insight about the real-world effects of achieving early dismissal of a contracts lawsuit on statute of frauds grounds. They could also begin to appreciate the practical difference between proving that one of the parties signed a writing and establishing that the parties had a fully enforceable contract.

## III. Contracts Beyond the Physical Classroom

If you are planning to teach Contracts entirely online, there are many elements that are likely to go into your course design. If you are teaching a blended course many considerations are likely to influence the balance between the in-person and the virtual aspects of your course. If you largely teach from the physical classroom, you may be thinking about ways to improve your students' experience by adding some limited online components. Whatever your goals and constraints, there are opportunities to evaluate if and how your Contracts course will help to support law student well-being. My hope is this chapter will provide some food for thought, and that both you and your students will strive to find a mix that allows you not just to survive the challenges of Contracts, but to thrive.

TWENTY-FOUR

# Teaching Civil Procedure Online with Active Learning

Cynthia M. Ho*

After reviewing this chapter, readers will be able to:

- Understand how a Learning Management System (LMS) can help provide formative assessment;
- Identify multiple types of formative assessment that can be used online;
- Understand the benefits of synchronous chat and asynchronous discussion boards;
- Know how to effectively use teaching assistants for online learning;
- Identify tools that can promote active learning and also inform faculty of student understanding;
- Understand how formative assessment can create opportunities for community building and collaboration;
- Understand how to use exam-type essay questions efficiently for active learning and formative assessment; and
- Understand the benefits of using pre-class data to promote active learning and use class time effectively.

The Civil Procedure course is jokingly compared to learning how to drive a car using only an instruction manual. Teaching the class online can exacerbate inherent difficulties in learning due to more distractions that compete with learning. However,

* Clifford E. Vickrey Research Professor, Loyola University of Chicago School of Law. Professor Ho began law teaching in 1997. She has taught fully online classes with both synchronous and asynchronous components, as well as blended and traditional classes.

I have found that promoting active learning[1] that incorporates different types of formative assessment can optimize learning for a fully online class in the same manner as a traditional or blended one. Although active learning need not incorporate formative assessment, I think that active learning is most effective when there is an assessment component. An online class can easily harness technology to achieve promote active learning and formative assessment.

The chapter begins with an overview of my class goals and my data-driven approach to teaching based on active learning that includes substantial formative assessment. The chapter then turns to the specific details. I hope this chapter is valuable for faculty interested in using formative assessment generally and with Civil Procedure in particular.

## I. Using Active Learning and Formative Assessment to Promote Course Goals

I teach a one-semester, four-credit Civil Procedure course with two goals. My first goal is ensuring students have a strong understanding of core concepts, including how to identify and properly analyze issues on an essay exam. My second goal is ensuring students are able to read primary material, especially federal rules and statutes, on their own. When met, these goals translate into strong knowledge for the bar exam and law practice.

To help students meet these goals, I leverage a Learning Management System and an online tool, Click & Learn: Civil Procedure (Click & Learn).[2] These tools supplant a traditional casebook to promote active learning of new material. In addition, I provide multiple feedback opportunities each week during class, as well as outside of class. Click & Learn provides many questions to actively engage students with cases and statutes, as well as provide automated feedback on their progress in learning the material. During class, I use polling questions and breakout rooms to promote feedback. Outside of synchronous class sessions, students are actively learning new material not solely with cases but with many multiple-choice and other short-answer questions to prime learning,[3] exam-type essay questions, review quizzes, discussion

---

1. Active learning is a broad category that can include any activity that directly engages students in their understanding of learning, rather than passively listening to an expert or reading, and often requires higher order thinking. Examples include voting on questions by polling devices, as well as think-pair-share, where students think about an answer, then share with a peer. *E.g.*, Robin A. Boyle, *Employing Active-Learning techniques and Metacognition in Law School: Shifting Energy from Professor to Student,* 81 U. Det. Mercy L. Rev. 1 (2003); Cynthia Braeme, *Active Learning: What Is It,* Vanderbilt University Center for Teaching (2016), https://cft.vanderbilt.edu/wp-content/uploads/sites/59/Active-Learning.pdf.

2. Angela Upchurch et al., Click & Learn: Civil Procedure, https://www.clickandlearnguide.com/ (last visited Nov. 19, 2020).

3. Nancy Falchikov & David Boud, *Assessment and Emotion: The Impact of Being Assessed, in* Rethinking Assessment in Higher Education: Learning for the Longer Term 144 (David Boud & Nancy Falchiko eds., 2007) (finding that when students were immediately tested after reading an article they performed better on a final exam than students not tested until three weeks later).

boards, and synchronous chat sessions. Moreover, I use teaching assistants to provide further formative assessment and guidance. Basically, all of these active learning tools promote student understanding of core concepts, how to read primary material and familiarity with how to succeed on a summative assessment (i.e. the final exam) that includes traditional essay questions, as well as multiple-choice and short answer questions concerning a "mystery statute" requiring them to apply their understanding to a statute not previously assigned or discussed in class.[4]

Using multiple forms of formative assessment can provide a rich source of data to better tailor class time. I use overall class data on multiple-choice and other short answer questions completed before class to determine what points of confusion need to be addressed and avoid wasting time on what students understand.[5] In addition, I require all students to answer essay questions on an almost weekly basis to promote active learning, but I only review a small sample of (anonymous) student answers to gain an understanding of what needs to be reinforced during class.

I have found this approach to work in both blended as well as fully online classes. Student performance in a fully online class was quite similar for both the midterm and final to prior years. The similar student performance seems to support the effectiveness of this approach for online learning. My experience is consistent with multiple studies that recommend repeated assessment to promote learning, especially assessment followed by prompt feedback.[6] After all, this will close any gap in understanding by providing immediate feedback on what a student has mastered.[7] In addition, given that students from blended classes have told me they easily retained the information when studying for the bar, I believe that will also be true for students from the online class.[8]

---

4. This may seem like a lot for students to do, but since I require them to read very few cases, I feel that on balance the workload is manageable.

5. This is discussed in Part III.

6. *See, e.g.*, Carol Springer Sargent & Andrea A. Curcio, *Empirical Evidence that Formative Assessments Improve Law Students' Final Exam*, 61 J. Legal Ed. 379 (2012) (empirical study finding that law students perform better on final exams with formative assessment); Sophie M. Sparrow, *Using Individual and Group Multiple-Choice Quizzes to Deepen Students' Learning*, 3 Elon L. Rev. 1, 3 (2011) (finding that using multiple quizzes within a course permits more coverage and reduces student stress). There is also extensive data beyond the law school context: Students can learn at a more rapid pace or in greater depth and scope than they would have without this feedback. Dai Hounsell, *Towards More Sustainable Feedback to Students, in* Rethinking Assessment in Higher Education: Learning for the Longer Term 101 (David Boud & Nancy Falchiko eds., 2007).

7. *E.g., How Feedback Loop Boosts Student Learning*, Educ. Tech. Insights (July 16, 2019), https://www.educationtechnologyinsights.com/news/how-feedback-loops-boost-student-learning-nid-722.html#:~:text=The%20concept%20of%20the%20feedback,focused%20on%20a%20learning%20target.

8. Although anecdotal, I usually get several emails every summer from students taking the bar that Civil Procedure is by far the easiest topic for them based on practice from their 1L class.

## II. Harnessing Online Assessment Options

Given the challenges of online learning, especially if students are also socially isolated, maximizing methods of interaction and assessment is important. This Part explains how a learning management system (LMS) such as TWEN or Blackboard can facilitate assessments, how to effectively use formative feedback, and then details specific assessments.

### A. LMS AS ONLINE ANCHOR AND ASSESSMENT PROVIDER

An LMS, which most instructors already use as an organizational platform for course documents like a syllabus, can provide a useful anchor for an online class, including multiple mechanisms for assessment.[9] An LMS may easily integrate with a platform for synchronous classes over video. In addition, most LMS platforms have discussion boards that allow students to respond to a prompt from the professor and each other's responses. An LMS typically permits students to upload assignments for which feedback can be provided as individual comments, a rubric, or a sample answer. Most LMS platforms also provide formative and summative assessment mechanisms for quizzes and tests, which can provide feedback to students.

Effective use of LMS assignment scoring can also help promote learning. In particular, if LMS assessments are scored to give students full credit for timely completion rather than accuracy, this encourages students to focus on learning. This can be done, for example, if the LMS permits a "check" for submission of an assignment or a set score if a quiz is completed by a particular date, regardless of the number of questions answered correctly. Sometimes the LMS may not provide a set score but may at least allow the professor to easily denote—such as in red font—scores that are late and thus not entitled to full credit (faculty may differ on whether the student should get no credit or partial credit). In such a situation, faculty can assign their own score with a simple online spreadsheet after a quick scan of which students were late.

Most importantly, focusing LMS scoring on timely completion enables re-use of the same questions year after year if students understand the point of formative assessment. Students should be told that the best way to learn material is to do it on their own, such that finding the "right" answer will not help them be able to identify and correctly analyze a new one on a final. I have found no problems re-using identical questions from year to year with this approach; given fairly similar student performance with the same questions, I believe that they are appropriately following guidelines.

---

9. For a more in-depth treatment of choosing and using an LMS, see Chapter 16: *A Millennial Law Professor's Guide to Learning Management Systems* by Verónica C. Gonzales-Zamora.

## B. INTERACTIONS DURING CLASS

### 1. Polling questions

One easy way to engage students is through polling the entire class. There are a variety of methods that can be used, including ones embedded in the online classroom platform (such as Zoom) and app-based polling that works in conjunction with an online platform.[10] Even the most basic free apps permit true/false or multiple-choice polling during class. Some also permit submitting text that can potentially show up as word clouds, and some even permit teams of students to compete against each other.[11]

Polling questions can be used to efficiently provide formative assessment to the entire class to help reinforce material just discussed. For example, after discussing a topic, a polling question can help assess whether students understand the material more effectively than Socratic dialogue with a single student whose understanding may not represent the class. In addition, because polling apps allow a professor to easily display how many students chose each answer, this can promote discussion of which answer is correct and why. I believe that soliciting the correct answer after students see the display is more effective than immediately revealing the correct answer. Seeing that they are not alone seems to promote discussion and embolden students to ask questions to better understand the flaws in their reasoning. In fact, when I solicit volunteers to explain what they think is the best reason and why, I sometimes have students say that they think they may be wrong since they are in the minority, but they are interested in explaining their reasoning to gain a better understanding of why they are wrong.

I find it useful to include polling questions throughout class. In a two-hour class period, I generally end up using six to eight polling questions. I often include a polling question after several content slides; I sometimes also include a polling question at the beginning of the class to recap information students should know. In addition, since it can be hard to predict the length of discussion with polling questions, I do not rigidly use every polling question I have prepared. After all, if students excel on a concept, I can skip a similar one. Sometimes I also ask students if they want another question on a topic before moving on and follow their lead. I also generally have extra questions at the end of my slides in case class proceeds quickly and there is time for review questions.

---

10. Examples include Poll Everywhere, Socrative, and Tophat. *See, e.g.*, SUSAN GILLES ET AL., INDIVIDUALIZED EDUCATION: USING ONLINE TOOLS AND VIDEOS TO REACH ALL STUDENTS 2 (2013), http://conference.cali.org/2013/sites/conference.cali.org.2013/files/slides/CALI%202013%20Handout-Final.pdf.

11. Socrative permits students to compete against each other with a feature it calls "Space Race." Carvin Palanca, *Deliver a Space Race*, SOCRATIVE, https://help.socrative.com/en/articles/2155306-deliver-a-space-race (last visited Nov. 19 2020); SOCRATIVE, SPACE RACE 1 (2012), http://eisdedtechs.weebly.com/uploads/1/3/1/9/13198293/socrative_space_race.pdf. In addition, Kahoot is a game-based learning platform, https://kahoot.com/.

The specific polling vehicle a faculty uses may depend on desired features. Personally, I prefer a system that permits students to redo questions on their own time outside of class and obtain the correct answer in "real time" because this provides additional formative assessment. Moreover, this can promote spaced repetition for students who do this with other topics. Since not all polling systems permit this, it is something to consider.[12] In addition, some polling systems require you to type questions into their platform whereas others will enable you to use questions you already have in your slides. So, this is another factor to consider.[13]

### 2. Breakout rooms

Small group discussions in separate breakout rooms can be beneficial in an online setting. They provide a sense of community in addition to providing the benefits of the power of group work. I have found it helpful to schedule time for breakout rooms during synchronous classes that give students the option of connecting socially, working on a problem, or potentially both within the same time period.[14]

Breakout rooms can be used to discuss a variety of substantive topics using different formats. Students can be assigned to work through a more challenging multiple-choice question or hypothetical. The professor could assign multiple groups to discuss the same question and then have the groups compare the results. Alternatively, to cover more ground with the groups, each group could be asked to focus on a different issue and then share with the entire class.

There are, of course, logistical decisions to be made in terms of breakout rooms. I personally like using breakout rooms roughly halfway through a two-hour class, and I tell students in advance not only that we will use breakouts but also when so that they know what to expect. I also use random groups to maximize opportunities for students to meet others. The size of the breakout rooms may depend on the goals. Small group work seems to work well for groups of two to five students. However, if breakout rooms are used flexibly to permit students to elect to socialize or discuss an assignment due later that week, I have sometimes included a few more students. Although faculty can monitor breakout rooms, I generally do not since one of my goals is to enable students to connect with each other. Students have told me that they

---

12. I have enjoyed using Tophat which has this feature. For some explanation on how to use this feature, see *Essentials: Adopting Interactive Content*, TopHat, https://support.tophat.com/s/article/Essentials-Flipped-Classroom-Interactive-Content (last visited May 20, 2021).

13. For additional treatment of polling systems, see Chapter 8: *From Ground to Cloud and Back Again: Modern Tactics to Improve Your Teaching* by Katherine Brem (discussing integrating polling questions to update a previously-taught course), and Chapter 20: *A Whole New Meaning to Cybercrimes: Teaching Criminal Law and Criminal Procedure in an Online Learning Environment* by Tonya Krause-Phelan (discussing using polling in online Criminal Law & Procedure courses).

14. For a more in-depth treatment of collaborative and team-based learning, see Chapter 10: *Team-Based Learning in an Online Teaching Environment* by Joy E. Herr-Cardillo and Melissa H. Weresh, and Chapter 14: *Effective Collaboration in Online Courses* by Darby Dickerson and Megan Bess.

look forward to these breakout sessions and the opportunity to meet their classmates. Moreover, some have connected outside of class with students that they initially meet in a breakout session.

Breakout sessions with small groups can be especially helpful in teaching first-semester 1Ls new, and likely foreign, concepts that would otherwise have been discussed in small groups in a traditional class. For example, to help students understand IRAC as an organizational principle, I have students work in breakout rooms during class to review about twenty sentences from a short IRAC essay answer, each of which is listed under a specific category such as "rule" or "analysis or conclusion." Their task is to determine the correct order using a mostly blank template that I provide that shows the overarching issue, as well as where sub-issues, rule, analysis, and conclusion statements belong.[15] During class, I give them seven minutes to discuss with a classmate the correct ordering, as well as questions concerning what things should be discussed. I provide a list of questions to consider based on points of confusion in prior years, such as whether an essay answer concerning whether there is federal subject-matter jurisdiction under section 1332 should discuss all rules concerning section 1332, even if there are no relevant facts in the scenario. Then I lead a class discussion about these issues and post the correct answer in the LMS to prepare them to write an essay in IRAC format on their own.

Along somewhat similar lines, I also have students collaborate to decipher the correct order of paragraphs for an actual personal jurisdiction opinion on the second day of discussing personal jurisdiction. At this time, they have been introduced to the overall framework of analysis. Still, they have not yet studied most of the components, including contacts via "stream of commerce" included in the opinion.[16] When done in person, students are given strips of paper that they can physically move around. However, the same scenario works online in that students in breakout rooms can be provided a document with randomized but numbered paragraphs and told to work through this. I typically email the students the document before class so that they can potentially print it out if that is helpful.[17] I tell students to skim through the numbered portions and then discuss with their groups (of roughly four students) the correct order. After a ten-minute period of small group discussion, I lead the class discussion on the correct order. I also post the correctly ordered opinion to students afterward on the LMS. This exercise helps reinforce the process of analyzing personal jurisdiction that students can understand even before they have

15. To prepare students for this exercise, I provide them a brief two page introduction to IRAC, together with the sentences and template before class. This material is available at: https://papers.ssrn.com/sol3/papers.cfm?abstract_id=3789103.

16. Although any opinion can be used, the one I have used is relatively short opinion that my colleague Angela Upchurch shared with me—Irizarry v. East Longitude Trading Co., 296 F. Supp. 3d 862 (N.D. Oh. 2003).

17. Another possibility I have not tried but could work would be to provide each group with their own Google document link and enable them to try to do the reorganizing online. Of course, the Google doc would need to be copied for each group.

learned all the nuances. I believe this also helps them understand how subsequent classes on these nuances fit in that process.

### 3. Teaching assistants

Teaching assistants can help with formative assessment during a synchronous class. As anyone who has taught a large 1L class online knows, it can be daunting to focus on delivering content and managing virtual hands, let alone address questions in chat. For faculty that do not want to personally manage chat, a TA can help to do so and potentially provide immediate formative assessment by responding to the chat during class. This may be especially helpful for students who feel uncomfortable asking their question to the entire class and who want to simply send a private message; this can roughly approximate a student asking a question privately right before or after class. Alternatively, the TA can collect questions and provide them to the faculty member during or after class for the faculty member to address.

Moreover, TAs can help with formative assessment based on submitted essay answers. I have found that two teaching assistants seem to be able to scan through about seventy submissions for serious issues in less than two hours. That permits the faculty to then personally follow up with just a handful of individual students. Alternatively, a faculty member can delegate follow-up to TAs.

TAs can also help with logistical issues that may prevent students from receiving material and engaging in formative assessment during an online class. For example, TAs can monitor attendance during an online class and let faculty know who is missing, as well as who had internet issues that prevented them from addressing a polling question, for example.

## C. INTERACTIONS OUTSIDE OF (SYNCHRONOUS) CLASS

### 1. Informal assessment through synchronous chat

While the chat function of an LMS or video conferencing platform is usually used as an adjunct to the video discussion, I have found benefits to office hours using "chat" without video in an LMS with this feature. One benefit of office hours via chat is that text-only connection may make for more secure, uninterrupted Internet connections in addition to potentially minimizing "Zoom fatigue." Using chat without video can remove some of the usual awkwardness during online sessions when students are unsure who should speak first without raising hands. And since text appears in the order in which people type, no one should feel interrupted. In addition, when the professor asks a question, students often enjoy trying to be the first to answer, and the professor can see all answers not just the first one. I definitely have some student devotees to this type of office hour over more traditional office hours. In addition, if the LMS generates a written transcript afterward, this can benefit all students regardless of whether they participated in that session.[18] Some students who say they can get confused by questions during a live session find it useful to read the transcript so that they can skim for questions that they had and ignore other questions that they find confusing. Accordingly, this format can accommodate an additional type of student engagement than traditional live discussion.

### 2. Informal assessment through asynchronous discussion

Discussion forums can be used by students to easily post questions 24/7 that can be answered by the professor and available to all as one type of formative assessment. One benefit of using a forum instead of individual emails to faculty is that students could reply to each other and try to test their knowledge before the faculty member chimes in. In addition, even if students do not do this, all students will benefit from seeing the answer. Admittedly, students may sometimes be shy about posting a response and seeming "dumb"; however, some LMS platforms like TWEN have an option to let students elect to make individual posts anonymous or to make the entire forum anonymous. From a faculty perspective, having all the questions in one place can be more efficient than emails, which can get lost in a teeming inbox. The one downside to the use of a forum rather than email for questions is that the faculty may not know when new posts appear unless the LMS setting notifies all about new posts or if the LMS gives individual posters the ability to notify all about a new post and students use that option. Without those features, the professor can regularly check the discussion boards for new posts.

### 3. Additional assessment with teaching assistants in structured office hours

To help provide more resources and assessment to students, I am fortunate to employ two teaching assistants, which is common at my school for 1L classes. Each TA has their own office hours that have a specific structure to help promote active learning and assessment. One student focuses on a review of material from the previous week via slides that I review and approve in advance. The other student will review an essay question with a "template"[19] that I also review in advance.[20] These office hours provide another means of active learning and formative assessment. For example, the slides or documents have blanks to prompt students to either insert key words or choose between two options. The TAs guide students to select the correct answers

18. TWEN provides this with the "Live Discussion" feature.

19. The "template" is a document that helps organize discussion of how to organize and analyze an essay answer.

20. Although it takes some time to review student materials, it is a relatively minor amount of time compared to how much time I would need if I did everything on my own. I would estimate that it usually only takes about thirty minutes and at most one hour to do so for about 25-30 slides that a student has created. It usually takes a similar amount of time to review an essay answer "template" that a student has drafted.

during their synchronous office hours. Although these can be recorded, I generally have not done so to encourage students to attend and obtain feedback. In addition, I believe that students may feel more comfortable asking questions if they know there will be no formal record of their questions.

For the TA focused on essay templates, I work with the TA to create a document that helps provide students a skeletal outline that shows how to organize a strong answer. Moreover, it includes tips based on issues that I have seen with some of the anonymous answers. For example, here's a portion of an essay template to the bolded question.

> **Discuss whether the court properly denied Dennis's motion to amend his answer.**
>
> The issue is whether the court was proper in denying Dennis's motion to amend his answer to add the defense of ______________ and a _________ claim against Johnny. A motion to amend should be denied if it is not procedurally proper or the Foman factors suggest that leave to amend should not be granted [in the interest of justice].
>
> - *Do you need to state the assumption that the period for making amendments as a matter of course has ended?*
>
>   The issue is whether Dennis's motion to amend was procedurally proper. A motion to amend is procedurally proper if made any time before trial.
>
>   ADD ANALYSIS
>
> - *At what point in the litigation was Dennis's motion made?*
> - *Is this analysis any different for adding claim versus defense? Given that, do you think you'll need to repeat this later?*

TAs may also pose discussion questions or short application questions for students to discuss in breakout rooms before the TA provides clarification. I work with the TAs about what to include, and I generally always share my data on what issues students are having trouble with. A TA can usually create a "new" question based on one that I have previously given in class by changing names and/or legal claims to help reinforce the material.

In addition to weekly office hours, I use my teaching assistants to help students process information and provide formative feedback in several stages. First, I have TAs do a weekly list of questions that students should know the answer to from class discussion. Second, my TAs explain how to outline and then provide individual feedback on portions of outlines over the course of the semester. I will briefly explain each of these.

The weekly list of questions that students should know the answer to is intended to help provide feedback on whether students are properly taking notes, and also provide a way for students to test their knowledge of the material. As with all other material,

I review the TA drafted document and sometimes add additional issues before it is posted on the LMS. Even though the document lists questions but not answers, some students find it helpful to use this to test their understanding. For any questions that they are not sure about, students can then ask about that during my office hours.

Outlines are obviously also an essential part of synthesizing course content. However, given that most students have never created an outline before law school, providing guidance is necessary. So at the first step, providing students with the goals of an outline—what to include or not, and some different partial examples—can be helpful. This seems to work well during a synchronous online session with TAs that permits students to volunteer how to complete the partial examples. I usually recommend the TAs provide two different versions for students to see that no single method of outlining ensures success. For example, a fill-in-the-blank flow chart or fill-in-the-blank textual outline could be used to further understanding of the material equally as well as the process of outlining. Students can be provided the slides (or a handout of the template) in advance for them to complete during the synchronous session. Importantly, students are provided with only a partial outline to encourage them to not only attend the session and participate in real-time, but also then to create the majority of their actual outline on their own.

Teaching assistants provide feedback on portions of student outlines over the semester to students that meet specific deadlines. Although students are not required to submit outlines, I always emphasize that students that take advantage of this assistance are more likely to do well since, without accurate understanding, students cannot excel. There are three submission dates for portions of outlines on various topics, with the deadline usually being about one to two weeks after the coverage of the last topic for that section. Having deadlines linked to feedback can help motivate students not to delay creating an outline. To keep the workload manageable, the TAs read three to five pages (single-spaced) for each student and comment on whether the stated rules are correct, as well as whether the format is likely to be helpful (or not) on a final.

As with all assessments discussed so far in this chapter, formative assessment can be effectively used by TAs in conjunction with the LMS. When the LMS is used instead of email, this can permit TAs and the faculty member to have access to the same information. So, for example, if a student having issues meets with their teacher, the teacher can easily see whether the student has ever submitted an outline, as well as what issues have already been noted for a student who submitted an outline.

Although this section has discussed the benefits of using TAs to provide more formative assessment, any of the above suggestions could also be used by an individual faculty member if TAs are not available. That said, it would likely be overwhelming to do all of these activities without the assistance of TAs since individual review of outlines is quite time-consuming. However, some of the other activities, like a weekly list of key questions students should know, as well as tips on how to outline, could be managed by an individual faculty member with minimal additional time.

## III. Effectively Using Online Assessment to Collect Data and Promote Collaboration

This Part explains some methods that provide data based on pre-class performance that can be effectively combined with in-class data (such as polling) to teach class efficiently. I will first provide an overview of online resources, including one that provides a wealth of data to faculty without the need for drafting questions. Then I will explain how to use essay questions to promote more formative feedback and a sense of community.

### A. AVAILABLE OPTIONS FOR PRE- AND POST-CLASS ASSESSMENT

Multiple-choice questions and answers have long been available to students and faculty. CALI lessons provide interactive online assessments to students.[21] Other questions also exist in hardcopy commercial supplements that can be useful, even if not interactive.[22] Some casebooks such as Casebook Connect also provide questions.[23] Recent years have seen more questions move online. Questions are available through platforms such as SeRiouS (Spaced Repetition), Quimbee, and Kaplan.[24] These questions can provide formative feedback after a topic has been covered in class without faculty needing to provide individual feedback.

In choosing among possible tools to use, consider the number of available questions, whether questions require students to integrate multiple topics, and whether questions help promote learning and understanding of essay exam answers. Another consideration is whether a tool permits the professor to monitor overall class and individual student performance.[25] Moreover, choosing a relevant resource may be a

---

21. *Lessons*, CALI, http://www.cali.org/lesson (last visited Nov. 19, 2020).

22. *See, e.g.*, JOSEPH W. GLANNON, CIVIL PROCEDURE: EXAMPLES & EXPLANATIONS (8th ed. 2018); *see also* JOSEPH W. GLANNON, THE GLANNON GUIDE TO CIVIL PROCEDURE: LEARNING CIVIL PROCEDURE THROUGH MULTIPLE-CHOICE QUESTIONS AND ANALYSIS (4th ed. 2019) (more recent Glannon book that has fewer questions, but focuses on helping students better understand how to answer multiple-choice questions). Other resources include: JOEL FRIEDMAN, CIVIL PROCEDURE: ESSAY & MULTIPLE CHOICE EXAMS (2009); LINDA MULLENIX, CIVIL PROCEDURE, SUM & SUBSTANCE, EXAM PRO. SERIES (2d ed. 2007); SIEGEL & EMANUEL, CIVIL PROCEDURE: ESSAY AND MULTIPLE-CHOICE QUESTIONS AND ANSWERS (5th ed. 2012); WILLIAM JANSSEN & STEVEN F. BAICKER-MCKEE, MASTERING MULTIPLE CHOICE FOR FEDERAL CIVIL PROCEDURE (3d ed. 2018).

23. This includes texts by Yeazell, Glannon et al., Subrin et al., and others. *CasebookConnect Catalog*, CASEBOOKCONNECT, https://www.casebookconnect.com/catalog (last visited Nov. 19, 2020).

24. SPACED REPETITION, https://www.spacedrepetition.com (last visited Feb. 4, 2021); QUIMBEE, *Civil Procedure Study Aids*, https://www.quimbee.com/study-aids/subjects/civil-procedure (last visited Feb. 4, 2021) (noting 30 essay exams, 428 multiple choice and over 700 flashcards); KAPLAN, https://www.kaptest.com/bar-exam/courses/1l-edge-program (last visited Feb. 4, 2021) (providing over 1000 questions tested on the multi-state, with some of these being focused on Civil Procedure).

25. There is growing recognition of the need to provide faculty feedback. CALI now offers an option for faculty to learn by using a lesson link. https://www.cali.org/faq-page/313-0#t313n15754. Click & Learn: Civil Procedure provides detailed feedback on overall class performance, as well as individual student performance.

function of whether a tool provides questions that are directed to help students better understand the basics of cases and provide feedback before class to further optimize class time.[26] The only online tool I am aware of with questions designed for pre-class use in addition to higher level review questions covering multiple topics, as well as essay tips is Click & Learn.[27]

Pre-class assessment, such as in Click & Learn, leverages the benefit of "failing."[28] Questions that prompt students to guess about what a rule or statute means *before* students have officially learned the material invoke the so-called "generation effect," whereby generating a guess promotes retention better than simply reading it.[29] So, for example, a student might be shown a specific rule in the FRCP and asked to speculate how it connects to other known concepts through reference to headers and other material before being provided the answer. Studies show information learned in this manner is better retained than if the student were simply told what the rule means and given time to study that.[30] In addition, it helps students better understand how to read new statutes and rules, a key lawyering skill that is generally not taught in casebooks or even other supplements. Studies show that pre-class assessment enhances final exam performance.[31] At the same time, the pre-tests can serve as asynchronous class time.

In addition to existing resources, faculty members can create assessments to use during synchronous class sessions or alternatively to do asynchronously using methods discussed in Part II. Faculty can readily create polling questions and/or quizzes

---

26. For an example, see Cynthia M. Ho et al., *An Active Learning Approach to Teaching Tough Topics: Personal Jurisdiction as an Example,* 65 J. Legal Ed. 772, 808–14 (2016) (providing example of questions relating to an assigned personal jurisdiction case).

27. Glannon's E&E has a chapter addressing the integration of subject matter, personal jurisdiction, and venue together. However, currently, Click & Learn is the only online platform that provides synthesis of these topics as well as questions that require mastery of joinder and preclusion. Moreover, Click & Learn provides guidance on essay questions, including how to identify issues, craft accurate and complete rule statements, and conduct rule to fact application. For example, students can read a short hypo on an easy subject-matter jurisdiction question and then be guided through how to analyze that with a series of questions. The same is true for a personal jurisdiction question involving breach of contract. In addition, there are questions to help students issue-spot for essay questions regarding joinder of parties.

28. *E.g.*, Benedict Carey, *Why Flunking Exams is Actually a Good Thing,* N.Y. Times Mag. (Sept. 4, 2014), https://www.nytimes.com/2014/09/07/magazine/why-flunking-exams-is-actually-a-good-thing.html. As of Fall 2020, Click & Learn: Civil Procedure (Click & Learn), provides a means to provide substantial formative assessment with over 2000 questions, as well as explanations using any web-enabled device.

29. *E.g.*, Norman Slamecka & Peter Graf, *The Generation Effect: Delination of a Phenomenon,* 4 J. Experimental. Psychol. 592, 601–03 (1978); Larry L. Jacoby, *On Interpreting the Effects of Repetition: Solving a Problem versus Remembering a Solution,* 17 J. Verbal Learning 649, 661 (1978).

30. *E.g.*, Veronica X. Yan et al., *Why does guessing incorrectly enhance, rather than impair retention?*, 42 Memory Cognition 1373, 1376 (2014).

31. *See, e.g.*, Macie Hall, *How Pretesting can Help your Students Fail Well,* Innovative Instructor (July 18, 2017), https://ii.library.jhu.edu/2017/07/18/how-pretesting-can-help-your-students-fail-well/. In addition, although anecdotal, students seem to find this true with Click & Learn as well. As one of the co-authors, I have received feedback from the publisher that faculty at other schools using it have found students did better on summative assessment than in previous semesters when they were more diligent in using this tool.

using issues that they know students have struggled with in the past. Especially for in-class polling, including a number of false answers that are common distractors can help promote discussion and clarify issues for students. Quizzes can be especially helpful for students to receive formative assessment since they can provide answers that students can review, as well as retake. Moreover, once polling questions and/or quizzes are created, they can be easily re-used year after year; thus, even if there is some investment of time initially, there are substantial time savings later.

### B. ASSESSMENT AND COMMUNITY BUILDING

Although I have long provided students with exam-type essay questions for formative assessment practice, I have used them differently when teaching a solely online course in a manner that not only provides assessment but also promotes community building and efficiency. In particular, I more often permit students to collaborate and jointly submit an assignment. I emphasize that the goal of collaborative work is to benefit from having two brains working on the problem rather than to split up the work and only learn half. Since each student is still ultimately graded individually on the final, I have not tried to police whether students are properly collaborating.

In addition, I have required student collaboration on most optional rewrites of exam-type hypo answers. I permit students an opportunity to rewrite the answer to a question previously discussed in class in teams of two by a given date. I instruct the students to each rewrite the answer on their own and then collaborate to produce the best possible answer to submit. This collaboration cuts down on faculty grading time, and some students have found it beneficial to see another student's approach when they effectively work as a team. For students who rewrite multiple answers, I often suggest working with different partners to get to know other students and learn different approaches.

Because weaker students may be intimidated to reach out to a classmate about doing a team answer, I set up a sign-up sheet on my LMS and nudge individual students to sign up with someone who has already signed up as looking for a partner. Using a sign-up sheet can also be helpful for placing limits if an instructor only has a certain amount of time to review such answers; for example, the instructor can limit review to the stated number of opportunities.

Another possible method of community building and formative assessment is to have students draft multiple-choice questions (and answers) together. This process can provide students an inside view of how such questions are structured and hopefully better understand how to approach them—especially after receiving feedback. For example, in reviewing a student-drafted multiple-choice question, I will typically tell them if the question is easier or harder than questions they can expect on the same concept on the exam. Students can also be incentivized to do this if they are told that draft questions may appear on the final exam. Although an individual student could obviously do this on their own, 1L students new to this task are more likely to produce a useful product by collaborating.

Another option for community building and formative assessment is to have students draft essay questions and sample answers, including with a given time limit to simulate an actual exam. This could be an extra credit project for students, perhaps focused on topics that the professor wants students to practice more. The final product with some potential tweaks after instructor review can provide a source of additional formative assessment to students. For example, just as my old prior exams (and sample answers) are available on the LMS, I include student drafted essay questions and sample answers. I believe that such a question—after any necessary instructor adjustment—is likely more helpful for students preparing for that instructor's exam than a random exam from another faculty member or from a commercial source. After all, there is a wide diversity in topic coverage and how material is tested. While students will not always draft strong questions, even a few can provide an additional source of formative assessment for students.

## IV. A Data-Driven Approach to Teaching with Formative Feedback

### A. WHY USE DATA

Class can be more efficient and effective using data about what the students understand to figure out what to focus on. For example, if data from questions before class reveals that 90% of students understand an issue, focus can be shifted elsewhere. In contrast, if 30% or more of students do not understand a concept, the concept needs further elaboration in class. Although certain concepts are perennially tough for all students, sub-issues of confusion may differ from year to year. Knowing what these issues are can help make limited class time more effective.

Admittedly, teaching this way requires time to review the data. However, the investment is worthwhile and need not be overwhelming. I have found that my class as a whole often has trouble with similar issues, even though the exact percentage may differ. Accordingly, I have not had to dramatically change slides from year to year, even though I may be tweaking some of the points of emphasis.

Beyond using data to decide what to focus on in class, LMS and polling platforms can easily identify students that need additional assistance if they perform sub-optimally compared to the rest of the class. For example, a faculty member may notice a student that repeatedly performs poorly. Some polling platforms make this task easier by providing not only comparative data but also emailing that data directly to the professor.[32]

Students themselves can also use class data to improve their metacognition. This is true for both data concerning quizzes in LMS and polling data. For example, if the LMS provides a breakdown of the class average and standard deviation on a quiz, students can see how they did relative to their peers. This helps them better prepare for

32. For example, Tophat, a polling platform, sends weekly emails on students who performed exceptionally well and poorly.

what to expect on the final as well as the reality of law school class ranks. In addition, providing data on how many students answered each question option (i.e., A versus D to a multiple-choice question) can also help students see if they are in the minority of students who do not understand an issue. If so, they know that they really need to focus more on that topic.

The available data can also provide faculty with another avenue to connect with students. For example, even though students who excel can see that information, they may still appreciate a personal note to congratulate them during the challenging situation of a fully online class. Similarly, a student who does poorly but receives an encouraging email from a faculty member may feel supported despite receiving a low score. An email acknowledging underperformance with some suggestions for how to do better can be empowering and motivating for a student who realizes that their faculty member is invested in their performance. Sometimes it can also help prompt a student to disclose struggles with personal issues that the faculty, potentially in conjunction with staff, can provide support for.

### B. HOW I USE DATA FOR CLASSES

Now that I have explained why data can be beneficial, let me explain my specific approach. I use three sources of data for my classes. Two of the three sources involve objective data. One is a weekly review quiz of mostly multiple-choice and some true/false questions concerning material that we have covered in class. The other is essentially data from pre-class questions from Click & Learn on information that was previously new to students. The final source of data I use to teach class involves anonymous student submissions to weekly exam-type hypos. As mentioned above, I provide feedback on a sample of answers, typically about three to five students out of a class of around seventy. I use the sample of anonymously submitted answers to get a sense of what students do not fully understand and thus know what to focus on during class. Then, during class, I may gather further data concerning essay questions with a polling question that asks which of the following issues the essay question should address.

In preparing for class, I spend time checking the objective data for class trends, as well as if individual students are having issues, although it generally is not realistic to check on all the individual students. Rather, when a substantial majority of the students have done the assignment, I can use the data to flag which questions/topics I need focus on. So, for example, with a recent short nine-question quiz, there were just three questions that I noticed needed substantial review (with 25%–40% getting them incorrect). So, I made sure to have bullets in my slides about these issues, included some in-class polls, and also incorporated questions about these issues for the next recap quiz.

In reviewing multiple-choice data, it is important to me not only if students get a question wrong, but which answers they are choosing since that can indicate different points of confusion. I usually start by looking for questions where at least 20–25% of the class answered incorrectly, and then I look at what answers they actually picked to try to discern points of confusion in a multiple-choice question. This data method works easily for systems that I have used that are available to any faculty member: TWEN quizzes as well as Click & Learn. Visual data from TWEN, as well as Click & Learn, is shown below (without full color) to help illustrate.

TWEN GRAPH OF CLASS DISTRIBUTION ON NINE-QUESTION QUIZ

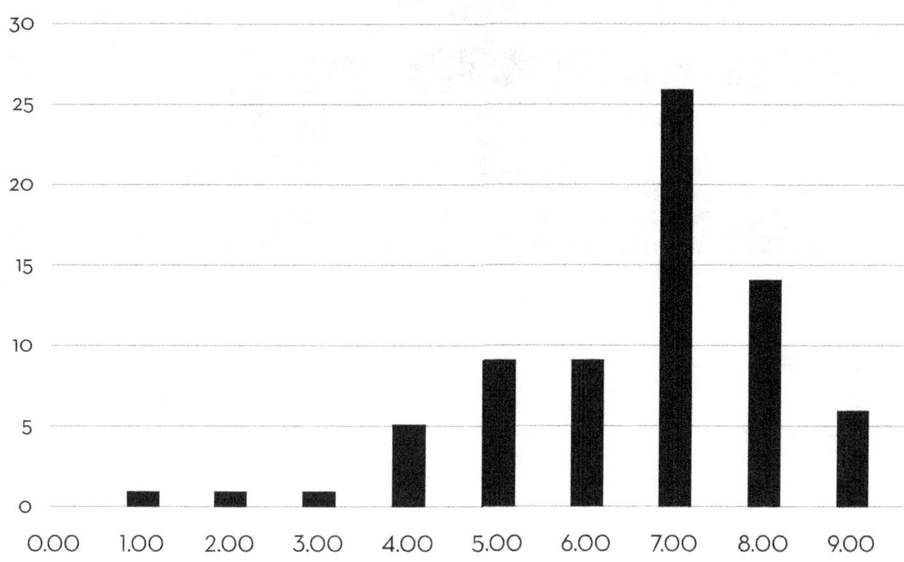


TWEN DATA ON BREAKDOWN FOR INDIVIDUAL QUESTIONS

| Question | Type | Answers | | | | |
|---|---|---|---|---|---|---|
| 1 | True/False | True: 11 | False: 61* | | | |
| 2 | True/False | True: 12 | False: 60* | | | |
| 3 | True/False | True: 13 | False: 59* | | | |
| 4 | Multiple Choice | A: 41* | B: 11 | C: 20 | | |
| 5 | True/False | True: 5 | False: 67* | | | |
| 6 | True/False | True: 53* | False: 19 | | | |
| 7 | Multiple Choice | A: 37* | B: 23 | C: 12 | | |
| 8 | Multiple Choice | A: 19* | B: 2 | C: 8 | D: 34* | E: 9 |
| 9 | Multiple Choice | A: 61* | B: 3 | C: 8 | | |

*Correct Answer

C&L DATA ON CLASS PERFORMANCE, AND ANSWERS FOR ONE QUESTION

Chapter Due date: 01-15-2020 9:00am CST

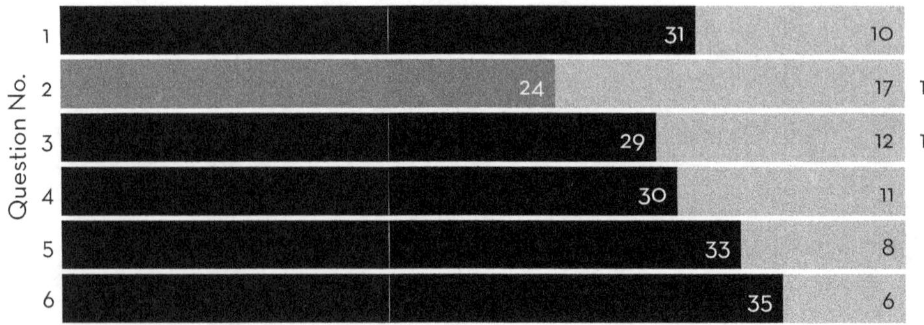


Number of Students Answering Question

Answer Breakdown
A: 24
B: 5
C: 11
D: 1

When I have time, I sometimes try to find out which students got certain questions wrong and then specifically cold call those students to ensure they have worked through their understanding and, if not, help them do so. Sometimes students will immediately respond that they remember getting it wrong and explain what they have learned. Other times the student seems unaware of what the answer should be. In those cases, I realize that the student needs additional reinforcement, which I can provide during class with some leading Socratic questions. Admittedly, I do not always have time to check on which students got which questions wrong. In addition, since I like to call on a number of different students to ensure that students can express themselves orally, calling on students who get a question correct is still useful. Nonetheless, I do think that can be an effective way to help individual students. Moreover, even if I do not try to cold call students during class who got a pre-class quiz question wrong, having data on individual students can help me identify very early in the semester who to recommend for additional academic support.

## V. Conclusion

I hope that this chapter has provided some useful ideas for how to incorporate formative feedback in an online Civil Procedure class. I personally enjoy a variety of techniques to engage students. I hope that faculty will find one or more of my techniques helpful for their own classes.

SECTION FOUR

# Beyond the First Year

TWENTY-FIVE

# Creating Practice-Ready Assignments: Low-Stake Assessments in Asynchronous Casebook Courses

Brad Desnoyer*

After reviewing this chapter, readers should be able to:

- Generate ideas for practice-ready assessments;
- Summarize the benefits and challenges of providing regular assessments;
- Create meaningful e-memo assignments that prepare students to write for practice;
- Create practical policy assignments that help prepare students to make informed and reasoned arguments; and
- Produce rubrics for each assignment.

Online learning offers the opportunity for a pedagogical reboot. The ABA and educational leaders have long criticized legal education for failing to effectively prepare students for practice.[1] Likewise, employers continue to lament that law school graduates lack the skills needed to excel as attorneys.[2] ABA Standard 314 partially answers

* Associate Clinical Professor, Indiana University Robert H. McKinney School of Law. Professor Desnoyer started teaching law in 2010 and began teaching Education Law as an asynchronous online course in 2019.

1. *See* A.B.A. Section on Legal Educ. & Admission to the Bar, Legal Education And Professional Development—An Education Continuum, Report of the Task Force on Law Schools and the Profession: Narrowing the Gap (1992); William M. Sullivan et al., Educating Lawyers: Preparation for the Profession of Law (2007) [hereinafter Carnegie Report]; Roy Stucky et al., Best Practices for Legal Education: A Vision and a Roadmap (2007) [hereinafter Best Practices].

2. *See* LexisNexis, *Hiring Partners Reveal New Attorney Readiness for Real World Practice* (2015), https://www.lexisnexis.com/documents/pdf/20150325064926_large.pdf.

these appraisals by demanding formative assessments throughout the curriculum.[3] But the ABA's allowance for distance education offers law schools an even greater opportunity to positively transform legal pedagogy—asynchronous courses that use multiple "practice-based" assessments.[4]

Per the ABA, distance education courses—including asynchronous courses[5]—must offer the opportunity for "regular and substantive interaction" between the professor and the students.[6] The ABA has not further defined this "interaction" or how to ensure it is equivalent to the interaction in live courses, but online formative assessments are now commonplace.[7] While some professors might grieve the opportunity to engage in Socratic dialogue, such questioning is simply not possible in asynchronous courses.[8] What is possible, however, is shifting away from an approach that fails to engage each student and can hinder the participation of women and minority students in the classroom.[9]

In 2019, I created the asynchronous course Education Law—an upper-level elective covering issues of school funding and equity, student constitutional rights, Title IX, and historic and modern segregation, among other topics.[10] Creating the course solidified my appreciation for strong online pedagogy. It made me value the behemoth workload requisite for designing a quality online course. And it instilled in me

---

3. A.B.A. Sec. Leg. Educ. & Admis. to the Bar, *Standards and Rules of Procedure for Approval of Law Schools*, Standard 314, at 24 (2020–21), https://www.americanbar.org/content/dam/aba/administrative/legal_education_and_admissions_to_the_bar/standards/2020-2021/2020-21-aba-standards-and-rules-for-approval-of-law-schools.pdf [hereinafter 2020 ABA Standards].

4. Practice-based assignments have the objective of solidifying a student's knowledge of the law and granting them the ability to apply that knowledge to solve legal problems. *See* Sherri Lee Keene, *One Small Step for Legal Writing, One Giant Leap for Legal Education: Making the Case for More Writing Opportunities in the "Practice-Ready" Law School Curriculum*, 65 MERCER L. REV. 467, 475 (2014).

5. *See* Yvonne M. Dutton & Seema Mohapatra, *COVID-19 and Law Teaching: Guidance on Developing an Asynchronous Online Course for Law Students*, ST. LOUIS U. L.J. (forthcoming 2021) (manuscript at 7) (on file with authors) [hereinafter *COVID-19*] (defining asynchronous courses as "time-shifted," where "students complete modules and assignments" within a set time but at their own pace).

6. *See* 2020 ABA Standards, *supra* note 3, Definition 7 (declaring distance education courses "use of technology to support regular and substantive interaction among students and between the students and the faculty member, either synchronously or asynchronously").

7. Yvonne M. Dutton & Margaret Ryznar, *Law School Pedagogy Post-Pandemic: Harnessing the Benefits of Online Teaching*, J. LEGAL EDUC. (forthcoming) (manuscript at 8) (on file with authors) (discussing these requirements under former ABA Standard 306) [hereinafter *Post-Pandemic*].

8. *See* Margaret Ryznar & Yvonne M. Dutton, *Lighting a Fire: The Power of Intrinsic Motivation in Online Teaching*, 70 SYRACUSE L. REV. 73, 75 (2020) [hereinafter *Lighting a Fire*]. *See generally* Yvonne M. Dutton, Margaret Ryznar & Kayleigh Long, *Assessing Online Learning in Law Schools: Students Say Online Classes Deliver*, 96 DENVER L. REV. 493, 514 (2019) [hereinafter *Assessing Online Learning*] ("[E]mploying the Socratic method is only one active-learning method ....").

9. *Post-Pandemic*, *supra* note 7, (manuscript at 16–17); Carol McCrehan Parker, *Writing Throughout the Curriculum: Why Law Schools Need It and How to Achieve It*, 76 NEB. L. REV. 561, 576 (1997).

10. For a discussion of teaching an Education Law seminar, see Chapter 26: *Designing and Cultivating Discussion in Online Seminars* by Kristen E. Murray.

an appreciation of the growing number of professors, both in online and in-person classrooms, who design their assessments to prepare students for practice.[11]

Low-stakes, practical assessments are more than a way of complying with ABA standards: They are a high-value means for supporting student learning.[12] By adopting practice-ready assignments, professors teaching asynchronous casebook courses can answer the Carnegie Report's call to seamlessly integrate the teaching of doctrine, skills, and values.[13] More importantly, such courses can spur a meaningful transformation for an academy and profession in need of reform.

This chapter begins by detailing the importance of practice-ready assignments and the need for regular assessments coupled with professor feedback. The chapter then discusses two types of assignments I have found useful in teaching Education Law: (1) e-memos and (2) policy assignments. Each section reviewing these assignments provides potential learning objectives, examples of assignments I used in class, and discussions of how I evaluated students.

## I. Practice-Ready Assignments

In asynchronous courses, students complete weekly "modules," which typically include reading assignments and video lectures supplemented with PowerPoints.[14] These modules can also include secondary sources, such as pertinent news articles, podcasts, or videos.[15] To ensure students are attentive to the readings and lectures, professors can include low-stakes multiple-choice quizzes during or after the lectures.[16] Further, professors can include a larger assignment at the end of each module to assess each student's learning.[17]

It is with these end-of-module assessments that professors can enhance their courses even further with practice-ready assignments: Assessments that have a student adopt the persona of an attorney and solve or evaluate a legal problem, often on behalf of a client.[18] For example, students might compose a legal document while adhering to accepted conventions (e.g., a risk assessment) or complete an exercise modeling how lawyers engage with others (e.g., participating in a mediation).

---

11. *See generally* Cynthia Batt, *A Practice Continuum: Integrating Experiential Education into the Classroom*, 7 Elon L. Rev. 119, 127 (2015); *see COVID-19*, *supra* note 5 (manuscript at 21–22).

12. Carnegie Report, *supra* note 1, at 164 (discussing the importance of formative assessment to "support opportunities to improve learning"). *See* John O. Sonsteng et al., *A Legal Education Renaissance: A Practical Approach for the Twenty-First Century*, 34 Wm. Mitchell L. Rev. 303, 408 (2007).

13. Carnegie Report, *supra* note 1, at 191.

14. *COVID-19*, *supra* note 5 (manuscript at 12).

15. *Id.*; *Post-Pandemic*, *supra* note 7 (manuscript at 4).

16. *See* Max Huffman, *Online Learning Grows Up—And Heads to Law School*, 49 Ind. L. Rev. 57, 83–84 (2015).

17. *Post-Pandemic*, *supra* note 7 (manuscript at 10).

18. *See* Keene, *supra* note 4, at 472, 475.

In addition to the specific exercises noted later in this chapter, professors have abundant options in creating practice-ready assignments based on each course's and module's learning goals and objectives. Potential assessment options include having students:

- Draft complaints;
- Write client or demand letters;
- Create or modify contracts;
- Counsel a client over a video service like Zoom;
- Negotiate with opposing counsel over a video service; and
- Present videotaped oral arguments.[19]

This is by no means an exhaustive list, and innovative professors have designed projects particular to their course topics. Professor Yvonne Dutton has students in Comparative Law write short comparative legal memoranda.[20] In Professor Seema Mohapatra's Bioethics and the Law, students invent "case studies" about bioethical conflicts, post those studies to the course website, review what others have uploaded, and detail how they would assist a client in the proposed situations.[21] Professors, therefore, must be creative in choosing what practice-ready assignments best fit their curriculum.

Further, in addition to preparing students to apply their knowledge, practice-ready assignments garner student engagement.[22] A thorough study of students taking online courses found students associate quality courses with regular, practice-ready assessments.[23] If the assessments are routine and low-stakes, students will develop an "intrinsic motivation" and perform better than they might with one or two high-stakes summative assessments.[24] Thus, rather than shirking from assessments and evaluation, students crave the opportunity to develop professional skills in a realistic but safe environment.

Assessments alone, however, are not enough. Feedback is crucial in the learning process,[25] and individual critiques allow students to evaluate their performance and

---

19. *See COVID-19*, *supra* note 5 (manuscript at 13, 22).

20. *Id.* (manuscript at 22).

21. *Id.*

22. *Lighting a Fire*, *supra* note 8, at 95–96.

23. *Assessing Online Learning*, *supra* note 8, at 527–28 (sharing the results of a study of student perceptions of online courses and finding students associate quality courses with regular, practice-ready assessments).

24. *Lighting a Fire*, *supra* note 8, at 84.

25. *See* Daniel Schwarcz & Dion Farganis, *The Impact of Individualized Feedback on Law Student Performance*, 67 J. Legal Educ. 139, 143 (2017) (presenting the results of a study suggesting individualized feedback improves student performance in law school exams, especially for "below median students").

improve both their practical and metacognitive skills.[26] Professors who have the time and ability can provide individual edits and comments on student papers; they might additionally offer model answers and rubrics.[27] If a professor does not have the resources to make individual comments, the professor can still offer general comments to the class and suggest students engage in group discussions and compare their work to the model answer.[28]

Regular assessments requiring feedback, or even necessitating professors review student papers for general class critiques, naturally raise the problem of overburdening overworked professors. To alleviate this drawback, professors and administrators will need to cap enrollment in casebook courses that have multiple practice-ready assignments.

## II. E-Memos

I have been teaching first-year legal writing since 2010. In that time, I have assigned students writing projects covering complex legal topics, including the First Amendment, the Fourth Amendment, and Title IX. Despite the complexity of these substantive areas, I am consistently amazed at how well students come to understand difficult subjects through writing about them.

Legal writing is, of course, a substantive class; legal writing professors do not teach writing in a vacuum.[29] To be successful, legal writing professors must become experts in doctrine and theory.[30] And by the time students complete first-year legal writing courses, the vast majority understand the discrete doctrinal areas that served as the foundations for their assignments. While part of their mastery can be credited to the time students spend with the material, much of their understanding comes from the simple and profound act of writing.[31] The recursive writing process is a forcing hand, demanding learners gain doctrinal clarity, articulate an analysis, and logically organize their points for an audience.[32] Writing is an ideal pedagogical tool.

---

26. *Assessing Online Learning*, *supra* note 8, at 498; Allison D. Martin & Kevin L. Rand, *The Future's So Bright, I Gotta Wear Shades: Law School Through the Lens of Hope*, 48 Duq. L. Rev. 203, 226–28 (2010).

27. *See* Martin et al., *supra* note 26, at 226–27.

28. Parker, *supra* note 9, at 576.

29. *See* Marie A. Monahan, *Towards A Theory of Assimilating Law Students into the Culture of the Legal Profession*, 51 Cath. U. L. Rev. 215, 219 (2001) ("[A]lthough a skills-oriented course, [legal writing] also presents an opportunity to teach fundamental legal concepts just as a doctrinal course communicates the substantive concepts and rules of a specific area of law.").

30. J. Christopher Rideout, *Knowing What We Already Know: On the Doctrine of Legal Writing*, 1 Savannah L. Rev. 103, 105 (2014).

31. *See* Syrene Forsman, Writing to Learn Means Learning to Think 162 (1985) (describing how writing assignments help students organize and critically think through an issue).

32. *See generally* Parker, *supra* note 9, at 566–68 (explaining how the process of writing helps students improve their analytical skills).

With this knowledge, when I set out to create Education Law, I wanted the course to incorporate writing assignments. Specifically, I wanted assignments that (1) gave students a chance to think through the materials critically, (2) emphasized practice-ready skills, and (3) were short yet meaningful assessments. In this way, the assignments would fulfill two of the educational goals stated by Professor Carol McCrehan Parker's groundbreaking article on writing across the curriculum: providing students with "writing-to-learn tools" for clarifying their thoughts and "teaching students to create effective professional documents."[33]

E-memos were my answer.

In modern practice, email is the primary method of communicating legal analysis.[34] Because of increased time and cost concerns, clients and supervisors have largely rejected traditional long-form memoranda in favor of condensed analyses in the body of emails.[35] According to my own empirical study of how attorneys write in practice, e-memos typically do not exceed two-traditional pages and are completed in under 48 hours.[36] Still, even though e-memos are short, quick turnaround projects, they demand a deep analysis of the law and a mastery of fundamental writing skills.[37]

E-memos compel a conciseness that can only come from a narrow focus on relevant issues, forcing students to show their true understanding of doctrine.[38] Longer writing projects can obfuscate a student's knowledge, with students taking a scattershot approach to answering a question. But with under two pages for an e-memo, students must crystallize their points and quickly reveal whether they comprehend the material.

---

33. *Id.* at 567–68.

34. Brad Desnoyer, *E-Memos 2.0: An Empirical Study of How Attorneys Write*, 25 Legal Writing: J. Legal Writing Inst. 213 (2020); Kristen Konrad Robbins-Tiscione, *From Snail Mail to E-Mail: The Traditional Legal Memorandum in the Twenty-First Century*, 58 J. Legal Educ. 32, 32–33 (2008) (presenting the results of a survey of Georgetown University Law Center alumni); Ellie Margolis, *Is the Medium the Message?*, 12 Legal Comm. & Rhetoric 1, 9 (2015).

35. Desnoyer, *supra* note 34, at 213–14; Robbins-Tiscione, *supra* note 34, at 32 (suggesting "the traditional memoranda is all but dead."). *See* Helene S. Shapo et al., Writing and Analysis in the Law 167 (7th ed. 2018) ("[Emails] are less expensive in terms of billing time and they accommodate the recipient's need for a fast response."); Kirsten K. Davis, *"The Reports of My Death Are Greatly Exaggerated": Reading and Writing Objective Legal Memoranda in a Mobile Computing Age*, 92 Or. L. Rev. 471, 473 (2014) (noting modern lawyers complain that traditional memoranda are expensive and time consuming).

36. *See generally* Desnoyer, *supra* note 34.

37. *See* Desnoyer, *supra* note 34, at 213–14.

38. *See* Keene, *supra* note 4, at 476 (defining "conciseness" as the ability to stay focused on pertinent information).

## A. LEARNING OBJECTIVES

Teaching writing skills is not separate per se from teaching doctrine.[39] Writing is a lawyer's primary rhetorical vehicle and an essential means of formulating knowledge of the law and showing that knowledge to the reader. Teaching students to write topic and thesis sentences, synthesize rules, reconcile seemingly conflicting cases, compare precedent to a client's facts, and effectively organize an analysis is teaching them to wield doctrine effectively. It is teaching them to be lawyers.[40] Having clear learning objectives aids me in creating e-memo assessments. Further, being transparent with students and sharing my learning objectives conveys the value of each assignment and garners student buy-in. I used the following learning objectives as my guide in creating the e-memo assignments:

1. To create a document meeting genre expectations;
2. To identify significant legal issues;
3. To analyze and synthesize cases, reconciling conflicting cases as necessary;
4. To separate relevant from irrelevant facts;
5. To decide on and implement an appropriate analytical structure;
6. To write thesis and topic sentences explaining how a particular legal rule applied in specific situations;
7. To apply the law to a particular fact situation and predict the outcome;
8. To identify and rebut counterargument;
9. To recommend appropriate next steps; and
10. To write clearly and concisely, with proper spelling and grammar.

## B. COURSE EXAMPLES

Students draft their initial e-memo during the second module of Education Law, which covers cases of when a public school teacher can be terminated or have their teaching license revoked. When students complete their readings and video lectures, the weekly assessment opens. I tell students they are now an attorney representing a fictional school district. Students then read an email from the district superintendent asking them whether a high school teacher can be terminated for a tweet belittling transgender students. The students must respond with an e-memo.

---

39. *Id.* at 579–80 (noting how writing assignments in casebook courses invites students to engage in a conversation with their writings and offers an opportunity for reflection and critical thinking); Joni Larson, *To Develop Critical Thinking Skills and Allow Students to be Practice-Ready, We Must Move Well Beyond the Lecture Format*, 8 Elon L. Rev. 443, 451 (2016) (arguing practice-ready skills are not separate from "content learning" but "part of the process of content, instruction, and learning").

40. Parker, *supra* note 9, at 580 ("Lawyers are professional writers.").

To engage students and make the assignment feel realistic, I include a screen capture of the tweet. Rather than simply giving the students a list of facts, the tweet provides clues about whether the teacher tweeted as a private citizen (invoking the First Amendment) or a public employee. In this way, the problem meets my objectives of having students identify legal issues and separate relevant from irrelevant facts.[41]

Because the e-memo must be under two pages, I am able to assess whether students can articulate the applicable legal rules and holdings. In other words, with an e-memo, students must be able to concisely and accurately state case holdings for their audience. Thus, rather than a student simply writing in their notes that "Munroe is that case about the teacher with a blog," the practice-ready prompt necessitates students think through their points, consider their audience, and write a topic sentence that instantly tells the reader the pertinent information. For example, a writer might state, "In *Munroe*, the Third Circuit held a teacher failed the Pickering balancing test because there was little public concern in her blog post mocking students and the post caused significant disruption."[42]

As I repeatedly tell my students, to efficiently and sufficiently explain a case, you must elucidate how the law applied to the case's specific facts—only then do both you and the reader truly understand precedent. The e-memo is, therefore, a better pedagogical tool for students than a case brief or exam outline because the e-memo necessarily reveals whether students can support conclusions with reasoning.[43]

As Education Law continues, my expectations grow and the problems become more complicated. A later e-memo assignment provides the students with the deposition of a high school principal. Based on the deposition, students write an e-memo to their law firm's partner about whether the principal's school district violated Title IX. As students read the deposition, they uncover several possible instances of actional harassment witnessed by various school employees. To effectively answer the partner's question, students should more than simply answer when the school definitely gained "actual knowledge" of the harassment: Students should address what facts still need to be uncovered, which employees to depose next, and what questions to ask in future depositions.[44]

The revised Bloom's Taxonomy classifies learning into a multi-tiered model of six cognitive levels, each more complex than the last: remembering, understanding, applying, analyzing, evaluating, and creating.[45] This particular assignment asks stu-

---

41. *See also* Larson, *supra* note 39, at 445 (stating a key skill legal employer's want is the ability to "weed through facts" and differentiate relevant and irrelevant facts, sometimes from documents not given by the client).

42. *See generally* Munroe v. Cent. Bucks Sch. Dist. 805 F.3d 454 (3d Cir. 2015).

43. Parker, *supra* note 9, at 570–71. *See also id.* at 574 (stating students will learn the difference between summarizing a case for class versus for a client when the summary is based on a client's problem).

44. This meets the assignment's seventh learning objective: providing appropriate recommendations for next steps.

45. A TAXONOMY FOR LEARNING, TEACHING, AND ASSESSING: A REVISION OF BLOOM'S TAXONOMY OF EDUCATIONAL OBJECTIVES 5 (Lorin W. Anderson & David R. Krathwohl eds., 2001).

dents to specifically focus on the highest level of the pyramid: "creating." By devising a plan and constructing recommendations, students are identifying themselves as legal counselors and preparing themselves for practice.

### C. EVALUATION

In keeping with the reality of practice, students should be able to complete their e-memos relatively quickly. And, in keeping with the pedagogical need for prompt feedback, I can typically assess students in under 48 hours. From my experience, approximately two days is enough time to complete my comments, edits, and assessments for 35 students.

When reviewing the e-memos, I focus on each student's overall understanding of the legal issues, how accurately they present relevant rules and holdings, and their application of law to facts. If a student is ready for further critiques, I can assess and comment on their writing—including organization and grammar.[46]

Future rubrics for professors wishing to incorporate e-memo assignments could be based on this model:

- Logically organizes the analysis;
- Clearly and accurately states rules upon which conclusions are based;
- Explains rules with appropriate amount of depth;
- Describes precedent by fully and accurately explaining the law and how it applied in specific circumstances;
- Applies rules of law to our facts by comparing facts of analogous cases to our facts and explaining how the relevant rule of law applies;
- Effectively presents and rebuts significant counterarguments;
- Effectively uses of topic and thesis sentences; and
- Contains accurate grammar, usage, punctuation, and spelling.

To facilitate sufficient interaction with students wishing to further understand my critiques, I set up meetings with students and hold virtual office hours.

## III. Policy Assignments

Judge Harry T. Edwards wrote, "A person who deploys his or her doctrinal skill without concern for the public interest is merely a good legal technician—not a good lawyer."[47] In creating Education Law, I wanted to address this point in the course's

46. *See COVID-19*, *supra* note 5 (manuscript at 22) (discussing a similar feedback strategy).

47. Harry T. Edwards, *The Growing Disjunction Between Legal Education and the Legal Profession*, 91 MICH. L. REV. 34, 66 (1992).

practice-ready assignments. And in doing so, I sought to fulfill Professor Parker's call to create writing assignments that afford students the chance to "resolve legal problems posed by... societal conditions" and ask students to consider "competing social policies" in their assignments.[48]

Preparing our students to be competent and ethical advocates requires supplementing our dissection of appellate decisions with an exploration of the policies that formed those decisions—and, in turn, the social realities those decisions form.[49] Assignments focused on public interest and policy can introduce students to the practice-ready skills of analyzing legislation, regulations, agency decisions, and primary documents related to policy objectives.[50]

Policy-based arguments are also critical in a more traditional legal setting: the courtroom. Courts are increasingly relying on independent research and non-legal materials in their opinions.[51] Problematically, law schools are not keeping up with this trend by adequately teaching students to advocate using non-legal sources.[52] If we wish to prepare our students to modern practice, we must introduce them to employing empirical research and established social theories in their arguments.[53]

Policy argument assignments fit well with Education Law, as the course deals directly with issues of public interest, such as, school funding, de jure and de facto segregation, and Title IX protections. Further, many of my students have public interest backgrounds or have expressed interest in pursuing such careers. These students in particular benefit from practice-based policy assignments, as attorneys in public interest settings often must be prepared to fully immerse themselves into practice earlier than their colleagues in traditional law firms.[54]

## A. LEARNING OBJECTIVES

Professors designing practice-ready policy assignments have a wide range of options.[55] Students might be assigned to write a variety of legal and non-legal docu-

---

48. Parker, *supra* note 9, at 568.

49. Fran Quigley, *Seizing the Disorienting Moment: Adult Learning Theory and the Teaching of Social Justice in Law School Clinics*, 2 Clinical L. Rev. 37, 41 (1995).

50. Margaret B. Kwoka, *Intersecting Experiential Education and Social Justice Teaching*, 6 Ne. U.L.J. 111, 129–30 (2013).

51. Ellie Margolis, *Beyond Brandeis: Exploring the Uses of Non-Legal Materials in Appellate Briefs*, 34 U.S.F. L. Rev. 197, 208–09 (2000). *See generally* Michael R. Smith, *The Sociological and Cognitive Dimensions of Policy-Based Persuasion*, 22 J.L. & Pol'y 35 (2013) (discussing the importance of policy arguments, categories of policy arguments, and exploring strategies for improving policy arguments).

52. Margolis, *supra* note 51, at 201.

53. *Id.* at 208–09. *See generally* Smith, *supra* note 51 (discussing the importance of policy arguments, categories of policy arguments, and exploring strategies for improving policy arguments).

54. Kwoka, *supra* note 50, at 123.

55. *See generally* James Heller, *The Required Law & Public Policy Course in the College of William & Mary's Master of Public Policy Program: 25 Years of Lessons*, 9 Wm. & Mary Pol'y Rev. 73, 88–89 (2017) (describing how roleplay assignments teach students about policy and how to influence lawmaking).

ments, from legislation,[56] to legislative review papers or think tank "white papers," to op-eds or blog posts.[57] All of these options allow professors to bring trending topics into the classroom, illustrating to students a practical application of theory and the real-world effects of policy decisions.[58]

Policy assignments have the added benefit of fostering empathy for individuals and respect for legitimate sources in a world beset by tribalism and misinformation. Empathy is a critical practice-ready skill,[59] but one that is difficult to teach in the abstract.[60] Hard data and statistics help me provide context to judicial opinions and lay a foundation for building empathy and compassion. I can then construct on this foundation by sharing marginalized voices underrepresented in law school classrooms—voices that show the direct impact of the policy choices often made by law school graduates.[61] I find supplementary videos and podcasts are especially useful cornerstones in this endeavor.[62]

For example, before having students read *Brown v. Board of Education*,[63] I assign them a C-SPAN clip overviewing the groundbreaking "doll tests" relied on by attorney Thurgood Marshall.[64] And, towards the end of the course, after students read *Parents Involved in Community Schools v. Seattle School District No. 1*[65] (where the Supreme Court prohibited voluntary desegregation programs), I ask students to listen to a pod-

---

56. *See generally* Ann L. Schiavone, *Writing the Law: Developing the 'Citizen Lawyer' Identity through Legislative, Statutory, and Rule Drafting Courses*, 55 Duq. L. Rev. 119, 129–30 (2019) (listing course goals and objectives for an experiential legislative course).

57. *See generally* Jodi S. Balsam, *Law Blogging Engages Students in Writing That Connects Theory to Practice and Develops Professional Identity*, 23 Perspectives Teaching Legal Res. & Writing 145 (2015) (providing an excellent summary of the benefits of blogging assignments as practical assessments).

58. *Id.* at 146.

59. *See generally* Marjorie M. Shultz & Sheldon Zedeck, *Predicting Lawyer Effectiveness: Broadening the Basis for Law School Admissions Decisions*, 36 Law & Soc. Inquiry 620, 630 (2011) (naming "able to see the world through the eyes of others" as one of the 26 factors of lawyering effectiveness.); Kristin B. Gerdy, *Clients, Empathy, and Compassion: Introducing First-Year Students to the "Heart" of Lawyering*, 87 Neb. L. Rev. 1, 15 (2008) ("[C]aring actually makes analysis stronger.").

60. *See* Gerdy, *supra* note 59, at 30 (discussing how legal education fails to provide students with context and gives "little or no discussion of how the legal concepts . . . actually impact the lives and emotions of real people").

61. *See generally* Quigley, *supra* note 49, at 40 (noting that law schools should teach social justice concepts because, among other reasons, law school graduates have "created a society with the highest level of income stratification and incarceration of any industrialized nation").

62. *See generally Lighting a Fire*, *supra* note 8, 94–95 (noting that students find supplementary videos "helped them stay motivated and interested" in online courses).

63. 347 U.S. 483 (1954).

64. "The Doll Tests" were a series of experiments by Drs. Kenneth and Mamie Clark. The tests presented children age three to seven with dolls that were identical except for color. The majority of children, including African-American children, preferred white dolls, leading the doctors to conclude a sense of inferiority among African-American children and damaged self-esteem. NAACP Legal Defense Fund, *The Significance of "The Doll Test"*, https://www.naacpldf.org/ldf-celebrates-60th-anniversary-brown-v-board-education/significance-doll-test/ (last visited Nov. 14, 2020).

65. 551 U.S. 701 (2007).

cast from *This American Life* about the history, successes, and complications of school integration programs.

Only then, after providing students with both legal and non-legal sources, do I assign assessments that might build the skills they need to excel as informed advocates—both inside and outside the courtroom. My learning objectives for students are as follows:

1. To identify competing policies;
2. To understand and identify how policies differ and their potential societal outcomes;
3. To evaluate the strengths and weaknesses of differing policies;
4. To apply secondary and non-legal sources;
5. To recommend which policy should prevail and why;
6. To create new policies and explain their societal outcomes; and
7. To write clearly and concisely, with proper spelling and grammar.

### B. COURSE EXAMPLES

The first Education Law policy assignment unilaterally elects each student to the Indiana state senate. The student-senators are emailed by a coalition of school districts and parents who want to know the student-senator's views on the goals of school funding, the merit of Indiana's funding system, and the benefits and problems of relying on state funds over local property taxes. In addition to primary legal authority, successful students will apply non-caselaw resources touched upon in class: a news article, an NPR audio report, and a recent report from the U.S. Commission on Civil Rights about funding inequalities and race.

There is no "correct" conclusion, but students should reply to the email by articulating competing goals of education funding, demonstrating their knowledge of different funding models, and relying upon credible sources to conclude what model Indiana should adopt. Many of the students responded by creating their own funding models, signifying their understanding of the materials and their creativity. Further, a particular strength of this assignment is that it allows me to have students write about potential legislation without teaching students the nuances of legislative drafting, which is beyond the scope of the course.

A later assignment asks students to write an op-ed for *The Indianapolis Star*, arguing why a local school district should not adopt a proposed drug testing policy for middle and high school students. In addition to legal arguments about the program's constitutionality, students should use non-legal sources to argue about the program's consequences and whether the program would be effective in protecting students. In many ways, this assignment reflects the same objectives of having students use non-legal sources in a "Brandeis brief."[66] But because the op-ed is for a nonlegal audience, the assignment requires students to oblige the general public and explain complex principles in plain but memorable terms.

Other professors have used blogging to bring practice-ready assignments into their classrooms.[67] Legal blogs are a growing means of sharing a practitioner's expertise and can increase the blogger's professional visibility—leading to new business, invitations to deliver presentations and give media interviews, and relationships with other legal bloggers.[68] Further, like writing an op-ed, blogging allows lawyers to sensibly add to public discourse and shape public policy.[69] As a practice-based assignment, blogging has the added benefit of motivating students for publication in blogs maintained by their professor or school—or even outside blogs seeking guest contributors.[70]

## C. EVALUATION

An important criticism of the Socratic classroom is its power to devalue student contribution and demean individual beliefs.[71] Practical policy assignments, however, can awaken students from legal pedagogy's moral relativism and empower them to raise their unique voices to advance social, economic, and racial justice.[72] Therefore, to ensure student voices are respected, I make it clear that my goal is not to inculcate students to my values. Students do not need to parrot back my beliefs. But I also am clear that students must consider their ethical responsibilities and make reasoned arguments based on credible sources, sound logic, and thoughtful policy. With this goal in goal in mind, my focus in reviewing policy assignments remains on providing feedback about how to form reasoned arguments.

A rubric for policy assignments might mirror the following model:

- Identifies relevant policy arguments;
- Clearly and accurately explains differing policies;
- Effectively presents arguments using appropriate sources;
- Effectively presents and rebuts significant counterarguments;

---

66. A "Brandies brief" is named after a brief submitted by future Associate Justice Louis D. Brandeis and that heavily relied on social and medical data. Margolis, *supra* note 51, at n. 12; Noga Morag-Levine, *Facts, Formalism, and the Brandeis Brief: The Origins of a Myth*, 2013 U. Ill. L. Rev. 59, 60 (2013).

67. Balsam, *supra* note 57, at 148.

68. Douglas E. Abrams, *Writing in Law Reviews, Bar Association Journals, and Blogs (Part II)*, 72 J. Mo. Bar 88, 89 (2016).

69. *Id.*

70. Balsam, *supra* note 57, at 146–47.

71. Carnegie Report, *supra* note 1, at 170; Best Practices, *supra* note 1, at 102–03; Lauren Carasik, *Renaissance or Retrenchment: Legal Education at a Crossroads*, 44 Ind. L. Rev. 735, 750 (2011) (stating the Socratic method can require students to divorce morality from their professional identity).

72. *See* Carasik, *supra* note 71, at 751.

- Contains accurate grammar, usage, punctuation, and spelling; and
- Contains concise and readable sentences.

## IV. Conclusion

Practice-ready assignments provide a means of engaging students, improving their skills, and modernizing legal education. Such assignments work especially well in asynchronous casebook courses, which by their nature require multiple assessments. But with practice-ready assignments also comes the need for enrollment caps, substantial time investments, and administrative support.[73] Professors, administrators, and institutions considering adopting practice-ready assignments must grapple with whether the investment is worth the reward. Students, on the other hand, already know the answer.

---

73. Administrative support can come from reduced teaching loads, stipends, and general appreciation. *See* Jennifer E. Spreng, *Suppose the Class Began the Day the Case Walked in the Door: Accepting Standard 314's Invitation to Imagine a More Powerful, Professionally Authentic First-Year Learning Experience*, 95 U. Det. Mercy L. Rev. 421, 455–56 (2018).

TWENTY-SIX

# Designing and Cultivating Discussion in Asynchronous Online Seminars

Kristen E. Murray*

After reviewing this chapter, readers will be able to:

- Appreciate the unique challenges of teaching asynchronous online seminars in the upper-level curriculum;
- Design a seminar that encourages student participation through different modalities; and
- Evaluate student participation both quantitatively and qualitatively.

Even as there has been an increase in research and scholarly work on law school teaching, there is not as much written about the law school seminar as one might expect. Much more has been written about large lecture classes in law schools than law school seminars. This is perhaps because it seems easier to discuss lectures as a cohort; broadly speaking, law school lectures have a shared (if flawed) pedagogical default (the Langdellian case method and Socratic dialogue) and most law schools have a fair amount of overlap among core course offerings in both the first year and upper-level curricula.

In contrast, the law school seminar may vary wildly based on subject matter and pedagogical approach. One definition of "seminar" in the law school context is: "a group of advanced students studying under a professor with each doing original research and all exchanging results through reports and discussions."[1] This inclusive definition is a good starting point, but variations on this theme can take many forms,

* Professor of Law, Temple University, Beasley School of Law. Professor Murray began law teaching in 2004 and began teaching courses online in 2018. She has designed and taught synchronous and asynchronous courses.

1. Margaret Moore Jackson, *Constructing a Seminar*, Best Prac. for Legal Educ. (Nov. 25, 2013), https://bestpracticeslegaled.com/2013/11/25/constructing-a-seminar/.

for both professor and student. Seminars can be a way for faculty to connect their research interests with their teaching, a reward in the form of "extra time and fewer students," a hoop for students to jump through in fulfillment of a graduation requirement, or a deep dive into a niche subject that might never appear as part of the core curriculum.[2] In the modern law school classroom, they might be clinical, or skills-focused, or introduce an advanced look at a particular topic.[3]

Still, there are some commonalities. Seminars are almost exclusively offered as part of the upper-level curriculum. They are almost always capped at a size much smaller than a lecture/exam class, though even the cap can have substantial variations; at my own institution, courses classified as "seminars" can range in size from a maximum of six to twenty students. Classroom pedagogy in seminars is generally non-Socratic and the deliverable for the students is usually a writing project (or projects) rather than a final exam. Taken together, this means that a successful seminar relies on student engagement and discussion in a unique way when contrasted to law school lectures and exam-based classes.

Moving an upper-level seminar to an asynchronous, online format then starts with a fundamental question. How does the professor preserve the robust engagement and discussion that are the hallmarks of the law school seminar?

This was the biggest challenge I faced when I created an asynchronous version of my upper-level Education Law seminar. I have taught my Education Law seminar for many years. I had experience varying the course format; I had previously modified the course as an offering in the undergraduate General Education program. In 2018, when my dean asked if anyone would be interested in experimenting with an asynchronous, online format, I volunteered.

This chapter will discuss my experience planning and teaching this asynchronous seminar while trying to preserve the goals and outcomes of the in-person version of the course.[4] I will discuss my decision to teach the seminar, the course design plan, cultivation and assessment of discussion in the seminar, and some broader considerations related to teaching asynchronous seminars.

---

2. Philip C. Kissam, *Seminar Papers*, 40 J. Legal Educ. 339, 339 (1990).

3. More has been written about teaching skills-focused seminars than topical seminars. *See, e.g.*, Margaret Moore Jackson, *From Seminar to Simulation: Wading out to the Third Wave*, 19 J. Gender, Race, & Just. 127 (2020); Roberta Rosenthal Kwall, *Teaching an Intellectual Property Seminar Through the Legal Literature*, 52 St. Louis U. L.J. 813 (2008); Julie D. Lawton, *Teaching Social Justice in Law Schools: Whose Morality Is It?*, 50 Ind. L. Rev. 813 (2016); Nancy A. Millich, *Building Blocks of Analysis: Using Simple 'Sesame Street Skills' and Sophisticated Educational Learning Theories in Teaching a Seminar in Legal Analysis and Writing*, 34 Santa Clara L. Rev. 1127 (1994).

4. For a different look at teaching Education Law asynchronously, see Chapter 25: *Creating Practice-Ready Assignments: Low-Stakes Assessments in Asynchronous Casebook Courses* by Brad Desnoyer.

## I. The Decision to Teach an Asynchronous Seminar

The decision to offer an asynchronous upper-level seminar was consistent with any decision to offer a law school class in an online format. The goal was to increase flexibility for students, especially evening students, by offering a class that did not require them to convene on campus at a particular time (or at all).[5] Seminars seem particularly important in this regard; seminars at my home institution are one of the ways students can fulfill one of our upper-level requirements, such as a writing, skills, or experiential requirement. My personal motivation to try teaching an online seminar was twofold. First, I wanted to support the initiative to provide our students with both additional course offerings and increased flexibility. Second, I like experimenting with form, especially when it comes to technology.

Mine was the first law school-created asynchronous, online class to be offered at our law school. I was fortunate to have the support of the Office of Digital Education at Temple throughout the planning process.[6] I had many resources related to online teaching at my fingertips, including a full production studio and the advice of experts. However, my concern from the moment I started planning the class to the moment I started teaching it was how to create an asynchronous seminar that did not compromise the heart of the in-person version of my seminar: discussion and interactivity from all students.

Much of the literature on online learning is focused on transmitting content rather than encouraging discussion; this is particularly true for the scant amount of literature specifically focused on law schools.[7] Margaret Ryznar and Yvonne Dutton have discussed engagement in asynchronous law courses in the context of motivation, though in their framework "motivation" is more of a broad view of capturing the students' attention and encouraging them to complete the work, whereas I was particularly concerned about the "work" of class participation and discussion.[8]

To help answer the question of how to encourage and assess class participation, I spoke to a colleague at a different school at my university who has taught many online undergraduate classes. Her advice was: "participation is not better or worse, it's just different." I took this to heart, along with the commonly-offered advice that online

---

5. Yvonne Dutton & Seema Mohapatra, *COVID-19 and Law Teaching: Guidance on Developing an Asynchronous Online Course for Law Students*, St. Louis U. L.J. (forthcoming 2021) (manuscript at 7), https://papers.ssrn.com/sol3/papers.cfm?abstract_id=3604331&download=yes ("The flexibility inherent in online courses helps students balance other competing interests, such as work, family, and child-care commitments.").

6. Temple Univ. Off. Digital Educ., online.temple.edu (last accessed Nov. 22, 2020).

7. Margaret Ryznar & Yvonne M. Dutton, *Lighting A Fire: The Power of Intrinsic Motivation in Online Teaching*, 70 Syracuse L. Rev. 73, 74–75 (2020) ("The scholarly literature also has not yet comprehensively addressed how to best motivate students in the online classroom, especially in law school.").

8. *Id.* at 77.

teaching—especially asynchronous teaching—cannot be successful if the course attempts to precisely replicate the elements of in-person, synchronous course design.[9]

## II. Designing an Asynchronous Seminar

Generally speaking, across the law school curriculum, "[c]ourses are effectively designed if the teaching, assessments, reading and other assignments, and learning objectives are congruent with each other, and if the delivery of instruction is efficient, effective, and appealing."[10] According to a cohort of law students who had been enrolled in asynchronous courses, the "components of a quality online course included (1) organization, (2) engaging presentation of course content, and (3) opportunities for assessment and professor feedback."[11] Most of this felt familiar to me, even when adapting my course for an asynchronous setting. But the questions of what was organized, efficient, engaging, and appealing in this context posed more of a challenge.

As a starting point, I thought concretely about the design and goals of the in-person version of the seminar. In my in-person seminar, each class starts with a short lecture where I introduce the main themes of the reading and/or points of law from the major cases. I list questions on the classroom whiteboard to frame our discussion and over the course of the class meeting, we work our way through the questions in an organic order. Sometimes we don't get to all of the questions; occasionally we focus the discussion on a single one. The course meets once per week for two hours, so I try to vary teaching methods in each session; this often includes small-group work including drafting exercises. I end most classes with a recap and/or a "one-minute paper" where I ask students about what they understand, what seems murky, and what they would like to discuss more or again in the next class.

Generally speaking, because this is an upper-level seminar, I choose breadth of coverage over depth, and each week focuses on a different topic in education law. I replicated this structure in my asynchronous course; I divided the class into fourteen modules that tracked the fourteen-week semester structure. I decided that the course would not be self-paced.[12] Self-paced courses maximize flexibility, but pacing felt like a necessary prerequisite to encouraging and managing interactive discussions.

---

9. *See, e.g.*, Linda B. Nilson & Ludwika A. Goodson, Online Teaching at Its Best: Merging Instructional Design with Teaching and Learning Research at x (2014) ("online teaching methods often diverge from live ones"). *See also* Chapter 2: *The Art of Cutting Yourself Some Slack: Reinventing Yourself as an Online Teacher* by Meredith A. G. Stange (discussing adapting your teaching from in-person to online); Chapter 8: *From Ground to Cloud and Back Again: Modern Tactics to Improve Your Teaching* by Katherine Brem (describing the process of adapting an in-person class for online delivery).

10. Michael Hunter Schwartz, *Towards A Modality-Less Model for Excellence in Law School Teaching*, 70 Syracuse L. Rev. 115, 132 (2020).

11. Yvonne M. Dutton et. al., *Assessing Online Learning in Law Schools: Students Say Online Classes Deliver*, 96 Denv. L. Rev. 493, 525 (2019).

12. In this context, "self-paced" would mean that I made all fourteen modules available to students at the start of the semester and that they could work their way through the materials on their own schedule. Instead, I launched one module per week, as discussed below.

I assigned many of the usual foundational readings but also added in different modalities, including video content, podcasts, and articles from the popular press. With the help of our instructional designers, I created scripted introductory videos—the equivalent of the short lectures I gave at the start of the live class. Each video was no more than seven minutes long and some modules included multiple videos. The course satisfied our serial writing requirement, which requires students to write "a series of short papers;" I mostly adhered to my standard set of short papers, with some modification for the online course (discussed below). Eighty percent of the course grade is based on the writing assignments.

The remaining 20% of the grade is based on class participation. In my in-person seminar, I make both quantitative and qualitative assessments of class participation and I keep track of the participation in each class session. I preserved these percentage allocations for the asynchronous course, but the biggest challenge in designing this asynchronous seminar was determining how to cultivate and assess participation in online discussions.

## III. Cultivating Discussion in an Asynchronous Seminar

"Professor Murray," asked one of my students at my office hours during the first week of class. "What is the optimal amount of discussion you would like to see for this class?"

I answered honestly: my IDEAL level of participation would be the equivalent of a group chat I have with a group of friends, with every participant checking in periodically to see what was new and what they might add to the conversation. But I knew this was a lot to expect. So I clarified for the student (and later the class) that I hoped the discussion would be "organic but organized." I knew that this would require some management on my part.

In my research about online instruction, I encountered some research about a concept I think many educators deploy instinctively: pattern teaching, in which each class has a pattern or structure.[13] I determined that successful discussion in my asynchronous class was more likely to occur (and occur in a way that could be fairly assessed) if each week had a clearly-defined pattern that was known to the students.

Instructional design principles suggest that pattern teaching helps set student expectations,[14] and I thought this was particularly important in an asynchronous format where the student work was mostly self-directed. During the first week of the semester, in my course overview video, I introduced the workflow for a given week: the

---

13. Christine Tulley, *How to Avoid Overprepping for Your Classes*, Inside Higher Ed (Jan. 15, 2019), https://www.insidehighered.com/advice/2019/01/15/how-save-yourself-overpreparing-your-classes-opinion.

14. *See id.*

module would "launch" on Saturday, initial contributions (in whatever form) were to be submitted by Wednesday, and any follow-up (again, form varied) was to be done by Friday, in time for the launch of the next module.

To keep the discussion lively and to encourage participation, I employed a variety of discussion formats. I also varied my own participation. I monitored the discussions daily and contributed when a specific response or comment was warranted. I chimed in more robustly at the end of a module, with a written or video recap of the week's work.

By using a standard pattern plus variations in form, I was able to achieve my goal of "organic but organized" discussions. Ultimately, I used five different types of discussions: professor prompts, hosted cases, small group activities, guest speakers, and student presentations.

### A. PROFESSOR PROMPT

This type of discussion is the most similar to what I would offer in my in-person seminar. The workflow for the week started with a "reading" assignment[15] and an introductory video.[16] Students then had to respond to a specific prompt on the week's discussion board; the prompt would ask one or two questions about the material. On these discussion boards, students could not see the contributions of others until they wrote their first post. The follow-up was either a second, sequenced question from me, or a request that they respond to their colleagues' posts.

These were usually introductory modules (the start of a new "unit," usually), in contrast with weeks where the anchor of the discussion was a specific case. These also included occasional case studies that complemented a hosted case discussion.

### B. HOSTED CASE

In seven of the fourteen modules, I had students "host" the weekly discussion. The core reading/prompt for discussion was a major education law case, and two students were assigned to each case.[17]

The instructions for these posts included the following:

- Each student wrote a post about the case and presented 1–2 discussion questions for the other students in the class to answer.
- The suggested length for these posts was 750–1000 words.

---

15. "Reading" here includes not only articles and commentary but also other media such as podcasts, videos, and news articles.

16. This included videos created by the instructional designers and narrated PowerPoint presentations.

17. In five of the modules we discussed a single case; two of the modules included two cases.

- The post required the host students to do at least some additional research and reading beyond the case itself.
- The general prompt for this assignment was: how is this case relevant to or what does this case tell us about public education today?
- The host students then had to moderate the discussion that followed.

This post and the discussion that followed was one of the graded, required assignments for the course. The rest of the class read only the unedited case.

### C. SMALL GROUP ACTIVITY

Small group work is an important part of my in-person seminar. I thought it would be impossible to replicate in an asynchronous format, but I wanted to offer opportunities for non-discussion board interactions.

Some work was collaborative on a class-wide level—for example, one week we created a wiki of state constitutional education provisions. Other group work was done in smaller, three-student cohorts that I assembled randomly. This usually involved a problem set or case study.

Where students were to convene in small groups, I allowed them to do so asynchronously or synchronously—I assigned the students to groups and they had to decide how they wanted to proceed. Synchronous groups had to find a mutually-agreeable meeting time for their discussion and then assemble a summary for my review. Asynchronous groups had a dedicated discussion board to do the group work and had a choice of form (written discussion or video comments). Surprisingly, all the students in the class exercised the synchronous option for the first small group project. In fact, students asked for more opportunities for this kind of collaboration, which I provided when the opportunity arose.

### D. GUEST SPEAKER

I devoted two modules to guest speakers. I do this frequently in my seminars; I try to engage experts and practitioners to talk to the students about specific course topics.

I used two different formats for the speakers I invited to the online version of the course. First, I recorded interviews with two experts who hold opposing views on charter schools, and posted the interviews (as both video and audio files) as part of the module. The recorded interviews were a follow-up to the previous week's module on school choice. The discussion for this module involved an initial "reaction" post that also had to include follow-up questions for classmates.

Second, I had one live, synchronous meeting with a guest speaker who is an active practitioner and relatively recent alumna of the law school. I did not mandate that students attend the synchronous guest speaker session. The session was scheduled before the class was listed and the single synchronous session was part of the course description so students were aware pre-registration, but I still wanted to offer a fully asynchronous option for students who could not commit to attending the synchronous session. I asked students who could not attend the synchronous class to submit questions in advance for me to ask the speaker on their behalf. All students then had to post a "reaction" to the talk, though this prompt did not require any follow-up questions.

### E. PRESENTATIONS

The final assignment—a critique of an education law case—included both a paper and a presentation. Again, this is similar to what I would require in my in-person seminar. Here, I allowed for student creativity: they had to find some way to "present" their written critique to the class using audio or visual media (the audio or visual critique was submitted separately for my review). They also had to review each other's presentations in small groups, similar to those I had constructed for small group activities. Again, all of the groups chose to meet synchronously, and several groups reported that they were glad to have the option of closing out the class with a synchronous discussion. The student presentations were especially creative; one student who critiqued a First Amendment case involving MySpace created a one-page handout on the case that was formatted to look like a MySpace user page.

## IV. Assessing Participation in Discussions

In my in-person class, I take notes about both the quantity and quality of student contributions to the discussion. I developed a rubric to evaluate class participation in this online setting. The rubric applied to all forms of class participation; I did not vary it based on form. But it, too, was meant to set student expectations. I recommend a course-specific rubric for class participation as a way of communicating your standards for quantity and quality of contributions to the course.

I used the rubric to track class participation each week, and notified students whose participation seemed to be flagging (based on substance and/or timing) over a number of weeks. Students also had a standing offer to boost their class participation by posting to non-module discussion boards.[18]

I recognize that even in the small group setting that a seminar provides, some students are less comfortable speaking out in class. I also noted that "speaking" in an online discussion forum could feel both easier and harder than speaking in class—easier because the "speaker" has a chance to hone and edit her views but harder because it might take longer to craft and writing out a point can feel higher stakes than talking

18. I set up one for general current events and one specifically for news about education and COVID-19.

through something in class. This was part of my decision to vary the types of participation available in the course.

Still, even with these variations, discussion board-based conversations posed two significant challenges: originality and fatigue.[19] I attempted to mitigate problems with originality in some discussions by requiring students to post before they could see their classmates' contributions. Fatigue might be inevitable, and some students participated less in some weeks than others, but the same is also true in the in-person version of the class. One student helped me think differently about this: the discussion contributions, though in writing (and thus more formal and thought out than classroom contributions might be) were an opportunity to talk about the law without the constraints of formal legal writing. To the extent this is an opportunity not often offered in the upper-level curriculum, I now see this as an asset.

Another asset is the way that the discussions allowed the students to learn from each other at a deeper level than they typically do in the in-person version of the seminar. I attribute this to two things. First, my facilitation of the discussion was less visible than in the in-person seminar, so students directed most of their responses to each other instead of to me. Second, each student had ample time and space to share their own observations and experiences, in contrast to a time-limited in-class discussion. Several students told me that they both noted and appreciated this dynamic.

This dynamic was enhanced by my decision to use pattern teaching in the weekly discussions. Asynchronous discussions are often frustrated by timing-related limitations: either there is too much time between contributions to the discussion for an engaging dialogue to occur or the discussion takes place without enough time to reach resolution.[20] Neither of these problems occurred in my course. I can point to three reasons why our discussions were not frustrated in this way: the pattern balanced structure with flexibility; students were aware of the pattern and my expectations about participation; and the large majority of the eighteen students in the class followed the pattern every single week so that discussion never flagged.

One other potential challenge—also not one I encountered when I taught this course—is maintaining civility in online discussions. In the first two sessions of my in-person seminar, I always tell the students that the course depends on our ability to share personal experience and opinion but also to be respectful of classmates. I included this sentiment in my video introduction to the asynchronous course. I was confident that this would be enough to set the tone in an online format, especially

---

19. *See* Ryznar & Dutton, *supra* note 7, at 99 (noting the "challenge of being creative and original in overcrowded discussion boards").

20. Jennifer C. Richardson & Phil Ice, *Investigating Students' Level of Critical Thinking Across Instructional Strategies in Online Discussions*, 13 Internet & Higher Educ. 52, 57 (2010); Richard Schreck, *Continuing Education, Critical Thinking, and Virtual Collaborative Learning* (unpublished) at 7 (2011), https://courses.worldcampus.psu.edu/canvas/sp20/22011---8213/content/01_lesson/corefiles/SchreckDraft.pdf.

among our law students, but I included the university's suggested language[21] about "netiquette"[22] on the course syllabus as well.

In the end, I was pleased with the quality of discussion in the seminar. I believe this is the result of careful planning, clearly-communicated instructions and expectations, and good faith effort by the students.

## V. Other Course Elements

Some seminars might require or benefit from two elements I did not include in my own seminar: quizzes and peer review of written assignments.

Assessment is important in online classes, when the professor cannot "read the room" to ascertain whether students are understanding the material. I felt confident that my students would understand the doctrinal concepts in the course; in fact, I assumed most of them would have encountered the content before, in other classes like Constitutional Law. In courses where professors want to more concretely assess student understanding, there are many tools available to do so. For example, most learning management systems include a quiz function. Standalone quizzing applications allow for more creative, dynamic quizzes.

In some skills-based seminars, in-class drafting or peer review of assignments might be fundamental to the course. The writing assignments in my course were sequential but took different formats: the final grade was based on the hosted case discussion, a personal experience paper, an op-ed (and letters to the editor based on their classmates' op-eds), and a critique and presentation. Thus, I provided detailed instructions on these papers, but we did not discuss them in class, other than my initial introduction into what was required and the relationship(s) among them. Professors who wish to do so can find a variety of tools for collaborative writing and/or peer review platforms online.[23]

---

21. The policy stated:

> Your instructor and fellow students wish to foster a safe online learning environment. All opinions and experiences, no matter how different or controversial they may be perceived, must be respected in the tolerant spirit of academic discourse. You are encouraged to comment, question, or critique an idea but you are not to attack an individual.
>
> Our differences, some of which are outlined in the University's nondiscrimination statement, will add richness to this learning experience. Please consider that sarcasm and humor can be misconstrued in online interactions and generate unintended disruptions. Working as a community of learners, we can build a polite and respectful course atmosphere.

22. For an example of "netiquette" language for synchronous discussions, see Chapter 29: *Training Effective Virtual Oral Advocates* by Susie Salmon.

23. This can include commonly-used products like Google Docs, https://workspace.google.com/features/, or more specialized services like Peerceptiv, https://peerceptiv.com/, or EliReview, https://elireview.com/.

## VI. Other Considerations

In addition to the considerations laid out elsewhere in this chapter, I think it's important to keep several things in mind when planning and teaching an asynchronous seminar.

First, give students time to get to know each other and the course. I had students post video introductions to a discussion board during the first week of class, so they (and I) could pair names with faces and learn a little bit about who was in the class. I tried to structure the first module so that the students were exposed to all the different modalities the course would use, but I also jumped right into the course content and probably should have left a little time for students to settle into the course, especially because during the first week of the semester there is always some add/drop movement.

Second, give students the chance to get to know you. I posted my own video introduction, but also tried to find other points of connection during the course—video or written recaps of a weekly discussion or posts to the non-module discussion boards. The module-based discussion boards required less moderation from me than I expected, which was a good thing. But I also tried to make all my points of contact as authentically "me" as I could, because some of the scripted video content I developed early lacked my voice—I leaned toward formality, which is the opposite of what I do in my in-person seminar.

Third, give students the chance to offer feedback about the course. I was candid about the fact that this was a new form for me, and encouraged students to reach out with feedback; I got some, but mostly from students I happened to already know well. I gave all the students the chance to fill out an anonymous midsemester evaluation. And at every point of contact I told students I was attempting to make my instructions as clear as possible but that they should let me know if they had any questions.

Note that even with best efforts in all three of these categories, it is likely that you will feel a certain amount of disconnect from the students in an online class. To me, it is strange to feel both that our class discussions were rich in personality and personal experience but also that I might not recognize some of the students if we passed by each other in person.

Nevertheless, it is possible to teach an asynchronous law school seminar that does not compromise the goals and outcomes we usually associate with this type of upper-level course. As with all online courses, this is only possible with thoughtful and thorough course design that also allows for some flexibility while the course is underway. The rewards for students include increased flexibility and the potential for different (and potentially richer) engagement with the course materials.

TWENTY-SEVEN

# Blasphemy! Skills-Based Constitutional Law Online

Kathleen M. Burch*

After reviewing this chapter, readers will be able to:

- Understand the benefits of asynchronous learning;
- Understand evidence-based learning techniques;
- Use evidence-based learning techniques to design formative assessments;
- Understand how focusing on the skills relevant to constitutional law creates opportunity for students to access and acquire competency in the course material; and
- Scaffold asynchronous activities to model complex problem solving.

Most students approach their constitutional law course with excitement and trepidation. Excitement because it is constitutional law, the sexiest course in law school, and trepidation because of the myth that constitutional law is one of the hardest subjects to master. For many years, I approached teaching constitutional law with both excitement and trepidation. Excitement because I was providing students with skills and knowledge to better understand how our government operates and how society and the law impact each other. And trepidation because there is so much material to cover, and students often lack knowledge of history and of how government works. Creating a blended course has relieved our trepidation over constitutional law, has allowed me to move historical and background material online, and to use synchronous time to model more complex problem solving.

* Professor, Atlanta's John Marshall Law School. Professor Burch began teaching in 2001, began teaching parts of her Constitutional Law course online in 2015 and began teaching fully online in January 2020. Professor Burch has designed and taught blended courses.

This chapter highlights my journey from teaching a traditional classroom course to designing and teaching a blended course. Part of my course is delivered asynchronously through an online learning management system and part of my course is delivered synchronously either in the classroom or via a video-conferencing platform. In my blended courses, students are better prepared for class, are more actively engaged, and have better retention of the material.

In determining what and how to move portions of my constitutional law courses online, I started by identifying the skills I wanted my students to acquire competency in. I developed a series of formative assessments centered on the identified skills. By focusing on skills, students were provided opportunities to practice how to use the material in the way attorneys do. Formative assessments were designed to assess one or more skill and were scaffolded so that students had an opportunity to practice a foundation skill before having to use the skill in conjunction with other skills. Students were better able to attain competency because they understood why they were learning the material and how they would use the material, creating longer lasting learning outcomes.

## I. The Benefits of Asynchronous Learning

By labeling the traditional law school model as completely synchronous, we ignore the reality that law school has historically been a blended learning model. Requiring students to read cases and prepare case briefs prior to class shifts some of the learning from the classroom (synchronous) to outside the classroom (asynchronous). For decades law schools have posted first assignments before the semester begins, highly recommended that students create their own outlines, and recommended that students study from old exams. With the American Bar Association's recent requirement that law schools provide students with formative assessments,[1] many faculty have created formative assessments that are completed outside of class time, shifting even more learning to asynchronous time.

Labeling traditional legal education as blended may sound like heresy but consider your own law school experience. Either during Orientation or shortly thereafter, someone told you—either a faculty member or more likely an upperclassman—that you needed to find a study group. While that first semester may have felt like the blind leading the blind, the purpose of that study group was for students to practice what they were learning in class. Faculty did not oversee your study group or assign a grade for work completed in study group. But, most, if not all, law schools fostered an environment where study groups were deemed essential to academic success, implicitly fostering a blended model.

---

1. A.B.A. Sec. Leg. Educ. & Admis. to the Bar, *Standards and Rules of Procedure for Approval of Law Schools*, Standard 314 (2020–21), https://www.americanbar.org/content/dam/aba/administrative/legal_education_and_admissions_to_the_bar/standards/2020-2021/2020-21-aba-standards-and-rules-for-approval-of-law-schools.pdf [hereinafter 2020 ABA Standards].

There is nothing inherently wrong with a blended education model. The traditional law school model is often not effective because the asynchronous portion is not intentionally designed to scaffold learning or to focus on the development of specific skills. Study groups function autonomously, creating their own agenda, with the work of each group varying widely and the academic performance of the members of the group varying widely. This result is not surprising because individuals are "*poor judges* of when we are learning well and when we're not."[2]

Both the synchronous and asynchronous portions of a course need to be intentionally designed using learning theory, and the design of each portion should be integrated with the other. The asynchronous assignments must be relevant to and support the learning taking place in the synchronous portion of the course. This symmetry is needed to create the most effective learning model.

## A. LEARNING THEORY

We know that re-reading material and re-listening to a lecture are not effective study tools.[3] But, students are not aware that the study techniques they grew up using and that they believe made them successful are not the study techniques that will make them successful law students. I have found that students are more likely to complete assignments and fully participate in formative assessments if they understand why they are required to complete the assignment. Students need to be convinced that their old study habits are not effective. I take time at the beginning of each course to teach students evidence-based learning techniques,[4] to explain how the course employs evidence-based learning techniques, and why I have made certain course design choices.[5] Once students understand the science behind what I am trying to accomplish, they understand that each assessment aids in their attaining competency in a particular skill or doctrine leading to success in the course.

The learning techniques that I incorporate into my course include: retrieval practice, spaced retrieval practice, elaboration, and generation. I provide individualized comments on mid-term and final exams to encourage reflection (students assess what

2. Peter C. Brown & Henry L. Roediger III, Make It Stick: The Science of Successful Learning 3 (2014).

3. *Id.* My students have reported that having materials available to consult if they miss class, being able to re-listen to the portion of the lecture that covers material they did not understand, and being able to review faculty created PowerPoint slides alleviates stress. This has been particularly true in 2020 when classes moved online due to COVID-19.

4. Evidence-based learning techniques are learning techniques and strategies that improve memory and learning whose efficacy is based on scientific data from the fields of Psychology and Cognitive Neurosciences.

5. Students are required to read portions of *Make It Stick* and to identify at least one learning technique that they will use during the semester. At the end of the semester, students perform a self-assessment on whether they used one of the learning techniques and whether using the learning technique helped to improve their performance.

they did well and what they can change or improve to attain better results in the future)[6] and calibration (aligning their perception of their performance with reality).[7]

Retrieval practice is "self-quizzing," the recalling of facts, concepts, or events from memory.[8] Retrieval practice is more than questioning the text through critical reading, although critical reading is a necessary foundation to retrieval practice. Retrieval practice is more than creating a case brief, although case briefs support the learning that takes place through retrieval practice. By engaging the text through critical reading, students sort and rank information, and by creating a case brief with the ranked information, students organize the information in a uniform, logical format, making that information easier to retrieve. Students need to engage in retrieval practice to test their ability to recall the information. Retrieval practice can be fostered by having students complete online quizzes, particularly quizzes that focus on the skills and doctrinal concepts the faculty knows are necessary building blocks to attain competency in skills and doctrine that will be introduced later in the course. In my constitutional law course, students complete a quiz on the definitions of the canons of constitutional construction and a quiz where they identify the canon being used in an opinion before drafting an essay that requires them to use the canons to interpret a provision of the Constitution.

Spaced retrieval practice "means studying information more than once but leaving considerable time between practice sessions."[9] Spaced retrieval practice can be intentionally built into the course by periodically including concepts and skills taught earlier in the course in quizzes and other assessments assigned later in the semester. Spaced retrieval practice works well when you want students to understand the relationship between the skill or doctrine learned earlier in the course and the new skill or doctrine being taught.

Elaboration is "the process of finding additional layers of meaning in new material."[10] Elaboration works well in assessments where students are provided autonomy to decide how they would like to complete the assessment. The instructions and grading rubric for the assessment need to provide the students with sufficient guidance to know that they have satisfied all of the requirements for the assignment, but leave students sufficient freedom to own the assessment and encourage creativity in completing the project. Current event projects that require students to link constitutional law doctrine to a pending case or current event allows students to engage with the material in a way that is relevant to them.

---

6. *Id.* at 209.
7. *Id.* at 210.
8. *Id.* at 201.
9. *Id.* at 203.
10. *Id.* at 207.

Generation is "an attempt to answer a question or solve a problem before being shown the answer or the solution."[11] Generation can be accomplished through assessments that are completed before the class in which the assessment will be reviewed or material tested in the assessment will be covered. An easy and common generation assessment is to assign hypotheticals for students to complete and submit prior to class.[12] Generation assessments provide students with the opportunity to figure out what questions they have about the material so that they can then ask those questions during the synchronous portion of the course.

## B. DEVELOPING A BLENDED COURSE

The key to developing a blended course is to identify what you want to accomplish during your synchronous time. Synchronous time is limited and thus, precious. My synchronous time with students is an opportunity for me to model the skill I want students to learn and to confirm that students understand the material. The synchronous portion of my course has two components, the review of the assigned material and the learning activity. During the first part of my class, I review the doctrine, charting the rules of law.[13] During the second half of class, I focus on skills working through problems that grow more complex throughout the semester. I usually have students work on problems in small groups before working through the problem as a class.[14]

The asynchronous portion of my course has two components, the lecture and the learning activity. To ensure that students have a sufficient understanding of the material to meaningfully participate in class, I provide students with online lectures. When I developed my first blended class, I posted audio lectures on TWEN. Knowing that students would not sit through long lectures, I limited each lecture to twenty minutes.[15] Students were able to download the lectures and listen to them at any time; some students saved the lectures and used them to study for the bar exam. Students were also assigned a short activity that required them to apply the law. When I first assigned these activities, students complained bitterly. These complaints all but disappeared when graduates studying for the bar exam reported that they remembered the rule of law or how to solve the problem because they remembered the activity they were required to complete.

I continue to post lectures for my students but have graduated to video. With video, I can highlight important passages in a case or use PowerPoint slides to illustrate

---

11. *Id.* at 208.

12. When written submissions are not required, students are less likely to work through the hypothetical prior to class. Written submissions can be uploaded as an assignment or discussion post in the course learning management system.

13. These charts are the skeleton for the student's course outline.

14. In the small groups, students use retrieval practice and generation learning techniques.

15. Optimally, lectures should be between seven to ten minutes.

important concepts.[16] I can also integrate the lecture and assessment by embedding questions in the video.[17]

### C. ASYNCHRONOUS LEARNING ACTIVITIES IN CONSTITUTIONAL LAW

My approach to asynchronous learning activities is to start small and build throughout the semester. Before I begin to design a learning activity, I identify the skills and doctrine that I want students to learn; I determine whether an identified skill is a composite skill, meaning does the student need competency in a sub-skill or component skill before students can attain competency in the skill that is the subject of the learning activity; I determine the logical order that the skills and doctrine need to be taught; and I determine what competency looks like. This groundwork assists me in drafting the student learning objectives for my course,[18] to determine the best learning technique to use for the assessment, and to develop a grading rubric for more complex assessments. The grading rubric communicates to students the expected level of competency for the skill or doctrine being tested. The grading rubric contains sufficient detail for the student to use the grading rubric to self-assess their work providing the incentive and opportunity to improve work prior to submission.[19]

## II. Practical Tips

A blended course is a partnership between you and your students. Communicate with your students. Let them know what to expect, including when you are available to respond to questions. Model for students the healthy habit of creating boundaries to respect work/life balance.

Make sure you know why you are developing a blended course. If you are only teaching online for a semester, consider using publisher prepared materials rather than creating your own material. If you are developing a blended class to accomplish specific andragogical goals, then start by deciding what you want to accomplish in your synchronous time. Knowing what you want to accomplish in your limited synchronous time will help you to identify the material and skills practice you want to move to asynchronous time.

---

16. I use Screencast-O-Matic which allows me to record over a screen capture. SCREENCAST-O-MATIC, https://screencast-o-matic.com/ (last visited Feb. 22, 2021). I can easily move between my e-casebook, PowerPoint slides, or other material as I record.

17. I upload my video to EdPuzzle. EDPUZZLE, https://edpuzzle.com/ (last visited Feb. 22, 2021). EdPuzzle allows me to embed questions and audio comments at any point in the video. EdPuzzle will automatically grade objective, non-essay questions.

18. 2020 ABA Standards, *supra* note 1, Standard 315.

19. The ability to assess one's own work is necessary to the practice of law and translates into knowing when one's work is ready to be presented to a supervisor or client or filed in court.

Only once you have identified what you want to accomplish in both your synchronous and asynchronous time are you ready to start creating the material for the asynchronous portion of the course. Before you can create the material, you need to research the best technology to use. Take time to learn the learning management system before you start to move your course online. What are the limitations of the system? What are the capabilities of the system? What technology is available to deliver different material? Will you use audio or video? Will you embed questions?

In determining the best way to deliver material, you must consider not only whether your delivery is the best andragogy, but whether your students have access to the technology needed to access the material. If your students do not have access to reliable broadband internet, you may need to provide alternative delivery methods. You must decide how students will receive feedback on each assessment, and the amount of time it will take you to provide that feedback. Use technology to assist you with grading assessments and providing feedback.

The amount of time students spend on your course should be the same regardless of whether the course is a traditional course or a blended course; the ABA requires that online and blended courses meet the same standards as traditional law school courses.[20] You need to determine the amount of time students will spend on each asynchronous assignment. Avoid assigning too much material asynchronously—the course and a half syndrome. Avoid assigning too little material asynchronously, especially if you have reduced your synchronous time. Use an Alternative Instructional Equivalencies chart[21] to calculate how much time the asynchronous portion of your course will take, and then determine whether the synchronous portion of your course should be reduced. Because of the amount of asynchronous work I assign, the synchronous portion of my three credit hour blended constitutional law course is two hours.The most important thing to remember when you start to develop your blended course is to be kind to yourself. If you can, introduce only one new technology a semester.[22] Avoid using too many platforms. Make it easy for you and your students to find course material.

Remember it's a partnership. Communicate with your students. Set boundaries. Be creative.

20. 2020 ABA Standards, *supra* note 1, Standard 310; 2016 Guidance Memo on Standard 310: Determination of Credit Hours for Coursework at 4, https://www.americanbar.org/content/dam/aba/administrative/legal_education_and_admissions_to_the_bar/governancedocuments/2016_standard_310_guidance_memorandum.pdf.

21. Most universities have policies for determining instructional equivalencies.

22. April Dawson, *The Paperless Prof*, AALS Section on Technology, Law, and Legal Education 2020 Summer Webinar Series (May 27, 2020), https://www.aals.org/sections/list/technologu-law-and-legal-education/2020techwebinar-paperless-law-prof/.

## III. Constitutional Law as a Skill

Every course in law school requires students to master skills necessary to become competent lawyers. Some of these skills, like legal analysis, are general skills practiced in every law school course. Other skills are specific, even exclusive, to a particular course. Constitutional law has skills that are exclusive to it. Even in a traditional constitutional law course, most professors expect students who have completed the course to know how to interpret the Constitution. It is assumed that somewhere over the course of the year or the semester, students will acquire this skill. It should not be assumed that students are teaching themselves this skill or even that students know that they are supposed to teach themselves this skill. Constitutional interpretation, as well as other skills, should be intentionally designed into the course.

Using student-centered course design makes it easier to intentionally include skills training in a course, even for faculty who have never taught a "skills" course. In developing my course, I start with two questions: 1. What do my students need to be able to *do* to pass the bar and/or be competent attorneys? 2. What do my students need to *know* to be able to pass the bar and/or be competent attorneys? By starting with what students need to be able to *do*, my focus changed from purely doctrinal, to skills based. Now I teach the skill within the framework of the doctrine, and students are able to attain competency by not just knowing the doctrine but also by using the doctrine.[23] Practicing the skill reinforces the doctrine, improving retention of the doctrine while honing the skill.

### A. SKILLS SPECIFIC TO CONSTITUTIONAL LAW

Identifying the skills I need to teach my students required me to question how each case assigned could be used to teach one of the skills specific to constitutional law:

1. Applying the canons of constitutional construction to interpret the Constitution.
2. Using the process of analysis that the United States Supreme Court uses for constitutional analysis.
3. Identifying when the law is a fact for purposes of analysis.[24]

The first skill I teach is constitutional interpretation, applying the canons of constitutional construction. As is common in most Constitutional Law I courses, I assign

23. I identify the doctrines I emphasize based on the types of jobs graduates usually obtain. For example, because most of my students go into solo, small firm, and civil service jobs, I have chosen to include a robust section on standing in my Constitutional Law I course. Students complete the course knowing how to determine whether their client has standing and how to assist their client to gain standing.

24. In most courses, students are asked to apply a statute, regulation, or case law to a set of facts. In constitutional law, students are asked to determine whether the statute, regulation, or holding of a case is constitutional, making the law, or language of the law, a fact for purposes of analysis.

*Marbury v. Madison*,[25] *Martin v. Hunter's Lessee*,[26] and *McCulloch v. Maryland*.[27] I tell students that they already know the holding of these cases; they learned this in their high school history or government class. We read the cases not to learn the holding but to learn how our federal court system developed. We read these cases to understand the canons of construction and process of constitutional analysis that the United States Supreme Court uses to interpret the Constitution. Students need to deconstruct the cases to learn to how to identify when a canon of construction is used so they can model that analytical process, applying the canons of construction to interpret the Constitution—on the course exam, the bar exam, and in practice. We practice this skill when we read other cases throughout the year.

I assign *Baker v. Carr*[28] to teach students the second skill, the process of constitutional analysis. In a constitutional law course focused on doctrine, Justice Brennan's majority opinion in *Baker v. Carr* is usually assigned to introduce students to the political question doctrine. A course focused on skills will take the "rule of law" articulated in Justice Brennan's opinion and show students that the "rule of law" is not only a rule of law but also sets out the process of analysis that must be applied when answering every constitutional law question.[29]

Because the canons of constitutional construction are applied during the process of constitutional analysis, students must learn the canons of construction before the process of constitutional analysis. These skills must be scaffolded.

By focusing on the skill of constitutional analysis, students learn the process of analysis, which is then practiced throughout the rest of the course, allowing students to internalize and practice applying the skill in different factual settings. Students know where to start the analysis of every constitutional question, which relieves their anxiety in approaching the rest of the semester, the exam, and the bar exam. The focus on the process of constitutional analysis provides a natural point to review the canons of constitutional construction and provides students additional opportunities to practice using the canons to interpret the Constitution.

The third skill specific to constitutional law is the ability to identify when the law is a fact for purposes of analysis. In constitutional law, the question is always whether the action taken by the government or government official is constitutional. When the

25. 5 U.S. 137 (1803).

26. 14 U.S. 304 (1816).

27. 17 U.S. 316 (1819).

28. 369 U.S. 186 (1962).

29. 369 U.S. at 217. Students learn to apply the following Process of Analysis: Always start by determining who acted. If a co-equal branch of government acted, then determine whether the action taken is authorized by a provision of the Constitution. Once the constitutional provision is identified, the scope of the power granted and whether the power is discretionary or non-discretionary must be determined by applying the canons of constitutional construction. Once you know the scope of power, you know whether there is a "judicially manageable standard," a rule of law. If there is a judicially manageable standard, then that standard is applied to determine whether the action taken is constitutional.

question is whether the statute is constitutional, then the actual words of the statute are facts for the purposes of analysis. Constitutional law courses are the only courses that regularly require students to use the law as a fact. Students struggle with this concept and need to be provided opportunities designed to practice identifying when the law is a fact.

## B. GENERAL LEGAL SKILLS

In addition to the three skills specific to constitutional law and the ubiquitous skill of legal analysis, I also emphasize three general skills:

1. Reading the case as a set of instructions.
2. Identifying how a case decided by the United States Supreme Court has changed the way society operates.
3. Identifying constitutional law issues in current events.

Because I want my students to be able to advise their clients before a law violation occurs, I create opportunities that require students to read the assigned case as a set of instructions—what to do, and what *not* to do, in future cases. This type of exercise forces students to think about how they will use the doctrine they are learning both inside and outside of a litigation setting. An added benefit of this type of exercise is that students can more easily identify when the court is creating a standard that is virtually impossible to satisfy, which, in turn, leads students to be better able to identify the policy choices the court has made in a particular case.

To understand the role of the United States Supreme Court and the Constitution within our society and culture, I create opportunities that require students to identify how a specific Supreme Court decision has changed how our society operates. This skill is more than identifying whether the Court is opening or closing the door to a particular set of litigants. This skill requires students to understand how a Supreme Court decision changes the behavior of businesses and ordinary people. An example of this skill is recognizing that the prescription drug commercials on television and in print media are a direct result of *Virginia State Board of Pharmacy v. Virginia Citizens Consumer Counsel.*[30]

The third skill I emphasize is the ability to identify constitutional law issues in current events. Students often view constitutional law as historical. Lawyers, however, need to be able to identify the constitutional law issues that arise in everyday life. I use news stories as the factual basis of hypotheticals that I ask students to analyze in a discussion post or that we discuss in class.

---

30. 420 U.S. 971 (1975).

One series of online assessments that I use assesses students' competency in the three skills particular to constitutional law courses and provides students multiple opportunities to practice each skill.

### 1. Constitutional Law I: *Marbury* through the Essential Functions Doctrine

The series of online assessments starts with multiple choice questions embedded in the video for *Marbury v. Madison*[31] that require the student to identify the canon of constitutional construction used by Chief Justice John Marshall. The video for *McCulloch v. Maryland*[32] starts with similar multiple choice questions and then moves to open-ended questions that require the student to identify the canon of construction used and explain why their choice is correct. The video for *District of Columbia v. Heller*[33] includes only the open-ended style questions. In a discussion post, students are required to compare the opinions of Justice Scalia and Justice Stevens in *Heller* identifying the canons of construction each uses and analyzing how that canon is used by the Justice to reach his conclusion. With each case, the retrieval practice becomes more sophisticated. This series of assessments models the retrieval practice I want students to start to do independently either on their own or with their study group.

After we complete the material on judicial review and the standing doctrine, I introduce students to the political question doctrine using Justice Brennan's opinion in *Baker v. Carr* to explain the process of constitutional analysis. In the videos for *Nixon v. United States*[34] and *Powell v. McCormack*,[35] the embedded quiz questions require students to identify the canons of construction the Court is using. This spaced retrieval practice requires students to apply the skill and knowledge from the *Marbury* through *Heller* assessments. During the synchronous time, I use *Nixon* and *McCormack* to walk students through how the rule Justice Brennan sets out in *Baker* is the process of analysis. From this class forward, students always know to start the analysis of each case and each hypothetical by asking who is acting and then what power granted in the Constitution is being exercised.

This series of assessments culminates in the students analyzing whether a statute that restricts the jurisdiction of both the lower federal courts and the appellate jurisdiction of the Supreme Court is constitutional. In the one sentence statute, Congress is exercising two separate powers. The assessment requires students to identify in which part of the sentence Congress is exercising which power. Once students have identified the power being exercised, students must then apply the canons of construction to determine the scope of the power granted and whether the power granted is dis-

31. 5 U.S. 137 (1803).
32. 17 U.S. 316 (1819).
33. 554 U.S. 570 (2008).
34. 506 U.S. 224 (1993).
35. 395 U.S. 486 (1969).

cretionary. Once students have determined the scope of the power, students can then determine whether there is a judicially manageable standard. Students need to identify the effect of Congress exercising the two powers and determine whether the combined exercise of power violates the essential functions doctrine. In this one assessment, students must demonstrate a minimum competency in the three constitutional law course skills, competency in the skill of using the language of the statute as a fact for purposes of analysis, and competency in knowledge of the power of the federal judiciary, the power of Congress to limit the power of the federal judiciary, and the essential functions doctrine.

This series of assessments is all completed asynchronously online. By creating assessments that are intentionally scaffolded and require students to continually practice the building block skills, I can use my synchronous time to work through more complex problems. Students arrive to class better prepared to engage with the material and better able to complete small group work without extensive oversight.

### 2. Constitutional Law II: Free Speech

By the time I cover free speech in the spring semester, I have been working with students for 8 months, and most students have acquired some competency in the constitutional law course skills identified above. My focus is on creating opportunities for students to practice the constitutional law course skills within the context of the nuanced free speech doctrine. My secondary goal is to require students to make the connection between the law and current events by using the learning techniques of elaboration and generation.

Students are assigned a short activity/assessment for each rule of law we study in the free speech doctrine. Some of the activities I assign are:

1. Identify a recent statement in the media that if made in 1800 would have led to prosecution under the Sedition Act of 1798 as that Act has been enforced.
2. After listening to the *Bradenburg v. Ohio*[36] lecture, watch the YouTube video of Michael Brown's stepfather's reaction to the Grand Jury's failure to indict.[37] Can the stepfather be prosecuted under the *Brandenburg* test?
3. Analyze whether Edward Snowden's release of U.S. government documents to *The Guardian* and *The Guardian's* publication of the documents violate the rule of law for confidential information.
4. Find an example of commercial speech which would have been unprotected prior to the Supreme Court's decision in *Virginia State Board of Pharmacy v. Virginia Citizens Consumer Council*.[38]

---

36. 395 U.S. 444 (1969).
37. This assignment should be updated on a regular basis, so students are familiar with the event.
38. 420 U.S. 971 (1975).

5. Take a picture of yourself in a public forum.
6. Take a picture of yourself on or find a picture of government property not open to the public for speech.
7. Complete one of the following: (a) Obtain your public library's filtering policy and determine whether it complies with *U.S. v. American Library Association*;[39] or (b) Obtain your town or city's parade permitting requirements and determine if the requirements are a constitutional time, place, and manner regulation.
8. Either find a picture of symbolic conduct or take a picture of yourself engaged in symbolic conduct.

These assessments require students to engage in retrieval practice. To complete the assignment, students must question their knowledge of the rule of law being studied. Students are engaged in elaboration because they are required to apply the rule of law to current events or to their own behavior. Students are also engaged in generation because they must complete the assignment prior to the class where we discuss the material.

These assessments are all completed asynchronously. Students submit their work through the learning management platform. I use the student submissions to create hypotheticals or as a basis for discussion during the synchronous class time. Students often come to class having researched other current events and excited to discuss how the law relates to those events.

### 3. Group Project: The Constitution in current events

The purpose of the project is to create a student driven vehicle for the discussion of current issues in the areas of constitutional law studied in that semester. This assignment began as an effort to force students to recognize the constitutional law issues in current events and to take ownership of their learning. I initially assigned the group project only in Constitutional Law II (individual rights) but have recently started assigning the project in Constitutional Law I (structure and powers).

The project has three parts: (1) a presentation on the students' chosen topic using their chosen software,[40] (2) a project log and group assessment, and (3) comments on peer presentations. Students must work in a group, must obtain approval for their chosen topic,[41] and must create original content. Students have full creative license on the format of the presentation. Students have submitted presentations in the form of mock talk shows, puppet shows, cartoon animations, and mock oral arguments. The presentation portion of the group project requires students to use retrieval practice,

39. 539 U.S. 194 (2003).

40. The software must be free to viewers and able to be uploaded to the learning management platform.

41. The purpose of approval is to avoid duplication of project topics. Part of the goal of the third part of the project is to provide the students with a course review.

elaboration, and generation learning techniques. Students are assessed on their understanding of the law and their application of the law to current events.

The project log is the equivalent of the time records that practicing attorneys maintain. The group assessment is a critique of both how the group worked together and a critique of the student's own work and participation. Students are asked to assess what worked well, what could have been improved, who contributed to the final project and the extent of the contribution. This part of the project requires students to engage in reflection and calibration. It also requires the students to use organizational, interpersonal, and intrapersonal skills that are necessary for practice but often not taught or assessed in law school. Most important, this part of the project provides me the information I need to ensure that grading is fair and to prevent free loaders.

In the final part of the project, students must view and post a substantive comment on the other groups' presentations. The substantive comment requirement forces students to engage in spaced retrieval practice at a time when they are beginning to prepare for exams. In their comments, students often engage each other in a substantive discussion on the topic of the presentation which provides the added benefit of elaboration. The presentations are submitted the last month of classes; so, this part of the project acts as a course review.

The group project is completed asynchronously through the learning management platform. Most students enjoy the group project as it is one of the few times in their legal education that students are able to direct their own learning.

## IV. Grading

Students need to receive feedback on formative assessments, but not all formative assessments need to be graded. The purpose of formative assessment is to provide students an opportunity to practice. If there is no correction during the practice period, then bad habits are formed and internalized. The best form of correction is individualized feedback. This is easy to provide for multiple choice questions as most learning management systems are designed to both grade the student's answer and to provide an explanation of the correct answer. Essay questions take more time and effort to provide feedback. It is not always possible to provide individualized written comments on every assignment. Alternatives include model answers, peer review, comment sheets that identify common errors, and in-class discussion.

Because I want to incentivize my students to make the most of the learning opportunities provided, I count all formative assessment toward the final grade.[42] I do not, however, grade each assignment. Most formative assessment grades are completion

---

42. If you want the formative assessment to have a positive impact, i.e. a slight boost for the student, then having it account for 30% of the final grade is the sweet spot. If it counts for less than 30%, the student's final grade is the exam grade. If it counts for more than 30%, the final grade may not accurately reflect student competency.

grades. If a student makes a good faith effort to complete the assignment and submits the assignment on time, they earn the points. Assessments that take more effort to complete are assigned more points. The mid-term exam and the group project are graded assignments, with students receiving individualized comments. These individualized comments provide students guidance on improving their performance prior to the exam.

The amount, format, and timing of the feedback you can provide is inversely proportional to the number of students you have in a semester. When you are designing your formative assessments keep in mind not only the amount of work you are assigning the students, but how and when you will provide students with feedback. Assign only those assessments that you can provide feedback on; be realistic when making this determination. An assignment without feedback is busy work, not a formative assessment.

## V. Conclusion

It is now time to create your own blended constitutional law course. Identify those skills that your students are most likely to use in practice. Develop asynchronous formative assessments that allow your students to practice these skills within the context of constitutional law. As students practice these skills, they will develop confidence in their ability to retain, recall, and apply the information, leading to better student outcomes. Create formative assessments that you will enjoy reading and assessing. Developing a blended constitutional law course allows you to be more creative and to make course material relevant to each generation of students you teach.

TWENTY-EIGHT

# Creativity, Community, and Content in Evidence Online

Lynn Su*

After reading this chapter, you will:

- Appreciate the importance of student-to-professor, student-to-student, and student-to-content engagement in an online Evidence course;
- Know how to connect with online learners;
- Know how to use collaborative projects and synchronous group work to promote student-to-student engagement in an online Evidence course; and
- Know how to cultivate student-to-content engagement in an online Evidence course.

The virtual law school classroom can be an incubator for innovations in community building and collaboration.[1] Abandoning the brick-and-mortar learning environment, professors must reimagine how to deliver content and inspire students to embrace a new way of learning. The transition to online legal education motivated me to think deeply about why I teach, how I connect with my students, and what is important in a virtual Evidence classroom.

Although I have been teaching for a long time, I still marvel at my good fortune having a job that allows me to share my passion for and knowledge of the law with others. Mentoring students, learning about teaching pedagogy, creating course materials, and collaborating with my colleagues has, over the years, given me much professional and personal satisfaction. My strength as a law school professor is my nurturing approach to

* Professor of Law, New York Law School. Professor Su began law teaching in 1992 and began teaching courses online in 2020.

1. *See* Michael Hunter Schwartz, *Towards A Modality-Less Model for Excellence in Law School Teaching*, 70 Syracuse L. Rev. 115, 130 (2020) ("[P]rofessors teaching online classes need to develop and, in fact, have developed tools for connecting with students and building community.").

teaching. I set high expectations for my students, but I do not subscribe to the Professor Kingsfield teaching model premised on intimidation and fear.[2] Rather, I encourage students to approach their studies with a growth mindset,[3] celebrate their achievements, and provide constructive critiques that focus on the quality of their work.

My reflections about teaching during the pandemic led me to conclude that while subject matter knowledge, organization, preparation, and feedback are indispensable, the ingredient that makes teaching exceptional, whether in-person or online, is the human dynamic.[4] Even though students and professors, who may be in different states or even countries, interact through the magic of technology in an online classroom, the human dynamic can nonetheless thrive in a virtual learning environment.[5]

Creating a "human-centered learning experience"[6] is the driving force behind the design of my synchronous online Evidence course. The course, which examines the Federal Rules of Evidence ("FRE"), is fundamental for several reasons. First, lawyers must know the rules of evidence to be effective in the courtroom. Second, Evidence is a subject tested on the bar exam.[7] Finally, a well-rounded lawyer benefits from having a solid understanding of Evidence. Simply put, Evidence should be a part of a lawyer's professional DNA.

My virtual Evidence course is informed by the Community of Inquiry ("CoI") paradigm.[8] CoI recognizes three types of engagement—student-to-professor, student-to-student, and student-to-content—as integral to human-centered learning in an online environment.[9] "Each of the elements [teaching presence, social pres-

---

2. *See* John Jay Osborn Jr., The Paper Chase (1971).

3. *See* Carol S. Dweck, Mindset: The New Psychology of Success 7 (2016) ("*[G]rowth mindset* is based on the belief that your basic qualities are things you can cultivate through your efforts, your strategies, and help from others.").

4. *See* Janet R. Buelow et al., *Supporting Learning Engagement with Online Students*, Online Learning J. 313, 327 (2018) ("An overarching thread in the qualitative findings [in an online learning engagement survey] suggests that what students in online classes seek is *connection*—to oneself, to others, and/or to course material.").

5. *See* Hunter Schwartz, *supra* note 1, at 130 ("A number of our students have friends all over the world whom they have never met in person, and they experience those connections as meaningful.").

6. Sharon O'Malley, *Professors Share Ideas for Building Community in Online Courses*, Inside Higher Ed (July 26, 2017, 3:00 AM), https://www.insidehighered.com/digital-learning/article/2017/07/26/ideas-building-online-community (quoting Michelle Pacansky-Brock, http://brocansky.com/) ("In our digital age of knowledge abundance, an educator's value is no longer derived through delivery of content. Rather, our new focus is on designing human-centered learning experiences.").

7. *Understanding the Uniform Bar Exam,* Nat'l Conf. Bar Ex., https://www.ncbex.org/pdfviewer/?-file=%2Fdmsdocument%2F209 (last visited Oct. 28, 2020).

8. For a further discussion of the Community of Inquiry, see Chapter 15: *Using the Community of Inquiry Framework to Make the Most of Assessment in Online Learning* by Audrey Fried.

9. Noelle Wall Sweany, *From Theory to Practice: Evidence-Based Strategies for Designing and Developing Engaging Online Courses*, 70 Syracuse L. Rev. 167, 172 (2020) (citing D. Randy Garrison et al., *Critical Inquiry in a Text-Based Environment: Computer Conferencing in Higher Education*, 2 Internet & Higher Educ. 87, 88 (2000) ("The [CoI] framework assumes that learning takes places [sic] through the interaction of three core elements within the online community—social presence, teaching presence, and cognitive presence.").

ence, and cognitive presence] overlap and interact to support the online educational experience."[10]

The first part of this chapter discusses cultivating student-to-professor engagement in an online setting—it is critical that the professor reveal her authentic self[11] and provide online learners with individualized attention. The second part focuses on student-to-student engagement, highlighting collaborative projects and synchronous group work that build community in an online Evidence course. The chapter concludes with a discussion of ways to engage online learners with the content in Evidence, the powerful but often perplexing rules whose purpose is to promote fair and just outcomes in court proceedings.[12]

## I. Professor-to-Student Engagement

In my early years of teaching, I was hesitant to reveal too much about myself, fearing that familiarity would diminish my authority as a professor. I shared only basic information about my legal career and an occasional anecdote from practice, believing that any further revelations would blur the professional student-teacher boundaries. My perspective has, however, evolved—while professional boundaries are important, the most effective law professors open their hearts, allowing students to get a glimpse into their lives outside the classroom.[13]

In online classrooms where computer screens separate participants, it becomes especially important for learners to get to know instructors as real people.[14] To connect with online learners, professors may send welcome emails, share biographical introductions, conduct check-ins, engage in class follow-up, host small discussion sessions, and meet with students individually.[15]

### A. WELCOME EMAILS AND INTRODUCTIONS

Establishing a personal connection with online learners can be challenging, but it is not impossible. Before the semester begins, I send my students a welcome email to

---

10. *Id.* at 174.

11. *See* Michael Hunter Schwartz et al., What the Best Law Teachers Do 47 (2013) ("Students reflect that authenticity significantly contributes to teachers' effectiveness.").

12. Fed. R. Evid. 102 ("These rules should be construed so as to administer every proceeding fairly... to the end of ascertaining the truth and securing a just determination.").

13. *See* Hunter Schwartz et al., *supra* note 11, at 45–48 (observing that effective law teachers are genuine and open).

14. O'Malley, *supra* note 6; *see also* Michelle Pacansky-Brock, Best Practices for Teaching with Emerging Technologies (2017).

15. *See* Wall Sweany, *supra* note 9, at 174 (discussing welcome emails); *see* Hunter Schwartz, *supra* note 1, at 137 (discussing welcome videos); Jean Dimeo, *Take My Advice*, Inside Higher Ed (Nov. 15, 2017, 3:00 AM), https://www.insidehighered.com/digital-learning/article/2017/11/15/peer-advice-instructors-teaching-online-first-time (offering advice for novice online instructors including check-ins).

break the ice. The course syllabus acknowledges possibilities and challenges inherent in online learning:

> Classes will be on Zoom.... Although this online format is a departure from the traditional classroom, it presents a unique opportunity to develop new skill sets and ways of communicating that will be invaluable when you enter legal practice. . . .
>
> Despite the exciting possibilities of this new virtual world, there inevitably will be times when internet connections are interrupted, when one of our furry friends decides to bark or meow, or when a roommate or family member is chatting in the background. We ask that you be supportive and kind in these circumstances. We will work through the challenges.... Please embrace the online learning experience as an exciting part of your journey in becoming effective, empathetic lawyers![16]

In my first Evidence class, I express gratitude for my "three" careers—the first as an assistant district attorney, the second as associate in civil practice law firms, and the third as a law professor. I announce that I am available to discuss the joys and challenges of being an attorney and to answer questions about different career paths.

After describing my background, highlighting my practice experience working with evidence, I show a decades-old photo of me and other newly hired assistant district attorneys and then project a recent holiday photo of me with several of the same people with whom I have enduring friendships. Starting on day one, students learn about my life outside the classroom.

## B. DAILY CHECK-INS

To advance student-to-professor engagement and encourage a mindset of tranquility in online courses, professors may conduct check-ins at the beginning of class. I began this practice in spring 2020 when the death, illness, and economic strife resulting from the COVID-19 pandemic invaded our lives. I wish everyone well and share a photo sending positive energy. Students appreciate the daily check-in, so I have made it a staple of my teaching. I show and describe pictures that I have taken, including snaps of soothing ocean waters, golden sunsets, snowcapped mountains, and my tabby cat asleep in a peaceful pose. A calming, personal launch into class allows professors to share more about themselves, and it also gives students a moment to focus on the beauty in the world before diving into class content.

## C. CLASS FOLLOW-UP

The ability to linger online immediately after class is a plus of virtual teaching—students have face time with the professor as well as the opportunity to dig deeper into

16. The Fall 2020 Evidence syllabus is on file with the author.

the subject matter of the day. I remain online for up to a half hour after class to field questions. A post-class discussion may attract many students. In contrast, after the conclusion of an in-person class, students who have to hurry to other classes and activities may not be able to linger.

### D. DISCUSSION SESSIONS AND INDIVIDUAL CONFERENCES

Small group discussion sessions allow professors to interact with online learners in a more intimate setting and also promote student-to-student engagement. And individual student conferences are, of course, essential to creating student-to-professor engagement in both online and live courses.[17] A professor who encourages individual meetings shows that she is committed to helping her students reach their full potential.[18]

## II. Student-to-Student Engagement

The in-person law school experience offers a variety of opportunities for students to engage with each other socially and intellectually—they chat in the halls before and after classes, share meals in the cafeteria, and participate in extracurricular and co-curricular organizations. The law school campus is where many lifelong friendships take root. Even though they do not share a physical space, online learners may collaborate and develop a "social presence" [19] and esprit de corps, albeit in a new way.[20]

Professors teaching online can facilitate student-to-student engagement by creating breakout discussion groups,[21] conducting team-building games, and assigning collaborative projects. And upper-level students, serving as teaching assistants, can be an important resource for online learners, providing the student perspective on study skills and exam-taking strategies.[22]

---

17. *See* Hunter Schwartz et al., *supra* note 11, at 273 ("Students value meeting with teachers to talk about their performance and feedback. . . .").

18. I use Microsoft Teams, an online conferencing platform, for individual meetings.

19. O'Malley, *supra* note 6 (Professors teaching online courses "are embracing the notion that 'social presence,' a concept promoted by the researchers D. Randy Garrison, Terry Anderson and Wally Archer in the early 2000s, is critical to the success of the online learner. Together with cognitive presence and teaching presence, social presence occurs when students can connect on a human and emotional level.").

20. *See* Caroline Haythornthwaite, *Facilitating Collaboration in Online Learning*, 10 J. Asynchronous Learning Networks 7, 11 (2006) (Fostering collaboration "is particularly important for distributed students who cannot meet in the conventional on-campus classroom, hallways and coffee shops.").

21. *See* Pacansky-Brock, *supra* note 14, at 92 (discussing the Zoom breakout room feature).

22. *See generally* Julie M. Cheslik, *Teaching Assistants: A Study of Their Use in Law School Research and Writing Programs*, 44 J. Leg. Educ. 394, 411 (1994).

## A. TEACHING ASSISTANTS

Teaching assistants participate in my online Evidence course; they play an invaluable role in spearheading student engagement.[23] Very personable and approachable, my teaching assistants attend classes and share study tips at the end of most classes. The more than twenty study tips focus on note-taking, outlining, time-management, resilience, and self-care. A consistent message is that while learning the requirements of the FRE is essential, knowing how to apply the rules in different factual situations is a sign of true mastery. In addition to participating in classes, the teaching assistants host discussion sessions and are available to meet with students one-on-one. I frequently solicit their advice on how to maximize student engagement, and I collaborate with them to create synchronous team-building review games and ungraded quizzes. The contributions of teaching assistants humanize the online learning experience and energize the virtual classroom.

## B. BREAKOUT ROOMS

Breakout rooms allow the host of the meeting to create discussion groups during a synchronous class.[24] This feature provides a venue for small groups to exchange ideas and answer questions. It is a convenient way to promote student-to-student engagement, as well as student-to-content engagement, in an online class. Breakout rooms offer a more comfortable forum for students who are hesitant to speak in a large group to participate in the conversation.[25]

Breakout room discussions are a regular component of my online Evidence course. Most classes include one or two breakout room sessions in which students work together to answer hypotheticals involving evidentiary rules introduced during the lecture. The breakout rooms include about four to eight students, and each breakout session lasts for up to ten minutes. Teaching assistants and professors may travel between the breakout rooms to check progress and answer questions.

After the breakout rooms close and students rejoin the main class session, the breakout groups share their analyses of the hypotheticals. Each group may designate a reporter to share the group's answer. The class discussion that follows the breakout room sessions may reveal gaps in comprehension. This feedback provides insight into students' understanding and helps professors adjust their teaching to improve learning.[26]

---

23. I want to extend my heartfelt thanks to the following NYLS students: Francesca Rogo and Tyler Wilkerson, the teaching assistants for my Fall 2020 Evidence course, and Saraya Ivanova, my research assistant whose help was invaluable in writing this chapter.

24. *See* PACANSKY-BROCK, *supra* note 14, at 92 (discussing the Zoom breakout room feature).

25. *See* Heidi K. Brown, *The "Silent But Gifted" Law Student: Transforming Anxious Public Speakers into Well-Rounded Advocates*, 18 LEG. WRITING 291, 326 (2012) (presenting recommendations for "fostering a healthy communicative classroom dynamic" for quiet law students); *see also* Chapter 4: *Understanding and Lifting Up Our Quiet Students: Reimagining "Participation" in the Remote Classroom* by Heidi Brown.

26. For additional discussion on using formal and informal teams in online courses, see Chapter 10: *Team-Based Learning in an Online Teaching Environment* by Joy E. Herr-Cardillo and Melissa H. Weresh, and Chapter 14: *Effective Collaboration in Online Courses* by Darby Dickerson and Megan Bess.

## C. TEAM-BUILDING GAMES

The social distancing requirements and quarantines triggered by COVID-19 physically separated families, friends, and co-workers. To nurture relationships and alleviate loneliness, many people began playing online games during the pandemic.[27] Educators and businesses have recognized the use of games to promote camaraderie and engagement.[28]

Law school professors have increasingly embraced games as a teaching tool, bringing games into the classroom to reinforce concepts and enliven learning.[29] Games may be especially useful in a virtual law school classroom,[30] providing online learners, some of whom may be sitting alone in front of computer screens in childhood bedrooms, with an opportunity to interact with their classmates.

To help students review for the midterm and final exams in Evidence, I worked with my teaching assistants to create Evidence Jeopardy games.[31] Evidence Jeopardy encourages team building by requiring online learners to work together to reach a consensus.

Evidence Jeopardy consists of several rounds, each with three or four questions. The categories for the midterm review are relevance and prejudice, categorical exclusions, character evidence, and impeachment, and the categories for the final exam review are hearsay, experts, and authentication. The questions, which test students' understanding of the FRE, call for true or false, fill in the blank, and multiple-choice responses.

To play Evidence Jeopardy, the class is divided into teams, each consisting of up to eight students. Before the game begins, the teams meet in their breakout rooms to select a team name and a captain. The team names in my Fall 2020 Evidence class were amusing and clever—Learned Hand-Sanitizers, The Probatives, Confrontation Clauses, and Evidence is the Fly—to name a few. After selecting team names and captains, the students return to the main online class to start the game.

---

27. *See generally* Ruchir Sharma, *People Aren't Reading or Watching Movies. They're Gaming*, N.Y. Times (Aug. 15, 2020), https://www.nytimes.com/2020/08/15/opinion/fortnite-epic-apple-gaming.html.

28. *See generally* Matthew Farber, Gamify Your Classroom: A Field Guide To Game-Based Learning (Colin Lankshear & Michele Knobel eds., 2015); John Newstrom & Edward Scannell, The Big Book Of Team Building Games: Trust-Building Activities, Team Spirit Exercises, And Other Fun Things To Do (Richard Narramore et al. eds., 1997).

29. *See generally* Daniel M. Ferguson, *The Gamification of Legal Education: Why Games Transcend the Langdellian Model and How They Can Revolutionize Law School*, 19 Chap. L. Rev. 629 (2016); *see generally* Jennifer L. Rosato, *All I Ever Needed to Know About Teaching Law School I Learned Teaching Kindergarten: Introducing Gaming Techniques into the Law School Classroom*, 45 J. Leg. Educ. 568 (1995).

30. *See generally* Jordan Friedman, *Explore the Pros, Cons of Gamification in Online Education* (Feb. 17, 2016, 9 AM) US News & World Report, https://www.usnews.com/education/online-education/articles/2016-02-17/explore-the-pros-cons-of-gamification-in-online-education.

31. In designing the Evidence Jeopardy games, one of my teaching assistants drew on her experience playing a team-building Jeopardy game during a summer internship.

My teaching assistants created visually engaging Evidence Jeopardy PowerPoints that include instructions, questions, and answers. The questions are projected in the PowerPoint, read out loud, and shared in the group chat in the main online classroom. After a round of questions is published, the teams reenter their breakout rooms and have five minutes to answer the questions. To ensure confidentiality, each team emails their answers to a teaching assistant.

After the teams submit their answers for a round, the class reconvenes. I then reveal and explain the answers, referring to specific provisions in the FRE. The review provides students with immediate feedback. After the review, the class moves to the next round and repeats the process. The overall winners—first, second, and third place—are announced at the end of the game. Professors may send winners gift cards for coffee or office supplies. And bragging rights may suffice if swag is cost prohibitive in a large online course.

## D. COLLABORATIVE PROJECTS

Collaborative projects promote teamwork and esprit de corps in online courses. I developed an optional assignment titled "Collaborate, Learn, and Teach: The Evidence Video!" in which small groups create short videos based on hypotheticals in the course textbook or other fact patterns.[32] The vignettes bring the Federal Rules of Evidence to life, demonstrating how complex rules apply in practice.

Before filming a video, the groups write scripts which I review and edit. Each video includes an introduction, a mock argument on the admissibility of proffered evidence, and a ruling on its admissibility. Working in separate locations, students may individually film their parts on cell phones, share the videos, and edit the videos with iMovie.[33] I show the videos in class, and I also post them online. Students who complete the project receive extra credit on the midterm exam.

The video project showcases students' ingenuity and technological know-how. The Fall 2020 videos, which featured students playing attorneys and judges, highlighted evidentiary rules relating to relevance (FRE 401), prejudice (FRE 403), subsequent remedial measures (FRE 407) and character evidence offered by the accused in a criminal case (FRE 404(a)(2)). After watching the videos in class, the chat exploded with compliments and thanks to the creators of the videos. Not only did the videos heighten classroom engagement, but students also reported that the videos helped clarify their understanding of the rules.[34]

---

32. *See* Wall Sweany, *supra* note 9, at 176 (noting that video assignments encourage student creativity).

33. One group edited their video with TikTok. Although my assignment instructions address only the content and structure of the videos, professors may also offer guidance on filming.

34. While the video project was successful, participation was not widespread. In the future, I may make the project a course requirement.

Online learners may also collaborate outside of class to write answers to practice essay questions. Resembling a multi-part question on a final exam, the practice question in my online Evidence course presents facts in a hypothetical criminal case involving charges of robbery, burglary, and attempted murder. Working in small groups, students analyze issues relating to hearsay, witness competency, relevance, prejudice, and the admissibility of prior convictions. The assignment, which is ungraded, requires students to grapple with the issues, debate the applicability of the rules, and decide the admissibility of evidence. The question is reviewed in class; groups share their analyses and outline the collaborative process they engaged in to reach a consensus.

## III. Student-to-Content Engagement

The study of Evidence is action-packed—the FRE include more than 60 individual rules, many of which are interrelated.[35] To engage online learners with the content in Evidence, the classroom presentation should be clear, well-organized, and attention-grabbing[36]—PowerPoint and videos are impactful online tools. The class content may be reinforced with in-class hypotheticals, homework assignments, and assessments that require students to identify issues and apply rules.[37]

### A. POWERPOINT

In every Evidence class, whether live or online, I share a PowerPoint and I also post it, usually before class, on the course LMS. The PowerPoints include a recap of prior material; an introduction to the topic of the day; a presentation of rules, including the policies and rationales on which they are based; and hypotheticals to illustrate how the rules work.[38]

Vibrant pictures, graphics, and charts tell a visual story of Evidence. For example, a scale weighing the probative value of evidence against the danger of unfair prejudice represents the FRE 403 balancing test,[39] and a FRE 609 chart breaks down tests for determining the admissibility of prior convictions. Eye-catching imagery energizes the online classroom, and simplified charts provide students with alternative ways to conceptualize the rules.[40]

---

35. FED. R. EVID.

36. Yvonne M. Dutton et al., *Assessing Online Learning in Law Schools: Students Say Online Classes Deliver*, 96 DENV. L. REV. 493, 525 (2019) ("According to the focus group students, the components of a quality online course included (1) organization, (2) engaging presentation of course content, and (3) opportunities for assessment and professor feedback.").

37. *See* Wall Sweany, *supra* note 9, at 174 (offering strategies for "enhancing cognitive presence").

38. I want to thank Professors Heidi Brown (Brooklyn Law School) and Daniel Warshawsky (New York Law School) for sharing their Evidence class PowerPoints with me. I relied on their material when designing my Evidence course.

39. The Rule 403 visual was included in Professor Brown's materials.

40. PACANSKY-BROCK, *supra* note 14, at 12 ("Each of the senses enhances learning, but the human brain particularly loves images.").

### B. VIDEOS

Evidentiary rulings shape the trajectory of legal cases and play a significant role in determining the fate of people charged with crimes[41] and those prosecuting or defending civil actions. Evidence, therefore, is powered by emotion. Courtroom scenes from movies, television shows, and real cases, along with student-created videos, can bring that emotion into the online classroom and illuminate confounding evidentiary requirements.[42]

What no doubt is a favorite of many law school professors, an entertaining courtroom scene from the movie *My Cousin Vinny*, demonstrates, for example, that knowledge and experience can be an adequate basis to qualify a witness as an expert.[43] Scenes from television shows involving legal drama, such as *Law & Order*, *Suits*, and *The Undoing*, also depict how witnesses may be examined at trial. Hollywood's obsession with lawyers in the courtroom has generated a treasure trove of material that can enhance learning in an Evidence classroom.

Playing excerpts from real-life courtroom proceedings is another way to capture the attention of online learners. When discussing the use of leading questions on cross-examination, the class may view a cross-examination in the trial of Conrad Murray, who was convicted of involuntary manslaughter in connection with the death of the singer and songwriter Michael Jackson.[44] After watching the clip, the discussion may focus on FRE 611, which permits leading questions on cross-examination. Studying real cases helps students appreciate the power of evidentiary rulings.

## IV. Hypotheticals

Online Evidence class should be interactive, requiring students to engage with course content by working through hypothetical case scenarios. Students can determine the applicability of evidentiary rules in different factual situations and predict whether a court would admit proffered evidence.[45] Professors may use textbook hypotheticals

---

41. *See generally* Anna Roberts, *Reclaiming the Importance of the Defendant's Testimony: Prior Conviction Impeachment and the Fight Against Implicit Stereotyping*, 83 U. Chi. L. Rev. 835, 856–60 (2016) (discussing how evidence of an accused's prior conviction may contribute to an unjust result in a criminal case).

42. *See generally* Miguel A. Méndez, *Teaching Evidence: Using Casebooks, Problems, Transcripts, Simulations, Video Clip, and Interactive DVDs*, 50 St. Louis U. L.J. 1133 (2006) (discussing innovative ways to teach Evidence).

43. Movieclips, *My Cousin Vinny (5/5) Movie CLIP—Automotive Expert (1992)*, YouTube (Aug. 4, 2015), https://www.youtube.com/watch?v=3nGQLQF1b6I&t=78s.

44. HLN, *Defense Witness: Don't Put Words in My Mouth*, YouTube (Dec. 3, 2012), https://www.youtube.com/watch?v=TA3Xy53hMMY&t=210s.

45. At the beginning of the Fall 2020 semester, class participation was robust and anxiety related to the pandemic was no doubt high; therefore, after consulting with my teaching assistants, I decided not to assign on-call student panels, a system I have used for ensuring participation in large in-person classes. However, because the level of participation varied as the semester progressed, I will likely assign on-call panels in future online courses. *See* Jacqueline D. Lipton, *Distance Legal Education: Lessons from the "Virtual Classroom,"* 60 Idea 71, 89 (2020) ("One big concern many teachers have about online education is

and create others, including fact patterns based on legal cases making headlines in the news.

Relating course content to news events, my class examined a criminal case brought against Paul Manafort, a former political campaign manager, analyzing whether the danger of unfair prejudice would, under FRE 403, substantially outweigh the probative value of proffered evidence.[46] We also discussed the use of expert testimony in the Harvey Weinstein sex crimes trial; the defense called an expert who testified about the fallibility of human memory.[47] Showcasing the real-life implications of evidentiary rules provides context for the course content.[48]

The class analyzes hypotheticals in either breakout rooms or the main online classroom. Students may play attorneys who advance legal arguments and judges who issue rulings. Zoom polls allow breakout groups to share their answers to questions on the admissibility of evidence.[49]

## A. HOMEWORK ASSIGNMENTS

Work outside of the classroom, whether completed in groups or individually, draw online learners deeper into the world of Evidence, sharpening their knowledge of the rules. The practice essay group assignment and evidence video project do double duty, bringing students together in the virtual learning environment and challenging them to master the intricacies of rules. Those who desire additional practice may write answers to essay questions from previous final exams; these questions can be reviewed in class and sample answers may be posted online.

## B. GRADED AND UNGRADED ASSESSMENTS

Assessments measure comprehension and motivate students to engage with course content.[50] A multiple-choice midterm and a final exam, consisting of essays and multiple-choice questions, are the graded assessments in my online Evidence course. I

---

how to ensure adequate student participation. In class, you can adopt a 'panel system' or a general class participation requirement. . . .").

46. CourtListener, https://www.courtlistener.com/docket/6183591/united-states-v-manafort/?page=2 (last visited Jan. 8, 2021) (court docket including motions in limine to preclude evidence).

47. *See* Brent Lang & Gene Maddaus, *Weinstein Defense Expert Testifies That Memories Can Be Contaminated*, Variety (Feb. 7, 2020, 8:20 AM), https://variety.com/2020/film/news/weinstein-defense-memories-contaminated-1203496279/ (explaining that new information can become incorporated into memory and cause a contamination of memory).

48. *See generally* Méndez, *supra* note 42.

49. *Active Learning for Your Online Classroom: Five Strategies Using Zoom*, Colum. U. Center for Teaching and Learning, https://ctl.columbia.edu/resources-and-technology/teaching-with-technology/teaching-online/active-learning/ (last visited Oct. 30, 2020).

50. *See* Michael Hunter Schwartz et al., Teaching Law By Design: Engaging Students From The Syllabus To The Final Exam 155–70 (2017) (discussing assessments).

review the midterm in class, and I am available for individual meetings with students who want to review their performance on the midterm and final.

Quizzes, graded and ungraded, and online polls are additional assessment tools that enrich online learning.[51] Quizzes, which may be posted online, give students practice identifying and applying evidentiary rules. Online polls with multiple choice and true or false questions provide immediate feedback on learners' understanding and retention of course material.

## V. Conclusion

The shift to online law school instruction during the pandemic has been the impetus for institutional dialogue[52] and self-reflection about best practices in legal education. My most profound take-away is that delivering a human-centered learning experience is the hallmark of excellent law school teaching, whether in-person or online. To achieve excellence, professors teaching online should embrace new technologies and methods of instruction that nurture "social presence, teaching presence, and cognitive presence."[53]

Moving forward, I plan to redouble my efforts to use technology in my online Evidence course and to create authentic, meaningful connections with my online learners. Because Evidence involves courtroom drama, it is especially ripe for innovative online simulations that engage students and deliver content—I look forward to my continuing journey in the online world of Evidence and hope to use the lessons I have learned and continue to learn to become a more effective teacher.

---

51. *See* Dutton et al., *supra* note 36, at 527 (discussing the use of quizzes in online courses).

52. NYLS formed a partnership with Columbia University Teachers College Instructional Design Team to support NYLS professors teaching online courses.

53. *See* Wall Sweany, *supra* note 9.

TWENTY-NINE

# Training Effective Virtual Oral Advocates

Susie Salmon*

After reviewing this chapter, readers will be able to:

- Evaluate whether and how to implement virtual oral-advocacy activities into a variety of skills courses;
- Implement fundamental best practices in all skills and advocacy classes to help students become better virtual oral advocates;
- Identify and weigh key considerations in designing virtual oral-argument activities in a 1L legal-writing course;
- Design and implement effective virtual oral-argument activities in a variety of skills courses for both synchronous and asynchronous online students;
- Effectively prepare students for virtual moot court competitions; and
- Effectively coach teams at virtual moot court competitions.

On Monday, May 4, 2020, the United States Supreme Court heard remote oral arguments for the first time.[1] The arguments took place by teleconference, and that audio-only argument was live-streamed online.[2] By that date, federal appellate courts had been hearing oral argument virtually since March, often through videoconference applications, and some state appellate courts had been hearing virtual arguments as well.[3]

---

* Director of Legal Writing and Clinical Professor of Law, University of Arizona James E. Rogers College of Law. Professor Salmon began law teaching in 2008 and began teaching online in 2017. She has designed and taught synchronous and asynchronous courses.

1. Associated Press, *Supreme Court Broadcasts Oral Arguments for the First Time Ever*, MarketWatch (May 4, 2020), https://www.marketwatch.com/story/supreme-court-broadcasts-oral-arguments-for-the-first-time-ever-2020-05-04.

2. *Id.*

3. *Courts Deliver Justice Virtually Amid Coronavirus Outbreak*, U.S. Courts (Apr. 8, 2020), https://www.uscourts.gov/news/2020/04/08/courts-deliver-justice-virtually-amid-coronavirus-outbreak.

Throughout the COVID-19 pandemic, SCOTUS continued to hear oral arguments telephonically,[4] and many other appellate courts conducted the majority of their oral arguments remotely by video.[5] Even before the pandemic, alternative dispute resolution and some court proceedings started shifting to the online format.[6] Once the pandemic began, courts quickly began changing rules to permit even party depositions to be conducted online, and many of those rules have become permanent.[7] Now that most lawyers and judges have become comfortable with virtual interactions, and clients have seen the cost savings they reap when they no longer have to pay travel costs for attorneys to attend far-flung hearings or witness interviews, the trend toward virtual practice is bound to expand and continue.[8] Thus, it behooves us as legal educators to train our students to succeed in this brave new world of virtual oral advocacy.

To assist in those efforts, I will first outline some basic best practices that will help you train students to be better virtual oral advocates, whether you are teaching in the first-year legal-skills classroom, conducting oral-argument activities in the doctrinal classroom, or coaching students in moot court competitions. I will then provide more specific advice for virtual oral argument in the 1L legal-skills classroom and for preparing a team to participate in a virtual moot court competition.

## I. Basic Best Practices for Virtual Oral Advocacy

Simply teaching students online, particularly in the synchronous online classroom, presents opportunities to train them in skills that will make them better virtual oral advocates. By teaching, modeling, and reinforcing netiquette and other fundamental best practices in the online classroom, we also build habits and practices that will make our students more successful in the online courtroom.

---

4. Press Release, Supreme Court of the United States, Media Advisory Regarding November and December Teleconference Argument Audio (Oct. 22, 2020), https://www.supremecourt.gov/publicinfo/press/pressreleases/ma_10-22-20.

5. *See, e.g.*, Press Release, United States Court of Appeals for the Ninth Circuit, COVID-19 Update (June 29, 2020), http://cdn.ca9.uscourts.gov/datastore/general/2020/06/29/covid%20update%20june%2025.pdf.

6. Elizabeth B. Juliano, *The Evolution, Benefits, and Challenges of Alternative Dispute Resolution and Online Dispute Resolution*, LITIG. MGMT, INC. (June 10, 2020), https://lmiweb.com/article/evolution-benefits-and-challenges-alternative-dispute-resolution-and-online-dispute; Peter Halprin & Andrew Nadolna, *Is Virtual ADR the "New Normal"?*, LAW.COM (July 30, 2020), https://www.law.com/newyorklawjournal/2020/07/30/virtual-adr-the-new-normal/. Some courts shifted select proceedings to videoconference before the pandemic. *See, e.g.*, *Videoconferenced Arguments Guide*, U.S. COURT OF APPEALS FOR THE TENTH CIRCUIT, https://www.ca10.uscourts.gov/clerk/videoconferenced-arguments-guide (last visited Nov. 19, 2020).

7. *US Remote Deposition and Oath Status*, PERKINS COIE (Nov. 10, 2020), https://www.perkinscoie.com/en/news-insights/us-remote-deposition-and-oath-status.html.

8. Frank Ready, *Keep It Virtual: Some Hope Remote Depositions, Court Hearings Continue Post-COVID*, LAW.COM (June 2, 2020), https://www.law.com/legaltechnews/2020/06/02/keep-it-virtual-some-hope-remote-depositions-court-hearings-continue-post-covid/.

## A. NETIQUETTE

Netiquette refers to internet etiquette, the rules of professional behavior that govern online conduct.[9] Syllabi for synchronous online classes should include a section on netiquette—practices you expect your students to follow to facilitate successful, professional online interactions—covering topics ranging from civility in oral and written communication, to applying a duty of confidentiality to classroom communications, to devoting one's attention to the task at hand and not to outside distractions.[10] In crafting the netiquette section of your syllabus, consider including the following provisions, which also reflect best practices for online oral advocacy:

- Set up a videoconferencing account through your institution with the platform your institution uses. Upload a professional-looking profile photo and enter your full name.
- Keep your microphone muted when you are not speaking.
- Keep in mind your appearance and that of your surroundings. Dress as you would if you were appearing in person. Consider what others can see or hear in the background and do your best to eliminate distractions. Position yourself before a blank wall, if possible, or use a neutral online background. Silence mobile phones and other alerts. Restrain pets in other rooms or outside. To the extent possible, work in a room where you can exclude other people.

If students violate any of these provisions or seem unclear on the boundaries of appropriate online behavior, gently coach them during office hours or after class. If you use teaching assistants, consider having a teaching assistant approach the student first; sometimes students are less intimidated by—and thus are more receptive to—advice from near peers.

## B. TECHNOLOGY TIPS AND BEST PRACTICES

The online classroom also presents opportunities to have students learn and implement good habits in interacting over videoconferencing platforms. You may wish to share these tips in an addendum to your syllabus or in a post on the course page in your learning management system.

- Rather than looking at the onscreen face of the person with whom you are conversing, practice looking at your webcam. While it may feel awkward at first, you will become more comfortable with this over time, and looking at the webcam consistently will create the illusion of natural eye contact.

---

9. *Netiquette*, Merriam-Webster Dictionary, *https*://www.merriam-webster.com/dictionary/netiquette (last visited Nov. 19, 2020).

10. For "netiquette" language that can be used for asynchronous discussions, see Chapter 26: *Designing and Cultivating Discussion in Asynchronous Online Seminars* by Kristin E. Murray.

- Place your webcam (or your laptop, if you are using a laptop's embedded camera) at or slightly above your eye level and approximately arms-length distance from your face.
- If you are not using an external microphone, know where the embedded microphone on your computer is located. Make sure not to cover it with hands, papers, or other objects while you are speaking.
- Consider using headphones or a headset to ensure that you and your audience can hear.
- Note that the online environment amplifies the impact of distractions. For professional presentations, dress simply and professionally in subdued, solid colors. Avoid rustling papers and tapping surfaces.

Conventional wisdom dictates that when delivering oral presentations online, one should stand, just as attorneys generally would in the courtroom. I resist that advice. First, delivering an effective argument from a standing position often is logistically difficult from home. Most people do not have in-home podia or even standing desks, much less ones that make it easy to mount a camera and microphone at an effective height or distance or make it easy to access written notes. Moreover, standing at such a distance from a normal monitor or laptop screen makes it even more difficult to see the judges and read facial expressions or body language. Second, viewing standing as a manifestation of formality and deference is a relic of the Classical ideal of the male warrior as the paradigm of effective advocacy, which unnecessarily disadvantages individuals with mobility disabilities, among others.[11] I suggest embracing the partial move to virtual arguments as an opportunity to reexamine that tradition, and I would not require first-year law students to find a way to stand while presenting.[12]

## II. Introductory Oral Argument in First-Year Classes

Many law schools have students engage in some form of oral argument in their first-year legal-skills courses, from in-class exercises to a formal 1L moot-court competition. All of these activities can be adapted for the online classroom.

11. *See* Susie Salmon, *Reconstructing the Voice of Authority*, 51 Akron L. Rev. 143, 154 (2017).

12. It seems that at least some of those running virtual moot court competitions agree. The rules for the Pace Environmental Law Moot Court Competition explicitly give advocates the option of sitting or standing during oral argument (although they encourage advocates to stand). Jeffrey G. Miller National Environmental Law Moot Court Competition, 2021 Official Rules for Virtual Competition Rule VII(F) (2020), https://law.pace.edu/sites/default/files/nelmcc/2020/2021/2021_Official_Rules_Sept_29.pdf. The rules for the National Online Moot Court Competition are silent on whether advocates must sit or stand. *See* National Online Moot Court Competition, 2021 Rules, https://drive.google.com/file/d/122MjQR0HgFzLm-WfbBWtgRhTEgrt873n/view. And it seems that courts permit advocates the option of sitting. Virtual Oral Advocacy 2 (2020), http://www.adi-sandiego.com/practice/mcle/MCLE_Virtual_Oral_Argument_Presentation.pdf.

But given the logistical difficulties of teaching online and the already litigation-heavy first-year curriculum, why add oral argument to the 1L classroom, when many law graduates will never argue before a court and still more will never deliver an appellate oral argument?

Oral-argument activities have benefits beyond preparing students for litigation practice. For example, scheduling an oral-argument activity after students have submitted a first draft but before they have submitted a final draft can help students refine and revise their arguments and develop stronger counter-analysis. Often, students who struggle putting complex legal analysis into words on paper have an easier time articulating those ideas orally. Responding to questions from a mock judge can help students identify inconsistencies in their reasoning or augment policy arguments. Research suggests that oral argument may have particular benefits for students for whom English is an additional language.[13] And oral argument activities provide students whose oral communication skills are stronger than their written communication skills an opportunity to shine.

If you decide to have students present oral argument in your online first-year classroom, you will need to weigh a number of options in designing that exercise, including:

- Should students present individually or in pairs or teams?
- Should students argue against one another?
- Who should serve as judge for the argument? How many judges should you have? Should the judges ask questions during the argument?
- Should the arguments be graded? If so, how much of the final grade should the oral argument score comprise?

The answers to these questions depend on the learning objectives you target with this activity and the limitations of your online student population. If all of your students attend class synchronously and have access to reliable internet and high-quality microphones and webcams, the playing field is reasonably level, and you can feel more comfortable having them argue against one another, grading the arguments, having the oral argument grade make up a meaningful percentage of the final course grade, and asking questions during the arguments. Because you likely are not using oral argument primarily to train oral advocates but rather to achieve broader learning objectives, however, it may be better to create a lower-stakes, lower-stress exercise that either is ungraded or makes up a minimal portion of the final grade—just enough to make sure that students invest enough effort to obtain the desired benefits.[14]

---

13. *See generally* Larry Ferlazzo & Katie Hull Sypnieski, The ELL Teachers Toolbox: Hundreds of Practical Ideas to Support Your Students (2018).

14. In my experience, the fear of embarrassing oneself in an oral argument before peers or their professor is often—although not always—enough to motivate students to prepare adequately.

One option for a synchronous, lower-stakes exercise is to devote a class period to team arguments. A couple of days before class, post the exercise instructions and assign students to teams and each team to a side. You can use a problem the students are working on in class or a simple new scenario. Begin class in plenary session with a brief lecture reviewing key oral-argument formalities—introductions, a short theme statement, and a brief roadmap of the argument—and the logistics of the argument. Then put the students into breakout rooms[15] by team to prepare. Teams should divide the argument among the team members.[16] To conduct the actual arguments, you can either pull one team into the other team's breakout room, or you can move pairs of teams into the main room. You can ask questions designed to achieve your learning objectives,[17] you can have teaching assistants do the same, or you can assign a set of students to be the judges and ask a set number of questions and deliver the final "opinion."

## A. ORAL ARGUMENT WITH ASYNCHRONOUS STUDENTS

In conducting oral-argument activities with asynchronous students, although you can schedule times when pairs of asynchronous students can argue against one another and before you, this may be impracticable with larger classes and where students reside in various time zones. Instead, you may wish to have students argue individually and just before the professor or teaching assistant rather than before a panel.

In a mixed class, where some students attend asynchronously and others synchronously, you may wish to have students record[18] their oral arguments in pairs, with each student serving as judge and asking questions while the other student argues. If you choose this option, provide the students with clear instructions in writing, including things like (1) how long the arguments should be, (2) how long a student should be allowed to deliver an introduction and roadmap before being interrupted with questions, (3) roughly how many questions the "judge" student should ask the "advocate" student, and (4) criteria on which the students will be graded.

---

15. This works quite well on Zoom, but you can do this with any platform that supports breakout rooms.

16. How they divide the argument depends on your learning objectives. I often conduct this exercise after the first draft of the final memo is due but before the revised, final draft is submitted. I use it to reinforce the CREAC organizational paradigm and to encourage students to develop stronger counteranalysis, so I have the students divide the argument by the parts of CREAC—one student delivers the opening with roadmap and theme, a second student delivers the rule and rule explanation, a third delivers the primary application of rule to fact, and the fourth delivers any counteranalysis and rebuttal of that counteranalysis.

17. For example, to reinforce the CREAC paradigm, I might ask questions designed to keep a student from straying from her assigned portion of the paradigm (e.g., from rule into application), or to encourage her to deepen her discussion (e.g., to discuss the facts and reasoning of key cases in rule or to compare the case at hand to the facts of relevant precedent in application).

18. Most videoconferencing platforms like Zoom allow people to record sessions and download the resulting videos as MP4 files. Students can then upload those files to an assignment folder on your course page on your learning-management system, or they can email you the files.

If you only have one or two asynchronous students, you may consider having those students record themselves delivering individual arguments, and they can then upload the arguments for your evaluation. Be sure to provide feedback just as you would if the student were delivering the argument before you in real time.

## III. Coaching Teams for External Moot Court Competitions

Even in the absence of a pandemic, virtual oral argument competitions are likely to continue. They are less expensive to run, less expensive to attend, and less burdensome on students and coaches. Removing travel from the equation creates opportunities for students who otherwise might not be able to attend competitions, and schools may be able to stretch budgets further and provide opportunities in more subject-matter areas by adding virtual competitions to their rosters.

In determining whether to send a team to a virtual competition, you will weigh many of the same factors you do in considering whether to send a team to an in-person competition: (1) the quality and reputation of the competition, (2) the availability of a qualified coach with the time to prepare students appropriately, and (3) the match between the competition subject matter and your institution's particular areas of strength or focus. Cost should be less of a concern; thus far, virtual competitions have tended to be significantly more affordable than in-person competitions, offering reduced registration fees and eliminating travel expenses. And a few competitions have maintained normal registration fees but provide competitors with technical equipment like quality microphones and webcams in return.[19]

In assessing the quality of the virtual competition, you may wish to peruse the competition rules—most competitions post rules on the competition website—to evaluate likely proxies for the competition's level of preparation for virtual argument, such as how thorough those rules are, how well they provide for likely contingencies, and whether they adhere to best practices like those outlined in this chapter and in the guidance document developed by the National Association of Legal Advocacy Educators.[20] By the time this book is published, most competitions will already have run at least one competition virtually; queries on the various moot-court and legal-skills listservs should give you a good sense of how well those went.[21]

---

19. For example, the National Online Moot Court Competition, created by a consortium of law schools and designed from the outset to be a virtual competition, provides all competitors with a kit of technology to level the playing field. Kent Streseman, *Developments in the Law School Advocacy Community*, App. Advocacy Blog (July 29, 2020), https://lawprofessors.typepad.com/appellate_advocacy/2020/07/developments-in-the-law-school-advocacy-community.html.

20. *See* Guidance for Conducting Moot Court Competitions (2020–2021), https://drive.google.com/file/d/159dpAtBy-MjnN_QBOCltuz-QD5de4QMb/view.

21. *See* Legal Writing Inst., New Member Information Guide 7 (2018–2020), https://www.lwionline.org/sites/default/files/New%20Member%20Information%20Guide%202018-20.pdf.

## A. PREPARING TEAMS

The first key to preparing students for a virtual competition is setting and maintaining a positive tone and a focus on the key learning objectives. Moot court is fun, especially when it involves traveling with a group of colleagues who have become friends. And winning a moot court competition is even more fun. But ultimately, participating in moot court competitions should be an educational experience. Competitions provide opportunities not just to enhance oral-argument abilities but also to achieve other key learning objectives, like developing listening skills, forming professional identity, practicing professionalism, enhancing resilience, rehearsing nimble thinking, and building subject-matter knowledge.[22] Students (and the coach) may be disappointed to be participating in a virtual competition rather than an in-person one, so it is important to emphasize—and exploit—the potential advantages of virtual competition.

In preparing students for competition, you should conduct all but one or two practices under simulated competition conditions. Just as with in-person competitions, for all but the very earliest practices, you should invite outside lawyers to serve as mock judges to ask questions during the argument and provide feedback, and students should present their arguments under timed conditions and just as they plan to do at the actual competition. For virtual competitions, simulating competition conditions also means holding all practices online—even if conditions otherwise permit you to meet in person—using the videoconferencing platform the competition itself uses and following any protocols dictated by the competition rules.

Before teams begin formal practices, you should dedicate at least one session to preliminary matters:

- Review competition rules regarding how oral arguments will be conducted, including any guidelines regarding team members communicating with one another during rounds. Plan to adhere to those rules in all practices.
- All team members should test their microphones and webcams, and teams should troubleshoot any technical issues.
- If the competition rules and any other applicable conditions permit team members to participate in the competition from the same location, like a courtroom or classroom at the law school, discuss whether you wish to do so. Whichever mode you choose, you should conduct all future practices in that mode. On the one hand, having the teams participate from the same location on campus better simulates the in-person competition experience. If the competition requires advocates to present from a standing position, this may be easier in a classroom or courtroom, where you may have access to a podium and to convenient locations to set up the camera and microphone at appropriate heights and distances. It may be easier to insure access to competent IT support on campus. Teams may

22. James Dimitri et al., The Moot Court Advisor's Handbook (2016).

have better control over outside distractions. And having a team member in the same room during argument can provide helpful moral support. On the other hand, eliminating the need to travel to campus may reduce stress and make the advocates more comfortable, and advocates may actually have more control over interruptions and outside distractions at home than they do at the law school.

Online practices present many advantages, not least of which is the opportunity to cast your net wider in recruiting practice judges. Alumni, including former team members, who practice in different cities and even different states can join practices from their homes or offices. Faculty with subject-matter expertise may be more willing to serve as judges if they can do so from home instead of remaining on or returning to campus. You can tap into your entire network of professional colleagues to build a roster of practice judges who can thoroughly prepare your students for the competition experience.

As you would for an in-person competition, you should provide judges with materials to help them prepare to ask questions and provide meaningful feedback. Those materials may include the competition problems, team briefs, a team-created bench memo, prepared questions, and even a video reviewing the key facts and authorities. With a virtual competition, because your judges are unlikely to have experience with judging or participating in a moot-court competition online, you also should provide the judges some written tips. To the extent that you know the guidelines the competition itself will provide judges, share those guidelines with your judges. At minimum, you should provide the judges tips regarding assessing students in the online context. For example:

- Because online communication is not instantaneous, judges should be more forgiving if a competitor does not immediately stop talking when a judge begins asking a question. Judges should also understand that technology glitches may elongate pauses or affect speech cadence.
- Competitors who maintain good eye contact are looking at the webcam rather than the judges' onscreen images and thus may miss physical cues like opened mouths or raised hands. Judges should incorporate some filler language at the beginning of questions (such as "counsel, I have a question for you") to permit the advocate time to pause and listen to the substance of the question.[23]
- Like competitors, judges should speak more slowly than they normally would to ensure that advocates can understand questions.

Online practices also make it easier to record practices for focused coaching. Instead of grappling with cameras and tripods, you can simply hit "record" once the formal portion of practice begins. Coaches and judges can provide oral feedback at the end of the practice, just as they would with in-person practices, but coaches can also

23. Guidance for Conducting Moot Court Competitions (2020–2021), *supra* note 20.

review the recordings afterward to identify and analyze both examples of excellence and opportunities for improvement. Schedule regular individual meetings with team members to review those examples and opportunities.

Participating in a moot court competition presents the opportunity to enjoy one of the most satisfying aspects of law practice: building a bond with a group of people dedicating their talents to success in a shared endeavor. Because building this bond may be more challenging online, coaches must be deliberate in creating opportunities. In planning practices, budget time at each practice for chitchat, either before or after your outside judges join you. Similarly, in your individual debriefing meetings, allot time at the beginning and end to touch base with team members about their wellbeing, their classes, and any personal challenges. To the extent that time permits, schedule non-practice times to gather online. Consider holding an online viewing party where you watch and discuss videos of previous final rounds of the competition, if the competition makes those available, or selected oral arguments from other competitions or similar appellate arguments; you can find many such videos on YouTube and elsewhere. As the competition date nears, perhaps hold one or two "happy hour" or "coffee break" gatherings online.

### B. COACHING TEAMS AT COMPETITION

Once the virtual competition begins, the coach serves as cheerleader, moral support, and educator. To the extent the competition rules permit, coaches should attend all team meetings and oral arguments.[24] Use online conferencing—rather than phone calls or texting—for a brief pep-talk and any final questions before arguments and to debrief arguments and discuss judge feedback after each round. The coach can put judge comments in context and help the students determine which feedback is useful and how and whether to implement it in future rounds, and often it is helpful to be able to see the student's physical demeanor—and for the student to see yours—to ensure open, effective communication. And teams should build in time to celebrate successes and commiserate over frustrations.

## IV. Conclusion

Oral argument is an essential component of law school, and it can add variety and even fun to the classroom. Since some form of online law practice is here to stay, legal educators should incorporate some form of virtual oral argument into the curriculum, even in an in-person class. With planning and thoughtful effort, professors and coaches can use the virtual oral argument experience to train students to be effective advocates in both the in-person and the online setting.

---

24. National Online Moot Court rules allow coaches to be in virtual courtroom, muted, with video off. NATIONAL ONLINE MOOT COURT COMPETITION 2021 RULES 5.016, https://drive.google.com/file/d/122MjQR0HgFzLm-WfbBWtgRhTEgrt873n/view.

THIRTY

# Backward Design: Course Design for Online Simulation Classes

Christine Church*

After reviewing this chapter, readers will be able to use backward design techniques to create a simulation course as evidenced by:

- Drafting learning outcomes focused on fundamental skills;
- Creating assessments for each learning objective, both formative assessments for introductory skill levels and summative assessment demonstrating competency;
- Creating assessments that provide evidence of compliance with ABA Standard 304(a) on simulation classes;
- Designing learning activities to support each learning outcome (fundamental skill) maximizing student engagement, whether in the classroom, in the virtual classroom, or in a hybrid environment; and
- Creating additional learning resources for supplemental learning to support each learning outcome, whether in the classroom, in the virtual classroom, or in a hybrid environment.

Designing a course should always begin with the end of the course in mind, by defining the students' learning goals or objectives.[1] The instructional design/assessment mantra goes like this: "*at the end of this unit/course, students will be able to* [fill in the blank with the learning objective] *as evidenced by* [fill in the blank with the assessment that demonstrates mastery of the objective]."

---

* Tenured professor, Western Michigan University, Thomas M. Cooley Law School. Professor Church began teaching law in 2006 and began teaching online skills classes in 2015. She has designed and taught synchronous online courses and hybrid courses, and created asynchronous learning materials used for classroom, online and hybrid law school courses.

1. For a discussion of using backward design for different modalities of course delivery, see Chapter 8: *From Ground to Cloud and Back Again: Modern Tactics to Improve Your Teaching* by Katherine Brem.

For too long, legal education has focused on a different mantra: "*But I taught them* [the learning objective]—*so they obviously learned it*." Adopting a backward design focus demands proof. It shifts from an observation ("*But I taught it*") to the key question ("*Did they learn it?*") As professors teaching lawyering skills, we want proof positive that our students have mastered the art and the disciplines we teach.

Additionally, our accreditors demand clear student learning outcomes in our syllabus and want to see clearly identified formative and summative assessments tied to each learning outcome as our evidence that the students mastered the learning outcomes. This is the culture of outcome-based education—including using data-driven decisions to make improvements in our courses based upon the premise "*what did they learn?*"

Backward design means starting with the end in mind, with a focus on what students will be able to do at the end of the course. For each learning outcome, we develop formative and summative assessments to provide evidence of mastery. Finally, we articulate the learning activities and student resources that facilitate student learning. This chapter focuses on backward design for simulation courses.

Begin by creating a course map. This map can be created using the table feature in Word or as an Excel spreadsheet. Excel gives you more space to write without worrying whether your table fits on a printed 8.5 x 11 page. For simulation courses, the map will have five columns, as shown in the table below.

| Unit Outcomes<br>*...at the end of this course, students will be able to* | Assessments<br>*...as evidenced by ...* | Standard 304 | Learning Activities | Learning Resources |
|---|---|---|---|---|

By completing this course design map, we create simulation courses designed to facilitate learning professional skills with clear evidence that students mastered the course learning outcomes. In the process, the map provides concrete proof that the simulation course meets the requirements of ABA Standard 304 to count as experiential learning credits.[2]

This method can be used for any simulation course, whether taught in-person, online, or using blended (hybrid) learning. This chapter suggests online tools to demonstrate student mastery of learning objectives for simulation classes. To illustrate the method, this chapter takes you step-by-step through the process of designing an online trial advocacy course.

---

2. A.B.A. Sec. Leg. Educ. & Admis. to the Bar, *Standards and Rules of Procedure for Approval of Law Schools*, Standard 311(e) (2020–21), https://www.americanbar.org/content/dam/aba/administrative/legal_education_and_admissions_to_the_bar/standards/2020-2021/2020-21-aba-standards-and-rules-for-approval-of-law-schools.pdf [hereinafter 2020 ABA Standards].

## I. Start by Drafting Unit Outcomes

Think of a "unit" as a particular learning outcome. It might be a topic that takes one week to cover. It might be a topic that stretches over several weeks to fully cover. Sometimes, there could be more than one unit covered in a week. But this is a learning outcome that every student in your course should be able to master by the end of the course. For simulation courses, the question of units typically boils down to mastery of the fundamental professional skills developed in the course.[3] Learning outcomes for mastery of professional skills must include integration of the "doctrine, theory, skills, and legal ethics" that underlie the professional skill under ABA Standard 304(a) and (b).[4]

Chasing perfection in drafting the perfect learning outcome bogs down the process. Drafting effective learning outcomes typically requires choosing the right verb to demonstrate the level of learning (or higher order thinking skills), using Bloom's taxonomy.[5] The task can be daunting, and you can easily get bogged down in drafting. To avoid being sidetracked, begin by drafting learning outcomes "off-the-cuff." Professors know the outcomes they intend to teach, so begin by listing those topics in the grid. Perfect them after choosing assessments and completing the overall course design.

Typically, the unit outcomes for trial advocacy follow the chronology of a trial and the typical Table of Contents in a trial advocacy textbook. Notice that the topics are general, leaving perfection of the learning outcome using the right verb to a later step in the process.

| Unit Outcomes<br>*... at the end of this course, students will be able to* | Assessment<br>*... as evidenced by ...* | Standard 304 | Learning Activities | Learning Resources |
|---|---|---|---|---|
| Opening Statements | | | | |
| Direct Exams | | | | |
| Cross Exams | | | | |
| Closing Arguments | | | | |

3. ABA Standard 302(b) defines professional skills as "Legal analysis and reasoning, legal research, problem-solving, and written and oral communication in the legal context." Standard 302(d) includes the catch-all "Other professional skills needed for competent and ethical participation as a member of the legal profession." Interpretation 302-1 defines other professional skills as "interviewing, counseling, negotiation, fact development and analysis, trial practice, document drafting, conflict resolution, organization and management of legal work, collaboration, cultural competency, and self-evaluation."

4. 2020 ABA Standards, *supra* note 2, Standard 304.

5. To explore more about Bloom's Taxonomy in the context of teaching skills, see Paul D. Callister, *Time to Blossom: An Inquiry into Bloom's Taxonomy as a Hierarchy and Means for Teaching Legal Research Skills*, 2 LAW LIBR. J. 191 (2010).

After reviewing these basic fundamentals, I added *Storytelling and Theme*, *Making Objections*, *Laying Foundations*, and *Trial Notebooks* to the list.

By looking at the full list, the chronology of the class changed. Once I list the basic course objectives, I can arrange the chronology of the course to increase student learning. If I had simply followed the Table of Contents in the accompanying textbook, I would not have thought about unfolding trial advocacy concepts in the most effective chronology for teaching. After all, a good litigator always starts by creating a closing argument—incorporating necessary elements, theme, and evidence and creating a blueprint for the trial. Why begin with *Opening Statements*?

For my class, *Storytelling and Theme* came first, after introducing the fact pattern and jury instructions identifying the necessary elements and defenses. The second unit, *Closing Arguments* reinforced the lessons taught in the storytelling and theme unit, and students learned to weave the law and the facts to create a blueprint for the trial. Students learn to ask, "How will I best tell the story?" while including the evidence (testimony and exhibits) needed to blend the law and the facts to persuade.

The third unit became clear. All litigators must think about the evidence—how to prove each necessary piece. What evidentiary issues could we encounter? Trial Skills is a perfect medium for application and reinforcement of evidence concepts. We must not limit the evidence review to objections in the courtroom but require students to explore how to prove a point with admissible evidence.

As I explored the chronology of the course, the order of the unit outcomes changed considerably:

| Unit Outcomes<br>*...at the end of this course, students will be able to* | Assessments<br>*...as evidenced by ...* | Standard 304 | Learning Activities | Learning Resources |
|---|---|---|---|---|
| Storytelling and Theme | | | | |
| Closing Arguments | | | | |
| Marshalling Your Proof | | | | |
| Direct Exams | | | | |
| Cross Exams | | | | |
| Opening Statements | | | | |
| Evidence: Authentication | | | | |
| Evidence: Admissibility | | | | |

By using backward design, I could clearly see the flow of the learning outcomes to better facilitate student learning. After working through the trial blueprint (*Storytelling and Theme, Closing Arguments)* and the evidence (*Marshalling your Proof)*, building a direct examination makes much more sense. After practicing *Direct Examinations* in class, *Cross Examination* follows neatly. Once students constructed the trial blueprint, crafted direct exams, built outlines for cross exams, and thought about possible exhibits—then creating *Opening Statements* followed naturally. Finally, we work through evidence units on introducing exhibits and objecting to exhibits based on *Authentication* (laying required foundations) and *Admissibility* of evidence (testimonial and exhibits). The students are ready to demonstrate mastery of these fundamentals.

## II. Evidence of Mastery

Step Two creates both formative and summative assessments as evidence that students have mastered each learning outcome.

How do students demonstrate that they have mastered the learning objective? Two distinct types of assessments help a professor determine mastery. Formative assessments help the student understand what they know and what they do not know, while informing the professor about areas where students display confusion or struggle. Formative assessments help students improve their learning, and help professors understand student problem areas needing further instruction. Comprehensive summative assessments demonstrate that students have mastered the learning objective at the end of the course.[6] Most simulation courses plan summative performance opportunities at the end of the course to demonstrate student mastery of the professional skill. In my trial advocacy course, students complete at least two complete jury trials in the final quarter of the course.

In simulation classes, professors rarely rely on tests or quizzes to assess student learning. ABA Standard 304 requires multiple opportunities for performance in simulation classes.[7] Students engage in class exercises and performance of the skill. Other types of formative assessments, particularly in online classes, include answering discussion board questions after reviewing materials (particularly performance videos), or self-reflections on a student's strengths or weaknesses to increase metacognition regarding mastery of the skill.

---

6. Thus demonstrating compliance with ABA Standard 314: "A law school shall utilize both formative and summative assessment methods in its curriculum to measure and improve student learning and provide meaningful feedback to students." 2020 ABA Standards, *supra* note 2, Standard 314.

7. *Id.* 304(a)(3).

When designing a course, pay particular attention to when a learning objective is introduced, when it is reinforced, and differentiation in the mastery of the skill expected. What assessment or performance opportunity demonstrates whether each student understands and has begun developing mastery of the fundamentals?

The online environment creates unique opportunities for formative assessments. For example, after introducing the theory, practice, and legal ethics involved in a direct examination, my students paired up in breakout sessions to work on a direct examination. Some students complained that they were not ready—they wanted more time to work on their direct exam before performing. But formative assessment stretches students out of their comfort zone and asks them to demonstrate developing competencies (not mastery) of the skill. Each student performed a direct examination as their partner role-played the witness and they recorded a video. Then they switched roles. Both students were online. They watched their video after the class and completed a self-assessment using a standardized rubric. I also watched each video and gave each student individualized feedback using the same rubric. The student could compare their self-assessment with my assessment. The videos could be shared with other students for possible objections or for feedback from peers. After watching the student videos, I could see that my students needed help breaking up a big overarching question into smaller bites. Without watching these formative assessments, I could have simply assumed—"I taught it, so they learned it." As a result, the next week included additional exercises on step-by-step narratives to better tell the story in a direct examination.

As learning objectives are reinforced, student mastery of the skills should increase. After completing the first attempt at a direct examination, students turned in a written outline of their direct, and received professor feedback. The following week students performed the direct examination again during the class on cross examination. After watching the direct examination, the class discussed the cross examination of the witness—what evidence must be elicited from the witness in cross and what weaknesses in the direct testimony could be exploited. Each student turned in a bulleted outline for a cross examination. The next week, the class entered breakout groups where the students practiced the direct examination of the same witness (with improvements) and others would attempt the cross examination. These small groups were recorded for review. And, of course, the summative assessment demonstrating mastery of direct examination are the video trials near the end of the semester.

The course map begins to fill out. Not only can you see where each student's beginning performance is assessed, but you can also see opportunities to reinforce learning as evidenced by subsequent performances. Summative assessment then occurs through external reviewers, bringing in lawyers or judges through video conferencing to act as the judge in the trial and to provide feedback to students utilizing a class rubric. The completed course map documents compliance with ABA Standard 304.

| Unit Outcomes<br>*...at the end of this course, students will be able to* | Assessments<br>*...as evidenced by...* | Standard 304<br>• *Multiple opportunities for performance;*<br>• *Self-assessment;*<br>• *Faculty feedback.* | Learning Activities | Learning Resources |
|---|---|---|---|---|
| Direct Exams | • Introduction: class exercise in crafting open ended questions.<br>• Reinforcement: recording direct exams in pairs<br>• Drafting outline of direct exam<br>• Reinforcement: direct exams followed by cross<br>• Reinforcement: three full trials | • Peer review and faculty feedback on class exercise.<br>• Self-assessment and faculty assessment using rubric<br>• Faculty feedback on outlines<br>• Peer assessment, self-assessment, faculty feedback.<br>• External assessment (lawyer/judge) at trial using rubric and providing feedback. | | |

Once you add the methods of assessment to the course map, it is time to rewrite the learning outcome. Using the chart of verbs and higher orders of thinking in Bloom's Taxonomy,[8] the learning objective changes from "*Direct Exams*" to "At the end of this unit, students will be able to construct and perform effective direct examinations, using open ended questions." The verbs "construct" and "perform" connect with the highest order of Bloom's Taxonomy, as students combine knowledge, skills and legal ethics to create an effective direct examination.

The completed course map for the online trial advocacy class, showing all detailed learning objectives and the formative and summative assessments used throughout the course is found at the end of this chapter.

---

8. *See* Patricia Armstrong, *Bloom's Taxonomy*, Vanderbilt University, https://cft.vanderbilt.edu/guides-sub-pages/blooms-taxonomy/ (last visited Jan. 25. 2021); Nelson Miller, Teaching Law: A Framework for Instructional Mastery 99–107 (2010).

## III. Learning Activities and Learning Resources

These last two steps are the easiest. After finetuning the learning outcomes and the assessments that evidence student mastery of the outcome, thinking about learning activities in the classroom (virtual or physical) comes naturally. Identify how each learning outcome will be introduced, and where each outcome is reinforced, and fill in the learning activities planned to teach these concepts.

In an online simulation class, technology provides a number of tools to create learning activities to integrate the "doctrine, theory, skills, and legal ethics"[9] underlying the professional skill.

- *Slide Decks.* Traditional teaching or lectures using presentation technology to keep students oriented to a topic can be effective in online learning. Create planned opportunities for engaging *every* student in the material presented. Student attention span is much shorter in a virtual classroom than in a physical classroom. Plan a question after every four or five slides, asking the entire class for an answer. Require every student to respond using either the chat feature, or a polling feature.
- *Videos demonstrating performance.* The professor can create a video demonstrating excellence in performance of the lawyering skill or engage colleagues to create a video. Students can record videos demonstrating their performance of the skill.[10] The professor chooses one or more effective videos for teaching. The video may be required viewing prior to class with discussion board questions to follow.[11] The video can be shown during class, pausing at key points to illustrate or engage the class in discussion.[12] Students could be required to watch the video demonstration after class, and identify key points included in the lecture. Videos can include classic movie clips—either as examples of excellence or those with obvious mistakes.[13]
- *Breakout rooms* with fact patterns for practice. Assign roles (performer, role player), including the role of being an observer who will give feedback to the

9. 2020 ABA Standards, *supra* note 2, 304(a)(1).

10. Students should record their own performance to identify their strengths and weaknesses. Professors might play excellent demonstrations of the skills. Do not play videos to demonstrate poor performance to the entire class, as this causes embarrassment and anxiety for all students in the class.

11. For example, professors record a direct examination, followed by an excellent cross examination incorporating the key skills being taught. Students identify excellent illustrations of closed ended questions, or where the professor demonstrated taking small bites with short succinct questions. If your school uses Canvas for your Learning Management System, students can pause the video and create comments visible to the professor.

12. For example, the professor teaches about the ethics of closing arguments, incorporating Rule 3.3 Candor Toward the Tribunal and Rule 3.4 Fairness to Opposing Party and Counsel. Then the professor plays a video where the professor demonstrates what NOT to do as an illustration.

13. There are many great movie clips to demonstrate trial work. A personal favorite are clips from *Anatomy of a Murder* (1959).

performers based upon a rubric. Roles should rotate. Some breakout room technology permits recording, increasing student accountability during the breakout session and allowing the professor to provide individualized feedback after the class.

- *Fishbowl demonstrations* before the entire class in the virtual classroom. A fishbowl demonstration requires two roles: 1) active participants in a discussion by asking questions, giving feedback and comments, and 2) observers standing "outside" the fishbowl listening carefully to the ideas being presented. A performer demonstrates the skill at the center of the fishbowl. In a classroom, the active participants form a circle around the performer. The observers form a second circle. In an online environment, the active participants turn their videos on. The observers turn their videos off.[14]
- *Debriefing* after performance, emphasizing the primary learning objectives. The debriefing can occur during the classroom or could also be one-on-one virtual meetings with students. Debriefing includes individualized feedback and student self-assessment and reflection on performance.

Student resources include materials students must review prior to class for class preparation or following the class for review. List each item provided to students for each learning objective. Examples of student resources include reading material, video material, audio recordings, websites, etc. Do not worry over which activity belongs in which category.[15]

The following is an example of the completed course map for the direct examination outcome:

14. *See Teaching Strategies—Fishbowl*, Facing History & Ourselves, https://www.facinghistory.org/resource-library/teaching-strategies/fishbowl (last visited Jan. 25, 2021).

15. Generally, learning activities take place in the classroom, whether virtual or physical. Student resources are materials shared with students before or after class.

| Unit Outcomes<br>*...at the end of this course, students will be able to* | Assessments<br>*...as evidenced by...* | Standard 304<br>• *Multiple opportunities for performance;*<br>• *Self-assessment;*<br>• *Faculty feedback.* | Learning Activities<br>*Integrating doctrine, theory and ethics underlying the professional skill* | Learning Resources |
|---|---|---|---|---|
| *At the end of this unit, students will be able to* construct and perform effective direct examinations, using open ended questions. | • *Introduction:* class exercise in crafting open ended questions<br>• *Introduction*: rubric for effective direct exam<br>• *Reinforcement*: recording direct exams in pairs<br>• Drafting outline of direct exam<br>• *Reinforcement*: direct exams followed by cross<br>• *Reinforcement*: three full trials | • Peer review and faculty feedback on class exercise.<br>• Self-assessment and faculty assessment using rubric<br>• Faculty feedback on outlines using rubric<br>• Peer assessment, self-assessment, faculty feedback using rubric.<br>• External assessment (lawyer/judge) at trial using rubric and providing feedback. | ✓ Lecture on direct examinations, emphasizing open ended questions.<br>✓ Class exercise reframing leading question into open ended question.<br>✓ Breakout groups in pairs, recording direct exam.<br>✓ Class debrief<br>✓ 2nd attempt at direct exam in following week after feedback (with class debrief)<br>✓ 3rd attempt at direct exam in following week after feedback (with class debrief) | **BEFORE CLASS**<br>*Read* chapter 6 on direct exams.<br>*Read* unit learning outcome<br>*Watch* YouTube videos (links provided on LMS)<br>*Answer* discussion board questions about video<br>**AFTER CLASS**<br>*Review* copy of PowerPoint presentation<br>*Watch* Recordings of student video with professor feedback.<br>*Reflect* on your own video identifying strengths and weaknesses |

Once each cell of the course map is filled in, the course design is complete. Determine which weeks of the semester the class will be covering each unit outcome, and build the class, week-by-week. If your institution uses a Learning Management System, the course map provides a complete course blueprint for each class and for the materials to post to the course page. Remember to post the unit learning outcomes to the Learning Management System for transparency with students.

## IV. Conclusion

Once your course map is complete, share your learning outcomes with your students at the beginning of each unit. Consider creating rubrics that identify what a "developing" skill looks like, what a "progressing" skill looks like, what "competence" looks like, and what "exemplary" looks like. Remember that your goal is for all of your students to reach "competence." Transparency about outcomes and competent performance is essential.

As experiential learning professors, backward design creates a game-plan to build "practice-ready" lawyers. Our role in the class shifts from lecturer to coach. The backwards design method identifies the performance skills and the level of performance expected at the end of the course. Every student possesses the tools to self-assess their competence in each fundamental skill. Most importantly, the professor has evidence to demonstrate competence (or exemplary performance) in these fundamentals for each student and has a framework for continuous improvement in teaching.

| Unit Outcomes<br>*…at the end of this course, students will be able to* | Assessments<br>*…as evidenced by…* | Standard 304<br>• *Multiple opportunities for performance;*<br>• *Self-assessment;*<br>• *Faculty feedback.* | Learning Activities<br>*Integrating doctrine, theory and ethics underlying the professional skill* | Learning Resources |
|---|---|---|---|---|
| Craft and present their client's **story** throughout a trial showing a strong connecting **theme**. | • *Introduction*: class exercise in talking with a classmate and telling their story<br>• *Introduction*: first outline of closing argument from storytelling point of view<br>• *Introduction*: telling the story to a high school student.<br>• *Reinforcement*: Continued work on closing argument and opening statement to tell the story.<br>• *Reinforcement*: performing at least one opening statement and one closing argument in the two jury trials. | • Students reflect on how effective their storytelling is after first draft of closing argument.<br>• Students reflect what they learned from telling the story to a high school student.<br>• Student self-assesses the connection between opening statement and closing argument and the strength of their theme.<br>• Faculty feedback on first classroom exercise.<br>• Faculty feedback in writing on first outline of closing argument.<br>• Faculty feedback and external reviewer feedback on storytelling and theme in two jury trials. | ✓ Lecture<br>✓ Storytelling exercise<br>✓ Storytelling fishbowl<br>✓ Working through fact pattern for story and theme. | *Read* chapter 1 on storytelling and theme<br>*Read* unit learning outcome<br>*Read* Fiction 101: a Primer for Lawyers on How to Use Fiction Writing Techniques, 32 Rutgers L.J. 459 (2001).<br>*Watch* Videos on storytelling for lawyers.<br>*Answer* discussion board questions about video<br>*Preview* Storytelling slide deck on LMS |

| | | | | |
|---|---|---|---|---|
| Construct and perform effective **closing arguments** that weave the law and the facts, and that create a blueprint for the trial. | • *Introduction*: Draft outline of first closing argument.<br>• *Introduction*: Rewrite after feedback.<br>• *Reinforcement*: Upload written planned closing argument to LMS.<br>• *Reinforcement*: Perform closing argument.<br>• *Reinforcement*: Upload revised closing argument after trial reflecting changes made based upon trial testimony and evidence presented | • Student reflection on final closing argument and changes made.<br>• Faculty feedback on outline of first closing.<br>• Faculty feedback and external reviewer feedback on closing argument in at least one of two jury trials | ✓ Lecture<br>✓ Working through jury instructions and creating blueprint for trials.<br>✓ Breakout groups working on closing arguments followed by group discussion<br>✓ Movie clip of effective closing argument. | *Read* chapter 8 on closing arguments<br>*Read* unit learning outcome<br>*Watch* Videos on closing arguments.<br>Video on professionalism<br>*Preview-Review* Closing argument slide deck on LMS |
| Construct and perform effective **direct examinations**, using open ended questions. | • *Introduction*: class exercise in crafting open ended questions<br>• *Reinforcement*: recording direct exams in pairs<br>• *Reinforcement*: Drafting outline of direct exam<br>• *Reinforcement*: direct exams followed by cross<br>• *Reinforcement*: three full trials | • Peer review and faculty feedback on class exercise.<br>• Self-assessment and faculty assessment using rubric for effective direct exam<br>• Faculty feedback on outlines using rubric<br>• Peer assessment, self-assessment, faculty feedback using rubric.<br>• External assessment (lawyer/judge) at trial using rubric and providing feedback. | ✓ Lecture on direct examinations, emphasizing open ended questions.<br>✓ Class exercise reframing leading question into open ended question.<br>✓ Breakout groups in pairs, recording direct exam.<br>✓ Class debrief<br>✓ 2nd attempt at direct exam in following week after feedback (with class debrief)<br>✓ 3rd attempt at direct exam in following week after feedback (with class debrief) | BEFORE CLASS<br>*Read* chapter 2 on direct exams.<br>*Read* unit learning outcome<br>*Watch* videos on direct exams<br>*Answer* discussion board questions about video<br>*Preview-Review* slide deck on direct exams on LMS<br>*Watch* Recordings of student video with professor feedback. |

Continued

Continued

| Unit Outcomes | Assessments | Standard 304. | Learning Activities | Learning Resources |
|---|---|---|---|---|
| Construct and perform effective **cross examinations**, using tightly constructed closed ended questions. | • *Introduction*: class exercise in crafting closed ended questions<br>• *Reinforcement*: Practicing cross exams in front of class.<br>• *Reinforcement*: Drafting outline of cross exam<br>• *Reinforcement*: practicing cross exams for trials.<br>• *Reinforcement*: performing at least one cross exam in three full trials | • Peer review and faculty feedback on class exercise.<br>• Self-assessment and faculty assessment using rubric for effective cross exam<br>• Faculty feedback on outline of cross<br>• Peer assessment, self-assessment, faculty feedback using rubric.<br>• External assessment (lawyer/judge) at trial using rubric and providing feedback. | ✓ Lecture on cross examinations, emphasizing tight, controlled closed ended questions.<br>✓ Class exercise creating cross exam questions<br>✓ Breakout groups in pairs, recording.<br>✓ Class debrief<br>✓ 2nd attempt at cross exam in following week after feedback (with class debrief) | *Read* chapter 7 on direct exams.<br>*Read* unit learning outcome<br>*Read* Written materials on cross exams.<br>*Watch* Videos on cross exams. |
| Construct and perform an effective opening statement, demonstrating story and theme, and previewing the evidence. | • *Introduction*: class exercise on crafting effective opening statement<br>• *Introduction*: Drafting outline of expected evidence.<br>• *Reinforcement*: Drafting outline of opening statement<br>• *Reinforcement*: practicing opening statements for trials.<br>• *Reinforcement:* performing at least one opening statement in three full trials | • Student reflection on final opening statement and changes made during term.<br>• Faculty feedback on outline of opening statement<br>• Faculty feedback on practice of opening statement.<br>• Faculty feedback and external reviewer feedback on opening statements in at least one of two jury trials. | ✓ Lecture<br>✓ Working through how to weave expected testimony into opening statement.<br>✓ Connecting story and theme in opening statement<br>✓ Breakout groups working on opening statements followed by group discussion<br>✓ Video clip of effective opening statements | *Read* chapter 2 on opening statements<br>*Read* unit learning outcome<br>*Watch* Videos on opening statements<br>*Watch* Video on professionalism<br>*Preview-Review* Opening statement slide deck on LMS |

| | | | | |
|---|---|---|---|---|
| Lay proper foundations for photos, documents, diagrams, and tangible items of evidence and demonstrate the proper procedure for admitting the item into evidence. | • *Introduction*: Class exercises in laying proper foundations<br>• *Reinforcement*: performance – laying foundations for specific trial exhibits.<br>• *Reinforcement*: Objecting when a step is missed<br>• *Reinforcement*: Each student will lay a foundation for at least one item to be entered into evidence at jury trials. | • Peer review and faculty feedback on class exercise.<br>• Self-assessment and faculty assessment using foundations doc<br>• Peer assessment, self-assessment, faculty feedback on objections<br>• External assessment (lawyer/judge) at trial using rubric and providing feedback. | ✓ Lecture on basic foundations for typical trial exhibits and authentication issues<br>✓ Class exercises in laying foundations.<br>✓ Fishbowl on laying foundations and objections<br>✓ Practice on laying foundations with trial exhibits | *Read* basic foundations.<br>*Read* Evidence at a Glance<br>*Read* unit learning outcome<br>*Watch* Videos on laying foundations<br>*Preview-Review* Foundations and objections slide deck on LMS |
| Apply the Federal Rules of Evidence in a courtroom setting, both in submitting evidence and objecting to evidence. | • *Introduction*: Go through closing arguments and identify evidentiary issues<br>• *Introduction*: draft motions in limine<br>• *Introduction*: class exercises on hearsay, character, and relevance<br>• *Reinforcement*: identifying type of objections during direct exam and cross exam practice.<br>• *Reinforcement*: performing as trial lawyer in three trials. | • Faculty feedback on motions in limine<br>• Peer review and faculty feedback on class exercise.<br>• Self-assessment and faculty assessment on objections<br>• External assessment (lawyer/judge) at trial using rubric and providing feedback. | ✓ Lecture on types of objections during trials<br>✓ Class exercises in identifying, planning for, and responding to evidentiary issues | *Read* Evidence at a Glance<br>*Read* Evidence Flow Chart<br>*Read* unit learning outcome<br>*Watch* Videos on working with evidence, admissibility and objections |

*Continued*

*Continued*

| Unit Outcomes | Assessments | Standard 304. | Learning Activities | Learning Resources |
|---|---|---|---|---|
| Create a trial notebook for use during a trial. | • *Introduction*: draft outlines for each part of the trial notebook as the class covers that part (opening, direct, cross, closing, motions in limine)<br>• *Reinforcement*: create trial notebook for final trial. Use during trial | • Faculty feedback on trial notebook with emphasis on ethical issues.<br>• Student reflection on use of trial notebook during trial. | ✓ Lesson on parts of a trial notebook and how to construct. | Sample trial notebooks |

THIRTY-ONE

# Strategies for Remote Clinical Supervision

Emma Sokoloff-Rubin*

After reviewing this chapter, readers will be able to:

- Summarize the benefits of a clear structure for delivering assignments and feedback in a remote clinic;
- Draft clinic policies that enable clinic supervisors to provide this clarity;
- Identify concrete ways to foster mentorship relationships between students and between students and supervisors who don't see each other regularly in person;
- Identify concrete ways to foster strong relationships between students when some or all are learning remotely; and
- Consider how many remote social events will enhance the clinical community without provoking Zoom fatigue.

The clinic I co-teach is by design a cross-country partnership. The students and I are based at Yale Law School in New Haven, and we partner with the San Francisco City Attorney's Office to litigate cutting-edge public interest cases. Because of the distance, we have found creative ways for students to build relationships with their supervisors, produce strong work product, and receive meaningful feedback with phone, video, and email as the primary means of communication. These strategies served us well during the COVID-19 pandemic and are also applicable to clinics and externship programs looking to strengthen partnerships between students and supervisors who are not based in the same place.[1]

* Clinical fellow and lecturer in law, Yale Law School. Professor Sokoloff-Rubin is in her second year as clinical fellow and oversaw her clinic's transition to online-only during the Spring of 2020 and then to a hybrid format for the 2020–2021 academic year.

1. Students in the San Francisco Affirmative Litigation Project—SFALP for short—work directly with deputy city attorneys through every stage of the litigation process, from dreaming up new lawsuits to filing complaints, from motions practice to appeals. The clinic's assignments are wide-ranging and fast-paced, and the attorneys rely on the students to produce top-notch work. The program has become a model for

## I. Clarity Is Key

Clarity surrounding expectations for students and supervisors matters more than ever for a clinic operating remotely. Clear policies and expectations free students and supervisors alike to focus their energy on the substance of the collaboration—the relationships and the cases. In short, a well-organized clinic allows us to focus on the work. It also means that when things are not working, when phone calls are awkward, or a memo misses the mark, we have a clear sense of what we have been doing and can better pinpoint areas that need change.

Of course, what works for us will not work for all clinics. Because we partner with in-house counsel,[2] we do not need to navigate remote client interactions to the degree that many direct services clinics do. Likewise, we do not face the unique responsibilities and tight deadlines that come with being an individual client's only attorney. But like any clinic, and like many externship and internship programs, we aim to teach through practice and produce meaningful work. Strong relationships between students and supervisors are at the heart of what makes that possible. Below, I describe structures and policies that work when students and supervisors cannot be in the same room.

### A. WORKING GROUP CALLS ARE SACRED

Each semester, students are divided into working groups based on their interests, with each group focusing on one case or issue area. One group is always devoted to developing new case ideas. There are usually two to four students in a group, with two supervising deputy city attorneys. Most groups have an hour-long call every other week, and the group decides whether to use phone or video. Whenever possible, a recurring call time is set far in advance. This time is precious, and, barring emergencies, students and attorneys are expected to attend each one. This consistency would be important even if the meetings were in person, but it is particularly essential when students and supervisors do not have the ability to connect informally in a clinic office or the halls of the law school and answer questions or just touch base. Students and supervisors alike also communicate something important by showing up consistently for working group calls: That they are committed to the project and value each others' time. Of course, some cases and projects will call for more frequent, last-minute meetings, but it still makes sense to have a recurring call time as a baseline.

---

other city attorneys' offices and law schools, with many of SFALP's cases making national news. I spent two years in SFALP as a student, and now I help run the clinic alongside Dean Heather Gerken, who founded it in 2006. I bring the perspective of both student and teacher, and I've seen what works and what doesn't from both sides. I also get to build on the hard work of the many clinical fellows who came before me and developed many of the strategies I describe here. For a discussion of setting up a blended externship program, see Chapter 33: *Blended Learning Externships* by Leanne Fuith and Denise Roy.

2. The San Francisco City Attorney's Office, tasked with representing the city and county of San Francisco.

## B. CLARIFYING ASSIGNMENTS IN WRITING LEADS TO BETTER STUDENT WORK

After each working group call, students are expected to send a follow-up email within twenty-four hours summarizing their assignment to make sure everyone is on the same page. This allows supervisors to intervene early if the summary does not reflect the assignment they envisioned. Sometimes what the student heard is different from what the supervisor said, but just as often, students' efforts to summarize their understanding of the assignment help supervisors clarify for themselves and for the students what they had in mind. The back-and-forth might clarify, for example, whether the supervisors envisioned a persuasive memo or a more neutral analysis of a potential claim; whether they wanted a formal memo or a bulleted list of key findings; whether they are interested in persuasive authority or just looking for binding precedent on a particular issue.

We also encourage students to call and email their supervisors with questions as they work rather than waiting until the next working group call. It usually takes some prodding to get students to let go of concerns about bothering their supervisors and realize that the attorneys enjoy hearing from them and that asking questions allows the students to produce better work. We enlist returning clinic students to emphasize that the supervisors really want to hear from students and that students can simply pick up the phone and call a supervisor when a question arises. If that does not work, the next step is to send an email and arrange a time to talk.

## C. MENTORSHIP REQUIRES INTENTION

We look for attorneys who are eager to get to know law students and who see mentorship as part of what they are giving in exchange for having students collectively spend thousands of hours per semester helping to litigate and develop cases.[3] Crucially, the deputies have the support of *their* supervisors, who recognize the time spent mentoring students as an essential part of the office's work.[4]

Our usual practice is to have several of the supervising deputy city attorneys come each semester to co-teach one of our seminar meetings. Topics vary widely, from "the ethics of negotiating settlement agreements" to "movement lawyering inside and outside government." These classes give students the opportunity learn from the attorneys outside of case-specific supervision and to create a natural opportunity to build and deepen mentorship relationships. In addition to teaching a class when they are on campus, we ask the visiting deputies to hold open office hours with students

3. We work with the Chief of the Complex and Affirmative Litigation team at the San Francisco City Attorney's Office to select as supervisors the deputy city attorneys who are most invested in getting to know the students and mentor them.

4. Special thanks are due to City Attorney Dennis Herrera, who has supported the partnership from the start, along with Ron Flynn, Senior Chief Deputy City attorney, Yvonne Meré, Chief of the Complex and Affirmative Litigation team, and the many deputies who have supervised students over the years.

during the day and join students for pizza after class. Over time, students have the opportunity to meet most of the attorneys who directly supervise them and to build relationships with attorneys staffed on different cases.

Going forward, I expect that we will resume in-person visits when it is safe to do so, but also permit supervising attorneys who are not able to travel to join remotely. While this is not a perfect substitute for a lively in-person visit, our experience has shown that students can still build strong relationships with supervisors they never get to meet in person. This also opens the door to inviting multiple guests to one class, which might otherwise not have been logistically or financially feasible. For example, we might invite a panel of past clinical fellows to join a class by Zoom to share their varied experiences working in and around local government. While we have found that students are generally less likely to sign up for one-on-one office hours with seminar guests over Zoom than in person, there may be other ways to help students engage with virtual seminar guests.[5] A more attractive alternative may be small-group discussions with attorneys focused on particular topics—underrepresented perspectives in the legal field, experiences in private versus public lawyering, etc.—rather than open-ended one-on-one conversations.

Mentoring *between* students is also central to our clinic's work. At the start of each semester, we pair new clinic students with returning students for one-on-one conversations. When clinic application season rolls around, we encourage prospective students to reach out to students already in the clinic to learn more about the workload and clinic structure. And students in their third or fourth semester in the clinic often volunteer to share specific expertise with newer students, such as strategies for attacking thorny questions around standing when proposing new case ideas. Students adjusted quickly to doing this remotely, via Zoom coffee dates or phone calls, perhaps in part because we have always recognized the time they spend on these conversations as an essential contribution to the clinic. We take care to highlight this mentoring work in our syllabus, in information sessions for prospective clinic applicants, and during clinic meetings.

This approach has a practical effect—busy students are more likely to make time for mentoring when they feel that the clinic values it—and also communicates an important lesson about law practice: building relationships and talking about cases and ideas counts as work and is part of what we are doing together. It's all part of lawyering and learning. Clear avenues for mentorship between students also allow students in different working groups to get to know each other outside the confines of the clinic seminar. There are usually between two and four students in each working group, so two students can easily go several semesters without working

5. We tried remote office hours with one of our guests during our first hybrid semester, Fall 2020, and only two students signed up as opposed to the usual seven-to-ten. Students had already spent so much time on Zoom that more time online was a hard sell, no matter how amazing the guest. This reluctance to attend online office hours may be different in a semester in which students are able to attend in-person classes.

together directly. Often, mentorship relationships develop naturally between newer and more experienced students in a working group, but the buddy system and the other structures we have in place for mentorship help students build relationships across working groups as well.

While our emphasis on mentorship between students pre-dated the COVID-19 pandemic, it proved particularly important to maintaining a strong clinic community when students were dispersed around the country. Programs in which students are learning remotely, or learning in person but working on different case teams or at different externship sites, could use similar strategies to build and maintain a strong sense of community.

## D. STUDENTS BENEFIT FROM A CLEAR STRUCTURE AND TIMELINE FOR FEEDBACK

In most cases, students are required to submit memos forty-eight hours in advance of their working group call to allow supervisors time to read their memos thoroughly before the call. This deadline is particularly important given the time difference and the many constraints on supervisors' time, from other case deadlines to childcare responsibilities. The period between memo submission and the working group call also gives students time to read their teammates' work. Prior to the COVID-19 pandemic, students often read each others' work, but doing so was not a formal policy or expectation. We realized that with students calling in to their working group calls from their homes, rather than congregating in the clinic work room to call their supervisors together, they were less likely to have informal conversations about their research before and after the call. So we added to the syllabus an expectation that students read their teammates' work prior to each working group call.

In addition to providing oral feedback during working group calls, supervising attorneys automatically redline one of the first two assignments that students complete for a working group. Supervising attorneys will decide which assignment to redline unless students reach out with a preference. The redlines get emailed directly (and only) to the individual student and to me, the clinical fellow. We call this the "quick edit," designed to bolster the substantive feedback that attorneys regularly give students and provide an opportunity for students to remedy relevant legal writing or research issues early in the semester.

We ask supervising attorneys to make edits in track changes. This helps ensure that the feedback is concrete and specific, based on the text on the page rather than only general impressions. Quick edits are usually both stylistic and substantive. As an example of a stylistic edit, one supervisor noted in a comment that "active voice is usually better than passive, except when you're deliberately trying to distance the actor from the activity (e.g., 'mistakes were made')." Later in the same document, the supervisor provided guidance on when to capitalize "court." In a different quick edit, a supervisor flagged a part of the memo that was missing a transition. "Think about including a transition sentence here to link with the rest of the brief," the supervisor wrote. "Something like: 'Other courts have reached similar conclusions to the Ninth Circuit's.'"[6]

When supervisors send students their quick edits, they usually include in the email a high-level summary of the edits. The following examples show the types of edits made as well as how supervisors framed them, often by identifying one of the student's strengths as well as areas for improvement:

- "Overall, you did a great job identifying some potential hearsay exceptions, but I think the memo could have been stronger if you'd matched the facts to the law more and analyzed whether the exceptions applied for our materials."
- "I thought that you found really great case law, but the initial discussion kind of buried that. I would keep your audience in mind when writing. Generally, a litigation memo is not going to rely on academic articles, except for in discussing more abstract or theoretical concepts which are unaddressed by the case law. So I would lead with the cases, even if you found them through academic sources."
- "My edits are mainly stylistic.... For instance, I made a few changes to tighten up sentences that I thought were perfectly clear but could be shorter. We're often dealing with word limits in briefs, so it's good to get used to saying things with fewer words when possible."
- "A recurring problem for me was your combining two conclusions in a single paragraph—leaving it unclear what circumstances would support which conclusion. I appreciate that the analysis whether each of the materials you considered could be entitled to immunity depends on facts that you did not have. Under these circumstances, it might be best not to begin by stating a final conclusion, but rather to posit the conclusion whether immunity applies as being dependent upon factors one through XX, and then go on to discuss the impact that each of the factors has on the immunity question."

In addition to the quick edit, each student is entitled to one "deep edit" per semester. This is a more in-depth edit that students initiate by reaching out to a super-

6. Another common theme is comments reminding students to lead with their main conclusions rather than burying them at the end of the memo. "This section probably could have been a little shorter and more streamlined to provide the top-line take-away first," one supervisor wrote. "This reads like it was written as you researched it, starting with the statutes. Usually it's helpful to have more of the topline analysis upfront." Another supervisor recommended that the student provide "some kind of indication of context/question presented," in the summary section of her memo. In addition to flagging the need for context, the supervisor provided an example of what this might look like: "for example, 'You asked me to think about ways to respond to arguments by [redacted] that the trial court did not properly consider certain evidence or arguments because the court's order allegedly did not discuss them . . .' or something like that. It's often helpful to include that context, especially when we look back on these memos further in time from when they were initially assigned." Supervisors also raise case-specific questions and identify gaps in students' legal analysis.

visor. The supervisor provides written feedback on one piece of work product, often including suggestions for further student research and written work, and schedules a one-on-one call with the student to discuss the edits. When I was a student in the clinic, the feedback I got through the deep edit marked a turning point in my legal writing. At that point I was often using large block quotes from cases, with minimal introduction. Rather than picking out the most salient quote, framing it, and incorporating the quote into the paragraph, I was setting it aside as a block quote far more often than was warranted. As the attorney told me during our one-on-one call, she was able to get the information she needed from my memos, so flagging my over-use of block quotes wasn't a top priority on working group calls. She may also have been hesitant to highlight a flaw in my writing in front of my clinic teammates, who were already strong legal writers. The deep edit invited her to step back and help me think about how to improve my writing. Now that students and supervisors alike are so familiar with Zoom and screen sharing, these deep edit conversations might be served by having the pair review the edits together in real-time via screen share.

Feedback also needs to go the other way, from student to supervisor. We do not yet have a formal mechanism for this, but we encourage students to come to me or their supervisors with any suggestions or concerns. We select supervisors who are thoughtful about pedagogy and open to feedback. Among many benefits, this gives students the opportunity to practice "managing up" with supervisors who are open minded and eager to create a positive learning environment.

## II. Building Clinic Community Without Regular, In-Person Contact Is an Ongoing Challenge

I do not mean to paint an overly rosy picture of remote supervision or suggest that we have it all figured out. Until the pandemic hit, Dean Heather Gerken, the students, and I were together in New Haven and saw a lot of each other on a regular basis. Even during the spring of 2020, we had a couple of months of normalcy before the world seemed to change overnight. We worked with our student directors to host a community dinner and happy hours, organize small group conversations, and encourage informal collaboration and conversation in the clinic workroom. The Fall 2020 semester was the first one that started without our usual community touchstones. The clinic seminar and social events are in some ways separate from the "fieldwork" component that is supervised remotely. But the strength of students' relationships with each other and with Heather and me is part of what makes it work to have their legal supervisors so far away.

If anything, it felt more important coming into the Fall 2020 and Spring 2021 semesters that the students get to know each other, in order for the work to go smoothly and to combat the loneliness social isolation brings. In her application to serve as student director, a leadership position in the clinic, one student wrote in December 2020 that "[t]he clinic has also given me a deep sense of community, one that I have come to hold especially close during these past 8–9 months.... In an environment where it is easy to become fixated on individual achievements and one's own professional future, SFALP repeatedly encourages us to take a moment to connect, reflect, and then engage."

Among many benefits of a strong community, students who feel connected to each other are more likely to bounce ideas off each other without worrying about being judged, run memos by each other, and approach me together when something is not working. I often coach pairs or small groups of students on strategies for reaching out to their supervisors. That is an important professional skill and one that takes courage to learn. When students have strong relationships with their teammates and can discuss concerns with each other first, they are more likely to raise them with me rather than simply muscle through. And the concerns they raise often allow them to produce better work. For example, in one group working on a particularly fast-paced and wildly complex case related to the gig economy, students felt that they did not have a strong grasp of the bigger-picture strategies into which their assignments fit. I arranged an optional hourlong call with their supervisors, who were happy to give them additional context and have a broader discussion about the case. I would not have known students were craving more background if they had not brought it to my attention.

There have also been times when an individual student needed some time off from clinic for health or other reasons. Often they first come to me for help on the urging of a clinic teammate. This proved to be more common during the pandemic but is not limited to pandemic-related challenges. We try to make clear from the start that we see students as people, not just producers of work product. We encourage them to come to us as soon as they are struggling or anticipate needing an extension, rather than trying to drag themselves to the finish line or disappearing without notice. When we know, we can help. This might mean connecting the student with resources and filling the gap in their working group by "borrowing" a student from another group or asking for volunteers to take on an ad-hoc assignment.

Bottom line, a strong sense of clinic community serves students on many levels, and allows them collectively to produce strong work. Here are three ways we use seminar and virtual social events to help build community.

### A. REGULAR SEMINARS HELP BUILD CLINIC COHESION

Each fall, SFALP offers an ethics seminar that explores the unique obstacles confronting municipal lawyers. The seminar has always served to build a sense of cohesive clinic community so that students aren't totally siloed in their working groups. This fall, regularity was particularly important for building a sense of community. It gave us a regular touchpoint, a time and place to connect. The seminar was required for the ten new clinic students, and all but one of the ten returning students opted in as well. We used a blended format: The seminar met four times in total, with six online-only classes, and four concurrent classes. For the concurrent classes,[7] Heather taught in person, I joined via Zoom, and the deputy city attorneys we invited to guest lecture Zoomed in from San Francisco. About half of our students attended in person and the others via Zoom.

The concurrent classes were tricky at first, particularly with one instructor in person and the other online. Heather and I made on-the-fly decisions out loud that ordinarily might have required no more than a glance or brief aside around the seminar table. Should we take the break now, or wait? Pose a question for everyone to answer round-robin style, or continue building the queue based on hands raised? But the awkwardness was worth it. Just seeing everyone's faces on the screen was a reminder that we were all in this together, working on cases and thinking about similar practical and theoretical questions despite the distance. In addition to the rich substantive discussions we have always had during seminar, we took care to build into seminar some of the more informal conversations that would usually happen before or after class or during chance encounters in the hallways.

## B. ICEBREAKERS ACTUALLY WORK

We intentionally built in a little more class time than was strictly required so we had time to start most classes with an icebreaker. Icebreakers helped us form informal bonds within the confines of online or hybrid learning. And they are effective throughout the semester, not just at the start. They helped build inside jokes, light-hearted banter, and a sense of knowing each other beyond purely academic interests. During the first class of the fall semester, we asked students to share their hometown and favorite food. Hometown quickly evolved into "places you claim," since many students have called multiple places home. Other icebreakers included "something that drives you crazy" (answers: humidity, people who wear masks below their noses, lukewarm iced coffee, and more), your favorite sports team or TV show, something that brings you comfort, and the most surprising job you've ever had.

Starting class with an icebreaker also helped students and instructors alike be a little less polished throughout the class. This allowed for more genuine engagement with the substantive questions we discussed, and more moments when students thought out loud and tried out new perspectives and ideas. My favorite icebreaker, borrowed from a colleague in a different clinic, was "your smallest problem today." The answers ranged from the serious to the hilarious, and the question itself was a way of acknowledging that small things get to us and have big impact even amid the much bigger problems facing us and our world. I was surprised, without having seen the students in person all semester, and never having met some of the new students at all, by how connected I felt to them and by the chemistry and connection

7. "Concurrent" is a general term often referred to as the specific iteration called "HyFlex." A concurrent class is one in which the professor simultaneously teaches students online and in the physical classroom.

among the whole group. This sense of community also made possible more serious conversations about what's happening in our country as it relates to clinic work, career goals, and more.

### C. LESS SEEMS TO BE MORE WHEN IT COMES TO VIRTUAL SOCIAL EVENTS

Our student directors—two veteran students selected to help steer the clinic—felt strongly going into the Fall 2020 semester that less is more when it comes to Zoom social events. They predicted that after spending so much time on Zoom for classes and extracurriculars, optional social events would start to feel draining even if the in-person equivalent would have been energizing. In pre-COVID times, the student directors and I hosted a couple of social events per month, everything from happy hours to pizza dinners to brown bag lunches with clinic alumni. This felt like the right number of in-person events, and most were optional. During Fall 2020, in contrast, we hosted only two large-group social events, a student-only welcome chat and a virtual cooking class led by our own Heather Gerken. Both were optional, but turnout was strong, and a number of roommates and significant others joined for the cooking class.

Some of the students based in New Haven were eager for safe in-person interactions. We encouraged them to get together outside (always in line with University policy), and the student directors held open office hours outdoors one day in October. Heather also facilitated three informal hour-long conversations about the future of local government law with interested students, two at the law school for local students and one over Zoom for students learning remotely. Finally, we held an end-of-semester celebration over Zoom using rotating breakout rooms to simulate the kind of small-group conversations that usually happen at our in-person celebration. Heather and I circulated among the groups. The event was on our syllabus from the start of the semester and all students were expected to attend. We leaned into the inevitable awkwardness of a Zoom party by acknowledging it from the start, so that we could all laugh about it together. The event provided a sense of closure that was missing the previous semester when we had skipped the end-of-semester celebration, unsure of how to provide a meaningful experience over Zoom. During Spring 2021, we continued to use the concurrent seminar model and experimented with a mix of small, socially-distant in-person gatherings and larger-group Zoom events, with about one of each per month.

## III. Conclusion

All of this is a work in progress, and we look forward to continuing to collaborate with and learn from clinicians across the country. In SFALP, we'll continue building on strategies we already used for remote supervision and finding new ways to build community without our usual in-person classes and clinic gatherings. Even when we can all safely gather around a crowded seminar table again, what we've learned will stick with us. By pushing us to be even more attuned to creating clear systems for feedback and mentorship, and to find new ways to build community, the circumstances brought on by COVID-19 are making us more creative and flexible teachers and practitioners. They have certainly heightened the desire we share with our students to use law to protect vulnerable consumers, promote civil rights, and create lasting change.

THIRTY-TWO

# I Want to Hold Your Hand: Better Clinics Through Technology and Student-Driven Innovation

Melina A. Healey*

After reviewing this chapter, readers will be able to:

- Craft enriching simulations and role plays to duplicate the challenges posed by remote client representations;
- Harness technology to bring interdisciplinary approaches and collaboration with experts into the classroom and case work;
- Use remote platforms to provide clinic experiences to students who might not otherwise be able to participate, and to provide legal services to client communities with no alternative access to legal services; and
- Identify moments in representation where in-person experience is indispensable.

On a chilly night in March of 2020 I left my husband behind in a COVID war zone. I packed our car full of toys and diapers and stuffed our kids into their car seats. We drove off as he waved in the moonlight.

I was gone from Ross and our home for much longer than we imagined. Ross, a resident physician, became one of his hospital's "COVID Warriors," toiling long hours in the ballooning COVID-ICU in our nation's first coronavirus hotspot. Our children and I were taken in by brave friends and family all over the East Coast. Our odyssey lasted for five months.

* Director of Clinic Programs and Assistant Clinical Professor, Touro College, Jacob D. Fuchsberg Law Center. Professor Healey has been teaching clinics since 2014, and her clinic courses have ranged from partially to fully remote in case work and instruction.

During those months away I, along with so many others all over the world, had cause to reflect on, and to grieve, the sudden loss of in-person experiences and connections we had taken for granted in all aspects of our lives. In those early weeks, when transmission of the novel coronavirus was acutely mysterious, my family spent only one heartbreaking weekend with Ross but "social distancing" from him. I will never forget the anguish of my 3-year-old, desperate to hug her father who scrupulously maintained a 6-foot distance.

My clinic work and teaching became physically isolated too. For many months, my students, our clients, and I did not see one another in person. My colleagues in the clinical program that I direct did not see each other, their students, or their clients. We had messy virtual mediations and awkward court hearings and garbled conversations. Meanwhile, in heartbreaking contrast, Ross's work kept him in intimately close contact with those he served. He held patients' hands as they died, their loved ones tuned in to say goodbye forever via video chat because no hospital visitors were allowed.

The physical isolation of the pandemic underscored the sacred importance of physical touch and presence in our personal and working lives. But it also presented an opportunity to identify those aspects of legal education and lawyering that truly depend on in-person experience from those that can benefit from reimagining our methodology. In many ways, the forced conversion of legal representation and education to virtual platforms provided an occasion to address systemic inequities in our profession and to increase access to both learning and justice.

In this chapter, I share lessons from several years of partially remote client representation in clinics I have taught, as well as from my experience directing the abrupt conversion of the Touro Law Center Clinical Program from an intensively in-person law office to a temporarily fully remote program of instruction and legal services during the COVID pandemic. I lay out strategies to help clinics identify the kinds of instruction and legal representation that can improve with new technology and remote work, and those for which in-person presence is too valuable or simply indispensable to our obligations as lawyers and teachers ever to forego.

## I. Adopt a Clinic Mindset

I start most clinic work by developing devices to engage my students in working through the dilemmas and challenges posed by our lawyering and learning. "Nondirective" supervision is a foundational method in clinic pedagogy.[1] When done well,

1. It is beyond the scope of this Chapter, but nondirective supervision methods should not lead the clinician to turn over the process entirely to students, allowing then to make and execute all decisions on case work. Careful modeling and opportunities for specific and thematic learning must be strategically presented. Ann Shalleck describes one such dynamic approach to supervision in *Clinical Contexts: Theory and Practice in Law and Supervision*, 21 N.Y.U. Rev. L. & Soc. Change 109, 178–182 (1994). See Serge A. Martinez, *Why are We Doing This? Cognitive Science and Nondirective Supervision in Clinical Teaching*, 26 Kan. J. L.& Pub. Pol'y 24 (2016), and Wallace J. Mlyniec, *Where to Begin? Training New Teachers in the Art*

the careful deployment of nondirective modes of supervision gives a student the personalized tools and habits she needs to be reflective about goal setting and strategic planning and to feel confident that she can be an effective professional.[2] The method also encourages students to bring fresh ideas and perspectives to our work and improves client representation. Students may come from the communities that the clinic serves, may share culture, race, age, or other common ground with clients, or may have had other relevant prior professional experiences from which to draw insights and propose creative approaches.[3] In the context of new technology and tools for communication, the relative youth and ease with technology of clinic students can be an advantage in identifying new modes for working with clients.[4] Student ideas may well run up against ethical and professional norms, of course, so they also provide opportunities to learn the professional rules and to engage with the norms.[5]

Clinics should create opportunities for clinic students to take the lead in adapting to new technology and updating the profession. Below are some ways to approach new technology and student-driven innovation in the three main areas of clinic work: seminar instruction, case rounds/supervision, and case work design.

## A. ENCOURAGE STUDENT INNOVATION THROUGH SIMULATION

Clinic seminar meetings should include robust simulation of lawyering challenges. Simulated activities are not bound by the time and opportunity constraints of actual client representation. They carry no risks other than to the student performers. Unlike real-life situations, they can be perfected to sequence and present the clinic's curricular "skills" learning goals. And they fill in the practice gaps that inevitably open up in real client representation. They are a critical component of experiential learning and work in perfect partnership with the learning from client representation.[6]

---

*of Clinical Pedagogy*, 18 CLINICAL L. REV. 505, 518 (2012), for more recent critique of a fully "nondirective" style of clinic learning.

2. Harriet Katz explores the educational benefits of various forms "collaboration" by students in client representation and "modelling" of good lawyering by supervisors in *Reconsidering Collaboration and Modeling: Enriching Clinical Pedagogy*, 41 GONZ. L. REV. 315 (2006).

3. While clinic students are usually beginners in law practice, they bring valuable insights to client representation even as they learn. Thus, in addition to students' work on cases and in simulation benefiting their own education, it also can benefit the client. For discussion of how these benefits come to light in "case rounds" clinic seminar session, see Susan Bryant & Elliott S. Milstein, *Rounds: A "Signature Pedagogy" for Clinical Education?*, 14 CLINICAL L. REV. 195, 210–11 (2007).

4. *See* Emily A. Vogels, *Millennials Stand Out for Their Technology Use, but Older Generations also Embrace Digital Life*, PEW RES. CTR. (Sep. 9, 2019), https://www.pewresearch.org/fact-tank/2019/09/09/us-generations-technology-use/.

5. I also encourage open conversations about how extensively we can challenge professional norms or perceived biases in the legal system while still fulfilling our obligations for zealous client-centered representation. Students often have brilliant ideas about navigating this.

6. For a brief overview on designing effective simulations within clinic seminar, see Susan Bryant & Elliot Milstein, *Planning and Teaching the Seminar Class, in* TRANSFORMING THE EDUCATION OF LAWYERS: THE THEORY AND PRACTICE OF CLINICAL PEDAGOGY 57, 77–80 (Susan Bryant et al. eds., 2014).

Drawing on the extensive experience clinical law teachers have in learning through simulation, the method can also help clinicians to explore newly emerging challenges in remote client representation and technology and to engage students in developing strategies to deal with these challenges. Below are some ideas for simulations involving virtual platforms or remote work:

### 1. Client interview simulations using videoconference software

In this exercise, students conduct simulated video conference client meetings with an actor playing a "client." The session is recorded for review and critique. The actor-client embodies many of the behaviors and responses that clinicians have found commonly challenging in video conference client meetings. So, for example, the client has difficulty accessing the link to gain entry into the session, she requires additional guidance with the technology set up (and reacts poorly to complicated instructions), or she shows up to the meeting grumpy. She might challenge the student's authority or display her discomfort by turning her camera to face the top of her head or the ceiling while talking. Family members may interrupt her during the meeting, compromising confidentiality requirements.

The students must face these challenges in role and then debrief their own and others' performances by reviewing the recordings. The critiques incorporate, among traditional metrics for client interviews, the quality of the student's instructions to clients for accessing the meeting and videoconference body language, tone, and professional presentation on screen. The exercise works well as a prerequisite to initial videoconference client meetings because it allows students to plan for these additional difficulties on top of the rapport building and other richly complex work of any client interview or meeting. I recommend incorporating a critique from the actor-client as well as peer and instructor critique.

### 2. Client text or social media message simulation

Clinics typically prohibit or strongly discourage students from texting or exchanging electronic messages with clients in non-email platforms. Despite these restrictions, clinic students often rely on text, SMS, or social media messaging, especially when working with lower-income clients that many clinics serve. Many clinic clients lack their own dedicated phone number or reliable internet access. Clients request or expect students to use texting for comfort, convenience, or out of necessity; for example, if they work or live in a crowded environment and cannot communicate confidentially because other people are present. Simulations can engage students in identifying a secure platform for communication that ensures confidentiality and continuity of representation after the clinic student leaves. The simulation can then give students a chance to practice using their chosen platform with a client and encourage students to meet client needs while maintaining ethical and professional behavior. Students also must consider how to communicate professionally in their written communication with clients while also ensuring that clients with varied ability levels and language barriers can understand.

In a "messaging" simulation, a student is presented with a simulated client who does not have a phone number or personal mobile device and insists on texting over an internet-based messaging system for routine communications, which she accesses on a friend's phone. The student must research whether the messaging app is a secure platform for client communications and has appropriate levels of encryption. The student then engages in a simulation of texting with the client, in which the client may misinterpret or take offense to the text, seek legal advice in text message form, or share important confidential information that they are not willing to disclose in person. Students must grapple with questions such as:

- How do I verify that the person I am messaging with is the client?
- Is my communication with the client being recorded?
- Might the client understand my words as legal advice in this context?
- Should I use informal language to mirror the client's communications?
- What about emojis?
- How do I deal with disclosures of alarming information when I cannot see the client with whom I am messaging?
- Given the risks of written text, what should I put into written form and what must be discussed by phone or in person?

## B. SIMULATION OF VIDEOCONFERENCE PROCEEDINGS

The Touro clinic program has a growing volume of virtual hearings and mediations; our approach to these events is preceded and informed by the simulations we have devised to prepare for a videoconference setting. Videoconference court proceedings are a rapidly emerging practice, and our students have contributed great insights into how to litigate and negotiate effectively while on videoconference. Many of these insights were developed through simulation. Clinic programs that have to handle videoconference hearings, conferences, and trials should prepare students for this work, and for their future work as attorneys, by designing robust simulations that situate them in the challenges of videoconference representation. A clinic's academic setting is a good laboratory for novel methods.[7]

When planning for an online trial or hearing simulation, students should make explicit preparations relevant to the virtual format. The simulation should encourage students to consider questions in advance:

---

7. For additional coverage of online advocacy skills, see Chapter 29: *Training Effective Virtual Oral Advocates* by Susie Salmon.

- How will you structure your presentations or arguments in order to account for videoconference fatigue?[8]
- How will you maintain virtual "eye contact"?[9]
- How will you "read" reactions in your audience?
- How will you present exhibits and other demonstrative evidence on the screen?
- What will you do to account for the possibility that opposing counsel has easy but improper access to witnesses through virtual messaging platforms?
- What will you or a judge do if a witness appears to be impermissibly reading from something while testifying?
- If you cannot be in the same room as your client, how will you have instantaneous and confidential communications with them to check in on goals and strategy, or provide comfort and reassurance?
- What virtual or real background and attire are appropriate?
- How will you avoid distractions in your and others' environments?
- What feedback do you want from jurors or others judging a simulation?

### C. USE TECHNOLOGY'S REACH TO ENRICH CASE ROUNDS SESSIONS AND SEMINAR DISCUSSION

When clinic seminars are hosted on video platforms, clinicians have rich opportunities to bring in otherwise geographically distant or busy expert visitors to participate in clinic seminar classes and, even better, to consult with students in real time on case work. Guests are frequently deployed in clinic seminar as a tool for exposing students to diverse styles and professional voices or to people from client communities. These visitors may develop into resources for clinic case work or mentor clinic students.[10] In my own clinic, during our first pandemic semester, I hosted a tribal leader and a young tribal member from the Assiniboine and Sioux tribes to discuss case work that we had done together and to engage students in related simulations. The tribal guests reside on a remote reservation more than 2,000 miles away. Because they and the class members were all on the same shared videoconference, we occupied the same space and status in the conversation in a way that would have been impossible had the class members been in a traditional in-person seminar setting. For our trial simulations, I was able to bring in both local and national trial attorneys to consult

8. Liz Fosslien & Mollie West Duffy, *How to Combat Zoom Fatigue*, HARV. BUS. REV. (April 29, 2020), https://hbr.org/2020/04/how-to-combat-zoom-fatigue.

9. I encourage students to review footage of their favorite newscasters and video bloggers to think about how to perform with dynamism and style when addressing and audience on a screen.

10. *See* Stephen R. Miller, *Field Notes from Starting A Law School Clinic*, 20 CLINICAL L. REV. 137, 159 (2013); Janet Weinstein & Linda Morton, *Interdisciplinary Problem Solving Courses as a Context for Nurturing Intrinsic Values*, 13 CLINICAL L. REV. 839, 866–67 (2007).

and give feedback on our simulated hearings.[11] A word of caution, however: we should use "experts" intentionally and avoid spending too much clinic time with them rather than on planning and facilitating the critical dialogue that can only happen among students in the seminar.

Clinicians can also consider the use of videoconference class technology to join forces across distances and institutions for case rounds. Case rounds, a "signature"[12] clinic tool, are clinic discussions that focus on specific cases, projects, or themes that are current in a clinic's case work.[13] They are usually facilitated by faculty and ideally are driven by student exploration and peer insight. The clinic identifies a critical decision point or challenge in the work and discusses possible approaches to the "problem" and explores related ethical, professional, personal, or social justice issues. Case rounds enhance student presentation skills and capacity to effectively seek insight from colleagues. I also occasionally invite the interdisciplinary professionals whom I partner within my clinic to provide insights in case rounds, provided they are appropriately within our attorney-client privilege.[14]

Videoconference technology enables even more expansive approaches to case rounds. During the pandemic remote teaching, my clinic and a number of other education and juvenile law-related clinics across the country gathered for a series of inter-clinic case rounds by videoconference. Rather than focusing on individual clients (which of course we could not do for confidentiality reasons), we identified common themes, challenging aspects of representation in our field and social justice issues, and we engaged in collaborative dialogue. The conversation was rich and enlightening for all of us and, during a very isolating period of education, it connected us. Our clients were suffering acutely in many similar ways, and we shared strategies and renewed our commitment to social justice movements to seek systemic reform or revolution. Inter-clinic case rounds involving broader themes or challenges in legal work can mitigate the risks associated with overreliance on case rounds or hyper-focus on specific cases as a teaching tool in clinic.[15]

---

11. A fully remote synchronous videoconference classroom is the ideal setting for a guest speaker. It is far less engaging to invite guest speakers to occupy a screen when the remainder of the class is in-person. Challenges of the concurrent model specific to having some classroom participants in person while others access the classroom or discussion through videoconference, apply to an arrangement in which the students are in person, but a guest is on the screen. *See* Edward J. Maloney and Joshua Kim, *Fall Scenario #13: A HyFlex Model*, Inside Higher Ed (May 10, 2020), https://www.insidehighered.com/blogs/learning-innovation/fall-scenario-13-hyflex-model.

12. *See* Bryant & Milstein, *supra* note 3, at 214.

13. For an overview of case rounds and valuable strategies for implementing them, see generally Bryant & Milstein, *supra* note 6, at 113–50.

14. For example, my clinic collaborates with social workers and social work students and educators and education students, to give our young clients "holistic" services, and also to enrich the students' professional development and conversations about our approach to legal work.

15. The risks of failing to cover lawyering skills in a clinic due to overreliance on case-specific case rounds for training is explored by David A. Binder and Paul Bergman in *Taking Lawyering Skills Training Seriously*, 10 Clinical L. Rev. 191, 208–09 (2003). The authors analogize to case rounds in medical educa-

One word of caution: Inter-clinic case rounds among multiple clinics, or case rounds with invited experts or consultants from other disciplines, are valuable. But these sessions do not substitute for in-house clinic case rounds. The intimate setting of classic rounds, with only a clinic's students and supervising professor, facilitates important clinic community-building. These sessions elevate clinic student voices that might otherwise be drowned out by "experts" or other student communities from other schools. They also provide the safe insular space for the vulnerability necessary to make progress in learning and client work.

### D. SELECTIVE DEPLOYMENT OF TECHNOLOGY TO ENHANCE CLINIC CASE WORK

Clinics are not only critical to a law student's professional education, they also help to fill unmet needs for legal services in underserved communities and pursue important social justice missions.[16] There are significant advantages to integrating law school clinics into local communities, particularly those communities the clinic's clients are part of and those with which the clinic partners in seeking to make systemic change. A robust in-house clinic program can be a welcoming space where clients can receive holistic legal assistance in a variety of practice areas, a warm cup of coffee, and the resources of eager students and an academic institution, including the benefit of interdisciplinary partnerships.[17]

The importance and advantage of serving local communities is clear. But some communities in grave need are not near any law school. Remote or quasi-remote clinic work with these communities can sometimes provide both effective representation

---

tion: "Interestingly, the deficiencies that led medical school educators to take skills training more seriously echo those that exist with the case-centered approach to clinical legal education. For example, medical schools realized that their heavy reliance on the case rounds approach often: Failed to expose medical students to common but important medical problems. That is, as with clients in clinical legal settings, working with actual patients was often a hit-or-miss method of exposing medical students to a range of common problems." *Id.* Clinicians can address the limitations of case rounds by introducing simulation into clinic work and by taking care to guide students from the "specific" to the "general." *See* Bryant & Milstein, *supra* note 3, at 216 ("Teaching in rounds, like all clinical teaching, involves a series of judgments about how to get from the practical questions and descriptions that students often bring to the discussion to identifying, naming and developing theories that will inform not only particular questions but practice itself.").

16. *See* Phyllis Goldfarb, *Back to the Future of Clinical Legal Education*, 32 B.C.J.L. & Soc. Just. 279, 302 (2012).

17. My clinic values interdisciplinary partnership and inter-clinic collaboration in order to provide clients with holistic services. We have a social worker in my clinic as well as partnerships with health and education organizations, and often refer clients to our other in-house clinics for legal support. For guidance on "Multi Disciplinary Practice" or interdisciplinary collaboration models in clinics, see generally J. Michael Norwood & Alan Paterson, *Problem-Solving in A Multidisciplinary Environment? Must Ethics Get in the Way of Holistic Services?*, 9 Clinical L. Rev. 337 (2002). There are great benefits to education, client advocacy, and community activism when services are provided out of one in-person geographic space. For example, in addition to our in-house clinic program, at Touro we also host a well-established "Public Advocacy Center" that provides office space and resources to public interest organizations from the local community. *See William Randolph Hearst Public Advocacy Center*, Touro Law https://www.tourolaw.edu/StudentResources/william-randolph-hearst-public-advocacy-center.

and excellent learning opportunities. My own clinic work with students has involved representation of distant tribal nations and individuals and of people in faraway prisons, in which most of the work was accomplished using remote methods. Below is a set of criteria to help law teachers identify when and how to use remote technology to enrich student learning and to make possible access to justice for communities and people who have few other options.

1. Does the individual or group I propose to represent have access to viable local representation with whom they can have more regular in-person contact, and who might be more in tune with local dynamics, legal systems, and resources?

Clinicians should be open to and creative about leveraging technology to serve communities in dire need of legal services. For example, the tribal community that I have represented in my clinical work has no access to free or low-cost legal services of any kind within 500 miles of their community.[18] Additionally, local attorneys were unwilling to undertake the civil rights and racial justice work we did because of the risks of retaliation from both the white local community and the local legal system. It was clear that if a clinic would not represent them, no one would. But the challenges are significant when the lawyer is not present "in" a community. My students and I were not able to closely discern local shifting allegiances, politics, and attitudes within this small-town world. We could not address the spreading rumors about our work except by phone, videoconference (for those clients who had access), or written virtual messages. We were working across great geographic divides as well as across great cultural divides. This posed many powerful learning opportunities for all of us. And it helped us to appreciate more deeply the real value of having an attorney who engages directly, consistently, and in-person.[19]

2. How will I ensure that I have sufficient understanding of my remote client's life and world to provide competent representation?

A clinic that pursues remote or partially remote client representation or project work should use local partnerships and technology strategically to understand the clients' community and context. Clinics always do best in teaching and serving when collaborating with trusted community partners. But this is even more critical when the work is done across geographic and cultural distances. For example, when working with tribes, I engage tribal elders and community-based organizations and grassroots

18. *See* Annie Waldman & Erica Green, *'I Feel Invisible': Native Students Languish in Public Schools*, N.Y. Times (Dec. 28, 2018), https://www.nytimes.com/2018/12/28/us/native-american-education.html (describing how at Wolf Point High School in rural Montana, Native American students face the same neglect native students across the U.S. do as they navigate a school system that has failed American Indians).

19. Of course, clinics should only undertake representation in jurisdictions where the supervising attorney is authorized to practice law, or where the relevant student practice order which authorizes supervised representation of clients by law students covers the work.

groups and hold virtual meetings and "listening circles"[20] with these groups. I have my students develop plans for how to elicit these groups' voices.[21] We also spend time exploring the limits of our ability to fully understand another community and the ways our biases and assumptions may affect our conception of their needs and goals, their legal issues, our translation of their personal stories into legal frameworks, or our proposed strategies.[22]

Many clinical professors would surely agree that their students are more adept than the teachers at identifying social media and media platforms that may provide insight into a community. These platforms emerge and evolve constantly, and while social media profiles and postings and local news stories do not provide a complete or necessarily factually accurate portrait of an individual or community, they can reveal patterns and issues. They may also be places in which community members are more comfortable sharing opinions than they would be in person.

Knowledge of popular media and social media platforms in client communities also facilitates a clinic's online outreach and messaging work. My clinic has worked with individual and organizational clients to use local and national news outlets, as well as social media campaigns, to effect changes in discriminatory school systems when our legal strategies were limited.

### 3. How will I build trust and avoid misunderstandings in my videoconference meetings or written communications?

Written postal mail, email, text exchanges, and videoconferencing all risk miscommunication between client and attorney. An attorney sending a written text cannot view or respond to the client's reaction in real time. We cannot see the client's nonverbal expressions or hear their voice. We cannot immediately correct misunderstandings. A client may be reluctant or unable to handle a misunderstanding in either written form or by phone call. These kinds of problems arise with frustrating frequency, for example, with clients in prison, with whom the only reliable and confidential way to communicate between legal visits is via snail mail. Some young clients have difficulty reading; some elderly clients have difficulty using technology. Clinics must create strategies to deal with these challenges. The first step in ameliorating these

---

20. "Essentially about community, listening circles are entirely voluntary processes that allow each participating individual an opportunity to tell his or her personal story as a key element of community connectedness and conflict resolution. The circle is more than a mere hearing process; it is conceived of as a sacred space with power beyond the sum of the individuals." Alison Peck, *Identity-Based Conflicts in Public Policy: Hydraulic Fracturing in Pennsylvania*, 79 U. Pitt. L. Rev. 437, 476 (2018).

21. My clinic's strategy of elevation of client voices and collaboration for systemic change (or revolution) is also often discussed among clinicians in the context of "movement lawyering." Gerald P. Lopez's Rebellious Lawyering: One Chicano's Vision of Progressive Law Practice (1992), is seen as the foundational text for this vision of law practice.

22. Susan Bryant's *The Five Habits: Building Cross-Cultural Competence in Lawyers*, 8 Clinical L. Rev. 33, 34 (2001), provides an essential framework for clinicians working with law students to build cross-cultural awareness, empathy, and humility.

problems is to work with a client to explore the best forms of communication. Where possible, videoconference interactions should be used.

4. How can I use technology to provide enhanced services to clients and better educate more diverse groups of students?

There are advantages to the use of remote work technology for increasing access to justice. Before the COVID pandemic, our clinic program hosted weekly sessions at local libraries where community members with legal questions related to our clinic's area of expertise could obtain basic information, referrals, or advice and counsel, and, in some cases, engage the clinic for further representation. We have converted this community program onto a videoconference platform. This method allows more clinic students to work with clients in private settings using secure breakout rooms than was possible when we occupied the library, and allows more students to be supervised by a single clinic faculty member, who can circulate easily among the breakout rooms responding to questions.

Remote technology for client representation also increases access to clinical legal education for a wider population of law students. We can accommodate and train law students in clinics who otherwise had limited ability to participate in clinics, such as part-time students or those who have caregiver responsibilities.

5. What protections have I put into place to ensure secure and confidential communication and record keeping?

This is a critically important component of remote representation that clinicians must address and is beyond the scope of this chapter to explore fully. However, relevant considerations include: level of security in the clinic's digital file sharing system and student adherence to that system; integration of the file-sharing system with case management software to facilitate universal access to updates in cases and client documents; use of end-to-end encryption in videoconference software, chat, and messaging platforms; use of unique passwords; and waiting room functions for all clients for their videoconference meetings. Additionally, many universities require that remote classes be recorded, and access to those recordings is often open to several administrators. Clinics cannot avoid discussion of case work during class, so clinicians must seek a waiver from this policy or take care to turn off the recording when client information is being discussed.

6. When is it important for me to be there to hold my client's hand?

Despite the many advantages that new technology affords for increasing access to justice and the quality of representation, the COVID pandemic made clear that there are times when remote conversation cannot substitute for an in-person experience with a client. Clinicians must identify those key moments and be sure to provide them when possible, both for the benefit of their students and their clients.

I began my legal career working with child clients on education cases. I visited them at their homes, went with them to their schools, saw their classrooms, and met their teachers. This allowed me to understand the singular richness of their lives, their support systems, and some of the injustices they faced. It also demonstrated to them that I had a genuine interest in their life. I was their advocate, not a figure on a screen. I showed up for them.

In the midst of the pandemic my clinic continued to represent young people. Some clients have embraced videoconference and other technology, but often we have had difficulty forming viable connections with them on screens. We know that when children were assigned to attend schools remotely many simply did not show up. Our clients "ghosted" us too. I suspect that this was because our interactions were virtual. One clinic student was able to connect with a disappeared client. This student had himself struggled in high school and ultimately received a high school equivalency test. This experience helped the student connect with the client who had also dropped out of high school. The clinic student said, "I know what I need to do. I need to get into a room with this young man and walk him through this. He needs to see my face and know I am here for him." And through meeting in person with the client, the clinic student was able to resuscitate and prevail on his client's case in family court.

Clinicians spend a lot of time working with students to understand their clients in context. The students build empathy and commitment, learn how to communicate more effectively, and work to develop more client-centered strategies. Seeing a client's home, family, and community, allows students to more closely understand the client's lived experience and so enhances the quality of their lawyering.

One of the tribal elders I work with has said of her remote reservation in eastern Montana, "You have to experience this place to understand the injustice." She is right. The generous spread of plains give way to sacred badlands. The landscape stretches out endlessly under the bright glare of open and unrelenting skies. Small dusty homesteads and trailers dot the landscape. Horses and cattle huddle under scarce, scrubby cottonwood trees, escaping the sun in the summer, or hunched against the epic wind when the season turns. Tiny hardscrabble towns, half Native and half white, lean against the wind, brutalized by the harsh plains weather. Nearly every car carries spidery cracks through its windshield. One has to witness the visual majesty of this place, and its climactic extremes, to begin to understand the lived experience of people who occupy it, and to begin to decode the interactions among Native and non-Native people who share the space. The in-person experience of the landscape itself is important to the work my clinic has done with the tribes.

For my clinic students who have worked with clients in prison, the experience of visiting them in person has been equally significant to the students' education. Even in the sanitized context of a legal visit, students not only connect and communicate with their clients but also witness the relentless dehumanization of prison life. These visits are necessarily disturbing. But even small glimpses of life inside bring critical insights that helps us to understand how and why our clients' goals may be different than what we might otherwise expect. It also strengthens the students' commitment to undoing, either in individual representation or through systemic change strategies, the brutal system of mass incarceration.

## II. Conclusion

Increasing legal, instructional, and communication technologies hold genuine promise for clinic teaching and representation. Clinicians should be open to and should generate these ideas, particularly when informed by student innovation, while remaining committed to our most sacred professional obligations to maintain client-centered advocacy, keep client communications effective and confidential, and pursue social justice. There are many ways that technology's capacity for widespread access increases our profession's reach to clients in need and helps provide more equal opportunities for those of us in legal academia. As a junior faculty member with two young children, pre-pandemic I struggled to attend the conferences and faculty workshops that I wanted very badly to be a part of because of my caregiving obligations. Working remotely let me access this content and more through the wide deployment of videoconference technology. I was able to teach, meet with, and support my students who have similar obligations. But in the end, I remain mindful that to be there, in person, for my clients has been critical to my development as a lawyer and that it is my obligation to provide this opportunity to my students as well. Being creative about how to do this well sets out a new path for clinics to follow in order continue to innovate to improve legal education and provide needed and effective service.

THIRTY-THREE

# Blended Learning Externships

Leanne Fuith*
Denise Roy**

After reviewing this chapter, readers will be able to:

- Appreciate the unique importance of blended learning externships in meeting the diverse and specific needs, interests, educational goals, and career goals of students, many of whom may live significant distances from the law school;
- Understand the need for flexibility at many levels in developing and operating a blended learning externship program;
- Appreciate the value of integrating student advising, career planning, and employer and alumni relations in a blended learning externship program;
- Appreciate the need for and benefit of broad cross-departmental collaboration in designing and executing a blended learning externship program;
- Anticipate the ways in which technology will play a central role in organizing, approving, and supervising blended learning externships; and
- Identify and implement key components of a blended learning externship program that accomplishes the above objectives.

* Associate Professor and Dean of Career and Professional Development, Mitchell Hamline School of Law. Dean Fuith began law teaching in 2012 and has been designing and teaching synchronous, asynchronous, and blended courses since 2017. Dean Fuith helped lead the team that designed and launched the school's Blended Learning Externship program in 2017.

** Professor and Externship Director, Mitchell Hamline School of Law. Professor Roy began law teaching in 1992 and began teaching blended learning HyFlex courses in 2013. She has designed and taught blended learning courses involving various combinations of in-person, synchronous remote, and asynchronous remote instruction. Professor Roy helped lead the team that designed and launched the school's Blended Learning Externship program in 2017.

With technology that allows students to attend a law school wherever it may be located from wherever they may be located, students no longer need to move away from their communities or uproot their families to receive a legal education. Working law students can stay where they are—in the jobs on which they depend and in the communities where their children go to school. Perhaps most importantly, in rural parts of the United States, where legal representation is most sparsely distributed, members of those rural communities can now attend law school from home and remain as practicing lawyers serving the legal needs of their home communities. Making law school accessible to these students can be effectively accomplished by a blended learning JD program; that is, one that combines remote—ideally asynchronous remote—and in-person learning opportunities.[1]

This chapter describes the unique and flexible requirements of a blended learning externship program. The program that inspired this chapter was developed for law students who cannot or do not want to relocate to attend law school, usually because of work, family, or community ties. These students are likely to work full-time, in some cases leading businesses or other organizations. For most, the law may be a second or third career. They may also have significant additional obligations outside of work and law school such as raising children, caring for elders, and serving as leaders in their communities. The students live in nearly every state in the United States as well as internationally and most are not within commuting distance of the law school. The students represent both urban and rural parts of our country and a broad cross-section of our country's people, including communities of color, tribal nations, religious faiths, and communities of varying economic wealth and resources. The long-term professional interests of these students are as deeply varied as their geography and backgrounds.[2] The suggestions in this chapter are essential for a program that serves such students.[3]

A blended learning externship program that works for remote students also offers significant benefits for in-person students. Many in-person students also have work,

---

1. Mitchell Hamline School of Law was the first U.S. law school to offer an ABA-approved JD degree through a blended curriculum that made attending law school a possibility regardless of location. The class that entered in Fall 2020, with a total of 246 blended learning students, represents 42 states and 197 undergraduate institutions. First generation students make up 43 percent of the class. Students of color make up 24 percent of the class. The median age of students in the class was 35, and 102 of the students came to law school already holding other advanced degrees. Thirty students are in the military. Email from Anne Gemmell, Vice Pres. Enrollment, Mitchell Hamline L. Sch. to Leanne Fuith (December 31, 2020, 06:45 PM CST) (on file with Leanne Fuith).

2. Blended learning students make up more than half of the student body at Mitchell Hamline School of Law and the school's blended learning externship program has been popular among those students. In the first two semesters of the program, 76 blended learning students completed externships. Over the next three years, blended learning students completed externships at 704 sites in 46 states, plus the District of Columbia and several countries (including Canada, Germany, and Malta). This information comes from internal records of the school's Blended Learning and Externship programs on file with Denise Roy.

3. For additional discussion of blended experiential programs, see Chapter 31: *Strategies for Remote Clinical Supervision* by Emma Sokoloff-Rubin.

family, and community obligations that present challenges for structuring externships or they may commute long distances to attend classes on campus. With increasing access to online courses, a blended learning externship program could allow students to spend a semester or more away from the law school by combining local externships with online courses. Students spending summers experimenting with jobs in different communities far from the law school could earn externship credit while doing so. A student planning to relocate after graduation could transition to practice by spending a semester working full-time in their future home community. A blended learning externship program can meet the diverse needs of these students as well.[4]

## I. A Blended Learning Externship Program

A flexible blended learning externship program is critical to (1) making externships feasible alongside existing work obligations or financial needs, (2) arranging placements for students who may live far from any relevant externship site, and (3) allowing students to take full advantage of opportunities to use externships as a bridge to practice that may involve a new role with an existing employer or transitioning to leadership in a family law firm.

Students who are second and third-career professionals may also need to demonstrate to prospective employers the value of hiring someone with prior professional experience transferrable to legal work. They require externship placements in their home communities, where they can demonstrate those skills while simultaneously developing the professional connections that will be critical to their long-term success. The skills, interests, and needs of these students are both specialized and customized, and the process of developing externships for them may need to be entirely bespoke. A flexible blended learning externship program can enable these students to secure offers for post-graduation full-time employment from their externship sites, make connections that lead directly to post-graduation full-time work, or develop skills and expertise at their externships that advance them in their current professional roles.[5] Here are three examples:

Patti Buhl is a member of the Cherokee Nation who came to law school after serving twenty-five years in law enforcement, including twelve years as the first female

---

4. Because the structure of the blended learning externship program that inspired this chapter was intentionally designed to serve many students who live remotely from their law school and who, upon graduation, plan to transition into practice in their home communities, the discussion will continue to focus on the advantages for those students, but the principles discussed may also benefit law schools with working students and students who live or plan to relocate a significant distance from their law school.

5. In a recent survey of Mitchell Hamline School of Law blended learning externship alumni, 49 percent reported receiving a post-graduate job offer from an externship placement site. Another 22 percent reported receiving a post-graduate job offer from connections, skills, or references developed during an externship. The survey was sent to 234 blended learning students. Fifty-eight responded, of whom 50 were former externship students. This information comes from internal records of the school's Blended Learning and Externship programs on file with Denise Roy.

chief of police for a state university and as a Cherokee Nation Tribal Police officer. While a law student, Patti externed with the U.S. Attorney's Office for the Northern District of Oklahoma where she worked, which allowed her to gain valuable litigation experience and develop in-depth knowledge in new areas of law.

Similarly, Caleb Carr is the owner of a company that develops innovative hardware solutions for safety problems in aerospace, construction, and other dangerous industries—a business he founded after he watched a friend die when a helicopter was unable to use its hoisting system due to high winds. Caleb intends to use his law degree to further his legal expertise in the aeronautics industry and advance his business. While in law school, he externed on legal projects for his business and under the supervision of a private practice attorney who served as an advisor to Caleb's business.

Finally, Ruthann Deveraux-Gonzalez, a part-time law student and stay-at-home mom who homeschools her five children, sought out a remote externship with the National Association on Counsel for Children (NACC) in Chicago, Illinois, a national non-profit organization with staff in the Washington DC area, Denver, and Chicago. Ruthann worked as a paid extern for one semester and has continued in a paid position working remotely from her home.

To serve students such as these, Mitchell Hamline developed its blended learning externship program. The following is a step-by-step view of how a blended learning externship program may be organized and operated to meet the diverse goals and circumstances of students who live remotely from their law school, as well as students who attend school far from their destination communities, with features of this school's program used as illustration.

1. **Encourage early planning.** Because of their busy and complex lives, students in a blended learning program may need more encouragement and assistance than other students to plan for and take advantage of experiential learning opportunities. As early as their first semester, students should begin planning for externships to gain critical legal experience further along in their legal education. Students looking for externships far from the school's location, especially those in rural communities, may not have access to existing externships and may need to get started earlier identifying and securing placements.

In Mitchell Hamline's blended JD program, students may participate in externships beginning the summer after their first year of law school. Externships are prominently featured in curriculum advising materials and programming. Early in each term beginning in the spring semester of their first year, students are invited to consider developing an externship proposal for the following term. Students are provided information about externship goals and requirements, and a centralized email address makes it easy for students to get answers to their questions.

2. **Be open to flexible placement sites.** A blended learning externship program must be flexible, collaborative, and open to new ideas, beginning with supporting its students in setting up placements. Students can be proactive in lining up their own

placements. Schools should consider providing students with general guidance about how to seek a placement and supporting materials to help acquaint potential sites with the externship program.

Ideally, students should also have access to one-on-one support for finding placements such as by assigning every student to work with a career advisor when they matriculate. The career advisors become familiar with their students' individual career plans and professional needs. In Mitchell Hamline's Blended Learning Externship Program, students receive this support through the Career and Professional Development team as well as the Externship Program itself, the Blended Learning program, the Alumni Development team, and individual faculty members, who can suggest possible placements for students.

Flexibility in identifying placements may include allowing students to set up externships in their existing workplaces, in a family firm, or in a business the student owns. This may also involve working with students to establish supervision arrangements that avoid or mitigate the risks of having family members or subordinates involved with externship supervision and of having students externing at their place of employment. For instance, students externing at their own place of employment might work on matters in an area of law that is not part of their regular work responsibilities or work with an attorney supervisor who is not their regular work supervisor. They may also carve out specific hours that are devoted to externship work only. Students working for organizations in various non-legal departments may also set up externships within their employers' legal departments.

The ability to earn academic credit for paid externship work is critically important to giving students the flexibility to organize externships at existing workplaces and to fit externships into their crowded and varied schedules. For the most part, the same supervision requirements will be effective for both paid and unpaid externships but maintaining close contact between the school and paid externship site is particularly important. One way to do that is to require a synchronous (ideally in-person) meeting among the student, site supervisor, and faculty supervisor mid-way through the semester. Such a meeting is an opportunity to revisit and adjust externship learning goals and allows students to show off their workplace.

3. **Vet proposed externship sites.** Once students have secured placement commitments from sites, they should submit a proposal with preliminary information about the student's learning goals and field activities. At Mitchell Hamline, students submit an online proposal using a form developed by the Externship team in collaboration with the IT team.[6] The proposal aids in the process of vetting proposed sites as well as the maintenance of centralized and easily searchable data on externship placements. Students must submit the form by a deadline that allows sufficient time for the site

6. Students are in control of their own online proposal forms and only they can correct or update the forms if need be (a very intentional design choice!).

vetting process; how much time is needed will depend on the number of externship proposals and size of staff available to work on vetting. Requiring submission of an online proposal form is an efficient way to trigger the law school's externship vetting process and can initiate all the remaining steps in the process of organizing the externship, from vetting to enrollment to assignment of a faculty supervisor.

Career advisors or other staff who have JDs can conduct the initial vetting. Career advisors are copied on the automated emails confirming submission of an online proposal by their assigned students. The career advisor reviews the student's online proposal and contacts the potential site to discuss the proposed externship. The career advisor speaks with potential site supervisors about externship requirements, gathers information to ensure that supervision will meet the school's standards and ABA Standards, and discusses the student's preliminary learning goals and hopes for fieldwork activities with the site supervisor. During this conversation, the career advisor refers to the online vetting form which includes a checklist of items to review with potential site supervisors and comment fields for the career advisor to record plans for supervision, fieldwork activities, and access to resources. The online vetting form facilitates the conversation, provides a means of memorializing it, and identifies any necessary follow-up on-site supervisor questions.

With placements in multiple jurisdictions, one of the challenges is assisting sites and students with the varied state student practice rules. In the vetting process, site supervisors should be asked whether they would like more information about those rules. If requested, the law school can send the site supervisors links to and documents taken from appropriate state web sites. The law school does not need to purport to be an expert on student practice rules for every state, but it should provide students with certifications or other documentation needed to meet state student practice rules.

4. **Organize coursework and faculty supervision.** Once a site has been vetted and approved, the career advisor "locks" the online vetting form, which automatically sends an email notification to the student and alerts externship staff to enroll the student in an appropriate externship course. Students are assigned to faculty supervisors through the course, up to twelve students per supervisor.

Mitchell Hamline offers three remote asynchronous general externship courses. The courses may be taken in any order and are cleverly labeled the Spring, Summer, and Fall General Externship courses. Having multiple courses that can be taken in any order is an important flexibility to consider in designing a blended learning externship program. Even greater flexibility is needed to accommodate students' diverse summer schedules, so the summer course offers rolling start dates from the time the course opens in May through the end of June.[7] The school also added

7. Students are provided with tools to help them plan their summer externship coursework over whatever period they will be working at their externship sites, which typically ranges from ten weeks down to five. It is possible for students to work out longer or shorter externships depending on their needs.

three "independent" externship courses (Fall, Spring, Summer) that may be taken by students who have already completed the General Externship course for a particular term.[8]

The General Externship courses are monitored by a tenured faculty member, the externship director, but taught by a talented, dedicated, and diverse team of adjunct professors who are trained, supervised, and supported by the externship director. For the most part, adjunct faculty supervisors are generalists, but students in solo or very small firm placements are assigned to an adjunct faculty member who is passionate about mentoring students interested in solo practice. One of the adjunct professors serves as the lead instructor, and the externship director serves as a liaison between the teaching team and all other departments of the law school. This structure has been instrumental in developing a dedicated and enthusiastic adjunct faculty team that has been with the program from its beginning.

Each General Externship course is organized in five modules. The first and last are devoted to getting started and wrapping up the externship, and the middle three focus on a variety of skills and topics related to learning on the job. Each General Externship course (Fall, Spring, Summer) focuses on a different set of skills and topics so that the learning is new for students who take multiple externships during their law school experience. Students are assigned readings and learning exercises from *Learning from Practice*,[9] which allows students to purchase just the three to five chapters assigned each semester. Over the three General Externship courses, students work on developing and improving skills related to working effectively with supervisors, observation, reflection and journal writing, active listening, collaboration, cross-cultural communication and other relational skills, and writing. Students also address topics relating to professionalism and ethics, including professional identity formation and diversity, equity, and inclusion.

The coursework in each semester is different, but the learning activities are familiar to those who teach in the externship context, including:

- Planning for the Externship
  - ✓ Learning Goals
  - ✓ Field Activities
  - ✓ Site Supervision
  - ✓ Faculty Supervision

---

8. As an alternative, blended learning externship students are also invited to "remote in" to on-campus externship courses focused on specialty topics when the synchronous class meeting time fits with their schedules.

9. Learning from Practice: A Text for Experiential Legal Education (Leah Wortham et al. eds., 3d ed. 2016).

- Observations
- Reflective Writing
- Discussions with Site Supervisors
- Debriefing and Troubleshooting with Classmates
- Meetings with Faculty Supervisors
- Meetings with Site Supervisors
- Self-Evaluation
- Supervisor Evaluations

One of the challenges of an asynchronous online externship course is finding ways for students to work with each other when their schedules and time zones are so varied. Asynchronous discussions are one workable solution. Other exercises can require students to collaborate by finding synchronous meeting times or by peer reviewing other written or video-recorded student work. When students are together on campus, externship gatherings can give students and instructors time to strengthen connections, share experiences, and troubleshoot problems. Those in-person gatherings also feature discussions about racial justice and other diversity, equity, and inclusion topics that relate to what the students are experiencing at the placement site and benefit from in-person, real-time conversation.

5. **Work with remote sites.** Working with sites in different states and sometimes in different countries presents unique challenges. Law schools cannot rely substantially on their long-standing relationships with regional legal employers to connect students with remote, high-quality placements. Additionally, visiting all sites in person is not feasible.

The program features described above, including the vetting process, reflect this reality. In addition, site supervisors working with remote students should be encouraged to be even more intentional than usual in discussing learning goals with the students and determining how the site supervisor can help achieve those goals. Site supervisors should also be asked to check in with students more frequently than usual to ensure learning goals are being met and to communicate with the law school regularly about plans for and progress with remote work. In remote externships, shorter, more structured work experiences can be particularly beneficial.

## II. Program Takeaways, Challenges, and Successes

Through the unique pedagogy and practical nature of a blended learning externship program, all students gain legal work experience that meets, complements, and even builds upon their diverse scheduling needs, professional backgrounds and experiences, geography, and professional interests. Faculty, staff, and administration leading the externship program also gain from encountering and resolving many challenges.

## A. STAFFING AND CROSS-DEPARTMENTAL COORDINATION

Particularly given the necessarily bespoke nature of blended learning externships, achieving the right level of staffing, information flow, data sharing, and process coordination across faculty and staff can be a significant challenge. At Mitchell Hamline, eight distinct departments are involved in administering the blended learning externship program and the launch of the blended learning externship program increased cohesiveness across faculty, staff, and administration.[10] That cohesiveness extended to other programs within the law school and led to a broader and more coordinated effort inside and outside the classroom in the areas of professional identity formation, skill development, and career and academic advising.

## B. A UNIQUE OPPORTUNITY FOR ADJUNCT FACULTY

An asynchronous blended learning externship course also offers a unique opportunity to engage adjunct faculty, including alumni, in teaching. Supervising asynchronous coursework and meeting with students at times arranged for convenience suits the busy lives of adjunct faculty and students alike. Teaching the skills both of practice and of learning from practice plays to the professional strengths of these lawyer/teachers. Adjunct faculty are not subject-matter experts, but they bring their legal practice skills and knowledge to bear in teaching and mentoring students working in the field. They get to know the students well and help fulfill the law school's promise to be a resource and support for alumni throughout their careers.

## C. INNOVATION IN LEGAL EDUCATION

Externships allow law students to gain hands-on legal experience serving clients in urban and rural communities around the country, including communities that are typically underserved or otherwise have difficulty accessing legal services. This innovation is a key part of developing practice-ready lawyers who are well-equipped to deliver justice to clients with diverse legal needs. The development of flexible, collaborative, and creative blended learning externship programs challenges the traditional norms of legal education and establishes a new framework for educating lawyers facing challenges that had previously gone unanswered by the legal profession and law school educators.

---

10. The program is a collaboration of faculty and staff from Academic Technology, Alumni Relations, Career and Professional Development, Externship Administration, Instructional Design, Information Technology, and Student Services offices.

THIRTY-FOUR

# A Virtual Lesson: Creating Community with Collaboration in Law School Bar Preparation Programs

Brittany L. Raposa*

After reading this chapter, readers will be able to:

- Summarize the benefits of combating isolation in bar prep with collaborative online learning;
- Understand the importance of collaboration and community in bar exam preparation;
- Plan bar exam preparation programs online;
- Incorporate collaborative teaching and learning into bar preparation courses; and
- Design an entire bar support program online.

When most people hear the word "collaboration," they normally would not associate it with bar exam preparation. In fact, many people's memories of the bar exam trigger feelings of not only stress, but also isolation. Being isolated has somehow become normalized when studying for the bar exam. Graduates think that they must work alone—there is only so much time in a day and there are a lot of tasks to complete. So, therein lies the standard image of bar preparation: closed-off desks that sprout off of lonely hallways in a library, or a bar studier locked alone in a room for hours in front of a stack of books and an illuminating computer screen. Cell phones are silenced and

* Professor and Associate Director of Bar Support at Roger Williams University School of Law. Professor Raposa began teaching in 2017 and was teaching courses online since 2015 as a private bar exam tutor prior to working in a law school setting. She has designed and taught synchronous, asynchronous, and blended courses in the areas of bar exam preparation and support.

friends are put on do-not-disturb, both in-person and virtually. Much social interaction is halted because there simply is no time for idle chit-chat.

Then, we have students who have no choice but to study alone in an isolated setting. Many students simply cannot afford to pay rent, utilities, and living expenses without working to stay close to law school to study for the exam. So, they move back home, making a study space in their childhood bedroom, a basement, or a Starbucks, away from the law school community.

However, this chapter challenges this normalized view of bar preparation by fostering and incorporating collaborative learning and social interaction online in bar preparation programs. With the increased use of technology, bar support professors can, and should, move toward more collaboration in their programming. I have taken advantage of our new online space in legal education to create a program that increases access, student support, and sense of community.

This chapter will first briefly describe what collaborative learning is and how collaborative learning works in an online environment.[1] Then, this chapter will focus on how bar support professionals can create a collaborative online space in bar preparation programs.[2] Although some of this programming was created out of necessity due to the pandemic, many of these strategies can continue, as they were extremely effective in not only preparing students for the bar exam, but also for creating a supportive and strong sense of community.

## I. Planning to Incorporate Collaboration in Bar Review

In simple terms, collaboration is when two or more students work together on a particular task to achieve a common goal. Specifically, collaboration has been defined as "an interactive process that engages two or more participants who work together to achieve outcomes they could not accomplish independently."[3] When assignments are created with the intention for students to collaborate, the objective is for students to learn from and with each other. Consequently, collaborative learning is defined as "constructing knowledge, negotiating meanings and/or solving problems through mutual engagement of two or more learners in a coordinated effort."[4]

Collaboration involves both individual and group effort. The key to successful collaborative learning is to maintain both individual accountability, where students are

---

1. For a more in-depth treatment of collaborative learning generally, see Chapter 14: *Effective Collaboration in Online Courses* by Darby Dickerson and Megan Bess.

2. For additional discussion of converting academic success programs to an online format, see Chapter 7: *Using Blended and Online Learning Strategies to Provide Innovative Academic Support to All Students* by Susan Landrum.

3. Janet Salmons, Learning to Collaborate, Collaborating to Learn 5 (2019).

4. *Id.*

held responsible for their own learning, and positive interdependence, where students reach their goals if and only if the other students in the learning group also reach theirs.[5] In order to ensure individual accountability and positive interdependence, the professor must assess both individual and group learning.[6] Although students work together to achieve common goals, students are also working towards achieving their own personal goals.

In collaborative learning, the common goals are educational and culminate in the creation of an educational product. "Small group collaborative learning has been shown to result in higher achievement, less stress and greater student satisfaction, and greater appreciation for diversity."[7] In addition, small group collaboration is critical in an online environment because it incorporates the social aspects of learning into a virtual environment.[8]

Creating online programs ultimately takes a lot of planning and time upfront. I suggest the following planning strategy considering three main questions:

1. Write down your goals for your bar preparation programs, both before and after graduation.
2. Brainstorm how online learning can facilitate these goals. Answer the question: which type of online activity will best achieve my stated goal?
3. Write down your resources. Which resources can you utilize in an online program? How can programming online make up for a lack of institutional resources?

After you consider these issues, then you will be ready to create course content and exercises.

## II. Incorporating Collaborative Online Learning in Bar Preparation Programs

How can we incorporate online collaboration techniques and exercises into our bar exam preparation programs in law schools? Below I outline and explain all of the components and the goals of the online bar preparation program I created, together with how it incorporates collaborative learning to foster community online. In addition, I offer specific tips and suggestions on how to incorporate this programming, along with sample assignment and assessment language.

---

5. Karen Swan et al., *Assessment and Collaboration in Online Learning*, 10 J. of Asynch. Learning Networks 45, 47 (2006).

6. *Id.*

7. *Id.* at 51.

8. *Id.*

## A. PRE-BAR PREPARATION WORKSHOPS PRIOR TO GRADUATION

Goal: Building a sense of trust and comfort with all students and their instructor.

Effective collaborative learning typically includes a preliminary orientation to the group. A preliminary gathering lays the foundation in trust and interpersonal connections that sustains students at a distance.[9] This trust and connection is important to develop, especially when students can get vulnerable during bar preparation as they begin to realize and discuss their weaknesses.

To create a sense of trust and comfortability with the students, I created a program called Kick-Start to Bar Review. For four weeks prior to graduation, the students and I met on Saturday mornings for a coffee hour and to discuss bar preparation. We also discussed practice multiple-choice questions, essay writing, and performance test writing. These informal gatherings not only helped get students a bit more familiar with the bar exam, but they also allowed for trust building. The students began to trust me and trust each other for a positive and shared bar exam study experience to come.

Doing this online is rather simple and incredibly accessible to students no matter where they are located. I used the Zoom platform to hold meetings, and began each session with a poll in order to ask the students how they were feeling. Poll questions varied from "What are you most worried about when thinking of studying for the bar exam?" to a simple "How are you doing?" If there was a large attendance, I would move the students into breakout rooms, giving them discussion questions. Some of the discussion questions I asked that promoted fantastic conversation were the following:

- What are you looking forward to after the bar exam is over?
- What is your dream job after you become a licensed attorney?
- What are your fears about studying for the bar exam, and how can you work as a group to come up with ways to conquer those fears?
- What do you perceive as your weaknesses, and how can you work as a group to come up with ways to deal with those weaknesses and turn them into strengths?

When the students are in their virtual breakout rooms, I would enter each one for about five minutes to engage in the discussion with the students and then would move to the next room.

During the 2020 bar exam season after implementing these virtual workshops, my participation in the rest of my bar preparation program was much higher than it had

9. *Id.*

been in the prior two years. Before implementing this part of the program in 2018, attendance averaged at 38% and in 2019 it averaged at 46%. In 2020, after I implemented these workshops, attendance averaged at 71%. Giving the students an opportunity to get to know each other and get comfortable with one another created comfort and trust that allowed them to want to keep working together throughout their bar review study.

## B. INITIAL BAR EXAM BIG PICTURE WORKSHOPS

**Goal**: Introduce students to bar exam substantive material while allowing them to work collaboratively on problems solving exercises.

In 2020, with a prolonged and extended bar exam period, students had almost four months to study for their exams, and commercial bar preparation courses pushed back official course start dates. Consequently, I wanted to create workshops that introduced students to the law topics that they needed to master for the bar exam and to ease them into bar study mode, especially given the stress of the pandemic and bar study. Then came the idea for initial bar exam big picture workshops.

This program took the term "collaboration" literally in many ways. First, I created workshops that covered each subject taught on both the MBE and the MEE. These workshops would include bar-style introductory lectures for each subject. Second, I reached out to our faculty to get volunteers to teach the subjects. This created a sense of collaboration between the students and our faculty, and created a sense of community—we were all in this together. Instead of just having strangers lecture for commercial bar preparation courses, faculty who students have developed relationships with were also involved in their bar preparation and teaching them substantive material. We were able to create this community because we were all accessible to one another online.

In addition to substantive law lectures, the workshop series also included skills workshops that I taught. We went over skills such as MBE question taking, MEE and MPT writing, mind mapping, time management, and effective study strategies. Table 1 (following page) shows the schedule I used over the course of the summer of 2020 as an example of how I structured the workshops.

TABLE 1

| Week | Day | Topic | Faculty |
|---|---|---|---|
| 1 | 1 | Introduction to the Program<br>Introduction to Legal Writing for the MPT | Legal Writing Faculty Member |
| | 2 | Evidence<br><br>**SKILLS WORKSHOP**<br>**MBE Fundamentals; How to Study for the MBE** | Evidence Faculty Member<br><br>**ASP Faculty Member** |
| | 3 | Criminal Law & Procedure | Criminal Law & Procedure Faculty Member |
| 2 | 4 | Torts<br><br>**SKILLS WORKSHOP**<br>**Bar Study Skills: Mind Mapping & Spaced Repetition** | Torts Faculty Member<br><br>**ASP Faculty Member** |
| | 5 | Real Property 1 | Real Property Faculty Member |
| 3 | 6 | Contracts & Sales | Contracts Faculty Member |
| | 7 | **SKILLS WORKSHOP**<br>**MEE Fundamentals; Studying with MEE Questions** | **ASP Faculty Member** |
| | 8 | Secured Transactions | Secured Transactions Faculty Member |
| 4 | 9 | Constitutional Law<br><br>**SKILLS WORKSHOP**<br>**MPT Walk-Through** | Constitutional Law Faculty Member<br><br>**ASP Faculty Member** |
| | 10 | Wills and Trusts | Wills and Trusts Faculty Member |
| | 11 | Business Organizations | Business Organizations Faculty Member |
| 5 | 12 | Civil Procedure | Civil Procedure Faculty Member |
| | 13 | Conflict of Laws<br><br>**SKILLS WORKSHOP**<br>**Spaced Repetition; Studying with MBE and MEE Questions** | Conflict of Laws Faculty Member<br><br>**ASP Faculty Member** |
| | 14 | Family Law | Family Law Faculty Member |

In a post-pandemic world, when bar review is not extended, how can we keep this type of programming? At my law school, we are keeping the program and incorporating it with just slight differences. First, the faculty have recorded the lectures that will be available to students studying for the bar exam or for use by students who would like to begin early preparation prior to graduating. Second, during bar study, each faculty member will hold a live question and answer session online where students can come and ask substantive law questions. In this way, we plan to still foster that sense of community in the standard ten to twelve-week bar preparation.

## C. BAR EXAM DISCUSSION BOARD

Goal: Students can collaborate with the professor and each other engaging in asking and answering questions about substantive material and bar exam study.

Since during the pandemic most law schools could not incorporate an in-person discussion component to their programming, an online discussion board became critical for student interaction and access to me, the professor, to create a sense of community and allow the students to discuss bar exam progress and ask questions. With an online discussion board, students may be instructed to post any questions about substantive content, skills, or general study questions, rather than asking a professor individually via email.

In my discussion board, I had discussion threads for the following substantive topics: Real Property, Evidence, Criminal Law and Procedure, Torts, Contracts, Federal Civil Procedure, Constitutional Law, and MEE subjects. I also had threads for how to approach MBE questions, MEE writing questions, MPT writing questions, and general study questions.

For the 2020 bar exam season, a total of 402 questions were posted in the discussion board. Students not only asked questions that were answered by me, but students also engaged in a discussion with each other about what was working for them and what was not working regarding their bar study. Again, this not only fostered a sense of community, but it also allowed students to work with one another to develop a deeper understanding of the material and study strategies. The discussion board also created more access for students who were not on campus. Normally, any student studying for the bar exam could walk into my office and ask me questions. However, those students studying away from school and by themselves at home did not have as much access to me or even each other. The online discussion board created a more inclusive bar study environment for all, regardless of their financial status, privilege, or individual circumstance.

## D. SMALL GROUP COLLABORATION

Goal: Have students learn from one another and collaborate to solve analytical problems in bar exam questions.

Each week, I held small group collaboration workshops completely facilitated by students. Students would sign up for these workshops in advance on a Google sign-up sheet. The groups consisted of about five to ten students, and this program was completely voluntary. During the workshops, the students worked together to answer multiple-choice or essay questions. Students had the opportunity to sign up for these workshops every two weeks.

For the multiple-choice workshops, I provided students with twenty questions on heavily tested topics in mixed subjects. The instructions told students to answer questions together, not only discussing which answer was correct but verbalizing why the other three answer choices were incorrect. This workshop incorporated collaboration to the fullest by having students work together to achieve a particular result—the correct answer to a multiple-choice question. After the students completed the twenty questions, I made the answers and explanations to the questions available. The students were instructed to then review and discuss the answers and explanations with one another.

For the essay workshops, I provided students with one essay question that they needed to collaboratively write together. After the essay was written, they submitted it to me for written feedback. Students were instructed to answer the essay together in any way they want to—either entirely together or separating the essay by issues. These workshops allowed students to not only work together to produce an essay answer, but it also allowed them to critique and engage with each other's writing, making this skill stronger.

Essentially, these workshops acted as virtual study groups for students. Students were able to engage with each other and work together to solve a problem or to write an answer. They were also able to benefit from learning from each other.

## E. COLLABORATIVE EXAM GRADING

Goal: Collaborate with other students to critique and grade bar exam essays and performance tests.

In live sessions on a video-conferencing platform, I broke students up into groups to critique actual student bar exam essays. Students read prior essay and performance test answers and graded them on a zero to a six bar exam scale. Students were required to work together not only to come up with a grade, but also to critique the writing, organization, rule statements, and analysis of the essays and performance tests. The students were given (1) rubrics created by me and (2) sample answers that were actual answers from students who had taken a bar exam previously.[10]

10. These essays have been collected by me over the years and are used with the permission of students. The sample student essays can also be obtained from jurisdictions' bar exam websites.

After this, we come back as a group, and one student from each group reported on the given bar exam score with their reasoning for that score looking at the following categories: (1) structure and organization; (2) issue identification; (3) rule statement writing; (4) analysis writing; and (5) overall writing clarity.

We also discussed the strengths and weaknesses of each essay. I revealed the actual bar exam score the student received, and then I explained why while enforcing important writing or performance test skills and strategies. We were able to do this online much more effectively than we would be able to in person. Each of the groups was able to be in its own space for discussing and critiquing the essays using shared screens.

## F. ALUMNI MENTORSHIP PROGRAM

Goal: Bar studiers can learn from those who have recently taken and passed a bar exam, and further gain a sense of collaborative community.

One of the most successful programs I started during the pandemic was the alumni mentorship program. I paired students with an alumni mentor who was successful on the bar exam, preferably in the same jurisdiction that the taker was sitting in. I created mentor guidelines, which stated the following:

- The mentor needs to check-in with the mentee once per week at a minimum, either by email or by phone.
- The mentor needs to video chat with the mentee at least once throughout the mentee's bar study.
- The mentor's role is to provide guidance and support throughout the mentee's bar study—it is not a substantive law role. Mentors are not expected to teach the law, but are instead expected to provide guidance on study strategies to assist students with increasing their scores.
- The mentor may, but is not required, to give the mentee guidance and/or feedback on essays or performance tests.
- The mentor is expected to be responsive, within reason, to questions posed by the mentee via email or any other medium.

The mentors and mentees were paired strategically. The students in the bottom quartile of the class were paired with mentors who graduated and were successful in the top or second quartile of the class. In this way, lower performing students could collaborate with former students who were higher performing. This created a knowledge exchange, and the students at the bottom of the graduating class could learn and get strong study strategies from those who performed well. Students in the third and second quartiles were paired with mentors who were similar to them—mentors that had lower GPAs or similar grades in certain classes, but succeeded on the bar exam the first time despite those obstacles. It was also a knowledge exchange, but it also fostered a sense of motivation. If their mentor could do it, and if their mentor could guide them through how they did it, then the students could do it too.

The mentorship program also fostered a strong sense of community. Typically, the bar preparation program was centered on the instructor and the students. Now, alumni were also invested in their success, and the students could make connections in the broader law school community, which they were about to join. This further gave students the "we're all in this together" approach and diminished the feelings of isolation that bar preparation brings.

### G. ELECTRONIC OFFICE HOURS

Goal: The ability for a professor to work one-on-one with students studying for the bar exam, fostering collaboration through knowledge transfer.

Throughout bar preparation under normal circumstances, students would pop into my office to meet with me one-on-one. In an online world, this could not happen. I did not want students to think I was any less accessible or not accessible at all. Therefore, I established virtual office hours. Two days per week, I set a particular time frame where I would be on Zoom so students could work with me one-on-one if they wanted to. I had a waiting room set up and I would let students into my virtual office in the order they entered the waiting room. I increased my accessibility online and was able to work with students one-on-one through their bar preparation, teaching them either doctrine they were confused on or working with them on their writing.

### H. VIRTUAL MONDAY MOTIVATIONAL MESSAGES

For each Monday during bar preparation, I created a video of myself giving the bar studiers a motivational message. This online presence and part of the programming was not only the most enjoyable to create, but one of the most important. If you work with students during the bar exam, then you know that it is difficult to sometimes reach students. They are graduated, so your classes are not mandatory, and sometimes emails go unanswered. Despite that, we also know that bar study is exhausting, and is a process that can really make you question your abilities and your worth. Recording motivational messages and sending them out to bar students reminded them that everything is within their power, and that power is within themselves. It reminded them that they could do this. It reminded them that they can and will pass this exam. These videos create that accessibility and outreach that we just do not have in-person, and further created the essence of a bar exam community.

## III. The Virtual Lesson: The Importance of Collaboration and Community in Bar Preparation

The COVID-19 pandemic presented many challenges and obstacles to overcome, but it made me realize that one challenge of bar prep always exists: the feeling of isolation. Although I worked hard to incorporate community and collaboration into the bar preparation program in a purely online environment, these components are still critical after the world returns to "normal." In fact, these components were what was missing from my bar preparation program all along.

After the dust settled in October, when all of the bar exams were finally finished, I sent a survey to my now former students, asking for their feedback on the components of the law school's bar preparation program. All of the components that fostered collaboration and community written about in this chapter, received tremendous positive feedback. For example, one student commented, "The opportunity to come together and be with other people each week was so good for me. I was feeling depressed and lonely, but seeing other students and studying with them really helped me."[11] Another student commented, "I was feeling really nervous about the bar exam and definitely thinking I would not pass with everything going on. I definitely don't feel like that anymore. I feel like I studied hard, and that reassurance came from everyone involved in the preparation."[12]

Academic success and bar preparation professionals, as well as faculty and staff at law schools, know that when a student reflects on their bar exam experience, they remember the loneliness. The feelings of isolation and seclusion tunnels into them and leaves a lasting memory. As such, creating a sense of community and belonging is so critical for our bar exam takers. They certainly need to study, and they certainly need their individual performance to grow, but they also need motivation and support. Incorporating collaboration and community into our bar preparation fosters motivation and drive, and it also shows that we are truly all in this together. An online environment allows us to do just that.

So, let's change the standard image of bar preparation. Let's replace the closed-off desks and lonely rooms with the sharing of ideas, learning, and interaction in an online space. Let's embrace the opportunities the online space gives us to interact more with our students and to create access and opportunity. Let's create community with collaboration.

---

11. On file with author.
12. On file with author.

# Acknowledgments

It certainly takes a village to complete a book, especially during a global pandemic. This book would not be possible without the help of so many over the past year. First, to Carol McGeehan and Linda Lacy at Carolina Academic Press—thank you for being not just supportive, but enthusiastically supportive, of this project and promptly answering our questions. To Ryland Bowman, Jennifer Hill, Steve Oliva, and Arthur Iannacone, also at CAP, thank you for your help in making this book a reality.

To our chapter authors—you are heroes! We had a tight publication schedule, and you met every deadline. We have learned so much from the experiences you share, and we have certainly made new friends. It will be nice to meet, someday, in person.

To the students who helped with cite-checking—Daniel Bowman, John McKelvey, Zeke Peterson, and Tyler Stine—thank you for your diligent work.

And now for a few personal thanks.

*Professor Dysart*

Thanks first to Tracy for joining this project and providing so many key insights—especially on terminology. This book needed your online expertise, and I have learned so much from you.

Thank you to my colleagues for your support as I have been busy with the book. A special thanks to Susie Salmon and Diana Simon for your thoughtful comments and, Diana, for taking on an extra load with *The Journal of Appellate Practice and Process* while I worked on this manuscript.

To my husband Andrew—I know it was a crazy year with a global pandemic, a newborn, a toddler, and home renovations. Adding a book project only made it even more crazy, but your encouragement (and meals and kid wrangling) made it possible. And to my parents Bryan and Valerie, who also helped with meals and the kids while I was busy—thank you. I could not have done it without you. Finally, to my children—James and Vera—thank you for the smiles, the laughs, and the sleepless nights that gave me time to ponder this book. I hope that this project will lead to a better education system when you enroll in law school (no pressure!).

*Professor Norton*

My biggest thanks go to Tessa for inviting me to participate in this project. Tessa's vision and organization have shepherded this book from an idea to a fully-realized, indispensable resource. During a pandemic. In less than a year. With two small children. She is a force, and I have been fortunate to work with her on this.

My world for the last year has been my husband, Michael, and our three daughters: Emma, Kate, and Lizzie. All three "girls" attended virtual school—college, high school, and first grade—while I worked below in the basement. Thank you to Emma for basement deliveries of coffee, Diet Coke, and sandwiches. Thank you to Kate for providing a plant-filled oasis when I needed a change of scenery. Thank you to Lizzie for comic relief and words of wisdom. And thank you to Michael for everything always.

# Index of Applications & Platforms*



* "Free" indicates a limited or full edition for free. "$" indicates availability of a paid version with premium features. "$$" indicates a platform only accessible as a paid version.

# Index